Nietzsche and Modern Times

Nietzsche and Modern Times

A Study of Bacon, Descartes, and Nietzsche

Laurence Lampert

Yale University Press   New Haven and London

Designed by Sonia L. Scanlon.

Set in Bembo type by Tseng Information Systems, Inc., Durham,
North Carolina.

Printed in the United States of America by BookCrafters, Inc.,
Chelsea, Michigan.

Library of Congress Cataloging-in-Publication Data

Lampert, Laurence, 1941–

Nietzsche and modern times : a study of Bacon, Descartes, and
Nietzsche / Laurence Lampert.

p.   cm.

Includes bibliographical references and index.

ISBN 0-300-05675-3

1. Nietzsche, Friedrich Wilhelm, 1844–1900.   2. Bacon, Francis,
1561–1626.   3. Descartes, René, 1596–1650.   4. Philosophy and
civilization.   5. Philosophy and science.   I. Title.

B1198.L36   1993

193—dc20   92-27259

CIP

A catalogue record for this book is available from the British Library.
The paper in this book meets the guidelines for permanence and
durability of the Committee on Production Guidelines for Book
Longevity of the Council on Library Resources.

10 9 8 7 6 5 4 3 2 1

To my parents

Contents

Acknowledgments

Timely grants from a friend of Nietzsche who prefers to remain anonymous and from the Earhart Foundation freed me for long periods of study in which to work on this book. I am grateful for their support.

Abbreviations

In the text, citations to the works of Bacon and Descartes provide the volume and page number of the standard edition, with the following exceptions: Bacon's *New Organon* and Descartes's *Principles of Philosophy* and *Passions of the Soul* are cited by book and aphorism number. Nietzsche's works are cited in the text by aphorism number, except for *Nachlass* citations which refer to the Colli and Montinari *Gesamtausgabe* by volume, notebook, and section number—for example, volume VIII, notebook 15, section 30 appears as VIII 15 [30].

Bacon
GI	*Great Instauration*
NO	*New Organon*
PFB	*Philosophy of Francis Bacon*, Farrington
WA	*Wisdom of the Ancients*
Works	Spedding, Ellis, Heath edition

Descartes
AT	*Oeuvres,* Adam and Tannery edition
PW	*Philosophical Writings*, Cottingham, Stoothoff, Murdoch, Kenny edition

Nietzsche
A	*The Antichrist*
AO	*Assorted Opinions and Maxims (HH,* vol. 2, pt. 1)
BGE	*Beyond Good and Evil*
BT	*Birth of Tragedy*
CW	*The Case of Wagner*
D	*Daybreak*
EH	*Ecce Homo*
GM	*On the Genealogy of Morals*
HH	*Human, All Too Human*
JS	*The Joyous Science*
KGW	*Kritische Gesamtausgabe,* ed. Colli and Montinari
NCW	*Nietzsche Contra Wagner*

Nietzsche and Modern Times

Chapter 1

Introduction

This book is an installment in the new history of philosophy made possible by Friedrich Nietzsche.

The three main principles of this history can be expressed in Nietzsche's direct pronouncements: "The greatest thoughts are the greatest events" (*BGE* 285). "Genuine philosophers are commanders and legislators" (*BGE* 211). "The difference between exoteric and esoteric [was] formerly known to philosophers" (*BGE* 30).

Such sayings are familiar to readers of Nietzsche but in my opinion they have not been treated seriously—they have not been treated as if they could be true. For if they are true they must revolutionize the way we view the history of philosophy and consequently the spiritual history of humankind. "The greatest thoughts are the greatest events"—if this is true then thoughts are a primary agent of historical change and have governed our history by governing our shared convictions about what is worth doing; if this is true we have to abandon plausible fashions that have long prevailed and that have taken thoughts to be the lightest and most changeable of things, mere foam thrown up by more substantial motions. "Genuine philosophers are commanders and legislators"—if this is true, thinkers, those whose life is thought, have been primary actors in history and have influenced the course of events through teachings; if this is true we have to abandon the notion that thinkers are merely products of their time and place and that their thoughts are derivative from the real events that actually move human beings. "The difference between exoteric and esoteric [was] formerly known to philosophers"—if this is true then philosophers have practiced arts of dissimulation that put persuasive speech in the service of their legislative ends; if this is true we have to read philosophers differently, abandoning the notion that—like us—they tried to make everything as clear as possible to everyone, and we have to entertain the unpalatable and unwelcome possibility that they hid their real meaning and that they had good reasons for doing so.

Nietzsche's three pronouncements are typical of his abbreviated style for he does not attempt to persuade by providing the arguments and examples that would make such pronouncements plausible. Nevertheless, although a master of the art of pronouncement, Nietzsche is very far from wanting to be accepted on authority, and such statements as these are invitations, even provocations, meant to incite to inquiry. Nietzsche's positive views may fail to take any initial hold on the reader, but they are embedded in writings that command attention by the flamboyance of their language and by the pleasure and shock of their critiques—like his Zarathustra, Nietzsche knew how to draw a crowd. But behind all the enticements and calls for attention lie steady and affirmative views that are unconventional in the extreme. And if those views are more than simply flamboyant exaggerations or one man's willful creations—if they are true, they must change the way we look at the history of philosophy. Could they be true? This book will argue that they are.

But how can this argument be served by reading Francis Bacon and René Descartes? Bacon, Descartes, and Nietzsche mutually illuminate one another. Bacon and Descartes, often enough considered in some sense the fathers of modern philosophy, seem to me to share in all essentials the view of philosophy set out in Nietzsche's three pronouncements. Confirmation of Nietzsche's three principles is beautifully accessible in their writings; they are "Nietzschean" philosophers, legislators who mastered an esoteric style and whose thoughts are among the greatest modern events. Nietzsche's pronouncements provide entry to their writings, and their writings reciprocate: reflection on them and their revolutionary consequences prepares the reader to enter Nietzsche's writings with a clear sense of what is possible for a philosopher. Once Bacon and Descartes come to light as legislators of modern times in a specifically Nietzschean sense, Nietzsche can come to light as the first thinker to have understood modern times comprehensively, to have encompassed and transcended them in his thought. The actuality of the Baconian and Cartesian revolution prepares the reader for the possibility of the Nietzschean revolution.

"How to philosophize with a hammer"—does this nice Nietzschean phrase imply that Bacon and Descartes can be hammered into Nietzschean shapes, that the history of philosophy is so malleable that it can, under the force of powerful views, be shaped and drawn into ever new configurations? No. Nietzsche's views on the history of philosophy hold that there is something firm and unyielding in history that can well be ignored or covered over but that can also be heard for what it is. Nietzsche's hammer leaves things intact. It touches them lightly as a hammer touches a tuning fork forcing them to yield their characteristic tone: things have characteristic tones and what one needs to hear them is a hammer and an ear. The Nietzschean hammer does not do violence to the thought of Bacon and Descartes but allows it to come to our ear as what it is.

Nietzsche, so famous for his relativism or for being its cause in others, is not a complete historical relativist himself, for he aims to recover the past as it really was—though, as he says, all conclusions must be kept under the police supervision of mistrust (*JS* 344). "Genealogy" is the Nietzschean science, and for all Nietzsche's emphasis on the unavoidable bias of interpretation, his own genealogies aim to uncover our actual family history and not merely relate some likely or entertaining tale. Applied to Bacon and Descartes, Nietzschean genealogy affords a new perspective on just what it means to say that they were founders of modernity. But it affords a new perspective on another, still broader matter, for Nietzschean genealogy links these revolutionary moderns to the ancients in an amazing way. Both Bacon and Descartes flaunted the impression that their innovations required a wholesale break with the philosophical tradition, with "ancient pagans" as Descartes seems to sneer. But when read with the attention due philosophers who state openly that they respect the difference between exoteric and esoteric, it becomes clear that both knew they were not simply innovators. They acknowledge in the appropriate ways that the problem of innovation—the problem of introducing novelty into the settled ways of a people—had already been thought through to the bottom by Plato. As befits radical innovators they mask and seem to disown their debt to Plato. But the debt is there and they repay it in the fitting way.

A Nietzschean perspective allows modern revolutionary thinkers to come to light as "Platonic" philosophers—"Platonic" in an uncustomary but basic sense that will be developed throughout this book. A coherent Platonism in the philosophic tradition from Plato through modern times—this is the view of Western thought that Nietzsche advances. And in making possible the recovery of early modern philosophy in all its grandeur and ambition, Nietzsche makes a still deeper recovery possible, the recovery of Plato as the fundamental teacher of the West, the philosopher with "the greatest strength any philosopher so far has had at his disposal" who set "all philosophers and theologians on the same track" (*BGE* 191).

Contexts

A history of philosophy in the Nietzschean vein requires contextualizing a philosopher's thought. But setting the philosopher in context does not entail the supposition that thought is a product of its context in some mechanical way as Hegel or Marx or Freud argued; contextualizing in Nietzsche's sense is not enslaved to some reductionism that explains thoughts as a reflex of the non-thought. Nietzsche's contextualizing takes seriously what Bacon expressed in his fable of Cassandra: a genuine philosopher is a Cassandra reformed, a prophet who knows where he is and who has learned how to speak to his times in a way that will be persuasive and make a difference. Contextualizing in Nietzsche's sense presupposes that the genuine philosopher has comprehended his times and thus transcended them; he has passed from being a child of his times to being their stepchild (*SE* 3).

The context for Bacon and Descartes involves not simply the contemporary state of philosophy, as important as that is, but also fateful events like the assassination of two French kings or the trial of Galileo, events referred to at important points in their writings. This immediate political context broadens out to a more comprehensive political context, the war of the Christian sects which had drastically altered the spiritual atmosphere in Europe during the bloody century prior to their writings and that continued without signs of abatement. But broader still than these intra-Christian squabbles is the one great fight that lies at the foundation of Western spiritual life and that Nietzsche refers to as "Rome against Judea, Judea against Rome" (*GM* 1.16), the fight between the classical heritage of Greece and the biblical heritage of Israel. That long fight had just seen one of its periodic outbreaks end with the collapse of the Renaissance in a frenzy of religious zeal. This great event gave impetus to the revolutionary work of Bacon and Descartes. Protracted things are hard to see whole, Nietzsche said (*GM* 1.8), and these immensely protracted things are made even more difficult to see whole by the fact that we still live in their midst as partisans of a particular understanding of them, the understanding that advertises itself as a melding of the two inheritances, Greek and Hebrew, in a Hegelian *Aufhebung,* that act of magic which preserves what is good for us in each inheritance while letting the junk fall away. The recovery of Bacon and Descartes reestablishes a radical and sober perspective on our spiritual heritage; in their work our philosophic and religious inheritances come to light as spiritual opponents harboring starkly different dispositions to life, and their efforts, so far from harmonizing opposites, kindle spiritual warfare between them, the warfare Nietzsche advances and brings into the open.

But the context for understanding philosophy must be broader even than this whole sweep of our Western inheritance, according to Nietzsche, for philosophy arose as an event within what he calls the "moral period" of human history, the last ten thousand years or so in large regions of the globe (*BGE* 32). Within the moral period, Greek philosophy and biblical religion are local events, although decisive local events for us who live within them. Nietzsche is a more revolutionary thinker than Bacon and Descartes, more revolutionary even than Plato, because his work occurs at what he regarded as the end of the moral period and plots its overcoming. Being a revolutionary of such proportions—an overthrow of *morals?* But how will we treat one another?—puts Nietzsche in a delicate situation and almost all have judged that he handled it badly, that his chosen rhetoric for initiating and advancing this unexampled moral revolution is either rash or evil. But I say at the beginning what I hope to make evident throughout, that the work of the first "immoralist" is no atavism, no wild outbreak of the premoral or submoral. It is postmoral and takes its guidance necessarily not from some divinity or some law of nature but from the refined sensibility and taste of a human understanding schooled in the discipline of science, as Nietzsche said (*BGE* 230), and heir to ten thousand years in the development of conscience. As Gilles Deleuze says, "a book about Nietzsche must try hard to correct the practical or emotional misunderstanding as well as re-establishing the conceptual analysis."[1] Many still fear for their children when they hear Nietzsche's views and such fears are not illegitimate: Nietzsche does want to win them to a new perspective shocking to their parents.

Yet even the ten thousand year moral period is not a broad enough context for Nietzsche's thought. The philosophy that arises at the end of the moral period is attuned to its place in the universe: a place on earth. The broadest context for Nietzsche's thought is the broadest possible context, the natural history of the universe as brought to light by science of which Nietzsche is the friend and advocate. "Hooray for physics!" Nietzsche says in the *Joyous Science* (335) while making clear that he does not praise Baconian and Cartesian science for its end of technological dominance and its method of supposed certitude. Nietzsche's advance-

1. Deleuze, *Nietzsche and Philosophy,* xii.

ment of science is keenly aware that our hopes and fears incline us to take as true what our inquiry forces us to judge as false. And when he entertains the suggestion destined to become one of the standard canards in the dismissal of his work, that it is a *sacrifizio dell'intelletto* (*BGE* 23), he responds quite simply and quite devastatingly: "On the contrary." The contraries set forth in the aphorism are heart and mind: Nietzsche's work sacrifices the heart to the intellect. Nevertheless, Nietzschean science still draws from hearts used to sacrificing the intellect the ridiculous charge that *he* sacrifices the intellect. "On the contrary," Nietzschean science, joyous science, attempts to train the heart to delight in the earth as illuminated by intellect, to be loyal to the earth as a haven of life that has appeared and will perish within the deep and mysterious immensities of space and time. Nietzschean science is ecological science in the most comprehensive sense. And as such it tethers the heart to the mind.

"Philosophers are commanders and legislators." If philosophy is contextual, as it always is for Nietzsche, commanding and legislating are not acts of creation that call something into being out of nothing—Nietzsche does not imagine that nature and history are simply at the disposal of a powerful mind as a simplistic reading of his edict could conclude. Rather, commanding and legislating molds and fashions what is already given by nature and given by history; it is always attentive to its materials. The "historical sense" that Nietzsche celebrates as the sixth sense of the nineteenth century (*JS* 357) is a sense possessed by all genuine philosophers: they knew where they were and they knew how to speak in order to make a difference. Recovery of their thought depends upon restoring that context as far as it is possible to do so.

Science

The theme of this book is science, Baconian-Cartesian science and Nietzschean science. Its argument is that Nietzsche came to recognize the dangers attendant on modern science and set about to remedy them with a new understanding of science based on a more adequate understanding of nature. Nietzsche's perspective on modern science is a long one: modern science is one form of science as such, the passionate desire to understand the whole rationally. But Nietzsche criticizes modern science as in part a narrowing of horizons in the service of a political goal.

Is Nietzsche in any position to criticize science? Has he *understood* science? Typical of the dismissals of Nietzsche's assessment of science is the claim that "Nietzsche had no first-hand acquaintance with any scientific discipline."[2] Such claims betray by their very wording their surrender of science to a popular Cartesianism; they understand *Wissenschaft* to be *Naturwissenschaft* and the paradigmatic science to be modern mathematical physics. To suppose that Nietzsche had no training in a scientific discipline is false: he was acknowledged the most promising man of his generation in the discipline of philology. Philology? Is philology a science? Not only had philology developed the instruments of textual criticism that were making possible a more adequate public recovery of the two literary traditions on which the West was founded, Greek and Hebrew; not only had philology long since adopted the ascetic canons of objectivity and collective, collaborative procedure made standard by the Baconian model; but philology as Nietzsche understood and practiced it staked a claim to being the paradigmatic science. Philology is the science of interpretation, the discipline schooled in the subtleties of good and bad interpretation by constant exposure to the elusiveness of texts and the bias of interpreters. And as a historical science providing access to the origins of Western culture and culture generally, philology had proved a liberating, subversive science, as shown again and again by the renaissances in Islamic and Christian cultures based on the recovery of "the science of the Greeks." Philology is a school of caution and suspicion directed toward the whole of the human past, and in its highest form it is moved by what it is literally: love of the logos.

Nietzsche's scientific training as a philologist prepared him to raise the fitting objection to modern science: is modern mathematical physics the proper paradigm of science with its Cartesian conviction that an absolutely certain account of the laws of nature is accessible to the inquirer stripped of interests and perspectives and rendered all eye? It has long since dawned on many more than five or six minds that physics too is only interpretation (*BGE* 14). And if the question of the epistemological status of physics is so much as *raised*, then no matter how the question is answered, philology assumes its proper role as the fundamental science, the adjudicating science that confers legitimacy on the various fields and modes of interpretation. Modern mathematical physics cannot justify its procedures simply by practicing them; it cannot put its justification in the language of physics but only in the language of interpretation; its legitimation depends on philology, on a reasoned account of its own canons of interpretation.

But the Nietzschean science of philology not only judges the inter-

2. Brinton, *Nietzsche*, 81.

pretive status of canonical science, it judges the great philosophical texts. And the philological study of philosophy rediscovers the difference between exoteric and esoteric. As a science of textual interpretation it brings the history of philosophy into a new and at first extremely compromising light. For Nietzsche's history of philosophy makes clear that the great philosophers were not above lying, *noble* lying to be sure, *necessary* lying, to use the two words Plato used to excuse his most famous endorsement of the lie (*Republic* iii.414b–c). This is far from being an idiosyncratic judgment on Nietzsche's part; he shares it with Bacon and Descartes, who not only understood the history of philosophy this way, but practiced their own forms of esotericism. This at first unbelievable and unwelcome conclusion about philosophers, lovers of truth, becomes more plausible when the grounds for such a practice are understood, grounds as far as possible from the frivolous or perverse or accidental. Nietzsche sets out the grounds with great clarity when he speaks of "the deadly truths," namely, "the doctrines of sovereign becoming, of the fluidity of all concepts, types, and kinds, and of the lack of any cardinal distinction between man and the animals" (*UD* 9): if these doctrines are "true but deadly" as Nietzsche holds, then truth is at odds with life and lovers of truth find themselves in a perilous situation as traffickers in a deadly substance. From a Nietzschean perspective on the history of philosophy, Plato is the first philosopher to face up to the most profound practical question facing philosophy: can society be built on the truth known to philosophy? Nietzsche's Plato judges that the answer is no, that it is necessary to lie, lie nobly on behalf of the well-being of society. Beginning with Plato, philosophy pursued politics on a grand scale that required sheltering society from the deadly truths known to philosophy, and—not incidentally—sheltering philosophy from the noble lies that sustained society. That philosophic politics was shared and advanced by Bacon and Descartes, thinkers who provide some of the finest specimens of esotericism in the history of philosophy and who therefore confirm this aspect of a Nietzschean history of philosophy.

Nietzsche's treatment of esotericism breaks with previous philosophers on the question of its necessity, for Nietzsche is not simply a philological detective who catches philosophy in the act of deception: he brings it into the open. This is not the rash and isolated act of an imprudent philosopher who never learned how to curb his tongue, for in Nietzsche's view, the science stemming from Bacon and Descartes radically altered the setting for philosophy by making science a public enterprise of first importance. The discipline of science is the discipline of

[8]

truth and that discipline has now become public. In Zarathustra's words, honesty is the youngest virtue and because virtues are jealous masters, honesty fights to win supremacy (Z 1.3,5). Noble lying now has the public conscience against it. Modern society cannot recapture what Gibbon saw as characteristic of Roman society where "the various modes of worship, which prevailed in the Roman world, were all considered by the people, as equally true; by the philosopher, as equally false; and by the magistrate, as equally useful."[3] It is precisely our share in the new public conscience, our "intellectual probity" as Nietzsche calls it, "our virtue" (BGE 227), that makes it so unpalatable for us to think that the great thinkers engaged in massive deceptions that we could never think of indulging in ourselves. Nevertheless, it belongs to our own probity to acknowledge the presence of such deception in the history of philosophy. Montaigne is the pre-Nietzsche thinker who describes its presence perhaps most openly,[4] but even that paragon of enlightened truth-telling, Kant, acknowledges its necessary presence in predecessors who had the misfortune of not living in an age of enlightenment.[5] But Kant was not really running a risk with truth because he so believed in the moral law that he could postulate God, freedom, and immortality: he had no reason to fear enlightenment with truth so benign.

After Nietzsche, philosophy's esotericism need not be felt as scandalous. Its great modern practitioners like Bacon and Descartes employed it as the indispensable instrument of philosophy to liberate philosophy from severe religious repression. Much of what their esotericism hides was criminal in their own times but, thanks in part to them, is neither criminal nor hidden in our times: the general worldview of inquiring science from Democritus to the present. Bringing such esotericism into the open provides a bracing and uplifting perspective on the philosophic tradition, and it enables us to side intelligently with advocates of reason who found it necessary to appear, temporarily, to side with reason's enemies. So far from spreading scandal, the recognition of esotericism spares us scandal: the scandal of a history of philosophy content to judge the greatest advocates of reason inattentive to contradiction, the contradictions of Descartes's supposed dualism, say. When permitted his strategic speech on behalf of his world-altering program, Descartes shows himself to be wholly consistent, his provisional compromise necessary

---

3. Gibbon, *Decline and Fall*, chap. 2.
4. See, e.g., Montaigne, *Essays* ii.12, "Apology for Raymond Sebond," 376, 379f.
5. Kant, *Critique of Pure Reason*, B776–78. See Rosen, *Hermeneutics as Politics*, 27–40.

for the sake of permanent victory. And not only that: an unexpected but most enjoyable comic element in Descartes comes to light when his esoteric style is appreciated. Similarly with respect to Bacon: recognizing the necessities under which he labored would facilitate the revival of his ruined reputation. Esotericism of their sort, so far from being a vice, needs to be seen as a virtue, "the intellectual virtue of honest dissimulation," to use the words of a historian who defines and defends its practice by an embattled Galileo.[6] My book will attempt to make this virtue evident in the grandeur and nobility of its practice in Bacon and Descartes.

According to Nietzsche, a new setting for philosophy has been created by the public discipline of science, a pursuit of the truth based on the conviction that the truth will set you free. But Jesus' dictum is far from what most philosophers have held: they held that truth chastens and saddens, and while leading some to cynicism or despair, it leads others to indulge impulses once restrained by respect or reverence or fear, for if God is dead everything is permitted. Such philosophers have held that truth is deadly because society can flourish only on the edifying fictions that it is permanent and select. Can a human community be built on the truth? That question animates what Nietzsche calls his "great politics," a politics which echoes the philosophic politics of its great predecessors, but which runs a monumental risk by making an experiment with the truth. And not for the fun of being risky but because it has recognized the new conditions created by a public science. Is society compatible with science? Or, as Nietzsche asks in his typically more flamboyant, profound, and open way: why has life favored ignorance and the lie?

Nietzsche's incurable flamboyance, plus a host of accidental factors like the incompleteness of his work, or the ascension of Heidegger to the position of Nietzsche's most authoritative student, have led to the deeply ingrained misconception that Nietzsche is an enemy of science. An enemy of science and a friend of art—for are not science and art warring opposites? The answer for Nietzsche is no; they are not opposites and though they have been at war, a proper understanding of each leads to an armistice which endorses science from the perspective of art, or from the perspective of perspective (*BT* Preface 2). The science

6. Redondi, *Galileo Heretic,* 283. A useful introduction to esotericism is John Toland's 1720 essay, "Clidophorus, or the Exoteric and Esoteric Philosophy," a detailed demonstration of the esoteric writing of ancient philosophers; in Toland, *Tetradymus,* 61–100. See also Strauss, *Persecution and the Art of Writing,* and Zagorin, *Ways of Lying.*

Nietzsche advances is inquiry that has broken with both of its two great historic predecessors, the Platonic science of the transcendence of nature and the Baconian science of the mastery of nature. Nietzschean science is a pure immanentism or naturalism wholly consistent with the naturalistic worldview of contemporary cosmology and biology. The highest aim of Nietzschean science is an understanding that affirms beings and lets beings be. Its complement is Nietzschean art that celebrates and beautifies the world disclosed by science. Can a future society be built on a complete immanentism? Nietzschean politics keeps that question open while assuming that it is necessary to try.

Philology

Nietzsche shows how the whole trajectory of Western spiritual life can now be mapped from pre-Platonic Greece, through Platonism, to the long warfare against Platonism of which we are, as Nietzsche says, the tensed and expectant heirs (*BGE* Preface). As an installment in the mapping of this spiritual drama, my book focuses on two great events. The first is the rise of modern science with its attendant technology. I hope to cast new light on our origins as moderns by examining a few key writings that stand at the fountainhead of our age. They are marvelous, almost magical documents written to justify the new undertaking: the mastery and ownership of nature for the human good is, these works argue, a necessary project at this point in human history. The second great event is Nietzsche's thought itself, for Nietzsche is not only a philosopher who set the whole of our tradition into the light of a new sun (*JS* 34), he too is forced to take part and fight (*BT* 15). Nietzsche's work presents itself as warfare on behalf of a new human stance toward nature which overcomes the now apparent dangers of Platonism in both its ancient and modern forms and which makes possible a human affirmation of all beings in their transitory passage. Nietzsche, the thinker best known for his negations, grounds a new affirmation of the earth, the eternal return of all beings.

In Nietzsche we find an enthralling tale enthrallingly told. For in presenting his understanding of our spiritual history Nietzsche practiced his own form of the art of writing: the art of the aphorism even when the books are long. That art is meant to appeal to a particular kind of reader and in that appeal to form and mold, to educate, make Nietzschean. Nietzsche's art allows for the fact that at first everything will sound strange because there are no readers not already molded to another, alien perspective; there are, to begin with, no Nietzscheans but Nietzsche. The introduction of unwelcome novelty into ways already set is one of the great problems faced by every innovative teacher. Nietzsche's study of the problem made it clear to him that not everyone would like him, that he would be branded a teacher of evil, for in the literal sense he *is* a teacher of evil: "Evil is what goes against tradition" (*HH* I.96)— "what is new is always *evil* . . . only what is old is good" (*JS* 4). How to introduce an "evil" teaching? By a conspiracy. By seduction. By the arts of "the genius of the heart . . . the tempter-god" who knows how to "descend into the underworld of every soul" (*BGE* 295).

In its own way, my book is an introduction to Nietzsche and his evil teaching, to the radical and comprehensive civilizational problem that Nietzsche faced and, in my opinion, solved. "Too little philology"— that was the crime of which the old philologist Nietzsche convicted his contemporaries. "Too much philology"—that is the crime of which many readers will likely convict my book. Who will want to bother with the minutia of the texts of Francis Bacon when the goal is something as great as understanding the origins of modernity? Worse, who will want to pore over Bacon's *Advertisement Touching an Holy War* hoping to discover in its little nooks and niches Bacon's reasons for launching a holy war against Christianity? And while everyone reads Descartes, not everyone will think that his *Discourse on the Method* is worth such a minute analysis or that it is the necessary entryway into Descartes's whole project. My book leaves the beaten path to explore such neglected works from a Nietzschean perspective. My excuse is that in these little works a magnificence lies encapsulated that can be folded out of them only with persistent study. Moreover, it seems to me that only in such works and in such study do the philosophic origins of modern times become accessible. Philology, the art of interpretation, hermeneutics: I would like to have begun with an invocation to Hermes but even if I knew how to do that, it would only have made things worse.

In the part on Bacon, I concentrate on two brief writings, both post-humous, both apparently fragments, but both, it seems to me, utterly essential as Bacon's reasoning on behalf of the project of science and technology that he initiated. His longer works set out that project; they teach the new goal of understanding nature to conquer nature and they teach the experimental method as the means to that end. The two little works, *New Atlantis* and *An Advertisement Touching an Holy War,* come later and come quietly, and they explain in their enigmatic way just who Bacon is and just what his reasons were for embarking on this task.

My account of Descartes concentrates on the brief writing with which he introduced himself to the world, *Discourse on the Method,* a preface setting out, for the single time in his writings, Descartes's whole rationale. In an uncanny way, this work also acknowledges Descartes's debts for it shows how the thinker who presents himself as sui generis can be Socratic Platonic Montaignian Baconian. For Nietzsche I focus on two writings, one from relatively early in his career, *On the Use and Disadvantage of History for Life,* and one from relatively late, *Joyous Science,* Book Five. Juxtaposing the two works displays an essential progression in Nietzsche's thought from an early profound concern to a later almost confident solution. "Whither science?" could be the title for both the concern and its solution, if science is thought of in a broad enough way. What are the human prospects given the now evident consequences of Baconian and Cartesian science, the public science that opens all of us to the "deadly" truths? How can deadly science become joyous science and provide the human community with an affirmative disposition to transient beings? In the great event of Nietzsche's thought a legislative philosopher entices his reader to an affirmation of beings that engages both heart and mind.

Part 1

Philosophy's Lord Chancellor

Chapter 2

Why Read Francis Bacon?

We are very far from knowing enough about Lord Bacon, the first realist in every great sense of that word.—Nietzsche (EH Clever 4)

Lord Bacon was a realist, as Nietzsche said, but he was also a fabulist. He told tales on behalf of his realism, and perhaps by paying closer attention to those tales we can get somewhat closer to knowing enough about Bacon. For in his tales and fables Bacon shows the extent of his ambition and the grounds of his responsibility—there it is fully visible that Bacon is a philosopher in Nietzsche's sense.

Appreciating Bacon as a philosopher in Nietzsche's sense would recover his now almost evaporated reputation. Rousseau said that perhaps the greatest of philosophers was Lord Chancellor of England. French Enlightenment thinkers saw him as their essential forebear. Kant and Darwin honored him by using mottoes drawn from his writings to stand at the head of their chief works. But high repute has now given way to the judgment that Bacon was at best an energetic publicist and a mediocre thinker whose contribution to the history of philosophy is so marginal that it can be omitted without skewing that history. A different view of Bacon and his place in the history of philosophy becomes available through his fables, for they reveal a Bacon at once more fabulous and more sober, more ambitious in his ends and more calculating in his means, an indispensable figure in the history of modern times.

While many factors contributed to Bacon's current diminished stature, the one that seems most to blame is what Nietzsche called "the unseemly and harmful shift in the respective ranks of science and philosophy." Just here, Nietzsche said, where we should be strict about giving "each his due," far too much is given the scientist and far too little the philosopher (*BGE* 204, 211). Bacon is the philosopher whose program is the advancement of science and the elevation of science in the eye of the public to a status worthy of the highest public esteem. Bacon's reputation has fallen victim to his own success; Baconian science, forward-looking, ever-advancing, world-mastering science, seems to outstrip the need for mere philosophy. But the philosopher Bacon understood the respective ranks of science and philosophy in the way Nietzsche did. Not only is philosophy the supreme undertaking as inquiry into the truth about nature and humanity, that inquiry, carried far enough, invests the inquirer with responsibilities that can only be called imperial. His ambitions and his achievement make Bacon a "genuine philosopher" in Nietzsche's sense, a "commander and legislator" who has determined "the Whither and For What of humanity" (*BGE* 211). Bacon himself is more circumspect in the words he chooses to describe both philosophy and himself. His restrained speech is, however, accompanied by reasons for restraint and when one reflects on those reasons it becomes clear just how unrestrained Bacon's ambitions for philosophy and for himself really are. Restraint required of Bacon "that impish and cheerful vice courtesy," the art, Nietzsche said, of successfully appearing more stupid than you are (*BGE* 284). Bacon's enforced courtesies now serve no useful purpose; instead, they hinder the recovery of Bacon's role in our history. And recovering Bacon as one of the philosophic founders of modernity serves the larger purpose of recovering philosophy's role in our history.

The philosopher Bacon can be recovered, it seems to me, through a careful study of *New Atlantis* and *An Advertisement Touching an Holy War,* and the two following chapters aspire to that recovery. *New Atlantis* is overtly a fable, the account of a fabulous island in the Pacific whose possession of Baconian science made possible its long history of peaceful progress and its harmony of science and religion. The *Holy War* is a dialogue on the present state of Christendom and its ripeness for holy war, but it too is a kind of "feigned history" or fable because the holy war for which it enigmatically argues is the war on behalf of Baconian science.

Of course, not everything is in these two short fragments, and a full understanding of Bacon requires, in addition, close study of works that give a more detailed expression of Bacon's program. Bacon's own most extensive account of his works is given in the dedicatory letter prefacing *Holy War,* where he makes two works most prominent, *The Advancement of Learning* and *The Great Instauration* (*Works* VII.13–14). The *Advancement of Learning* is described as a "preparative, or key, for the better opening of the Instauration." As Bacon's account of the present state of learning and the task at hand, it is indispensable for an appreciation of Bacon's "historical sense," his view that the history of Greece, Rome, and Christianity had altered philosophy's setting and given him his task. *The Great*

Instauration and that part of the instauration that is *The New Organon* set out the new method in the natural sciences that is lacking in the fables and that Bacon took to be indispensable to his task.[1]

Nevertheless, the two fables seem to me to occupy a pivotal place in Bacon's work because they provide the reasons for Bacon's actions, the philosophic rationale for his break with the ancient writers he knew so profoundly and with whom he shared the deepest sympathy. Each of these works, however, is a fragment, each breaks off at a point where the reader has been led to expect more. Initially therefore, they suffer from an impression of haphazardness that seems to diminish their importance. Are they uncompleted projects dashed off by a harried writer, occasional entertainments begun but dropped because more important projects required attention? Studying the works themselves can correct this initial impression, for each reveals the reasons for its apparently unfinished character. They are fragments composed by a writer who had long reflected on the strategic uses of the fragmentary.

One reason for the fragmentary character of these two works can perhaps be glimpsed in a small aside in *De Augmentis Scientiarum,* where Bacon refuses to speak of "the art of government." This art requires an "art of silence" which he had forgotten to mention earlier (*Works* V.31). When he finally arrives at "the art of empire or civil government" he repeats his vow of silence while giving his qualifications to speak, and he adds: "But if my leisure time shall hereafter produce anything concerning civil knowledge, the work will perchance be either abortive or posthumous" (V.78–79). And Bacon produced two such works, each abortive and posthumous, the *Holy War,* composed at just this time (1622–23), and *New Atlantis,* composed a year later (1624). In these two works, Bacon's vow of silence on the art of government or empire is, in a certain fashion, broken. Each was planned to be both abortive and posthumous, and each treats of the deepest secrets of civil rule. Each exhibits philosophy's place in the world and shows why action must be initiated on behalf of both philosophy and the civil world.

Bacon knew as well as Nietzsche the uses of fragments or aphorisms in selecting readers and setting them to work: aphorisms are "knowledge broken" and "invite men to inquire further" (*Advancement, Works* III.405). Bacon and Nietzsche share the Socratic conclusion regarding

---

1. That method is compatible with contemporary standards of scientific method and is not outmoded as earlier twentieth-century critics supposed. See Urbach, *Francis Bacon's Philosophy of Science,* Perez-Ramos, *Francis Bacon's Idea of Science,* and Wheeler, "Invention of Modern Empiricism."

the most important matters: what needs to be learned cannot be taught—but it can be learned if inducements are fittingly arranged. Artfully constructed fragments do not say everything but say enough to initiate inquiry, giving it impetus and direction. Transforming the fragment into a whole depends upon the reader. Bacon is, of course, no postmodern; his fragments are not paradigms of the fragmentary character of all understanding, nor are they inducements to a play of interpretation that taunts readers to invent their own fragmentary misreadings. Completing the fragments requires an interpretation that accords with the whole of the Baconian project, a project that is in its own way, "a work unfinished." The fragments all serve Bacon's teaching, part of which is the new science of nature, and the whole of which is a philanthropic undertaking on behalf of humanity that accords with Plato's understanding of philosophy. Completing the fragments therefore requires understanding them in the light of Plato. As I will argue in the following chapters, Bacon displayed his comprehensive perspective in his fragmentary fables; they show how his own project related to its own time and to the philosophical model that counted most, the model of Plato. They also show his own understanding of his place in the history of philosophy; they could be arrayed under the Nietzschean title "What I Owe to the Ancients." For although Bacon was so adamantly a modern that it was impolitic to acknowledge openly too great a debt to ancient philosophers, he was, nevertheless, in their debt and he acknowledged it.

These tales make apparent one of the great senses in which Lord Bacon is a realist: Bacon is no utopian. He is the progenitor of a utopian dream, the founder of the modern faith in the technological conquest of nature as the means to prolong our lives and make them easy; but Bacon is not himself—the fables show us—a simple believer in that faith.[2] What Bacon owes to the ancients is realism. His realism led him to believe in the need for a new belief; and his fables let it be known just why he believes a new faith is necessary. Establishment of that faith requires a holy war on its behalf. This is the "crime" to which Nietzsche refers when he speaks of Bacon: "The strength required for the vision of the most powerful reality is not only compatible with the most powerful strength for action, for monstrous action, for crime—it even presupposes it" (EH Clever 4). This "crime" is the Baconian program for science: the greatest crimes in Nietzsche's sense are novel teachings that change the way

2. See Weinberger, *Science, Faith, and Politics*. My interpretation of Bacon owes much to the writings of Jerry Weinberger and Howard White.

human beings look at things (see *D* 496), they go against custom, they overthrow a whole way of life. A Nietzschean perspective brings the whole criminal history of philosophy into a new light. One could say with respect to Bacon that the criminal Bacon is visible from the perspective of the criminal Nietzsche. Nietzsche goes against custom—he has no faith in modernity's Baconian dream. And his lack of faith or his breaking faith helps make it possible to recover Bacon's own stance toward his teaching.

Bacon's Enigmatical Style

Stylistic caution:
A: But if everyone knew this, most would be harmed by it. You yourself call these opinions dangerous for those exposed to danger and yet you express them in public?
B: I write in such a way that neither the mob, nor the populi, *nor the parties of any kind want to read me. Consequently these opinions of mine will never become public.*
A: But how do you write then?
B: Neither usefully nor pleasantly—to the trio I have named.—Nietzsche
(WS 71)

"But how do you write then," if you write publicly of things that would be harmful to most? In "enigmatical, folded writing"—the words Bacon's mother applied to her son's writings (*Works* VIII.245), a description that certainly fits *New Atlantis* and *Holy War*. Before entering these tales it may be useful to study Bacon's account of the means and ends of rhetoric, for he wanted it known that he practiced a method of writing "used among the ancients, and employed with discretion and judgment" (*De Augmentis, Works* IV.450), a method "not to be laid aside" (*Valerius Terminus, Works* III.248).

Bacon does not do as builders do: "After the house was built they removed the scaffolding and ladders out of sight" (*NO* I.125). Bacon's discussions of the methods of discourse leave the scaffolding and ladders partially in sight and call attention to his aims as a builder. In the most elaborate of these discussions (*De Augmentis, Works* IV.448–50, a later version of *Valerius Terminus, Works* III.247–49, and *Advancement, Works* III.403–4), Bacon refuses to place the art of transmitting knowledge (the "Method of Discourse") under logic or rhetoric as had previously been done; he allows it to stand by itself as "a substantive and principal doctrine" of its own with the title "Wisdom of Transmission." He then lists six different methods for the transmission of knowledge, each method being a pair. The first and second pairs are of special relevance.

The first pair divides the transmission of knowledge into "Magistral or Initiative": the magistral teaches, the initiative initiates; the magistral transmits in a way that requires belief, the initiative in a way that elicits examination; the magistral is appropriate for the crowds of learners, the initiative for the few sons of science; the magistral has as its end the use of knowledge as it now is, the initiative has as its end the extension and progress of knowledge. Bacon judges the initiative method to be "a road abandoned and stopped up" and he aims to open it again, for the advancement of science depends upon generating followers or sons who outstrip their fathers and whose manner of working goads them to do so. This method "discloses and lays bare the very mysteries of the sciences" and is called "the handing on of the lamp." Bacon elaborates this image in the fable "Prometheus" (*WA*) where he urges reestablishment of the competitive games of the Greeks but with a Baconian twist: the games are now dedicated to Prometheus and the burning torch is to be carried forward by those committed to the goals of science.[3]

This first pair is indispensable to progress in science; the second pair has a different purpose. This pair, "the Exoteric and Acroamatic" (or esoteric), has an affinity with the first pair "in intention" but "in reality" it is almost contrary. The affinity is that each pair represents a selection process singling out special audiences from the crowd of learners. But they are contrary in the means of selection and in the content of what is transmitted to the select. The initiative method selects by being *more open* than the common method of delivery whereas the acroamatic method selects by being *more secret*. "Knowledge gained by induction" can be transplanted according to the order of its discovery; initiation into the

3. In a brilliant essay that cannot fail to give pleasure to every serious student of Bacon, Stanley Fish demonstrates how Bacon's *Essays* exemplify the "initiative" method over the "magistral," how they practice Bacon's scientific method by breaking the mind's passivity, its propensity to recline in common opinions, and by forcing activity upon it. Describing the "strenuous and disquieting reading experience" (162) required to study one of the essays, Fish likens the process to reading one essay, Bacon's, and composing another, our own, but with Bacon in control of both (147). Fish compliments the *Essays* by calling them "works unfinished" (151) whose negative instances subvert the moral and edifying discourse and goad to further inquiry. Quoting Bacon's statement, "we are much beholden to Machiavel and others, that write what men do and not what they ought to do" (79), Fish shows how we are much beholden to Bacon for the same service (Fish, *Self-Consuming Artifacts*, 78–155).

new method of Baconian science requires such a presentation and it will train initiates to make further progress in science—these initiates will be the sons of science nurtured by their fathers in the method that will enable the sons to surpass the fathers in discoveries and inventions. The initiative method seems to be the method practiced in the aphorisms of the *New Organon* where the whole plant of the new science is transplanted into the minds of select scientists; the selection process is passive: the presence of talent and interest selects to the open methods of science.

The acroamatic method of delivery is quite different. It is not original to Bacon but was used with judgment and discretion by the ancients. It has suffered disgrace by being employed to transmit counterfeit merchandise, presumably alchemy, astrology, and magic; in recovering this old practice Bacon has to free it from its misuse. But the sole means available to the acroamatic method is "obscurity of delivery" and Bacon must leave obscure what kinds of obscurity might be employed, and what subject matters might be appropriate for its employment. He describes only the intention fulfilled by obscurity: to keep out and to lure in. Those kept out lack what those lured in possess: the privilege of having been given the means of access either by their teachers through the interpretation of the enigmas, or by possession of "wits of such sharpness and discernment" that they were capable of piercing the veil on their own. Talk of such obscurity is of course an incitement or provocation for those whom Nietzsche came to call "nutcrackers." While *De Augmentis* gives no reasons for such a procedure, *Valerius Terminus,* Bacon's earliest account of the uses of obscurity, gives two: to avoid "abuse in the excluded" and to strengthen "affection in the admitted," or as Plato says, to harm no one, and to do good to those who are good (*Republic* i.331e–336a).

Bacon limits himself to approving the acroamatic method: how *could* one approve the method of obscurity but obscurely? Just what it is that is obscured will become apparent in *New Atlantis* and *Holy War* but a preliminary glimpse is afforded by what Bacon says about the use of fables or similitudes in his sixth and final pair of methods of discourse: "For it is a rule, whatever science is not consonant to presuppositions, must pray in aid of similitudes" (*Works* IV.452; see *Advancement, Works* III.407). Bacon is a teacher of things not consonant to presuppositions, and *New Atlantis* and *An Advertisement Touching an Holy War* seem to be answers to prayer, similitudes in aid of the science least consonant with presuppositions. The differences between "initiative" and "acroamatic" make it obvious that these similitudes are *not* used by Bacon to initiate into the mysteries of the new science. *New Atlantis* displays some of the results of the new science and the administrative structures necessary to achieve those results, but it does not initiate into the Baconian method; and the *Holy War* is almost silent on the new science. *New Atlantis* and *Holy War* are not themselves concerned with giving birth to the sons of science. As instances of the acroamatic method, they are fables or similitudes that initiate their readers into something that is *always* not consonant to presuppositions. Even if Bacon's new science itself becomes presupposition—as Bacon clearly anticipated—these works will not be consonant with it; they will retain their acroamatic character for they intimate mysterious deeds that will always be thought of as an "Impossibility," to employ the sign Nietzsche put over the way taken by his Zarathustra to his own mysterious deeds. Such acroamatic works initiate into philosophy; in Bacon's case, into the compelling philosophic reasons behind the new science. By using an old method to solve an old problem, Bacon suggests his own affinity with the old. The revolutionary advancement of science presupposes a return to philosophy in an older, perennial sense.

Just how fables can serve the acroamatic method is discussed in the Preface to *On the Wisdom of the Ancients,* where Bacon argues that fables are the traditional means of introducing innovation, the old way of introducing the new. His argument ends on the point made in *De Augmentis*: "And even now if any one wish to let new light on any subject into men's minds, and that without offense or harshness, he must still go the same way and call in the aid of similitudes." Bacon calls in the aid of ancient fables on behalf of his own novelties. And he makes great claims on their behalf, including the fabulous claim that the most ancient times were the most enlightened times whose wisdom comes down to us as sacred relics only partially preserved by the Greek poets who retold them. How fine of Bacon to begin his fables by asserting one of the hallmarks of fable, that an irrecoverable golden age stands at the head of time, peopled by gods and heroes so unlike ourselves that we can only admire them and never duplicate them. One has to forcibly remind oneself that the speaker is Francis Bacon, the philosopher who argued (with Giordano Bruno) that we who come later are older than the ancestors and hence more deserving of the honor accorded age, wisdom,[4] Francis Bacon, the philosopher who in these very fables, tacitly assents to the view of

4. *NO* I.84: "For the old age of the world is to be accounted the true antiquity; and this is the attribute of our own times." See also *Advancement, Works* III.291. See Rossi, *Philosophy, Technology and the Arts,* 77.

Democritus that human origins are poor and penurious and devoted to survival.[5]

Toward the end of his Preface, Bacon acknowledges that his fabulous claims for the authority of fable may well be refused by someone whose excessive sobriety prompts the judgment that fables are merely frivolous. Forbidden fable in the defense of fable by someone excessively sober, Bacon undertakes to "attack him, if indeed he be worth the pains, in another matter upon a fresh ground." The fresh ground is a defense of fable for two traditional and contrary uses. The second use is to clear and throw light upon the meaning, the only use described because Bacon announces that the first use, "to disguise and veil the meaning," he has given up. Given up? This simple disavowal nicely disguises and veils his meaning for the excessively sober. Meanwhile, his own interpretations regularly point to disguised and veiled meanings. And he says frequently that the disguising and veiling of meaning is *not* to be given up. And in the parallel passage in *De Augmentis* introducing three fables (*Works* I.520; IV.317), he offers the three as examples of the use of disguise. The disguising use of fable serves subject matters whose dignity requires that they should be seen through a veil—religion, policy, and philosophy—the three pertinent subject matters not only of *On the Wisdom of the Ancients,* but of *New Atlantis* and *Holy War* as well.

Bacon's accounts of his esotericism accord with the description of esotericism made by Nietzsche, a philosopher schooled in the ancient texts and no longer subject to Kant's faith in Enlightenment. Nietzsche rediscovered "the difference between the exoteric and the esoteric formerly known to philosophers" (*BGE* 30). His statement of the grounds of this practice updates Plato's paradigmatic account of the grounds for a philosophical art of writing: when the highest insights of the philosophers are "heard without permission by those who are not predisposed or predestined for them," they no longer sound like high insights, Nietzsche

5. By making the fabulous claim that a superior wisdom preceded the Greeks, Bacon is presumably doing what he had described as possible for himself two years earlier: he had admitted that "if he chose to act with less than absolute sincerity, it would not be difficult to convince men that among the sages of antiquity, long before the Greeks, a Science of Nature had flourished, of much more potency than theirs and sunk in deeper oblivion" (*PFB* 86–87). Precisely the same claim is made eleven years later in *NO* I.132. Benjamin Farrington, Bacon's translator, believed that Bacon acted with absolute sincerity when he alleged that he now really believed what he had earlier (and later) said he could say without believing. Farrington explains these shifts as Bacon serially changing and rechanging his mind (*PFB* 121). A more reasonable account is given by Stephens, *Francis Bacon,* 137–53.

says, but "like follies and sometimes like crimes." In Plato's wording, the philosopher will be judged useless, and insofar as he is not useless, dangerous (*Republic* vi.487b–502c). Because they would be judged useless or dangerous, follies or crimes, Bacon had to dissimulate his thoughts, not the thoughts necessary for handing on the lamp of the new natural science, but the thoughts behind those thoughts, their reasons or grounds. Bacon's necessary dissimulation has, in part, cost him his reputation. The sons of science outstrip their fathers through the initiative method which hands on the lamp: publicly authoritative in matters of the mind, the sons of science neglect the obscurities of the acroamatic method or see themselves morally superior to it. In this way too they outstrip their fathers, particularly that father of modern science who maintained the need for obscurity for views not consonant to presuppositions.

In his fables, similitudes that both show and hide, Bacon conveyed what was fundamental to his task as a philosopher, showing and hiding both the responsibilities of the philosopher and the character of his own times, the two most basic grounds of his one great action, the establishment of a new science of nature. *New Atlantis* retells the fable of Atlantis invented by Plato. Bacon calls attention to the Platonic origins of his own fable by entitling it *New Atlantis,* and by having one of his characters demean Plato and ridicule his account as "all poetical and fabulous." What is the relationship of new Atlantis to old Atlantis, of the fabulist Bacon to the fabulist Plato? The character who demeans Plato is a Christian priest who takes himself to be in possession of a higher knowledge than that afforded by philosophy, biblical religion. What is the relationship of the new science to biblical religion, of Bacon to the Bible? *New Atlantis* answers these questions in a specific if enigmatical way and the answers point to *An Advertisement Touching an Holy War*. That dialogue is a complex treatment of Bacon's times focusing on the warfare of the Christian sects. That warfare is made fundamental to the times and is viewed against the long preparatory background provided by Greek philosophy and biblical religion. Out of that background an imperative for present action is shown to arise. Bacon grounds the new holy war, spiritual warfare on behalf of the new science, in the unique extremity of his times and in the perennial responsibility of the philosopher.[6]

---

6. All page references to *New Atlantis* and *Holy War* are given in the text and refer to *Works* III (*New Atlantis*) and *Works* VII (*Holy War*).

Chapter 3

Who Rules in Bensalem?

*Not around the inventors of new noise but around the inventors of new values
does the world revolve; it revolves inaudibly.*—Nietzsche (Z 2.18)

Rule, says Bacon in the *Advancement of Learning,* "is a part of knowledge secret and retired" and he seems content to leave it that way,
thinking it decent that he be known as the philosopher who "knew
how to hold his peace" (*Works* III.473–75). Has Bacon held his peace?
Has he held his peace in *New Atlantis,* that feigned commonwealth
which was from the beginning accompanied by a foreword written by his chaplain which stated that the subject of rule was absent
from it? Bacon lost interest in this part of his little fable, Rawley
says, and turned instead to what Rawley thinks he thought more
interesting, collecting his natural histories. But one ought to hesitate before taking one of Bacon's valets as the guide to his work; as
Howard White said, "One may not be perfectly understood by one's
chaplain."[1] The art of rule is secret and retired, Bacon said, in "both
respects in which things are deemed secret; for some things are secret
because they are hard to know and some because they are not fit to
utter." Bacon does not make it a secret that he has penetrated the
hard-to-know secrets of rule; his apparent silence is therefore adequately explained by their not being fit to utter. If at first it seems
that in *New Atlantis* Bacon held his peace, closer study of this work
shows that he uttered the secrets of rule in a way befitting them, a
way that is hard to know. He disclosed the ruling art in the only
way appropriate to a master practitioner of that art.

New Atlantis, it seems to me, is the work that most completely
reveals Bacon's thoughts on the secrets of rule. Coming to light in
a way that does not violate Bacon's claim to have held his peace,
they appear as the secret rule of the philosopher over the apparent
rulers. *New Atlantis* links the secrets of such rule to the first Atlantis,

1. White, *Peace among the Willows,* 15.

Critias, Plato's unfinished work that provides the contrast for Bacon's "Work Unfinished." But no work of Bacon's seems to me more finished than *New Atlantis,* for the study of its details forces an encounter with an almost incredible density. And yet that density does not mar the polish of its entertaining surface but augments it in wholly unexpected ways. What at first simply pleases, later, with more careful study, leads and instructs and pleases more deeply. It is, I think, a paradigmatic work for a Nietzschean history of philosophy, for its esoteric style leads one quietly into the amazing place of philosophy in the world, the inaudible revolving of the world.

To investigate the question of rule in *New Atlantis* I begin with the surface, the rule exercised by science and technology in the Baconian society of Bensalem. It becomes apparent, however, that this rule is not autonomous, that one must wonder how these rulers are ruled. They are ruled by their natures, it turns out, natures described by Bacon in the *Wisdom of the Ancients,* and they are ruled by opinions, by "values" they did not give themselves but that were first given by King Solamona, the founder who rules in Bensalem through the tradition that lauds and magnifies him. But Bensalem is not simply a traditionalist society, for great innovations have been introduced since Solamona. Who had authority to introduce those revolutions? Or who *took* authority? The fable shows how the wise took authority, how the philosopher rules.

Fathers of Salomon's House

After science has with fortunate success fought off theology whose "handmaid" it was for too long, it is now prepared with complete recklessness and lack of understanding to legislate for philosophy and play the "master" itself—what am I saying?—to play the philosopher.—*Nietzsche (BGE 204)*

Bensalem is a monarchy. In addition, it has "governors" of its cities and places and of its various institutions (147–48, 154, 135, 155). But even a cursory consideration of *New Atlantis* makes it apparent that the actual rulers of Bensalem are the scientists of Salomon's House, either all thirty-six or the three Interpreters of Nature who seem to stand at the pinnacle of its internal hierarchy. In his single explicit reference to the relationship between the scientists and the "state" Bacon says that the scientists have the right to keep secret what they know and what they can do not only from the public but also from the state itself (165). While the powers of the scientists are made explicit, the powers of the monarchy are kept obscure except for a single occasion: when the words of the absent king are read at the Feast of the Family, he appears in his dependency as debtor to his subjects, and after the reading of the king's charter it is not the king who is hailed but the people.

The king is shown to depend on the people, but the people depend on the Fathers of Salomon's House: in their "circuits" throughout the kingdom the Fathers dispense gifts which could more efficiently have been granted immediately after their invention by the political system of governors. Their chosen means of direct dispensation through personal visits enables them to milk what Machiavelli called the one dependable political sentiment, gratitude. And they do it in accord with Machiavelli's strictures that their gifts never be ordinary or expected but always startle and that the benefactor always present them to the beneficiary in person. Knowing their benefactors enables the people to properly direct their loyalties. But Machiavelli noted another facet of gratitude's political dependability: while binding the people to the prince, it binds the prince to the people, assuming that the prince has some need for the gratitude the people give.[2] As will be seen, a need for gratitude makes the Fathers of Salomon's House dependable rulers in Bacon's island kingdom. Gratitude may be a political virtue but in Bacon *in*gratitude also has an essential role as the fable of Prometheus makes emphatic: "Conceit of plenty is one of the principle causes of want" (*Works* VI.749). The Bensalemites are to be grateful but they are to expect more, and the Fathers of Salomon's House exist to give more and to encourage the belief in ever more.

When the Father appears in person toward the end of the tale, his coming prepared dramatically through the elevation of Salomon's House by all the main speakers, he comes "in state" and he comes with the trappings of rule. Those trappings are most prominently the symbols of spiritual rule, passed to him from their original religious source: not only the crosier and the staff and the papal blessing, but the chariot resembling the Ark of the Covenant with its precious cargo of sacred authority. And he comes in the stark black-and-white garments reminiscent of Dominican friars who came on matters of Inquisition. But the trappings include as well the symbols of temporal rule, for he comes at the head of all the officials of the city to a people arranged like an army to welcome his coming.

For his audience with the strangers the Father is seated on a throne

---

2. Machiavelli, *Discourses* I.28–32.

raised on "the state" and adorned with "a rich cloth of state over his head" (156).[3] At the end of his speech he relates that on such visits the Fathers "publish such new and profitable inventions as they think good." On this visit he publishes "the greatest jewel" he has, for he allows the narrator to make public what he has been told. This act shows just who the actual rulers are, for the Fathers seem to have decided on their own authority that the time has come to rescind one of "the fundamental laws" established nineteen hundred years earlier by the lawgiver of their nation, King Solamona, the laws of secrecy that have, till now, been indispensable to their well-being.

The Fathers rule not only the state but religion as well, and Bacon indicates this through the Governor of Strangers' House, a Christian priest and state functionary. The priest has been trained to meet strangers and although he seldom uses this skill—these are the first strangers in thirty-seven years—he exhibits his training through his use of duplicity: knowing them to be in fear for their lives he tells them at their first meeting that the state has granted them permission to stay for six weeks, with perhaps more time available before they sail. He is lying, for he tells them two days later, when they are better prepared for it, that strangers are given every encouragement to stay forever and that the Bensalemites have been so successful in this encouragement that they have no memory of a ship *ever* returning from Bensalem. He had said "the law in this point is not precise" but in fact the law is both precise and fundamental and he knows it. But the priest's duplicity, his diplomacy perhaps, is bettered by the strangers' for they know how to "knit [his] heart" to them with their strategic first question. "How did Christianity come to this island?" they ask the Christian priest who seems to hold their fate in his hands. And they reserve for later their real first question: "What is the fate of strangers on this island?" In this battle of diplomatic wits the strangers seem to come off decidedly better, for their questions elicit answers that make it possible for them to piece together the truth about Bensalem, the truth about their fate, and the truth about the coming of Christianity to the island.

The priestly answer to the pious question of the coming of Chris-

3. Bacon seems to play with various senses of the word *state* in contexts where authority is prominent. The coming of the Father of Salomon's House is "in state." Whereas he sits on a throne "under" which is "the state" (156), the *Tirsan* at the Feast of the Family sits on a chair "over" which is a "state" (148), "state" being a platform in the former case and a canopy in the latter. The Father of Salomon's House has a rich cloth of state "over his head."

tianity is sufficient to demonstrate to a skeptical listener what it demonstrates to a skeptical reader, that Christianity was introduced by a wise scientist as an instrument to lead the sheep. Skepticism may begin with the name of the Bensalemite city where Christianity first appeared: Renfusa. Renfusa is a combination of two Greek words that mean of the nature of sheep, sheeplike: quietly, beautifully, uttering a single word, Bacon suggests the perspective to be taken on the pious tale of Christian origins told by its advocate. Or skepticism may begin with the one non-sheeplike person present at the founding event: a Father of Salomon's House just happened to be there and took charge, certifying the marvel a miracle without any of the cautions proper to a Baconian scientist. We learn later that Merchants of Light had existed for over three hundred years with the purpose of bringing back to Bensalem anything that might be useful. We also learn, in the last paragraph describing the wonders of Salomon's House, that they have houses of deceit in which they practice feats with light on which they "labor to make them seem more miraculous" (164). The tale of Christian origins is told by a believer, a Christian priest; a different perspective on such origins will be provided by one who does not believe them but knows their uses, the wise Joabin, and it is especially through Joabin that Bacon will show that skepticism regarding the priest's tale is warranted. In the introduction of Christianity, therefore, Bacon has treated us to the spectacle of an authoritative scientist introducing a religion of a holy God and immortal souls to the sheeplike, a religion that will become the dominant religion of their society more than three hundred years after the introduction of Baconian science. In this and other ways yet to be seen, Bacon lets it be known that religion in Bensalem, like the state, has passed into the care of science. With this transforming shift, religion and the state do not lose their authority, only their independence, and that only covertly. Religion and monarchy retain their traditional roles, religion as "the chiefest bridle of all vices" (153), monarchy as a venerable link in the chain of patriarchal authority that sustains Bensalemite society.[4]

But if the scientists rule in Bensalem, are they the ultimate rulers? When these thirty-six consult in secret are they guided by standards they give themselves? Are they wise? Joabin is the only character in *New Atlantis* said by the narrator to be wise. But is the narrator in a position to know? Our confidence in the narrator is given firm grounding in his

---

4. On the rule of the scientists in Bensalem, see Wheeler, "Francis Bacon's *New Atlantis*."

first direct speech, for he introduces himself there as a philosopher: his first words are "Let us know ourselves," a repetition of the Delphic injunction identified with Socrates, and his speech shows that he is in fact a knower who has understood their situation and can tell them precisely what to do. He knows that things are not as they appear to others, for he is not taken in by appearances; he knows that they are all in mortal danger while seeming to have been saved. Based on what he alone knows, he is able to provide the counsel that may well save their lives, for while not taken in by appearances he knows how to appear. He instructs the others to maintain a strict Christian appearance for the sake of their Christian keepers who hold their lives in their hands. The narrator thus exhibits his wisdom in the appropriate Baconian way: he is a knower who is a master of seeming. He is the "one" in this company of "one and fifty" (133) and the fifty come to recognize it, for at the end they elect him to have the private audience with the Father of Salomon's House. Authority thus passes from "the first man among us"—the captain—to the narrator, from the powerful to the wise. One final indication of just who the narrator is occurs when the wise Joabin makes his first speech reported by the narrator, a speech following many unreported ones and made after their close acquaintance: "You have reason" are the first words Joabin is heard addressing to the narrator. Yes, the narrator is in a position to know if Joabin is wise.

When announcing that Joabin is wise the narrator provides grounds for his judgment. Joabin's wisdom is revealed in his stance toward religion. With respect to Christianity, Joabin "would ever acknowledge" and "would tell" what the Christian majority would be pleased to hear (151). With respect to his own people, he was "desirous, by tradition among the Jews there, to have it believed" that they were a chosen people whose founding lawgiver, Moses, was ultimately responsible for the foundational laws, the laws believed by the Christian majority to have been given by King Solamona. After showing how Joabin encouraged beliefs he did not himself hold, the narrator passes to the decisive sentence identifying Joabin as wise: "But yet setting aside these Jewish dreams, the man was a wise man . . ." The narrator sets aside these Jewish dreams, but read without a dangling participle, the sentence says that Joabin does too. Joabin, the only important Bensalemite apparently not described with respect to his dress, is after all described with respect to his dress: being a wise man he dresses in the beliefs that will be seen to become him.

The "Jewish dreams" that a wise man sets aside all the while desiring that they be believed by others, believed by tradition, are convictions about the founding laws of Bensalem, its noble origins. But the strangers have just heard a different account of these traditions given by one never said to be wise, the Christian priest and state functionary. It is clear that the priest's tales are the corresponding *Christian dreams* and that they will have to be set aside in order to discover the truth of Bensalemite history. Like Joabin, the narrator will have understood that it is desirable "by tradition . . . to have it believed" (151) by the Bensalemites that Bensalem has divine origins and a divine mission; they will both know that such a "noble and necessary lie," as Plato called it, can no more be abandoned by the Bensalemites than it could be abandoned by the inhabitants of the feigned commonwealths founded by Plato's Socrates (*Republic* iii.414b–415e) or his Athenian Stranger (*Laws* ii.663d–664c).[5]

Joabin and the Governor-priest thus provide a most instructive contrast in their stance toward their respective dreams. Joabin is a knower while the Governor is a believer. The believer is shown fully immersed in body and mind in the symbols of Christian and Bensalemite authority; religion and state coalesce for him into a harmonious unity. And if he has to engage in duplicity in his bureaucratic function, if he has to lie, he lies for the good of the state and for the ultimate good of those lied to. As a believer in religious and civil authority, the Governor-priest stands under it as its servant, ruled by beliefs he takes to be simply true. But if the contrast between the Governor-priest and Joabin is the contrast between the dependent servant of tradition and its independent observer and student, then an inference suggests itself that is far more important for understanding the secrets of rule in Bensalem: precisely the same contrast can be drawn between the Father of Salomon's House and Joabin. Decked out in the symbols of Bensalemite and Christian authority, the Father too is immersed in those traditional symbols as a believer, as their servant. Believers of two sorts thus frame the wise knower in the narrative of *New Atlantis*. Believing fundamentally in science, the scientist apparently believes too that religion has its proper place and authority in a scientific society; believing fundamentally in religion, the priest believes too that science has its proper place and authority in a Christian society. Harmony between science and religion is achieved in

5. Two others in *New Atlantis* are said to be wise by the Governor of Strangers' House whom the narration shows not to be wise. Still, the reputedly wise scientist who introduced Christianity and the reputedly wise Altabin who saved Bensalem from the Atlantians can be judged wise by virtue of their deeds.

Bensalem by a proper acknowledgment of the spheres and roles of each by their respective believers.

That the Father is a believer and not a knower is suggested by his dependence upon appearance. The pomp and symbols of his coming raise him to the highest honor with the people; from that pinnacle he looks down on others with "an aspect as if he pitied men"; he does not attempt to mask his sense of the distance separating himself and others as Joabin does, but in his elevation bestows an ostentatious blessing on the pitiable beneath him. Appearances distance him from the strangers as well: he stands above them blessing them, and he permits them to kiss the hem of his garment as the Governor of Strangers' House had not. He draws no distinctions among the strangers, addressing as "my son" the one selected by them for the private audience, the wise narrator. His report on the ceremonies and honors of his house shows that appearances are fundamental to it too: statues are raised to immortalize the inventors, and circuits are made to receive the honor due them. Nothing in his speech suggests that these appearances are *mere* appearances and that he shares with Joabin a knowledge of their utility. His address to the narrator, though given to a wise man in absolute privacy after he has dismissed the pages, is a monologue that brooks no discussion—a kind of revelation granted dogmatically to a recipient expected to be only awed and grateful. Joabin, on the other hand, engages in a dialogue with the narrator, a form of speech that can be a give-and-take between equals and that can reveal without having to say everything.

The contrasts between the wise Joabin and the Father of Salomon's House suggest that the Father is a servant of belief. But if the actual rulers of Bensalem are ruled by belief they cannot be the ultimate rulers; they cannot be ruled by standards they give themselves; they cannot be wise. Who are these nonwise rulers and why has Bacon handed them power in the new age knowing them not to be wise? Bacon exhibits what they are in the fable of *New Atlantis,* but he analyzes what they are in his book of fables, *On the Wisdom of the Ancients,* in the fable of Daedalus.

Daedalus

Let us look more closely: what is the scientific man? A type of man that is not noble; he has an instinct for his equals and for what they need; for example, that claim to honor and recognition, that constant attestation of his value and utility which is needed to overcome again and again the internal mistrust which is the sediment in the hearts of all dependent men. He is rich in petty envy and has lynx eyes for what is base in natures to whose heights he cannot attain. Their sense of the mediocrity of their own type instinctively works at the annihilation of the uncommon man and tries to break every bent bow or, preferably, to unbend it.—Nietzsche (BGE 206)

Daedalus is the ancient hero fit for the Baconian tasks of invention and engineering for the public good. But Daedalus lacked the public spirit-edness essential to Bacon's undertaking; he was treacherous and lawless, serving only himself in his apparent service of others. How can Bacon dare to entrust the rule of Bensalem to the Daedaluses?

In retelling the Daedalus fable, Bacon emphasizes the ancients' failure to bridle the genius of invention and mechanical skill. He notes that the ancients often attempted to curb the Daedaluses by Minos, or the laws, by condemning their inventions and forbidding their use, but he calls attention to the futility of such legal prohibitions and quotes Tacitus's reference to a similar case (that of mathematicians and fortune-tellers): they are "a class of men which in our state will always be retained and always prohibited." But Bacon omits the central part of Tacitus's charge, the part that puts the ancient case against the Daedaluses most tellingly: they are the ones "whom the powerful cannot trust and who deceive the aspiring."[6] Untrustworthy and deceptive, the geniuses of mechanical invention put their skills to work for evil ends of passion and tyranny rather than the decent ends of a decent people. As Bacon presents the ancient wisdom, their emphasis on Daedalus's villainy has its positive complement in the assurance they offer that a well-ordered society can get along very well without him. Ancient wisdom, recognizing how corruptible the talents of a Daedalus were, flaunted that corruption and tried to establish the view that his talents were virtually superfluous.

This is Francis Bacon speaking. *The Wisdom of the Ancients* here repeats a most un-Baconian rhetoric: inculcation of the belief that the common good is not served by the inventors, that communal well-being comes from different sources and can be threatened by the innovations of Dae-dalus. This ancient wisdom with respect to the Daedaluses is a Greek wisdom and, as Bacon omits to say here but says frequently elsewhere when it serves his own rhetorical ends, it differs from Egyptian wisdom, the *most* ancient wisdom with respect to the inventors, for Egyptian wisdom magnified the inventors and "rewarded inventors with divine

---

6. Tacitus, *Histories* 1.22. This observation is made by Heidi Studer in her dissertation on *The Wisdom of the Ancients* (see p. 201) that she kindly made available to me.

honors and sacred rites" (*NO* I.73; see I.129; *Advancement, Works* III.301). Bacon is not acceding to Greek philosophical wisdom about Daedalus; he is not acknowledging its superiority to his own. He grants its basic point: the Daedaluses *are* most dangerous, and not simply because of their genius but because of their natures. But he highlights its greatest weakness: Daedalus is not successfully curbed by the salutary lie of his dispensability, or by laws, or by banishment. And at the very end of his fable he allows his own advance to be glimpsed: the Daedaluses cannot be bridled by the old means, but they can be "convicted by their proper vanity"; they can be made to bridle themselves, Bacon hints, if attention is paid to their nature, to what they are rather than what they ought to be. The ancients knew the nature of the Daedaluses: they are, of all men, those most troubled by envy. Their envy is the most bitter and the most implacable kind. And their envy never lets them rest. The ancients attempted to reform or repress that ineradicable envy and to make the Daedaluses superfluous. Bacon attempts to use that envy, to direct it by nurturing it in a society that thinks the Daedaluses indispensable.

The Father of Salomon's house is a Daedalus tamed, a Daedalus convicted by his own proper vanity. Bacon brings the envious Daedaluses under Minos by allowing them to be the envy of all. More exactly, he allows the Daedaluses to usurp the powers of Minos and ascend to the positions of rule because he has found a way for their vanity to channel their powers. The vanity of the Daedaluses, the product of their envious natures, requires that they be acknowledged as the singular geniuses they think they are. Uneasy in their self-regard, they crave recognition both by the many and by the few who are like themselves. They are lovers of honor consumed by the passion to be looked upon as marvels and to outstrip those already honored, and in Bacon's *New Atlantis* they are given what looks like free rein.[7]

Bensalemite society is calculated to feed the envious natures of the Daedaluses. Supreme place for the Fathers of Salomon's House is re-

7. The very next fable, "Ericthonius, or Imposture," continues the Baconian way of subduing the inventors. Ericthonius, the imperfect offspring of Vulcan's attempted rape of Minerva, invented the chariot to display his well-made parts and hide his deformed parts. The meaning Bacon attributes to this fable suggests the improved way of Bensalem over the ancient way. Vulcan, or the artisan, left to himself, tries to force nature to yield to him and, although some imperfect products spring from his impassioned effort, they lead to imposture. As in the Daedalus fable, the very end heralds Bacon's way. The fault is Vulcan's, not Ericthonius's, and Vulcan can easily be directed to pursue nature with due observances and attentions; through him and his forge, a nature obeyed can become a nature conquered (see *Advancement, Works* III.325).

quired even at the Feast of the Family where the natural father, even on this one day of his greatest esteem, cannot be esteemed more highly than a Father of Salomon's House: if one is present he sits next to the natural father (150) on a day when the king himself acknowledges that he is in the father's debt. The ascendant place of Salomon's House is recognized too by the religious official who acknowledges it to be the "very eye" of the kingdom (137) and who (unknown to himself presumably) allows it to be seen that the religion he serves was itself instituted by a scientist he esteems as wise. These new "Fathers" have appropriated the priestly designation once used by Christian priests like the Governor-priest; they are the ones who now get to call all men "my son" (156). And these envious natures are fed by the galleries that are a part of Salomon's House, for the Bensalemites do not allow an inventor to be forgotten; they immortalize both the invention and the inventor if they are great enough, with the inventors being accorded statues in an order of rank topped by gold (165–66).

But to be fed in their vanity these Daedaluses must put their genius to one use only: the common good. There is no statue to Daedalus himself whose gifts to Pasiphae and to rival kings did not serve the common good by relieving the human estate. Daedalus himself, the very symbol of invention for a wisdom that wanted to diminish him, seems to have been forgotten by the society that magnifies invention and the inventors. Bensalemite society must forget Daedalus and his wicked ways for it satisfies the Daedaluses only when they satisfy others, when they turn their pliable talents to the well-being of those not driven by implacable envy, the great majority driven by nothing higher than a desire for well-being and ease. The envious natures of the Daedaluses are turned to the common good when those natures are fed on all the honor and gratitude their beneficiaries can bestow. And Salomon's House administers punishments as fitting as these rewards: behavior inappropriate to their powers brings "ignominy and fines"—wounded pride and diminished wealth (164). Such rewards and punishments channel the genius of the Daedaluses by satisfying their natures; they are domesticated, made virtuous or civil by that novel, Baconian form of society that believes Daedalus's gifts to be worthy of the highest public esteem. By attending to what the Daedaluses are and yielding to their needs, Bacon is able to ensure that they will make themselves what they ought to be, public benefactors.

Baconian society is not dependent on hope or prayer: Bacon's Daedaluses have *not* been transformed in their natures; they have not become philanthropists who, out of some newfound goodness in their natures, suddenly desire the well-being of others. Treated as a superfluous ornament by an ancient wisdom leery of his powers, ancient Daedalus must revenge himself in the ways Bacon describes in his fable; subject to a nature flawed by ineradicable envy, Daedalus must take whatever means are available to flaunt his unappreciated greatness. Bacon's Daedaluses continue to be marked by a deep "malignity" that places them among the misanthropes, "the very errors of human nature" who, Bacon holds, "are the fittest timber to make great" rulers (*Essays,* "Of Goodness and Goodness of Nature"). Bacon constructs a society in which their passionate natures, once vainly curbed by law or banishment, are permitted satisfaction. The coincidence of their private good with the public good is dependent neither on their moral virtue nor on miracle, the "divine goodness" that Bacon nevertheless finds it prudent to call upon for assistance. Bacon conscripts the rare Daedaluses for service as dependable tyrants to whom the new enterprise can be entrusted without having to pray for their trustworthiness. The nature of the Daedaluses cannot be conquered except by being obeyed (*GI, Works* IV.32).

Bacon's new wisdom conquers the Daedaluses as the ancient wisdom could not because Bacon promulgates a new highest good—the ease and longevity of everyman. As the ones who make this highest good actual, how could the Daedaluses not be held in highest esteem? But the Daedaluses have not themselves promulgated the new highest good. And by emphasizing this fact, Bacon makes clear that the actual rulers of Bensalem are themselves ruled. They are ruled by their natures and ruled by a system of recognition and reward that is not of their own making but to which they must yield if they are to satisfy rather than torment their natures—to which, therefore, they readily and gladly yield, and come to believe, as do the great majority their genius serves, that all other social orders of rank, like those that exist among foreigners and in earlier ages, are primitive and inhumane. The ruling scientists, those "of great place" in Bensalem, are thus "thrice servants"; "they have no freedom, neither in their persons nor in their actions nor in their times" (*Essays,* "Of Great Place"). The actual rulers are merely apparent rulers for they are ruled by that prudent legislator who established not only the house of which they are members but the new good to which they are subject, relief of the human estate through the mastery of nature.

Who rules in Bensalem? King Solamona rules and he rules in the way that the fundamental or founding rulers have always ruled, by the instauration of authoritative opinion that rules the apparent rulers. In

Nietzsche's words, King Solamona is a genuine philosopher, the commander and legislator who determined the Whither and For What of his society (*BGE* 211).

Solamona

The ideal scholar in whom the scientific instinct blossoms and blooms to the full is certainly one of the most precious instruments there are, but he belongs in the hand of one more powerful.—Nietzsche *(BGE 207)*

"Since custom is the principal magistrate of man's life," and since "custom only doth alter and subdue nature," it is the establishment of new customs, especially the custom of honoring the Daedaluses, that makes King Solamona the "lawgiver" of Bensalem, its great innovator and revolutionary founder whose novelties could come to have the authority of the sacred for later generations (*Essays,* "Of Custom and Education," "Of Nature in Men"). But custom has authority precisely because it is *not* novel, because it has always already been practiced. How did King Solamona solve the problem of introducing novel customs and make himself the unseen spiritual ruler of Bensalem?

King Solamona's prudent legislation is memorialized in *New Atlantis* by the Governor of Strangers' House, a pious antiquarian whose accounts can be expected to be skewed by his loyalty. Nevertheless, his tale of two great innovations—the laws of secrecy and the founding of Salomon's House—make it possible to reconstruct the strategy of the revolutionary founder.

The first great innovation, the laws of secrecy, transformed an open and maritime power into a sealed society. According to the Governor, Solamona had three arguments for this monumental transformation, each appealing to the Bensalemites' pride in their own things (144). Each of these arguments loses force upon examination. The second—restricting their shipping to local voyages—is simply a consequence of his measure, not a reason for it; the first and third—their complete independence and their faithful perpetuation of the past—are transparently dubious, the first because they continue to depend on Merchants of Light sent forth to steal light from foreigners, and the third because the scientific institution aims above all at *change,* being the novel ground of novelties. The revolutionary change that insulates Bensalem from all other peoples of the earth is introduced under the pious cover of a people's pride in its own resources and its own old ways.

These laws of secrecy are alleged to be a mixture of humanity and policy, but the priest's way of formulating the policy raises deep suspicions that Joabin will acknowledge to be justified, for he will intimate that the ostensible mixture of humanity and policy is a pious fraud. Masking policy by humanity is an ancient practice in Bensalem as indicated by the remembered deeds of the twice-lofty Altabin (142); Solamona has made use of an already existing and historically justifiable pride in Bensalemite difference. That sense of difference is endangered by contact with outsiders who will, of course, if too much is known of them, prove not to be so very different after all. An edifying sense of difference can be preserved by the radical novelty of isolation, and by tales told of the inferiority of strangers such as Europeans. Bensalemite superiority will be confirmed for the Bensalemites by the humane way in which they think they treat the exceptions, those accidental travelers from inferior societies who, they think, are freely given the choice between enjoying the benefits of Bensalem or returning home. Solamona's first great innovation, therefore, depends on skillfully exploiting the natural fiction of the distinctiveness and superiority of one's own people and ways. Skill is necessary because the need for isolation seems to be based only on vulnerability or weakness, the suspicion that Bensalem could not withstand open contact with strangers.

The second great innovation, Salomon's House, is introduced by Solamona as something other than the world-transforming novelty it is. Having established his character as one who seeks "to give perpetuity to that which was in his time so happily established," Solamona is able to introduce a revolution—the perpetual revolution of superior technique—under the illusion that it serves the conservative propensity of a proud people. To further this illusion, Solamona presents his work as a kind of instauration, a reestablishment of a great program already begun by King Solomon.[8] The successful revolutionary founder yields glory to the already glorified, to God and Solomon, by naming his own creation "The College of the Six Days' Work" and "Salomon's House." His most revolutionary innovation requires that he submerge his own name under ancient names, apparently submitting to the already existing purposes of God and the wise.[9] Solamona was moved by something other than the love of glory that moves the Daedaluses whom he put to use for his own

8. On "instauration" see Whitney, *Francis Bacon and Modernity,* 23–54; and "Francis Bacon's *Instauratio,*" 371–90.

9. Solomon was not already as honored a figure in Bensalem as he would become with the later introduction of the Hebrew Bible as the forerunner of Christianity. While afforded

ends. He "knew well what solemnity it would add to new discoveries to connect them with remote antiquity in the same way as self-made men invest themselves from the dubious traditions of the genealogists with the glory of some ancient stock" (*PFB* 87).

Solamona's loyalty to Solomon can be adequately assessed only after a closer look at Joabin because only then will it become clear why Bacon has named his pivotal characters after just these biblical figures. But for now it is necessary to look further into Solamona's great innovations because there, in Solamona's founding, we begin to see the rationale for Bacon's great instauration.

Great novelties, once introduced, must be carried forward by others after the legislator's death, and not even Solamona can alter the nature of time: "Time is like a river that carries down what is light and empty and drowns what is solid and substantial" (*PFB* 80; *Advancement, Works* III.291–92; *NO* I.71; *GI, Works* IV.15). Solamona knows the unalterable nature of time and uses it for his purposes: not being able to trust to the accidental and irregular appearance of the very few wise who are capable of appreciating what is solid and substantial in his innovation (the Joabins, as we will see), Solamona entrusts his program to the accidental but regular appearance of the relatively many Daedaluses, elevating their station by making them the focus of light and empty adulation. Solamona's gift of adulation to the hitherto unappreciated and ostracized Daedaluses ensures that they will carry forward what is solid and substantial as its beneficiaries rather than as its knowers.

Solamona's revolutionary new polity is based on knowledge of human nature and knowledge of time and on something more—a new knowledge of nature that will supplant the ancient interpretation of nature. According to Bacon, the fable of Pan presents the ancients' interpretation of universal nature. In Bacon's retelling of the Pan fable, "there are no amours reported of Pan, or at least very few," namely, amours with Echo and Syringa. Pan chose for his wife Echo, or philosophy, as a form of discourse that simply repeats him. The marriage of Pan and Echo, nature and philosophy, was barren except for a putative daughter, Iambe

---

the highest honor only among the Jews then living in Bensalem (141), Solomon could still be thought to be that one of the available ancient wise with whom Solamona's own program best accorded. In spelling the name as Salomon rather than Solomon, Bacon followed the Greek of the Septuagint and the Latin of the Vulgate as well as the early English versions of the Bible such as the Tyndale and the Cloverdale. Thus the shift from Solamona to Salomon is not a compromise between Solamona and Solomon but a complete yielding to Salomon.

or vain babble. And Pan's pursuit of the nymph Syringa was also almost barren, surviving only in the sad sighing of Pan's pipe constructed from the reeds into which Syringa transformed herself to successfully escape from him. Also, ancient Pan, though sacred to a kind of hunter, was not a hunter of discoveries, and Bacon relates that Pan's discovery of Ceres was only an accident. If the Pan fable recounts the ancient philosophy of nature then the great god Pan must die and nature must be construed in an entirely new manner for Solamona's polity to be established. Nature must be viewed as malleably female and philosophy as a virile male for that marriage to take place whose offspring are the line and race of inventions (*GI, Works* IV.15) described by the Father of Salomon's House. Solamona founds a new science that is more than a wifely echo and more than a mournful piping for a lost true love—the Socratic turn from an unattainable natural philosophy to a second-best political philosophy whose only issue, vain babbling, will be supplanted by the new science of nature, a systematic and methodical investigation of nature in which few vestiges of Pan survive.

But if the ancient teaching about nature must be supplanted, not all ancient teachers must be abandoned: Solamona's work as a founding legislator shows that he is, after all, a follower of one ancient teacher, Plato. By giving the name *New Atlantis* to his fable, Bacon suggests that Plato's old Atlantis supplies the primary model, and comparison of the two tales of Atlantis reveals just how much Bacon owes to Plato. The priest of Bensalem who relates their Atlantis tale does not deign to name Plato, condescendingly calling him a "great man with you." The biblical loyalist thus makes this great man with us seem like nothing with them, a false teacher whose Atlantis tale is full of self-serving lies and ill-informed policy twisted dubiously to inflate the Athenians, a people less powerful and less merciful than his own Bensalemites. Bacon thus makes his Platonic point in what passes for a criticism of Plato: disallowing Athens its mythic past, Bensalem asserts its own and for the very same reasons of self-inflation and national pride. Bacon doubles Plato's Atlantis to confirm Plato's point: salutary invention of a national past scorning *them* and magnifying *us*. The loyalist's critique of Athenian self-praise is wholly applicable to his own but he would not know it: other societies are founded on lies, his alone on the truth. Further guidance about Plato's role in *New Atlantis* will come from a more dependable source, Joabin who calls attention to a book by one whom he too names "one of your men," a book dealing with a "Feigned Commonwealth," Plato's *Laws*. Furthermore, Plato's feigned commonwealth, the *Republic*, provides what will come to light as the ultimate model of rule in *New Atlantis,* the rule of the philosopher. Plato, "a great man with you," provides the fundamental instruction without being explicitly identified in this role. Solamona's strategy is exemplary here, an indication of how Bacon himself had to proceed: in a project like Solamona's which aims at reconstituting a whole people on the basis of a new science of nature, discipleship to an alien philosopher is of no practical public use while feigned discipleship to God and the acknowledged wise is. Solamona strategically masks his actual dependence on Athens with apparent dependence on Jerusalem and allows his people to believe that his novelties arise out of the Bible and oppose the alleged wisdom of pagan philosophers. When viewed without the pieties of the believer in the Bible, *New Atlantis,* so far from being "the only major Baconian work which is directed primarily against Plato,"[10] comes to light as Platonically anti-Platonic, trans-Platonic, Platonic in an enigmatic way.

This, it seems to me, is a matter of capital importance: Bacon's relationship to Plato. Is there more to that relationship than Bacon's characteristic criticisms imply? The criticisms focus on Plato's coupling of philosophy and theology, a radically different issue in Bacon's times than in Plato's because of the rise of revealed religion. *New Atlantis* suggests there is a great deal more to Bacon's relationship to Plato, for it points to Plato as the fundamental mentor. Through Solamona, the wise founding legislator of Bensalem who learned the basic measures from Plato, Bacon points to Plato as his own mentor—and Solamona's reasons for reticence on this matter would be Bacon's own: expedience demands that feigned dependence on the Bible mask real dependence on philosophy. Of all the issues that display themselves through a close examination of *New Atlantis* this seems to me the most important in itself and the one most fruitful for a Nietzschean understanding of the history of philosophy. For in Nietzsche's view, the philosopher's role is far grander than has been imagined, and Plato's role is grandest of all. Through Plato, Socrates becomes the one turning point of all so-called world history. And Bacon, it seems to me, takes a part in that history as a Platonic philosopher.

How does Plato enter *New Atlantis?* Furtively, in a way recognizable only to those who know Plato to be a great man among us and who have read not only the Atlantis tale of *Timaeus* and *Critias,* but the book referred to by Joabin, Plato's *Laws.* While seeming to reduce himself to

10. White, *Peace among the Willows,* 112.

a faithful follower of God and God's Solomon, Solamona actually follows Plato, for as a lawgiver he follows Plato's anonymous lawgiver, the Athenian Stranger. The two great measures Solamona institutes, reduced contact with strangers and a new ruling council, modify somewhat two prominent measures of the final Book of Plato's *Laws*.

Regarding contact with strangers, the Athenian Stranger knows, as Solamona does, that a noncommercial state has less need of others (*Laws* xii.949e). Therefore, "doubting novelties, and commixture of manners" because a good city "might be a thousand ways altered to the worse, but scarce any one way to the better" (144; *Laws* 949e–950a), the Athenian recommends restrictions on contact with strangers that are strict if less strict than Solamona's (949e–950d). Still, contact with strangers exists for both societies, and its two main consequences are the same in Magnesia as in Bensalem: a sense of superior morals and a means of acquiring the useful. The Athenian permits groups of selected citizens to participate in the games conducted at the oracles and when they return, these groups "teach the young that the legal customs . . . of the others are in second place": however the Magnesians fare in other contests they always return with the report that they won the laurel for virtue. The Merchants of Light perform the same function if in a different way, for Joabin relates the zeal with which Bensalemites compare their own chaste sexual practices with those of Europeans. But no Bensalemites except a very few Merchants of Light have ever seen a European: they have been taught to scorn these strangers as moral inferiors and elevate themselves as supremely virtuous. No wonder they bridle themselves "in so civil a fashion" when some of these sexual degenerates actually appear in their midst (132–33).

In addition to the groups of travelers, Plato's Magnesia recognizes that "certain citizens desire to observe the affairs of other human beings at greater leisure" (951a). Such citizens are "spectators" who seek out "certain divine human beings—not many—whose intercourse is altogether worthwhile" and who appear as frequently in bad regimes as in good. These individual spectators, like the divine ones they seek out, are concerned not simply with legal customs but with their foundations (951c), for they are the few philosophers. Such a traveler reports back to the ruling council both what he has found and what he has thought out for himself (952b). The Athenian thus acknowledges that the founding laws are not by themselves simply sufficient and unalterable but that they are open to alteration and supplement by what these wise travelers discover and think out. Solamona too seems to have adopted this measure for this reason: though the pious loyalist thinks the Merchants of Light search especially for "sciences, arts, manufactures, and inventions of all the world" (146), the tale he tells makes it apparent that they sought out and introduced a new civil religion as well, his own.

The second measure, the ruling council, confronts a fundamental difficulty, the final, obscure topic of the *Laws* after the legislation proper has been completed: "the perfect and permanent safeguard" for what has been founded that will ensure its faithful transmission.[11] That perfect and permanent safeguard requires that even the foundational laws be open to alteration, for "what almost amounts to a prohibition against change" acknowledges the necessity of change under certain circumstances.[12] Thus, when the Athenian lists the membership of the Nocturnal Council a second time (961a–b; see 951a–952b), the returned travelers replace the Supervisors of Education. Education on the foundational matters belongs to those returned travelers who are—as the Athenian suggests when he mentions the constitution of the Nocturnal Council a third time[13]—"the interpreters, teachers, and lawgivers, the guardians of the others" (964b). The returned travelers are the piloting intellects whose inquiry includes the idea of virtue, the noble and the good, and the gods, this last topic being the highest inquiry which investigates the soul and the stars without falling into atheism. The returned travelers, the very few philosophers, are therefore the true guardians of the law and the only ones properly designated by the term *Nocturnal Council;* the other council members, those piloted by them, are now referred to simply as "the Council."[14] Future piloting by these intellects cannot be set out in the founding legislation because that legislation must have the aura of the unalterable and also because the times within which these future guardians will find themselves and the measures for those times cannot be determined in advance. Nevertheless, there are preparations that can be made and the Athenian undertakes to assist in those preparations. Thus they set up the "divine council" to which they hand over the city (969b).

King Solamona can be seen to have followed Plato in setting up a new "divine council," the thirty-six Fathers of Salomon's House supplanting the thirty-seven Guardians of the Law (752e). This new divine council consists of those who most excel in Bensalemite virtue: service to the

---

11. The interpretation of the last topic of the *Laws* is derived from Strauss, *Argument and Action of Plato's Laws,* 169–86.

12. Ibid., 177.

13. Ibid., 181.

14. Ibid., 184–85.

common good through the technological mastery of nature. They are accorded virtually divine honors as befits the authors of inventions in the judgment of former ages (*NO* I.129). The institutionalized inventor, the tamed Daedalus who is the Father of Salomon's House, shows in his speech that they have imitated the thunderbolt and are therefore worthy of the honors once accorded Zeus, the singular keeper of the thunderbolt alleged by the ancients to be inimitable. In Plato's *Critias,* the gods gather at the end to hear Zeus's speech on why Atlantis must be punished for its fall away from its original godly ways, a fall into human pride which challenges the gods. But Zeus does not speak. *Critias* is a work unfinished. Before *New Atlantis* ends, before this "work unfinished" modeled on *Critias* ends, a long speech is given to an audience of one, a speech which could be heard as the speech of the new Zeus, representative of the collective possessors of the thunderbolt, and in his speech he gives the reasons why Bensalem has not been punished but blessed. The incomplete *New Atlantis* is relatively more complete than the incomplete *Critias* on which it is modeled.[15]

Possessing Zeus's thunderbolt, the new Atlantians are spared Zeus's judgment, and its leaders receive the honor once accorded him. The actual forms of the honor accorded the Father seem to merge the biblical and the Greek. On the Ark of the Covenant containing the tablets of the law stood two gold cherubins with wings displayed; on the chariot containing the Father of Salomon's House stand one gold cherub with wings displayed and one gold sun "upon the top, in the midst," perhaps the sun that in the *Laws* is given such prominence in the celebration of the Auditors, the judges of the judges who are accorded highest honors (945b–948b)—the Greek or pagan sun thus taking precedence over the biblical cherub.[16] These "Fathers" are high priests of a new religion that

15. See White, *Peace among the Willows,* 112–34; Weinberger, "Introduction," xiv–xv.

16. Did Bacon know Maimonides's explanation (*The Guide of the Perplexed,* 577) concerning why there were two Cherubins rather than one? It occurs in the context of an account of how the multitude are made to think of authority, especially the authority of the law. Belief in law's authority depends on a prior belief in prophecy which in turn depends on a prior belief in the existence of angels which rests on the fundamental belief in the existence of God. God commanded that two angels be placed over the ark in order to fortify the belief in the existence of a multitude of angels. One cherub instead of two would have had the consequence of misleading the multitude in a specific way: they might have taken one cherub to be the image of the deity itself and so become idolaters. Display of a single cherub to the multitude of Bensalem could encourage a kind of idolatry, a belief that could focus on the scientist himself as the angel of God who brings the law the people are pleased to obey.

has captured the hearts and minds of the Bensalemites. As will be seen, Bacon is acutely aware that the battle for the new science will have to be fought on the level of religion, though not—at any costs—over the issue of religion.

In reconstituting the divine counsel, wise Solamona handed the city over to envious lovers of honor suspected and feared by the ancients. But he did not give them free rein, for he knows the ultimate secret of government tended by Plato and made most accessible in the *Republic,* the secret rule of the wise or the philosopher. Plato had argued that the philosopher has no desire to rule as king and that the people could never be persuaded to compel him to become their king (*Republic* vii.519c–520d; vi.494a). But even though it is impossible and undesirable that the philosopher rule in the way of the king, Plato shows how the philosopher rules in his own piloting way through the establishment of a new fundamental good; he rules in the way Socrates came to rule Glaucon and Adeimantus, by an art of persuasion that led them to believe again in the worthiness of virtue. In the *Republic,* their belief in virtue is made possible by a series of deepening accounts that first ties virtue to the good of the city, then grounds virtue in ideas and in the idea of the good, and finally reinforces virtue with watchful gods and immortal souls. In similar persuasive ways the philosopher in the *Laws* comes to rule the lawgivers responsible for Magnesia's laws. The philosopher rules by providing the actual rulers what they cannot provide for themselves, the purportedly ultimate or sacred standards that they apply to the particulars they are called upon to decide. The marvelous irony at the end of the *Laws* thus becomes clear: Megillos comes to life to compel the Athenian Stranger to stay in order to provide the perfect and permanent safeguard of the laws—one of the two conditions of the philosopher's rule is thus fulfilled. Will the Athenian philosopher let himself be compelled? Not only would it be against his desire, he has already done everything that can be done regarding what they want to compel him to do. He is the Nocturnal Counselor who instructs the counselors; he rules the rulers in the way befitting a Platonic philosopher and he can go.

The secret of government that philosophers are "commanders and legislators" is present throughout Bacon's work. The philosopher, that fortunate traveler who proceeds on his own solitary way, rules the counselors by providing the goal or the good that informs all their deliberations. The "genuine philosopher" rules as the inventor of values around which the world inaudibly revolves.

King Solamona is the founding legislator of Bensalem who invents and introduces the charitable science of nature three centuries before his successors introduce the charitable religion of Christianity. There is no need to harp on the obvious parallel of King Solamona and Francis Bacon except to call attention again to the one basic matter. Plato, the philosopher who instructed Solamona, instructed Bacon, and Bacon's need to distance himself from that instructor can itself be understood as obedience to his instruction. But to understand more clearly Francis Bacon's place in post-Platonic history we must look to Joabin, a wise and politic man who finds himself in the polity established by Solamona.

Joabin

Are there [genuine] philosophers today? Must *there not be such philosophers?*
—Nietzsche (BGE 211)

Wise Solamona laid the foundations of a stable society pursuing the mastery of nature for the relief of the human estate and ruled by the lovers of honor most driven by the most importunate and continual passion, envy. But has Solamona made provision for those few, very few, driven by the highest passion, an eros for wisdom? Has Solamona made provision for Joabin?

Joabin is the only contemporary given a name rather than a title derived from his office. His private dialogue with the narrator seems to concern only customs regarding the sexual passion and what the Bensalemites (or as Joabin always says, "they") believe about those customs. They pride themselves on their superior virtue in controlling the passions and this pride grounds their self-respect which is, "next religion," as Joabin says, "the chiefest bridle of all vices." But the private dialogue of the wise makes it possible to learn the truth about Bensalem hidden behind its superior virtue—the truth about their policy as well as their passions.

Bensalemite hospitality, that marriage of humanity and policy with respect to strangers that seemed all humanity when told by the Governor, is in fact all policy, including the politic mask of humanity. The truth comes to light in allusions Joabin and the narrator make to the Bible, incomplete allusions befitting men who do not have to spell everything out to each other. Joabin alludes to "Lot's offer," and the narrator to what Elijah said to the widow of Sarepta. As Jerry Weinberger has shown, when one reflects on what Lot's offer actually was—an offer of virgin daughters for the good of strangers—and what the narrator leaves out of his citation—the words of the widow, "and kill my son" [17]—it becomes clear that the hospitable Bensalemites offer their virgin daughters for the good of the strangers but if that offer is spurned and the strangers desire to return home, policy dictates that they be killed under the guise of return. The unlucky thirteen taken home "in our bottoms," according to the Governor-priest, are in fact killed. That fate had already been obvious in the words of the credulous priest: "But you must think," says the priest, "whatsoever they have said could be taken where they came but for a dream" (145). On the contrary, we must think that tales told of a secret and advanced civilization by sailors who had been there and who could tell exactly what it was and where it was would be most readily believed. And we must think that wise Solamona would know it and would not have entrusted Bensalem's secrecy to anything so transparently foolish as confidence in people's skepticism.

Joabin and the narrator also make it possible to see the truth about Bensalemite passions, control of which grounds their pride. Joabin's final allusion to the Bible opens a new perspective on this theme, for, as Weinberger has also shown, Joabin's account of the Adam and Eve pools alludes to an instance not of controlled but of uncontrolled sexual passion, one in which Joabin's namesake Joab played a decisive role: David viewed Bathsheba bathing naked and took her for himself after having Joab see to the murder of her husband, Uriah.[18] In this reference Joabin most clearly touches Joab and forces the reader to ask why Bacon names the wise and politic man of Bensalem Joabin, or "Joabs." As King David's most trusted and ruthless captain, Joab committed the crime that enabled David to satisfy his passion for Bathsheba and continue the royal line. For David married Bathsheba and after their first-born son (conceived in David's illicit passion) was taken as an offering to God's anger, Bathsheba bore him Solomon, David's successor. Joabin's allusion thus brings into view a whole constellation crucial for understanding New Atlantis: the biblical House of David compared to the Bensalemite House of Solamona. How has Bacon's Solamona achieved what the biblical David could not, secure rule wisely guided over centuries of stable governance?

In pointing to Joab, Joabin may seem to point to a ruthless minister of terror indispensable to prudent rule, for his dialogue with the nar-

17. Genesis 19:1–11 and I Kings 17:18; Weinberger, "Introduction," xxv–xxvii.
18. II Samuel 11–12; Weinberger, "Introduction," xxvii–xxix.

rator makes clear the connection between prudence and ruthlessness in Bensalem. But that Joab is in fact much more than this can be seen even in his act of having Uriah killed: that ruthless deed was not undertaken on behalf of prudent rule, but on behalf of imprudent and impassioned rule. What was Joab's role with respect to the ruler David? Consideration of all his deeds as David's general makes Joab appear much closer to a prudent counselor and independent actor who succeeded in tempering the imprudent and passionate rule of David, sometimes through ruthless deeds, sometimes through refusing them. What comes to light from consideration of all Joab's deeds in fact puts the focus on David: here is a ruler ruled by private passion to the peril of his kingdom, a ruler in need of being curbed by someone like Joab, or someone still more prudent.

But Joab, who provided at least some prudent curbs on the impassioned rule of David, was killed by Solomon at the instigation of his dying father, and, as king, Solomon did not think he needed counsel because he thought himself wise. Solomon is presented as the wisest man in the Bible, a view of himself he promulgated. But *New Atlantis* with its tacit Platonic standard provides a startlingly different perspective on Solomon. When judged by the Platonic standards of Solamona, the wisest man in the Bible is foolish: rather than cut off contact with foreigners he enlarged contact and flaunted his riches, making his kingdom vulnerable to the envy of his neighbors; rather than make chastity an honorable end he flaunted his seven hundred wives and his three hundred concubines arousing the passionate instincts of his own people; he built a temple to God while leaving unbuilt the temple Solamona had to allege that Solomon intended to build, the temple to science; and he killed Joab. For the sake of a few years of personal and national splendor, foolish Solomon sold his people's well-being and unity, leaving them no future stability but only a past to romanticize. Wise Solamona learned from Solomon's folly while preserving the fiction of his wisdom. By following a policy precisely opposed to Solomon's, Solamona secured the succession in his kingdom and enabled his people to prosper and achieve a future that outstripped even the myths of their own noble past. Solamona seems invented by Bacon in part to measure Solomon and not to honor him, to measure what passes for wisdom in the Bible with a wisdom derived from Plato. In other writings too, Bacon employs Solomon as his ostensible guide while actually taking his guidance from philosophy; as James Stephens states with respect to Bacon's account of rhetoric: "It is typical of [Bacon's] ethos that these practical rules [of rhetoric] are associated with the Christian figure Solomon rather than the 'anti-Christ' [Aristotle] who is his real source."[19] Feigned allegiance to Jerusalem veils actual allegiance to Athens.

The problem of rule is not the ruthless Joabs but the passionate Davids and the foolish Solomons, one favored with tempering counsel, the other thinking himself above it. But in the stable dispensation established by Solamona the Joabs or Joabin are faced not with a David or a Solomon but with collective rule by the Fathers of Salomon's House, the apparent heirs of the wise Solamona who rule for the common good made co-incident with their own. Can these rulers dispense with guidance? Have wise counselors become superfluous in the Solamonaic age?

It is evident on the surface of *New Atlantis* that Joabin is a wise observer who knows the truth. But reflection on the biblical and Platonic parallels that are beginning to become evident makes it apparent that he is more, that he is an observer who acts, a worthy heir to Joab in a kingdom heir to wise Solamona rather than foolish Solomon. The very name Joabin for the wise man in the Solamonaic kingdom suggests that rather than kill Joab, Solamona found a way to tie the Joabs to Salomon's House. Not the biblical but the Platonic parallel, the *Laws,* helps explain Joabin's role, as it helped explain Solamona's. Joabin is said to be a "merchant," a word in Bacon's time used almost exclusively for those engaged in *foreign* trade. But Bensalem has no foreign trade—except in "light" and that trade is undertaken by merchants, Merchants of Light. Joabin seems to have traveled widely for he is acquainted with the customs of the world, and although the narrative must seem to base his knowledge on books only, his wisdom and his actions suggest that Joabin, who says he has read the *Laws,* is one of those special travelers in Plato's *Laws,* one of those who has gone on "observation missions" and sought out "cer-tain divine human beings—not many—whose intercourse is altogether worthwhile" (*Laws* 951a–c). In the *Laws,* such a returned traveler is treated by the ruling council to which he reports as if he were corrupted by his travels, corrupted into wisdom (952c), whereupon he is to live a private life and not claim to be wise. The returned traveler, now a wise spectator in his own land, has knowledge that carries him beyond the ruling council, but he remains loyal to the noble and necessary beliefs that are regarded as themselves the foundation by the ruling council. Just so, Joabin remains loyal to the beliefs of Bensalem, desiring that it be be-lieved that Bensalem had sacred origins, and making no end of praising it. There are necessary restrictions on such knowers, but they are per-

19. Stephens, *Francis Bacon,* 50; see the chapter, "The Debt to Aristotle," 36–54.

mitted to have contact with strangers if they do not become busybodies concerning education and the laws (952d). Just so, Joabin leads a private life but is permitted contact with the stranger who is the wise narrator. Joabin's praise of Bensalemite belief is worded in such a way as to allow that stranger to learn the truth about Bensalemite virtue and the merit of its mix of tradition and innovation. And the narrator himself? He seems to be one of those rarest of strangers described by the Athenian Stranger as the counterpart of Magnesia's solitary travelers: a visitor to Magnesia worthy of witnessing what it normally keeps secret, both its wisdom and its wealth (953c–d). In the private conversations between Joabin and the narrator, one Platonic stranger learns from another Platonic stranger the secrets of a Platonic society wisely founded and wisely guarded.

If *New Atlantis* is in this way modeled on Plato's *Laws,* Joabin is one of those wise men whose future role could not be set out by the Athenian legislator but whose participation in governance is the sole possible guarantee of a "complete and lasting safeguard" (*Laws* 960b), one of those Nocturnal Counselors to whom the legislator handed over the city while seeming to hand it over to the Council as such, one of those entrusted with fundamental changes the character of which could not be anticipated by the founding legislator. It is to the Joabin that Solamona entrusted fundamental change in Bensalem. Solamona's Bensalem follows Plato's Magnesia in feigning to spurn innovation while being open to innovation by wise successors, the necessities of whose times the founding legislator could not know. The two fundamental, post-Solamona innovations recounted in *New Atlantis* demonstrate this: the introduction of Christianity and the revoking of the laws of secrecy. These deeds bespeak a combination of wisdom and power that cannot be attributed to the thirty-six Daedaluses. These deeds bespeak the effective presence of Solamona's like.

Christianity has apparently been introduced by one of those special travelers, a Merchant of Light, who saw to it that a novel and foreign religion of a just God tending immortal souls appear in Bensalem under the cover of the appropriate divine signs. Such a religion is, in Nietzsche's words, "a Platonism for the people" that makes universal and more terrible Plato's own religious Platonism for the people, the just gods and immortal souls whose utility to public life after the old gods are dead is made apparent in the ministering poetry of Book Ten of the *Republic.* Joabin's conversation helps to explain the rationale of the momentous event which changed Bensalem's "religion, the thing that has most power over men's minds" (*NO* I.89). This new religion of hope controls the private passions for the public good—especially the sexual passion, the passion that eventually destroyed the civil realm brought into being by Orpheus's ordering music. The new religion thus takes special pains to remedy the second of the two failures of Orpheus, the ancient who may pass "for philosophy personified." Though "wonderful and plainly divine," Orpheus failed in both branches of philosophy, first in "natural philosophy" and second in "moral and civil philosophy" to which he turned in sadness after his first failure (*WA* "Orpheus").

The whole of the single reported conversation between Joabin and the narrator concerns domestication of the sexual passion which makes men burn with complete madness (*Laws* vi.783a). The conversation is initiated by the narrator's curiosity about the marriage customs—the narrator did not himself attend the Feast of the Family but asked the wise man to relate its significance. Joabin's response reveals the degree to which Bensalem is successful in forcing private passions to serve public interests. Plato's solution is called to mind by Joabin's allusion to the practice recommended in the *Laws* of having public nakedness serve private marriage choices: Plato aimed to render public and open what is characteristically private—nakedness, mating, and child-rearing. The Bensalemite solution as related by Joabin reverses the procedure of the *Laws*. Instead of making the private as public as possible, it allows the public to enter the private through the medium of conscience. Privacy can be more extensive in Bensalem than in Magnesia because privacy is compromised by an unseen seer from whom nothing can be hidden—an ambiguous power which one can interpret as divine or demonic (140). Two italicized sentences in Joabin's speech record Bensalemite sayings on how the sexual passion is bridled: by religion and by reverence for oneself. The innovation introducing Christianity introduced an all-seeing and just God to whom the most private is fully visible and who rewards or punishes the immortal soul on the basis of all its deeds, including its most private thoughts. The injunction "that no one, male or female, should ever be without a ruler" (*Laws* xii.942a) is in this way realized without it being necessary that "everyone should in every respect live always in a group" (942c). Even the individual alone is now a group. "Religion being the chief band of society" (*Essays,* "Of Unity in Religion"), a post-Solamona wise man introduced a foreign religion based on inward beliefs rather than rites and ceremonies and carrying the most stringent standards of public decency into the no longer secret places of heart and mind. Body and mind are no longer, strictly speaking, one's own.

It is, however, not religion itself but the most important bridle "next religion" which Joabin emphasizes as the means to control the sexual passion: reverence for oneself. This reverence, the dictates of that seemingly most private possession, one's own conscience, internalizes an external standard of pride and shame. Through the developed conscience, public restraints are privately exercised. Should Joabin actually mean by "next religion" *the* next religion, he could be alluding to a historic step in the genealogy of morals whereby religion is seen progressively as a stage in the process of making humankind civil, and the development of conscience—that fundamental Nietzschean theme—could here be portrayed in that step through which it outgrows its dependence on external agency, God's agency. Bensalemites would have advanced to the exercise of self-control out of their own power to be decent, with God's status as an observer maintained as a courtesy. However that may be, Joabin presents the people's reverence for themselves as requiring collective admiration for their own exaggerated virtues and collective contempt for the exaggerated vices of others. For the Bensalemites, those others include Europeans whom they are taught to think of as dissolute, their own image of "the Spirit of Fornication" (152). The public enters the most private activities in the form of a collective image of what befits a Bensalemite, the internalized spirit of the fathers whose paternal authority comes to seem like nature itself (148). Nature tamed by religion and custom can thus come to seem like nature itself presiding—as the narrator indicates in the words that open his dialogue with Joabin (151).[20]

The House of Solamona thus introduced of its own accord the religion which rent the House of David, the religion of Jesus which presents itself as the spiritual heir to the temporal kingdom lost by the successors of David and Solomon. Introduction of moderated Christianity as the civil religion of Bensalem extends the wise governance of Solamona in a way shown by the *Essays:* "the part of Epimetheus might well become Prometheus"—hopes retained by the improvident brother who has not learned what to wish can be put to good use by the brother with foresight. Christian hopes, vain hopes, the hopes of an Epimetheus supplement the material hopes introduced by Solamona's science; wise government is thus able to "hold men's hearts by hopes" (*Essays* "Of Seditions and Troubles"). Domestication of the sexual passion tames Dionysos by incorporating Dionysos, his ivy and his grape, into a bound fruitfulness that serves a foreign God and the Bensalemite state. The

---

20. The conversation with Joabin on taming nature occurs in the seventeenth paragraph, and in Pythagorean number symbolism, seventeen is the number for nature.

Bacchanalian women, whose horn of Dionysos drowned out Orpheus's finer, gentler music and led to his demise, are brought under control by the new Orpheus.[21] A foreign Platonism for the people supplants Plato's failed Platonism for the people. By managing hopes and giving evidence of their fulfillment, Bensalem ensures its own hope of longevity, its own hope of mastery over the natural decay of societies.

Bacon's fable presents history inverted. Solamona's charitable science, which came to political and spiritual authority during three centuries of benevolent rule, introduces the charitable religion of Christianity. Why has Bacon inverted the actual historical succession of charitable religion and charitable science? With this question of the precedence of science over religion we arrive at what seems to me the core of Bacon's program for rule. It is quite obviously a matter not fit to utter, too delicate to address openly, too important to be left unaddressed. For a complete and satisfying answer to this question, one "abortive and posthumous" work of political philosophy, *New Atlantis*, needs to be supplemented by the other, *An Advertisement Touching an Holy War*. What is suggested in *New Atlantis* is confirmed in *Holy War*, whose whole point, it seems to me, is to provide the argument that charitable religion must now be brought under the control of charitable science. Here is a theme most congenial to a Nietzschean history of philosophy: the warfare of modern times between philosophy and religion seen at its very beginnings in the monumental aims of a genuine philosopher. *New Atlantis* and *Holy War* show how philosophy planned to establish its rule over religion after society had "paid dearly and terribly" because religion had insisted on having its own sovereign way over philosophy (*BGE* 62).[22]

Bacon's historical inversion in *New Atlantis* suggests an inversion in authority: charitable science can introduce charitable religion without fear of falling captive to it, without fear of duplicating the actual rule

21. Perhaps the unseen and unacknowledged presence of the mother at the festival celebrating the father for what was at least equally her doing indicates the continued presence of a nature thought tamed by the males. The mother's observation of these male rites, which include Dionysian symbolism, could be seen as a pale reversal of the crime of Pentheus.

22. Jerry Weinberger's rewarding study of the *Advancement of Learning* is particularly helpful on this crucial aspect of Bacon's work, his reasonable opposition to Christianity. "Bacon's impiety is enormous," Weinberger says (*Science, Faith, and Politics*, 99), and he shows just how deep that impiety goes: how Christianity altered the world philosophy occupies, how Bacon took his bearings from standards first arrived at by Plato and Aristotle, how the technological mastery of nature arose as a strategic endeavor on behalf of philosophy. "In the age of ferocious Christian charity, the best that Bacon can do is to turn its avarice against nature rather than against men" (143).

of religion over philosophy characteristic of Bacon's times according to *Holy War,* times in which Christianity had subverted Aristotle and taken the whole of philosophy captive. If Bacon's inversion of the historic order of Baconian science and Christian religion is an argument for the re-establishment of the rule of philosophy over religion, perhaps it can help explain the date of the most crucial event in Bensalem's history, the reign of King Solamona. The date of Solamona's reign is said to be "about nineteen hundred years ago" or around 288 B.C.E. according to the reasonable chronology established by Howard White.[23] This date of his reign would put the date of his birth roughly contemporary with Aristotle's death in 322 B.C.E. The birth of the philosopher of Bensalem who carries forward the natural science already well begun by pre-Aristotelian Greeks would then correspond roughly to the death of the philosopher who "did not think he could reign secure until he had slain his brothers" and whose fratricides could seem to have cost the West its heritage in natural science, a deed that makes him in a way "the Prince of imposture, the Anti-Christ" (*PFB* 110, 112–13; *Advancement, Works* III.352; *NO* I.63, 67). Solamona is born after the full legacy of Greek natural science has been secured and the political philosophies of Plato and Aristotle have instructed the wise. And he is born after Aristotle's scholar, Alexander, had carried Greek culture to a wider world. Solamona's Platonic laws of secrecy, promulgated at this point in the development of philosophy and when every maritime nation of the world is open to every other, ensure that Bensalem will follow a different course from the one fated for Europe by Alexander and by the subsequent empire of Rome. For Bacon argues (in an extended and crucial historical argument to be considered later), that *Rome* was ultimately responsible for the loss of the greatest treasures of Greek natural science because it could not forever thwart its rivals; Rome and not Aristotle cost the West its scientific heritage—the argument does not breathe a word about Christianity but surely implies it (*PFB* 113–14). Knowing both Plato and Aristotle, knowing the whole of Greek natural science, and knowing the course chosen by Aristotle's scholar, Solamona had the luxury of striking out on his own course as Plato's scholar: using the political wisdom of Plato and the natural science of the earlier Greeks, Solamona founded a new society by conscripting a novel aristocracy to manage it in a way that would both preserve philosophy and serve the well-being of the multitude. Bensalem would represent the fancied history of a Europe

23. White, *Peace among the Willows,* 121.

spared Europe's fall into Christianity, a Europe in which Baconianism became the reigning Platonism for the people, a Europe spared the periodic ebb and flood of science and learning that had condemned it, as Bacon said, to three brief periods of learning (*NO* I.78). Such a society would even be capable, eventually, of introducing a novel and useful religion without running the risk of having philosophy fall under the rule of religion, as had occurred, unforeseeably, with "Aristotle's incarceration" by Christianity.[24] Bensalem, distant home of the miraculous preservation of Greek wisdom, would itself be capable eventually of imperial rule, of returning to Europe to call it back to its Greek heritage and bring under philosophic control the religion that had insisted on having its own sovereign way.

But does not the very idea of universal charity spring from Christianity, thus making Bacon's historical inversion spiritually anachronistic? Bacon will go out of his way in *Holy War* to deny the Christian paternity of universal charity or philanthropy. Its roots are to be found in Greek philosophy. As Timothy Paterson has argued, Baconian science was established so much earlier than Christianity in Bensalem to show that it "must have roots quite independent of faith."[25]

Though it was necessary that charitable science be legitimated rhetorically by the charitable religion that already prevailed, Bacon aimed in fact to win control over it. As the argument of this book proceeds, the grounds for this claim will be augmented and extended, for not only will Bacon's *Holy War* state this historic necessity, Descartes will be seen to take up Bacon's campaign for precisely Bacon's reason, and Nietzsche will make the profound differences between Greek philosophy and biblical religion an open polemical theme. Nietzsche claimed that modern philosophy was covertly or overtly anti-Christian (*BGE* 54). Covertness can not be surprising in a campaign of this magnitude and gravity, and Bacon's covertness is merely the elementary prudence of not informing his victim of his plans of attack. Bacon did not have to learn from Machiavelli that an assailant does not say "Give me your gun, I want

---

24. Weinberger, *Science, Faith, and Politics*, 169.

25. Paterson, "On the Role of Christianity in the Political Philosophy of Francis Bacon," 419–42. Paterson's perceptive article gathers the arguments which show "that Bacon was indifferent and even hostile to Christianity" (419) and that Bacon's writings exhibit "a profound inner distance from Christianity" (441). His article performs an important service because "belief in the essentially Christian inspiration and intention of Baconian science is, in my opinion, the single greatest contemporary obstacle to understanding Bacon's . . . political philosophy as a whole" (421).

to kill you with it" but says at most "Give me your gun." Bacon does not even say that; he takes the gun without asking permission: charitable science that serves the common good of earthly well-being will displace in authority a charitable religion that serves some unseen future of immortal souls, and it will displace it through its own rival gospel or propaganda.

If Joabin's words make it possible to understand the great post-Solamona innovation that brought Christianity to Bensalem, Joabin's deeds make it possible to understand that other great post-Solamona innovation, revoking the hitherto fundamental laws of secrecy and bringing science to Europe. For Joabin seems to be responsible for this great innovation.

Joabin and Salomon's House are mysteriously related. Joabin is secretly informed of the pending arrival of the Father of Salomon's House whereupon he informs the narrator and arranges a place for the arrival to be viewed. He is given responsibility for entertaining the Father. He arranges for the whole company to meet the Father and for one of their number to hear his speech and receive permission to make Bensalem known to Europe. These actions must be interpreted in light of both biblical and Platonic precedents: Joab's ability to act for David's good irrespective of David's wishes, and the ability of the returned traveler or Nocturnal Counselor to determine the actions of the Council.

After viewing the spectacle of the Father's arrival in the company of the narrator—"after the show was past"—Joabin informs the narrator of his own responsibility to entertain the Father. His exact words (155) state a preference for attending the wise over entertaining the powerful, but his duty prevails over his preference. As the wise entertainer of the powerful, Joabin cannot be a mere spectator of the great events unfolding in his presence, some Epicurean viewing human events from a safe distance. His namesake, Joab, and his model, the Nocturnal Counselor, make such a role impossible, as does Bacon's repudiation of the Epicurean form of the contemplative life, for the Epicureans are a philosophical sect "inferior to the rest" (*Essays,* "Of Truth," "Of Love"; *Advancement, Works* III.420–23). Therefore, although the means are not exhibited in *New Atlantis,* it seems necessary to regard Joabin as responsible for that momentous change which breaks Solamona's policy of secrecy. But is it imaginable that the august Father of Salomon's House, in all his pride and arrogance, will accept advice on a fundamental matter from a Jewish merchant? It is if Joabin is a former Merchant of Light, known to the Father as one of his own company, a returned traveler retired to private life. And it is when the opening of the *Laws* is considered: Is it imaginable that an old Cretan and an old Spartan will accept advice on their fundamental legislation from an old Athenian, advice that alters their laws and introduces novelties and comes from a citizen of a city they must suspect as treacherous owing to old animosities and conflicts? It is if the Athenian knows how to win their confidence through his entertaining talk, an intoxicating mix of praise and blame that prepares old patriots for innovation and change. Joabin's act would be consistent with the Platonic model: an altering of the fundamental laws by a wise man whose place in the law-making process cannot be set out in advance.

But Joabin must not only rule the apparent rulers he must prepare the narrator. Joabin has sought out the narrator, not the narrator Joabin, as indicated by Bacon's repeated use of "again" when Joabin comes to the narrator (154, 155). He initiates the narrator into the secrets of Bensalem after he has learned that he can say to the narrator, "You have reason" (152). In the single reported conversation between the two, Joabin initiates the narrator overtly into the Bensalemite customs of marriage and covertly into Bensalemite secrets of rule, thus allowing the narrator to view the hidden secrets of "the virgin of the world," his odd name for fruitful Bensalem. Given the image of the Adam and Eve pools, one could say that Joabin allows the friend to view the virgin bride naked, knowing he will not betray that with which he is entrusted, knowing that the report he makes to Europe on the virgin bride will be silent on her hidden defects. In the image of a different fable, viewing the nakedness of the virgin of the world initiates the narrator into the crime of Acteon who viewed the virgin Diana bathing naked.[26] The narrator avoids Acteon's fate by the two discretions Bacon suggested in interpreting the Acteon fable: he will keep his new knowledge secret from the prince, and he will avoid giving his own servants any occasion to betray this knowledge to the prince—with both the Father of Salomon's House and his own fifty shipmates he will cover his dangerous knowledge with the piety of belief, desiring to have it believed that Bensalem is the model the rest of the world should follow.

Through their conversations, Joabin reveals to the narrator Bensalem's mastery of the natural passions; and through Joabin's arrangements the Father of Salomon's House reveals to the narrator Bensalem's mastery of nature as a whole. In these two ways Joabin sees to the narrator's education, enabling him, when he brings the Bensalemite teaching to

26. See White, *Peace among the Willows*, 184.

Europe, to avoid the two failures of Orpheus, that perfect symbol of philosophy who failed to control either the Dionysian passions or the infernal powers. Framed in the narrative by two fathers, one natural and one spiritual, whose secrets of mastery are known to him but not to them, and hiding his own knowledge in the conventionality of beliefs, Joabin sets out to become the teacher of the new Orpheus, the narrator cured of the defects of Orpheus and fit to bring to Europe the two "relations" (151, 166) he had heard, the new teaching that will remake Europe.

The last events that at first looked like accidents thus come to light as the consequence of design—the narrator's "falling into straight acquaintance with Joabin," the coming of the Father of Salomon's House, the narrator's private audience with him, and the publishing of the news of Bensalem now that the time has come. The final deed revokes a foundational law in the way said to be appropriate by the one who gives the foundational law in the *Laws*. In accord with the irreversibility (*Laws* 960d) naturally implanted in the laws by the original lawgiver, a change is introduced by the subsequent wise to accord with times that could not have been anticipated and therefore not legislated for. The wise Joabin sees to it that the wise narrator departs "as a friend leaving friends, honored with gifts and fitting honors" (953d). Joabin performs his deed in a way that honors Solamona. Just so, exactly so, has Bacon honored Plato.

Bacon and Unfinished Rule

The philosopher as we understand him will make use of religion for his project of cultivation and education.—Nietzsche (BGE 61)

Joabin and the narrator are not, as the Father of Salomon's House is, natures tamed, convicted by their own proper vanity into the pursuit of socially useful projects. Such natures seem to lack vanity: Solamona assimilates himself to Solomon, Joabin seems only a Jewish merchant, the narrator subjects himself to the paraded superiority of the Father of Salomon's House, ostensibly becoming his paid servant spreading his message.

What moves such men? Here for the first time we touch a fundamental issue for world-historical thinkers like Bacon, Descartes, and Nietzsche: what moves the philosopher to undertake his history-making labors? Why not just watch, just contemplate the amazing spectacle of human affairs on a transitory planet? Why take part and fight? Many have wanted to convict Francis Bacon of mere love of glory, passion to be immortalized in the minds of men as their benefactor. *New Atlantis* argues against that interpretation in the characterization of Solamona, Joabin, and the narrator, each embodying an element of Francis Bacon. And Descartes will indicate his agreement when speaking of what moves him in the final paragraph of his *Discourse on the Method*. Can we believe such protestations of modesty in the most immodest of men? It seems to me that we can, based on the psychology of the philosopher set out most clearly in Nietzsche's *Thus Spoke Zarathustra*, a fable relating the philosopher's self-discovery as the discovery of responsibility that falls to him unasked. Nietzsche's fable argues that the genuine philosopher acts out of a philanthropy that is a love of the highest in humanity, a love of reason or the logos. As Nietzsche put it in his first book, the contemplative man stands deeply moved at the gates of present and future, a witness to tremendous struggles and transitions; charmed by those struggles he must take part and fight (*BT* 15).

One must be skeptical about such a virtuous depiction of the philosopher and at every step Nietzsche invites skepticism. But skepticism may be tempered by the recognition that Bacon and Descartes claim a similar motive and by a further recognition they force on their students: this is the *Platonic* psychology of the philosopher. Platonic philosophy requires the philosopher's engagement in the affairs of the city: "You must go down," Plato says to the philosopher in the *Republic*. But why must the philosopher go down? Plato's reasons will be examined later;[27] they are substantially the same as those given by Bacon, Descartes, and Nietzsche. It is one of the core theses of this Nietzschean history of philosophy that the Nietzschean psychology of the philosopher is present in the works of the great philosophers as their own understanding of their actions. With respect to Bacon, a more complete account of this claim will be possible after examining *Holy War*.[28]

27. See the section, "The *Republic* and Responsibility," in chapter 5, pp. 127–32.

28. Interpreting Bacon's "psychology of past philosophers," Timothy Paterson merges the motives of scientist and philosopher in a way Bacon never does: "The case for the rule of scientists rests not on the assumption of any extraordinary benevolence of scientists *qua* scientists, but rather on an argument that the good of scientists requires of them a certain degree of attention to the good of society, and that the domination of nonscientists by scientists will be nobler, milder, and more compatible with the fundamental desires and interests of the ruled than are other forms of political or economic exploitation" (477–78). Paterson draws no distinction between the motives of the "mechanic" and the "philosopher," Daedalus and Orpheus. Bacon himself is seen as a Daedalus moved by love of fame. "The Secular Control of Scientific Power in the Political Philosophy of Francis Bacon," 457–80.

Any adequate interpretation of what moves the great philosophers must confront the problem of their masks, an omnipresent problem from Plato, who wrote only dialogues, to Nietzsche, who talked incessantly of masks. Bacon simply assumes that the philosopher's actions require mastery of the art of seeming. As wise men who know how to seem, Solamona, Joabin, and the narrator all seem to be less than they are. They possess the art described most luminously by Nietzsche, irony or courtesy, the art of appearing more stupid than they are (*BGE* 284). That art frequently employs fable, a device that allows philosophers to depict their heroic aims and motives without making themselves laughable. Bacon made the necessity of that art emphatic by putting it at the beginning, middle, and end of his book of fables, *Wisdom of the Ancients,* and he emphasized as well that that art takes a specific form in times dominated by Christianity.

"Cassandra, or Frankness of Speech," the opening fable, shows that a wise man must learn how to speak his potentially harmful truth in a way that will be believed: he must know where he is, that he is never in Plato's *Republic* or in any other "feigned commonwealth." Bacon knows where he is: in a world created and framed by Christian belief and now turned frenzied in the pursuit of belief. *Holy War* makes clear what must be done in the face of that frenzy, and "Diomedes, or Zeal" makes clear that the ancient world could never have fallen prey to it.

"Juno's Suitor, or Disgrace," the central fable, shows how a wise man will act now that the ancient world has been forever supplanted by new gods. In a Christian world the natural nobility which is philosophy is judged vain pride because all men are equal before God, all blighted irremediably by the common depravity. The naturally superior, even Jupiter himself, will find it wise to feign abjectness, to appear not as a bull or an eagle or a swan or a shower of gold, as he could and would in a world aroused by such spectacles, but as a wretched cuckoo. A wretched cuckoo will seem appealing to the new Juno taught to be aroused by the spectacle of abjectness. The philosopher dressed as wretched cuckoo presents himself as at the mercy of nature, bewildered, frightened, and half-dead, in order to sway the object of his suit, Juno who loves the pitiable. This central fable displays the necessity governing the writings of Francis Bacon. The times dictating his art are marked by a disorder unforeseen by the wise whose wisdom he inherits: the transcendence and eclipse of philosophy by a universal religion of pity. In the *Advancement of Learning* (*Works* III.281–82), Bacon gives three examples of the "morigeration" of philosophy or the subjection of the wise to the powerful, and in each case he approves the philosopher's defense of his subjection. Such stooping "may have some outward baseness," Bacon says, but "they are to be accounted submissions to the occasion and not to the person."[29] The wise man who aims to make a difference will follow the narrator in his first recorded speech to his fellow shipmates and practice an art of seeming; he will know how to seem to those schooled in the virtue of abjectness.

"The Sirens, or Pleasure," the final fable, touches with proper circumspection one final aspect of the philosopher's art of seeming. Solomon is accorded the courtesy of teaching the view present in philosophy from Democritus and Socrates to Nietzsche that philosophy is the highest and most intense pleasure, pursuable for itself and providing power to resist all the lower pleasures including the most dangerous, the counsels and flatteries of followers. Deaf to all such indulgences while attentive to a siren song inaudible to others, the philosopher will have to surpass Odysseus to become a new Orpheus. Instead of stopping his friends' ears with wax, he fills their ears with a new song that reorders civil society to his own music. Instead of needing to be strapped to the mast, he partakes of the pleasures of philosophy which exceed the pleasures of the senses not only in power but also in sweetness. This is what Francis Bacon hides. For all his trumpeting of ambitions as the one who rings the bell to call the wits together, he veils his most far-reaching ambition to be the philosophic lawgiver of a new religion that will supplant the old. For this, it seems to me, is the meaning of the final deed in *New Atlantis:* to bring news of Bensalem to Europe is to subvert Europe's religion in its time of crisis.

With the rescinding of Solamona's fundamental law of secrecy, the narrator is given leave to make Bensalem known to the world and set Europe on the path to a new future. New Atlantis does not, like old Atlantis, itself set sail to conquer the world. Its conquest of the world exhibits what the House of Solomona has learned from the House of David: it sends not arms but emissaries, missionaries who have glimpsed it.[30] Bensalem itself remains "in God's bosom." The New Testament puts Jesus in God's bosom and magnifies Jesus as the one who reveals the un-

29. See Weinberger, *Science, Faith, and Politics,* 146.

30. When the Father assigns the narrator and the others a large bounty to perform this task, it is not, as Weinberger has argued ("Introduction," xiv), an instance of Bensalem's excess. Those paid the bounty are the workers given the responsibility to tell the world of Bensalem. A glimpse of Bensalem, while a kind of bounty, is not payment for a labor performed. They are paid not for receiving the message but for spreading it—once paid.

seen God: "No man hath seen God at any time; the only begotten Son, which is in the bosom of the Father, he hath declared him" (John 1:18). By invoking this passage in the very last words spoken by the Father of Salomon's House, Bacon quietly suggests that what now goes forth from God's bosom is a new way of salvation, the way of Bensalem, "the perfect son." [31] Jesus, formerly regarded as the perfect son (Hebrews 2:10, 5:8–9), now stands revealed as an imperfect son bringing an imperfect redemption. If the perfect son remains a land unknown, in God's bosom, new apostles go forth with the new universal redemption, the gospel of Bensalem which subverts the gospel of Jesus.

The new unarmed prophet directs the science of Bensalem to be disseminated throughout the world by its missionaries as Christianity had been. And the true order of rank between these two powers is suggested in a subtle manner by what Joabin "would tell" of Jesus: how God made Jesus ruler of the Seraphim, the angels of love given first place in the hierarchy of angels by Pseudo-Dionysius, second place going to the Cherubin, angels of light (*Advancement, Works* III.296). But Bensalem reorders the ranks of angels, light taking precedence over love while wrapping itself in love. Jesus is free to rule the Seraphim if Bensalem rules the Cherubin. As symbols of Bensalem, the Cherubin stand with wings hanging downwards, as if at rest (130), as if they no longer need to guard Eden with outstretched wings against intruders from east of Eden. The new religion masters the old religion by adopting and improving on its measures. It adopts the message of Christianity but gives it a new focus as earthly good effected by the mastery of nature. It adopts the universal character of Christianity, for if it springs from a single chosen people, it now makes its salvation available to all. And it adopts the means of Christianity, a message of salvation spread by believers who have glimpsed its promise for themselves. Like its predecessor, it offers everything to everyone for almost nothing, for belief in a land unknown. In this way religion passes into the care of philosophy; Baconianism supplants Christianity by making its promises worldly. [32]

In Bensalem, Christianity is clearly subdued by science. Although

---

31. See White, *Peace among the Willows,* 152–53.

32. Frances Yates, in her fascinating and useful studies linking the occult and early modern science, draws the conclusion that Bensalem is governed by a Rosicrucian Brotherhood whom she identifies with the "priest-scientists" of Salomon's House (*Rosicrucian Enlightenment,* 118–29, and *Giordano Bruno,* 450). While the parallels she notes may well prove that Bacon knew the Rosencreutz story, they do not, I think, require the conclusion that Bensalem is ruled by a Rosicrucian brotherhood. Yates's interpretation of a number of parallels seems to me forced into the service of her thesis: the Governor of Strangers' House who wears the red cross is not one of "the governors of the country" and the priest-

religion plays an important role in bridling the passions, science commands the highest symbols of social life. But science succeeds in subduing Christianity because it represents a set of beliefs that are themselves best viewed as religious. As befits "a land unknown," they are unconfirmable beliefs, based on authority, regarding questions of the ultimate meaning of human life. They accord with the definition of Christian belief Bacon offers in *The Characters of a Believing Christian:* "A Christian is one who believes things his reason cannot comprehend; he hopes for things which neither he nor any man alive ever saw; he labours for that which he knoweth he shall never obtain; yet, in the issue his belief appears not to be false; his hope makes him not ashamed; his labour is not in vain" (*Works* VII.292). The major tenets of the new faith adjust the traditional teaching on God and the soul: in place of belief in God and dependence on God as all-efficacious, Baconianism fosters belief in man's own capacity to master nature or even the whole universe; in place of careful tending of the immortal soul, Baconianism fosters belief in man's capacity to engineer the longevity of the body.

New Atlantis, a popular fiction depicting a future society living the Baconian religion, is one of the most important tracts for the new faith. It is a city set on a hill as the light of the world, the inspiring model of what is possible for a society committed to "enlarging the bounds of human empire" (156). Such enlargement requires active belief in the human capacity to master nature, a capacity exhibited by the listing of "we haves" indulged in by the proud Father. (Bacon's own perspective on the list may be gained from a comment published with the *New Organon* in 1620: "I care little about the mechanical arts, only about those things which they contribute to the equipment of philosophy" [*Works* IV.271].)[33] In addition, Baconian religion requires belief that the ebb

---

scientists who are wear no such cross; Bensalemites refuse payment for their service to the sick not because they oppose being paid for such service but because they oppose being "twice paid"; dress with no distinguishing mark is worn only abroad by the Merchants of Light while the officials of Bensalem are distinguished by their dress; the cherubins' wings which she regards as symbolic of the Rosicrucian sign, "Under the Shadow of Jehova's Wings," have wings pointing downwards in Bensalem and not outwards as in Rosicrucian emblems, and wings pointing downwards cast no shadow. If there is a Rosicrucian symbolism present, it seems to point not to secret rule by Rosicrucians but much rather to what the Rosicrucian movement itself served according to Yates's account: a freer Europe achieved by manipulation of the more or less tyrannical participants in the current religious warfare by those not themselves religious zealots (*Rosicrucian Enlightenment,* 25). Here as elsewhere, Yates's writings have the unfortunate consequence of assimilating Bacon to the intellectual currents he mimicked in order to subvert.

33. A contemporary assessment of the devices of the House of Salomon, and of the

and flow of science and learning in history is merely accidental and that history can be continuously, linearly progressive as Bensalem's history has been.

Baconian religion thus requires new beliefs regarding being and time: faith in the malleability of nature by man and faith in the linearity of time from primitive beginnings to a perfect end. For the inculcation of these beliefs, *New Atlantis* forms one important piece of the Baconian program set forth in the *New Organon* as the reconstitution of hope. In the *New Organon* itself (I.92–114) a major part of Bacon's rhetorical effort aims to give a reason for that hope. Without hope the rest of his scientific program "tends rather to make men sad (by giving them a worse and meaner opinion of things as they are than they now have, and making them more fully to feel and know the unhappiness of their own condition)" (*NO* I.92). How can a society welcome what saddens or pursue actively what Nietzsche called "the deadly truths"? By being taught new hopes, Bacon seems to answer, a new faith in things unseen that gives human beings a new sense of what to wish (*PFB* 96).

The new religion of scientific technology is bound to come into conflict with the old religion it imitates in order to supersede. While feigning religious harmony, *New Atlantis* necessarily initiates holy war, the spiritual warfare that became the actual warfare of modern times between two great camps of believers. Why incite Europe to holy war? Why turn the engines of Bensalem against Europe? It seems to me that Bacon regarded this as a most important issue and that he took great pains to justify his warfare in a little writing whose complexity and depth matches *New Atlantis, An Advertisement Touching an Holy War.*

---

whole culture of Baconian science, can be found in Klug, "Lab Animals, Francis Bacon and the Culture of Science," 54–72, where Bacon is arraigned for the crimes of modern science against nature. From this important perspective Bacon is to some degree recovering his reputation—but as the one to blame. See also Merchant, *Death of Nature,* 164–90; Leiss, *Domination of Nature,* 45–71. Such assessments of Bacon and the scientific-technological enterprise he helped set in motion are, in my opinion, timely and valuable, but are best made from the perspective of Nietzsche's comprehensive reevaluation of modern times. Rebukes for our flagging Baconianism are voiced by Dewey, *Reconstruction in Philosophy,* v–xli and Medawar, "On 'the Effecting of All Things Possible,'" 119–38.

Chapter 4

Why Incite a Holy War?

One always pays dearly and terribly when religions do not want to be a means of education and cultivation in the philosopher's hand but insist on having their own sovereign way. —*Nietzsche* (BGE 62)

Bacon's *Advertisement Touching an Holy War* is, to say the least, odd. The only dialogue in the Baconian corpus, it presents six characters arguing the merits of a holy war pitting Christian Europe against the Islamic Ottoman Empire. The work begins on one day and plans an elaborate set of speeches for the next, but it ends abruptly in the first of the promised speeches. Despite this unfinished appearance, Bacon equipped it with a crucial preface, saw to its translation into Latin, and planned its posthumous publication in both languages.

The characters allowed to state their arguments are the two most inflamed by the desirability of holy war, more moderate voices being permitted only a few interruptions and the merest hints of what they would have said had they been given space to say it. Arguments on behalf of holy war are reasonably seen today as discrediting the one who advances them and that Bacon should have advanced them is an embarrassment even to Spedding who would like to dismiss them as Bacon's surrender to a blindness of the times.[1] Must we believe that Francis Bacon fell prey to zealous blindness, that the philosopher was overtaken by zeal for his religion? But why else allot the stage to the zealots and plan for that stage a prominent place in the posthumous writings?

Suspicions about Francis Bacon's holy war could have an external source: Bacon's lifelong concern for religion uniformly expressed itself in arguments for moderation in religion; and the Christianity of Bacon's future society in *New Atlantis* is wholly incapable of waging Christian holy war for it has grown tolerant and civil, acknowledging the power of science and the state and the privilege of other religions to exist. Suspicions about Francis Bacon's holy war

1. See Spedding, preface to *Holy War, Works* VII.5–6.

could have an internal source: what if the character who seemed to oppose holy war had had a chance to deliver his speech? And what about the citations that at first seem to point to the desirability of a religious holy war but when probed seem to point against it? Once our suspicion is aroused, questions arise about just who these six characters are, why they bear the names they do, why the dialogue ends where it does. And once the questioning starts, Bacon's little dialogue unfolds as a document of uncanny intricacy and extreme historical gravity.

Written in the terrible opening years of the 1620s, as the co-religionists of Bacon's zealot Zebedaeus marched victoriously not only over the co-religionists of Bacon's zealot Gamaliel, but over any moderate forces such as Erasmianism that still survived in Europe, the dialogue's many allusions force one to reflect on events of the preceding hundred years of Protestant and Catholic warfare, on the centuries of Crusades and Inquisition that preceded them, on the martial establishment of Christianity within the Roman Empire, and on the very different temper of Greek philosophy in contrast to Christian religion. What we witness most overtly in the dialogue is a religion which, in Nietzsche's words, had come to "insist on having its own sovereign way." But many of the dialogue's allusions, as well as its action, and its interruptions, suggest just how "dearly and terribly" Europe has had to pay for that sovereignty. The dialogue seems to invite a Nietzschean conclusion that one should well be chary about drawing: Bacon seems to pit philosophy against religion with a view to bringing religion under philosophy's control.

This conclusion is at first "adverse to common sense"; but so is all "such knowledge as is digged out of the hard mine of history and experience" (*Works* III.503). What Bacon dug out he seems to have reburied for easier mining in *An Advertisement Touching an Holy War*. And the conclusion is clearly compatible with *New Atlantis,* for if incapable of Christian holy war, Bensalem wages holy war on behalf of the ideas most dear to it, technological and scientific advancement. And this is the actual holy war fought out in Europe in the coming centuries, the warfare of science against religion that tamed sovereign religion and at whose head stands one man above all others, Francis Bacon. How to *begin* such warfare against sovereign religion in times ruled by the very zealots against whom one must fight? How else but covertly, enigmatically, in the acroamatic manner practiced so beautifully in *Holy War?*

As I see it, Bacon's little dialogue demonstrates just why it is necessary to initiate the spiritual warfare that Nietzsche identified as fundamental to modern philosophy: "Modern philosophy . . . is, covertly or overtly, *anti-Christian" (BGE* 54). In an "advertisement," a public notice or announcement made by the town crier, Bacon covertly justifies that most monumental of steps, holy war or war on behalf of the propagation of faith, a faith to compete against Christianity and tame it, faith in science. As the work arguing for the necessity of the holy war actually kindled in Bacon's other works and fought out in the modern world, *An Advertisement Touching an Holy War* is a document of stunning historical significance. Here, the acknowledged father of modern technological science shows that he undertook his revolution with the clear intention of curbing the religious fanaticism that had gripped Europe for a century and threatened another dark age. Spedding recognized that the *Holy War* "deserves a conspicuous place among Bacon's writings" (*Works* VII.6) but he completely ignored the best part, the argument itself: "The argument of the dialogue has but little interest for us today" (5). On the contrary, the argument is of the greatest interest, for it demonstrates in an amazing way why Bacon set himself at the head of new orders that made war on the prevailing Christian orders. In grounding the new spiritual warfare, the *Holy War* is Bacon's apology for philosophy in the ancient mode; like *New Atlantis,* it derives from philosophy the grounds for a break with traditional philosophy. The small drama of the conversation mirrors that greatest of dramas, spiritual warfare on behalf of philosophy Platonically understood.

The Setting

The *Holy War* begins with a letter of dedication to Lancelot Andrewes, bishop of Winchester and (according to T. S. Eliot) the man who holds "a place second to none in the history of the formation of the English Church."[2] The letter is of great importance: it contains what Spedding calls "the fullest account of Bacon's own personal feelings and designs as a writer" (6). All serious students of Bacon would be drawn to the *Holy War* to study Bacon's own thoughts on his writings—and those thoughts single out the *Holy War* for a most important task.

The letter opens elegantly, likening Bacon, as a man once mighty now fallen into disgrace, to three elevated classical examples, Cicero, Demosthenes, and Seneca. Seneca provides the example from which Bacon draws his own resolve to spend the rest of his life writing, for

---

2. "Lancelot Andrewes," in *The Private Devotions of Lancelot Andrewes,* xxii. Bacon described Bishop Andrewes as his "inquisitor" (*Works* X.256; see also IX.141).

Seneca "spent his time in writing books, of excellent argument and use for all ages" (13). Bacon's resolve to follow this example causes him to reflect on the books he has already written, emphasis falling on *The Great Instauration* and the way in which his previously written books fit into that project. At this reflective turning point in his life, "revolving with myself my writings," both those already published and those already written but not published, Bacon arrived at a conclusion that assigns the *Holy War* immense importance. This writing fulfills a function none of his other writings attempts: "They went all into the city, and none into the temple." The *Holy War* goes into the temple.

How does *Holy War* enter the temple? With an "argument mixt of religious and civil considerations, and likewise mixt between contemplative and active." The civil and active components come to predominate, for Bacon enters the temple in the same way that he enters those regions described in *The Great Instauration* as omitted or deficient: not "like an augur taking auspices" but "like a general who means to take possession" (*Works* IV.23). Bacon's dialogue is, as he says, a "poor oblation" for it is no oblation at all: it does not enter the temple to make an offering, but to seize possession. Having described the purpose of his *Holy War,* Bacon asks enigmatically, "For who can tell whether there may not be an *Exoriere aliquis?*"—but the rising up that Bacon incites is something quite different from what the temple itself would dictate. Drawn to the *Holy War* by Bacon's reflection on his writings, the student of those writings will study it as the work that remedies a deficiency in them by engaging in an action.

In the Latin translation Bacon entitled the *Holy War* a "dialogue." In addition to the six characters, Bacon himself is present as the narrator who provides the setting and who interrupts the dialogue with his own authoritative observations. The dialogue promises a very long discussion, so long that the speeches planned and assigned on the first day are postponed to the next in order to allow time for their uninterrupted continuance. But the dialogue then breaks off in the midst of the first of the promised speeches. The *Holy War* is a fragment that calls attention to its fragmentary character.

But is it incomplete? Did Bacon abandon his dialogue and leave it in a state of incompleteness bound to diminish its importance by making it seem "abortive and laid aside" (in the words of one of its rare commentators)?[3] Significant items point to its completeness: translation into Latin

3. Patrick, "Hawk Versus Dove," 159–71.

overseen by Bacon himself; revisions Bacon made after completing the only manuscript version that survives (5–7); its singular place in Bacon's writings as asserted in the letter of dedication; the importance of the letter of dedication as Bacon's most extended reflection on his writings; the care with which Bacon made a place for it in the planned posthumous work *Opera Moralia et Civilia;* the remark made at about the same time in *De Augmentis Scientiarum* (*Works* V.78–79) that any work of his on "the art of empire or civil government" would "perchance be either abortive or posthumous"; and, finally, the fact that apparent incompleteness is a device employed by Bacon for that other work on the art of empire and civil government written in English, translated into Latin, and set aside to be published posthumously in *Opera Moralia et Civilia: New Atlantis.* More telling still than all such external considerations is the internal evidence of the dialogue itself: it ends just when all the planned topics have in fact been covered; and it ends just when Bacon enters the temple. Seemingly conventional in appropriating a parable told by Jesus, yet daring and radical in altering that parable to serve Bacon's purpose, the ending of the dialogue attests to its perfection. Yet the *Holy War* is, in one sense, like *New Atlantis,* "a work unfinished": a complete argument, it testifies for a work only now beginning, the rising up of something great, the holy war itself.

Two characters in the dialogue have Hebrew names, two have Greek names, two have Roman names. The two Hebrews are zealous divines, the two Greeks are a politique and a moderate divine, and the two Romans are men of action, a soldier and a courtier. The Latin version adds that all but Gamaliel are Roman Catholics. The two Hebrews, Gamaliel and Zebedaeus, bear New Testament names. Gamaliel was a Pharisee, head of the school of Hillel and the greatest Jewish teacher of his day; he enters the New Testament as the teacher of Saul of Tarsus (Acts 22:3). Zebedee was the father of James and John, the two disciples whom Jesus rebaptized "the sons of thunder" (Mark 3:17) and who exhibit their zeal by asking Jesus to call down fire upon the Samaritan village that refused them entry to preach (Luke 9:54).[4] The namesakes of Gamaliel and Zebedaeus were, each in his own way, "fathers" of Apostles, fathers of zealots.

The characters with Greek names, Eupolis and Eusebius, are literally

---

4. On Gamaliel, see Acts 5:34ff.; 22:3; see also Num. 1:10; 2:20; 7:54, 59; 10:23. On Zebedee, see Matt. 4:21; 10:2; 20:20; 26:37; 27:56; Mark 1:19, 20; 3:17; 10:35; Luke 5:10; John 21:2.

"good," "good city" and "good worship" (= pious, devout). Eupolis is the host in whose house the dialogue occurs and he gives the order to the speeches of the second day. Bacon forces a question about Eusebius's role by the curious title he gave his list of characters: "The Persons that speak." The very first person named, Eusebius, never speaks. Why does a moderate divine have nothing to say on the question of holy war? Eupolis assigns him "a great part," a part fit for a moderate, the comparative part of measuring the relative claims of the actions proposed and assigning them a rank order. But "Eusebius hath yet said nothing" and will continue to say nothing. The mute moderate forces us to ask about the role of moderation and to focus on Eupolis, the moderate who is not mute—and who is not a divine. But reflection on moderation and speech is given a most surprising twist for mute "Eusebius" does, in a certain fashion, speak: that most garrulous of ancient authors, Eusebius, Bishop of Caesarea, turns out to be the source of a statement admired by Martius and of a classical reference used by Pollio in the crucial speech.

The two with Latin names are Martius the military man, and Pollio the courtier. Martius's military zeal moves the whole discussion, for while the theme is "the affairs of Christendom at this day" (18), the explicit theme is the Christian holy war incited by Martius's speech. But Pollio interrupts and contradicts Martius until he is forced to appeal to others to provide a reasoned foundation for the actions he passionately advocates. As the dialogue proceeds the central question becomes, who will direct Martius? And from what grounds? And for what ends? The confederacy of Eupolis and Pollio, a Greek and a Roman, quietly rises against the two Hebrews, Zebedaeus and Gamaliel, with the might of a tractable Martius as the prize—and Eusebius, apparently silent, looking on.

The dramatic date of the dialogue seems to have been left a mystery. At first, a precise dating seems possible because Martius's speeches twice point to 1621 as the *latest* possible date: in describing the worthy martial undertakings of Christian Europe, Martius speaks of events that have occurred within "the space now of half a century of years" (18) and "within the space of fifty years" (19) and the first of these events was the naval victory over the Turks at Lepanto in 1571.[5] (It may not be incidental to the consideration of the argument of the *Holy War* that Bacon in the *Essay* "Of the True Greatness of Kingdoms and Estates" says that the battle of Lepanto "arrested the power of the Turk," for if their power had been arrested fifty years earlier, one of the reasons for war against them would have been eliminated.) In addition, Pollio's de-

5. See Weinberger, "On Bacon's *Advertisement Touching a Holy War,*" 191–206.

scription of the present pope makes 1621 the *earliest* possible date: the "decrepit" Gregory XV was elected pope in February 1621. But mystery is then added because Pollio refers to an event that occurred in August 1623, the election of the new pope. Pollio has knowledge of that event: the new pope's name: Urban; his reason for taking that name: to honor the first pope to declare a Crusade (Urban II); and the pope's age, "between fifty and three-score": Urban VIII was fifty-five when elected. Because Martius's speech places the date no later than 1621, and because Pollio's speech requires that the decrepit pope be still alive, Pollio's speech on the new religious leader is cast as prophecy by Bacon. Pollio is made to appear as some latter-day Isaiah able to prophesy by name the new Cyrus, the new alien ruler destined to rebuild Jerusalem and restore the Temple (Isaiah 44:28–45:4).[6]

Bacon leaves no doubt about the place: "Paris (in the house of Eupolis)."[7] Paris is the capital of an uneasy kingdom shaken by the consecutive assassinations of kings thought disloyal to Catholic policy, Henry III and IV. In his *Essays* (§39), Bacon refers to the two assassins, Friar Clement and Ravillac, as a kind of conspirator unknown to Machiavelli, Christian conspirators secure in the absolute privacy of their conscience that their regicides are tyrannicides. In the summer of 1621, Louis XIII, twenty-one and dreaming of greatness, was in southwestern France at the head of the army attempting to reduce the Huguenots. The dialogue takes place in the house of Eupolis both literally and figuratively. "Temperate and without passion," he is fit to be "the Fifth Essence" housing the other four Elements who differ and yet are friends under his harmonizing influence.[8] But if Eupolis houses a world of warring elements, that world must be remade in the way prophesied by Pollio.

The First Day
The Opening Scene
The dialogue opens suddenly as Pollio arrives late at a private conference already underway. The first exchange—between Pollio and Eupolis—serves as an essential supplement to the "Characters of the Persons" be-

6. Pollio's speech puts the composition date—at least of this part of the speech, dramatically *the* turning point of this dialogue—after August 1623 and not in 1622 as Rawley stated on the title page of the first (1629) edition.

7. Another of Bacon's works with a dramatic setting is placed in Paris: "The Refutation of Philosophies" (1608) where a nameless sage passes judgment on philosophies for fifty assembled European dignitaries. See PFB 103–33.

8. See White, *Peace among the Willows*, 15: "Recalling that Bacon means by 'passion' perturbed affection, not all emotion, to be without passion certainly would be a divine goal."

cause it identifies all six while singling out for special attention Eupolis and Pollio. The other four characters are "the four Elements" that "were able" to make a world, even "a good World," though they are as different as earth, air, fire, and water. Eupolis stands apart from the four elements as "the Fifth Essence." Surrounding and enclosing the other four, he brought them into a harmony that made "the Great World."

And Pollio? He stands still further apart for he alone makes "the Little": he stands outside the constituted world as a whole. But he does so as one who takes its measure: "Because you profess and practice both, to refer all things to yourself." But to refer all things to oneself, to find in oneself the standard of measure, is, Bacon says, "a desperate evil in a servant to a prince," a courtier (*Essays,* "Of Wisdom for a Man's Self"); it is the practice of "the corrupter sort of mere Politiques, that have not their thoughts established by learning in the love and apprehension of duty, nor never look abroad into universality" (*Advancement, Works* III.297). Is this a description of Pollio? Does he take his measure of the Great World from mere self-interest? Who *is* Pollio?[9]

He is a *courtier* who professes to refer all things to himself. As a courtier he affects that *grazia,* that nonchalance or easy grace which Castiglione prescribed as essential to the courtier, nonchalance as art, an art that conceals its artistry in contrived and calculated naturalness; as permissible deception, nonchalance is art that looks like nature. Always artful, the courtier seems always natural. In particular, a courtier's nonchalance requires always being well-briefed and prepared for everything he has to do or say while giving the impression that everything is extemporaneous.[10] Part of Pollio's artfulness could well be the profession of referring everything to himself, a profession easily held in suspicion in a courtier. Could Pollio be a courtier who in fact serves something other than himself by masking his loyalty and seriousness of purpose in artful self-centeredness?

And he is *Pollio:* Asinius Pollio was a great Roman who participated independently in the events of Rome's fall from a republic to a tyranny. Consul in 40 B.C.E., he retired early from public life in order to devote himself to the advancement of learning. He established the first public library in Rome, wrote tragedies and a history of the civil war, none

9. Unpublished writings by Mary Frisby have helped me to a better understanding of Pollio's role.

10. Castiglione, *Book of the Courtier,* 66–70, 147–50. John Briggs provides an interesting discussion of Castiglione and Bacon, though without reference to *Holy War,* see *Francis Bacon and the Rhetoric of Nature,* 118–28.

of which survive, and became the patron of Horace and Virgil. Virgil dedicated to him the first writing in classical times to look ahead to a golden age in a human future brought in by human beings (the *Fourth Eclogue*), a most Baconian theme.

Professing to refer all things to himself, does Pollio measure the Great World by some selfishness? We are invited to doubt this by his being a courtier and by his being Pollio. It is much more probable that the courtier Pollio wears "the helmet of Pluto, which maketh the politic man to go invisible" (*Essays*, "Of Delays"), though not absolutely invisible, for what he professes in the coming speeches will make it possible to glimpse the actual grounds of his practice—and the sense in which he does *not* refer all things to himself.

If Eupolis's description of Pollio prepares us for Pollio's part, what of Pollio's description of Eupolis?[11] Pollio identified Eupolis as the Fifth Essence which held the other four together in the harmony of the great world. But the speeches that follow will show that great world to be breaking apart in a way that could perhaps not be stemmed by a *politique*. In France in 1621 a politique was a member of the moderate political party that arose out of France's religious and civil wars, in particular the Saint Bartholomew's Day Massacre in 1572. At first a term of contempt thrown at those who presumed to place the interests of the nation above religion, "politique" became the honorable term for the successful politics associated with Henry of Navarre, friend of Montaigne, the politics that tempered the zealots of Reformation and Counter-Reformation, the Gamaliels and Zebedaeuses. As a politic moderate in the inflamed extremes of European religious wars, Eupolis would act on historic precedents which aimed to subordinate ecclesiastical interests to civil power and ultimately to rational control, "Ghibelline" or, more narrowly, "Erasmian" precedents.[12] Moreover, a politique who is a Fifth essence would surely resemble "the greater and deeper politique" whom

11. The historical Eupolis was an Athenian comic poet (445–410 B.C.E.) regarded, with Aristophanes and Cratinus, as one of the three masters of Old Comedy. In the *Demes*, called by a modern commentator, "the most important political comedy of all time," Eupolis summoned four great Athenian statesmen from the dead to remedy "the spectacle of our present public life." The tale was told, falsely according to Eratosthenes, that he was drowned by Alcibiades on the way to Sicily in 415 in revenge for the attack on Alcibiades in the *Baptai*. See Norwood, *Greek Comedy*, 178–201.

12. For an account of Ghibelline politics in the setting of European philosophy see Caton, *Politics of Progress*, 122–33, and Yates, *Astraea*, 1–28; on the history and meaning of Erasmian in the Christian wars see Trevor-Roper, *Crisis of the Seventeenth Century*, 24–28, 41–43, 204–36.

Bacon described as sharing a quality with divine providence: he "can make other men the instrument of his will and ends and yet never acquaint them with his purpose" (*Advertisement, Works* III.359).

What would be required to recompose the warring elements of the great world into a harmonious whole? Certainly Bacon himself did not simply rely on the old methods of moderating religious zeal. And his Pollio will show—in the crucial speech that breaks the suggested order— that there is a way in which the warring elements might be composed into a new harmony. Pollio thus seems to be much more than a courtier: he seems to be the philosopher who takes the decisive step required by the new conditions. Pollio would thus succeed Eupolis as the giver of harmony, though they remain confederates, united against an immoderate religious politics.

Pollio professes and practices to refer all things to himself, but he asks, "What do they that practice it and profess it not?" What of those who in fact take their measure from themselves while not acknowledging it? They are, Eupolis answers, "the less hardy, and the more dangerous." Who are they? Less hardy and more dangerous will, in the course of the dialogue, come to fit one character above all others: Zebedaeus. He will profess to take his measure from a source other than himself but he will, in a way, practice referring all things to himself by misusing a universalism in the service of a narrow self-centeredness.

This little opening exchange sets the great contrast under which the dialogue will now unfold: Who can take the measure of the world? Can it be taken by a professed selfishness that may in fact look to universality? Can it be taken by a professed universality that in fact practices selfishness? What, precisely, *are* these two in the dialogue? It is too early to prove it but the dialogue will answer: philosophy and religion. Practice and profession are exhibited in one way in the dialogue by Pollio: professing to refer all things to himself, he seems in fact to draw his measure from universality. Practice and profession are exhibited in another way by Zebedaeus: a mere element, one-sided and disharmonious in himself, he professes to refer all things to a measure beyond himself but he is in fact less hardy and more dangerous because he refers all things to his own narrow ends. The outcome of the dialogue will be the devastating measure taken by philosophy of the Great World now dominated by religion. Can a new world be formed out of the broken and polarized parts of the old world whose measure is taken by philosophy? What form could such a new world take? It is necessary to keep forcibly before us the salient fact that this is the dialogue written by Francis Bacon, maker of a very specific new world only hinted at in this dialogue but, in the event, the successful rival to the warring Christian world here depicted.

Eupolis breaks off the opening exchange by inviting Pollio to join them in discussing "the affairs of Christendom at this day." This will be the theme for the whole dialogue and Pollio will do what he is invited to do: give his opinion.

Pollio has come directly from court, but he has "journeyed this morning" and is now weary: the speechmakers must be interesting enough to make him keep his eyes open. But having implied his own drowsiness he accuses their speeches in advance of a drowsiness to which he will wakefully call attention. He asks permission "to awake you, when I think your discourses do but sleep." From a wakeful perspective which refers all things to himself, Pollio will measure the perspective of a drowsing world. "You cannot do us a greater favor," Eupolis says of Pollio's promise to keep watch over the discourses that may sleep, but he voices a "fear" that Pollio may take as a mere dream incapable of realization "the trumpet of War" just sounded by Martius. Pollio, thus warned, will attend to Martius's speech as summoning to war sleepwalkers with the power to realize their dreams.

The setting is now complete. Pollio's arrival can hardly have been an accident. Given the evident confederacy of Eupolis and Pollio, it is plausible to conclude that Pollio has been summoned by Eupolis to hear a call to war and to prepare an intervention against it. Martius will begin again for Pollio's sake—his speech deserves to be heard twice, says Eupolis. His "auditory is not a little amended by the presence of Pollio": he will be interrupted three times by wakeful Pollio and the interruptions will provide the perspective from which to measure the dreaming world he calls to war.

Martius's Speech

Martius's call to action is an indictment of Christendom: the recent military ventures of Christendom shame a military spirit because of their meanness. But Martius's standard of martial nobility is a product of Christianity: the wars unworthy of Christian princes would have befit the heathen. The heathen peoples named are Athens, Sparta, and Rome—"exemplar states," Bacon himself calls them (*Advancement, Works* III.225). Their wars fell short of what Martius most admires because they did not aim at the propagation of faith by arms. The Christian standard of warfare has altered the nature of war. Martius traces the new militarism to "our Lord" who said on earth to his disciples, "go and preach," and proclaimed from heaven to a Roman emperor, "In hoc signe vince." Gibbon calls this sign from heaven to Constantine, "the Christian fable of Eusebius," the sign and related dream Eusebius presented as the occasion for Constantine's conversion and his successful entry into Rome as emperor.[13] As a character in Bacon's dialogue Eusebius says nothing, but he speaks here, in a way, as the Bishop of Caesarea, the Christian historian who recorded the Christian conquest of Rome through the Blessed Emperor Constantine.[14] With Constantine, the Christian sign appeared for the first time at the head of armies, and the Christian religion became the civil religion of a great empire. Drawing his inspiration from words addressed to Constantine, Martius speaks for the "Christian soldier" moved now to "religious emulation" in his own art, not only by the original example of Constantine but by later examples of aggressive zeal in militant religious orders. If Christian soldiers now lack a Constantine, they do not lack the will to carry out the command given to him or examples of zeal among the religious.

Martius can remember only three "noble and memorable actions" in the last fifty years in which "the Christian hath been the invader." The first was a victory and the other two defeats which Martius blames on a lack of Christian unity, a lack exemplified by the reaction to Pollio's first interruption.

Pollio's First Interruption

Pollio stops Martius with an emphatic no to his list of "noble and memorable actions" and then invites him to continue by asking, "What say you to the extirpation of the Moors of Valentia?" Martius says nothing to that, for Bacon's own first interruption into the narrative states that Martius was at a loss for an immediate reply to the "sudden question." Martius will have a ready response to only one of Pollio's interruptions; others fill the gap created by his inability to respond on the other two occasions; in doing so they reveal their stance towards Martius's trumpet of war.

Pollio's no seems to challenge Martius's standard of noble and memorable: why not include the extirpation of the "Moors of Valentia" in 1609 as a noble and memorable Christian action?[15] Two of Martius's own examples had pointed to Christian differences regarding the particulars of

13. Gibbon, *Decline and Fall,* chap. 20.
14. Eusebius, *Life of the Blessed Emperor Constantine* I.28–32.
15. See Lea, *History of the Inquisition of Spain,* III.388–98.

holy war, but the example Pollio now forces them to confront occasions a flare-up of the deepest hatreds dividing Christian Europe, for Gamaliel and Zebedaeus speak out on behalf of Protestant and Catholic views respectively. This verbal conflict between Protestant and Catholic is the first sign of the holy wars fomented by these two parties within Christendom, the wars which had ravaged France and the rest of Europe for the fifty years in question. Just once, but at the beginning and over a recent European event, does the warfare represented by these zealots flare into the open in the dialogue. Their fierce opposition can be assumed to be present throughout the sequel despite Eupolis's ability to deflect them into a continuation of civil dialogue. This brief outburst goaded by Pollio shows that the great world made harmonious by Eupolis is rent by differences between sectarian zealots. "The principle of discord was alive in their bosom," as Gibbon said of earlier Christians,[16] and we will hear a continuing litany of references to historic events in their warfare.

Gamaliel, the Protestant zealot, makes his only speech to disapprove of the expulsion of the Moors. He bases his disapproval on signs he reads of God's disapproval—the fate of the principals, Philip III and the Duke of Lerma, looks to him like God's punishment on them and he warns of further punishment to follow. His speech at first seems temperate but it contains submerged threats against "you catholics," "whose fortunes"—like the Duke of Lerma's—"seemed to be built upon the rock"—the rock St Peter—but may, like Lerma's, be "ruined," perhaps by those who yield to "the thirst of revenge."

Zebedaeus's response brings the warfare among Christians into the open. He challenges Gamaliel not to make "hasty judgment" of "that great action," for it was like "Christ's fan," a winnowing fan, separating out the "cursed seed." Zebedaeus calls in a Biblical precedent: one could object to the extirpation of the Moors only if the Moors could point to a contract, a Spanish covenant permitting co-habitation, similar to the covenant Joshua made with the Gibeonites. But Zebedaeus's precedent subverts his argument. Joshua's covenant swore God's people to spare the Gibeonites (Joshua 9 and 10), but the covenant was broken by Saul "in his zeal for the people of Israel and Judah" (2 Samuel 21:1–9). Zebedaeus's model of contractual moderation is a covenant betrayed by a zealot on behalf of God's people. Zebedaeus is not content to defend a zealous act by his own party; his final sentence is a provocation attacking the Protestant Gamaliel: the expulsion and killing of the Moors, he says,

16. Gibbon, *Decline and Fall*, chap. 47.

"was done by edict and not tumultuously; the sword was not put into the people's hand"—militant actions by us Catholics are defensible in a way that militant actions by you Protestants are not, for in appealing to the tumultuous mob and putting the sword in their hand, you threaten an order held together by our edict and sword.

Pollio's interruption opened the question "What is noble in religious warfare?" but that opening is closed by the judgment of zealots. These judgments not only exhibit the warfare within the Christian camp, they prepare its escalation in Zebedaeus's accusatory reply. Gamaliel could surely have replied in kind but why cannot Eusebius speak, the Christian moderate tempering the zeal of his co-religionists? His silence, made conspicuous by being called twice to our attention, could be a silence intrinsic to his kind: Christian moderation has no authority to which it can appeal when Christian zeal captures the rival camps. The actual drowning out of Christian moderation in the warfare of Reformation and Counter-Reformation zealots makes Bacon's character historically authentic.[17] Not Greek Eusebius but Greek Eupolis, not "piety" or Christian moderation but "good city" or classical moderation, tempers the world threatened by escalating zeal.

Eupolis defuses the potential conflict between Gamaliel and Zebedaeus by recalling a distinction drawn earlier by Martius—a distinction Martius himself could not call to mind quickly enough to answer Pollio. The conflict can be set aside for now because the example that caused it to flare up "sorted not aptly with actions of war" as Martius had defined them, being an action "upon subjects, and without resistance." But Pollio's interruption has served its stated purpose: Martius's discourse on Christian warfare sleeps by ignoring the warfare within the Christian camp which wakeful Pollio forces into the open. Eupolis praises Martius as an encouragement to continue: "Methought he spoke like a divine in armor," like the god Mars, perhaps, for whom he is named, the raging god scorned by the Athenians for his barbarian lack of cultured speech.

Martius Continues

Martius turns now to a different consideration: though his principal object is "piety and religion," he can make his case strictly as a "natural man." Holy war against the Turks can be likened to the wars of conquest by Spain and Portugal which have given Europe a global empire, even though those wars were conducted first for "secular greatness" and

17. See Trevor-Roper, *Men and Events,* 35–60, and *Crisis of the Seventeenth Century,* 193–236.

only secondarily for "the propagation of the Christian faith." A war against the Turks could serve "both the spiritual and temporal honour and good."

Pollio's Second Interruption

Pollio's central objection occurs at a pause in Martius's speech. It accords with Martius's promise to "speak only as a natural man" for it derives its point solely from temporal or civil considerations. The objection is decisive for it determines the rest of the dialogue: Martius tries to meet its demands but his failure forces him to call in assistance; Zebedaeus answers that call on the next day and reveals the true weight of the objection by natural man.

Where has the discourse fallen asleep this time? Judging from the exchange, Martius is asleep to the distinction Pollio introduces: asked to "remember" this distinction, Martius says, "I know no such difference amongst reasonable souls." Pollio distinguishes "wild and savage people" from "civil people": the former "are like beasts and birds," wild or fierce nature which can be made the property of those who subdue them, whereas civil people cannot. Pollio's standard distinguishes relative civility among peoples and justifies possession of the relatively uncivil and not of the relatively civil—a standard reminiscent of Aristotle's argument in the first book of the *Politics* (chap. 8, 1256a–b). Martius knows no such distinction and introduces another: "Whatsoever is in order to the greatest and most general good of people may justify the action, be the people more or less civil." Here are the two great standards under which the rest of the discussion will be carried out and the implicit question always is, how can such standards be known and how can they be applied? Who can judge relative civility? Who can determine the greatest and most general good? On these supreme questions Martius is willing to take instruction. And Zebedaeus is eager to give it: on the basis of divine authority, the greatest and most general good of people is consistent with their annihilation if we can satisfy ourselves that they are utterly wild and savage. But Zebedaeus himself will concede that he cannot know these great standards except by deferring to divine authority. Can they be known in any other way? He will, by default, show how they can.

Martius Continues

Having denied that reasonable souls know Pollio's distinction, Martius employs it nevertheless. He supposes that he has deciphered Pollio's intention even though Pollio gave no intimation of how he himself would interpret the distinction between wild and civil. Supposing that Pollio would hold the people of Peru or Mexico to be "brute savages," Martius argues for their civility, implicitly judging the Spanish conquest unjust by Pollio's standard. Martius has presumably already heard those who justify the slaughter and enslavement of Peruvians and Mexicans on the grounds of their incivility—Zebedaeus makes that argument on the next day. Martius seems to react gallantly to what he thinks is Pollio's slur on the civility of the conquered peoples of the Spanish dominions. His defense of their worship and government would make Christian cruelty against them still more unjustifiable. But for Martius, the civility of these now subdued peoples serves a single point: to illustrate the incivility of the Turks and foment Christian holy war against them. He thus launches the vehement denunciation of the Turks that Pollio interrupts "in the midst" and terms an "invective." Zebedaeus, the next day, explicitly rejects the description "invective" in favor of "the true charge." And solely on the basis of this allegedly true charge, Zebedaeus will suspend all six points that he had enumerated as possible limitations on holy war. Here is the breaking point of the dialogue. After Martius's description of the Turks, the reader is forced to side with Pollio or with Zebedaeus because Martius is about to retire from the field, his trumpet of war sounded. And in siding with Pollio or Zebedaeus in the interpretation of Martius's call to holy war, the reader is forced to draw a conclusion regarding Bacon's intention in the dialogue.

Pollio's Third Interruption

Calling Martius to wakefulness for the final time, Pollio again appeals to him to remember something: "Do the Turks this right, as to remember that they are no idolaters." Pollio demands that Martius honor the standard he had himself drawn from the *Wisdom of Solomon* chapter 13 to defend the worship of the Peruvians. If degrees of civility are to be measured by a people's view of the gods, then the Turks must be regarded as civil for the God of the Turks is the first person of the Christian trinity. Martius is silenced by having his own argument turned against him. But Pollio's theological latitudinarianism draws Zebedaeus's immediate ire as he fills the gap created by the silencing of Martius. And for the only time in the dialogue, Bacon describes the bearing of one of his characters. Zebedaeus speaks with "a countenance of great reprehension and severity" to rebuke Pollio for falling "at unawares into the heresy of Manuel Comnenus." One can doubt that Pollio, a nonchalant courtier always well-briefed, has fallen unawares into the theological controversy cited by Zebedaeus. That controversy casts a penetrating light over the whole dialogue. When Manuel Comnenus, the Byzantine Emperor (1143–1180) during a period of war with the Islamic Turks, announced the view that Pollio here defends, it was not only rejected and condemned by the patriarchal synod, Zebedaeus says, but was "imputed to the Emperor as extreme madness." And the condemnation as Zebedaeus reports it went still further, for the bishop of Thessalonica, the learned Eustathios, issued a threat that Zebedaeus ostentatiously refuses to repeat, pointing only to his "bitter and strange words as are not to be named." What were those words?

They are in fact the almost insane words of a religious zealot who lost control of himself over a moderate proposal by the emperor aimed at tempering relations with Islamic Turks. "My brains would be in my feet and I would be wholly unworthy of this garb," says Archbishop Eustathios, "were I to regard as true God the pederast who was as brutish as a camel and master and teacher of every abominable act." [18] The chronicle reporting this event describes Eustathios as shouting these words, "visibly shaken by pious zeal."

Bacon has been very assiduous in finding an occasion in the history of Christian relations with Islam directly relevant to his dialogue. And to climax his reference to that occasion, he has his inflamed character allude to certain words "not to be named." Surely Bacon expects a complementary assiduousness on the part of his reader. When the obscure *Annals* containing the words are finally located, we find ourselves treated to a spectacle of religious zeal in conflict with civil authority directly parallel to the situation of the dialogue. In the historic example Bacon forces us to consult, civil tolerance is met with religious intolerance. But there is something more, for the example is slightly distorted in Bacon's retelling because the synod in fact did not accuse the emperor of "extreme madness." That description best fits Eustathios, the religious authority rebuked and chastened for his lack of control by civil authority, the emperor. This little adjustment to the tale forces the reader to raise the question of madness in the conflict between religious and civil authority, mirrored in the dialogue as the conflict between Zebedaeus and Pollio. Whose proposals border on extreme madness? Pollio himself will make a decisive reference to madness in his next speech, and that reference illuminates this one.

18. Choniates, *O City of Byzantium, Annals of Niketas Choniates*, 122. See Meyendorff, "Byzantine Views of Islam," 115–32; Kedar, *Crusade and Mission*, 95.

It is a dramatic moment when Zebedaeus "with a countenance of great reprehension and severity" threatens Pollio with heresy. Zebedaeus is one of the authorities to whom Martius will shortly appeal for grounds, the one to whom Eupolis will assign the crucial speech on the lawfulness of holy war. The debate opened by Pollio's final interruption concerns the relation between civil and religious power and the right of each to give direction to Europe, the debate crucial to the politics of Reformation and Counter-Reformation Europe but reaching much further back into European religious and political history. By having Zebedaeus refer to a much earlier and distant outbreak of the conflict between priest and prince, one that occurred in another part of Christendom altogether and that pitted civil moderation against an almost mad religious frenzy in relation to the Turks, Bacon succeeds in raising the central issue of the dialogue without seeming to take sides among his characters. And he succeeds in giving a premonition of what is to come: moderating religious zeal is Europe's great political problem.

Martius Pauses

To the civil-religious debate opened by the final interruption Martius offers no comment but only a confession. He confesses an opinion so absolute and so extreme as to reveal perfectly the dream in which he sleeps and from which no prudent objection by Pollio can ever awaken him: holy war against the Turks is the most worthy military undertaking in the history of the world. Whether the standard be drawn from religion or from honor, its absolute merit is evident to Martius. Given this opportunity by history to perform the most sacred and most honorable duty ever offered to human beings, how can one hesitate? Martius's self-induced trance of martial glory is now fully evident, but his speech is not finished. He means to proceed after the company has made good on what he now requests, and the speech Eupolis assigns him will in fact "resume" the speech now broken off. The dialogue ends before that speech is given, but everything that now transpires is an interlude in Martius's call to holy war.

Martius gives three reasons for pausing: he would be glad to catch his breath; he desires that others speak who can speak better; and the chief reason, itself divided into three parts: he knows he is in the presence of "excellent interpreters of the divine law, though in several ways"; he distrusts his own judgment as "weak in itself" and as easily overpowered by his "zeal and affection to this cause"; and he thinks it would be an error on his part to proceed before seeing "some foundation laid of the lawfulness of the action, by them that are better versed in that argument." He is not asking the interpreters of the law *whether* an argument can be provided to support his martial zeal but *that* they provide it. His hesitation is not based on uncertainty but on prudence: it would be an "error" to proceed before they supply the arguments. Zebedaeus's arguments on the next day are given obediently to the military spirit that demands reasons for actions it has already decided are the most pious and most honorable in the history of the world. Zebedaeus grounds in divine law the strong prejudice that already exists in favor of holy war.

Eupolis's New Order

Eupolis commends Martius for his "great moderation" but the commendation is for one thing only—that a man of his profession seeks to ground his action in law. As for the action itself, Eupolis describes only its effect and one of its appearances: it "warms the blood and is appearing holy."

Eupolis now gives a new direction to the dialogue by making "some motion touching the distribution of it into parts." He assigns the parts as follows:

Zebedaeus is assigned the main question: "Whether a war for the propagation of the Christian faith, without other cause of hostility, be lawful or no, and in what cases?" But Zebedaeus's actual speech makes "the propagation of the Christian faith" disappear completely as the ground of holy war: it is replaced by a new ground: curbing an enemy of humankind.

Gamaliel is assigned the question of whether such warfare is not only lawful but obligatory. This speech becomes superfluous when Zebedaeus argues its obligatory character.

Eusebius who "hath yet said nothing" is assigned as punishment the long "comparative" part on the relative merits of holy war compared to other sacred and civic duties. Pollio's speech will leave Eusebius nothing to say.

Pollio is assigned a special part. Out of keeping with the rest of the speeches, it is in keeping with Pollio's nature, now described through the addition of one new feature: he "hath a sharp wit of discovery towards what is solid and real and what is specious and airy"—he possesses a philosophic nature capable of distinguishing the true from the false. Given Pollio's philosophic character, Eupolis "doubts much" that he will "esteem all this but impossibilities, and eagles in the clouds." Pollio's coming speech is heralded as the decisive speech on the possibility or impossibility of their dreams by one who is no dreamer. Eupolis had already explicitly warned Pollio not to take these discourses as dreams but Pollio himself will suggest a somewhat different dream whose solidity must be measured in part at least by the fact that he is its source. In assigning Pollio his task, Eupolis makes a most remarkable appeal in the name of all the others, of the whole "Great World" which Pollio has entered as an observer: "We shall all intreat him to crush this argument with his best forces." Would Martius or Zebedaeus wish to have their arguments for holy war crushed? Whoever Eupolis speaks for, himself or all of them, Pollio obeys literally. Speaking early and out of order, he shows exactly how to crush their argument. And Eupolis's curt rejoinder acknowledges his assent to Pollio's manner of crushing. But now, as his final charge to Pollio, Eupolis shows the high task that will follow his success in crushing their argument: "By the light we shall take from him," from Pollio, they will either abandon Martius's project or free it of what is vain and hopeless. Pollio is the giver of light who will show how Martius is to be redirected.

Eupolis assigns himself the task of showing how any impediments to the enterprise raised by Pollio could be overcome. It may be a "hard encounter to deal with Pollio," but for Eupolis no encounter will be necessary because Pollio not only gives his own invited speech one day early, he gives Eupolis's as well: Pollio and Eupolis know that holy war is possible and how it is possible.

Martius is assigned the resumption of his earlier speech: the "means, preparations, and all that may conduce unto the enterprise."

At the end of this distribution, Bacon states that each accepted his part and agreed to defer the speeches till the next morning, "because the day was spent." But a final speech is made by Pollio—and this speech, the decisive speech, signals Bacon's intent as clearly as is ever done in the dialogue, for it prepares an unexpected interpretation of Zebedaeus's speech on the next day: advocacy of holy war becomes a different matter after Pollio speaks.

Pollio's Advocacy and Prophecy

Pollio does not need to wait till the next morning or till his assigned turn, for his preemptive speech properly precedes all the others. He acknowledges the truth of Eupolis's characterization of him: "You take me right." Pollio does distinguish the solid from the specious, and he would take all this talk of holy war for "impossibilities and eagles in the clouds" except for one thing: he knows the solid and real means that will turn these eagles into omens of real war. His means fulfill Eupolis's invitation to "crush this argument with his best forces": "For I am of opinion that except you could bray Christendom in a mortar, and mould it into a new paste, there is no possibility of an Holy War." Pollio has taken Eupolis's part and stated the conditions under which the enterprise would be possible: by means of a broken and remolded Christianity. This could be taken to mean a Christianity refired with the zeal of a Zebedaeus, but it could also be taken to mean the breaking and remaking of the Christian religion evident in Bensalemite Christianity, Baconian Christianity whose charity has turned practical and technological. The rest of Pollio's speech confirms this latter possibility.

Pollio's second sentence reports what was "ever" his opinion: "That the Philosopher's Stone, and an Holy War, were but the *rendez-vous* of cracked brains, that wore their feather in their head instead of their hat." Here, in Paris, at this little *rendezvous,* are there only cracked brains in pursuit of mad dreams, the cracked brains of alchemical philosophers and of religious zealots bent on holy war? Or is Pollio *no longer* of this opinion? Has he perhaps seen that there is a way that the philosopher's stone and a holy war can become "solid and real" precisely when they rendezvous in the way suggested in his first sentence, in a Christianity brayed and molded into a new paste? That he holds this possibility under one condition only is stated in his third sentence, a complex mix of conditions and consequences that must be analyzed in all its parts:

"Nevertheless believe me of courtesy . . ." Despite what Pollio has just said was ever his opinion, they are to believe him capable of altering it.

". . . that if you five shall be of another mind . . ." You five are "the Great World" of four elements and "the Fifth Essence" housing them. If they are all of "another mind," Pollio could alter his mind. But only one arrangement of the five could alter Pollio's considered judgment: if the one mind that brings the four disharmonious elements into the accord that makes a great world were of another mind, if Eupolis were of another mind, then Pollio the small world, could reflect it, referring it to himself and professing it in the appropriate way.

". . . especially after you have heard what I can say . . ." What he can say he is saying, and it will, in part at least, help to make "you five" of "another mind." This condition being met, Pollio is ready to draw the consequence:

". . . I shall be ready to certify with Hippocrates, that Athens is mad and Democritus is only sober." This is the decisive conclusion toward which Pollio's compacted argument for holy war has been leading, and it makes Bacon's own case with amazing brevity and inventiveness. For

Pollio with practiced nonchalance here invents a classical saying to fit the present circumstances and explain with exactitude just why he can alter what was ever his opinion on holy war. No such saying exists in the classical corpus but each of its elements can be traced and each contributes to Pollio's meaning. ". . . to certify with Hippocrates . . ." ties Pollio's diagnosis to ancient Greek medicine though Hippocrates says no such thing. A holy war can be medicinal, a Greek antidote to heal a sickness not otherwise susceptible of treatment. ". . . Athens is mad . . ." Abdera, Democritus's city, ought to be the reference says Spedding but the Latin too has Athens and Bacon knows the difference. Expecting Abdera instead of Athens, we also expect "only Democritus is sober" as the appropriate contrast to the first part of what is certified, madness. When Pollio says "Democritus is only sober," he implies that sobriety is a defect in contrast to Athenian madness. Read literally, Pollio's conclusion implies that for a sickness whose proper antidote is holy war, Athenian madness must be taken in conjunction with Democritean sobriety. Bacon often affirms the atomism of Democritus as the most probable teaching on the ultimate nature of things,[19] but here Democritus is assessed as defective in a single respect: he is sober where madness is called for. If Athens possesses the medicinal madness that the truest teaching on nature lacked, it can only be the philosophical madness of Plato, "the divine madness that grants a divine release from the customary habits" (*Phaedrus* 265a–b). The Hippocratic antidote combines Plato and Democritus, adding Platonic madness to the sober teaching about nature.

When one finds the sources of Pollio's conclusion, an arresting fact comes to light that clarifies just what Athenian madness is in this context: Pollio has invented his classical authorization but not out of whole cloth, for his judgment adjusts a judgment rendered by Philo of Alexandria, "one of Plato's school" (*Advancement, Works* III.267). In the *Contemplative Life* (14–17), Philo criticized the Greeks who praised Democritus for abandoning his fields to the sheep in order to take up philosophy. Philo argued that philosophy does not require such lack of concern for others because with no less ardor for philosophy a philosopher can benefit others: he contrasts Democritus with a group of his own acquaintance who combine philosophy for themselves with magnanimity for their kin

19. On Democritus see esp. *WA* "Coelum," "Cupid," "Prometheus"; *Advancement, Works* III.358; "Thoughts on the Nature of Things," *Works* V.419–23; "On Principles and Origins," *Works* V.461–68; "Description of the Intellectual Globe," *Works* V.514–15; *NO* I.51, 57.

in that they donate their fields to their kin to be used rather than to fall waste; these "therapeutae" philosophize while tending the sick. Comparing the two actions, Philo says Democritus's act was "thoughtless" and he adds that he would have gone further: except for the fact that the Greeks admired it, he would have called Democritus's action "mad." The action of the others, he could call "sober." And the superiority of the sober way combining philosophy with magnanimity is supported by Philo with a quotation from Hippocrates, an aphorism often quoted by Bacon, "Life is short but art is long." The main elements of Pollio's sentence are present in Philo: Hippocrates, Democritus, madness, sobriety. But Bacon has given the elements his own mix and added one item, Athens.

By tampering with an ancient judgment in this very precise way, Bacon forces his reader to interpret his changes and track their consequences. When this is done, it seems to me that Bacon's strategy emerges into full visibility as a staggering task for philosophy against religion. The holy war Bacon advocates through Pollio combines Athenian madness with a truer teaching on nature to combat religious extremism: Plato and Democritus combine to crush Christendom into a new paste. The precise form that Athenian madness will take becomes apparent through Zebedaeus's speech, but on the basis of Philo's *Contemplative Life* it can be said to be a philosophic philanthropy which takes in hand a teaching for the people: whereas Democritus lacked "foresight and consideration for the interests of others," leaving them defenseless in the face of the seemingly hostile nature he uncovered, Platonic philosophical magnanimity benefits others through a teaching that gives solace. Athenian madness includes the magnanimity, in Bacon's teaching, of charitable science, the means of curbing Christian rule. Athenian madness grants Bacon divine release from the customary habits and permission to establish new ones. That madness is far from the religious madness of a Eustathios or a Zebedaeus, hot for holy war. Their holy war is crushed by Pollio's best forces, an argument for holy war derived from philosophy; religious madness is brought under control by Athenian madness.

This interpretation of Pollio's speech is confirmed and augmented by what happens later in the dialogue, especially in Zebedaeus's speech, but this much can be said already: the interpretation accords with *New Atlantis* and the relationship between philosophy and religion set out there.

Pollio has usurped Eupolis's part in the coming day's speeches, for he has proven how the enterprise is possible. But he seems to have usurped another part as well for there is one more little fact to be noted about

Bacon's use of Philo. Philo's *Contemplative Life* with its defense of philosophy is, its translator says, "better known and more discussed than any other work of Philo" [20] for one reason: it was discussed and elaborated by *Eusebius* in his best known work, *Ecclesiastical History* (ii.17). Our "Eusebius," one of "the Persons that speak," "hath yet said nothing" when Pollio speaks and almost quotes Philo. Eusebius's namesake had already spoken, for his tale of Christ's martial words to Constantine provided Martius with inspiration. Now the seemingly mute moderate divine "speaks" a second time in a similar way. But this time his namesake speaks to preserve a Greek wisdom passed down through Philo, the first thinker to attempt to reconcile Greek wisdom with biblical revelation. And Eusebius argued that Philo's *therapeutae* were actually early Christians. Moderate Christian divinity praises and preserves a Greek wisdom praised and preserved by Philo. In Philo the school of Plato began its attempt to reconcile the politic wisdom of Plato with the Bible, an attempt carried forward by moderate Christian divinity. Perhaps Bacon is suggesting that moderate Christianity has had the beneficial effect of preserving Greek antiquities by assimilating it to Christian teachings. In the last of his *Essays*, "Of Vicissitude of Things," Bacon challenges Machiavelli's view that "the jealousy of sects doth much extinguish the memory of things." Bacon does not modify Machiavelli's reference to the destruction of pagan things by Pope Gregory and "other heads of the Christian religion";[21] instead, he simply cites a counterexample, Gregory's successor, Pope Sabinian, under whom, Bacon alleges, Greek antiquities were revived.[22] Suitably moderated, Bacon seems to imply, Christian sects can be a means of preserving the philosophic heritage.

If Eusebius speaks out of Pollio's reference, moderated divinity speaks out of Plato's school. As Nietzsche says, "Christianity is Platonism for the people" (*BGE* Preface). While one "pays dearly and terribly" when this religion "insists on having [its] own sovereign way," it can nevertheless be a "means of education and cultivation in the philosopher's hand" (*BGE* 62). Perhaps, in now being wordless in the face of Pollio's argument for holy war, moderated divinity accedes, ignorantly or knowingly, to its necessity. The *Holy War* was a gift for Bishop Andrewes, a founder of the moderate English church.

20. Loeb Classical Library, *Philo* vol. 9, p. 106.

21. Machiavelli, *Discourses* II.5.

22. Sabinian is best known for reviving the moderate clerical party in place of the zealous monks brought to power by Gregory.

No Greek or Roman need speak after Pollio has spoken for he has usurped the speeches assigned to Eupolis and Eusebius, and Martius will do what he is told. Only Hebrew zealots are left to speak. And they will speak in Zebedaeus's hotter zeal for he takes over Gamaliel's part by arguing that holy war is obligatory. Contained in that speech of religious zeal will be the excess that convicts it, making necessary a confederation of Greece and Rome against it.

Pollio, then, seems ready to suspend the doubting sobriety that "ever" judged the philosopher's stone and holy war to be the coming together of cracked brains; he seems ready to certify that Athenian madness linked to Democritean sobriety could mount a holy war that would be the classical cure for the historic problem posed by Christian zeal. Spedding reports that the rest of Pollio's speech is not in the manuscript version; it seems therefore to have been added later, after the August 1623 events it prophetically names. Pollio's reason for speaking further is to avoid being misunderstood as "altogether adverse" to the project they all favor; he therefore assists them by stating just how it will be possible. He shows how the holy war is to be conducted before any of them even state their arguments on whether it should be conducted. His avowed frankness, however, is compromised both by its very avowal, and by the mysterious form of prophecy in which it is cast.

Pollio knows that the others will devise many solemn matters, but he simply commands them to take orders from him. Holy war is determined by the leadership of Christendom and for the new crusade to have any hope of success the leadership must be changed. "This Pope is decrepit and the bell goeth for him." Pope Gregory XV, already old and frail when elected in February 1621, must be replaced and Pollio gives orders for what they are to do when the pope is dead: see to it that a pope is chosen "of fresh years, between fifty and three-score," fifty-five, as was Urban VIII when elected on August 6, 1623, to succeed Gregory XV, "and see that he take the name of Urban," the first Pope to institute a crusade or to "stir up the voyage for the Holy Land." This voyage, under the new leadership of Christendom, will be the voyage to the holy land of Bensalem.

Full display of the historic necessity of holy war and the means at Bacon's disposal will not be complete until the next day when Zebedaeus reveals the full ferocity of civil authority grounded solely in sacred right. Nevertheless, the essential matter has been stated in Pollio's speech: they must alter the leadership of Christendom. Pollio, no dreamer, dreams that they can elect the new pope and, as a token of his own powers, prophetically provides the age, name, and goal of that new leader. Some new young Urban must sound the trumpet of a new crusade, not Maffeo Barberini, of course, the future Urban VIII, but a leader capable of braying Christendom in a mortar and molding it into a new paste which will cement a new society: a philosophic leader like Bacon who will lead a crusade for Bensalem.

In the character of Pollio, Bacon himself shines forth, for Pollio knows where he is and he knows how to speak. Knowing "the affairs of Christendom at this day," he knows that Christianity must be broken and remolded to moderate its goal, and he knows as well that this great undertaking must be spoken covertly in masking or sporting speeches that hide their high ambition in allusion and suggestion.

Pollio's speech receives a two-fold response from Eupolis, praise and blame that acknowledge the confederacy between them. "You say well." Eupolis grants the truth of Pollio's statement without qualification: he at least is of another mind having heard what Pollio can say. "But be, I pray you, a little more serious in this conference." Does Eupolis need to remind Pollio that this conference calls for a seriousness he has not exhibited? When the content of Pollio's speech is considered in the light of Zebedaeus's coming speech, Eupolis's attribution of levity serves to mask its actual gravity: the grave matters it proposes are best kept from the others by apparently rebuking it as the frivolous speech of a witty and pleasant courtier. We never hear Pollio again, but Bacon reports that Eupolis's call to be more serious has not curbed him: next morning Pollio reports his own dreams in "sporting speeches" announcing, in confirmation of the present speech, that the holy war has already begun in his dreams.

We must pause over Pollio's speech, invited but out of order, impetuously and with apparent levity settling conclusively just how the holy war must be fought now that it has been determined to be necessary. The pause can be made here where a pause is built into the dialogue: the speakers have till the next morning to reflect on what has been said and prepare what they will say.

In giving orders to change the decrepit leadership of religion, Pollio echoes the new papal doctrine of tyrannicide fostered by the Jesuits. Under this doctrine, regicide was tyrannicide if the regent was not ours, and tyrannicide not only justified the killing of the regent but sanctified it. Pollio leaves the initial part to nature—this pope is decrepit; the other part he assigns to secret councils he dreams they can determine—"Take order, that when he is dead . . ." Such thoughts about replacing the pope inevitably bring to mind the new thoughts of the popes about replacing monarchs opposed to their ends. England had experienced this new doctrine directly when Pope Gregory XIII released the Catholic faithful from obedience to the "tyrant" Elizabeth and invited her murder (1580): writing to two English nobles who planned to kill the queen but fretted over their deed being a sin, the papal secretary informed them that with respect to "that guilty woman . . . whosoever sends her out of the world with the pious intention of doing God service, not only does not sin but gains merit . . ." France, where Bacon's dialogue is now unfolding, had experienced the new doctrine still more directly in the blessed assassinations of its two previous kings.

What did Francis Bacon think of holy war in this papal vein? It seems to me that *An Advertisement Touching an Holy War* can answer that question quite completely: he thought such a holy war demanded a holy war against it using a broken and remolded Christianity of the sort exhibited in Bensalem. But a very useful supplement to the *Holy War* appears in a speech Bacon made on 17 May 1615 as Attorney General (*Works* XII.152–68). The speech provides telling confirmation of the interpretation of the *Holy War* given here for it is an explicit condemnation by Bacon himself of matters advocated by his Zebedaeus in the speech to be given tomorrow. Though only a supplement to what the *Holy War* says on its own, it is a most pleasant supplement as Bacon's commentary on his Zebedaeus and what he advocates. The occasion for Bacon's speech was the prosecution of a young Roman Catholic named Owen indicted on charges of high treason for speeches advocating the lawfulness of killing a king who has been excommunicated. Bacon's speech reviews the papal doctrine in detail and concludes that "this opinion is of all high treasons the highest" (165). The reasons he gives are that this form of regicide is based on religion, "a trumpet that inflameth the heart and powers of a man (above all things) to daring and resolution," that it has no limit concerning conspirators but appeals to "any son of Adam whatsoever to kill the King," and that it has no limit concerning time but "is a perpetuity of conspiracies." The seriousness of this crime, its absolute ground and limitless permission, leads Bacon to a noteworthy conclusion: "It deserveth rather some holy war or league amongst all Christian princes of either religion for the extirpating and rasing of this opinion and the authors thereof from the face of the earth" (157). This holy war is to be made against those Bacon calls "the common enemies of mankind" (165). Bacon's speech compares the doctrine of tyrannicide with other examples of murderous policy and finds the Counter-Reformation doctrine to be in all particulars the worst. The examples Bacon offers as *less* criminal than the Catholic doctrine are the very ones the Catholic Zebedaeus will cite to justify holy war against those who hold them.

In the *Essays* Bacon makes clear that he thinks Machiavelli was wrong in his description of the Christian soldier because Machiavelli did not give proper due to the absolute privacy of the Christian conscience which can persuade itself, or be persuaded by the authority to which it defers, that crimes like those of Ravillac and Friar Clement in killing the king of France are deeds that bring heaven's blessing (*Essays,* "Of Custom and Education"). And in writings directly concerned with Elizabeth's reign, Bacon consistently presents the view that the popes' policy of tyrannicide is a crime. "On the Fortunate Memory of Elizabeth, Queen of England" (1608) praises the moderation of Elizabeth's response to "the excommunication pronounced against her by Pius Quintus" ("that excellent Pope," Martius had said, "whom I wonder his successors have not made a saint" [19]) and condemns the bloody consequences it set in motion as "examples scarcely to be named among Christians" (*Works* VI.305–18; see also VIII.146–208, esp. 178–80, 187–89).

The more one considers such words by Bacon, the more the *Holy War* becomes a clear apology for a program against the common enemies of humankind, religious authorities who recognize no curbs on their actions because they are favored with privileged access to divine guidance. The second day's speech by Zebedaeus, the cool, considered speech of a fanatic who had all night to reflect on it, comes to light as self-indicting. A staggering conclusion but one pleasing to a Nietzschean perspective seems to be confirmed: in the writings of Francis Bacon the modern project of science and technology becomes visible as a civilizational fate set in motion by philosophy to wrest control of the human future from fanatics who take their instructions directly from God.

The Second Day

Bacon does not report Pollio's "sporting speeches" made at the opening of the conference the following morning. But in calling attention to them he shows that Pollio continues to hide his seriousness in sporting speeches. Pollio's war has already begun; it is present in his dreams, and he is one who can distinguish "the solid and real" from "the specious and airy" (24). Zebedaeus's speech will justify and ground what Pollio dreams.

[94]

Before the planned speeches begin, three amendments are made to the distribution agreed upon the night before.

Martius's Amendment

On sober reflection, Martius is moved to object that the order of the parts seems inappropriate to him because his part—the means—often determines an action's possibility or impossibility—Pollio's and Eupolis's parts. Martius is oblivious to what transpired the night before, the settlement by Pollio and Eupolis of the possibility of the holy war and the means to it. He cautions them far too late "not to speak peremptorily or conclusively touching the point of possibility, till they have heard me deduce the means of the execution." Martius quite naturally magnifies the importance of his own part, but Pollio and Eupolis do not take counsel from Mars on how he is to be used. They no more need instruction from Martius on means than they do from Zebedaeus on legality. Martius's objection seems to be moved by a fear that Pollio and Eupolis will decide too hastily on the impossibility of the enterprise. He seems to have spent the night worrying that the most worthy military enterprise in the history of the world could be derailed by those ignorant of his means.

The second day of *An Advertisement Touching an Holy War* begins with a "solid and grave advertisement" regarding the means. Possibility and impossibility are dependent upon means, Martius declares; the parts assigned to Eupolis and Pollio depend upon Martius—according to Martius. While Martius's claim of the dependence of ends on means was "much commended by them all," Eupolis speaks next and what he says makes the means depend upon the end.

Eupolis's Amendment

Why would Eupolis amend his own proposal? His amendment is something "more than a misplacing" of the sort that elicited Martius's amendment because it concerns "an omission" relevant to Zebedaeus's part, namely, "how far an Holy War is to be pursued." Eupolis's amendment is the appropriate one after Pollio has spoken: now that the holy war has been shown to be possible, and now that its means have been disclosed, the question of its extent or end becomes acute. Eupolis presents three degrees of extremity in the ends of holy war: first, the displanting and extermination of people; second, the enforcement of a new belief; third, the subjection of a people in order to prepare the way for a new belief "by persuasion, instruction, and such means as are proper for souls and consciences." Zebedaeus argues immediately that no new part is necessary to deal with this question of the ends of a holy war, because he, the most extreme advocate of holy war, father to the sons of thunder, will settle it; and in fact the most extreme possibility, "displanting and extermination of people," becomes the legal *obligation* of Zebedaeus's war. The end embraced by Zebedaeus requires that the full fury of Martius be put at the disposal of the spiritual sword. But the most moderate of the three ends, that which uses "the temporal sword to open a door for the spiritual sword to enter, by persuasion, instruction, and such means as are proper for souls and consciences," is the only one that would be consistent with what Bacon elsewhere uniformly endorses with respect to religion: in his praise of Elizabeth's moderate policy on the religious question, for instance, or in his fable "Diomedes or Zeal" where he introduces into the ancient fables a matter quite foreign to them, known to the ancients only by "reflection and imagination" and not by experience—religious wars. Holy wars, Bacon says there, did not exist among the ancients because their gods were not jealous gods, jealousy being "the attribute of the true God." Diomedes wounded Venus but he was incited by Pallas because of her rivalry: rivalry among gods is essentially different from the jealousy of the one true God (see also *Essays*, "Of Unity in Religion"). For Martius, what is worthy of "the wars of the Heathen" is "not worthy the warfare of Christians" (18) and the fable of Diomedes shows this to be a difference of kind: servants of a jealous God admit no limits to their martial zeal on his behalf. Zebedaeus will expound a war worthy of the servants of the jealous God; nevertheless, his argument and examples will enable Bacon himself to make a case for the most moderate end of holy war suggested by Eupolis.

Zebedaeus's Amendment

Zebedaeus makes the most extreme amendment for he changes the very nature of the speech he was assigned. When he seeks their approval for the change (28), "he perceived nothing but silence and signs of attention to that he would further say": they neither approve nor disapprove but simply attend to what he is going to say. How has Zebedaeus amended his assignment?

He interprets Eupolis's amendment as encouragement "to take that course which I myself was proposed to do." He even adds Eupolis's amendment as the sixth of the "particular cases" determining the lawfulness of a holy war. But then he proposes to *ignore all six* because of what he calls "a point that precedeth all these points recited." Not only does his new point precede them, it "dischargeth them." "Dischargeth" is ambiguous, suggesting either fulfilling them or dismissing them, but it is unambiguous in the important respect: the new point alone need be considered. The new point might have escaped Zebedaeus's attention, he says, if it had not been for Martius's "representation of the empire of the Turks." That speech is the "true charge," the true indictment that moves Zebedaeus to bring sentence against those charged—though for Pollio that speech was "invective" unjust to the Turks (22). The more Zebedaeus thought about the indictment, the more he settled into the opinion that "a war to suppress that empire, though we set aside the cause of religion, were a just war." Therefore, instead of the speech Eupolis distributed to him on "whether a war for the propagation of the Christian faith, without other cause of hostility, be lawful or no, and in what cases?" (23), Zebedaeus will make a wholly different speech advocating war against one particular people, a war that *sets aside the cause of religion.* And the more Zebedaeus thought about it the more he became persuaded that with respect to the Turks all limiting cases can be ignored because the issue is not sectarian but universal. This is Zebedaeus's amendment: setting aside the cause of religion and arguing solely from the cause of humanity with an assist from philosophy, he will claim that human considerations alone necessitate holy war against some humans who have fallen to a subhuman state that threatens real humans.

Just here, it seems to me, Bacon prepares his own case through the words of his zealot. Not Zebedaeus but Bacon sets aside the cause of religion; not Zebedaeus but Bacon makes an appeal to philosophy. Zebedaeus appeals to what is in fact his authority, his own interpretation of his sacred texts; but his theological argument for the purported depravity of the subhumans will stand exposed as a partisan's fraud, exposed by his own invocation of universal human grounds in philosophy. Two standards operate simultaneously in Zebedaeus's speech, one drawn from philosophy, the other from religion. Zebedaeus thinks they cohere; reflection on their content shows that Bacon knows they do not. Zebedaeus's amendment aims to *remove* the argument for holy war from sectarian narrowness. It both does and does not. While showing how one kind of holy war can in fact be based on philosophy, Bacon has Zebedaeus reveal that his is based wholly on religion. Zebedaeus's invocation of philosophy serves Bacon and subverts Zebedaeus. Philosophy does not justify Zebedaeus's cause, it convicts it. Here is the conflict between those who "profess and practice both, to refer all things to [themselves]" and those, "less hardy and more dangerous," who "practice it, and profess it not." In Zebedaeus's speech Bacon presents his case for a true charge against Zebedaeus's cause, philosophy's case against unbridled religion. The tension between philosophy and the Bible, Athens and Jerusalem, allows Bacon the prosecutor to enter the temple with its indictment.

The break for a night has had this result: Martius has been moved to inflate his role, Eupolis to moderate it, and Zebedaeus to ground it in reasons that abolish all moderation. So far from growing more moderate with time to reflect, Zebedaeus falls further into the grip of an opinion to which he inclines. Observation of the three characters who speak on the next morning, and consideration of the informative report on Pollio's speeches, provide a possible explanation for Bacon's introduction of a long break into a short dialogue. Bacon even induces a question about the night-long break by making the timing seem inappropriate: Pollio arrived in midafternoon (18, "the heat of the day") but after the short discussion which admits of no pauses, Bacon announces the recess "because the day was spent" (24). On the following morning both Martius and Eupolis refer to the discussion of "yesternight" (25–26). Why does Bacon draw out the time covered in his little dialogue and force a night to intervene? "It were better that in causes of weight the matter were propounded one day and not spoken till the next day" (*Essays*, "Of Counsel"). Pollio did not need to wait, for this is a matter on which he is well briefed and the night can be spent dreaming of the holy war he initiates. The intervening night helps to reveal the character of the other participants: it has been a night of self-inflation for Martius, of moderating thoughts of ends for Eupolis, and of immoderating passions for Zebedaeus. In Zebedaeus's speech we hear the zealot's justification of the warrior's "invective," cool reasons in the service of hot blood. He too seems to have spent the night dreaming of nothing but "Janizaries and Tartars and Sultans" and his dreams lead him to argue that "though we set aside the cause of religion" a war against them is just. Setting aside the cause of religion wholly changes the perspective of the previous day: justification for holy war switches from the intrinsic good of the cause to the intrinsic evil of the enemy. In this, it seems to me, Bacon's purpose is revealed: Zebedaeus's speech is a self-indictment, a "true charge" that reveals the enemy and justifies Bacon's war against it.

Zebedaeus's Speech

Zebedaeus speaks uninterruptedly to the end of the dialogue, giving not a "treatise" but a "consultation"—a brief speech of advocacy aimed to stimulate action. His authorization for war is rooted in two sources: "The law of nature and nations," whose authority is Aristotle, and divine law, "the perfection of the other two," whose authority is the Bible.

Any war, not only holy war, must make evident the justice of its cause, Zebedaeus argues, and he sets out to make evident the justice of the war he advocates. But his exhortation to clarity is carelessly worded for it sounds as if he is going to "make a Moloch or an heathen idol of our blessed Saviour"—though as Martius knows and Zebedaeus will show, Moloch never caused wars as bloody as the wars of the blessed Saviour. Three criteria are given for the justice of an action: the merits of the cause, the warrant of the jurisdiction, and the form of the prosecution. Zebedaeus will address all three. "As for the inward intention," he asserts, "I leave it to the court of heaven." In fact he assumes he has a window on the souls of his enemies and that his knowledge of their wickedness warrants jurisdiction over them to the most extreme form of prosecution.

Zebedaeus dismisses Scholastic debates on holy war as based on the inadequate resources of Roman positive and civil law.[23] The argument is thus simplified to two authoritative sources, Aristotle and the Bible.

Zebedaeus's philosophical argument for the law of nature and nations is drawn from a single passage in Aristotle, the first substantive discussion of rule in the *Politics* (bk. 1, chap. 4–7, 1253b–1255b): "That from the very nativity some things are born to rule, and some things to obey." Zebedaeus lists three interpretations of the passage, the first he calls a "brag," the second a "wish," and the third, the one to which he assents, a "truth." The brag makes the distinction Aristotle's warrant for Greek dominion over barbarians, the wish makes it a speculative platform that the best should govern, while the truth makes it a distinction of rank. Is Zebedaeus's interpretation Bacon's interpretation? Before considering Zebedaeus's interpretation, it is useful to consider the "wish," the central interpretation, for this seems to present with astonishing exactitude Bacon's own interpretation of classical political philosophy and to form the core of his own argument for warrant:

> Some have taken it for a speculative platform, that reason and nature would that the best should govern; but not in any wise to create a right.

23. The Scholastics are said to lack the gift of Navius, a gift of miracle in support of augury that made a doubting and cautious king believe in his ability to succeed in a war without fundamentally altering his forces. Livy, I.xxxvi; See Cicero, *De Divinatione* I.xvii.

Does "not in any wise" mean, not in any *way?* It makes perfect sense to understand it literally: not in any wise *men*. The final clause would then mean that none of the wise have a "right" to govern created by reason or by nature. Nevertheless, "reason and nature would that the best should govern." There exists a rational and natural warrant for the rule of the best, the wise, but this warrant is not translated into rights by human conventions. As constituted, political regimes do not accord with reason and nature by granting the wise the right to rule. Zebedaeus brands this interpretation a mere "wish," as if it hid the secret passion of the wise to rule. But Zebedaeus's dismissal accords perfectly with Plato's expectation, and it was Plato who first propounded in the *Republic* the view here summarized. Plato acknowledged that men do not desire to be governed by the wise, though that is what both reason and nature "would." But for Plato, the wise do not "wish" to rule in the ordinary way, and it is he who teaches the way in which the wise actually rule as legislators. Zebedaeus states that those who interpret Aristotle's account of rule as advocating the rule of the wise, take it "for a speculative platform." That "some" excludes Zebedaeus but includes Francis Bacon: not only is this the view of rule expressed in *New Atlantis,* it is the view intimated at the end of the letter of dedication to the *Holy War.* Describing his dialogue Bacon says, "Great matters (especially if they be religious) have (many times) small beginnings: and the platform may draw on the building." The central interpretation of Aristotle's account of natural rule presents that "platform," the speculative platform that reason and nature would that the best rule. "Platform" in Bacon's time was a word used for a plan to build by, or a plan of action, more specifically, a scheme of principles made on behalf of a religious party. The platform that reason and nature would that the best rule is dismissed by the zealot, but it is the ground of Bacon's rule, of Bacon's intervention in a world that requires, when measured by reason and by nature, that the rule of the wise become active, as it did in Joabin. Bacon takes his warrant from the Greeks and he shows it through an interpretation rejected by one who takes his warrant from the Bible. These small beginnings, this platform carefully constructed in a dialogue that rivals Plato's for subtlety, may "draw on the building"; it may inspire those deeds that will be an *Exoriere aliquis,* an uprising that will become a general uprising or turn European society to Baconian ends via Baconian means.

Zebedaeus's interpretation of Aristotle is different from this but in his interpretation too, Bacon's central point is echoed, for Bacon can do what Zebedaeus acknowledges he cannot do: measure from the perspective of the highest. Zebedaeus argues that the way Aristotle limits the claim to natural rule makes it "a truth": if there can be found an inequality between man and man such as evidently exists between man and beast or between soul and body, then that inequality would grant a right of government of the higher over the lower. But can such an inequality be known? Zebedaeus states that "men will never agree upon it, who is the more worthy" and that "fitness to govern is a perplexed business." Zebedaeus surrenders in the face of this difficulty of agreeing upon the high. But lacking knowledge of the high, men have been granted assistance, Zebedaeus holds, and to interpret his authoritative philosopher, he abandons philosophy in favor of the Bible. His way of demonstrating inequality will not exhibit the worthy but the unworthy; abandoning the notion of natural governors because of endless disputes, he embraces instead a notion of the naturally unfit whose unfitness can be authoritatively known. The rest of his speech will justify this claim; it will exhibit human unfitness, the forfeiture of the right to rule and the warrant for being ruled. From this point on, Zebedaeus's speech depends upon a principle of governance drawn solely from the Bible, for only on that basis can forfeiture or depravity be exhibited. Zebedaeus's interpretation of Aristotle's assertion of a natural distance separating human beings depends decisively on the Bible; because the Greek measure of the high is inaccessible to him, Zebedaeus replaces it with a biblical measure of the low. But Bacon does not share Zebedaeus's inability. Like Pollio, he possesses "a sharp wit of discovery towards what is solid and real and what is specious and airy." Able to distinguish the true from the false, Bacon is not disarmed by the fact that "men will never agree upon . . . who is the more worthy."

The trajectory of Zebedaeus's speech has now become fully visible and so too has Bacon's strategy. Zebedaeus turns to the Bible to warrant his holy war because of a self-confessed inability to provide a positive measurement of the inequality separating man and man, the inequality based on nature and reason. Unable to discern natural excellence, he fixes on an authoritative account of natural depravity. Pollio professes referring all things to himself, but in practice he is open to a universal standard of nature and reason; Zebedaeus professes a universal standard but in practice refers all things to himself, to a private standard derived from authority. Structuring Zebedaeus's speech as this precise move from Aristotle to the Bible, Bacon not only exemplifies in miniature

Christianity's illicit capture of philosophy, he prepares its release. Bacon is present henceforward in Zebedaeus's speech with the measure drawn from philosophy.

Before turning to the Bible to prove the inequality between man and man, Zebedaeus seeks to "confine ambiguities and mistakings," of which he mentions two. It is "idle" to say that the more capable have a right to govern because men will never agree on who is more worthy. Besides, "fitness to govern is a perplexed business" because it is most unlikely that the requisite qualities will all appear together. For not only is wisdom required, so too is "courage to protect," and "above all, honesty and probity of the will, to abstain from injury." Wisdom, courage, moderation, and justice are all required lest rule by the high or purportedly high turn into tyranny. Thus, Zebedaeus argues, it is impractical to look to the high because of the inability of men to agree on what it is, because of the improbability of its appearing, and because of the risk of abuse by those who claim it. Despairing of the "comparative," the ideal drawn from philosophy, Zebedaeus turns to the "privative," the absence of the ideal. The privative case will be "an heap of people . . . that is altogether unable or indign to govern"—the emphasis will fall not on "unable" but on "indign," on unworthiness measured by Zebedaeus's standard. Existence of the wholly unworthy will be just cause for war, assuming only that the subduing nation is "civil or policed," "though it were to be done by a Cyrus or a Caesar, that were no Christian." This standard for war reverses Eupolis's assignment: "A war for the propagation of the Christian faith" (23). Christianity has disappeared as a relevant criterion in the subduing nation; now the criterion is the civility of the subduing nation and the incivility of the nation to be subdued. This great shift requires but one more step for the reversal to be complete: identification of the nation to be subdued with Christendom. As Zebedaeus unwittingly supplies the evidence for this step too, Bacon's argument for holy war becomes complete. Reason and nature require the intervention of some Cyrus or Caesar to temper Christian incivility.

"The second mistaking" cleared up by Zebedaeus distinguishes tyrannical individuals from tyrannical political orders: holy war is justified not when the state of Rome happens to be ruled by a personal tyrant (Caligula, Nero, Commodus) but when the very constitution of the state and its fundamental laws and customs "are against the laws of nature and of nations."

Zebedaeus is now ready to give his speech. It is to have three parts:

First: are there any nations against which it is lawful to make war without provocation?

Second: what breaches of the law of nature and nations forfeit all title to govern?

Third: are these breaches found in any nation today, specifically in the Ottoman empire?

But after this clear announcement of the structure of his speech, matters grow obscure for Zebedaeus treats the second point prematurely (30–31) and then says he will postpone handling it: does he ever return to it? and is the third point ever discussed? Of course, the second and third points could be thought to be in the part of the speech not reported. But once a question about the announced structure is raised, attention is drawn to another three-part structure made apparent only as the speech unfolds: Zebedaeus differentiates three kinds of evidence, "proofs," "examples," and "arguments." What is the relationship between the three parts of the speech and the three kinds of evidence? When examined in detail the two sets of three merge: the first point is satisfied by the proofs, the second by the examples, the third by the single argument. Given this latent structure, Zebedaeus's speech is complete as a set of proofs, examples, and a single argument.

The Proofs. Is there "any nation or society of men, against whom it is lawful to make a war without a precedent injury or provocation?" In answering this question Zebedaeus turns to the Bible. Bacon very nicely makes his own point about what grants a right to rule by having Zebedaeus say, "Observe it well, especially the inducement or preface." Obeying this command, one observes that the apparent preface, "Let us make man after our own image," is itself preceded by a preface: "Saith God." The preface to Zebedaeus's proofs is a claim about what God says. Such a preface to the laws is of course not unknown to the philosophers, for Plato states that law stands in need of prefaces that ground the authority of the laws in the gods (*Laws* iv.722c–724a). The question implicitly raised by Zebedaeus's speech is this: is there harmony between what the gods now say—what God says—and the law of nature and nations?

Zebedaeus's proofs unfold in two stages, both dependent upon biblical texts. The first establishes that there is an "original donation of government" that can be forfeited, the second "that there are nations in name, that are no nations in right." But while deriving what God says about the right to rule from biblical texts, Zebedaeus concedes that his texts have to be interpreted: the seat of authority is not the Bible but one interpretation of it. On the fundamental point of the original donation of government, given in the Genesis account of man's creation and his relation to the animals, Zebedaeus follows the interpretation offered by Francisco de Vitoria, elevating his words to special authority—"a most true and divine aphorism": Rule is not founded unless it is in the image of God. But giving divine authority to Francisco de Vitoria quietly subverts Zebedaeus's proof, for Vitoria is the interpreter famous for his account of just wars and for his judgment that Spanish warfare against the natives of America was unjust, a conclusion contrary to Zebedaeus's. The words Zebedaeus cites are used by Vitoria, their author, to prove that the Indians *had* a natural dominion and were *unlawfully* deprived of it by their Spanish conquerors.[24] Furthermore, in this very context, Vitoria refers as well to the Poor Men of Lyons, and to Genesis, chapter 1, and Hosea, chapter 8—all in order to prove the contrary of what Zebedaeus will use them to prove.

After securing the "charter of foundation" that allegedly gives a right to rule, Zebedaeus moves to his second point by showing how that right is forfeited: by defacing the image of God on which it is based. Just what constitutes defacement is disputed, but Zebedaeus makes a single matter decisive: defacement of natural reason. Among those who interpret the forfeiture of dominion differently, Zebedaeus names "the poor men of Lyons." This is the first of many references in Zebedaeus's speech to Christian victims of Christian persecution. The Poor Men of Lyons or the Waldensians had sold all they had to follow Jesus into a life of poverty and piety, but they were hunted down and persecuted wherever their teaching broke out because of their denial of the authority of Rome.[25] The reference to the Poor Men of Lyons seems especially significant because they hold the distinction of being the first group of Christians in Medieval times to attempt reform on principles that would become basic to the Reformation: reading the New Testament in vernacular translation, comparing early Christian practices with contemporary church practices, challenging the efficacy of church rites for salvation. These practices made them the first to bring down upon themselves a crusade against heretics or fellow Christians, as an adjunct of the Albigensian Crusade against the Cathars. Under Innocent III, the whole apparatus of the Crusade, developed for war against the infidels, was applied to war

24. Vitoria, "On the American Indians," in Vitoria, *Political Writings,* 239–43.
25. See Lea, *History of the Inquisition of the Middle Ages,* I.76–88, 123–79.

against fellow Christians whose views were heretical. With the prospect of two years of indulgence and eternal salvation if killed, Christian warriors were set against Christian heretics. Then, with the failure of that crusade to stamp out heresy, the Poor Men of Lyons became the group of reformed Christians against whom the Inquisition was first developed, again in conjunction with the attempt to stamp out the Cathars. For decades and then centuries, small pockets of Poor Men of Lyons experienced the full ferocity of Christian holy war. By his seemingly gratuitous reference to the Poor Men of Lyons, Zebedaeus calls attention to the origins of Christian holy war as it was still being fought in Bacon's time. Repeated use of such references enables Bacon to point quietly to the history of Christian violations of the law of nature and nations.

Zebedaeus's proofs now turn to two additional biblical texts to prove that nations exist that have forfeited their right to rule. The first, Hosea 8:4, makes the chosen people of the Bible the people who have forfeited their right to rule. The second is another judgment against God's chosen people, made this time by their founder Moses (Deuteronomy 32:21). When Zebedaeus draws his conclusion from these proofs he states that there are nations outlawed and proscribed "by the law of nature and nations, or by the immediate commandment of God." This "or" makes it possible that the law of nature and nations and the law of God are alternative sources of condemnation, rather than the law of God being the perfection of the other two as had been claimed earlier (28). In addition, it is not easy to understand how either of Zebedaeus's two biblical proofs concerns the defacement of natural reason; the biblical standard declaring forfeiture seems nothing but "Saith God." How is that commandment to be measured by the law of nature and nations? This question takes on special importance as Zebedaeus passes from his proofs to his examples, for his examples include condemnation of those professing immediate access to God's commandment.

The Examples. What breaches of the law of nature and nations forfeit all title to govern? The examples, we are told, prove as much as the proofs and illustrate more than the proofs can. Judging by this introduction, the examples are at least as important as proofs based on the Bible. But the power of examples had already been attested in Bacon's letter of dedication, where he cited his own "examples," Cicero, Demosthenes, and Seneca. And the letter also spoke of arguments, anticipating Zebedaeus's third kind of evidence as well. In speaking of his own case did Bacon offer "proofs" from the Bible? The Bible is mentioned once in the letter, for Bacon opens by bringing the Bible into contact with examples and arguments: "Examples give a quicker impression than arguments; and besides, they certify us, that which the Scripture also tendereth for satisfaction, that no new thing is happened unto us." When Bacon himself brings together Zebedaeus's three kinds of evidence, arguments appear at the center and examples, rather than being "put after" biblical proofs (32), certify what Scripture "also tendereth": Bacon himself assimilates the Bible to the category of example.

Zebedaeus gives nine examples. The first four all illustrate "terror of danger" as grounds for holy war. The next three illustrate "error of nature" as grounds. The eighth example justifies the Spanish conquests in America. The final example does not illustrate Zebedaeus's "privative" case at all but refers to the fabulous example of Hercules to justify a singular kind of warfare.

"The true received reason" for the lawfulness of war against pirates —the first example—is the "natural and tacit confederation amongst all men against the common enemies of mankind." The same "law of nature" holds for the second example, "rovers by land." The third and fourth examples refer to enemies "now destroyed": the kingdom of Assassins and the Anabaptists of Munster. When Bacon used these two examples in his 1615 speech as Attorney General in the high treason trial against Owen, they served as examples of crimes illustrating the still greater crime of political assassination advocated and practiced by the Counter-Reformation church (*Works* XII.158, 166–67). What Bacon said explicitly there seems implicit here. If the views of the Assassins and the Anabaptists of Munster justify war against them, greater still is the justification of war "for the extirpating and razing of this opinion and the authors thereof from the face of the earth, as the common enemies of mankind"—where Bacon is referring explicitly to Counter-Reformation papal policy (*Works* XII.165). Zebedaeus describes the Assassins this way: "There the custom was, that upon the commandment of their king, and a blind obedience to be given thereunto, any of them was to undertake, in the nature of a votary, the insidious murder of any prince or person upon whom the commandment went." Such wording would surely remind readers of the doctrine and practice of political assassination that had appeared within the past fifty years—the papal bull of Pope Pius V against Queen Elizabeth in 1570; its intensification by Pope Gregory XIII in 1580; the outlawing of William of Orange by Philip of Spain in 1580 and his subsequent assassination (1582); the assassinations of Henry III (1589) and Henry IV (1610) by Christians following their conscience schooled by Counter-Reformation doctrine.

Bacon dealt explicitly with Christian assassins in the *Essays,* expanding Machiavelli's famous chapter on conspiracy to commit assassination.[26] Bacon praises Machiavelli's rule for "the achieving of a desperate conspiracy": do not entrust such matters to nature, to natural fierceness or resoluteness, but to custom, to one who "hath had his hands formerly in blood." The rule still holds, Bacon claims, but now there exists a noteworthy exception taught by recent examples: "Machiavelli knew not of a Friar Clement, nor a Ravillac, nor a Jaureguy, nor a Baltazar Gerard." These four Christian assassins, whose deeds were performed in 1589, 1610, 1582, and 1584, respectively, demonstrate that "superstition is now so well advanced, that men of the first blood, are as firm, as butchers by occupation." The essay as a whole attests to the supreme power of custom—"custom is the principal magistrate of man's life"— but Bacon's conclusion makes "votary resolution" a power that can now rival "custom even in matter of blood." "Votary resolution" is the extreme danger now represented by private Christian conscience released into assassination by God's regents. After drawing attention to "the force of custom copulate, and conjoined, and collegiate," Bacon concludes: "But the misery is, that the most effectual means, are now applied, to the ends, least to be desired." Least to be desired are the ends of assassins steeled in the private resoluteness of fanatical Christian conscience by collegial custom unknown to Machiavelli, recent Christian assassination doctrine.[27] Zebedaeus of course is forbidden the mention of such examples, being himself a Catholic zealot, but by mentioning similar examples which Bacon himself used in contexts that refer to Christian assassins as the most acute danger of all, Zebedaeus provides access to Bacon's own case.

Could hope for the moderation of Christian conscience lie in Protestantism? The namesake of the Protestant zealot Gamaliel is synonymous with moderation, and Gamaliel speaks moderately in his single speech— but Zebedaeus's account of the Anabaptists of Munster suggests that the offspring of the Reformation cannot be moderated, any more than Gamaliel could moderate his pupil Saul of Tarsus. With the Anabaptists, it is not so much their actions that make them guilty as the principle of their actions, a claim of privileged access to binding law transcendent to any law of nature and nations. But Zebedaeus's indictment seems to indict him as well, for in saying that "this is indeed no nation, no

26. *Essay* 39 "Of Custom and Education"; Machiavelli, *Discourses* III.6. Montaigne, *Essays* ii.29, "Of Virtue," discusses the Assassins along with Jaureguy and Balthazar Gerard, and other Christian assassins.

27. See Weinberger, *Science, Faith, and Politics,* 150–64.

people, no signory, that God doth know," he too claims to know what God knows and to base his actions on that. According to Zebedaeus, "any nation that is civil and policed may (if they will not be reduced) cut them off from the face of the earth." The Anabaptists of Munster were cut off from the face of the earth, as Bacon's readers well know, by a combined Catholic and Lutheran army, but whether those forces represented the "civil and policed" is questionable given the ferocious vengeance with which Christian annihilated Christian in that terrible episode of holy war.

When Bacon spoke in his own name of the Anabaptists, he judged their teaching second in dangerousness to the papal doctrine of assassination (*Works* XII.166–67). His reason is Zebedaeus's reason, but he carries its application further: the Anabaptists chant a Bible verse (Psalms 149:8) to warrant their overthrow of kings and nobles; but Bacon calls this claim of immediate access to an authority higher than the civil "a very express image of the Pope's authority." And while the two doctrines are akin, Bacon finds greater criminality in the papal doctrine on which Zebedaeus of course remains silent: whereas the Anabaptists (Bacon says) are "a furious and fanatical folly," the Consistory of Rome is "a sad and meditated tyranny. The one imagines mischief as a vain thing, and the other imagines mischief as a law." Though the Anabaptists and papal assassins can be ranked with respect to orders of danger, no hope can rest in either when the aim is the moderation of Christian conscience grown ferocious and unreachable in the war of the sects. Zebedaeus's examples prove as much as his proofs and they illustrate more. Nevertheless, they do not yet suggest just how the holy war against holy war is to be conducted—later examples illustrate that.

Zebedaeus turns from the "terrors of danger" represented by the first four examples to the "errors of nature" represented by the next three examples (nations where women reign over men, slaves over freemen, and sons over fathers) and argues for the right to subdue them too in the name of nature. He then turns to the example discussed on the previous day by Martius and Pollio, the Spanish conquest of Mexico and Peru. Pollio had called attention to the philosophical distinction between nature and convention and Martius had defended the conventions of the West Indies as in keeping with nature. Zebedaeus, addressing Martius directly, argues that their conventions were *contrary* to nature and therefore invited and justified their conquest by the Spaniards. But to view the Spanish conquest of Peru and Mexico as justified by the laws of nature, is to repudiate Francisco de Vitoria, the authority whose "most true and divine aphorism" Zebedaeus had earlier cited as the foundation of legitimacy; Vitoria deduced from his aphorism the illegality of Spanish conquest, Zebedaeus deduces from it the legality of that conquest, indeed its moral necessity. In making his case, Zebedaeus explicitly excludes propagation of the faith as a ground and bases his conclusion solely on what he regards as the law of nature and on the "policy and moral virtue" of the conqueror—qualities put in question with respect to the Spanish conquerors by Zebedaeus's own disavowal of Spanish cruelties at the end of this example. Zebedaeus says his conclusion rests not upon "nakedness," "idiocy," and "sorcery," but upon cannibalism "joined with the rest." For Zebedaeus this is such an "abomination" that "a man's face should be a little confused" to deny that it gave the Spaniards the right "either to reduce them or displant them"—this is, however, just what his authority Vitoria denied, and it is just what Montaigne denied in his famous essay "On Cannibalism" where he compared this custom favorably with European customs, including the custom of religious warfare (*Essays* i.31; see also "Of Coaches" iii.6).

"Of examples enough," Zebedaeus says, but then adds one final example, "the labours of Hercules"—not exactly an example then but a fable, the device used so tellingly by Bacon to disclose the most secret matters of government, religion, and philosophy. Hercules illustrates a single point: exhibiting "the consent of all nations and ages"—though Hercules is a Greek of ancient origin—"in the approbation of the extirpating and debellating of giants, monsters, and foreign tyrants, not only as lawful but as meritorious of divine honor." So the English version. Significant changes are introduced in the Latin version—"foreign tyrants" become "enormous tyrannies" and "not only as lawful, but as meritorious even of divine honor" becomes "but just as with excellent deeds; which deserve divine or at least heroic honors." The changes show how close Zebedaeus's English words are to the well-known words of Pope Pius's charge against the "foreign tyrant" Elizabeth inviting her assassination. The Latin translation of the *Holy War* seems governed by the same principle as the translation of the *Advancement of Learning:* in a letter to King James accompanying the latter, Bacon said, "I have been . . . mine own *Index Expurgatorius,* that it may be read in all places. For since my end in putting it into Latin was to have it read everywhere, it had been an absurd contradiction to free it in the language and to pen it up in the matter" (*Works* XIV.436).

Zebedaeus says the example of Hercules shows the legitimacy of the deliverer coming "from the one end of the world unto the other."

This point had already been made by his second example, illustrated by Rome's deliverance of Greece. Here, the opposite deliverance seems implied: a Greek journey to deliver Rome. For Zebedaeus refers to the special labor of Hercules that Bacon had made prominent in *On the Wisdom of the Ancients* in the fable of "Prometheus, or the State of Man." Hercules is celebrated for a labor not listed among the customary twelve, a labor in the service of humanity's great benefactor, Prometheus: Hercules sailed across the sea in a cup to deliver Prometheus from the punishment inflicted by Zeus. To explain this punishment, the daily tearing of Prometheus's entrails by an eagle, Bacon altered the original fable as he had reported it; it was not Prometheus's many earlier crimes on behalf of humanity and against Zeus that caused Zeus to inflict this terrible punishment on him, but one crime only, "that last crime of Prometheus," his attempt on the virgin Minerva, goddess of wisdom. Bacon's interpretation of the fable suggests that Hercules's great journey delivers philosophy in the person of Prometheus from the chains in which ignorant Zeus had placed it for its attempt to possess the wisdom Zeus had accounted his own offspring. Prometheus's last crime was "trying to bring the divine reason itself under the dominion of sense and reason." Prometheus's crime is Bacon's crime, one that inevitably brings "laceration of the mind and vexation without end or rest." These cares and solicitudes are precisely the ones to which Hercules brings relief, for he represents a virtue that comes from without, the virtue of courage in the face of great responsibility, a virtue that "is not a thing which any inborn or natural fortitude can attain to." Coming from afar, brought from the sun by the deliverer Hercules, the virtue of courage is said to be a consequence of wisdom: the sun, not Zeus and his virgin Minerva, represents wisdom. Though it stems from the sun, courage comes from across the sea in a cup, from "meditation upon the inconstancy and fluctuations of human life, which is as the navigation of the ocean." Such philosophic courage, springing from a natural wisdom, neither curbs wisdom nor gives it a new charge but calms the cares elicited by its audacity in bringing divine reason under the dominion of sense and reason, bringing Zeus and Minerva under the sun. Just how Bacon effects that subjection of religion to philosophy is told in his final point prior to the reinstitution of the games to honor Prometheus: "Men must soberly and modestly distinguish between things divine and human, between the oracles of sense and of faith." Men like Bacon must maintain that there are two separate kinds of truth-seeking, one adequate for divine matters and incompetent for all others, the other adequate for all others but incompetent for divine. This anti-Platonic strategy for philosophy is the one means of now avoiding "a heretical religion and a fabulous philosophy."

Zebedaeus's last example points to Bacon's own attempt on Minerva, his own combination of Prometheus and Hercules, wisdom and courage, his own refusal to refrain from bringing "strange fire to the altar of the lord." But if the final example suggests that Bacon's task constitutes Greek deliverance of Rome, the argument with which the dialogue ends suggests a more comprehensive journey of deliverance: from Athens to Jerusalem with the aim of capture.

The Argument. Are these breaches of the law of nature and nations found in any nation at this day? The proofs, examples, and arguments justifying holy war now come to their culmination in one argument only, an argument that completes Bacon's case and makes its opponent evident. Here Bacon shows that he is able to do what his Zebedaeus is unable to do, measure from the perspective of the high. Bacon's own case, unlike Zebedaeus's, does not rest on the privative or low but on knowledge of the high. *An Advertisement Touching an Holy War* comes to an amazing and perfectly satisfying conclusion. No more is said because no more need be said, the platform may now draw on the building.

Bacon's final argument involves an uncanny use of the Bible and sets out to reverse that most fateful capture in Europe's history, Jerusalem's capture of Athens. Fulfilling the promise of his letter of dedication, Bacon allows himself to be seen entering the temple, entering Jerusalem in the name of Athens.

There exist, the argument states, implicit bonds among nations that give one nation responsibilities toward others even where no explicit pact or league exists among them. Zebedaeus cites three forms of "implicit confederation": "Colonies, or transmigrants, towards their mother nation"; the union implied by a common language; and the still stronger bond conferred by having "the same fundamental laws and customs . . . as it was between the Grecians in respect of the barbarians." Zebedaeus refuses a fourth bond, the only bond referring directly to religion: "To be of one sect or worship, if it be a false worship, I speak not of it, for that is but *fratres in malo.*" (This sentence referring to "brothers in evil" was omitted in the Latin version.) The bonds among nations are completed by a fifth: "The supreme and indissoluble consanguinity and society between men in general." In support of this final point Zebedaeus refers first to a saying quoted by the Apostle Paul in his speech to the Athenians (Acts 17:16–34). In this speech bringing the Christian gospel to Athens, Paul approached the Athenians on their own grounds, quoting "the heathen poet," his fellow Cilician, Aratus: "We are all his generation." Then Zebedaeus quotes the words of another poet, saying that Christians ought "not to be less charitable than the person introduced by the comic poet." This vague reference prefaces the words "I am a man, I hold that nothing human is alien from me," words spoken by the old Athenian, Chremes, in Terence's comedy, *The Self-Tormentor* (i.77)—"the greatest sentence to emerge from the Hellenistic age" says one historian.[28] Chremes speaks these words when challenged with being a busybody for mixing in the affairs of others. Terence's play is an adaptation of a now-lost comedy by the Athenian comic poet Menander. One must again stand amazed at Bacon's ability to find references that display his case. Athenian madness had been the antidote suggested by Pollio, and here Athens reappears in a mix of references. The point that can be drawn from them all, the Apostle's speech included, is that universal charity and responsibility has *Athenian* origins. The charge of being a busybody and mixing in the affairs of others is one of the charges raised against philosophy (*Apology* 31c; *Laws* xii.952d; *Lovers* 137b). Bacon cannot avoid being a busybody and mixing in the most fundamental affairs that concern us all. As a man of Athens he must say, "I am a man, I hold that nothing human is alien from me."

If there is a tacit confederation among men, "it is against somewhat, or somebody: who should they be?" This is the final question of the dialogue and an answer needs to be sought because none is directly given: the dialogue does not end by applying its argument to the Ottomans as Zebedaeus had earlier promised (30). Zebedaeus says only that it is against "such routs and shoals of people, as have utterly degenerate from the laws of nature . . . and may be truly accounted . . . common enemies and grievances of mankind; or disgraces and reproaches to human nature." Who are these people? The final reference to the Bible suggests an answer.

The penultimate sentence is specific on the responsibilities for action but vague on those against whom the actions are to be directed: "Such people, all nations are interested, and ought to be resenting, to suppress; considering that the particular states themselves, being the delinquents, can give no redress." What states? We look to the final sentence.

It begins with a vague reference: "And this, I say, is not to be mea-

28. Ferguson, *Heritage of Hellenism*, 121.

sured." To what does "this" refer? It must refer to the general point of the previous sentences, responsibility for action by a confederation of men against the common enemies of mankind. This action and its grounds are "not to be measured so much by the principles of jurists"—though by those principles as well then—"as by *lex charitas: lex proximi.*" By citing the law of charity, the law of the neighbor, Bacon begins his use of Jesus' answer to the jurist who had asked "and who is my neighbor?" (Luke 10:25–37). The law of the neighbor "includes the Samaritan as well as the Levite." But where is the priest? Everyone knows that Jesus' story of the good Samaritan includes a priest. Bacon excludes the priest while including both the Samaritan who came to the aid of the beaten man and the Levite who did not. The extent of the law of the neighbor is repeated in the Latin clause added next: *lex filiorum Adae de massâ unâ* ("the law of the sons of Adam concerning a single mass"). Mass? Could the mass of the sons of Adam exclude the priests?—"mass" resonating with both senses: the great body of mankind as well as their religious service, the "mass" claimed as the exclusive right of priests?

The sentence continues: "upon which original laws this opinion is grounded." The law of charity grounds the responsibility to intervene and that law is original to Athens. The sentence ends: "which to deny (if a man may speak freely) were almost to be a schismatic in nature." May Bacon speak freely? Not entirely, but when a man can speak as Bacon speaks he can express his meaning under the very eye of the Zebedaeuses, no, with their very words. We have been told that those who refer all things to themselves and do not speak freely are the more dangerous, and Bacon's conclusion, not spoken freely, is dangerous in the extreme: to deny the law of the brotherhood of man is "almost to be a schismatic in nature." "Schism" is a word used in the Greek New Testament to apply to division in the Church (1 Corinthians 1:10, 12:25), and in English it was almost exclusively an ecclesiastical term referring to divisions that rent the Church. At the end of his case, Bacon appropriates an ecclesiastical term for far broader purposes: "Schismatic in nature." But this final phrase is ambiguous: it could mean that being schismatic almost belongs to the nature of those who deny this law; or it could mean that those who deny this law are almost schismatic among things governed by the law of nature, almost outside nature. Both senses seem to apply and in both senses the "almost" indicates a reserve that makes the judgment less absolute than it might be: this is a judgment against schismatics on which no anathema can be based. But it is a judgment nevertheless against those who are almost schismatics in nature because they deny the law of nature derived from the Greeks and pronounce anathema on all schismatics whose views take them outside their own notion of "Saith God." Apparently universalists, Christian latecomers to universalism, in their now uncontrolled zeal, are schismatics who divide what is naturally united.

Paul entered Athens using their poets selectively to introduce a new and strange gospel. Just so does Bacon enter Jerusalem. Paul entered Athens with the teaching of Jerusalem, purporting to bring knowledge of "the unknown God" or to replace Athenian ignorance about the gods—its "Socratism" one might say—with certain knowledge of the true God. Bacon enters Jerusalem with the teaching of Athens, feigning knowledge of the true God in order to win freedom from his regents guilty of crimes against the law of nature and nations. And Bacon enters Jerusalem to take possession as much as Paul entered Athens to take possession—and succeeded. The means to Bacon's success are alluded to only once in the *Holy War:* success will require a Christendom broken and molded into a new paste. The law of charity, that ostensibly Christian law already understood in a superior way by Greek philosophers as philanthropy (*Essays,* "Of Goodness and Goodness of Nature"), will have to be expressed in a new science of nature promising earthly benefit. The one writing of Bacon's that goes into the temple will have to be supplemented by the writings that go into the city: the project that takes possession of the city breaks the temple's dominance of the city and subdues it into service for its own ends. Bacon's holy war has the very purpose announced by Urban II at Clermont in 1095 when he called for the first Crusade: the capture of Jerusalem and the Holy Land. But Bacon's crusade is justified by teachings that arose in Athens and that serve a philanthropic and not a religious purpose.

Can Christendom be crushed in a mortar and molded into a new paste? Such an event would belong to "the greatest vicissitude of things amongst men . . . the vicissitude of sects and religions" (*Essays,* "Of Vicissitude of Things") and Bacon gives the rules governing such vicissitudes. A new sect can be expected to spring up "when the religion formerly received is rent by discords; and when the holiness of the professors of religion is decayed and full of scandal"—conditions more than met by the many events of Christian holy war alluded to in the *Holy War.* A further condition must be met, "if then also there should arise any extravagant and strange spirit to make himself author thereof"— a condition well met by that singular spirit who authored the new science of nature for the relief of the human estate. Success can come if the new sect contains within itself two further properties: "The supplanting or opposing of authority established; for nothing is more popular than that. The other is, the giving license to pleasures and a voluptuous life." Bacon's new sect is discreet in opposing authority but it can well afford to be because the license it gives to pleasures and a voluptuous life will make its opposition apparent and popular. The plantation of new sects takes place in three ways: "By the power of signs and miracles, by the eloquence and wisdom of speech and persuasion, and by the sword." Bacon's new sect employs the central means, but nothing forbids the other means: Bensalem controls signs and miracles and it holds a sword fashioned by the new technology it engenders. Nevertheless, it is moderated by knowledge of its own limitations: it knows the utility of the preface to laws that announces "Saith god," but it knows that no such preface stands at the head of its own laws. Study of *Holy War* enables us to say with Leibniz: "We do well to think highly of Verulam, for his hard sayings have a deep meaning in them."[29]

29. Cited by Robert Ellis, Bacon, *Works* III.71.

Chapter 5

Bacon, Plato, Nietzsche

I am a complete skeptic about Plato.—*Nietzsche (*TI *Ancients 2)*

Nietzsche's complete skepticism about Plato was not skepticism about his influence. On the contrary, Nietzsche attributed to Plato unparalleled sway over Europe, primarily because of Christianity's successful adaptation of philosophic Platonism into a "Platonism for the people." The greatest events have been events in the history of philosophy, in Nietzsche's view, legislative events that created the horizon of aspiration and opinion within which the whole of Western culture played itself out. But that philosophers are legislators is not usually the first and most prominent thing Nietzsche says about them, as the structure of *Beyond Good and Evil* exemplifies: first comes the attack "On the Prejudices of Philosophers" aiming to break their hold and clear our minds. Only after this liberation can philosophy be credited with its legislative, culture-making power. And only after that can training begin in a new perspective that springs from the new philosopher.

Bacon shares the basic features of Nietzsche's history of philosophy: recognition of the legislative power of philosophers, Plato at their head; attack on philosophers to free the mind of prejudices or idols derived from them; and promulgation of a new philosophic legislation. Such understanding and action require that the philosopher possess "the historical sense." Nietzsche found this "sixth sense" to be the particular possession of the nineteenth century (*JS* 357), but it is evident that Bacon too regards the historical sense or knowledge of the times as an essential possession of the philosopher.

Bacon and His Times: Cassandra Reformed

"Cassandra, or *Parrhesia*," the first fable of *On the Wisdom of the Ancients,* presents the essential lesson, exemplified in one way or another in all of Bacon's works, that the wisdom of insight must be accompanied by a wisdom of communication appropriate to the times. *Parrhesia* is the standard Greek word for frankness or freedom of speech, meaning literally, to say everything. The fable tells of the reproof dealt Cassandra for saying everything, for speaking her true insights too frankly or freely: not only was she not believed, she did harm precisely where she intended to do good, the destruction of her people hastened by her very gift of insight. Apollo, patron of philosophy, had been tricked into granting her insight, but he took revenge by withholding the further gift he might have granted, time and measure in discourse. Apollo's revenge deprived Cassandra of the Apollonian music that knows the difference between learned and unlearned, and between times to speak and times to be silent. Cassandra recklessly indulged in the *parrhesia* that Athenians later claimed as their birthright.[1]

The fable of Cassandra is augmented in Bacon's interpretation by the eminent example of Cato. Claiming that Cato was gifted with prophetic foresight into Rome's eventual fall into tyranny, Bacon argues that Cato succeeded only in hastening that fall because, as Cicero said of him, "he talks as if he were in the *Republic* of Plato and not in the dregs of Romulus." Cato spoke as if he actually inhabited the city founded by philosophy, but to speak this way is to betray the fact that one of the essential gifts of Plato's *Republic* has been withheld. For that dialogue shows how speech must accommodate itself to the actual cities or caves of men. Lovers of truth who have learned from Plato the necessity of enduring the lie of nobility on which every city is built (*Republic* vii.537d–539d) will not say everything; they will speak justly, doing good to friends who are good while not harming anyone (*Republic* i.331e–336a). Put first, this fable is the assurance Bacon gives that Apollo has favored him with both his gifts. Having learned from Plato's *Republic*, he does not talk as if he inhabits Plato's *Republic*. He knows where he is and he knows how to speak.

The fable of Cassandra is of capital importance for understanding the prophet of the "Kingdom of Man." Having foreseen the fall into tyranny that threatened his own times, the prophet Bacon attempted to overcome that fall by introducing into his own most troubled times a wholly new undertaking that would transform them by effecting "a total reconstruction of sciences, arts, and all human knowledge" (*GI, Works* IV.8). How did Bacon avoid Apollo's revenge? By a knowledge of the times, of

1. Euripides, *Hippolytus* 422. See Euripides, *Ion* 672; Plato *Republic* viii.557b; *Phaedrus* 240e; *Laws* ii.671b.

when to speak and when to be silent. And for Bacon, knowledge of the times requires knowledge of the history of philosophy, or an understanding of the degree to which the times have been framed by wisdom. In addition to the role of philosophy, another essential element in Bacon's understanding of his times is what Nietzsche called "the long and serious study of the average man" (*BGE* 26). Bacon goes so far as to say that the "judicious direction" of the "ordinary and common matters" of men is "the wisest doctrine" (*Advancement, Works* III.418) and that this study was deficient among the ancient authors. Philosophy seems to have neglected what religion, in particular Christianity, has studied, and in the face of threatening tyranny a reformed Cassandra will have to take over the direction of the common man from Christianity.

Bacon knows that he is not in the *Republic* of Plato but he knows as well that he is not in the dregs of Romulus. He is, as the *Holy War* makes clear, in the dregs of Moses and Jesus. Bacon described this problem of the times in *The Advancement of Learning*: where Christian law is "set down and strongly planted" it places itself in authority over philosophy, judging on its own terms the philosophic controversies that arose independent of it, even judging philosophy's idea of the highest good with its own (*Works* III.419–24). For philosophy to judge *it* and supplant *it* as ruling authority, philosophy must do as Joabin did and adopt its dress and speech. The result will be a new teaching of hope which folds itself into the old teaching to free itself to speak (III.419). Reformed Cassandra will possess a knowledge of the times granted by an understanding of the history of philosophy and an understanding of the average man formed by Christian belief. The new prophetic speech, having foreseen the ruin that threatens its times, will adapt itself to what has already been set down and strongly planted in order to choke it off.

Bacon's History of Philosophy

Bacon's most extensive account of the history of philosophy is given in Book One of the *New Organon*. But this history serves a polemical purpose, helping to make Bacon's case for the new science; a "refutation of the philosophies" (*GI, Works* IV.27; *NO* I.115), it aims to destroy belief in the adequacy of the reigning philosophy because "belief of plenty is one of the greatest causes of want" (*NO* I.85). While arguing that philosophy's apparent plenty is actual poverty, Bacon must also attempt to establish belief in the possibility of plenty if philosophy takes a different path. Destruction of confidence in the old philosophy and creation of confidence in a new philosophy must occur simultaneously because "the human mind is not like a wax tablet. On a tablet you cannot write the new till you rub out the old, on the mind you cannot rub out the old except by writing in the new" (*PFB* 103, see 132).

Rubbing out the old philosophy and writing in the new requires that Bacon sketch the history of philosophy. According to this sketch, philosophy flourished in three periods, all subsequent to Socrates, the one turning point because he turned away from natural philosophy to political philosophy. Bacon implies that his own thought is a return to the pre-Socratic philosophers, Democritus in particular, but his tale of philosophy does not surrender the gains of political philosophy: Bacon is politic in not explicitly tying either his natural philosophy or his political philosophy to a pagan source; like Solamona he acts as if the inspiration for philosophy came from Solomon. Nevertheless, Bacon's revival of pre-Socratic natural philosophy uses the politic philosophy traceable to Socrates.

Bacon's history of philosophy in *The New Organon*, occurring within his account of the "idols of the theatre," aims to disabuse his readers of illusions derived from the philosophers who composed the great stage play in which all now play a part. To achieve his own goals Bacon must overthrow the rule of Aristotle in natural philosophy. This act of philosophic insurrection depends on two main claims: that Aristotle has not enjoyed unbroken rule, and that the natural philosophy of the older Greeks was not refuted by Aristotle but yielded to the forces of empire.[2]

None of the three periods of learning—"the first among the Greeks, the second among the Romans, and the last among us . . . the nations of Western Europe" (*NO* I.78)—devoted itself to natural philosophy. In the latest period, "by far the greater number of the best wits have applied themselves to theology" rather than to natural philosophy (79), while in the second period, "the philosophers were principally employed . . . on moral philosophy, which to the heathen was as theology to us" (79). In the first period, natural philosophy flourished "but a brief particle of time," between the Seven Sages and Socrates. The eclipse of Greek natural philosophy occurred when "Socrates had drawn philosophy from heaven to earth." Bacon quotes Cicero's praise of Socrates[3] in order to state his own blame, because Socrates "diverted the minds of men from the philosophy of nature" (79). Socrates is therefore the one turning

---

2. See Weinberger, *Science, Faith, and Politics,* 177–78.

3. Cicero, *Tusculanae disputationes* 5.4.10.

point in the history of philosophy for, "if the truth must be told, when the rational and dogmatic sciences began"—with the Socratics, Plato and Aristotle—"the discovery of useful works came to an end" (85), the brief flourishing of natural philosophy, "the great mother of the sciences" (79, 80), came to an end.

Socrates and not the currently reigning Aristotle is the turning point in the history of philosophy. Moreover, with respect to the crucial question of the loss of the works of the natural philosophers, Bacon goes out of his way to say that Aristotle's attempted refutations were not responsible: "The common notion of the falling off of the old systems upon the publication of Aristotle's works is a false one" (77). Though he conducted himself like an Ottoman ruler killing all his kin the better himself to survive on the throne (67), Aristotle's attacks failed for the works of the Greek natural philosophers continued to survive through Cicero's time and beyond, threatening Aristotle's rule in natural philosophy (77). In a parallel passage Bacon emphasized that Democritus survived Plato's and Aristotle's attempts to obliterate him because his superiority in natural philosophy was well recognized by the Romans: "Democritus was held in great honor with the wiser sort, and those who embraced more closely the more silent and arduous kinds of speculation. Certainly in the times of Roman learning that of Democritus was not only extant but well accepted" (*Works* V.465–66. In an early work Bacon emphasized how assiduous he had been in his attempts to recover the lost teachings of the older Greeks [*PFB* 116].[4]). The works of the natural philosophers were lost not because of Aristotle's superiority but because Rome proved an incompetent steward of Greek natural science. In accounting for this great loss Bacon says only this: "When on the inundation of barbarians into the Roman empire human learning had suffered shipwreck, then the systems of Aristotle and Plato, like planks

4. On Bacon and pre-Socratic philosophy, see Sessions, "Bacon and the Classics." It is well worth noting for a Nietzschean history of philosophy that Bacon goes beyond simple reliance on Democritus. As Robert Ellis, one of Bacon's nineteenth-century editors argues, "Bacon had obtained deep insight into the principles of the atomic theory" and had abandoned the old notions that atoms had definite size and figure and were hard and unyielding. Like Nietzsche, Bacon advanced beyond the view of "the clod atom" (*BGE* 12) for in Bacon too, as Ellis states, "the atomic theory becomes a theory of forces only." Writing in the mid-nineteenth century, Ellis refers to Boscovich (1711–87) as the thinker whose theories of force accord with Bacon's views—and Boscovich was an important source for Nietzsche's reflections on atomism and his own theory of force, will to power: "Boscovich has taught us to abjure the belief in the last part of the earth that 'stood fast'—the belief in 'substance,' in 'matter,' in the earth-residuum and particle-atom" (*BGE* 12). See Ellis, preface to *De Principiis atque Originibus, Works* III.70–71.

of lighter and less solid material, floated on the waves of time and were preserved" (77). This asymmetrical sentence selectively mixes causes and contents; it names the cause of what was lost ("inundation of barbarians") while not naming what was lost (the works of Greek natural philosophers) and it names what was preserved ("the systems of Aristotle and Plato") without naming the cause of preservation. Why were the systems of Plato and Aristotle preserved? Given the characteristics Bacon supplies for the three ages—and given the arguments of *New Atlantis* and *Holy War*—these systems were preserved because they proved serviceable to the natural theology of Christianity, that greatest of inundations into the Roman Empire. The implication in Bacon's asymmetrical sentence therefore seems to be: the rise to power of Christianity within the Roman Empire cost us our heritage of Greek natural philosophy which had survived well into Roman times. Not "those innocent barbarians" (as Gibbon called the Goths and Vandals[5]), but Christianity brought the period of Roman learning to an end. This of course is Nietzsche's judgment as well, and Nietzsche's times required a strident and open rhetoric just where Bacon's required a restrained and masking one: "The whole labor of the ancient world *in vain:* I have no words to express my feelings about something so tremendous" (*A* 59).

Bacon's history of philosophy then, places the victory of the Socratic or the rational and dogmatic systems late in the Roman Empire, after a long period of co-existence with natural philosophy. The Roman Empire proved vulnerable to overthrow by Christianity, a popular movement that decided the fate of philosophy, or what would sink and what would float. In intellectual matters "the worst of all auguries" is popular consent (77) says Bacon, repeating Phocion's saying: "If the multitude assent and applaud, men ought immediately to examine themselves as to what blunder or fault they have committed." The fault here is a world-historical one, the capture within Rome of philosophy by religion and the consequent stamping out of Greek natural philosophy, continued pursuit of which could have generated the particular sciences (80) that Bacon now aims to establish.[6]

Toward the end of his long account (*NO* I.78–92) of the eclipse of ancient natural philosophy, Bacon notes that one of its perpetual enemies is superstition or blind and immoderate religious zeal; his examples from the three periods of learning put a special focus on the Christian fear of natural science (89), the attitude Nietzsche traced to the opening

5. Gibbon, *Decline and Fall*, chap. 71.

6. See Weinberger, *Science, Faith, and Politics*, 168–69.

chapters of Genesis as "the story of God's hellish fear of science" (*A* 48). Bacon emphasizes the fear of the loss of power by those who currently administer "the empire of faith over the sense." His own great task of rekindling hope in reason and in reason's power to give men dominion over nature (92–114) aims to destroy the power of the empire whose sway depends upon curbing natural science and defaming reason.

This current practical task occupies most of Bacon's public efforts, almost guaranteeing that he enter history as the philosopher who reversed the ancient order of rank between theory and practice, or contemplation and action. But at the end of his argument for a new practical philosophy Bacon affirms the ancient order of rank. "Now that hopes have been raised and unfair prejudices removed," Bacon can focus on the goal of his work. He elevates discoveries and especially that discovery "by means of which all things else shall be discovered with ease," the Baconian method. But just here, at this peak, Bacon allows the "whole truth" to be told, only a partial truth having as yet been told: "Assuredly the very contemplation of things as they are, without superstition or imposture, error or confusion, is in itself more worthy than all the fruit of inventions" (*NO* I.129). Bacon must act and his act elevates action to a higher plane than it had occupied hitherto. But Bacon's imperative to action comes from the need to defend contemplation, to defend philosophy.

Who is heir to Greece and Rome? In particular, who is heir to Greek philosophy? Bacon's third period of learning, his own age, was dominated by the empire of faith over the sense, and this empire interpreted history to accord with its victory. Christian learning took itself to be the rightful heir of Greece and Rome, preserving what it judged worthy while letting fall what it judged unworthy, preserving Plato and Aristotle while letting Democritus fall. So far from sharing Christianity's providential convictions regarding its victory over Greece and Rome or its judgment that it preserved what is best of them, Bacon stands much closer to Nietzsche's judgment: Christianity's victory is a triumph of the slavish and base over the noble, and its standard of what is worth preserving makes war against natural nobility. Bacon's times did not permit him Nietzsche's blunt claim that the fall of Greece and Rome into Christianity was the triumph of herd or slave morality, but "Renfusans" as the name for those to whom Christianity first appeared in Bensalem is a nice clue. And the case against Christianity stitched together in *An Advertisement Touching an Holy War* shows that Bacon acts on behalf of Greece and Rome.

Who is heir to Greece and Rome? There will be great confusion on this question, Nietzsche's Zarathustra tells his disciples, because the ancient inheritance has been skewed by Christian attempts to claim it (*Z* 2.7 "On the Tarantulas"). *Holy War* shows the violence with which Aristotle's teaching on the high was perverted to endorse a Christian teaching on the low. *New Atlantis* features a public history in which Bensalem dissimulates its actual dependence on Plato into apparent dependence on Solomon. Bacon lays claim to being the true heir of Greek philosophy, both pre-Socratic natural philosophy and Socratic civil or moral philosophy. The music of the new Orpheus both "propitiates the infernal powers and draws the wild beasts and the woods." Moreover, the new Orpheus acts because of the fate of ancient Orpheus: in retelling this fable, Bacon notes that Orpheus was torn to pieces by "certain Thracian women, under the stimulation and excitement of Bacchus," but he makes no comment on these details in his interpretation. However, when interpreting the fable dealing with Bacchus himself, "Dionysus, or Desire," Bacon returns to the fate of Orpheus. Frenzies are attributed to Bacchus's influence, he says, because every passion is a brief madness which, if vehement and obstinate, ends in insanity and "every insane passion grows rank in depraved religions." The "salutary and free admonition" that was Orpheus's civil counsel is "hateful and intolerable to an overpowering passion." The two fables dealing with Orpheus's fate point to the fate of Socrates, the model of Orpheus, but they point as well to the historic fate of Socratic philosophy at the hands of Christianity. That historic fate required that Bacon act.[7]

Bacon is heir to both Greek natural philosophy and Greek civil and moral philosophy; but the works of Greek natural philosophy did not survive while Plato's and Aristotle's did because of what is light and frothy in them. If Bacon distances himself from Plato by his prohibition on natural theology (see *NO* I.65), he follows Plato on the crucial issue of civil philosophy by developing an apology for philosophy that is attuned to its times.

Bacon and Plato

Bacon's polemical history of philosophy cannot be a complete account of his predecessors; it emphasizes the prejudices of the philosophers as

7. For this interpretation of the Thracian women, see Paterson, "Bacon's Myth of Orpheus," 427–44.

a prelude to a philosophy of the future. Bacon himself plays the Ottoman ruler who slays his kin in order to prepare the way for the new
philosophy. But *New Atlantis* and *Holy War* show why such rhetoric is
necessary; the true greatness of these little works lies in their esoteric
disclosure of Bacon's loyalty to Greek philosophy: he does justice to
Greek philosophy in a way appropriate to an innovator. In *New Atlantis,*
King Solamona acts as if his inspiration were biblical all the while that it
is Greek, or, more specifically, Platonic. In *An Advertisement Touching an
Holy War,* the Greek law of nature and nations dictates that philosophy
enter the temple; Athenian madness combines with Democritean sobriety to provide the Hippocratic antidote to ills brought on by religion.
Overt opposition to Greek philosophy masks covert fidelity.

Plato is the fundamental figure. Bacon's characteristic opposition to
Plato is required by the times: Plato most effectively brought together
what Bacon was forced to separate, philosophy and theology. Bacon
forbids natural theology, one of the principal parts of Platonism for the
people, because it no longer serves philosophy's purpose to allege that it
has access to the gods, that it can serve the city by restoring the power
of gods gone dead. Bacon's times are not marked by a death of the gods
but by a God grown all-powerful, dominating even philosophy, a God
whose religion is now rent by discords that threaten European civilization. In such times, a Zebedaeus can expropriate universal philosophy for purposes wholly local to his religion and he can set Martius in
motion with reasons that are beyond Martius's grasp but that inflame his
already aroused passions. By giving "to faith only that which is faith's"
(*NO* I.65), Bacon makes room for knowledge invulnerable to correction
by faith. Opposing the natural theology of Plato and Aristotle, Bacon
alleged that there were two kinds of knowledge independent of one
another, each wholly competent within its own sphere while wholly incompetent in the other. This rational device is only an apparent limitation
on reason, for reason is fit to peer discreetly into the sacred mysteries
as Bacon made clear in modifying the Pentheus fable: in Bacon's version Pentheus's crime is followed not by death but only by confusion,
by the divided light of two suns and the divided loyalty of two Thebes.
(See *WA* "Acteon and Pentheus, or Curiosity"; in "Dionysus" Pentheus
dies for his crime.) But Bacon draws a further point in modifying the
Prometheus fable: Zeus's punishment for Prometheus's last crime, his
attempt to ravish Minerva or possess the divine wisdom, can be remedied by the gift Hercules brings from the sun. This most dangerous of
Promethean games captures the secrets of Zeus's self-generated wisdom

and uses them against him; it brings together philosophy and religion in a way kept secret from Zeus. Comfort is available for such high games but it is the comfort afforded by Hercules, not Zeus.[8]

In his strictures against Plato's natural theology, Bacon calls it "a certain rhapsody of natural theology" (*Advancement, Works* III.347), a form of philosophical poetry as Plato himself acknowledged in Book Ten of the *Republic*. The *New Organon* intimates that Plato's rhapsody covers a deeper skepticism, for Bacon credits "the school of Plato" with introducing *acatalepsia,* the skeptical doctrine advocated by the New Academy against the Stoics (*NO* I.67).[9] As Bacon presents matters, *acatalepsia* was introduced by Plato himself, "in jest and irony, and in disdain of the older Sophists, Protagoras, Hippias, and the rest" (67). Furthermore, Platonism itself is said to be reducible to a newer form of sophistry (71). Bacon too is a complete skeptic about Plato, his skepticism arising from appreciation of the rhetorical purpose of the dialogues.

For a Nietzschean history of philosophy it is crucial to understand that Bacon is no more the first to be a complete skeptic about Plato than he is the last. Bacon is preceded in this judgment by other philosophers of the highest rank, by Montaigne, for instance, and Cicero, and the Arabic philosophers Al Farabi and Averroes. Montaigne is willing to state his skepticism about Plato quite openly, for Montaigne's own skeptical purposes are served by betraying the skepticism behind Plato's rhapsody. The philosophers, Montaigne says, "wrote some things for the needs of society, like their religions . . . Plato treats this mystery with his cards pretty much on the table" (*Essays* ii.12, "Apology," 379). Montaigne picks through those cards to demonstrate that Platonism is "in fact a Pyrrhonism in an affirmative form" (376). Montaigne's skepticism about Plato and his philosophical theology is visible in Descartes as well, as I will argue in the next part, though neither Descartes nor Bacon can be as open about this as Montaigne.

A Nietzschean history of philosophy will have as one of its goals, it seems to me, complete openness about what was necessarily and for good reason hidden by the great philosophers, all of whom have known "the difference between the exoteric and the esoteric" (*BGE* 30), and all of whom have known what religions are good for (*BGE* 58). The *neces-*

---

8. For Bacon's separation of reason and revelation, see Anderson, *Philosophy of Francis Bacon,* 53–54, 58–59, 171–73, and *Advancement, Works* III.477–90. For his critique of Plato's natural theology, see *Advancement, Works* III.346–59 and *NO* I.62, 65, 89.

9. On *akatalepsia* as the means of demonstrating the impossibility of *katalepsis,* the Stoic criterion of truth, see Couissan, "Stoicism of the New Academy," 31–63.

sity of esotericism is a theme that arose early in Nietzsche's work and he returned to it constantly. But it is an embarrassing theme in a sincere age committed to the virtue of openness and to the abolition of any order of rank. In such an atmosphere, esotericism is bound to appear indecent; not only is it a form of lying, it insults everyone else's intelligence and strength, as if we could not all live in Democritus's sober world. My book aims to recover the honorable role played by esotericism in the history of our culture, a role that has its effective beginnings in the Socratic turn and especially in the writings of Plato. A Nietzschean history of philosophy could well be understood as the history of complete skepticism about Plato coupled with recognition of his unparalleled influence through the connection he forged between philosophy and public beliefs.[10]

For Bacon and other complete skeptics about Plato, opposition to some aspects of Platonism is wholly compatible with being schooled by Plato. *New Atlantis* points to dependence upon Plato's *Laws* where Plato as lawgiver teaches that necessity may, from time to time, require altering the fundamental laws while the manner of their alteration remains the same: through the intervention of the wise. Plato is the teacher not only of the nature of the city and its relation to philosophy but also of the philosopher's responsibility toward the city. The labor of the Athenian Stranger demonstrates that the Athenian Stranger is plural; more than simply Socrates or Plato, he is the Platonic philosopher as such, the one schooled by Plato to take in hand the instruction of the many Kleiniases and Megilloses, lawgivers to Magnesia, the greater city founded and sustained by philosophy. His name may be King Solamona, as implied by *New Atlantis,* or Pollio, as implied by *An Advertisement Touching an Holy War.*

What moves such men in their breathtaking resolve to alter the order of human affairs, to change the direction of history? Is it their love of the truth and their desire to impart it to others? Is it their love of fame or immortal glory, the motive for which Bacon in particular is often arraigned? Is it the notorious "will to power" understood as the passion to give one's imprint, any imprint, to history—a standard way of dismissing Nietzsche? What moves such men? This question seems to

10. Starnes, *New Republic,* argues that Thomas More's *Utopia* (1516) adopts an esoteric style to advocate a radical break with a Christianized Plato; More's ground for the break is similar to Bacon's: the political chaos into which Europe had fallen because of the conflict between spiritual and temporal rule.

me one of the cardinal questions of a Nietzschean history of philosophy and, as I think, it can be given a precise answer which shows that Plato, Bacon, Descartes, Nietzsche, and other genuine philosophers shared the same fundamental experience. That experience is made most accessible, it seems to me, in Nietzsche's writings about it, particularly *Thus Spoke Zarathustra,* a fable that tells the tale of the coming to be of the new philosopher. But it is accessible in Plato's dialogues in a special way because they proved exemplary for subsequent philosophers, so exemplary that one must include even Nietzsche among the Platonic philosophers when Platonic philosophy is understood as a psychology and sociology of the philosopher, or more simply, as an account of what moves such men. Because this issue is foundational to a Nietzschean history of philosophy, and because it helps to clarify not only Bacon's work, but Descartes's and Nietzsche's as well, it seems necessary to consider the Platonic paradigm, if only briefly. Plato's writings often address the issue of what moves the philosopher, but two writings seem of special importance, the *Republic* and the *Phaedo.*

The Republic *and Responsibility*

In the *Republic* the Platonic philosopher's responsibility is not only commanded in Socrates' words but exemplified in his manner of speaking them. The philosopher's responsibility becomes most apparent in the cave story, and while Bacon never treats this story in detail, he says explicitly when referring to one of its more superficial points, that he refuses "to enter into the exquisite subtlety of this allegory" (*De Augmentis, Works* IV.433). Entering at least some parts of that subtlety can cast light on Bacon's own assumption of responsibility, his own Platonic philosophizing.

The cave story introduces a great novelty by no longer permitting what was previously permitted (vii.519d): that the philosopher remain detached from the city to pursue the things that most accord with his nature as a passionate knower who desires to know everything (v.475c). Glaucon's objection is entirely fitting because Socrates has taught him that justice is doing one's own: the new requirement that the philosopher return to the cave does him an injustice for it deprives him of what is most his own or most natural to him (vii.519d). In response to this objection, Socrates prescribes the limits of the philosopher's new responsibility to return to the cave: only those philosophers whose cities have seen to their philosophical education are duty-bound to return; only philosophers raised by the city built in speech have such a duty. Philosophers who grew up of their own accord as if by grace or chance against the will of the city have no duty to go down. In describing these conditions Socrates invents a speech of admonition for philosophers schooled by the city built in speech: "You must go down" is the command which forms its core and theme (520b–d).

But just here, at the crucial elaboration of what is arguably the most important theme of the *Republic,* the relationship between the philosopher and the city, an odd contradiction has occurred. The one voicing the command "You must go down" and limiting it to philosophers raised by the city built in speech is Socrates, a philosopher who grew up by grace or chance against the will of the city. But if he now says, "You must go down," "I went down" was what he first said, the very first word of the *Republic.* The command at the center was fulfilled by the one issuing it in the first word and first deed of his narrative. Why has Socrates, that wild growth of philosophy, gone down? Why was the Socratic turn taken?

Socrates gave two reasons for his own going down, to pray and to observe (i.327a). Piety and curiosity satisfied, he meant to return but was constrained. Does Socrates stay only under constraint? The conversations of Book One occur under the original constraint, politely masked by the attraction of a dinner, a group of young men with whom to converse, and a torchlight parade on horseback for the goddess. By means of those conversations Socrates seems to have contrived his release and freed himself to return (ii.357a). However, he is immediately put under a new constraint by Glaucon and Adeimantus, a constraint with no suggestion of the brute force jokingly threatened by Polemarchus, the warlord. Instead, Socrates hears an appeal, almost a cry from the heart, by young men who know more clearly than Polemarchus that they have lost what they inherited from their fathers, that most precious gift of belief and practice that descends from the poets and still sends Cephalus to tend the sacrifice and tend his soul. "That's all over now," as Nietzsche says with respect to a later death of the gods (*JS* 357). Because that's all over now nothing stands between these young men and the temptations held out by Thrasymachus except a residual nobility that makes his allures unsavory and demeaning.

Why does Socrates stay in the Pireaus, his piety and curiosity satisfied and the constraint of mere force removed? The long conversation that now follows and that reschools Glaucon and Adeimantus seems to occur under a new constraint which Socrates places upon himself and expressly calls the constraint of avoiding impiety, the impiety of standing by and not defending justice when it is reviled (ii.368c). Socrates goes down for reasons of piety and curiosity but he seems to stay only for reasons of piety, piety for justice, having discovered in his descent new reasons to stay that appeal to his piety.

But piety in a Socrates is always suspect; such piety always seems to be accompanied by a second, more important motive like the curiosity of his original descent. In the *Apology*, Socrates' descent, his speechmaking in the marketplace, is based on piety to Apollo according to his first speech; but when he returns to the theme of why he speaks he says it is the greatest good for a man (38a); and when he alludes to his motive a third time—imagining his questioning of heroes in the underworld—he speaks of pleasure and happiness (41b–c).

What moves Socrates to stay in the Pireaus? Is it simply piety for justice? Exactly what it means for Socrates to be moved by piety for justice is made clear only by the long conversation itself. If at the beginning, solicitude for his young countrymen seems to be enough, in the depth of the night the true independence of the philosopher begins to be uncovered, and such solicitude is clearly shown not to be enough; the philosopher is not moved solely by love of his own city, his own cave. In the night, when they enter the cave, the fundamental motive for Socrates' staying seems to be revealed. The cave is always dominated by authoritative opinion, shadows and echoes traceable to those shadowy figures in the story who move behind a wall behind the prisoners' backs. The shadows they cast and the echoes they cause are the only reality accessible to the prisoners. Imprisoned within that reality and loving it as their own, the prisoners cannot welcome any inquiry into it or attack upon it. But the opening book has made it clear that in Socrates' times the old shadows and echoes lie exposed as the prisoners are led to look behind their backs at the source of the authoritative teachings. The authoritative teachings have lost their hold on the young who would, in normal times, have inherited them as Cephalus had from his father and his father's father before him. But now it seems as if only selfish advancement remains for the talented young, and they have, despite their noble inclinations, nearly yielded to the sway of teachers like Thrasymachus who, themselves lacking nobility, are ready to direct that advancement into tyranny.

But the nobility of the best young men leaves them open to persuasion by Socrates; they desire to be persuaded to virtue and they are persuaded. But if Socrates becomes authoritative for them, making the case for justice that they welcome, he shows too that he is not authoritative for the city. The cave dwellers generally must see him as useless and dangerous, as Adeimantus says on their behalf (vi.487b–d). In order for the philosopher's teaching on justice to take hold among those who despise and fear him, a transformation will have to occur in the city's disposition toward philosophy. Just how that happens is intimated by Socrates at the high point in the dialogue where he is goaded into saying just how the city built in the philosopher's speech can come into existence: either philosophers must become rulers or rulers philosophers. Outrage attends his announcement that men like himself ought to rule the city. Glaucon, a future ruler, shares that outrage when Socrates first makes his announcement and immediately, unguardedly, readies himself to strip and run at Socrates to do him harm (v.474a). But charmed by Socrates, Glaucon agrees to come to his aid and to protect him from the outrage naturally felt at his hubris. "Since you offer so great an alliance," Socrates says that he will try to make the case that the philosopher should rule the city. This alliance—Socrates and Glaucon, the philosopher who has gone down and the rising politically powerful who attend him—will make the city safe for philosophy by giving the city over to the rule of the philosopher. Allied with Glaucon, Socrates becomes useful to the city by founding its necessary virtues on ideas no one else can see. A new poetry of ideas replaces Homer's poetry, just as Homer's warring gods are replaced by gods who always agree; newly just gods watchfully administer a new justice, and newly immortal souls bear its rewards and punishments. In alliance with Glaucon, Socrates shows how philosophy has ceased to be useless and dangerous and become instead the city's true benefactor. This alliance creates new shadows and echoes; the cave is remade as a place friendly to philosophy, a place in fact ruled by philosophy and its salutary ideas.

This is madness. Athenian madness, the rule of the philosopher over the city. The Socratic turn away from Democritean sobriety that scorns its fellow citizens and drew their scorn. According to a Nietzschean reading of our tradition this madness succeeded; Socrates is the one turning point of all so-called world history; since Plato all philosophers and theologians have been on the same track (*BT* 15; *BGE* 191). The story of our civilization since Plato is the story of how the true world, Plato's world, "I, Plato, am the truth," finally became a fable (*TI*). Have there been genuine philosophers who have determined the Whither and For What of humanity (*BGE* 211)? The answer is obviously yes, for Platonism put Europe under the sway of its particular Whither and For What.

Is the Socratic turn which makes philosophy useful to the city really motivated by solicitude for the city, the piety Socrates avows? Not solely, it seems, for the Platonic Socrates has made the city safe for philosophy. "I went down" Socrates says and in staying down he schooled those who cast the city's shadows and cause its echoes. He schooled them to a new perception about philosophy as the benefactor of the city, the model and ground of the statesman's virtue. The alliance of the Platonic Socrates and Glaucon, of the new politic philosophy and the gentlemen, makes the cave safe for philosophy. In making respectable what had helped kill the city's gods and caused a turn against philosophy both by those who believed in the gods and by those who believed in the necessity of believing in them—both Strepsiades and Aristophanes—Plato found a way, an amazing way, to be of service both to the high which is the city and the highest which is philosophy.

The *Republic* seems to teach that Socrates went down out of piety and curiosity but that he stayed out of piety and responsibility. Staying, he argued the release not merely of a Socrates threatened by a community more powerful than he and guided by interests other than his own, he argued the release of philosophy as such from the completely appropriate suspicions under which it had fallen. Those suspicions culminated, in Socrates' own case, in execution; but those suspicions are soothed and settled by the Platonic Socrates, transformed into trust and gratitude by the young men who will always remember that night in the Pireaus and be elevated in their remembering. Perhaps one could even say (considering the great differences between the Socrates of Book One and the Socrates of Books Two to Ten) that the historic, executed Socrates freed himself to leave after humiliating Thrasymachus at the end of Book One and ruining everyone's feast. But the Platonic Socrates stayed after the appeal made by Plato's brothers, and he stayed in order to form an alliance with them by persuading them that philosophy can secure the virtue of the city. The Platonic Socrates thus distances himself from the Sophists and especially from the natural philosophers, Democritus and his band of giants (*Sophist* 247d–e). The Platonic Socrates has learned the lesson of the *Clouds*. In going down to rule, those few, very few, come to power who do not desire to rule but who desire still less to be ruled (i.347a), to be ruled, that is, by anything less than the great passion that defines them, the lust for knowledge, to know everything (v.475b–c).

Platonic philosophy, therefore, as it comes to light in the *Republic*, becomes civil and moral out of a responsibility owed to philosophy. The preservation of philosophy threatened by the city is effected by the rule of philosophy over the city. Plato, Nietzsche said, was beyond good and evil; but he was not, any more than Nietzsche was, beyond good and bad. Plato acted out of the judgment that philosophy was the highest good for humanity and that it was in need of shelter. Plato's Socrates won a stay of execution for philosophy itself in the city that executed its exemplar, the one Plato makes younger and more beautiful. The *Symposium,* that most beautiful of Platonic dialogues, makes Socrates literally more beautiful: he puts on his fancy shoes and his best clothes to go to Agathon's feast. But he also dresses in Diotima's garb by telling an elevating tale of the origins of Eros and of its passionate drive to the highest and permanent good. And he tells his tale to win over Agathon. But a rival for Agathon, drunken Alcibiades, tells a tale warning Agathon of an eros unrequited by Socrates. By describing a Socrates erotic only for wisdom, drunken Alcibiades beautifies Socrates into innocence: he corrupted the great Athenian criminal into nothing but moderation. And as this tale of the beautified Socrates is told, the descent of the *Republic* is reversed: the narration of the *Symposium* unfolds as narrator and audience ascend from the port up into the high city of Athens. The *Symposium* carries the beautified Socrates, philosophy's most persuasive advocate, up into the city that executed Socrates unbeautified.

The Phaedo *and Philanthropy*

The *Republic* emphasizes responsibility to go down for the well-being of philosophy; the *Phaedo* shows that the Socratic turn from natural philosophy to civic and moral philosophy is the turn from a dangerous way to a safe way. Phaedo recalls Socrates' dying day as a day mixed with pleasure and pain, laughing and crying. The absence of pity and the dispelling of fear show that this was a death but not a tragedy. But at the very center Phaedo turns to a death worthy of pity and fear, a death that would force both Socrates and Phaedo to cut off their hair in mourning were it to occur, the death of the logos (89c). Within the dialogue, the threat of that death appears when the argument for the immortality of the soul faces new objections raised by Simmias and Cebes. But that threat is the symptom of a more dangerous threat, a disease that might infect them all if they do not save the argument. Socrates must rally this little band of "defeated, retreating soldiers" and turn them around to follow him in attack (89a). And Socrates proves to be valiant, not only in retreat as Alcibiades had shown in the *Symposium,* but also in attacking this great enemy, for "no greater evil" exists (89d).

But to win their collective victory and to keep winning after the sun sets, Socrates must cement an alliance with Phaedo: Socrates, like Herakles, cuts off the Hydra's heads and Phaedo, like Iolaus, staunches the wounds lest two new heads grow, and together they hide the immortal head under a rock. For Phaedo, the survivor of that alliance, it is now "the greatest of all pleasures" (58d) to recall Socrates, and to retell the events and speeches of Socrates' last day, preserving the memory of Socrates' victory and making it memorable for others. Socrates' victory saves the argument and brings comfort not only to those present—those many founders of Socratic schools—but also to Echecrates and others to whom Phaedo tells the heroic tale (88c–e; 102a).

What was the fatal disease against which Socrates rallied his little army? Misology. Hatred of logos or reason. To explain misology Socrates links it to misanthropy, hatred of the human. Misology is like misanthropy in that each arises where there is a great deal of faith but no art or artfulness, no skill. When its faith is betrayed often enough, an unskilled love of the logos turns to a hatred of the logos, just as an unskilled love of humanity turns to a hatred of humanity. Misology and misanthropy grow out of their innocent opposites, philosophy and philanthropy, putting human beings in jeopardy to the one true tragedy, death of the logos.

Misology and misanthropy—these Greek words are less well known than the Latin word whose meaning now incorporates them and which was made famous by Nietzsche: nihilism. There is "no greater evil" than nihilism says Socrates on his dying day, the loss of faith in reason, in humanity as rational. If the logos dies, if hope in reason is lost, misanthropy must follow, for humans are the beings defined and dignified by logos. How can the little band attending Socrates on his dying day stay the misology and misanthropy bound to arise from an unskilled philosophy and an unskilled philanthropy? Socrates himself must perform the heroic deed, whether he assume the lion's skin of Herakles as here at the center, or the patriotic mantle of Theseus, the Athenian hero recalled at the beginning.[11] The heroic Socrates rallies his company like warriors for he confesses that in this hour he does not speak philosophically but like a lover of victory (91a). They are to have the courage to say, whenever the argument falters, that it is not the logos itself that is unsound but they as inquirers that are unsound; they must set out ever again to become sound, as Socrates has always done and does again now, the afternoon sun permitting a few hours still to make the unsound Socrates sound.

But how could misology ever befall these young lovers of argument?

---

11. See Klein, "Plato's *Phaedo*," 375–94. See also Burger, *Phaedo;* a number of points in my account of *Phaedo* derive from Burger's important commentary.

Socrates shows exactly how by recounting his own experience: excessive faith or trust in philosophy to uncover the causes of all things can lead to hatred of philosophy for its failure (96a). The failure of philosophy to fulfill the faith placed in it leads to the perception that neither words nor things have anything stable about them (90c). Socrates himself once wanted to believe in the capacity of philosophy to uncover the causes of all things but he learned to his dismay that mechanistic and teleological explanations of nature cannot give an adequate account of their own simplest categories of number and growth. Nor can they explain the real causes of why human beings do what they do, why Socrates is sitting in prison waiting for the sun to set on the last day of his life. How did Socrates avoid the misology and misanthropy consequent upon disillusionment with the promise of natural philosophy? By the Socratic turn, a second sailing in search of the cause, a second-best ship (99c–d). Socrates invented a new way of sailing to avoid the dangers of the first way; it is less heroic for it is a safe way attentive to the dangers of the first— Bacon records it as the way taken without gladness by Orpheus after he had lost Eurydice forever to the infernal powers. The second sailing remedies the unskilled faith of the first, for it is a *technē* of logos, an art of speech or reasoning that looks for the causes of things in the speeches about them. One does not sail alone on the safe way, for it is a dialogic way the end of which is persuasion rather than knowledge. The safe way is a way to satisfaction satisfied when the other is satisfied. And Simmias and Cebes are satisfied, and Phaedo and Echecrates are satisfied. One, however, seemed to remain dissatisfied; I forget just who, says Phaedo (103a). But the nameless one does not press his dissatisfaction. Perhaps at this point where the logos seems unsound, he will hold that it is not the logos but him. Dissatisfied with himself, he will be satisfied that Cebes is satisfied. If the safe way seems less than heroic, perhaps it is not heroic to risk the logos and risk one's fellows.

But the safe way is to be accompanied after all by astronomy, by continued inquiry into the highest things (*Laws* xii.966d–968a). Accompanied by the safe way, such risky study no longer leads to atheism as it once did, in that earlier period of rash philosophizing that led the poets to compare those who philosophized to howling bitches (967c–d).[12] Bacon often repeats this judgment: "A little philosophy inclineth man's mind

---

12. See Strauss, *Argument and Action of Plato's Laws,* 183.

to atheism, but depth in philosophy bringeth men's minds about to religion" (*Essays,* "Of Atheism").

The Socratic turn from the things to the speeches is a way of safety, the artful means of saving trust in reason. At the same time it is necessarily an act of philanthropy, for in preserving trust in reason it preserves trust in what is highest in humanity. The Socratic turn to speeches, or what seems to be the very core of Platonic philosophy, thus comes to light as the means to preserve what is in fact the very core of Platonic philosophy, love of the logos and love of humanity. Not innocent, unskilled love but love that is an art, an art that faces its highest task in times of misology and misanthropy and that devises a way to spare humanity that greatest of tragedies, nihilism.

Just here a Nietzschean history of philosophy reaches its bedrock: it is the story of the heroic effort to preserve the logos first brought to life by Greek thinkers prior to Socrates. Platonic philosophy arises as a cure to the innocence of that first impassioned moment, an innocence that threatened its life in the one setting that nurtured it. And Platonic philosophy continues as a series of comparable moments in which misology and misanthropy arise to threaten philosophy. Bacon's times are just such a moment and Bacon's response places him among the Platonic philosophers, not because he keeps to the second sailing but precisely because he does not: the fate of the second sailing forces Bacon to act, its capture by a misologic and misanthropic religion.

Plato's times are singular times because of the first ever presence of philosophy in the city. Plato's response makes all subsequent times post-Platonic in the specific sense anticipated in the cave story. The Platonic Socrates can issue the commandment "You must go down" and direct it realistically to all those raised to philosophy by the city built in speech in the forms in which it actually exists: Plato's recorded words in the dialogue the *Republic,* and the city transformed by philosophy's alliance with the gentlemen into tolerance for the philosopher. Educated by Plato to the truth of the city and philosophy, and educated in the city transformed by Plato's effective defense of philosophy, post-Platonic philosophers have a duty to go down. The Platonic philosopher goes down for precisely the reasons that the Platonic Socrates is shown to stay down in the Pireaus, piety and responsibility. "You must go down" to remake authoritative opinion and ground noble action on a foundation that will hold, as the Platonic Socrates did in the arguments he fashioned on behalf of the city's virtues. (The *Laws* provides another massive example of Platonic philanthropy: the Athenian Stranger does not travel to Crete to study the best laws but to introduce new laws and institutions. While acting the part of a patriot to win over patriots, he is a "civilizing philosopher who, being a philosopher, is a philanthropist." [13])

But the foundation that replaces Zeus's rule will be no more eternal than Zeus's was. It will in fact present itself as eternal by alleging the discovery of ideas that were always eternal. This Platonic tale satisfies what Bacon said "the nature of man doth extremely covet," namely, "to have somewhat in his understanding fixed and immovable, and as a rest and support for the mind" (*Advancement, Works* III.392). But Plato intimates near the end of the *Laws* that the fundamental laws of the city must be open to change in ways that cannot be anticipated by the founding legislator: "The opinions of human beings about gods having changed, the laws too must change" (*Laws* xii.948d). The Athenian who teaches the evils of innovation himself makes the greatest innovation and prepares the way for other innovations of great magnitude by the King Solamonas to come.

"I am a complete skeptic about Plato," Nietzsche says, "he's so moralistic." But the "first immoralist" does not differ fundamentally from the moralist Plato with respect to the philosopher's responsibilities. Nietzsche is no Epicurean standing aside and watching the city destroy itself while the philosophically inclined gather in a garden: "You dolts, you presumptuous, pitying dolts, what have you done!"—it is with such words that Nietzsche goes down, taking the divine hammer in hand and crying out in wrath, in pity, in horror (*BGE* 62). These are typical opening words of Nietzschean philanthropy. With Nietzsche too, philanthropy is philo-philosophy: love of humanity is love of what is best in humans. The action of the philosopher is a defensive action on behalf of philosophy. "You must go down" is the theme of *Thus Spoke Zarathustra,* which opens as the *Republic* opens, with the descent of the philosopher. How can the new philosopher go down to properly defend philosophy in the midst of a new nihilism? Not by trumpeting "I love humanity"— and when these telltale first words to a man after ten years of solitude slip past Zarathustra's lips, he covers them up immediately. Eventually he will name his going-down, "the gift-giving virtue" (*Z* 1.22), but this virtuous word for his philosophic philanthropy will itself be withdrawn. And calling it "the lust to rule," will also not do because it will be heard as base by those schooled in the reigning Platonism—even though the

13. Strauss, *What Is Political Philosophy?* 31.

Platonism in which they have been dyed is itself the consequence of the high philanthropy that properly bears this name (Z 3.10). Zarathustra leaves philanthropy nameless, a riddle for the coming nutcrackers, if an easy riddle, given that Nietzsche himself points to its being the most spiritual will to power.

Bacon's Platonic Responsibility and Philanthropy

Bacon is a Nietzschean philosopher in the sense just described. He is of course not permitted to shout "You dolts" but he is permitted to imply it everywhere, sardonically, trenchantly, through a thousand cagey quotes and learned allusions. Though he is not loud in Nietzsche's way, Bacon too intervenes on behalf of philosophy against its capture by religion. Such intervention marks Bacon as a Platonic philosopher, even though he must seem to disown Plato and pledge allegiance to the dolts.

Early in his life, in a private letter declaring his "vast contemplative ends," and asserting that he has "taken all knowledge to be my province," Bacon claims to be moved by "philanthropia" (*Works* VIII.109). Later, in the remarkable essay "Of Goodness and Goodness of Nature," Bacon identifies goodness or "the affecting of the weal of men" with what "the Grecians called *philanthropia*." The essay contrasts the Greek view that "the inclination to goodness is imprinted deeply in the nature of man" and the Christian view of man's inherent wickedness, and it culminates dramatically, if ironically, with one who wishes "to be *anathema* from Christ for the salvation of his brethren." Bacon's philanthropy is parallel to Socrates': in the *Euthyphro* Socrates avows his own philanthropy (3d) in contrast to the implied misanthropy of Euthyphro, a pious zealot whose willingness to try his own father reveals a misanthrope whose only thought is obedience to gods who might harm him and whose purposes he alone seems to know.

Bacon initiates a revolutionary scientific and technological project that turns humankind's energies away from the specific tasks of civic and religious virtue that the two previous periods of learning had held to be fundamental. He turns humankind to civic tasks that the older teaching had held to be of less value and greater danger. Plato, in his own fable of Atlantis, had discouraged the practical arts of technological advancement. Encouraging the very hubris punished by Plato's Zeus, Bacon invites a comparison with Plato that eventually reveals the reasons for his seeming betrayal of Plato. The *Holy War* locates the reason for this departure from the ancient teachings in an alteration of the Church described by Nietzsche. In a passage to be examined later, Nietzsche argues that the Reformation and Counter-Reformation had changed the character of what he called "the last construction of the Romans," the Roman church (*JS* 358). Nietzsche contends that the decisive alteration of this structure came not from thinkers and philosophers, for whom in fact it provided a haven, but from single-minded religious men, protesters in the name of religious zeal who elicited from their opponent a counter zeal. The new severity squeezed tolerance and latitude out of the church and threatened a new dark age: Luther is the new Alaric in Nietzsche's analysis, the new Germanic barbarian who forcibly altered the order of Rome for the worse.

Bacon responds to the new barbarism in its very midst. Viewed in light of the ancient political philosophy from which he takes his guidance, Bacon's response is a dangerous but not wholly rash undertaking. Acting to found a charitable science to break the sway of charitable religion, Bacon acts to re-establish the rule of philosophy over a tyrannical religion; he acts to forge an alliance that will serve philosophy. Plato had shown that philosophy stood in need of alliances and had brought the wise to the doors of the powerful in a new way: for the well-being of the logos, the Platonic Socrates forged alliances with Glaucon, with Phaedo, with Kleinias and Megillos. Platonic philosophy aimed to bring philosophy to rule by charming the rising power in Athens into its service. Young gentlemen, believing themselves wise because they attended the wise Socrates and pursued his edicts, were in fact only virtuous for they left to Socrates the task of seeing what they could not see, the ideas and the idea of the good that provided the foundation for their civic virtue. Roman philosophers attest to the success of the schools of Socrates in educating the gentlemen, and they celebrate Socrates' turn from natural philosophy to civil philosophy for educating the Romans too, the people of loyal Aeneas, to civic philosophy.

Bacon's employment of the scientists, tamed Daedaluses and Vulcans, forges a new alliance between philosophy and a rising power, the ascendant force of science and technology in his own time to which Bacon does not protest in the name of ancient virtue but to which he ties philosophy's fortune—also, if quietly, in the name of the ancient model. For Bacon recognized that "printing, gunpowder, and the magnet" or mariner's needle, as they had been developed and employed in western Europe, had already "changed the whole face and state of things throughout the world" (*NO* I.129). Precisely these three inventions had been made by the Chinese centuries earlier but they had been administered in a way that did not permit them to change the face even of Chinese society. Bacon allied philosophy to an ascending power in western Europe far greater than itself and already gathering strength in his time partly because of inventions it owed to China and put to its own uses. This new alliance kindled hope for recovering philosophy from the ruins of the Socratic alliance.

Bacon reverses the Socratic turn set out in the *Phaedo*, the turn away from natural philosophy to the *logoi* for reasons of safety. The safe way had become unsafe because the misology and misanthropy against which Socrates had warned his contemporaries had broken out in novel forms practiced by a prophetic religion. Because there is no safety in the once safe way for reason, Bacon returns to the pre-Socratics and especially Democritus. But he links that return to a social program whose benefits he can describe in virtuous words derived from Christianity. Success in this return depends upon what is uniquely Bacon's: the experimental method, and the construction of a society that will underwrite the new science and technology, a society not so much scientific as conducive to science because it believes in its beneficence. To mask the revolutionary character of his program, Bacon follows a lesson as old as Aristophanes' *Clouds*: new divinities must be introduced with the approval of the old. Bacon's theology avows loyalty to biblical traditions but he employs only a most convenient divinity: "God's self-restraining function in the Baconian system was to sanction whatever the New Science might permit human reason to produce."[14]

Bacon's complete project is breathtaking, a project befitting a new Orpheus, whose fable Bacon retells to make clear the extent of his ambitions for philosophy. Those ambitions are signaled as well by his adoption of the device and motto of Charles V, the emperor who revived in Renaissance Europe the Roman imperial theme of the Ruler of the World.[15] Sailing beyond the Pillars of Hercules, outer boundary of the ancient world, with the motto "Plus Ultra" instead of the ancient "Non Ultra," Bacon adopts the emperor's symbols of empire over the whole world. (See the frontispiece of *Great Instauration*; see also, *Advancement, Works* III.340.) What is already present in Europe as a mighty force with deep historical roots—the idea of empire and new inventions as the means to achieve it—is given a unique impetus by the philosopher Bacon.[16]

When the Baconian project is seen to arise out of the conflict between

14. Wheeler, "Invention of Modern Empiricism," 100.

15. See Yates, *Astraea*, 1–28, for the idea of European imperialism and how it might be adapted by a philosopher.

16. For some of the alliances later formed for Baconianism, see Jones, *Ancients and*

religion and philosophy, and when that conflict is understood from the perspective of Platonic philanthropy, it becomes impossible to believe that Bacon believed the more extreme formulations of the religion he was founding: belief is for the Glaucons of the new project, not its Socrates. As Nietzsche said: philosophers "simply do not believe in any 'men of knowledge'" (*JS* 351). Bacon's philosophers certainly do not: Joabin and Solamona know how to encourage efficacious dreams; Eupolis and Pollio know how to alter the dream that has crazed men's minds. One must follow Nietzsche's lead with respect to the philosophers and become a complete skeptic about Bacon—Bacon is not one of those contemporaries Nietzsche described who no longer know what religions are good for (*BGE* 58). The extreme beliefs of Baconianism—that man can master the universe and extend his days indefinitely—transparently appropriate powers assigned to God and the soul in the Christian teaching. Locating within earthly man powers traditionally held transcendent to him, Bacon sets the new beliefs into competition with the old. The new beliefs show how wise Prometheus can make use of his foolish brother Epimetheus by giving fear and hope a new content. Bacon, "the first realist in every great sense of the word," tied his project to the irreality of transformed Christian beliefs, to "things light and puffed up" that would be carried forward by time. This aspect of Bacon's project belongs within the warfare of the sects generated by Christian belief. Baconianism is a utopianism promulgated by a great realist.

Being a complete skeptic about Bacon requires abandoning the inadequate view that he fell prey unawares to the spirit of the age by becoming a believer in a secularized Christianity. *New Atlantis* and *Holy War* show that the reformed Cassandra knew precisely where he was—in the dregs but not the dregs of Romulus—and that he knew precisely how to speak in advancing a secularized form of Christianity. Christianity is his victim, not he its.

New Atlantis and *Holy War* yield an answer to the question, where does Bacon stand in the history of philosophy? And they do so by contributing to a new understanding of the history of philosophy from Plato to Nietzsche. Bacon helps bring Plato to light as the commander and lawgiver who helped to create a new popular tradition and to school subsequent philosophers in the way of philosophic rule. Plato teaches responsibility: we are not our own but owe our being to just gods to

---

Moderns; Webster, *Great Instauration*; Trevor-Roper, *Crisis of the Seventeenth Century,* 237–93; Caton, *Politics of Progress,* 15–109, 186.

whom we are ultimately responsible. And he schools those dubious of such a formulation to parallel responsibilities to an orderly and lovable cosmos to which we owe our being. And he teaches a different sort of responsibility to those of his own kind, a responsibility to philosophy and to the rare cities or societies in which it breaks out. *New Atlantis* and *Holy War* acknowledge acceptance of responsibility within this Platonic tradition.

Bacon begins what might be called an anti-Platonic platonizing, a platonizing which opposes a philosophic theology tying reason to what is given about the gods. Given an all-powerful Misologist and Misanthrope, a Tyrant who presumes to sell Plato into slavery (as Montaigne said in making the same point), Bacon runs the great risk of giving human beings prerogatives of the gods: dominion over all other beings, dominion over the universe, and immortality. Bacon is the "arch-heretic" described at the end of *Sylva Sylvarum*—one page before *New Atlantis*—in the one-thousandth aphorism, the millennial aphorism closing the ten "centuries." In an "experiment solitary touching the general sympathy of men's spirits," Bacon is one of those "great conquerors and troublers of the world" whose "introducing of new doctrines is . . . an affectation of tyranny over the understandings and beliefs of men." Philosophy is the "tyrannical drive itself, the most spiritual will to power, to the 'creation of the world'" (*BGE* 9). But the language of tyranny, of course, leaves open whether these rational men are benefactors or malefactors, philanthropists or misanthropes.

Nothing remains the same—as Plato's lawgiver acknowledged. The fantastic beliefs encouraged by the arch-heretic Bacon in imitation of Christianity cannot be maintained forever. The vain belief that man can be lord of the universe, or that the onward and upward march of time can continue until the end of history in some universal and homogeneous utopia—these and other Baconian fictions of modern times are first exploded by Nietzsche—"I'm no man, I'm dynamite" (*EH* Destiny 1)—the arch-heretic who questions the fundamental beliefs of modern times. And he too does so in order to overcome misology and misanthropy, the nihilism he diagnosed as the natural outcome of modern beliefs. But before considering Nietzsche, it is useful to look closely at that other arch-heretic of modern times who carried forward Bacon's themes, Bacon's worthy successor, Descartes.

Part 2

A Prudent Legislator

Chapter 6

René Descartes, Baconian

Bene vixit qui bene latuit [He lived well who hid well]—that is what is written on Descartes's tombstone—an epitaph if ever there was one!—Nietzsche (Letter to Brandes, 2 December 1887)

Descartes [was] the father of Rationalism and hence the grandfather of the Revolution.—Nietzsche (BGE 191)

Descartes a Baconian? Descartes who created the impression that he created himself out of nothing and was so thoroughly believed that he has been named "Father of Modern Philosophy"? Descartes's Baconianism would be completely evident, I think, if we followed Descartes's instructions and read his works in the order that he published them and read them all—presupposing, of course, that Bacon's writings too were as familiar to us as they were in Descartes's time.

A Nietzschean understanding of philosophy makes it possible to recover the actual relationship between these two strategic and world-transforming thinkers in a way that preserves the essential contribution of each. Reciprocally, a Nietzschean understanding of the high calling of the philosopher—the genuine philosopher, of whom there are very few—is exemplified and confirmed in these two thinkers once access is gained to their true grandeur by a proper appreciation of their style. The Baconianism of the Father of Modern Philosophy becomes evident when both are viewed from a Nietzschean perspective.

Descartes acknowledges his Baconianism in two very special

First epigraph: In fact, the motto does not appear on Descartes's tombstone. From Ovid's *Tristia* (III.iv.25), the "Sad Poems" protesting his exile, it is used by Descartes in a letter discussing the condemnation of Galileo: "I desire to live in peace and to continue the life I have begun under the motto *Bene vixit, bene qui latuit*" (letter to Mersenne, April 1634). The motto was popular among French *libertins érudits* of this period (Zagorin, *Ways of Lying*, 325).

places: the two occasions on which he most explicitly raised the question of why he must publish. One appears in his first book, the anonymous *Discourse on the Method,* the other in what was to be his last, *The Passions of the Soul,* and there too the acknowledgment is not in his own name for it is made by the Parisian friend whose letters serve as part of the Preface. These two crucial passages acknowledge Descartes's debt to Bacon while claiming advancement beyond him. Moreover, they provide an introduction to Descartes's own remarkable style, an introduction made necessary, perhaps even urgent, by the contemporary tendency to reduce Descartes to one of his facets, the author of the *Meditations* and part four of the *Discourse.*

Baconian Ends Cartesian Means

Only once does Descartes make the Baconian claim that his thought will "make us like masters and possessors of nature" (vi.62).[1] But once is enough because it is once and for all: the fabulous history of his life that is his *Discourse on the Method* has just arrived at a critical turn—why, the author asks himself, why publish anything at all in times like these when it is impossible to publish the book on which he has labored for years (vi.61–62)? He answers that his thoughts on the speculative sciences and on moral conduct do *not* need to be published but that his "general notions touching physics" do. Why? For a reason that is thoroughly Baconian in both style and substance: to keep these notions hidden away would sin against the law that obliges us to procure as best we can the general good of all men. The quasi-biblical tone continues for the rest of the argument, but the tone deflects attention only slightly from the anti-biblical substance. For the general good brought about by the new physics carries only an echo of the universal charity of the Christian religion while in fact advancing the charity first promised by Bacon: the general good is an earthly good, not the salvation of the soul, and the agent of the new well-being is man, not God. Descartes, like Bacon, seems to derive his imperative from the biblical story of the Fall from Paradise but only by transforming the story: the old tale of the loss of paradise becomes the occasion for promising its gain, and paradise is regained only by a reversal of roles that makes nature's subject nature's master. An irretrievable past becomes an achievable future in

1. References to the *Discourse* in the text will include the part and the page of the Adam and Tannery edition.

which humankind is redeemed from the fall by its own labor. Descartes has to publish because his physics will redeem humankind.

The new useful philosophy, Descartes says, will enable us to know "the force and the actions" of things: not their essences but what they do. Its scope will be universal, "fire, air, water, the stars, the heavens, and all the other bodies which surround us." We will know the universe "as distinctly as we know the various skills of our craftsmen" and this knowledge of all things will make it possible for us "to use them in the same way for all the purposes for which they are suited, and thus make us like masters and possessors of nature." Why is this unprecedented Baconian undertaking desirable? Descartes gives two Baconian reasons. The first is that the new practical philosophy will generate an unprecedented technology because of its knowledge of how natural things work. The resultant "infinity of devices" will enable human beings to enjoy without pain the fruits of the earth and all the goods one finds in it. What was once a mere dream of earthly paradise, a Garden of Eden placed at a lost and irretrievable beginning, can now be thought to be realizable on earth, not by grace but by human labor guided by insight into natural forces. In the earthly garden at the end of history, humankind may enjoy "all the goods one finds in it." *All* the goods includes what was once forbidden: the fruit of the tree of knowledge of good and evil, through whose taste men would become like gods (Genesis 3:3–5). The forbidden knowledge is disclosed in *The Passions of the Soul*: we become like gods when we know good and evil to be designations applied to things in accord with our experience of pleasure and pain. But will we surely die when we partake of such once forbidden fruit (Genesis 2:17)?

The second reason for the desirability of mastering and possessing nature concerns human mortality, the maintenance of health, "the first good and the foundation of all the other goods." Medicine, when directed by Descartes's general notions touching physics, will aim at the repair of both body and mind for Cartesian medicine recognizes that "even the mind depends greatly on the temperament, and on the disposition of the organs of the body." Applied to the allied sciences of body and mind, physiology and psychiatry, the new notions touching physics could rid humankind of an "infinity of maladies . . . and even perhaps also" of the enfeeblement brought on by old age. The longevity of the human race belongs not to some imagined golden age before the flood but to the future. The Bible may give a true report of the fundamental curses, that we are condemned to come forth on this earth in pain, to live by the sweat of our brow, and to die in uncertainty having been denied the fruit of the Tree of Life and the fruit of the Tree of Knowledge. But the means to undo the curses will be found in the new science. In this part of his *Discourse,* Descartes outfits the redeeming science with additional Baconian traits such as the need for an infinity of experiments and an army of workers to staff them, but rather than follow out those details now it will perhaps be better to turn directly to Descartes's other acknowledgment of his Baconianism.

Descartes names Lord Bacon only one time in his writings, in a place once prominent but now sunk into virtual oblivion: the first prefatory letter to *The Passions of the Soul.* [2] That book broke five years of near silence by Europe's most celebrated and most embattled philosopher; and, as Descartes said, it was bound to attract by its title many more readers than those few who could understand it. But most of the enticed readers could be expected to get through the Preface at least, the astonishing and entertaining correspondence between Descartes and some Parisian friend. In the key letter, the first, Descartes is praised for being the one thinker in the whole history of philosophy who can do the most to benefit humanity, but he is blamed for not saying so even though he well knows that saying so and being believed are necessary before humanity can reap the benefits offered by its greatest benefactor. Who is this Parisian friend and why is he saying these outrageous things about Descartes? And why is Descartes letting him say them in the first paragraphs of his long-awaited book? Hiram Caton has argued persuasively that the anonymous Parisian is Descartes himself. [3] The analysis that follows will, I hope, help to demonstrate the truth of this claim and show why Descartes's authorship could hardly have escaped his best contemporary readers. Under the cover of a friend loud in his abuse, Descartes is able to state true claims for himself "that decorum would not allow me to make known to the public myself" (Descartes's reply to the first letter); he is able to do what Bacon said a friend could do: "How many things are there which a man cannot, with any face or comeliness, say or do himself! A man can scarce allege his own merits with modesty, much less extol them; a man cannot sometimes brook to supplicate or beg." But a Parisian friend can: "All these things are graceful in a friend's mouth, which are blushing in a man's own" (*Essays,* "Of Friendship").

---

2. An excellent translation of this preface is found in Descartes, *The Passions of the Soul,* translated by Stephen H. Voss (Indianapolis: Hackett Publishing Co., 1989). This translation is far superior to the one which appears in *PW* and which omits the letters of the Parisian friend. All references to the *Passions* are to article numbers.

3. "Descartes' Anonymous Writings," 273–94.

Descartes's friend names Bacon in the midst of the most extensive acknowledgment of the Baconian character of Descartes's project in all of Descartes's writings: as described here, the core of Descartes's work is an experimental and mathematical physics which will create the technological devices necessary to secure the common good of all humanity. Decorum forbids Descartes from saying what his Parisian friend can say of him: he has made the essential contribution to the Baconian revolution, the indispensable method based on mathematics and applicable to all subject matters. The theme of the letter from beginning to end, the theme raised again in the letter-writer's brief second letter as his reason for writing the first, is that Descartes has not done all he could have done to solicit the necessary public support for the vast array of experiments now needed to carry his physics forward to its fruition in public weal. A friend therefore performs that very task once more—*once more,* because the friend makes perfectly clear that Descartes has in fact frequently made that request and made it in just the right way.

In its earnest and hectoring abuse of a Descartes it praises to the skies, this letter is one of the most enjoyable of all Descartes's literary performances, a comic scene worthy of a great philosopher: Descartes puts his fundamental public demand into the mouth of another as a chastisement of himself—that other being his *"charlatan,"* his mountebank, his entertainer employed by himself to address the crowd attracted by the title and by the reputation of the author. His entertainer delivers the old message as if it were new, as if Descartes had not already said that those who direct public affairs will have to align the public agenda to accord with goals set by a solitary philosopher.

That philosopher has been far too bashful, says his friend. He's had enough of Descartes's timid ways, his laziness, his lack of concern for the rest of us, and he won't stand for it any longer: if Descartes won't say who he is, he will. The friend has two complaints, one personal, one general. On the personal level, Descartes has refused to let him see the book on the passions that he promised him. Why? Descartes answers in his own name (in his first reply) by saying that it is one thing to address the capable privately on such matters (the private version was for his most capable reader, Princess Elizabeth) and another thing entirely to address everyone in public. Delay in showing his book to his Parisian correspondent results from the labor involved in transforming what he says privately to the most competent person he knows into something open to everyone's inspection: even though he did not change the content, Descartes says, and even though he added very little, he has nevertheless had to work longer on its present public form than on its previous private one.

Our letter-writer, however, had not waited for Descartes to provide his own reasons for the delay, for his letter gave his own account of Descartes's reasons based on what he took to be Descartes's motives. He had not wanted to seem unfair, however, and so had put his own speculations about Descartes's motives into the conditional form of what Descartes himself would perhaps say. But what "you will say, perhaps," is what Descartes will say in fact, but only in the book that the friend has not been allowed to see. Servility, virtuous humility, pride, modesty, glory are all employed in what "you will say, perhaps" and their use by the friend fully accords with the novel definitions Descartes later puts forward (§157, 158, 159, 204). Descartes's supposed failures are to be understood via the analysis of actions first introduced by Descartes's book. This is Caton's most telling argument: novelties introduced by Descartes's moral theory are the very items employed by his anonymous friend to explain Descartes's behavior.

This nice joke to reacquaint us with who it is we are reading is a prelude to a second and still finer joke. And here the friend makes his complaint general. Withholding the book from the friend hurt only him, but Descartes's failure to advertise himself properly hurts the whole Cartesian project and with it the whole of humanity which stands to benefit from that project. Descartes has been a negligent prophet for his cause. The friend knows what to do, however, and Descartes need only follow his advice to succeed where he has so far failed so miserably. What should Descartes do to advance his project? He should do what he did seven years ago in his letter to Father Dinet published with the *Meditations.* To "further your enterprise," "nothing seems to me more useful" than what Descartes has long since done. These instructions on what Descartes should do culminate in quoting Descartes to Descartes in Latin and then repeating to Descartes in French the audacious claim for his physics that he had already made in public and addressed to the Jesuit Superior of France as a challenge to the whole order. To best advance your project, you ought to do what you have done. And look at the results: seven years after your attack on the philosophical foundations of the Jesuits and not a peep out of them. What you should have done is directly challenge their physics, the very matter that they have chosen to make fundamental to their views, the very matter in which your supremacy in mathematics, acknowledged by everyone, will make you invulnerable to criticism.

Once is not enough for this fine joke of having his friend order him to do what he has done, and Descartes plays it again, elaborately and with modifications, correctly supposing that we were not sated the first time. Descartes, his friend says, the only way for you to succeed against the authoritative physics is to prove that physics is a part of mathematics, and to prove that a master of both is needed, and to prove that you are that master. It may do violence to your nature but you are going to have to bring yourself to say all that: you are going to have to bring yourself to say exactly what you already said in your *Principles of Philosophy* where these very points were proven four years ago. In 1649, looking back over his strategic battles with authoritative opinion, Descartes says through his Parisian friend: I should have done exactly what I have done.

Descartes failed in advancing his project yet the only way to succeed is to do what he did. Now we are laughing and we are laughing at the Jesuits, those educators of France and counselors of kings who for seven embarrassing years have been unable to answer the public challenge thrown down by their student. They silently endured not only the letter to Father Dinet but the performance that occasioned it: Descartes's amazing public rebuke of Father Bourdin S.J. Descartes had accused the Reverend Father of outright lying to ruin Descartes's reputation, and then of having lost control of himself and fallen into a hallucination for which he can be likened (in Descartes's long comic parody) to a poor envious bricklayer who hallucinates that no chapel exists on the spot where the great envied architect had just built one (the *Meditations*) but only the empty ditch of doubt which got the architect to the bedrock on which he built his chapel. At the end of his rebuke Descartes had reciprocated the friendship alleged by the Reverend Father and reported the lying hallucinator to his superior, Father Dinet, just as the poor bricklayer had been taken to a doctor by his friends. But the lying hallucinator is after all, Pierre Bourdin, a Jesuit professor of mathematics whose reply to Descartes (as Descartes suggests) is unlikely to be a merely private response but the response of the whole Jesuit order (*AT* VII.452–53; *PW* 2.303). The letter to Father Dinet had itself been a challenge to the whole Jesuit order. And now, in front of a large public drawn to his new book by its enticing title and the celebrity of its author, Descartes challenges the Jesuits again and taunts them for their telltale seven-year silence and does so from behind the back of some Parisian friend, does so inviolably.

The friend suggested at the opening that it may have been necessary for Descartes to leave the very best place to pursue his experiments, Paris, and work in a safe place, Holland. But the warfare can obviously be carried on from there against the spiritual powers that rule France. We are laughing, but the Jesuits were not—they will attempt to get his books banned. If he cannot be answered maybe he can be choked— as Descartes complained was happening to his *Principles of Philosophy* in another letter to Father Dinet (October 1644). This warfare where one side consisted of one man fighting alone with instruments of intelligent ridicule that included fictitiously multiplying his number, and the other side consisted of the instructors of the age and the counselors of the powerful—this warfare was won by the lone writer of comedy. And we are as glad as D'Alembert, who said one hundred years later, when the tide had turned, that Descartes had performed a service for philosophy far more difficult than that performed by all of his successors, calling together a company of conspirators to throw off the yoke of prejudice and barbarism.[4] No wonder Nietzsche prefaced his own book on enlighten- ment, *Human, All Too Human,* with a long quotation from Descartes's *Discourse* on the intense pleasure of philosophy.

Here we see a fine instance—there will be many—of another Baco- nian theme in Descartes, not the familiar Bacon of experimental science but the necessarily less familiar Bacon of revolutionary warfare against revealed religion, the Bacon of *An Advertisement Touching an Holy War,* the Bacon who entered the temple with a view to taking possession. In our tolerant age when the power of European religion has in fact been tamed by centuries of continual defeat at the hands of science, rumor of the marvelous beginnings of this historic warfare seems almost to have been lost and mention of it seems almost an embarrassment, an exercise in bad taste. If we take our measure from our own Jesuits and Calvinist rectors, it seems unbecoming of Descartes to conduct his battles with a Bourdin or a Voetius without putting all his cards on the table. But such a measure is a gross anachronism that wholly forecloses any possi- bility of understanding Descartes as an active player in the terrible age in which he actually wrote, an age marked in every facet of life by reli-

4. *Preliminary Discourse to the Encyclopedia of Diderot,* 80. The pleasant rumor that a Jesuit Father, Denis Mesland, was banished to Canada to minister to the Hurons and Iroquois be- cause he got too close to Descartes on the vital issue of transubstantiation is, unfortunately, false. This now widespread report is based on a marginal note written on the manuscript copy of one of Descartes's letters to Mesland (*PW* 3.278, see also the biographical sketch on Mesland, 388). In fact Mesland went to Martinique in 1645 and died in Santa Fe de Bogatá in 1672. See Pacheco, "Un amigo de Descartes en el Nuevo Reino." I am grateful to Father Charles E. O'Neill S.J. of the Institutum Historicum Societatis Iesu, Rome, for this reference.

gious zealotry that broke out again and again in holy wars engulfing a whole continent. To read Descartes in ignorance of the powers of a Father Dinet or a Rector Voetius is to deprive oneself of the setting to which Descartes himself regularly called attention. That setting does not explain Descartes's philosophy but it helps explain the form he gave it, and understanding that form helps one penetrate to the core of Descartes's philosophy. It belongs to a Nietzschean history of philosophy, it seems to me, to display as openly as possible earlier stages of the conflict that is so much in the open in Nietzsche's own writings: the conflict between philosophy and religion. That conflict is a constant theme in Descartes's writings. No single instance can tell the whole tale in its depth and intensity, not the attack on Father Bourdin, not the letter to Father Dinet, not their renewal in *The Passions of the Soul;* only the accumulation of instances can adequately present this fundamental issue and in the account of Descartes's thought in this and the following chapters the conflict between philosophy and religion will be a major theme.

To return to Descartes's Parisian friend: he makes Descartes's relation to Bacon's revolutionary experimental science an explicit issue near the end of his letter, but the fact that Descartes is a Baconian is present throughout his main argument: the experiments necessary to the new project will require the support of whole nations and eventually of all nations. The friend wants Descartes to emphasize three main points which, taken together, are the essence of Baconianism as modified by Descartes: first, an infinity of things that will be extremely useful for life can be found out through physics; second, there is good reason to expect you to discover these things; third, a great number of experiments are necessary and you will need assistance. In arguing the first point, the friend repeats a main Baconian lesson: "To prove that the excessive respect maintained for antiquity is an error which is extremely prejudicial to the advancement of the sciences." The Cartesian program requires new beliefs in the capacity of natural science to generate useful inventions.

In arguing the second point the friend introduces the Cartesian means to the Baconian ends, the mathematical foundations of physics with which alone it will be able to make all the discoveries useful for life. "Your eminence in [mathematics] is so well established" that it will be no trick for you to demonstrate that physics is nothing but a part of mathematics. In fact you have already done it in your *Principles.* "And inasmuch as no one doubts that you excel in [mathematics], there is nothing which is not to be expected from you in [physics]." Mathematical physics makes

Descartes the "Architect" who "has laid all the foundations and raised the main walls" of the new edifice.

In arguing the third point the friend explicitly invokes Bacon and states directly what has so far been implied: the Baconian project can succeed only with Cartesian means. As the architect who designed and advanced the modifications to the Baconian project, Descartes now needs assistants to complete it and the friend takes up the old appeal for assistance first made by Descartes in his first book. Just here Bacon is named for the only time in Descartes's writings: "I've also seen the *Instauratio Magna* and the *Novus Atlas* of Chancellor Bacon, who seems to me to be, of all those who wrote before you, the one with the best thoughts concerning the method that should be used to guide Physics to its perfection . . ." Bacon's method is not *the* method for rightly conducting one's reason and for seeking truth in the sciences. The friend does not praise Bacon's method but only his thoughts concerning the method and the two works he names present not his method but only his thoughts about the desirability of an experimental and technological science and the great ends it could achieve. Bacon advocates a program that his own method could never achieve: Descartes is the Baconian with the necessary means. The sentence on Bacon continues: "—but all the income of two or three of the most powerful kings on earth would not suffice to carry out all the things [Bacon] needs for this end." Descartes's means provide a less costly route to the Baconian ends they make possible. Nevertheless, you still need massive public support to achieve the Baconian ends you envisage. The friend thus asks Descartes to ask again for the support he has been asking for from the very beginning. Descartes thereby asks again, but this time he puts his case in its proper historic perspective: he is the Baconian philosopher who advanced over his preceptor by means of the mathematical foundation he provided for physics. Descartes has not usurped Bacon's place, nor is he Bacon's rival; he is a student who outstripped his teacher in the one essential way by contributing the essential means to the project first set forth by the teacher.

In his penultimate paragraph the friend continues in the now irresistible vein of comic enthusiasm: when rulers or their counselors get wind of this program not one of them will fail to embrace it and France will have to compete with all other countries in the race to do good through the new global project, devoting the ends of rule to the Baconian ideals of public good. Philosophy thus ascends to its proper place of rule, counseling the apparent rulers, and Descartes supplants the present counselors of those rulers, Jesuits who have not been able to answer Descartes's charges. Cartesian counselors replace Christian counselors in the global Baconian society built on Cartesian physics.

The final paragraph supplies the final comic touch to this Cartesian masterpiece in miniature. If I ever get to see the *Passions,* the friend says, I will myself compose a preface worthy of it. It will contain nothing that you could disapprove of and nothing not congenial to the feelings of every person of intelligence and virtue; just by reading it every such person will be turned into a zealous participant in the advancement of the sciences. Descartes reins in his zealous mountebank with the appropriate Whoa in his "Reply to the Preceding Letter" but the letter has served his purpose and there is nothing in it he would disapprove of: the Baconian project of spiritual warfare goes forward in the works of Descartes and if he had it all to do over again, he would do what he has done. Fate was cruel in robbing us of more such works by Descartes, but how fitting that Descartes now ends his work, his whole *oeuvre,* with this affirmation of what he had already done.

Other Baconian Signs

In continuing Bacon's rhetoric to advance Bacon's project, Descartes sets himself unmistakably within the Baconian succession. Once this kinship between the Baconian project and Descartes's own becomes clear, the sequence of events described in his *Discourse on the Method* becomes accessible in a new way. In part one of the *Discourse* Descartes had described his complete rejection of the tradition as following from a single criterion: his desire for "a clear and steady knowledge of everything useful for life" (i.4). This standard intimates that Descartes was a Baconian before becoming a Cartesian, a modern before discovering the general notions touching physics on which alone the Baconian project of the mastery of nature could be grounded. His discoveries in mathematics and physics mark Descartes's fundamental advance over Bacon and bring nearer to plausible achievement goals that would have remained mere dreams without them.

Because Descartes's advance over Bacon consists in supplying the method for the Baconian project that Bacon himself had failed to supply, Descartes implicitly criticizes the Baconian method for deficiencies that have long since become commonplace: a theory of experiment that diminishes the significance of hypothesis and deduction while relying on induction for the divination of essence, and a theory of method that posits as the goal of science the discernment of essences or natural kinds rather than the reduction of all essence to shared qualities of mass and motion subject to quantification. From Descartes's perspective, it could be said that while Bacon aimed to be a good bee he remained too much the ant and too much the spider, too much a busy gatherer and too much a programmed spinner still under the influence of the old categories or kinds. But instead of a mere critique of Bacon, Descartes remedied the implied deficiencies by supplying the necessary method.[5]

To side with Bacon while improving on him by providing the essential method is to aim definitively at the achievement of a scientific society grounded on the new view of nature and believing in the beneficence of science. Creation of such a society requires the establishment of scientific research institutions on a scale first imagined by Bacon but suggested by Descartes as well in part six of the *Discourse* and the prefatory letter to the *Passions*. Descartes states that several centuries will be required before the project can be fulfilled and that its success depends on attracting the best minds to its service by persuading them that their lives are best spent devoting all their abilities to it (*Principles,* "Preface," last paragraph). But Descartes's many references to the infinity of tasks involved in this project makes it seem that for him too the project will always remain "a work unfinished." Furthermore, Descartes also seems to follow Bacon in holding that only very few will have the inclination to read his writings in such a way as to discern which of the opinions expressed in them really follow from true principles (*Principles,* "Preface," penultimate paragraph). Others among the very talented (Descartes will single out the practitioners of a new medicine) will devote themselves to the tasks of science as the sons of science, believers in its humanitarianism and beneficiaries of the honor that accrues to it. The vast majority will honor science as the source of the technology that made possible their own lives of comfort and long duration. The order of society visible in Bensalem with its rare Joabins, its less rare Fathers of Salomon's House, and its contented many grateful to science, is thus visible in Descartes's view of philosophy, science, and society.[6]

In addition to Descartes's evident Baconianism regarding these central matters of a new science of nature and a society reordered to advance it, there are numerous other indications of the Baconian character of

5. See the references to Bacon in Descartes's letters to Mersenne, 23 Dec. 1630, 10 May 1632. On the role assigned to experiment in Descartes's philosophy of science, see Clarke, *Descartes' Philosophy of Science.*

6. See Kennington, "Rene Descartes," "Descartes and Mastery of Nature."

Cartesianism. Like Bacon, Descartes alluded to himself as the one master of the many masters of nature, the discoverer of the means by which all else shall be discovered (*NO* I.129; *Discourse* ii.11–13). Like Bacon, he presented the new philosophy as differing most from the old philosophy in its charitable concern for all humanity, veiling its actual dependence on Platonic philanthropy. Like Bacon, he called for an army of workers to help perform the observations and experiments essential to the new interpretation of nature (Bacon, *Works* IV.251 [*Parasceve,* 1620]; *NO* I.271, *GI, Works* IV.21). Like Bacon, Descartes anticipated that the philanthropy of science would include what Leon Roth called "the democratization of method,"[7] that leveling of wits which reduces the great range found naturally in human talent (*NO* I.61, 122). Like Bacon, Descartes resorted to fable to give an adequate account of the philosopher and his ambitions, Descartes choosing to tell his own life as a fable. Like Bacon, Descartes veiled the conflict of reason and revelation by alleging that there were two domains of truth independent of one another, each accessible by appropriate means and immune to conflict because each means was adequate only within its own sphere. Descartes too is a philosopher who knows where he is and knows how to speak and who takes responsibility for the future of philosophy.[8]

Before leaving the particulars relating Descartes to Bacon, I want to call attention to a little peculiarity in Descartes's *Meteorology* that seems to me to illuminate the relationship. At the end of the eighth discourse of the *Meteorology*, a discourse bound to become famous as the first ade-

7. Roth, *Descartes' Discourse on Method,* 54–55, 62ff., 69, 70.

8. On Descartes and Bacon, see Penrose, "Reputation and Influence of Francis Bacon," 117–52. Bacon was well known in France where his work circulated widely. The first biography of Bacon was written in French in 1631, Amboise, *L'histoire naturelle de François Bacon.* See Popkin, *History of Scepticism,* 84, 126. On Descartes's use of Bacon see Lalande, "*Sur quelques textes de Bacon et de Descartes,*" 296–311. In distinguishing between Bacon and Descartes, Paoli Rossi praises Bacon's modesty in contrast to Descartes's immodesty, supposing Baconian science to be wholly a cooperative effort in which no individual's contribution is decisive. Such praise of Bacon at Descartes's expense conveniently transforms into a modest fellow-scientist the one who said of himself, "if all the wits of all the ages had met or shall hereafter meet together, if the whole human race had applied or shall hereafter apply themselves to philosophy, and the whole earth had been or shall be nothing but academies and colleges and schools of learned men, still without a natural and experimental history such as I am going to prescribe, no progress worthy of the human race could have been made or can be made in philosophy and the sciences" ("Description of a Natural and Experimental History," *Works,* IV.252). See Rossi, *Philosophy, Technology and the Arts,* 103–09.

quate scientific account of the most famous sign in the sky, the rainbow,[9] Descartes demythologizes that sign of God's reconciliation by describing an apparatus for engineering one. Not only can Zeus's thunderbolt be imitated, so too can the heavenly sign of reconciliation offered by the God of the Bible to the species he had just cleansed by drowning. Ann Hartle and David Lachterman call attention to the significance of Descartes's act of showing how human beings can reproduce this sign that God's wrath has been assuaged.[10] If we know precisely how rainbows work as light refracted and reflected through drops of water, and if we can make them ourselves, causing them to appear whenever we want them to, then we have stripped them of that quality of wonder which inclines us to stoop before heavenly phenomena (first discourse).

But is there something else in Descartes's description of a device to produce rainbows, something that goes beyond mechanical reproduction of a sign in the sky? I think there is, and I think that readers of *New Atlantis* could hardly help but notice, because the setting Descartes provides for his rainbow machine suggests that he is demythologizing not simply an Old Testament miracle but a Baconian one: Descartes shows how to engineer the sign in the sky that introduced Christianity to Bensalem. That column of light topped by a cross appeared on a calm and cloudy night and moved the sheep-like to wonder; while they gaped in awe of this inexplicable light, one authoritative figure stepped forth from their midst, the scientist, and declared it a true miracle and Bensalem became Christian. *New Atlantis* appeared in English in 1627, in French in 1631, and in Latin in 1633, and in 1637, Descartes, demythologizer of the sky, showed how to build a device to reproduce that miracle in the Bensalemite sky. Bacon himself, of course, quietly indicated that his mighty sign in the sky was a hoax engineered to introduce a new civil religion to Bensalem by scientists who had ruled it for three centuries, and in showing how to make the device Descartes respects Bacon's reserve, for he does not flaunt his own unmasking of the hoax. He does not mention Bacon or *New Atlantis* but speaks instead in a vague way of an invention he remembers, a fountain whose water jets would create a sign in the sky inspiring wonder in those ignorant of its causes. But he adds many details that relate the sign to Bensalem, saying for instance, that such a

9. See Scott, *Scientific Work of René Descartes*, 71, 82; and Clarke, *Descartes' Philosophy of Science*, 183–85.

10. Hartle, *Death and the Disinterested Spectator*, 151, 187; Lachterman, *Ethics of Geometry*, 204f.

sign could take the shape of "a cross, or a column, or some other such thing which gives cause for wonder." And that a great deal of skill and labor would be necessary to create a device powerful enough to be "seen from afar by a whole nation" and refined enough to work "without the trick being discovered."

Descartes's mechanical trick does not quite fit Bacon's miracle for it occurs during the day and is a rainbow while Bacon's miracle is a white light at night. But these discrepancies are themselves explained, though not in the same place. At the end of the previous discourse (*Meteorology,* Discourse 7), Descartes gave an account of white lights that appear in the sky on nights that are calm and serene like that night in Bensalem when the sign appeared in the sky. He asserts that such lights can use the sun that has already set, but he does not complete the discussion. Instead, he refers ahead to the next discourse as its completion, the discourse on the rainbow which ends showing how to engineer a sign in the sky that "could be seen from afar by a whole nation" that would not discover the deception but be moved to wonder because they remained "ignorant of the causes."

If Descartes's device is a veiled reference to the miracle that introduced Christianity to Bensalem, as I think it is, then Descartes has shown in a very nice way that he understood Bacon on the crucial matter facing the introduction of the new science: how to introduce the new science into the world formed by the old religion, how to maintain that the new science and the old religion can be harmonized in a future society. Given the extreme delicacy that must govern such matters, Descartes does not say directly that the miracle introducing Christianity must be intended by Bacon to be interpreted as an engineering feat carried out by the House of Salomon. Nor does he say that the miracle shows religion passing into the care of the new philosophy. Nevertheless, the things not said are necessarily implied if this event is a mechanical trick engineered by the wise. If Descartes is alluding to Bacon's miracle, he is exhibiting his collusion in its purpose: the rule of philosophy over religion replaces religion's rule over philosophy. And the reserved manner in which he demystifies Bacon's miracle indicates that he too is a practitioner of the "enigmatical style" Bacon practiced.

Like the previous example from the *Passions of the Soul,* this example, arresting as it is and inexplicable as it is apart from *New Atlantis,* would not carry conviction as an instance of enigmatical style if it stood alone. In fact it does not stand alone, for as Hiram Caton says, Descartes is "full of pranks." [11] And his pranks follow Bacon's lead: they are all part of a multifaceted style of writing whose unified aim is revolution: in a world dominated by the warfare of the Christian sects, they incite to revolution while disavowing it. Descartes's rare discussions of style make this plain.

Cartesian Style

Posterity: Never believe the things said about me unless I have divulged them myself.—Descartes (Discourse vi.70)

The difference between exoteric and esoteric was formerly a commonplace among philosophers, Nietzsche said, arising automatically from their rank or difference (*BGE* 30). Descartes is no exception to the Nietzschean rule. Living well by hiding well he mixed candor and dissimulation to make himself the grandfather of the Revolution. As with Bacon and other masters of esotericism, Descartes gave clues to his hiding place by discussing the difference between exoteric and esoteric in the appropriate way, somewhat esoterically.

One such discussion of the esoteric style occurs at the end of the *Principles* (iv.205) where Descartes highlights the one problem that will unavoidably plague its interpreters: assuming a competent author, interpreters will not be able to prove the presence of esotericism in any direct way. The *Principles* is a Latin book meant to become an approved textbook and Descartes brings it to an end expressing concern lest some injury to the truth occur because of something he had had to maintain earlier: necessity had forced him to refer to the principles of his physics as false (*Principles* iii.44, 45; iv.1, 204). Responsibility falls to the interpreter if the evident is different from the true and to illustrate this responsibility, Descartes refers to an art of writing that practices a simple method of encoding: a message hidden in a Latin text that uses Latin letters in an uncustomary way. The true interpretation will be based on the conjecture that the Latin book is written in code and on the conviction that the code has been cracked. Good grounds exist for adhering to the interpretation if it is the simplest, the most consistent, and capable of prediction. Nothing, however, can ever remove the conjectural basis. The possibility always remains that the conjectured meaning is not the intended meaning, for the text might be written in a different and more complex code. But, Descartes adds, there is legitimate doubt that a more

11. Caton, *Politics of Progress*, 54.

complex code is possible especially for a long communication. Talk of a code illustrates Descartes's cracking of a complex code: the evident appearance of the natural world is best explained by the conjectured principles of Descartes's mathematical physics. But while the code of the world has been deciphered by the master interpreter on the basis of principles he had to present as false, communication of the decoded world is itself necessarily encoded. Deciphering that secondary code depends initially on conjecture which becomes persuasive when its simplicity, consistency, and explanatory power become evident—though it always remains a conjecture that there is an encoded message there at all. Ending the book this way illuminates the peculiar warning of its Preface not to accept as true any opinion expressed in it unless it can be very clearly seen to be deduced from first principles.[12]

Another discussion of the esoteric style occurs in an amusing setting: Descartes's public attack on the faulty rhetoric of his erstwhile disciple, Regius. *Comments on a Certain Broadsheet* exposes Regius's errors by discussing what Descartes calls the "Socratic style" or "speaking ironically." Practitioners of this style say one thing and mean another, leaving their interpreters the work of discerning their meaning. Faced with this work himself as the interpreter of Regius's book, Descartes proceeded in a way he recommends to his reader: he set forth "conjectures, not as true fact, but as mere conjectures, for I have nothing to say here that is certain" (*AT* VIIIB.355–56; *PW* 1.302). Descartes's main conjecture is based on an inference drawn from two mutually contradictory statements in Regius's discussion of the soul. One statement asserts that the soul is distinct from the body; the other implies that the soul is merely an instrument of the body. The contradiction is asymmetrical, an implication contradicting an assertion. Descartes detects a strategy here: the writer is addressing two different audiences with the same words. "These two statements are so manifestly contradictory that I do not think the author intended the reader to accept both at the same time; I think he deliberately muddled them together, with the aim of satisfying in some way

---

12. In the early and unpublished *Rules,* Descartes decried the rhetorical practices of ancient writers who were less than sincere and open, and who presented their discoveries wrapped in various obscurities. But a few pages later he described his own rhetorical practice as one that clothes his discoveries in an outer garment of mathematical method. If one attends closely to his meaning, he adds, one will see that ordinary mathematics is far from his mind and that he describes what is basic to all possible knowledge (*AT* X.366–67, 373–74; *PW* 1.13, 17. For an interesting resolution of the long debate over the term *Mathesis universalis,* see Van de Pitte, "The Dating of Rule IV-B."

his more simple-minded readers and fellow theologians by citing the authority of Scripture, while the more sharp-witted of his readers would recognize that he is speaking ironically when he says that 'the mind is distinct from the body', and that he is heart and soul of the opinion that the mind is nothing but a mode" (*AT* VIIIB.356; *PW* 1.302). Descartes thus concludes that the author intended something he did not directly state and did not intend something he directly stated. This conclusion applies a principle described three pages earlier concerning the relationship between faith and natural reason. At issue are matters of faith measurable by natural reason. Theologians have long encouraged philosophers to demonstrate such matters by natural reason. But what if natural reason and faith conflict?—as Regius suggested they did on the issue of the mind being distinct from the body. In a complex sentence Descartes states that he has never seen anyone who would maintain that the laws of nature could be different from what the Bible describes except for one reason only: an intention to show indirectly that one has no faith in the Bible (*AT* VIIIB.353; *PW* 1.301). Hiram Caton draws a hermeneutical rule that he thinks is implicit in Descartes's argument and that seems to me entirely correct: "We may say that the rule justifies resolving in favor of reason every contradiction in Descartes' writings between faith and reason." [13] Descartes speaks ironically in his description of ironic speech: his bold revelation of an opponent's strategic practices suggests he would never stoop to such practices himself. Descartes's discussions of the esoteric style must themselves be exoteric or open to a pious interpretation. Piety dictates the following reaction to Descartes's discussion of Regius: how treacherous of a former disciple of our philosopher to use a method that is tantamount to lying about his deepest views and how alert of our philosopher to have caught him.

Whether or not contemporaries drew the conclusion that Descartes himself practiced the "Socratic style" or spoke ironically—and many did draw this conclusion—the actual consequences of Descartes's method for religion were explosive. Richard H. Popkin, a leading historian of early modern skepticism and religion says that "one of the major factors, if not *the* major one, in the development of modern irreligion, was the application of the Cartesian methodology and the Cartesian standard of true philosophical and scientific knowledge." [14] Was Descartes him-

13. Caton, "Problem of Descartes' Sincerity," 366. Caton has written extensively and illuminatingly on the question of Descartes's dissimulation. See *Origin of Subjectivity*, 10–20; *Politics of Progress*, 25–32, 54–65.

14. "Cartesianism and Biblical Criticism," 61–81; quoted passage, 61.

self confused about the reconcilability of his science and his religion? His analysis of Regius's strategy suggests otherwise, for he shows that a writer may well refrain from stating the controversial conclusions he knows to be implied by what he does state. But on this important strategic issue we are not left simply with surmise, for Descartes describes his own strategy of silence in letters. Private communications to his own followers allow Descartes to be somewhat more open though even here, as he himself says in private, it is essential to keep one's deepest views slightly blurred. In the early 1640s when Regius's foolhardiness had already threatened to ruin Descartes's shaky reputation with Calvinist Dutch university authorities, Descartes instructed him on how to deal with the old views without rousing opposition (letter to Regius, January 1642). The strategy is Bacon's strategy of malign neglect. Descartes asks: "Why did you openly reject substantial forms and real qualities?" Do instead what Descartes himself had done in the *Meteorology:* "I expressly said I did not at all reject or deny them, but simply found them unnecessary in setting out my explanations." This strategy permitted his audience to do for themselves what they perhaps would not have done had he told them to do it: "If you had taken this course, everybody in your audience would have rejected them as soon as they saw they were useless, but you would not have become so unpopular with your colleagues." [15]

This is Descartes's strategy not only in the *Meteorology* but also in the *Meditations* as he tells Mersenne "between us": "These six Meditations contain all the foundations of my physics. But please, this must not be spread abroad, for those who follow Aristotle will find it harder to approve them. I hope that they will gradually get used to my principles and recognize their truth before they notice that they destroy the principles of Aristotle" (letter to Mersenne, 28 January 1641). Here is a key matter in Descartes's style: the most controversial implications of Descartes's method are expressly *not* drawn by Descartes. Knowing full well that his principles contradict the old ones, Descartes leaves it to his reader to see the contradictions and to draw the appropriate conclusions.

Additional light is cast on Descartes's esotericism by the not at all esoteric instructions he gave his young disciples Burman and Elizabeth,

15. Regius disagreed with what he took to be Descartes's public espousal of beliefs contrary to those he actually held. Speaking of others who hold this view of Descartes's strategy, Regius says they believe that Descartes did harm to his philosophy by publishing his obscure and unreasonable metaphysics. See *AT* IV.255; Caton, "Problem of Descartes' Sincerity," 364.

for to them he says explicitly what weight to give to the various themes of his work. In his conversation with his young Dutch devotee Burman that took place after he had written all the books he was to write, Descartes told him his own ranking of what was important in his writings. Focusing on his personal feelings and speaking of his cosmology (and of himself in the third person), Descartes "confesses that the few thoughts that he had concerning the universe are a source of the greatest pleasure for him to look back on. He values them most highly, and he would not wish to exchange them for any other thoughts he has had about any other topic." He would like the intelligent young enthusiast of his philosophy to share this judgment, especially with respect to one of those other topics: "Do not spend too much time on the *Meditations*." Unlike all Descartes's other comments in the conversation, this one piece of advice is volunteered with no connection to any particular passage; it is given spontaneously just after Burman had raised many of the issues in the *Meditations* destined to become the standard knots in interpreting Descartes's metaphysics. Descartes makes it emphatic: "Yet it is just these physical studies that it is most desirable for men to pursue." Young Burman became a theologian anyway, and an emblem of the course later taken by Descartes-interpretation: the *Meditations,* addressed in the first instance to "The Dean and Doctors of the Faculty of Sacred Theology of Paris"—France's Inquisitors—was read as if it addressed everyone in the same voice ("Conversation with Burman," *PW* 3.346–47).

Still finer is Descartes's explicit instruction to Princess Elizabeth (letter, 28 June 1643), a follower gifted with extraordinary perceptiveness and understanding. In an early letter in their long correspondence Descartes succeeds in making everything perfectly clear while sparing both of them the tedium of spelling everything out. How should the Princess spend her valuable study time? She should emulate her mentor in "the chief rule" he has "always observed in his studies": "Never to spend more than a few hours a day in the thoughts which occupy the imagination and a few hours a year on those which occupy the pure intellect," the latter having just been defined as "metaphysical thoughts which . . . help to familiarize us with the notion of the soul." A few hours a year. The Princess is the fitting recipient for such advice for she is, as Descartes noted in an earlier letter, schooled in the subtleties of reading and writing. Descartes is able to say to her that as a writer she commits only the traces of her thoughts to paper and while these traces at first sight seem perceptive, the more they are examined the more judicious and solid they appear. Furthermore, as a reader nothing can be concealed from her view (letter, 21 May 1643). Such a reader of such a writer would surely have permitted herself a smile at what her judicious counselor suggested she should do with his metaphysical reflections, for here—as Giorgio de Santillana says of a similar passage in a letter by Galileo—"the chuckle is almost audible." [16] A few hours a year. Given his knowledge of writing and reading it would surely come as no surprise to Descartes that the interpretation of his writings given by the learned came to be more Burmanesque than Elizabethlike. [17]

When Descartes's discussions of style are added to the few passages already examined, it should be clear that a rich vein in the Cartesian texts lies virtually untapped, the vein of comedy. Shining through the grave surfaces of Descartes's works, smiling through, leering through, is a comic strain that makes Descartes one of the great masters of comedy in the history of philosophy. Enjoyment of the funny parts depends on sensitivity to Descartes's esoteric style. When we see the difference between the esoteric and the exoteric as La Mettrie saw it a century after Descartes, we can join La Mettrie in defending "the great Descartes against all those who have taken to laughing at him for his silly errors." [18] We can stop laughing at him and begin laughing with him, because what look like Descartes's silly errors are silly errors of interpreters insensitive to Descartes's comedy.

Laughing with Descartes—the role such laughter can play in a Nietzschean history of philosophy can be seen in the opening aphorism of Nietzsche's book of laughter and remembering, *The Joyous Science*. Entitled "the teachers of the purpose of existence," it is a reflection on the ebb and flow of gravity and levity in human history. Nietzsche gives credit to the grave, the teachers of purpose who advanced humankind by persuading it, tribe by tribe, of some meaning for its existence. But in the long run every one of the teachings of purpose "was vanquished by laughter, reason, and nature: the short tragedy always gave way again

16. Santillana, *Crime of Galileo*, 172.

17. Maritain, *Dream of Descartes*, interprets Descartes's rhetoric as "only devices of policy: subtleties, perhaps—not lies; mental reservations at most" (44). Descartes himself was thus unaware of "the profound incompatibility of his philosophy with the whole authentic tradition of Christian wisdom" (44); he was "involuntarily ambiguous"; "at almost every point this philosophy places side by side a thesis and an antithesis equally extreme" (45).

18. Vartanian, *La Mettrie's L'homme machine*, 191–92.

and returned into the eternal comedy of existence; and 'the waves of uncountable laughter'—to cite Aeschylus—must in the end overwhelm even the greatest of these tragedians." Descartes found himself in the midst of a teaching of purpose and learned to turn against it the dread weapon of laughter. Of course Descartes himself does not laugh; only rarely, it seems, can he even be caught smiling. But what else could we expect? As Nietzsche says, the teacher of a purpose for existence "wants to make sure that we do not laugh at existence or at ourselves—or at him." Each such teaching holds that "there is something at which it is absolutely forbidden to laugh." Engulfed by such a prohibition and writing in a time of crisis for the prohibiters already a century old and still white-hot, Descartes knew that it would not do to laugh. Instead, he adopted the measures of the grave, pulling the mask of gravity over himself however ill the fit. Levity derives from that gravity, from the pose he adopts and which he allows us, in all caution, to view as a pose. He's not laughing. But we are. He forces us to laugh where it was prohibited to laugh and he does so with impunity because he is so grave.

But let's take our instructions from Descartes himself on laughing at the grave. In *The Passions of the Soul,* Descartes discusses a form of humor that Nietzsche makes central to philosophical method and of which he is himself a master: mockery or ridicule. "As for mockery," Descartes says, "which constructively admonishes vices by making them appear ridiculous, but in which one does not laugh at them oneself or express any hatred against anyone, it is not a Passion but a quality of a cultivated man, which shows off the cheerfulness of his temper and the tranquillity of his soul, which are marks of virtue, and often also the ingenuity of his mind, in that he is able to impart a pleasing appearance to the things he mocks" (180). "One does not laugh at them oneself"—but what about us, the audience enjoying this mockery? "It is not unseemly to laugh upon hearing another's mockery; it may even be such that it would be peevish not to laugh at it" (181). It is time to break out laughing, time to see Descartes as one of the great masters of comic ridicule in the history of philosophy.

"Laughter may yet have a future," Nietzsche says, as we discover and appreciate its past, its great role in overcoming all the teachings of purpose. "Do you understand me," Nietzsche says at the end of his aphorism, "Do you understand this new law of ebb and flood? There is a time for us, too!" The time of the joyous science of Nietzsche and his ilk is the end time of the teachings of purpose and the dawn of a teaching on the purposeless play of existence. Descartes is one of the teachers of laughter to whom we owe the most in overcoming the teachings of a purpose to existence.[19]

Descartes and the History of Philosophy:
The *Discourse on the Method*

The subsequent chapters on Descartes will all be concerned primarily with the *Discourse,* a book which occupies a special place in Descartes's writings for three main reasons. First, Descartes had long reflected on his public appearance and only after suppressing a whole series of projected first appearances, the *Olympica,* the *Rules,* the *World,* did he finally appear as the author of the *Discourse.* Second, the *Discourse* presents an outline of the whole Cartesian program and, to accompany and certify the program, a portrait of its anonymous author. The magnitude of the task and the singularity of its author are allowed to dawn on the reader more slowly than would have been possible had Descartes actually given his book the title he projected for it one year before its appearance: "The Plan of a universal Science to raise our nature to its highest degree of perfection. Plus the Dioptrics, the Meteorology, and the Geometry, in which the most curious matters which the author has been able to choose in order to give proof of his universal Science are explained in such a manner that even those who have never studied them can understand them" (letter to Mersenne, March 1636). Third, the *Discourse* is the preface to three "essays in the method." Though now widely ignored, this is, as Roth said, "the most important literary fact about the *Discourse*"; it is an introduction to treatises on scientific subjects which "bring us not to metaphysical but to scientific truth."[20] The scientific treatises, completed earlier without the metaphysical "foundation" (iii.29), could only be sent forth into the world when accompanied by a preface which made a place for them. By making that place, the *Discourse* serves as the essential prelude to all Descartes's work.

Ten years after the *Discourse,* when he reviewed his writings for the preface to the French edition of the *Principles of Philosophy,* Descartes emphasized that the *Discourse* remained the essential entryway into his work. His writings were systematically planned, he says, to prepare the minds of readers for his *Principles;* his series of books explains "all philosophy in

---

19. On the role of mockery as a weapon in the modern battle against revelation, see Strauss, *Spinoza's Critique of Religion,* 143–46, and *Philosophy and Law,* 11.

20. Roth, *Descartes' Discourse on Method,* 6.

correct order without having omitted any of those things which ought to precede the last things which I wrote."

Many years earlier than the *Discourse,* earlier still than all his other projected first appearances, Descartes wrote a fascinating note that chance has bequeathed to us as one of his earliest surviving fragments: "Actors, taught not to let any embarrassment show on their faces, put on a mask. So far, I have been a spectator in this theatre which is the world, but I am now about to mount the stage, and I come forth masked" (*AT* X.213; *PW* 1.2). When Descartes finally comes forth, he comes forth masked as the author of the *Discourse on the Method.* And within its autobiographical drama he allows his reader to witness a masking, for we see him entering the solitude of the *poêle,* that now famous south German "stove" or "stove-heated room" where he communed alone with his thoughts (ii.11). He remained in solitude not only for the whole day first reported but for the whole winter of 1619–20. When he finally emerged (iii.28), he emerged masked, for the revolutionary thoughts and revolutionary method he had legislated for himself were clothed, made invisible by the provisional code of morals with which he carefully outfitted himself while still in solitude. That masked revolutionary, looking just as he looked prior to his revolutionary thoughts in the *poêle,* takes up his wanderings again "more a spectator than an actor" (iii.28) in the great European events to which he refers. That spectator first became an actor with the *Discourse on the Method;* by publishing that book he mounts the European stage he will soon come to dominate.[21]

As the inviting preface to all Descartes's work, the *Discourse* gives a pleasing appearance of simplicity and candor. Descartes even hopes that his openness will be to everyone's liking (i.4). But that simplicity and openness seem to me to mask a complexity and density which are still more pleasing and which make the book an absolute marvel of philosophic writing. One strand of that complexity and density is Descartes's relationship to his philosophical predecessors and mentors. While acting as if he invented himself, Descartes shows how he was schooled by the great philosophers, especially, as it seems to me, Socrates, Plato, Bacon, and Montaigne. Descartes shows how he modeled himself on

21. The fascinating dreams and dream interpretation of Descartes's *Olympica,* when read as a conscious construction rather than as a record of actual dreams, appears as another early account of how Descartes answered the question, what way of life ought I to follow? It too seems to be an early attempt by Descartes to present his task and his fitness for the task. See Kennington, "Descartes' 'Olympica.' " The historicity of the dreams is defended by Cole, *Olympian Dreams and Youthful Rebellion.*

Socrates by duplicating famous Socratic deeds until finally his Socratic practice precipitated a turn in his life that forced a break with Socrates, an event described at the center of the *Discourse.* That break, as I will argue, prepared a turn to Plato, to a quite different politic style, an art Descartes shows himself learning in part six of the *Discourse.* He is related to Bacon because he takes over Bacon's project of the mastery of nature, grounding it in his own mathematical physics, and making that his sole reason for publishing anything. As for Montaigne, Descartes simply quotes many of Montaigne's singular opinions while never once breathing a word about their source, inviting readers to ponder on their own his debt to a modern skepticism that updates a Socratic and Platonic skepticism.

By pretending to invent himself while quietly displaying his dependence on his great predecessors, Descartes exhibits his kinship with the greatest minds who submit only to the wisest as their judges and who have no need to be held in admiration by the less learned (vi.78; i.6).[22] Similarly, those for whom Descartes writes, his true friends or kin, are the lovers of wisdom whom he invites to become his co-conspirators. They are to learn from his practice the guidelines for their own, for his practice claims membership in a long and noble line of fundamental teachers stretching back to Socrates; ironic speech was their indispensable instrument, preserving their privacy and their leisure while making their teaching accessible to those who combined good sense with study (vi.77–78). But Socratic speech must take different forms in different times and places; Cassandra must know where she is and know how to speak. Part of the irony of Descartes's speech is the illusion that this Socratic Platonic Montaignian Baconian invented himself. As I hope to make clear, the *Discourse,* a fabulous tale of the coming to be of the new philosopher, is a book bursting with allusions. Some are direct quotations from famous books like the allusions to Montaigne, some are repetitions of famous events like the allusions to Socrates or Galileo, some are brazen thefts of ideas like those stolen from Plato or Bacon.[23]

---

22. Plato, *Symposium* 194c; Bacon, *GI,* "Preface," last sentence; *Works* IV.21.

23. With respect to discerning influences on Descartes, a very valuable book on his mathematics argues that it is best to abandon the attempt as useless. Depreciating *Quellenforschung* as a useless *Ideenjagd,* David Lachterman argues that Descartes intended to cover all his tracks in order to leave the self-aggrandizing impression that he had invented himself: refusing to engage in *Quellenforschung* certainly helps that interpretation. And it can use help given the fact that Descartes opens his first book with a quotation from Montaigne for which very little *Quellenforschung* is necessary (Lachterman, *Ethics of Geometry,* 124–25).

But here a word of caution is in order. The *Discourse* appears to make absolute certitude the goal of philosophy, but attunement to allusions lacks absolute certitude; it depends upon the *esprit de finesse* and cannot even aspire to the *esprit géométrique*. At this remove in time and sentiment, it is not possible to identify all the allusions and a risk is always present that allusions will be falsely identified or their meaning misinterpreted. Nevertheless, it seems to me that Descartes has constructed his book in such a way as to force this labor on those who want to understand it, and that on the main matters he has made himself clear: who does not know the career of Socrates, or the writings of Plato, Machiavelli, Montaigne, Bacon, or the fate of Galileo? Descartes's appearance of self-generation as a rational man is wholly compatible with the acknowledgment of debts to the very few other wholly rational men and the way the debt is paid serves to make an important point for the rational ones for whom Descartes writes. Do not believe anything here that you do not know evidently to be true: do not believe on my authority any more than I believed on theirs. This, it seems to me, is Descartes's understanding of the uses of the history of philosophy. The great philosophers were his educators and they taught him participation in a cultural drama far greater than himself, a drama of human history that to a degree depends upon philosophy and in which he could aspire to play a part. Descartes teaches by showing how he was taught. He made himself by constant reflection on the great preceptors.

Chapter 7

Descartes and Socrates:
A Turning Point in the *Discourse*

We cannot fail to see in Socrates the one turning point and vortex of all so-called world history.—*Nietzsche (BT 15)*

And in fact Descartes did not fail to see in Socrates the one turning point of all so-called world history. His sole extended discussion of the history of philosophy—the letter introducing the French translation of his *Principles of Philosophy*—describes Socrates as the foundational teacher whose work was carried forward by his pupil Plato and Plato's pupil Aristotle and by all subsequent philosophy. But Socrates is not only the foundational thinker of Western philosophy, he is also the exemplary thinker who provided a model to emulate. Signs of the emulation of Socrates are to be found frequently in the first half of Descartes's *Discourse on the Method*. Nevertheless, there appears near its center a decisive turning point in its anonymous author's life where he suddenly ceased to emulate Socrates and chose a different course.

The Socratic model is evident in the means by which the author discovered his own ignorance: by an examination of the reputedly wise and by studying the customs of the world (i.4,10). Spurred by that acquired ignorance he took as his own rule of inquiry the Delphic injunction with which Socrates had become identified: "Know thyself" (i.10, 11). Following that Socratic path led to the Socratic conclusion that the life of philosophy gives the most intense satisfaction (iii.27) and that it is sufficient "to judge well in order to do well" or that virtue is knowledge (iii.28). Such suggestions of Socratic practice are confirmed at the end of part three where the author de-

Note: I owe many points in these chapters on Descartes to George Dunn. In particular some of the crucial arguments of this chapter on Socrates originate with his investigations of Descartes. I am grateful for his permission to put them to my own use.

scribes a turning point in his life when he abandoned his homeland and initiated a whole new field of inquiry for himself. That turning point meant a complete break with the way of Socrates.

To describe that break the author states explicitly for the first time just how Socratic his outward practice had been: for nine years he had followed the two principal points of Socratic practice: openly stating his own ignorance, he openly demonstrated the ignorance of those who claimed to be knowledgeable (iii.30). Socratic practice had a Socratic result: people started spreading the rumor around that he was wise, that his avowals of ignorance were merely ironic. Rumors of ironic ignorance and secret wisdom led eventually to Socrates' trial and execution. Similar rumors with a similar ground lead our author to an un-Socratic act: he cannot allow others to take him for something he is not; he must close the gap between his rumored wisdom and his flaunted ignorance. Rather than continue to follow Socrates and deny the rumor of his wisdom, he will take the opposite course and make himself worthy of the rumor. He will learn how to claim not ignorance but wisdom. Un-Socratic resolve requires an un-Socratic deed: he voluntarily exiles himself to a foreign country to prepare his demonstration of his wisdom for his countrymen.[1]

To claim wisdom rather than ignorance, our anonymous author has to change more than his location, he has to change his subject: the themes that will make him demonstrably wise are not what he has just spent nine years studying. They are the entirely new themes of part four, meditations on metaphysical matters which he described in the introductory summary as "the reasons by which [he] proves the existence of God and of the human soul, which are the foundations of his metaphysics." The author thus breaks with Socratic practice and spends eight years in exile to succeed where Socratic practice most obviously failed: to deal with public rumors of a secret wisdom he will show himself wise about the divine things and the human things, God and the soul. It seems to be of very great importance that people think well of him, for he gives only one reason for these radical steps of entering exile and taking up the new topics of God and the soul—his reputation. He will "try by every means" to make himself worthy of the reputation bestowed upon him by rumor. He changes his practice to change his reputation: it will

1. See Simpson, "Putting One's House in Order," 83–101.

be wise to be reputed wise on the very matters for which Socrates was executed.

By likening himself to Socrates has Descartes indulged in the "arrogance" of which he has been so often accused, comparing himself in his first book with the almost mythic hero of philosophy, and then improving on this hero by actually becoming wise? We must pause here to consider a fact about the *Discourse* that is often forgotten: it first appeared anonymously. It seems to me that this was not simply a prudent step on Descartes's part, for it befits the nature of the book that it be anonymous. The book is an autobiography, but whose? Who is the hero of this tale? The author never tells us his name but he does tell us how to think of his tale and consequently of him: think of it as a history—or, if you prefer, a fable (i.4). But he adds immediately that the aim of this history or fable is not to present a model for emulation, for "among the examples one can imitate, one also finds perhaps several others which one is right in not following." How should we think of this history or fable? The author answers our question by telling us what fables and histories are good for: the gracefulness of fables can awaken the mind while the memorable deeds of history can exalt it and when read with discretion they can aid in forming one's judgment (i.5). And he tells us too how to read with discretion: fables in their grand depiction of the acts of gods and heroes make us imagine many events to be possible that really are impossible (i.7). Has the hero of this fable undertaken the impossible? What *has* he undertaken? Will his history tell us? Even the most accurate histories, he says, distort in various ways so that what is included in them "does not appear as it really is" (i.7). Moreover, "those who govern their own conduct on the basis of the examples drawn from it are subject to falling into the extravagances of the knights of our novels and to conceiving plans that are beyond their powers." Discretion dictates that we not govern our own conduct on the examples of fabulous history—like the fabulous history of Don Quixote which had been published a few years earlier. But if the deeds portrayed in the *Discourse* are not exemplary because they are beyond our powers, are they beyond the powers of the knight of the *Discourse?* Just what are the fabulous deeds portrayed in the *Discourse* to awaken our minds to what is possible for a human being and to exalt our minds in its hero's attempt to perform them? As we will see, they are the deeds of a philosopher who takes his measure of greatness from the few philosophers of the past, the fabulous few who attempted what might be thought impossible.

[173]

The *Discourse,* to return to our place, is the fabulous history of a hero who for nine years made himself look like Socrates but then suddenly broke with the Socratic way in order to become worthy of the reputation for wisdom that had been bestowed on him. Why does the break with Socrates occur at just this point—the final paragraph of part three? The preceding paragraph casts light on the break because it corrects a misleading impression left earlier about the relationship between philosophy and the new method, discovery of which had been described in part two. When he first began to practice his method the author made a promise to himself to apply it to the problems of the other sciences just as he had first successfully applied it to algebra and geometry (ii.21–22). Being methodical, the method would have to be applied to the other sciences according to a principle of order derived from the method itself. That principle dictated that the treatment of philosophy be delayed because philosophy was the special case: till now, all the sciences had borrowed their principles from philosophy even though there was nothing in philosophy that was not doubtful. Philosophy's long-standing supremacy, the supremacy of the doubtful, made it necessary, above all, that something certain be established in philosophy; this was in fact "the most important thing in the world." But he was only twenty-three years old at the time, the author says, so the most important thing in the world would have to wait a bit. The expectation left by this chart of his future path is that nothing would be well-founded in the sciences until our author had applied his new method to philosophy, the old giver of principles to the sciences. But just before the break with Socrates we learn that this expectation is wrong.

The author kept his promise to himself and for nine years practiced his method both on mathematical problems and on other problems that he could render similar to those of mathematics by detaching them from all the principles of the other sciences that were not yet sufficiently firm, detaching them, that is, from philosophy in which nothing was firm. Made independent of the reigning philosophy and rendered mathematical, the problems of the other sciences proved soluble and our author refers us to the appended treatises as demonstrations of his claim: the *Dioptrics,* the *Meteorology,* and the *Geometry* are "essays in the method" that prove that the problems of the sciences are soluble when detached from philosophy and pursued by the new method. Nine years' work applying the new method to the sciences thus made clear what could not be clear at the beginning: the new method can *replace* traditional philosophy as the giver of principles to all the sciences. The statement of this claim contains a challenge: study the appended *Essays,* the author says, to see if the new method can succeed independently of traditional philosophy. *Prior* to the turn to metaphysics, then, the *Discourse* claims that complete success in the sciences is possible without philosophy as it has tradition- ally been understood; the old giver of principles can be replaced by a method whose principles are supreme for all the sciences even though those principles are not grounded in the old metaphysical way.

But that claim seems to be contradicted immediately because the fol- lowing paragraphs turn after all to the traditional themes of philosophy in order to obtain "foundations" that the author has just said are *not* nec- essary to succeed in the scientific endeavors of the *Essays.* Does the new science have to be founded in the old way, on a metaphysics of God and the soul, even if it can solve its problems without that metaphysics? How are the foundations of part four to be understood? The question is forced on the reader because these are not the only "foundations" in the *Discourse:* part one had identified "foundations so solid and firm" that the author had marveled that nothing had yet been built on them, the foundations of mathematics (i.7). This foundation had not yet provided the base for a noble building because their true usefulness had "not yet" been noticed. Had they *still* not been noticed after nine years of work on a mathematical method applicable to the other sciences?

The problem of foundations is perhaps the most important problem in the *Discourse,* and certainly one of the most complex—Hiram Caton calls it "one of the most intractable problems in Cartesian philosophy."[2] But now we can approach the problem of foundations from an unex- pected side, the side of a fabulous knight who had emulated Socrates but who emulates him no more, and whose erstwhile emulation—he now makes clear—had long been only a mask. For the sketch he has just given of his nine-year practice makes it obvious that he had been Socratic only outwardly, only while visible to others had he avowed his own ignorance and demonstrated theirs. Inwardly, invisibly, he had not been Socratic at all, for silently and alone he had pursued a method of his own discovery that had increasingly given him knowledge in the sciences. Flaunting ignorance, he had acquired knowledge of nature and its laws that no one before him had ever possessed, as the *Essays* demonstrate. So far from being Socratic in his solitude, he had been "pre-Socratic," he had sought a knowledge of nature of the sort Socrates had explicitly abandoned as hopeless and as dangerous to philosophy, according to the account in the

2. Caton, *Origin of Subjectivity,* 66, see 39–100.

Phaedo (88c–91c, 96a–102a, 105b). The way he had taken was no "second sailing" that begins with the *logoi* or the speeches of human beings in hopes of ascertaining from them the truth of the human things and of saving himself and his friends from despair at the *logos*. According to his own report, he had lost confidence in any method which examined the speeches of others for he had found them to be based largely on "example and custom," concerning which he had "learned to believe nothing very firmly" (i.10). It was *then,* at the end of part one, that he in fact broke with Socrates, in fact, though not in appearance. It was then that he plunged into solitude to examine himself quite alone. In solitude, as a consequence of his reflection on the sources of imperfection in human things, he struck upon a method that would allow him to achieve as much perfection as possible for himself. Perhaps it would not be much, perhaps he would never get beyond his skepticism about human judgments. But then his method gave him immediate and unexpected success in mathematics. Perhaps, though, mathematics would not prove useful, perhaps it would remain merely "solid and firm," a "foundation" on which nothing could ever be built, a foundation eschewed by "the ancient pagans" who built "magnificent palaces of morals" on nothing more firm than the sand and mud of opinions (i.7–8). But, as he continued to apply his method to problems that could be rendered similar to those of mathematics (iii.29), success continued. How far could this method carry him? Could the solid and firm foundation of mathematics turn out after all to be something on which a new palace of morals could be build? Could the knight of our novel be a builder capable of constructing a palace to challenge the magnificent palaces of those ancient pagans whose master had been none other than Socrates?

What our fable relates is no second sailing content with the sand and mud of opinion. Instead it revives the first sailing out of discontent with the second. Pre-Socratic natural philosophy had run aground on its own principles and, in Socrates' retelling of its fate, its demise threatened any trust in reason. In the face of nihilistic despair at reason, Socrates devised a safe way to rehabilitate reason, the way of the *logoi* extended by Plato and Aristotle into philosophical forms that had become authoritative. Behind his Socratic mask, our hero had pursued a decidedly un-Socratic course. But what he hid behind his Socratic skepticism was an increasingly successful means to knowledge based on a method of his own devising and now, after nine years of application, giving reasonable promise of being applicable to all subject matters as his *Essays* demonstrate.

What use could a Socratic mask be to him now, he who is preparing to come forth in the world as the discoverer of the method for rightly conducting one's reason and for seeking truth in the sciences? The mask of ignorance had to be discarded, for if it was a useful mask for a thinker like Montaigne, it could be of no use for a thinker like Lord Bacon, a thinker who had discovered a new kind of knowledge that could transform the world into a comfortable home for humankind. The one who had successfully devised a method applicable to all subject matters that could be rendered similar to mathematics would have to adopt a rhetoric appropriate to an optimism about reason rather than a skepticism about it. Reason's capacity would have to be exalted, not diminished; the way of Bacon would have to take precedence over the way of Montaigne and the way of Socrates.

Thus the knight of our fable surrenders the mask of Socrates. He retires to a foreign country there to prepare to come forth—How? Unmasked? He will labor to make himself worthy of the reputation bestowed on him, the reputation for having succeeded where all other philosophers had failed, in providing the "foundations" of a philosophy more certain than the commonly accepted one. And the result of "the first meditations" of his new solitude are the "metaphysical" reflections of part four (iv.31), "the reasons by which the author proves the existence of God and of the human soul, which are the foundations of his metaphysics." By these means the author makes himself worthy of a reputation that arose as mere rumor on the basis of his Socratic practice. Are the metaphysical reflections the unmasked truth authored by one who had previously hidden his real work behind a mask of Socratic ignorance? Or are they a more serviceable mask, one befitting a knower, a mask that permits the radical discoverer of a new method for knowing the world to come forth as one who can provide "foundations" for the new world that look so much like the foundations of the old world that they could seem not to threaten it?

In the *Discourse* confusion about foundations can in fact be reduced to a precise equivocation. Either the foundations are mathematics, solid and firm and till now ignored as a possible foundation for a palace of morals (1.7–8), or the foundations are the new themes of part four, the old themes of philosophers, themes introduced to serve the reputation of the new philosopher. The project taken up in part four to provide "foundations" can in no way alter the results of the nine-year project, for those results were attained quite independently of it, and that project alone carries forward the transformation of the sciences to which our author had dedicated himself and to which he will return in part five. The new project of part four, according to the precise way in which the author introduces it, does not arise out of any deficiency other than the reputation of its inventor. That reputation, however, is no small matter; the public success of the still only privately successful project depends in part on the reputation of the one who introduces it. To be seen as a wise man in the way that men are deemed wise, his wisdom will have to satisfy the standards of authoritative opinion.

Coming forth from exile the knight of our novel comes forth as wise, the first thinker ever to supply firm foundations for the world of concern to us, the daily world that surrounds us. Part four of the *Discourse* performs that most heroic of philosophic deeds, demonstrating that the ramparts of our world are firm, that it has "foundations" where foundations have long been sought, in God and the soul. But in exiting part four our author once again awakens our suspicions about the status of these foundations, for the opening paragraph of part five place its themes into a clear order of rank with the themes of part four. Now that he has solved "all the main difficulties commonly treated in philosophy," the author says he can begin to recount the "truths more useful and more important than anything he had formerly learned or even hoped to learn." These most useful and most important truths are the laws of nature, the laws of matter in motion basic to the evolutionary cosmology set out in part five. It is of course still necessary to allege that all the laws of nature could have been deduced from the infinite perfections of God. But our author refrains from doing so. He refrains from describing just how the world of concern to us, the changing world around us, is founded on what never changes, on the infinite perfections of God. Our knight says that he could have shown how that world is founded on the infinite perfections of God if he'd wanted to—but he didn't want to. He didn't want to? The philosophical mystery of the ages solved by the knight of our novel and he won't tell us how? We were warned: fables make one imagine some things to be possible that really are impossible.

Part five opens calling the laws of nature the most useful and most important truths, but then it ends calling the soul the subject "of the greatest importance" (v.59) and reintroducing the related question of God's existence. Once again we are faced with an equivocation like the equivocation on foundations, but once again Descartes provides a solution. The reason given for the importance of God and the soul turns out to have nothing to do with their truth, only with the consequences of their being believed. Their importance has to do with virtue and its link to the fundamental fear and hope of human beings. Because of the way we have been taught to think of ourselves and to distinguish ourselves from the animals, humans would be led away from the straight road of virtue if we were suddenly forced to believe that we had no more to fear nor to hope for after this life than have flies or ants. As Descartes says at the opening of the *Meditations,* "since in this life there are often more rewards for vices than for virtues, few would prefer what is right to what is useful, if they neither feared God nor hoped for an afterlife" (*A T* VII.2). The end of part five deals with what is useful for virtue, and it does not apply to human beings simply, but to "weak minds." God and the soul are of the greatest importance because weak minds need to elevate themselves above the animals and give themselves a special relationship to the deity in order to keep to the straight road of virtue. Knowledge is not virtue here, a particular kind of ignorance is virtue, ignorance of the natural origins and natural ends set out in part five. It being no part of the duty of a wise man to drive weaker men to despair, our author concludes his chapter on natural history by distinguishing man from the animals in the old unnatural or supernatural way. He offers in truncated form a variant of the argument Socrates had given for the immortality of the soul in the *Republic* (x.608e–611a) and the *Phaedo* (78b–82a). In the *Republic,* Socrates' inadequate and question-begging argument was presented just after he had explained the city's need for ministering poetry once Homeric poetry had been banished (606e–608b) and he linked his new, non-Homeric poetry on the immortality of the soul to just gods who reward and punish souls for their behavior. The ministering poetry of immortal souls and just gods, introduced by Plato's Socrates to keep Glaucon and the rest of the young men on the straight road of virtue, is used as well by the author of the *Discourse* out of deference to the morals of the weak-minded now raised on such beliefs.

Part four on God and the soul, introduced as serving only the author's reputation, serves the well-being of others. It is an act of decency, an act of justice by a student of Socrates: he practices the novel form of justice first defined by the Platonic Socrates in recognition of the benefit and harm a philosopher's words can bring. In the *Republic,* Socrates had criticized Polemarchus's statement of the traditional view that justice is doing good to friends and harm to enemies. The definition arising from Socrates' criticisms defines Socrates' practice throughout the dialogue: justice is doing good to friends who are good and not harming anybody. Our anonymous author explicitly appropriated Socratic justice in the hope he expressed for his book at its beginning: that it be useful to some, harmful to none and that its openness be to everyone's liking (i.4; *Republic* i.332a–336a). In order not to harm those whose virtue would be ruined by open advocacy of new views on the natural world, the teacher of those views is forced to practice an only apparent openness while making his views accessible to those few for whom they could be useful. In part four, where least open, he most avoids doing harm, for he seems to point to the things that endure; but where least open he is still of use to some, for he points in fact to the things that must be endured.

Will such feats of endurance be necessary in the new world set "somewhere in imaginary space" (v.42) by the author? *The Passions of the Soul* will answer no and ground its answer on the powers of habituation or conditioning: given the proper conditioning "there is no soul so weak that it cannot, when well guided, acquire an absolute power over its passions" (50). The *Passions* offers guidance that departs radically from traditional notions of God and the soul and redirects the fundamental fears and hopes.

The author of the *Discourse* has put himself on trial, presenting his life and occupation so that each person may judge them (i.3–4). In particular, he is "forced to speak" about the metaphysical matters of part four so that "one might be able to judge whether the foundations I have laid are sufficiently firm" (iv.31). Everyone can read his work and judge him, including authorities who have control over his actions and to whom he necessarily defers (vi.60). But at the end of his introduction of himself he says that it is "those who combine good sense with study to whom alone I submit as my judges" (vi.78). Socrates too had waited till the end of his *Apology* to identify as his true judges those who voted for his acquittal (40a). But the majority had voted that Socrates was guilty as charged. Flaunting wisdom rather than ignorance, our author broke with Socrates in order to begin his public life with a successful apology rather than end it with a futile one. After his break with Socrates he boasts of his wisdom, not of his ignorance. But so to doff the Socratic mask is to don the Platonic one. Just where does the knight of our novel stand with respect to Plato? Part six, it seems to me, helps answer that question.

Chapter 8

Descartes and Plato

I am a complete skeptic about Plato.—Nietzsche *(TI Ancients 2)*

Descartes too was a skeptic about Plato. He says so in the one place in his writings where he speaks of Plato's relationship to Socrates, the letter introducing the French edition of the *Principles of Philosophy*. But he does not quite speak of Plato even there, for in another of those wonderful pranks with which he entertains us, Descartes acknowledges the need for a preface as his book moves from a Latin to a French audience but says he cannot bring himself to write one. Instead, he will write what he would have written had he written one. A lay audience unschooled in Scholastic philosophy and suspicious of philosophy because of what professionals had made of it, should be told what philosophy is, why it is of the highest worth, how it has been conducted in the past, and how it can be conducted now, after Descartes. Had he written a history of philosophy, he would have said that "philosopher" is the name given to those who have sought the first causes and true principles from which one might deduce the reasons for everything we are capable of knowing. Descartes knows of no philosopher who succeeded in this project but he knows of two who acted as if they did, Plato and Aristotle, "the first and principal philosophers whose writings we have." There is no difference between the two except that Plato followed Socrates more closely by confessing that he had not been able to discover anything certain. Instead, Plato imagined some principles by which he attempted to explain other things—what the *Phaedo* describes as the safe way for philosophy when its failure to grasp the first causes of all things is recognized as leading to misology. We learn more about Descartes's ironic Plato from what he would have said about Aristotle: Aristotle was less candid than Plato, and although he had no principles other than Plato's, "he entirely changed the manner of presenting these principles and propounded them as true and certain, even though it is unlikely that he ever judged them to be so." Descartes was a complete skeptic about Aristotle too.

Nietzsche's Plato is beginning to become familiar, a skeptical Socratic whose skepticism is kept confidential by philosophers who recognize it. The philosopher Montaigne provides somewhat more open access to this private Plato for philosophers because he argues for a salutary skepticism; he has an interest in betraying Plato to the rest of us or in simply stating that Plato's integrity is not beyond question—as Nietzsche simply stated (*KGW* VIII 14 [116] = *WP* 428). With Nietzsche it all comes into the open because Nietzsche has no interest in preserving Plato's cover.

Descartes has such an interest. It would not have served Descartes's interests to flaunt his complete skepticism about Plato because he too came to adopt a Platonic art of writing—part of his artistry consists in not betraying its practice by the master lest he betray its practice by the pupil. Nevertheless, Descartes's practice is made accessible in the appropriate way in part six of the *Discourse* where he raises the question: Why write at all? Part five had reported on the treatise which had cost Descartes many years of labor but which "certain considerations" (v. 41) forced him to suppress. He had wanted to present everything he knew on "the nature of material things" but fear kept him from doing so (v. 42) and forced him to adopt the technique of a painter, highlighting one thing while darkening with shadows all the rest (v. 41). Despite these precautions, the treatise had to be withheld—not because of any failure in its foundations, its arguments, or its conclusions, for Descartes's summary of its contents makes clear that nothing needed to be corrected. Only after the summary, at the beginning of part six, does he turn to the "certain considerations" that were his sole reason for suppressing his treatise. Its only failure was a deficiency of caution and he discovered that deficiency in the nick of time: we see him preparing his treatise for the printer when suddenly he learns that a certain opinion expressed by "someone else" is condemned by the authorities. Immediately, he judged his own book insufficiently cautious and exposed to the same condemnation. Part six exists to show how Descartes remedied his failure of caution, how he learned a new form of artful speech, the Platonic form embodied in the book he is now making public.

The event that forced Descartes to alter the way he presented his thoughts on the nature of material things was a contemporary version of the trial of Socrates, the trial of Galileo, for "someone else" is Galileo, the most celebrated man of science of his day, the man whose public battles with religious authority had commanded the attention of everyone in Europe with the slightest interest in science. The power exercised by the Inquisition over Galileo made it all too apparent that it would not be sufficient for Descartes to allege that he was only describing some new world somewhere in imaginary space (v. 42), for Galileo himself had already done that, outwardly obedient to the Inquisition's distinction between discussing a view and holding it, between speaking hypothetically of what can save the appearances and speaking absolutely of what is physically true of the world.[1] The failure of Galileo's art of writing made clear to Descartes that a more elaborate exhibition of loyalty to authoritative opinions would have to be made. The writing that replaced the suppressed treatise would be one that learned from the fate of Galileo to attend more closely to Plato's strict lessons on how philosophy is to shelter itself.

Descartes's adoption of the Platonic shelter is explained in part six where he gives his reasons for writing as he now does. Plato's *Phaedrus* with its discussion of the dangers of writing comes to light as Descartes's model for his new way of making his thoughts public. Part six, Descartes's marvelous dialogue with himself on why he should publish anything and when, explains why the *Discourse* exists and why it takes the form it does. Because it explains the art of the *Discourse* and because it exhibits what is definitive in Descartes's project, part six can usefully be treated first. In order to proceed through the intricacies of this complex part, it will be necessary to follow the argument paragraph by paragraph.

A New Resolve (Paragraph 1)

Descartes begins part six by finally disclosing just what those "certain considerations" were that kept him from publishing *The World* three years earlier (v. 41). He relates those considerations with a mixture of vagueness and exactitude that forces the reader to reconstruct the situation on the basis of inferences. The main inferences are obvious enough but to draw them is to imaginatively picture Descartes being put on trial by the Inquisition as the Inquisition put Galileo on trial. Just what are the similarities between Galileo's crime and Descartes's book such that Descartes was forced to suppress the work that had cost him so many years of labor? Referring vaguely to "people to whom I defer," Descartes makes perfectly clear that these people may control his actions but he

---

1. See Galileo, *Dialogue concerning the Two Chief World Systems*, "To the Discerning Reader," 5–7, and 463–65; Santillana, *Crime of Galileo*, 149, 151, 171–72, 194, 207; and Descartes, letter to Mersenne, April 1634.

retains complete control over his thoughts. They had disapproved of a "certain opinion in the realm of physics" published by Galileo. It has long been supposed that Descartes is referring to Galileo's Copernicanism, the thought crime in physics for which Galileo was actually tried and convicted. But the possibility of a much more serious thought crime has been raised by Pietro Redondi in his marvelous book, *Galileo Heretic*. Because that possibility has weighty consequences for Descartes's actions it will be useful to investigate it.

What posed the greatest danger to Galileo, Redondi asks, his Copernicanism for which he was actually tried and convicted, or something else, something much more vital to Catholic orthodoxy in a time of war with powerful heretics? Three and a half centuries of interpretation have taken their bearings from the actual trial over astronomy but Redondi supplies evidence for a different danger: the physics of transubstantiation, the Catholic sacrament of the Eucharist according to which wine and bread are miraculously transformed into the blood and flesh of Christ's body. Redondi shows that heresy in astronomy was far less significant than heresy in physics; Copernicus's work was put on the Index in 1616, but the most zealous warriors policing Catholic orthodoxy after the Council of Trent, the Jesuits, developed a policing system which included openness to Copernican astronomy (287–90). Transubstantiation was another matter entirely. The issue was not something as relatively remote as the relation of earth and sky, but theories of the material make-up of everything, in particular the make-up of those material things that served as "the keystone of the entire faith of the Catholic Reformation" (207). In a historical reconstruction that recovers the Catholic context for Descartes's physics, Redondi demonstrates how the physics of transubstantiation had become the preoccupation of the whole debate over the new physics. In the presence of unprecedented heresy, the Protestantism that threatened the whole Church, and after centuries of debate on the physics of the Eucharist, the Council of Trent in 1551 defined the miracle in terms of Aristotle's physics of substance and accident and assigned its official defenders the highest responsibility: if someone advocates a physics unable to account for the miracle, "on him be anathema" (163). With their "theological philosophy," their doctrine of the rule of religion over philosophy, the Jesuits became the aggressive enforcers of this orthodoxy in physics; this entailed total opposition to the various forms of atomism, a physics unable to account for a thing having a different substance when all its sensible properties remained the same.

And Galileo? Redondi argues that the Jesuits had been threatened by political eclipse in 1623, the year in which Galileo published a book which singled them out for attack and spoke favorable of atomism. 1623 was the time of what Redondi calls "the marvelous conjuncture" of liberal and humanistic forces that promised to make the pontificate of Urban VIII, elected August 1623, a new renaissance freeing Catholic intellectual life from the narrowness of Counter-Reformation orthodoxy (68–106). Galileo was the official scientist of the new Pope (146, 147), and his new book, *The Assayer,* was a literary manifesto declaring a time of openness to the "new philosophy," a natural philosophy taking its guidance from "the great book of nature" whose signs were to be read mathematically (37, 53). In this setting, Galileo and his new physics looked almost invulnerable. And the centerpiece of Redondi's argument was that Galileo—at that moment—proved in fact invulnerable to an actual denunciation of heresy brought against him: almost by accident Redondi found a hitherto unknown document in the secret files of the Holy Office which denounces Galileo for the physics of *The Assayer* because it is heretical concerning the Eucharist. In the early years of Urban VIII's pontificate Galileo proved immune to the most grave charge of heresy.

But by 1632 everything had changed. The "marvelous conjuncture" had passed as Catholic fortunes declined with the Protestant victories of the King of Sweden. Urban VIII's pro-French, or anti-Spain, anti-Jesuit strategy seemed discredited and he faced the most serious crisis of his pontificate. Accused of being soft on heresy in the midst of a war against the heretics that the heretics were winning, the Pope had to compromise and one of those compromises entailed public demonstration of his intolerance of heresy. As Redondi argues, Galileo fell victim to a European politics broader than the new science. The Pope remained friendly toward Galileo, and if he was forced to condemn him it would be for his Copernicanism, not his physics, a reduced charge that enabled Galileo to be the beneficiary of special treatment. He was not tried before the Inquisition's own tribunal, and he was permitted to live out his life at home rather than be burned as Bruno had been burned in 1600.

Redondi's argument highlights an issue crucial to the interpretation of Descartes: the great intellectual events behind Galileo's trial become visible only on the supposition of a practice that Redondi calls "the intellectual virtue of honest dissimulation." His book is a sustained argument against those whose own scientific virtue makes this older virtue a vice. Against such anachronistic moralism—"deforming retrospective illusion" (323)—Redondi demonstrates that "what we have in *The Assayer* is an honest and rigorous dissimulation. Today we would call it hypocrisy. . . . In 1623, however, honest dissimulation was an intellectual virtue" (146). In 1637 too, when Descartes finally appeared in public, having been schooled by Galileo's fate.[2]

Redondi's enthralling reconstruction of this dismal chapter in religion's attempt to rule philosophy and science allows Descartes to be glimpsed briefly in Rome in 1625 during the early stages of the debate when Galileo was still invulnerable (69). Later, as an uncontrollable politics turned against Galileo, Redondi sees Descartes as a perfectly informed observer of the intricacies of religion and politics in relation to the new physics. Learning from Galileo's fate, Descartes became a more seasoned practitioner of "the intellectual virtue of honest dissimulation." Redondi's book thus provides an understanding of the trial of Galileo that makes entirely plausible Descartes's felt need to suppress his book on physics. The opening paragraph of part six with all its deliberate vagueness suggests that Descartes knew full well that the issue was joined over what the Jesuits held to be crucial: the Eucharist.[3] While many have followed Hobbes in condemning Descartes for treating a ridiculous miracle as if it had philosophical significance, Descartes's own strategic intentions forced him to view matters differently.[4]

What did Descartes learn from Galileo's trial? Nothing about physics of course, but a decisive matter in the contemporary politics of physics. The first paragraph of part six states explicitly that he had been ignorant

2. And in the 1660s and 70s as well, as has been demonstrated by Yirmiyahu Yovel who shows that Spinoza's rule of prudence required that he learn to speak one way to the multitude and another way to "the happy few." Yovel's book is a most effective demonstration of the necessities governing public speech in the age of Bacon and Descartes for it ties Spinoza's practice of dissimulation to the experience of a people grown accustomed to clothing their real thoughts in an acceptable public speech, the Marranos, the Jews of Spain and Portugal forcibly converted to Christianity and kept alive only by systematic dissimulation (Yovel, *Spinoza and Other Heretics*, vol. 1, *The Marrano of Reason*). Also interesting in this respect is the new light cast on the religious politics of Giordano Bruno by John Bossy, *Giordano Bruno and the Embassy Affair*.

3. Descartes argued that his physics could account for transubstantiation: *Replies*, (*AT* VII.248ff.; *PW* 2.173ff.); letter to Mesland, 9 Feb. 1645. See Watson, "Transubstantiation among the Cartesians," and Laymon, "Transubstantiation." Confirmation of the centrality of the Eucharist debate for Descartes's physics is found in Gabriel Daniel S.J., *A Voyage to the World of Cartesius* (1692), 28, 42, 126ff., 179.

4. See *Aubrey's Brief Lives*, "Descartes," 94–95: "[Hobbes] did very much admire [Descartes], but sayd that he could not pardon him for writing in the Defence of Transubstantiation, which he knew to bee absolutely against his judgement, and donne meerly to putt a compliment on the Jesuites."

of the necessary politics, for his earlier treatise contained nothing that he "could imagine to be prejudicial either to religion or to the state." The Inquisition's censure of Galileo's thoughts thus taught him that his own imagining of what could be taken to be prejudicial to religion and the state did not match what the enforcers took to be prejudicial and that he would have to tailor his writings to match their standards of the prejudicial. Descartes had described the function of these censors when he first intimated his own vast plans as a builder: they are "officials responsible for seeing that private buildings be made to serve as an ornament for the public" (ii.16). The trial of Galileo taught him that his ornamentation had not been elaborate enough and that he would have to look to his artistry for the ornaments the censors demanded. When he sent a copy of the *Discourse* to Cardinal Richelieu as soon as it appeared, he knew he was sending it to a vigilant inquisitor whose standards of the prejudicial were not less stringent than those of Cardinal Bellarmine and his successors. We can in a way be grateful for the Inquisition's trial of Galileo because it taught Descartes, just in time, to see the new standards of the criminal held by those with control over his actions. Recognition of the new standards forced Descartes to rethink the whole business of making books (vi.60) and part six shows how he perfected his art to meet their standards.

Descartes says that his reflections on the trial of Galileo made him change his resolution to publish despite the fact that he had powerful reasons to publish and despite the fact that resoluteness in keeping to a path once chosen is one of the maxims of his provisional moral code (iii.24, 25). What reasons for and against publication made the resolute Descartes irresolute? Not only does he have an interest in stating them, the public may have an interest in knowing them. Having sketched the setting dominated by the thought police, Descartes will not mention them again but will instead focus on his own reflections regarding the advantages to the public and the disadvantages to himself that would come from publishing. But one mention is enough: the reader will know that behind all the other considerations lie threats of persecution that dictate surface conformity.

Why Publish at All? (Paragraph 2)

Descartes differentiates three subject matters in his own work: his thoughts on "the speculative sciences," his attempts to govern his "moral conduct" on the basis of reasons derived from his method, and his "general notions in the area of physics" (vi.61). The *Discourse* treats the speculative sciences in part four, moral conduct in part three, and physics in parts two and five, as well as in two of the essays that constitute the bulk of the book, *Dioptrics* and *Meteorology*. Of the three subject matters, Descartes states that it would never have been necessary to publish his thoughts on the "speculative sciences" and on "moral conduct" for themselves alone, whereas his "general notions in the area of physics" *are* worthy of being published for themselves alone.[5] Then why is Descartes publishing in the *Discourse* what he explicitly says does *not* merit publishing on its own? The plausible answer is because of what *does* merit publishing on its own: the physics intrinsically worth publishing must be accompanied by thoughts on speculative sciences and moral conduct intrinsically *not* worth publishing in order that the physics be thought to conform to the new requirements of the prejudicial. Descartes's thoughts on the speculative sciences are not worth publishing for themselves— should that sentence by Descartes now be the motto accompanying all editions of the *Meditations* published for themselves?

Descartes's new physics alone warrants being published for its intrinsic worth. By what standard does Descartes judge intrinsic worth? His "general notions touching physics" are both novel and far-reaching but neither novelty nor comprehensiveness is given as the standard. Instead, Descartes says that not to publish them would be to sin against the law that obliges us to procure as best we can the common good of all humanity. The philosopher Descartes like the philosopher Bacon places himself under a law which echoes the universal charity of the Christian religion. But the common good as Descartes describes it follows Bacon in replacing the Christian good with an earthly good, not the salvation of the soul but the well-being of body and mind. And the agent of the new well-being is not God but man. Descartes makes the earthly good of all human beings the new standard of measure, that for the sake of which we do what we do (*Republic* vi.505d). Shortly after placing himself under this standard, Descartes invokes it as the new standard of virtuous action valid for all: virtue will come to be understood practically as useful service performed on behalf of humanity and the new standard of useful virtue will make the old standard seem like false pretenses (vi.65).

Descartes's general notions in the area of physics replace not just the old physics but the old speculative philosophy: the useless philosophy which gave its principles to all the sciences will be replaced by a useful

5. See Kennington, "Rene Descartes," 428.

philosophy based on physics. The new philosophy discovers what things do, their "force and actions," not their supposed essences; its scope is universal: "the force and the actions of fire, water, air, stars, the heavens, and all the other bodies that surround us," and its model of knowledge is the craftsman's knowledge, for its goal will be "the use of these objects for all the purposes for which they are appropriate." In the midst of this Baconian statement of his sole reason for publishing, a statement that the economical Descartes will make only once in all his writings, Descartes proclaims the new Baconian task for humankind: to "make ourselves, as it were, masters and possessors of nature."

The general notions of Descartes's physics must be published because they make possible the mastery of nature and the mastery of nature is desirable because it makes plausible the dream of immortal bodies inhabiting with ease a bountiful earth. A paradise inhabited by immortal bodies—how could a man obedient to the law of the common good not publish the means to that glorious end after discovering the means in his mathematical physics? Descartes brings this definitive paragraph to its conclusion by indicating his own place in the long process to realize the new Eden. Having found the means to succeed on the new route, Descartes would have traveled it to its end but for two impediments: the brevity of his life and the lack of experiments (see i.3). Because the new founder cannot himself enter the promised land he has glimpsed from afar, he must urge good minds to advance along the new route by taking up his project. Here is the theme that will become increasingly prominent as part six proceeds, the Baconian theme of an army of workers recruited to the new science and its task of creating a new society. Descartes ends the definitive paragraph on the goal of his work with a Baconian statement on the advancement of science: guided by his method, the progress of science will depend upon a multitude of experiments conducted by others and conveyed to the public so that later inquirers can begin where earlier ones left off. A chain of inquirers will be established that will stretch for generations into the future and realize for some distant posterity the Baconian and Cartesian paradise.

Progress in Cartesian Science (Paragraph 3)

In completing the reasons why he had to publish, Descartes gives a brief statement of the scientific method as he practices it, a statement that leads up to the conclusion already drawn that he cannot succeed alone and hence must publish in order to gain the necessary assistance. Descartes's statement of his method supplements what he had already presented in parts two and three regarding the steps of his method and these multiple presentations align Descartes far more closely with Bacon's experimental method than is usually supposed—but what is usually supposed takes its guidance from the *Meditations,* and the *Discourse* shows that the "meditations" were begun after the scientific method had already succeeded. Not universal doubt but the senses and the commonplace information they grant provide Descartes with his beginning point. He repeats here what he had stated earlier (ii.19): just after giving his four precepts Descartes had said that the beginning point is *not* a problem; he begins with the simplest and easiest to know, with the application of his precepts to geometry, algebra, and logic; he does not begin with the doubt of the meditations. This actual beginning point is exhibited again in the *Essays* as the method Descartes follows.

"The order I have held to" contains four steps. Descartes first tried to find in a general way "the principles or first causes of all that can be in the world" (vi.64). These are the kinds of matter and the laws of motion that would have been presented in the suppressed treatise, and that appear, if fragmentarily, in the *Meteorology;* they will eventually be presented in the *Principles.* Second comes the general cosmology which consists of the first and most ordinary effects deducible from matter in motion. Experiments become necessary as the third step in order to understand the more particular effects of matter in motion and to render this understanding useful. Here one proceeds from particular effects to their causes, as Descartes will state in more detail (vi.76–77) when introducing the actual procedure of the *Essays.* Fourth, seeing that he can explain all natural phenomena by means of these simple principles, Descartes recognizes the need for experiments that are like Bacon's "negative instances" (*NO* II.12) in that they aim at "outcomes that are not the same" or the disconfirmation of an hypothesis. This step is necessary in order to isolate the actual causes of particular phenomena from the many possible causes one can imagine, each consistent with the general principles of matter in motion.

Completion of an experimental science with the massive goal of mastering and possessing nature far exceeds the capacity of its founder. Though he can see the direction ahead for the multitude of experiments, he lacks the resources to perform them. The treatise he had written would have sounded the call for fellow workers and financial support but it had to be suppressed because of the censure accorded Galileo. Descartes could have been judged a criminal even though his project, as he now emphasizes, is the humanitarian project par excellence. Therefore, three years late and in a remade costume, Descartes comes forth to make the appeal he should have been able to make then. All those who really are virtuous—and not through false pretenses or reputation—should take up his humanitarian cause. The report on his treatise thus ends with a defiant claim of superior virtue over the keepers of public virtue who condemned Galileo.

Should He Wait till He's Dead? (Paragraph 4)

Despite the great goal and despite the necessity of attracting fellow workers, Descartes changed his mind and decided against publishing his treatise. He does not repeat the reason, but he explains his new resolve in a meandering, half-page sentence. Given the nature of his project he can of course not be spared the labor of making books: he does not excuse himself from that task as he earlier alleged he might (vi.60). Rather, he will write his books and correct them again and again as he sees the need, but he will keep them all to himself until he is dead. Then, beyond the reach of those with control over his actions, he will let them all be published. Waiting has two great advantages: the public will be benefited, if not right away, and he will be spared wasting his time on agendas other than his own. The new plan accords perfectly with the requirements of the common good under which he has placed himself: he is obliged to do good to others but those others are a very distant posterity that takes precedence over his own contemporaries.

What follows is Descartes's remarkable debate with himself regarding posthumous publication. In this private dialogue now being made public, Descartes takes both sides of the issue. One side says wait till you are dead. The other side says publish now. On the arguments, the wait-till-you-are-dead side wins. There seems to be no good reason for publishing now. But he *is* publishing now; readers hold the book in their hands and hear the author's appeal at the end to send him any objections they might have. Why this change of mind that runs counter to his whole reasoning? At the end of his dialogue (vi.74–75) Descartes provides two allegedly new reasons for publishing now, reasons that appear suddenly as if to overcome the arguments of the internal dialogue. The two reasons reduce to one: reputation. Once again at a main turning point in his life the resolute Descartes makes his choice on the basis of reputation. But meanwhile, within the dialogue, though without calling undue attention to it, Descartes has shown that waiting till he is dead is an unnecessary precaution for him because he has learned to mask himself. He can mount the stage still alive and the way he does it will certainly serve his reputation.

In this wonderful comedy of apparent irresoluteness the resolute Descartes makes himself look indecisive for a purpose: the reader will be forced to conclude that prior to 1633 Descartes was wrong in his evaluation of the precautions necessary for the presentation of a new teaching on the universe. 1633 made him think that conditions had grown so grave that he might have to wait till after his death to go public. But no, in writing as he now writes he can publish under the very eye of the thought police and still have control over his actions. His reputation is made: potential enemies will believe that he presents no danger; potential friends will see that he has no need of the coward's way of dying first and fighting later.

The first argument for publishing now is that waiting to publish till after he is dead would be a disservice to his contemporaries, that his own standard of the common good dictates publishing now. Countering this objection to waiting enables Descartes to show two things. First, that his method promises to bring its ultimate benefits only to distant generations. Second, that he himself still has a long way to go in the sciences. This second point focuses attention on Descartes's singular role; as the founder of a new way he must be especially attentive to the problem of beginnings, as Machiavelli taught.[6] Beginnings are small and difficult, but a project like Descartes's gathers energy as it proceeds, growing rich and powerful, as Descartes's examples indicate, until at last it has at its command an invincible army. At its beginnings, its originator must not waste his energy by bringing down upon himself unnecessarily the opposition of those who still have the laws on their side. Because greater leadership is required to maintain the army after a defeat in a battle, it is all the more necessary not to open with a defeat but with a series of victories that consolidate and inspire the army. The issue is "the foundations of his physics," not some specific conclusion in physics like Copernicanism. The foundations of his physics would engender hostility and hostility at the beginning would deflect his energies and jeopardize his project. Better to wait till he is dead.

6. *Prince,* chap. 4; *Discourses* bk. I.Introduction.

Would Waiting Be a Disadvantage to Him? (Paragraph 5)

Would he not be helped by public discussion of his views? Opponents could correct his errors and supporters buttress his work with their own, as happens "in the way of disputation as practiced in the Schools." Descartes's experience with his new method taught him otherwise; objections and suggestions have been useless whether they came from those he took to be friends, or those he took to be indifferent, or those he knew to be enemies. His method is so different that disputing his novel theses in the old way would waste his time. He does not need this sort of help. Better to wait till he is dead.

Would Waiting Be a Disadvantage to Others? (Paragraph 6)

Would the use to which others could put his work suffer if he waits? Descartes here raises the crucial question: How can he be of use to others (i.4)? How can he teach what he has learned? Descartes's answer begins and ends with declarations that he alone can bring to completion the foundations on which the useful sciences of mechanics, medicine, and morals can be built. In this respect, those whom Descartes teaches will necessarily be followers; the foundations (which still need to be expanded) are Descartes's own because he discovered them and only the discoverer can know what belongs to his discovery: "One cannot conceive a thing so well and make it one's own when one learns it from another as one can when one discovers it for oneself." Descartes's task is two-fold: expanding the foundations and communicating to others what he has made his own by discovering it. But how can others make their own what is already Descartes's own when making a thing truly one's own depends upon discovering it and Descartes has already discovered it? The paragraph sets out the only possible solution: Descartes must write in such a way as to induce others to codiscover, to discover on their own, what, till now, he alone has discovered. The problem becomes, *who* can make one's own what is Descartes's own, and Descartes singles out for special consideration "the greatest minds." In one sense therefore, Descartes is interested only in a very few readers whom he writes to instruct in the appropriate way. But he also writes for all readers because all are permitted to read what he writes, including those with control over his actions, and all will eventually benefit by his writings.

How can Descartes enable others to make their own what is already his own? He begins by describing his own experience in trying to explain his views to people with "great minds," but he passes immediately to the greatest minds, to those few thinkers memorialized in the history of philosophy. Descartes's conclusions about communicating his views arose from reflection on the history of philosophy, on the greatest minds and their followers. Before giving his examples from the history of philosophy Descartes issues the appropriate warning to posterity: do not believe what you are told about me, believe only what I myself have revealed. The question is not merely, how are we to read Descartes? but how is the history of philosophy to treat Descartes? It is to treat Descartes the way Descartes treated the history of philosophy: believe only what is revealed by the greatest minds themselves; be skeptical of all reports about them. Descartes now gives two examples of how he reads the history of philosophy skeptically; the first concerns the ancient philosophers whose writings we no longer possess, the second, one of the ancient philosophers whose writings we do possess, Aristotle. Descartes is not inclined to believe that the former thinkers actually held the extravagant opinions attributed to them. They were the greatest minds of their time and Descartes judges that their thoughts could not have been extremely unreasonable. Loss of their writings means that we now have only unbelievable accounts given by followers who were not the greatest minds; their actual thoughts are irrecoverable because we do not possess what they themselves actually revealed.

When he turns to an ancient whose writings have survived, Descartes is not as open as he later says he would have been had he been simply free to write a history of philosophy: he does not say that it is hardly likely that the Socratic Aristotle believed the opinions he propounded openly in his writings as true and certain. Instead Descartes points to the difference between Aristotle and his followers, leaving the impression that the latter have given a bad account of him. With Aristotle, however, as with Descartes, we have what he actually revealed. Aristotle's followers, Descartes says, lack the knowledge of nature that he had. All such followers of the greatest minds are like ivy that can ascend no higher than the trees that support it and that usually tends downward again after reaching the top. Descartes then describes how things stand in the history of philosophy as a result of Aristotle's ivylike followers, and he does so using images and warnings made famous by another of the greatest minds whose writings have survived, Plato. The downward tendency of the followers of Aristotle has carried them into a dark cave. Blinded by their obedience and practiced in the skills of the blind, they lure the sighted into their cave in order to fight on an equal footing. Philosophy itself has been accommodated to the cave of authoritative opinion by the mediocre minds of the followers of Aristotle, the only philosopher named in the *Discourse*. Misuse of Aristotle's writings has had the effect anticipated by the god who feared writing in Plato's *Phaedrus:* the writings of Aristotle have created a book culture inhabited by men who have lost their memories and substituted a supposed wisdom for a real one (*Phaedrus* 275a–b). That book culture is like a cave where the blind lead the blind but it is not identical to the cave of Plato's *Republic* for it is not a natural cave lying deep under the earth. The new cave is manmade, follower-made, made by the misuse of philosophy. The new philosopher still faces the old dangers at the hands of the voluntarily blind as Descartes's reference to the trial of Galileo makes clear, but Descartes modifies Plato's cave image in order to show the nature of the cave to which he goes down. It is an artificial cave constructed by ignorant followers of Aristotle's philosophy, it has windows and the new philosopher can throw them open and allow some daylight to shine on all by publishing the principles of his philosophy.

Voluntarily blind followers oppose the light that would shine into their cave were Descartes to publish the principles of his philosophy. But what about "the greatest minds"? Descartes states that even "the greatest minds" have no reason for wanting to know the principles of his philosophy. This is a startling statement. Why would the greatest minds *not* want to know these principles given the rank he has just attributed to them? They rival the principles of the pre-Socratic natural philosophers and the principles of Aristotle. To explain his startling statement Descartes describes the greatest minds. They are of two kinds. The first are lovers of fame and for them philosophy is a means to being held in admiration by the less learned (i.6). They have no reason for wanting to know Descartes's principles because only the reigning philosophy can provide the means to the recognition they seek. The second, however, are lovers of knowledge who may well "desire to follow a plan similar to [Descartes's] own." Why would *they* not desire to know the principles of Descartes's philosophy? Because, having the desire to know everything, they have no desire to be told everything, nor do they need to be told everything. Descartes says explicitly that they need to be told no more than he is going to tell them in his first book. Having been told that much about Descartes's principles, they will have the intense satisfaction of discovering the rest for themselves. Descartes writes in such a way as to necessitate what is desirable: the greatest minds must make their own what is Descartes's own by becoming its discovers or its codiscoverers. By making Descartes's discoveries with the aid of the enticements he has now provided, they will become his friends or accomplices, and he will have successfully made himself "the head of a group of conspirators."[7]

The principles of Descartes's philosophy can be discovered from the *Discourse* and its appended essays which make a calculated appeal to the greatest minds. Following a plan similar to his own, genuine followers will not become like ivy but will train themselves to search for further truths rather than remain content with the repetition of his. They will make the method their own by discovering it for themselves and Descartes offers himself as an example: he too would have become like ivy had he been taught from his youth all the truths for which he has had to seek demonstrations.

If part four exhibits Descartes's turn from the way of Socrates to the way of Plato, part six exhibits the extent of Descartes's kinship with Plato: his manner of presentation is dictated not simply by the question of his own reputation, nor is it dictated simply by the desire to avoid doing harm; it is dictated by the desire of the just man to do good to those who are good once it has become clear who the good are and how good can be done them (*Republic* i.335a). No wonder Descartes hoped that his book would "be useful to some, while harmful to none, and that my openness will be to everyone's liking." The things that need to be learned cannot be taught; they can however be learned by those fitted for them through the appropriate gifts of good sense and study. Seen from the perspective of Platonic philanthropy, Descartes merits the reputation for wisdom that he aims to acquire through his justice; his seeming to be wise is grounded in his being wise as he demonstrates in his manner of addressing both the unwise and the potentially wise.

The best way to be of use to the few for whom he really writes is to write in a way that both trains them and liberates them from the charms that now hold them. This is the cardinal matter in the Platonic art of writing. Descartes thus exhibits himself to be a student of Plato's *Phaedrus,* one who recognizes all around him the truth of Thamuz's warnings about a culture based on writing: a book culture will think itself wise without really understanding anything, it will be filled with the appearance of wisdom rather than with wisdom itself (*Phaedrus* 275a–b). Tradition stored in books passes down tales and stories without being able to pass down knowledge of their truth: Aristotle's tales have now

7. d'Alembert, *Preliminary Discourse to the Encyclopedia,* 80.

become traditional in just this way, for the truth known to Aristotle is denied his ivylike followers (*Phaedrus* 274c). The god's warning and its evident truth did not lead either Plato or Descartes to have done with the making of books; it led them instead to make books attentive to their dangers while exploiting their advantages. They follow not Thamuz but Theuth, a god more forgiving of the limitations of mortals, while at the same time more willing to entrust them with responsibility, a god who gives the civilizing but dangerous gifts of number and calculation, geometry and astronomy, checkers and dice—and writing. In the proper hands, Theuth's gift of writing can plant the seed that can mature into wisdom to the improvement of the human condition.[8]

Descartes's accomplices, having learned in the way appropriate to them how to search for the truth and carry the search further, may well surpass him along the way he has taken. Nevertheless, Descartes is the general who can win the present war by winning those two or three battles that would bring his own foundational work to completion, perhaps the very battles with the voluntarily blind that the publication of his work now initiates (vi.67–68).

This paragraph of Descartes's dialogue with himself has *not* provided an argument in favor of posthumous publication. It has instead shown that waiting till he is dead has become unnecessary: in a setting where he cannot say everything about the principles of his philosophy it has become clear that it is better not to say everything. To say what he has to say there is no need to wait till he is dead.

Would Waiting Be a Disadvantage to His Project? (Paragraph 7)

While posthumous publication would not present insuperable disadvantages to himself or to others, perhaps delay would damage the project itself inasmuch as its success depends upon experiments that he cannot possibly do himself. Must he publish now in order to advertise for help? Those moved by a love of gain could be employed to do precisely what he ordered. Those who volunteer out of a desire to learn would, however, have to be paid in other ways: because of their need for explanations or praise or useless conversations, they would waste his time. Those who only sent their experiments would also be wasting his time because their experiments, lacking the method now known only to him, would be faulty. The one way to assist would be to send money to enable him to

8. On the interpretation of *Phaedrus*, see Burger, *Plato's Phaedrus.*

hire help to further his experiments and to preserve his solitude. But he does not want to put himself in the position of accepting from anyone favors that someone might think he did not deserve—a condition that excludes all favors. Better to wait till he is dead.

Why Descartes Is Publishing the *Discourse* Now (Paragraph 8)

These were the considerations that led Descartes, in the aftermath of 1633, to resolve not to publish the book that had cost him so many years of labor. But in now reporting for a second time his resolve for post-humous publication, Descartes changes it. No longer is it a resolve to withhold all his writings till after his death, instead it is a resolve "never to make public any other treatise during my lifetime that was so general, or one on the basis of which one could understand the foundations of my physics" (compare vi.65–66 and 74). This more limited resolve is not altered by the publication of the *Discourse* and its *Essays:* it is not so general as *The World,* nor could "one" understand the foundations of his physics from it—although, as he has just indicated, some of the greatest minds could learn these foundations from it.

Descartes has made it obvious that even if he had waited till after his death to publish, he would have been just as careful about what he permitted in his books. His posthumous works would have been as guarded as any work he published while alive for the reason he has made apparent: Descartes *is* vulnerable even after his death. And not because the Inquisition could dig up his remains and burn them and anathematize his immortal soul, as it did as recently as 1624 with another heretic, Marco Antonio de Dominis, whose physics cast a question on how bread could turn to flesh and wine to blood. No, the delicate beginnings of a project as subversive as Descartes's require prudence of both the quick and the dead. He is vulnerable even after death because he is introducing a novel program that will require many generations to take root; and the success of the new teaching depends in part on the reputation of its teacher. His posthumous vulnerability is evident in the history of Cartesianism after 1650 in the zeal with which his enemies sought to ruin his reputation.

Descartes knows how to manage the introduction of his teaching while still alive. Furthermore, there are decisive advantages to beginning while alive. Therefore, in this paragraph which speaks about what he is now publishing, Descartes gives as the sole reason for publishing—his reputation. Waiting till he is dead is not desirable because his enemies could accuse him of having had something to hide; he had even handed them this weapon by not making a secret of his intention to publish. They could sully his reputation with suspicion and innuendo and it would be too late to answer. Reputation had earlier required that Descartes abandon his homeland and prepare teachings on God and the soul that would make him worthy of a reputation for wisdom. Reputation now requires that he publish before his death in order to demonstrate that his teachings do not need to be hidden away as if they were crimes. Therefore, with an openness that he can hope will be pleasing to all, he presents the world with a history of his life and three essays that show what he can do in the sciences. This is a beginning worthy of a great philosopher: he comes into the open in order to acquire the reputation that he has nothing to hide.

Descartes now adds as a reason for publishing the *Discourse* something he had already repeatedly emphasized: his need for fellow workers. Not only does he need helpers for the infinity of observations and experiments his project requires, he reports his daily-increasing awareness that his own plan of self-knowledge is suffering because he lacks such helpers. But this need too is immediately made secondary to that still more important matter, his reputation: he is determined to give posterity no cause to reproach him for failing to do all that he might have done to benefit them. For their sake he will even break his solitude and submit to becoming famous in his own lifetime. Descartes is not permitted to wait until he is dead.

Has Descartes's Art of Writing Succeeded? (Paragraph 9)

Descartes cannot be sure that his *Essays* will succeed as an exhibition of what he can and cannot do in the sciences. But he has done all he could to guarantee the success of his writings by composing a *Discourse* that follows the steps recommended in the *Phaedrus*. While a written work gets into the hands of everyone including those who have no business with it and to whom it is not addressed, Descartes's art of writing knows how to select its audience by distinguishing the kinds of souls there are and speaking in the appropriate way to each (*Phaedrus* 271d, 273d, 277b–c). Descartes himself properly desires to be left alone but the project devised and advanced in his solitude depends on its being taken up by others; it must therefore make use of a persuasive rhetoric, a tool of "incomparable power and beauty" (i.5), in order to show how the different kinds of souls (*Phaedrus* 271a–272b)—lovers of gain, lovers of honor, and lovers of wisdom—can each contribute to the new project in the ways appropriate to them. Writing is analogous to painting whose creatures maintain a majestic silence in the face of the questions put to them, but an art of writing, employing words that seem to say the same thing forever, in fact changes the way it addresses its reader the deeper its artistry is penetrated (*Phaedrus* 274d). And Descartes is willing to go a step beyond the *Phaedrus* because he has not waited till he is dead: as father of the discourse he will come to its aid as long as he is able by agreeing to answer questions put to it (*Phaedrus* 275e). In answering these questions he will not explain anything new but simply indicate the way in which the discourse itself can answer questions when they are properly put. Descartes's discourse thus proves that it is the legitimate form of written speech (*Phaedrus* 276a), for it can avoid the criticisms of its bastard brother raised by Thamuz, a jealous god insensitive to human limitations and desirous that human things remain as they are, wholly under his sway. Descartes's discourse is based on knowledge; it is written in the soul of the learner; it is able to defend itself; it knows to whom it should speak and to whom it should say nothing; and it breaks the hold of tyrannical Thamuz before his very eyes (*Phaedrus* 276a).

How to Read the Essays in the Method (Paragraph 10)

Descartes calls attention to certain "suppositions" found at the opening of the *Dioptrics* and the *Meteorology*. He appeals to his reader not to be shocked by the term *suppositions* or by his seeming unwillingness to prove them. It is only a *seeming* unwillingness for he in fact proves them in the only way possible. The "suppositions"—explicitly called such only in the *Meteorology*—are initial and incomplete statements of the fundamentals of Descartes's physics, the kinds of matter and the laws of motion. They are stated only to the degree necessary to explain the effects Descartes describes in each essay. Pay special attention to the procedure whereby these suppositions are confirmed—Descartes orders the reader to pay special attention to a procedure that goes to the heart of his method. The procedure is a sequence of reasons following this pattern: the last reasons, which Descartes calls "effects," are demonstrated by the first reasons, by the suppositions, which Descartes calls "causes." Reciprocally, the first, the suppositions, are demonstrated by the last, the causes by the effects. He is not committing the error of a vicious circle, he says; the reasoning is circular but not vicious because it is asymmetrical: the causes from which Descartes deduces the effects do not "prove" the effects for the effects are plain and need only the *explanation* the causes give; what is proven, in fact, are the causes which are not plain and which do stand in need of proof.

But why continue to call these causes "suppositions" if they are in fact proven by the arguments of the essays? The only reason Descartes gives is that he wants one to understand that he thinks he can deduce them "from the first truths I have explained above." The suppositions, therefore, while they are proven by the effects studied in optics and meteorology, do not originate as hypotheses from a consideration of these effects. They are called suppositions because they have been deduced from something still more primary than themselves: the kinds of matter and the laws of motion have been deduced from "the first truths I have explained above." But this is equivocal. Are these the "first truths" referred to in the opening sentence of part five, the truths of soul and God from which he alleges he could deduce all the truths of part five? Or are these "first truths" the truths arrived at first, the precepts of method given in part two as "the simplest and easiest to know truths" (ii.19) which gave him his actual beginnings in science?

Descartes's procedure is clear: the actual investigations in scientific subject matters begin with already formulated suppositions which are confirmed by the observational and experimental data, which they in turn explain. The suppositions themselves were arrived at as deductions from certain "first truths" and these Descartes leaves equivocal. More exactly, Descartes says that he purposely smudges this aspect of his method: "I have expressly not wanted" to deduce the suppositions from the first truths. Descartes has purposely left equivocal a crucial step in his method—and this in a discourse on the method. He gives a two-fold reason for choosing obscurity at this high point: first, he wants to prevent "certain minds" from building some "extravagant philosophy" on what they believe are his principles; second, he wants to prevent them from blaming him for this extravagant philosophy. He wants to make the interpretation of this point of his work difficult and he wants the blame for the interpretation to lie with the interpreter. He wants a certain immunity from the extravagant things that will be attributed to him— as they were to the greatest minds before him like the pre-Socratics and Aristotle. Without stating the opinions that are entirely his own, he ends the paragraph on method by characterizing them: they are "so simple and so in conformity with common sense that they seem less extraordinary and less strange than any others one could have on the same subject," and they strictly accord with reason.

Descartes's planned equivocation here resembles the equivocation on foundations: the "suppositions" his experimental method proves could be deduced from certain "first truths" which are *either* the "infinite perfections of God" (v.43) *or* the four precepts with which he began (ii.18–19). The latter possibility grounds the suppositions in the reasonable procedure laid out in parts two and three of the *Discourse* which culminated in the solution of the scientific problems of the *Essays* prior to the metaphysical additions (iii.29). The other possibility involves supposing that Descartes could have derived the kinds of matter and the laws of motion from his metaphysical "foundations" of God and soul. Why be coy about this if he can do it? If we choose this solution to the planned equivocation we are once again faced with the spectacle of Descartes implying that he could have shown how he based his physics on God and the soul if he had wanted to but that he did not want to. The choice that resolves the equivocation seems completely obvious—and shows once again that the metaphysical "foundations" are not in the least foundational to Cartesian science. (A related strategy regarding "suppositions" is followed in the *Principles* where the "suppositions" are even called "false suppositions" (III.44, 45, 47; IV.1) in relation to what everybody already knows, that God created the world in an instant. On the basis of these "false suppositions" all truths about the world can be discovered.)

The *Discourse,* therefore, *must* be accompanied by the *Essays* because they show what the author can and cannot do in the sciences: he can give an account of the world based on rational principles that are simple and in keeping with common sense, but he cannot base it on God and the soul. In the title, the *Essays* are said to be "essays in the method." Near the center of the *Discourse* (iii.29–30) "you" had been invited to consult the essays as examples of Descartes's successful application of his method to various problems which predate the foray into the old metaphysics in the name of his reputation. In the present paragraph introducing the *Essays* (vi.76–77), the reader is told their actual method: a method of hypothesis-testing complete within itself for it can demonstrate the truth of the fundamental hypotheses from the known effects and explain those effects in terms of the hypotheses. As for the hypotheses or "suppositions," the reader will have to determine whether they are derived from the infinite perfections of God or from the four precepts of the method. Descartes's physics, therefore, is a self-enclosed system that begins with the simplest and easiest to know, arrives at tentative suppositions about the physical universe as a whole, and proves these suppositions on the basis of effects readily known in the world. This is a "discourse" on the method, Descartes tells Mersenne in responding to Mersenne's prepublication objections (27 Feb. 1637), it is not a "treatise" on the method; it does not teach the method but as its "preface" or "notice" only talks about it. The method is a practice exhibited by the appended essays and the theory of the method is presented in such a way as to force the interpreter to reconstruct its particulars from Descartes's statement and Descartes's practice. Those who desire to follow a plan similar to Descartes's own do not need to be told anything more than he has told them in this book where he purposely does not tell everything.

Descartes's Judges (Paragraph 11)

Descartes is going to be judged; he is going to be put on trial. He begins his paragraph on being judged by referring to a particularly complicated new invention of his, an apparatus for grinding lenses to be employed in the telescopes and microscopes that make possible the demythologizing acts of seeing elaborated in the *Meteorology*. Skill and habit are needed to follow the instructions for building such machinery; no detail is to be overlooked; and no one should expect to succeed on the first try. As with building machines from exact instructions, so too with playing the lute from a good score—so too with reading books as exact as the *Discourse*: skill and habit, attention to every detail, success only after long trial. And Descartes's exacting book is written in the language of his country rather than the language of his preceptors, because he wants his opinions judged by natural reason in its purity and not by measures derived from belief in old books. At the end of the part that began speaking of deference to Galileo's judges, Descartes identifies those "to whom alone I submit as my judges." They are not the official judges and Inquisitors who appeal to the old books of Aristotle and the Bible, but "those who combine good sense with study." Descartes thus invites his reader to put the tribunal on trial through the exercise of natural reason.

Descartes's Platonic Philanthropy (Final Paragraph)

Descartes's manner of writing makes him a follower of Plato but his scientific project breaks with Plato as he shows again in his final paragraph in another allusion to the *Phaedrus*. Socrates tells Phaedrus, the lover of speeches, that scientific knowledge of nature is useful for providing a new knowledge that tends the soul because it can discern the various kinds of soul and the forms of discourse persuasive to each (*Phaedrus* 269c–272b). Descartes by no means ignores such soul-tending discourse, but he seeks a scientific knowledge of nature on which to base something that Plato explicitly placed lower in the *Phaedrus* (270b), a new medicine that tends the body. For the rest of his life, Descartes says, he will attempt to acquire a knowledge of nature from which others will be able to deduce rules for a new medicine. Descartes does not, as many have supposed, dedicate *himself* to the study of medicine,[9] even though he knows that those who actually deduce the rules for the new medicine will be the ones to receive the glory. Still, he and Bacon are the ones responsible both for the scientific method of medicine and for the new order of rank among the virtues that elevates to a higher rank the technical tending of body and mind. That new way of honor replaces "the proud and magnificent palaces" of morals built by "the ancient pagans," built by Plato and others who placed the tending of the soul higher than the tending of the body. Built on the solid and firm foundations of the new mathematical physics, the new Baconian and Cartesian palace of morals will be inhabited by those who are virtuous according to the new standard of virtue, the common good of all humanity understood as the earthly good accruing from the mastery of nature.

The new measure of virtue must pronounce a moral condemnation on the supposed nonhumanitarianism of the ancient philosophers, Plato included. But it does so—in Descartes as much as in Bacon—in full awareness of its debt to Plato. The break with Plato is a break with the Socratic tradition which received its paradigmatic description in the *Phaedo:* Socrates embarked on a second sailing because of the failure of the first sailing. The failure of natural science to give a rational account of itself and of the human things necessitated a second sailing for the safety of the logos, or of reason and philosophy. But that tradition was captured by the ivylike followers of Aristotle who perverted it into a cave of dogmatic opinion and made philosophy slave to religion. For the safety of philosophy or reason, "there was but one course left," as Bacon said, "to try the whole thing anew upon a better plan" (*GI,* Prooemium)— a new first sailing, a new natural science. But the new Baconian and Cartesian science does not surrender the gains of the second sailing: it uses the prudence with which Plato taught philosophy to speak, and it follows the fundamental Platonic injunction to philanthropy: "You must go down" out of love of humankind—love of *logos* or reason.

In his amazing final sentence Descartes reaffirms his kinship with

9. Roth, *Descartes' Discourse,* 15, 77–78, 88–89; Hartle, *Death and the Disinterested Spectator,* 152.

Plato and his aspiration to deeds worthy of a Plato. Descartes does not seek the popular acclaim that will be accorded the masters of medicine who use his method to ease the lot of others. He values his solitude and would feel more obliged to those who made possible his leisure than he would to those who offered him the most honorable positions on earth. "The most honorable positions on earth"—in the last words of the work that first introduced him to the world, Descartes politely declines any offers that would make this philosopher king. Do not offer me the kingship, Descartes says, to those who would be inclined, if they knew what he was doing, to offer him only the dungeon or the stake. Let me keep to myself. Like Joabin, say. Or like the Odysseus of Plato's *Republic*. Descartes too has chosen from all the available lives (iii.27) the quiet life of a private man, because, like Joabin and Plato's Odysseus, he has recovered from the love of honor (*Republic* x.620c). Like Plato, Descartes is a philosopher who does not desire to rule (vii.519c–520d), and he knows that the people cannot be persuaded that it is desirable that he rule (vi.494a). Still, he knows that the resolute philosopher, his actions guided by his judgments, can choose to take a hand in what rules human affairs. While ostentatiously declining the rule that the people think is the highest honor and that they would never offer him anyway, Descartes sets his mind to become the one master over the many future masters of nature, the secret spiritual ruler of the age, the father of modern philosophy.

By publishing his work in the way that he does, Descartes shows that he has learned the Platonic art of writing. By publishing it at all, he shows that he has learned that still more fundamental Platonic lesson to the philosopher given in the form of a commandment to those who have ascended out of the cave of opinion to the sun of knowledge: "You must go down" (*Republic* vii.520c).[10] Descartes too is a Platonic philosopher moved by philanthropy, by a love of humankind that can be made to look like Christian charity but that is a love of reason that traces its roots to Athens. Responsibility for the safety of reason now requires that action be taken to preserve philosophy from the rule of religion in the way pioneered by Bacon. Descartes too is a Platonic philosopher who knows where he is. As the analysis of the other parts of the *Discourse* in the next chapter will make still clearer, Descartes knows himself to occupy a world marked by warfare between the "great friends of God," as Descartes calls them, whose "righteous zeal . . . dictates to them the

10. See the section, "The *Republic* and Responsibility," in chapter 5, pp. 127–32.

greatest crimes man can commit, such as betraying cities, killing Princes, and exterminating whole peoples just because they do not accept their opinions" (*Passions* 190). In fulfilling the Platonic injunction, Descartes descends to the world Bacon described in *Holy War,* and he descends as a Baconian to carry forward Bacon's spiritual warfare.

When the resolute Descartes finally comes forth on the stage it is not from three months in the *poêle* sheltered by provisional maxims but from many preparatory years in exile sheltered by teachings on the speculative sciences and moral conduct that mask the foundations of his physics, the suppositions of matter in motion that are to be applied to all the other sciences. He comes forth as an actor who knows how to ground his actions in his judgments and he comes forth to war—spiritual warfare in deadly earnest against opponents powerful enough to exercise control over his actions though they have no power to control his thoughts. By enveloping the foundations of his physics in what look like the authoritative metaphysics and morals, by hiding it safely within such a vehicle, he offers his authoritative enemies a fatal gift like the gift the Greeks offered the Trojans that brought their war to a successful end. For just as the Trojans, tamers of horses, in breaching their wall and drawing into their citadel the horse sacred to Poseidon, drew in a gift shaped by Odysseus, Athena's favorite, whose contents would cause at last the fall of the citadel invincible to mere might, so too, the authorities to whom Descartes defers, in welcoming into the citadel of learning Descartes's gift of a new physics wrapped in the pious metaphysics of their Poseidon, draw in the instrument that demolishes their citadel from within. No wonder an English divine, a future Archbishop of Canterbury, could say, three-hundred years later, that if he were asked "what was the most disastrous moment in the history of Europe," he would be strongly inclined to say "that period of leisure when René Descartes, having no claims to meet, remained for a whole day 'shut up alone in a stove.'"[11]

---

11. Temple, *Nature, Man and God,* 57.

Chapter 9

Descartes and Montaigne:

The *Discourse* as Essay

Montaigne . . . the fact that such a man wrote has increased the joy of living on this earth.—Nietzsche (SE 2)

Part 1: Descartes and Everyman

We move from the last sentence of the *Discourse* to the first, from Plato to Montaigne, for while the last sentence is built on an allusion to Plato, the first sentence is a direct quotation from Montaigne.

"Good sense is the thing most evenly distributed in the world, for each thinks himself so well endowed therewith that even those who are most difficult to please in all other things are not wont to desire more of it than they have." This is surely the oddest sentence in the whole of the *Discourse* for it announces an equality regarding the very thing that the *Discourse* holds most precious and most rare, the qualities of mind for which a philosopher most yearns, the ability to distinguish the true from the false. And Descartes gives many reasons for thinking that his opening egalitarian announcement is false. The two considerations given in its favor—everyone thinks he has enough and no one is likely to be wrong—are less than persuasive because they purport to be universally true opinions based on nothing more secure than one's own opinion of one's own merits—and "I know how subject we are to delude ourselves in whatever touches ourselves" (i.3). Also, Descartes identifies himself as one who strives to improve his mind in its native wit, imagination, and memory, and so to improve his ability to distinguish the true from the false. Furthermore, Descartes only "prefers to believe" this opinion (i.2) which follows "the standard opinion held by philosophers"—but everywhere else he scorns their standard opinions. Eventually he just *tells* his reader that this is a false opinion, that almost all people are deficient with respect to distinguishing the true from the false. The world consists almost exclusively of but two kinds of people, Descartes says, and *both* are deficient in distinguishing the true from the false. One kind thinks too highly of its capacity, judging wrongly that it can properly distinguish true and false; the other kind judge rightly that they themselves are less capable of distinguishing the true from the false than are others (ii.15). Almost everyone is unable to distinguish the true from the false—therefore, Descartes argues, almost everyone ought not to imitate his method in its very first step for they ought not to detach themselves from the beliefs they have accepted as true. Almost everyone ought to follow those who *are* able to distinguish the true from the false, as the next paragraph shows. And not only is the opening opinion false, the reasons summoned on its behalf are later said to be inadequate, for the reasons appeal to majority opinion but "majority opinion is not worth anything for truths that are a bit difficult to discover" (ii.16).[1]

What audacity! After years of planning and many suppressed attempts, Descartes finally mounts the stage—and announces in his first public sentence an opinion he knows to be false. Those who desire to follow a plan similar to Descartes's own (vi.71) will doubt this opening announcement because they will do what Descartes says he does with every opinion: he never accepts as true anything he does not know evidently to be so (ii.18). Such cautious readers, alerted to caution by Descartes's odd opening, will have to distinguish the true from the false even in Descartes's book. By opening this way, Descartes's book promises to duplicate in miniature the deepest problem facing the would-be knower: yearning to distinguish the true from the false, the would-be knower is always already inserted into a setting of false but purportedly true opinions based on authoritative but inadequate inferences founded on self-love. Distinguishing the true from the false requires unremitting application by the few not given to trust their inclinations.

Descartes's book, though addressed to everyone, is addressed also to "you." Eight times Descartes uses the direct second person formal address to speak to his reader, and gradually the impression is formed that "you" are those very few whom Descartes identifies at the end as combining "good sense with study," those to whom alone Descartes submits as his judges (vi.77–78). These true judges of Descartes's thought— as distinct from the "judges" who have control over his actions—employ their native good sense in the toil of studying his book; they will distinguish the true from the false in it and for them his book will be

---

1. Burman's question about this odd opening receives a still odder reply; see *Descartes' Conversation with Burman*, 45.

especially useful (i.4). Such readers will have noted a remarkable fact about Descartes's opening sentence: it is a quotation from Montaigne. It is, moreover, the first of many unacknowledged quotations from Montaigne and it sets a pattern: in judging Descartes, those readers who combine good sense with the study of Montaigne will be in a position to understand his meaning much more readily.[2]

Descartes's opening sentence, both the opinion expressed and the reasons given on its behalf, are taken directly from Montaigne's essay "Of Presumption," an essay that almost begins by saying, "If a man be Caesar let him think himself the greatest general the world has ever known." But the theme of the essay is not the appropriate presumption of the few caesars but the appropriate presumption of the few philosophers. How are philosophers presumptuous, how do they think well of themselves? Montaigne makes an example of himself. Toward the end of the essay, after reflecting on philosophy and truth-telling, Montaigne situates himself: human reason is a two-edged and dangerous sword as one can see from the practice of reason's "most intimate and familiar friend," Socrates, and from the controversies sparked by Machiavelli. Given "the corruption of our morals" and the frail instrument of reason based on experience, prudent men who depend solely upon this instrument are obliged to keep their true opinions to themselves, while being suspicious of innovation. Thus explaining his strategy as a writer, Montaigne turns to his own presumption and concludes that he can think well of himself only in that thing in which no man ever thought himself deficient: "For who ever thought that he lacked sense?" Montaigne thinks well of himself not because he thinks he possesses sense but because he thinks he lacks it. He thinks he lacks what everyone else thinks they possess.

---

2. Many of the references to Montaigne are noted in Gilson, *Discours de la méthode*, see Index, 497; and Brunschvicg, *Descartes et Pascal*, but their discussions cast little light on why Descartes would quote Montaigne so extensively. See also Curley, *Descartes against the Skeptics*, 12–20, 38–40; Judovitz, *Subjectivity and Representation in Descartes*, 8–38; and Woodbridge, "The *Discours de la méthode*," 136–42. In *Montaigne's Deceits*, Margaret McGowan provides a persuasive portrait of Montaigne's practice of "the craftie and secrete methode." In addition to demonstrating the omnipresence of this intellectual virtue in Montaigne's work, McGowan exhibits "the traditions of defensive writing" among Montaigne's forebears and contemporaries. McGowan is especially effective in showing how the Religious Wars colored virtually everything Montaigne wrote and how his indirect style enabled him to speak relatively freely even in that oppressive context. Schaefer, *Political Philosophy of Montaigne*, provides a comprehensive reinterpretation of Montaigne emphasizing his break with the Socratic tradition and demonstrating on every page Montaigne's strategic writing.

That everyone else thinks they possess it is no evidence that they do, for to think one lacked it "would be a proposition implying its own contradiction." To think one lacks it is to possess it, not to think one lacks it is to lack it. "It is a disease that is never where it is perceived." "The wisest man who ever lived," Socrates, was not diseased for he thought he lacked it, whereas, "there never was a porter or a silly woman who did not think they had enough sense to look out for themselves." *This* is the presumption of philosophers: a superior modesty regarding knowledge, a modesty that comes from self-knowledge. They know they do not know. For Montaigne to think well of himself is to think himself deficient where no man ever thought himself deficient—except Socrates before him—and Nietzsche after him, for Nietzsche says that philosophers have always been suspicious of "knowers" (*JS* 351).[3]

Montaigne presumes to liken himself to Socrates, the wisest man who ever lived. And here is the sentence Descartes quotes: thinking himself deficient in good sense marks the philosopher for "it is commonly said that the most justly distributed thing that nature has given us is sense." In his very first public sentence, Descartes quotes Montaigne on what we all share just where Montaigne shows there are some few exceptions. Socrates is an exception and Montaigne follows Socrates in what makes him exceptional. And Descartes? What a way for a philosopher to mount the stage!

But this is not all, for in just this context Montaigne asks the crucial question, "For whom do I write?" and he answers that the world consists of but two types of people and for neither of these does he write. More explicitly, Montaigne says that he writes for neither the learned nor the common, the classification Descartes repeats when the time comes to ask for whom *he* writes (ii.15). Montaigne writes for a third class into whose hands he may fall, minds regulated and strong in themselves, a class so rare that it has neither name nor rank among us, the class, surely, into which Descartes falls. In learning that Montaigne wrote for him, Descartes learns his vocation as a philosopher from a philosopher. For Montaigne states in his most extensive account of the philosophers that they are the few human beings of the highest rank, that they have aspired to regulate the world with governments and laws, that they have had to write deceptively in order to shelter the pleasures of their own passion for learning and to shield others from conclusions neither "nourishing nor

---

3. Montaigne returns to this matter in his final essay, iii.13, "Of Experience," 823, again noting Socrates' difference from everyman. Hobbes makes the same point for the same reason (*Leviathan* chap. 13).

salutary," and that they have written for the needs of society especially on matters like religion (*Essays* ii.12, "Apology," 370–80; see iii.13, "Of Experience," 824). Montaigne further states that there are three kinds of philosophy and while Socrates, Plato, and Aristotle are to be named in none of the three, Socrates is the wisest man that ever was, "the master of masters," and the two Socratic masters, Plato and Aristotle, are Pyrrhonists sheltered in their writings. Montaigne too is a complete skeptic about Plato, and about Aristotle as well. Plato, while sprinkling his style with dogmatic cadences, aims to inquire more than to instruct, and Aristotle, "the prince of dogmatists," is himself no dogmatist but a teacher whose "Pyrrhonism took an affirmative form." This is the history of philosophy with which Descartes shows himself in agreement when he tells how he would have written his history of philosophy had he been free to write it (*Principles*, Preface). A Nietzschean history of philosophy will have to restore Montaigne to his rightful place.[4]

Montaigne emphasizes the philosopher's necessary employment of false opinion. Toward the end of an essay in which the love of glory is scorned as unworthy of a virtuous man, Montaigne recommends the love of glory as a useful tool in keeping people "roused to virtue." The example of Plato, Montaigne says, shows just how bold one can be on behalf of virtue, for Plato employed "every means" to this end, using not only the promise of glory but bringing in "divine operations and revelations" wherever human power failed, thus earning for himself the title "the great forger of miracles." Paying for virtue with counterfeit funds is a practice indulged in by "all legislators" especially with regard to the lie of sacred origins (*Essays* ii.16, "Of Glory," 477). "Plato treats this mystery with his cards pretty much on the table" (*Essays* ii.12, "Apology," 379).

In presenting himself to the world, Descartes follows Montaigne by giving a portrait of himself in the form of a history of his life and by writing "essays," though essays very different from Montaigne's. And in

---

4. In *Cosmopolis, the Hidden Agenda of Modernity*, Stephen Toulmin argues that the Renaissance humanists, especially Montaigne, were far more important for the rise of modernity than is generally recognized. He contrasts their perspective, more open and skeptical and more congenial to ourselves, with the "second stage" of modernity, the seventeenth-century rationalists, notably Descartes, who are generally credited with fathering modernity and who argued for a method of certainty uncongenial to ourselves. But the gains of Toulmin's effort to "recontextualize" early modern philosophy are, it seems to me, partially squandered by oversimplifying the context and giving it too much credit for dictating the philosopher's thought. Though far from reducing philosophy to its context, Toulmin nevertheless makes the thinker a victim of his times rather than a strategic actor in them (39–41).

his unacknowledged borrowings from Montaigne, Descartes seems to repeat Montaigne's invitation: "Let people see in what I borrow whether I have known how to choose what would enhance my theme." His borrowings from Montaigne follow Montaigne's way of borrowing from recent authors who write in the common language: he uses the reasonings and inventions that are best in them while deliberately not giving the author's name, and he does so in order to hold in check the hasty condemnations commonly directed at recent writings in the vulgar tongue (*Essays* ii.10, "Of Books," 296). Descartes thus takes permission from Montaigne for the crime of which an advocate of Montaigne has accused him: plagiarism of Montaigne.[5]

When Descartes quotes Montaigne again and again and never once says so, he quotes a teacher who may well be his initial and constant educator, though one from whom he has to keep a distance, Pyrrhonism being no useful part of the intellectual armory of a man with Descartes's aims. For Descartes it is better to acquire a reputation for making war on skeptics like Montaigne, and the reason could well be the reason stated by Nietzsche. In speaking of the philosopher as educator, Nietzsche gives Montaigne, "this freest and highest of souls," all but the highest praise: "The fact that such a man wrote has increased the joy of living on this earth. . . . I would side with him if the task were to make oneself at home on the earth" (*SE* 2). Making oneself at home on the earth cannot be Descartes's task either; he has to appear to disown Montaigne for the sake of his reputation: the Baconian project of mastering nature depends upon inflating confidence in reason, not diminishing it. Though they have a common enemy, as will be seen, Descartes and Montaigne adopt different strategies for disarming the enemy. Descartes steals from Montaigne while scarcely breathing a word about his own particular form of philosophic skepticism, but his very plagiarism helps lift the veil on this hidden dimension of his thought.

The Jesuits' scholar was Montaigne's pupil. And once this is realized, Descartes's account of his schooling in part one of the *Discourse* comes to light as the education of a Montaignian. Socratic lessons set forth obliquely in Montaigne's essays turned the young Descartes from reliance on his own time and place by teaching him to be skeptical about his authoritative teachers. They turned him to what Montaigne called "the great book of the world" (i.9) and finally they turned him inward, to the study of himself (i.10). And while teaching the radical detachment of the thinker from his own things, Montaigne's *Essays* teach obedience

5. Norton, *Influence of Montaigne*, 187–88.

to a "rule of rules," the maxim imprinted on the soul of Montaigne's singular friend: to obey and submit most religiously to the laws of his country though he would, had he had the choice, prefer to have been born elsewhere (*Essays* i.23, "Of Custom, and Not Easily Changing an Accepted Law," 86; i.28, "Of Friendship," 144).

If in addressing his own special reader, those who combine good sense with study, Descartes makes use of "you," he addresses "you" first with an invitation: what Descartes calls a "history" of his life, "you" may prefer to regard as a "fable" (i.4). "You" may be inclined to think that Descartes is writing fiction when he tells the history of his life. No matter. Histories and fables are both useful and they balance one another: the gracefulness of fables awakens the mind, the memorable deeds of history exalt it, and read with discretion, aid in forming one's judgment (i.5). The mind can be awakened to the great and monumental by the fabulous tales of gods and heroes, as Montaigne's mind was in the first taste he had for books, the fables of Ovid's *Metamorphoses*. Once awakened, the mind is exalted in its judgment of the great when it studies with discretion the memorable deeds of history, as Montaigne's mind was by reading Plutarch's *Lives* and Livy (*Essays* i.26, "On the Education of Children," 106–29). But fables have the disadvantage of making impossible events seem possible, and histories, even Montaigne's, have the disadvantage of omitting the basest and least illustrious details (i.7) so that what is included "does not appear as it really is." Descartes therefore ends his account of fable and history with a warning: those who govern their own conduct on the basis of them may fall into the extravagances of the knights of our novels and may conceive plans that are beyond their powers. Assuming that they are beyond *our* powers, what are the fabulous deeds portrayed in Descartes's history and are they beyond *his* powers? What will the *Discourse* portray of a hero whose deeds can both awaken our minds to what is possible for a man and exalt our minds in the portrayal of its achievement? Nowhere do these invited questions come more to the fore than in reflection on Descartes's first presentation of the fabulous task he set for himself as a young man.

Part 2: Fabulous Deeds

After years of preparation and many attempts that he came to judge as failures—*Olympica, Rules for the Direction of the Mind, The World*—Descartes finally introduced his thoughts to the world by introducing himself, by telling the fabulous history of his life. But Descartes's personal history is tied to the history of his place and time. His thoughts aspire to universality but they are not the thoughts of universal mind; they are the thoughts of a European, a Frenchman born into a continent at war. Descartes is very economical in referring to specific events of his place and time but his few references seem all the more telling for that reason. At the opening of part two, Descartes ties a signal event in his own life to a signal event in the life of Europe—"the wars" which were being fought when Descartes first had the thought that he reports, wars which "have still not stopped" seventeen years later as he introduces himself to the world. In a Europe torn by on-going wars, the thinker Descartes entered solitude and pursued unperturbed solitary thoughts. The other reference to the wars (iii.31) also emphasizes the contrast between public war and private peace: Descartes took up residence in Holland, in a Protestant part of Europe which he can praise for the privacy it permits a philosopher while being wholly mobilized for war. Whether temporarily in a south German *poêle* near Ulm or permanently in Protestant Holland, the solitary Descartes lives privately and quietly in a Europe torn by war: what is the relation between the wars and the thoughts of Descartes's solitude?

When Descartes entered the *poêle* for a whole day he was completely free to think. He had many thoughts but reports only one, a thought concerning perfection, specifically the perfection achieved by human making, manmade perfection. Two different routes to the elusive goal of perfection are contrasted throughout Descartes's paragraph-long thought: the route through the work of many masters and the route through the work of one. The trajectory of Descartes's thought carries him by an inexorable logic through five "thuses" each contrasting the relative imperfection of works on which many masters have labored with the relative perfection of a new work on which but one has labored. Descartes's thought expands in grandeur: the works considered advance from buildings to cities to peoples, and the master worker from an architect to an engineer to a legislator. Once the thought has achieved the grandeur of the legislator of a people it can ascend no higher; instead, attention focuses on the legislator himself and the qualities that belong to him and determine the perfection of his work, his people. Here is a tale fit for fable: a solitary young man retires from a people at war into the privacy of his thoughts and thinks of a more perfect people made anew by a more perfect legislator. If the greatest thoughts are the greatest events, and if philosophers are legislators, and if they write in a way that obscures their thoughts from the general view, then here is a thought that will bear a closer look.

The thought of perfection produced by human work seems to be structured around the five "thuses." Each stage contrasts works that have come into being over time and through many masters with works that have come into being more suddenly through one master. Buildings, cities, and peoples can either evolve over a long period acquiring a settled character through a history of change and adaptation, or they can begin through a plan devised by a single maker. And Descartes pauses to note that in cities what evolves over time comes to have an inertial resistance to novelty and innovation; loyalty develops to what has evolved even though "it is fortune more than the will of some men using their reason" that has given these cities their form. Loyal to what fortune decreed, citizens appoint officials to ensure concordance between old and new. And if a builder committed to novelty or innovation considers the standards of these officials, he will know that it is difficult to produce a finely executed work by laboring solely on the already existing buildings of others.

From this difficulty in reconstruction Descartes moves directly— "Thus I imagined"—to the most ambitious construction made by man, a people. Some peoples naturally evolve from savagery to civility, acquiring laws only to the extent that the inconvenience caused by crimes and quarrels forced them to do so. Other peoples, from the very beginning of their coming together, observe the constitutions of "some prudent legislator." Peoples of the latter sort are more perfect than those of the former because they are "better policed" or ordered. But they are still imperfect, and for this item in his paragraph on perfection, Descartes chooses to emphasize the imperfection even of the relatively more perfect. For the first time, specific examples of the relatively more perfect appear: two peoples, "the state of the true religion whose ordinances were fixed by God alone," and Sparta whose ordinances also have a single source. How perfect are these two relatively more perfect works? "Sparta flourished greatly in the past" but it has long since disappeared and many of its laws taken by themselves were strange and even contrary to good morals. Descartes evaluated his second example without evaluating his first. But if he "speaks of human matters" in order to follow his own precept of not subjecting revelation to his feeble reasoning (i.8), a precept Machiavelli also followed when reasoning about the founders of peoples,[6] Descartes leaves no doubt as to what he thinks. The state of the true religion "ought to be incomparably better governed than all the

6. Machiavelli, *Prince*, chap. 6.

others." Is it? States currently claiming governance by the true religion are engaged in the fanatical wars against one another to which Descartes has just called attention.[7] And the vague phrasing forces one to ask if these are the states Descartes means. Could he have meant ancient Israel? Surely he does not mean modern Islam, the Ottoman empire whose claims to be the state of the true religion have threatened Europe for two centuries? Which of the claimants to the state of the true religion is the true claimant?

And what about the source of the laws governing the state of the true religion? They were fixed by God alone, Descartes says, but he then speaks of the laws of Sparta as "invented only by one." One what? "God is it, or some human being, who is given the credit for laying down your laws?" These are the first words of Plato's *Laws,* his inquiry into the source of laws that begins with the source of Spartan and Cretan laws. "God of course, Zeus for us Cretans, Apollo for those Spartans"—so answers the one who lives under the laws fixed by God alone. And so answers Descartes by making God seem the source of the laws under which he and his countrymen live and mere mortals the source of the laws under which others live. The need for ornamentation in a city that has come into being over a long time and now has officials who jealously guard public structures requires that he answer "God of course" while speaking of his own state. But by speaking ambiguously of "one" as the source of the laws of others he raises the appropriate Platonic question about the source of all law. Descartes does not speak as freely as Machiavelli did in his chapter in the *Discourses* on the founding of a people as the work of one man only,[8] but his paragraph makes his Machiavellian point clear enough.

The imperfections of peoples relatively more perfect because founded by one prudent legislator lead Descartes to a reflection that at first looks quite different but that is in fact intimately related. Not simply "thus" but "and thus" introduces the last two stages of Descartes's thought as if they were the inexorable consequences of reflection on his two examples. And each introduces what Descartes *thought,* not just what he imagined. He thinks that when it comes to the possibility of drawing near the truth, the simple reasonings made naturally by a man of good sense are superior to "the sciences of the books, at least those whose reasonings are only probable." Traditions passed down in books are the

7. Kennington, "Rene Descartes," 427.
8. Machiavelli, *Discourses* I.9.

work of many masters and suffer the imperfection of such works, even the two book-based traditions that Descartes has just referred to: superior to what has evolved through time and been as subject to fortune as our heritage from Hebrews and Greeks is the simple reasoning made naturally by a man of good sense.

"And thus" Descartes moves to the final stage: natural reasoning is itself defective because it has been subject to development over time; the coming to be of our capacity to reason, like the coming to be of the relatively less perfect buildings, cities, and peoples, has left it subject to the work of many masters. Because we are all children before being adults, it is our lot to have been governed during the period of our formation by our appetites and our preceptors. Having been prey to these masters while we had no power to resist, our capacity for reasoning already has a determinate character when we first begin to employ it in our attempts to draw near the truth. History, in the form of our preceptors, and nature, in the form of our appetites, have shaped our natural reasoning before reason itself could undertake to shape us. What seems like the "teaching of nature" (*Meditations* vi.76–90) is in fact only the consequence of habit and schooling. The relatively more perfect side of the comparison of this final stage can be pictured only as a project: it is "almost impossible" for the judgments of a man formed by preceptors and appetites to be as pure and solid as the judgments of a man whose capacity for reasoning was fully formed at the moment of his birth and had served as the sole guide of his conduct ever since.

Descartes's thought on the perfection of human making comes to its culmination in a human being he can only imagine: a man born rational and subject solely to reason. That imaginable man would be most fit for perfect making, most fit to be the prudent legislator who founds a new people on rational laws that would supplant the heritage to which we are heir, a mixture of the ancient cities of Athens and Jerusalem transmitted to us through many masters. Such a legislator, working alone, would have to work on old materials cognizant of the fierce loyalties which had developed in the people heir to God and Greece. But prior to the transforming labor on the people formed in this way, the prospective legislator has a preliminary task, for nature and history have left *him* defective. His own long tutelage to appetites and preceptors has left his own reason impure. His first work will have to be himself. He will have to overcome his own natural history and make himself a wholly rational man, reborn with the full use of his reason and guided by nothing but his reason. Rebirth requires that he become his own preceptor and give himself the four fundamental precepts by which he is born again (ii.15–19).

The *Discourse* is the fabulous history of the coming to be of that rational legislator. Or, in the other image Descartes suggests we apply to his *Discourse,* it is a painting that paints the portrait of that man while attentive to painting as the art of light and shadow, of showing and hiding (i.4; v.41).[9] A painting, a history, a fable, the *Discourse* is a masterpiece of self-presentation that makes it possible to glimpse the heroic deeds performed by the one prudent legislator who frees himself in order to found the new people.

The immodesty of Descartes's thought of the legislator seems to be moderated immediately in the next paragraph where he acts as if his sole aim was to rebuild the house of his own opinions rather than pull down the houses of others. In fact, however, the second paragraph shows how the revolution of the first is to be conducted: wholly privately at first and never ever with any suggestion of a reformation that tears down the houses of others. Having begun his own liberation from customary opinion and set out on a road of radical innovation for himself, Descartes asserts the superiority of customary opinion and the danger of radical innovation, the philosophical revolutionary avowing a political conservatism that keeps to the old and well-worn roads. The campaign is conducted in accord with Montaigne's rule that seems to forbid speculation on "the best form of society" while stating that "not in theory, but in truth, the best and most excellent government for each nation is the one under which it has preserved its existence." In the midst of the convulsions ravaging France, Montaigne condemns reformers in words similar to those used by Descartes: "To undertake to recast so great a mass [as a state], to change the foundations of so great a structure, that is a job for those who wipe out a picture in order to clean it, who want to reform defects of detail by universal confusion and cure illness by death, who desire not so much to change as to overthrow everything" (*Essays* iii.9, "Of Vanity," 730–31). But such sentiments are completely compatible with the role of the prudent legislator, in Montaigne as in Descartes: Montaigne criticizes innovation in a way that seems complete, citing Livy that "no change from the ancient ways is to be approved," but he makes clear that such caution does not preclude there being "one who undertakes to control and change [the laws of his country]" and he cites Plutarch's praise of the legislator who knows how to command the laws

9. Nancy, *"Larvatus pro deo,"* 14–36.

themselves when public necessity requires it (*Essays* i.23, "Of Custom and Not Easily Changing an Accepted Law," 77–90).[10]

Descartes's second paragraph in part two revives all three stages of his first paragraph—houses, cities, and states—leaving the reader to ponder the question of just how revolutionary his rebuilding aims to be. Descartes says that we do not see that one pulls to the ground all the houses in a city but that we do see that sometimes people are forced to tear down their own houses because they are in danger of falling in on themselves and the foundations are not secure. This example persuaded him that it was not reasonable that a single individual undertake the design of reforming a state by changing all of the foundations and by toppling it in order to set it up again. But how *does* the single individual, the prudent legislator, proceed with respect to an already formed people? Descartes explicitly rejects the way taken by Bacon: reforming the body of the sciences and the order established in the schools for teaching them. But this is in fact the implication of his own reform of the sciences, though Descartes says privately that it is better not to say so. As he told Mersenne after informing him that the *Meditations* contains all the foundations of his physics: Do not tell anyone; let them find out on their own that his principles destroy Aristotle's; the reforms will follow the discovery of their necessity (to Mersenne 28 Jan. 1641). It is of paramount importance that the radical reformer Descartes not acquire a reputation as a reformer either of the state or of education in the state. "Reformer" is a word freighted with the most ominous implications because of the wars between reformers and counterreformers that had broken out again in Europe in 1619. Like Montaigne, whose whole life as a writer was spent in the midst of such wars, Descartes absolutely refuses the term in favor of judicious conformity; he must even appear to disown Bacon whose reform in the sciences Descartes grounds and furthers.

Descartes's rebirth requires replacing all the opinions based on appetites and preceptors with others built on the foundation of reason. "Foundations," the word that bears such close scrutiny in the *Discourse*, is used three times in this paragraph, and the uses are illuminated by its two uses in part one: the foundations of mathematics were so "solid and firm" that it was amazing that no one had built anything more noble upon them. Imagining firm foundations with no building makes Descartes think of the opposite: magnificent palaces of morals built by the ancient

---

10. On Montaigne's veiled radicalism see Schaefer, *Political Philosophy of Montaigne,* 153–76.

pagans on nothing more firm than sand and mud (i.7–8), the principles of their philosophy which have served ever since as the foundations of the sciences (i.8–9). Setting himself against the ancient pagans in a time of religious wars that put their still operative foundations into question, Descartes begins in utter solitude to lay new foundations on which a new palace of morals might be built, on which a new people might be founded. Again, are those foundations what he calls "the foundations of his metaphysics" in reference to part four (*Discourse,* introductory summary)? Or are they what he now describes in part two, the method which will supply the new principles for all the sciences? A prudent legislator, working with old materials, and knowing the hold exercised by loyalty to the old, will seem to keep to the old ways while putting entirely new foundations in place.

Before turning to the principles of his method, Descartes emphasizes his singularity. He is not a reformer bent on a reformation; he plans only a reform of his own thoughts. Why bother making them public then? "And if, my work having sufficiently pleased me, I show it to you here as a model, it is not for that reason"—it is not because of the pleasure Descartes derives from his work—"that I wish to advise anyone to imitate it." Why does Descartes write? To whom does he show his work as a model, and for what? There will be almost no imitators of his work because the world consists almost completely of but two kinds of mind and for neither is it at all suitable to take the first step with Descartes of resolving to detach oneself from received opinion (ii.15). The third kind of mind, the rare kind to which Descartes shows he belongs, is not *entirely* singular, and in a most pleasing way Descartes exhibits his singularity by intimating his dependence on Montaigne. As already noted, this passage follows Montaigne's account of whom he writes for in "On Presumption." Descartes singles out his own audience by referring to Montaigne's means of singling out his: setting right his own opening sentence and staying close to Montaigne, Descartes says that of the two kinds of mind that include almost everybody, one kind makes the mistake of judging its capacity too highly, thereby making premature judgments and lacking the patience for inquiry—Montaigne had spoken here of the learned, those who scorn everyone who does not know Aristotle (*Essays* ii.17, "Of Presumption," 498). These leaders are in fact followers, and if they were ever to doubt their accepted principles they would lose their way forever. The other kind make no mistake, they rightly recognize that they are less capable of distinguishing the true from the false than their instructors are—Montaigne had spoken here of ordinary minds who do not see the grace and weight of a lofty and subtle speech. Minds inappropriately vain and appropriately humble, followers minds, constitute almost the whole world.

Descartes himself was forced out of following and onto his own path for two reasons: he lacked a single master and he learned early the variety of opinion among the most learned, thus shaking his confidence in the intrinsic superiority of any opinions, including his own. But in spelling out these reasons, the one forced into independence depends on Montaigne. He follows a teacher who makes the very act of following an act of independence, a utilization of one's own reason. For Montaigne is a teacher who does not write for "the two types who fill the world" but for a third class whose minds are "regulated and strong in themselves" (Ibid.). He writes obliquely and does not draw the conclusions of his thoughts, leaving it to the resourcefulness of the reader to discover the richer and bolder matter to which the writing points. He even says that with respect to artful writing he has few equals: "I am much mistaken if many other writers offer more to take hold of in their material than I do" (*Essays* i.40, "A Consideration upon Cicero," 184–85). But the reader has to be very careful: "My ideas follow one another, but sometimes it is from a distance. . . . It is the inattentive reader who loses my subject, not I. Some word about it will always be found off in a corner, which will not fail to be sufficient, though it takes little room" (*Essays* iii.9, "Of Vanity," 761).

Descartes exhibits his independent dependence on this artful writer in a most witty way. "One cannot imagine anything so strange and unbelievable that it has not been said by some philosopher"—the philosopher Descartes quotes this strange and unbelievable opinion about philosophers from the philosopher Montaigne: the opinion that grounds his mistrust of philosophers is stolen from a philosopher. But Descartes's little joke is a stolen joke for the original opinion is Cicero's and Montaigne had made *his* case against the philosophers by citing a philosopher.[11] The other three reasons that forced Descartes into independence of customary opinion are also taken directly from Montaigne's school of skepticism about what one has taken over as one's own (*Essays* ii.12, "Apology," 325; i.31, "Of Cannibals," 150–59).

"Like a man who walks alone and in the shadows," Descartes has to move slowly and circumspectly. Circumspection requires that before

---

11. In the Latin version Descartes quotes Cicero word for word. See Gilson, *Discours de la méthode*, 178; Montaigne, *Essays* ii.12, "Apology," 408.

simply rejecting everything in his unsatisfactory training, he must satisfy himself that he possesses the proper method for testing the truth and falsity of opinions. Thus begins his account of the "search for the true method" (ii.17). Some of his training in philosophy and mathematics proved useful: logic, geometrical analysis, and algebra. In logic, separating the true and good precepts from the harmful and superfluous is almost as hard as drawing a Diana or a Minerva out of a block of marble. These virgin goddesses of political wisdom and wisdom as such punish those who view them naked, Diana punishing Acteon with death and Minerva punishing Teiresias with blindness. Before introducing the goddesses Descartes had distinguished a logic of explanation from a logic of discovery, emphasizing the priority of the latter. To make Diana and Minerva visible is to risk death for baring what one knows of political wisdom, and blindness, or the attribution of blindness, for baring what one knows of wisdom as such. Descartes thus seems to be indicating that his own logic of discovery must be presented in a way that respects the virgin goddesses.

In describing his search for a new method, Descartes returns to the high point of the first paragraph of this part, the laws that govern a state: just as a state is better governed by a few laws strictly observed, so Descartes replaces the many precepts of logic with four strictly observed precepts of his own. He legislates for himself, giving himself four precepts and the resolution never once to fail to observe them. These four precepts submit everything to the standard of Descartes's intellect. Neither mathematical nor metaphysical, they precede all subject matters as the strictly rational procedure to which all subject matters must submit if the mind is to gain freedom from its residue of tutelage to appetites and preceptors.

As Descartes says after listing his precepts, a model for them is supplied by geometry, and the success of geometry leads him to imagine a far grander success and to pronounce an extreme and quite un-Montaignian rational optimism: "There is nothing so far distant that one cannot finally reach nor so hidden that one cannot discover" (ii.19). Variants of this exuberant affirmation of reason's capacity will accompany all of Descartes's work and they have served as grounds for interpreting Descartes as a philosopher who affirms reason's capacity to unriddle all the mysteries of the universe, a philosopher for whom there is complete commensurability of thought and being, for whom mathematical reason opens one to the complete lucidity of the whole. But this first expression of confidence in reason is in fact limited in two important ways. First, it is what Descartes "was given occasion to imagine" by the success of geometry—and whether what he imagines accords with what he thinks will have to be seen. Second and more important is this precise limitation: "There is nothing so far distant that one cannot finally reach nor so hidden that one cannot discover," provided that one follow the method and provided that the subjects are "things that can fall within human knowledge." Descartes's rational optimism applies only to "the things that can fall within human knowledge" as ordered in obedience to the four precepts. But what falls *outside* human knowledge such that even the rigorous application of Descartes's precepts would leave it distant and hidden? To answer this question it will be necessary to watch Descartes's own application of his method to the various subject matters and in particular to attend to his equivocation on "foundations." In anticipation, it can be said that for Descartes, to fall within human knowledge means to be ordered according to a plan given by the mind rather than by things themselves. Descartes's rational optimism is grounded in what could be termed anachronistically a proto-Kantianism, and not in any correspondence between mind and the ultimate order of things. But if this is the case, Descartes's rational optimism is quite compatible with rational pessimism or skepticism of a certain sort: Descartes himself introduces the possibility that what appears certain to us may appear false to God or an angel, and his response is telling: Who cares? (*AT* VII.145; *PW* 2.103). Descartes knows full well that there are those who care very much that our certainties be identical to God's or an angel's but his account of perception in the *Optics* or of the activity and passivity of the mind in *The Passions of the Soul* shows that his conclusion—"Who cares?"—is the appropriate one for him.[12]

This epistemological issue is crucial for the *Discourse* but it is accompanied by a related, though nonepistemological issue. The two great modern masters to whom Descartes regularly points, Montaigne and Bacon, mix epistemological questions with the question of a fitting politics for philosophy. They take their bearings from the current state of European religion, not because the religious issue can advance the epistemological issue one iota but because confidence in reason bears on confidence in revelation. Montaigne emphasized the limits of reason and the modesty appropriate to relative ignorance, a modesty extendable to the immodest religious convictions which sent men to war knowing God's will.

12. Lachterman, *Ethics of Geometry*, provides a detailed argument for Descartes's constructivism with special attention to his geometry.

Bacon, on the other hand, inflated reason's capacity. But his unbridled affirmations of reason's capacity also serve a partially rhetorical purpose. Success in the scientific project depended on a belief in the capacity of reason, and as Bacon made clear in the *New Organon,* that belief depended on the ability of reason's advocates to recover the sole instrument for the investigation of nature from the various forms of skepticism which had cast doubt on its competence. This meant recovering human reason from the slanders made against it by those whose aim was salvation rather than understanding, and for whom the tentativeness natural to reason was to be replaced by an absolute certitude inaccessible to reason. In order to recover reason, Bacon not only separated reason from faith but elevated reason in an apparently literal way to capacities left mythical by Plato. But the rehabilitation of reason for the scientific project meant as well the recovery of reason from Montaigne's salutary skepticism. A skepticism familiar to genuine philosophers from Socrates to Nietzsche could be of no use in a program to reorder the world through belief in reason. With respect to the scientific project, Descartes sides with Bacon against Montaigne. The philosopher who adopted the Baconian ends had to adopt the Baconian means of encouraging confidence where confidence was both necessary and lacking. His method provided the grounds for that confidence. Nevertheless, subsequent passages in the *Discourse* show that Descartes advanced the Baconian strategy of fostering belief in the capacity of reason to render all being visible while holding a view of the limits of reason. Descartes was of course completely familiar with the possibility of a rational optimism masking a fundamental philosophical Pyrrhonism, for Montaigne attributes such a Pyrrhonism to the greatest teachers of rational optimism, Plato and Aristotle. And this "Pyrrhonism in an affirmative form" is precisely what Descartes himself attributes to Plato and Aristotle in his own substitute for a history of philosophy (*Essays* ii.12, "Apology," 370–76; Descartes, *Principles, AT* IXB. 5–9; *PW* 1.181–83). Descartes shows with great exactitude just where he stands on this issue of rational optimism and certitude in part four of the *Discourse.* In the midst of proofs for a God who will ratify absolute certitude, Descartes addresses the skeptical temperaments and gives them a reason to remain skeptical about all claims to metaphysical certitude.[13] The kind of certainty available from a mathematical science is different from the certainty claimed by the old metaphysics. Given the rhetorical needs of Descartes's program, and his exact

13. See the section, "Part 4: Certain Certainties" in this chapter, pp. 238–45.

words about certitude, it is necessary to be cautious in interpreting "Descartes against the Skeptics," or "Descartes conqueror of skepticism" while "Sceptique malgré lui." [14]

Clarity about Descartes's method requires watching how he actually proceeded once he had legislated his four precepts for himself. How to begin is *not* a problem because the precepts themselves require beginning with the simplest and easiest to know. There is a precedent for beginning in this way, because this is the way mathematicians have begun, and of all those who had already searched for truth in the sciences mathematicians alone had succeeded in finding certain and evident reasons for their demonstrations. But if he knows where to begin, Descartes does not know where he will end, because he still does not know if he can expect any utility from mathematics beyond accustoming his mind to truth (see 1.7). At this point then, certainty and utility are separate and Descartes is guided only by the resolution to pursue the certain, having no reason to expect utility from the certain except in training his mind. The true utility of this beginning point will become clear only underway.

But the utility of his method is not the only thing Descartes does not know as he begins: he does not know what subject matters it will eventually be applicable to. Will it be applicable to the traditional subject matter of philosophy? Philosophy has served as the giver of principles to all the other sciences (i.8): Descartes must set traditional philosophy aside in applying his own method to the sciences. As we watch Descartes's application of his method unfold in his narration, it will become apparent that his method *replaces* traditional philosophy as the giver of principles. The question therefore arises, how will the new source of principles relate to the old?

Before raising the question of the scope of his precepts, Descartes describes briefly their first great success, his invention of analytic geometry, which he describes as a reduction of relations to calculable proportions and a symbolization which abstracts from everything but the calculable. Descartes attributes his success to his strict observance of his four precepts and he likens the truths thus discovered to a truth in arithmetic learned by a child: having followed the rules of arithmetic to arrive at a simple sum, the child has found everything about the sum that the human mind can find about it. Descartes then draws a decisive conclusion: "The method which teaches one to follow the true order and enumerate exactly all the circumstances of what one is seeking, contains

14. See Curley, *Descartes against the Skeptics,* and Popkin, *History of Scepticism,* 172, 193.

everything which gives certitude to the rules of arithmetic." The method here *is* the four precepts; and the certitude achieved by following it does not depend upon making what Hume called "a very unexpected circuit" through "the veracity of the supreme Being."[15]

The method described in the four precepts predates the metaphysical meditations of part four just as the *Rules* of 1628 or perhaps earlier predate the metaphysics first outlined in 1629. Discovery and application of the precepts is independent of the "foundation" later supplied and the nature of the precepts shows that they can never stand in need of such a foundation. The *Rules* seems never to have been completed though it is clear from its content that it was intended to be a step-by-step introduction to the new method; the *Rules* is one of the projected introductions supplanted by the actual introduction, the *Discourse* and its appended *Essays*. It is uncertain whether Descartes would ever have made the *Rules* public but their public existence now makes it possible to view the method of part two of the *Discourse* in an earlier elaboration. The *Rules* make explicit the mathematicization of all problems through the depiction of the world as extensive magnitude via imagination. Rule twelve describes the process in the knowing subject whereby information passes from sense perception to intellect via the "common" sense and imagination. After elaborating the relationship of intellect to imagination, rule twelve gives an account of the known object ending with emphasis on how to begin with any matter to be inquired into. Taking the magnet as his example, Descartes indicates that one is to begin with all the available observations, "deduce" from these observations what mixture of factors is necessary to account for these effects, and then conclude boldly that one has grasped the true nature of the magnet as far as humanly possible on the basis of these observations. After describing the rule of abstraction from inessential particulars to essential ones in rule thirteen, Descartes describes the essential abstraction to extensive magnitude in rule fourteen. The aim is to arrive at perfectly determinate problems reduced to proportions whereby an unknown extension can be discovered on the basis of a comparison with the already known extension. Both the *Rules* and the four precepts of the *Discourse* show that Descartes's method is a mathematicized Baconianism not at all troubled by the two great dilemmas of his metaphysical meditations: where to begin? and how to proceed?

The final paragraph of part two is dominated by the word *method*.

15. Hume, *An Enquiry concerning Human Understanding,* sec. 12, pt. 1.

The word itself is used only at the beginning and end but it is referred to throughout by pronouns that force the reader to confirm the antecedent as in each case "method." Descartes uses the word only four more times in the *Discourse on the Method* (iii.27 [twice]; iii.29; vi.61) and each time he is clearly referring to "the method I prescribed for myself" (iii.27, 29) in part two. The earlier references to method are also unanimous in referring to the four precepts (introductory summary [twice]; i.3; i.4; ii.17; ii.18; ii.21). There is no equivocation in the *Discourse on the Method* about "method." The metaphysical meditations are never referred to as Descartes's method—and while "foundations" is used in connection with them, "foundations" is also used in connection with mathematics. How will Descartes's method apply to his metaphysical meditations? In the final paragraph of part two, Descartes promises to apply his method to the other sciences in accord with an order prescribed by the method itself. He says only one thing about that order: it forbids taking up the subject of philosophy just yet. But application of his method to the other sciences is accompanied by the awareness that he is encroaching on philosophy and its historic primacy, for he applies his method of certainty to sciences which have borrowed their principles from philosophy in which nothing is certain. Aware of the challenge his method represents to philosophy, Descartes thought that "above all" he ought to try to establish something certain in philosophy. "Above all." Descartes means it: this is "the most important thing in the world"—the world outside the *poêle,* the world at war because of what it thinks most important. What Descartes thinks most important will have to be delayed because the one who can perform the deed is not quite ready yet. Has the author of our fabulous history conceived a plan that is beyond his powers? Will the most important thing in the world fall within his powers after he has gathered himself for the deed? The order prescribed by the method now requires something quite different: a provisional morality that will enable him to appear in the world outside the *poêle* without drawing suspicion to himself as a revolutionary whose new method will ground a new people. His provisional morality makes him a master of the art of seeming and enables him to come forth from his solitude altered in every fundamental respect but unnoticeably so.

Part 3: Sheltered, Resolute, and Happy

Part three is directly linked to part two as the account of Descartes's solitude for it opens, "And finally . . ." And the introductory summary of the *Discourse* states that part three consists of "some of the rules of morality which the author has derived from this method." Those rules are a *provisional* code of morals. But Descartes raises the question of a *definitive* code of morals derivable from his method by returning to the metaphor of building: he likens himself to someone who has torn down his house and is in the process of rebuilding it. A prudent architect provides provisional shelter while rebuilding his dwelling. How will the finished building resemble the temporary shelter? More important, if the temporary shelter resembles the houses of the whole city, how will the finished building fit in? What will be its effect on the houses of the whole city—and on the laws of a whole people?

The opening paragraph orders the four following paragraphs by stating that the builder who destroys his own dwelling must find ways to be sheltered, resolute, and happy. Tearing down his house has deprived him of the means to these three things. Can reason alone provide a new means? Because reason's first provisions are called provisional, an adequate judgment must await the discovery of the definitive. Descartes says his *morale par provision* consists of three or four maxims which he wants to share with you. Those wanting to share them might ask, are there three or are there four? There are three, Descartes will answer, founded on a fourth matter neither provisional nor a maxim, but the self-legislation of the rational man who prescribes his own three provisional laws.

The first maxim legislates conformity—Caton calls it "a rule of seemliness." [16] It would be just as useful to the rational man, Descartes says, to adopt the moderate standards of the Persians or Chinese if he happened to live among them as it is to adopt the moderate standards of Christian Europeans among whom Descartes actually finds himself. In this spirit of conformity he obeys the laws and customs of his countrymen and holds on to their religion. Religion is mentioned only in the first sentence and with pious gratitude for "the religion in which, by God's grace, I was instructed since childhood"—but instructions since childhood are what reason forces him to suspend in order to be reborn as rational. Religion's hold on his obedience is clarified by what he says at the end of this maxim about law's hold on his obedience. He obeys the laws and customs as an observer of others: to discover people's true opinions observe what they do rather than what they say. Two reasons are given for discrepancies between actions and words, one external, the other internal. Owing to "the corruption of our morals" few people are

16. Caton, *Politics of Progress*, 84.

willing to say all that they believe; Descartes is decidedly not one of the foolish few. The second reason distinguishes believing and knowing: "The action of thought by which one believes a thing being different from the action by which one knows that one believes it, the one often occurs without the other." Belief often occurs without knowledge of belief. Belief is itself a form of obedience entailing submission to the believed; knowing what one believes liberates from that submission and from the actions it dictates. Rebirth as a rational being requires knowledge of one's beliefs, and to describe liberation from obedience to belief Descartes analyzes the phenomenon of obedience to law, obedience to religion kept safely out of the foreground.

Avowing that he always chooses the most moderate opinion, Descartes says he "placed among the excesses all of the promises by which one curtails something of one's freedom." Aiming to be absolutely free or governed by no law, Descartes states immediately that he approves of law: law is necessary to remedy the inconstancy of the weak-minded. Unable to legislate their own constancy, the weak-minded must have it imposed on them through policed obedience. Descartes has seen nothing that is constant in this world: the belief in constancy traditionally given as the ground for law is false. Furthermore, he is himself committed to change, to a radical transformation of himself into something not yet known to him. Capable of constancy, he lacks a knowledge of that to which he ought to remain constant, other than his rational precepts. Descartes is the precise opposite of the weak-minded: lacking constancy of will they believe they possess knowledge of the willable constant; possessing constancy of will Descartes knows he lacks knowledge of the willable. Just here Descartes reminds his reader of the apparent egalitarianism of his opening sentence: would it not be a grave indiscretion against good sense, that most evenly distributed thing, for him to bind himself by law as the weak-minded are bound?

In part six Descartes will claim obedience to "the law that obliges us to procure as best we can the common good of all men." Is this appearance of obedience to law *mere* appearance, or has something transpired in the seventeen years between the solitary reflections in the *poêle* and the publication of the *Discourse?* I think something has in fact transpired that enabled Descartes to move from a merely provisional morality to a definitive one derivable from his precepts. The law promulgated in part six represents Descartes's acquired knowledge of the choiceworthy, that to which constancy can now attach itself on the basis of knowledge. He has learned how reason can provide a new highest good, how the method of which he is the inventor can become supremely useful in a way that could not be anticipated at the beginning. The new highest good promulgated by Descartes—the new good under which the constant one can place both himself and the inconstant many—is the good of a humanitarian, scientific, technological culture. This move from provisional to definitive shows how the architect of his own house became the engineer of the new city and the prudent legislator of the new people. Obedient only to reason, Descartes legislates the new highest good, that for the sake of which one does what one does (*Republic* vi.505d).

The *Discourse* is a fable and therefore permissibly inflates the deeds of its hero but the reader who reads it with discretion will be able to temper the fable with part of the history left out: the highest good of the new people is a Baconian variant of Christian charity. It sounds enough like its Christian parent to appear pious while harboring a principle of worldly good that will break its parent's hegemony. The Baconian and Cartesian good is in its own way "parricide" (i.8). Apparently slaying the "ancient pagans" who are the actual fathers of its rational principle, it slays its apparent father, Christianity, in ways that will be made clear in *The Passions of the Soul*. It feigns judging the virtues of the ancient pagans in the way Christianity judged philosophic paganism: "insensibility" toward the hard lot of the rest of humanity: "pride" where humility alone befits the wretchedness of being human; "despair" at mortal existence where one might believe in redemption from it (i.8). But the *Passions* show how these judgments can be turned against Christianity.

Law-abiding, conforming, religiously proper Descartes places himself above law, custom, and religion as a thinker whose mind is free of mere loyalty. All the details of the first maxim follow Montaigne's "law of laws," that each man observe those of the place he is in, a law stemming from what Socrates had said about his obedience to the law and exemplified by Montaigne's own holding onto—"by God's grace"—the ancient beliefs of his religion (*Essays* i.23, "Of Custom," 86; ii.12 "Apology," 428, 436–37; in Plato's *Laws* the "law of laws" prohibits discussion of them and requires all to say in harmony that all the laws are finely made by the gods [634e]). For Montaigne, obedience to the local laws and the local religion is the teaching of Apollo who said that the true religion for each man was the one observed in the place he happened to live: what could teach more clearly, Montaigne asks, that religion is a human invention to bind society together (*Essays* ii.12, "Apology," 436)? But the law-abider who promulgates a new highest good is the law-breaker par excellence, the one who commands the laws by putting himself above them (*Essays* i.23, "Of Custom," 90; Nietzsche, *D* 496).

In the first provisional maxim Descartes looks to his appearance. Near the end of *The Passions of the Soul* (206) he again exhibits concern for his appearance and gives an illuminating reason. Having shown the roots of pride and shame and their true importance and function, Descartes states that it is good to adopt measures of the proud and shameful different from the true ones: adopt the common standards even though they are false. The reason for this duplicity is that Descartes must live among those whose judgment is false and must even be esteemed by them. Because their judgment of the proud or shameful determines what they esteem, one must seem to share their judgments in order to win their esteem. It will not do to be impudent (207). This is said with respect to the external aspect of actions: Descartes knows full well that it is not enough, given the corruption of our morals, to look to a person's actions to judge their beliefs. One who knows what he believes may knowingly act in a way that accords with beliefs other than his own, the beliefs of those whose esteem it is important to gain. Descartes too adopts the garb of "Juno's Suitor," abjectness. But the *Passions* shows that this garb is provisional and it elaborates a new palace of morals and the principles of conditioning that can make it universal.

The second provisional maxim states Descartes's resoluteness with respect to his actions while he remained necessarily irresolute in his judgments. He likens his resoluteness to the choice of a single direction that will eventually take a lost traveler out of a forest; perhaps this is the resolve to follow reason not knowing its eventual utility. But being irresolute in judgment does not preclude knowing "a very certain truth" about opinion: if we cannot discern the truest we ought to follow the most probable, and if we cannot discern the more probable we ought to follow some single course. This certain truth about the uncertain grounds of action delivered Descartes from all repentance and remorse. Once again, deliverance is contrasted with the bondage of the weak-minded. Thinking they know good and evil, their consciences are agitated by repentance and remorse for they do good and later judge it evil. Descartes's resoluteness delivers him alone from repentance and remorse, but the *Passions* show how this deliverance can be made general.

The third maxim is perhaps the most important because here the tension between provisional and definitive becomes most acute. The issue is happiness or the satisfaction of desire, and Descartes resolves "always to conquer myself rather than fortune and to change my desires rather than the order of the world." But part six makes clear that Cartesian physics promises to conquer fortune, to change the order of the world. The third maxim also makes philosophy prominent by contrasting the happy few and the miserable many: the happy few were the ancient philosophers whose intellect so mastered their desire that they achieved a happiness that rivaled the happiness of their gods while leaving to their misery the many whose intellect was incapable of curbing their desire. But part six promises a universal charity: by altering the world to meet our desires a worldly happiness is available to all. The third maxim opens a perspective on a crucial component in the program of the new legislator, one that will come into full view only very slowly and circumspectly. What begins here will be carried forward at the close of Descartes's sketch of his evolutionary cosmology in part five, a contrast between humans and animals that focuses on what has been required till now to make the human animal happy and good. That reflection on the uses of God and the soul leads to a new teaching on happiness and goodness in part six, according to which it is good to alter the world by means of the new physics in order to force it to meet our desires and make us happy. Happiness will no longer have to be the promised reward in some afterworld held out to the weak-minded in order to keep them on the straight road of virtue. Nor will happiness be the this-worldly result of a heroic mastery of desire attainable by some few geniuses of self-control. Happiness will be the result of the mastery of nature through technology: nature subdued and improved holds out the promise of meeting our deepest desires for a life of ease "and even perhaps also," Descartes says, for the postponement of death. *The Passions of the Soul* returns to this theme: opening with an affirmation of the Baconian mastery of nature, it affirms at its core a new way of mastering desire. In the first presentation of the modern psychology of conditioning, Descartes affirms the power of training to detach our natural attractions and repulsions—pleasures and pains—from their original objects and to reattach them to different objects. Human beings can be trained to be drawn to what naturally repels them and repelled by what naturally draws them (*Passions* 50), thus shrinking the distance between the happy few and the miserable many.

Descartes's third maxim trains him to believe that nothing is utterly within his power except his thoughts. Having done his best about matters external to his thoughts—but only then—anything in which he has not succeeded he will regard as absolutely impossible as far as his own bringing it about is concerned. This enabled him to stop desiring anything in the future that he would not acquire. Here in solitude, young and alone, having just framed ambitions for himself that are fit for fable, he severely curbs his expectations—with a provisional maxim. But the very method on which he has resolutely embarked holds great promise for the future. More than that, it will belong to the method to traffic in future hope, for it will promise to change the order of the world to accord with out desires. Descartes's private disciplining of hope will not prohibit him from kindling hope.

The third maxim contains a statement on contentment that is not in the least conditional: will tends naturally to desire only what intellect presents as possible. The intellect has control, even effortless control, over the will and its desires. The problem of desire is a problem of the intellect's construal of the possible. How can the intellect be schooled to present only the possible as possible, given that the intellect from its very beginning falls under the sway of appetites and preceptors which school it in false dreams of the possible?

The third maxim deals in extremes, contrasting a view that holds everything outside us to be equally impossible with various dreams of the possible. If the intellect could be trained to represent all goods outside us as equally beyond our powers then it is certain that "we should have no more regrets about lacking what seems owed to us at our birth when we are deprived of them through no fault of our own than we should have for not possessing the kingdoms of China or Mexico." We have no power at birth to give ourselves that one thing which the fable seems to emphasize is owed to us: reason. Our natural birth leaves reason subject to the appetites and preceptors it ought to master, but rational rebirth promises recovery from that fall, rational redemption. But if we can regret being deprived of reason at our birth, can we regret not possessing the ancient kingdoms of China or Mexico? China and Mexico, like most ancient kingdoms including the ancien régime of France itself, have long since been possessed by Cartesian modernism. Bacon quite explicitly imagined such conquests for his Bensalem and Descartes the Baconian seems to be anticipating the unprecedented global sway of Cartesianism in the very midst of parading Stoic restraints on his desires.

The continuation of the sentence seems to confirm this interpretation by showing what happens if we make a virtue of necessity: we surrender to alleged necessity what Cartesianism exists to overcome. "We shall no more desire to be healthy if we are sick, or free if we are in prison, than we would desire to have a body made of matter as incorruptible as diamonds, or wings with which to fly like birds." But Descartes's physics has medicine as one of its fruits: it refuses to make a virtue of the necessity of sickness. And the mechanics that is another of its fruits exists to break the bounds of natural prisons. Is it not precisely Descartes's physics that teaches us that it is possible to have bodies made of matter as incorruptible as diamonds and wings with which to fly like birds? Descartes's physics provides the intellect with new instructions on the possible and therefore disposes the will to new desires. Like Baconianism, Cartesianism is a new teaching on what to wish.

Ancient philosophers persuaded themselves that nothing was in their power but their thoughts. The new philosopher will teach new dreams of the possible, a new way to master fortune's domination: mastery and possession of nature is desirable because the earth will become a garden of Eden and our bodies immortal. This new dream takes one far from the ancient philosophers but not all that far from the dream taught the intellect by Christian preceptors. That dream taught the world to regret what was denied us at our birth into sinfulness; and it taught that it was possible to possess the ancient kingdoms of China and Mexico as Jesuit missionaries were in these very times attempting to possess them; and it taught that we could have new bodies made of matter as incorruptible as diamonds and a heaven into which we could fly like birds. By making the Christian dream seem possible on earth via the new physics, the new philosopher sets out to conquer fortune and change the order of the world.

To conclude this code of morals Descartes turns to the fourth matter—a fourth maxim in a provisional code of morals? It concerns the way of life he ought to follow (see i.3). He does not say to himself in the *poêle* what he says to the reader at the beginning of the *Discourse* that compared to philosophy all other ways of life seemed "vain and useless"—according to Plato the judgment all others make against philosophy (*Republic* vi.487b–d). Nor does he say that philosophy is the occupation most "solidly good and important" (i.3), but he does base his choice of philosophy on the same criterion: extreme satisfaction in his advancement in knowledge. The relation between his choice of philosophy and the three maxims is then made perfectly clear: advancement in knowledge gave him such satisfaction that "nothing else was of any consequence," and the three maxims were founded on his plan for advancement in knowledge. The three moral maxims are made necessary by the choice to pursue philosophy, to legislate for oneself as a rational man. When Burman referred to the provisional morality, Descartes told him, "The author does not like writing on ethics, but he was compelled to include these rules because of people like the Schoolmen; otherwise, they would have said that he was a man without any religion or faith and that he intended to use his method to subvert them." [17]

Descartes does what Socrates reported he had done at a turning point in his life: he examined the various vocations open to him and chose to remain with the one he had already taken up, philosophy (*Apology* 22e). And the reason Descartes gives, intense satisfaction, shows him to be like Socrates, a man experienced in the pleasures, one whose experience in their rank-order teaches him to spurn the pleasures of mere gain and mere honor and to pursue wholeheartedly the most intense pleasures of knowledge (*Apology* 38a, 41b; *Republic* ix.580d–583a). The three maxims hide Descartes's pleasure by his virtue; they show that he learned very early the Socratic practice of giving believable or virtuous reasons for his actions that differ from the real reasons founded on pleasure or intense satisfaction (*Apology* 37e–38a).[18] In Plato's *Apology*, Socrates gives two grounds for his choice. The first and much more elaborate ground is the injunction from the god at Delphi to which Socrates paints himself heroically obedient. The second is mentioned only once, after the jury had voted to convict him. Socrates gives this ground in response to an objection: his inability to keep silent or to live in exile, his inability to spare his countrymen philosophy. Mentioning the second ground requires stating why he had emphasized the first: his jury is likely to believe that he is dissimulating or speaking with irony if he says his practice is derived from the god, but it is even less likely to believe him if he says his practice is the greatest good for a human being, that it is based on the highest pleasure (*Apology* 37e–38a). And when Socrates addresses his friends in the final speech of the *Apology*, he tells a tale of travel to the underworld and the pleasure of speaking with the heroes he may encounter there (39e–42a)—in the underworld he would do exactly what he does in Athens though no god impels him and no city benefits. Like Socrates, Descartes grounds his practice on his private pleasure, but like Socrates he provides more believable grounds for those to whom philosophy is incommensurate with pleasure and who want to hear that practice is grounded in virtue. But while following Socrates, Descartes follows him in the still more politic way of Plato set out in the provisional maxim of Plato's *Phaedrus* (230a): self-examination requires accepting the current beliefs

---

17. *Descartes' Conversation with Burman*, 49.

18. See Strauss, *Platonic Political Philosophy*, 50. On pleasure and virtue, see Strauss, *On Tyranny*, 101.

about the traditional stories and exhibiting no envy for those who have to spend their time debunking those stories. Descartes even argues in favor of the current beliefs and attacks the skeptics who spend their time debunking those stories.

Nietzsche does not quote Descartes very often, but this statement on the pleasure of philosophy as a way of life and the consequent need to mask one's pleasure in virtue served Nietzsche as a preface to his praise of enlightenment, *Human, All Too Human*. Just here Descartes's text opens onto a vast and forbidden territory congenial to a Nietzschean history of philosophy but uncongenial, even offensive, to more customary approaches. For it harks back to the veiled inner life of the philosopher described by Plato in a veiled way that argued for the necessity of veils. That mix of high pleasure and vast ambition definitive of the philosopher is bound to appear as a vice if paraded in public. Descartes does not parade it any more than Plato or Bacon did—but Nietzsche does. Nietzsche's psychology of the philosopher, set out most clearly in the fable of *Zarathustra,* brings into the open what is carefully sheltered by previous philosophers. As if under the motto "It it important to find out from such people that they once existed" (*PTG* 8), Nietzsche takes the rash step of stripping the philosopher of his cover. Not only does Nietzsche find out that they existed, he judges that the times in which they existed were so different from the present times that it is now necessary to lift the veil on philosophy, to reveal its role in the formation of culture however much resentment or hatred or ridicule it causes.

Descartes's provisional code of morals reveals how he gained complete freedom while appearing to be bound in the ways others are bound. Each of the maxims aims at freedom from a particular kind of bondage: the general bondage to convention that rightfully subjects most people to law, custom, and religion; the general bondage to irresoluteness that subjects most to repentance and remorse; and the general bondage to fortune's domination that subjects most to sorrow and poverty because intellect gives will a poor idea of the possible. Only the rational man is free, and he is free because his intellect teaches his will what is desirable. This is the freedom of a Socrates: "It suffices to judge well in order to do well" (iii.28). Virtue is knowledge, if only for a philosopher; for the rest, for those whose intellects can never be fully guided by reason, virtue is law-abidingness fraught with repentance and remorse and prey to sorrow and poverty. The three maxims and their firm foundation thus indicate that for Descartes, as for Nietzsche, philosophy's freedom rests on its own bondage to the "strange and insane task" of knowledge, a task for which one is chosen by something unchosen, something deep down, unteachable, some granite of spiritual fate (*BGE* 230–31). And, as Nietzsche further says, "If one tethers one's heart severely and imprisons it, one can give one's mind many liberties" (*BGE* 87). The free mind can give itself a breathtaking liberty as both Nietzsche and Descartes did, the legislative liberty expressed in Descartes's first reported thought in the *poêle*. That same liberty is expressed in *The Passions of the Soul* §50, where Descartes says three times that it is "useful to know" that conditioning can break the natural bonds between thought and action formed "from the very beginning of life," that habit or custom can conquer what seems like nature in each of us, the imprint left by appetite and preceptors prior to the appearance of reason. If all can be trained, who trains the trainers? The ultimate trainer trains himself. However much Descartes aims at the common good or the happiness of all, he does not annul the radical difference separating the thinker and the rest of humanity on the possibility of freedom.

Descartes aligns himself with the ancient philosophers in the great distance separating the philosopher from the rest of humanity; but even though he is richer, more powerful, freer, happier, he sees to the well-being of others. The provisional points to the definitive: Descartes will introduce a new freedom as a hope for all, freedom from fortune's domination through the infinity of devices that master fortune; and he will introduce a new good for all: a life lived in service to the earthly common good. This is the finished structure to be built on the foundation supplied by the new philosopher, a structure that remedies what was said to be lacking in the magnificent palaces of morals built on sand and mud by the ancient philosophers: their virtues were transformed passions set on a high plateau with insufficient instructions on how to know them (i.7–8). Descartes's magnificent palace of morals will be erected on the solid and firm foundation of mathematics and he will supply instructions on how to bring the virtues within reach of everyone.

Descartes is now free to leave the solitude of the *poêle*, his provisional code of morals masking the most immodest ambition and the method by means of which it might be realized. He comes forth as a spectator on the "comedies" now being played out in the world, like the comedy of the most fanatical religious wars of history to date. For the spectator finally to become an actor on that comic stage required long preparation. Would he come forth as the dreamer of the *Olympica*? As the giver of *Rules*? As the creator of *The World*? No, he comes forth as the knight of a novel, speaking of method and showing what he can do in the sciences.

Exiting the *poêle,* Descartes invokes again the metaphor which has persisted throughout the two parts on his solitude, the house-builder (iii.29), and he affirms that he has saved the wreckage of his torn-down opinions for possible later use. Meanwhile, he continued to practice the method he had prescribed for himself, employing it to conduct all his thoughts. From time to time, he employed the method for particular thoughts which he identifies, the difficulties of mathematics and various other difficulties that he could render similar to those of mathematics by detaching them from the philosophy from which they had borrowed their principles. In the next two paragraphs, Descartes speaks of the "foundations" of a philosophy more certain than the commonly accepted one (iii.30) and invites the judgment whether the foundations he has laid are firm (iv.31). But he has just invited "you" to observe that his method can solve the problems of the sciences without the "foundations" he is going to supply in part four. Later, after having supplied the "foundations," Descartes will turn to the things more useful and more important than anything he has ever learned (v.40–41) and ostentatiously *not* connect this edifice of science and morals to the "foundations" of part four. No, part four must be the wreckage useful for making his temporary shelter conform to the standards of ornamentation supplied by the censors (ii.12). Descartes solves the problem that is "the most important thing in the world" (ii.22), the application of his method to philosophy, by liberating both science and morals from a foundation that has passed for philosophy. If his part in the comedy requires a reputation for wisdom, the way he wins that reputation shows he is worthy of it.

Part 4: Certain Certainties

"I do not know"—Descartes opens the part in which he gains absolute certitude not knowing whether he should relate it to "you." The reason given is that the first meditations he made after retiring to Holland "are so metaphysical and so out of the ordinary that they will perhaps not be to the taste of everyone." Why bother then? "In order that one might be able to judge whether the foundations I have laid are sufficiently firm, I find myself in some fashion constrained to speak." Part four will aid in judging the foundations of Descartes's philosophy. Later, he will clarify what constrained him to speak: forced to publish his physics to procure the common good of all men, he is forced to publish as their accompaniment his thoughts on the speculative sciences which are not worthy of being published for themselves (vi.61). If not to everyone's taste, Descartes seems to think these first meditations will be to the taste of those who will pronounce authoritatively on his reputation, like "the Wisest and Most Distinguished Men, the Dean and Doctors of the Faculty of Sacred Theology of Paris" to whom he addressed an elaboration of them, his *Meditations on First Philosophy*. The wonderful sophistries of what came to be regarded as "Cartesianism" include, *s'il vous plaît* (iv.34), the language of the Schools that must be explicitly dropped again before Descartes can give his scientific account of the world (v.43).

Rather than attempt a complete account of his meditations—Descartes said they would not be to everyone's taste—I want to consider only a single paragraph, the second last of this part (iv.37–39). It is addressed to those with a taste for skepticism, those "who have not yet been sufficiently persuaded of the existence of God and their soul by means of the reasons" just given. This amazing paragraph provides a definitive perspective on the whole issue of "foundations" and absolute certitude. Precisely here, where Descartes emphasizes absolute certitude and shows what is necessary to possess it, he shows that he lacks it. The affinity between Descartes and Montaigne becomes clear in their shared campaign on behalf of philosophy against an authoritative religion claiming absolute certitude.

The paragraph lifts a corner of the curtain covering the strings and pulleys of Descartes's metaphysics. It reveals in a most delightful manner his invention of what the scholars came very early to call "the Cartesian circle," for while Descartes does not "commit the error logicians call a vicious circle" in his scientific method (vi.76), he certainly does in his metaphysics. He was caught in the act by Mersenne and by Arnauld but he blithely sidestepped their objections in his replies. Father Daniel could call it "an antiquated objection" in 1690 while having some fun with it: during their layover before arriving at the sphere of the Moon on their voyage to the world of Descartes, the traveling souls meet the soul of Aristotle himself and it is he who points out that "Descartes made a circle in his method, which is the most vile and unpardonable fault that reasoning can be guilty of."[19] (The old Cartesian soul is not happy with this attack on his master and he revenges himself by shouting to the departing Aristotle: So where's the ring of fire you said lay between earth and moon?) In the long debate over "the Cartesian circle," *les doctes,* spending far more than the recommended few hours a year on these matters, have been forced to doubt Descartes's competence because

---

19. Daniel, *A Voyage to the World of Cartesius,* 82.

they cannot bring themselves to doubt his sincerity. But still more to be savored than the vicious circle which Descartes permits himself is the explanation of the possibility of certitude into which he inserts it. His own circular reasoning turns out to be an instance of the only way of achieving absolute certitude.

Descartes had proved the existence of God in an argument that has as its premise, the more perfect cannot follow from and depend upon the less perfect (iv.34)—a fine example of what Nietzsche called the metaphysicians' "faith in opposite values," their prejudice that the high and pure could never have originated out of the low and base (*BGE* 2). And now Descartes pauses to reflect on the whole matter of truth and certainty (iv.37–39). Addressing those whose skeptical temperaments make them doubt the existence of God and the soul, Descartes "would very much like" them to know that all other things are less certain—things like having a body and there being stars and an earth. The skeptical ones are told that it is possible to *dream* of a different body, different stars, and a different earth and that one will never be able to prove that such dreams are false and that our own bodies, our own stars, and our own earth exist as they seem to exist when we are awake. At just this point, Descartes introduces two kinds of certainty, moral certainty (*assurance morale*) and metaphysical certitude (*certitude métaphysique*). Moral certainty is possible about having a body, there being stars and an earth and the like—moral certainty is possible about the whole material world whose existence is in doubt at this point of the metaphysical argument. The *Principles* (iv.205) define moral certainty as "certain to a degree which suffices for the needs of everyday life, although compared to the absolute powers of God they are uncertain." It would be outrageous, Descartes says, to doubt the existence of the whole material world if it were not for a demand for a greater certainty, metaphysical certitude. This demand arises because of something we can imagine, namely, a dream of a different body, different stars, and a different earth. Imagining ourselves dreaming, we realize that our dream thoughts are no less "vivid and express" than our waking thoughts—"vivid and express" are near synonyms for clear and distinct and are used again in the final sentence of this part (iv.40). Imagining such dreams, we experience a need for a certitude greater than moral certainty. The only way to satisfy the heightened demand for metaphysical certitude is: presuppose the existence of God. On the basis of such a presupposition, and *only on that basis,* we can achieve metaphysical certitude: metaphysical certitude is *always only* the consequence of a presupposition. Inviting "the best minds" to "study this as much as they please" Descartes then makes the fatal announcement that destroys his own argument for God's existence: unless one *presupposes* the existence of God, clarity and distinctness cannot be taken as rules of certitude. This announces that Descartes's own procedure in demonstrating God's existence four pages earlier had been illegitimate: to prove God's existence he had taken as certain a proposition he could know to be certain only after he knew what the argument purported to prove.

This is the most grave matter concerning God and the possibility of absolutely certain human knowledge—and Descartes must be laughing. Are we to prefer a certitude based on a presupposition to a certainty it would be outrageous to doubt? Where do we get the outrageous doubt in the first place?—from a dream we can imagine about different bodies, different stars, and a different earth. Outrageous doubt arises because of the vivid and express dream that our whole civilization has been taught to entertain and in the pursuit of which our otherwise certain experiences of our actual bodies, stars, and earth fade into uncertainty. Descartes declares where he stands with respect to this dream: he will never be persuaded except by the evidence of his reason whether awake or asleep (iv.39). This is not the impossible claim to have brought under rational control the dreams that may trouble his actual sleep; it is the entirely reasonable claim to have brought under rational control that one dream that has most troubled our wakefulness.

The only way to achieve metaphysical certitude is to do what one committed to rebirth by reason would never do, presuppose the existence of God. This announcement, addressed to the skeptical and inviting the best minds to ponder it, makes metaphysical certitude contingent on a prejudice. In this fine way Descartes acknowledges that the new scientific worldview must unavoidably make do with truth claims whose status is lower than the status claimed by its authoritative opponent. Useful probabilities about our bodies, our stars, and our earth discovered by a wakeful science must oppose alleged certitudes about different bodies, stars, and earth that are the consequences of a dream based on a prejudice. Philosophy can never be metaphysically certain because it is not founded on a prejudice, but in its battle with the prejudiced, philosophy is free to co-opt their standard of certitude and feign it for itself. The weapons of philosophy's rhetoric are not confined to the actual limitations of probability and utility that it follows regarding its own subject matter, our actual bodies, actual stars, and actual earth.

It is a supreme moment in the history of philosophy when a philosopher takes over as his own the impossible truth claims of revelation in order to appear to ground science on those very claims. Not only does he capture the territory of the enemy, he says exactly how he does it, and he invites us to watch.

Heidegger is right: the need for certitude and the criteria of certitude are present in Descartes's work like the sacred relics of a way of salvation. But Heidegger is wrong: those sacred relics are not present in Descartes as the unconscious borrowings of a confused mind unable to transcend its historical horizons. Certitude based on clarity and distinctness represents Descartes's rhetorical appropriation of standards appropriate to a prejudice, and in this paragraph he shows those who do not simply accept him at his word how a science based on the probable and the useful can best oppose a religion based on certitudes derived from its prejudice. This paragraph shows how little Descartes depends on Medieval categories in the way argued by Gilson and others. It also shows how little Descartes is guilty of the "Calvinism" attributed to him by Richard Popkin who argued that the standard of certitude based on clear and distinct ideas was a specifically Protestant element in Descartes's metaphysics, the objectification of subjective certitude through attaching it to God.[20]

What Descartes invites the best minds to ponder is that religion as authoritative revelation is irrefutable by philosophy. It is based on an act of will that does not take its guidance from the intellect's determination of what is possible; its wisdom is founded on a passion: fear of the Lord is the beginning of its wisdom. But philosophy too is based on an act of will as Descartes's rebirth shows: prior to knowing how such a birth will mature, it chooses to accept intellect's guidance in all matters. This choice cannot be simply rational because it precedes the rational clarifications its choice makes possible. Descartes wills to submit his will to his intellect; his own choice to be rational repeats on an individual scale what Nietzsche sees as general: "How did reason come into the world? As is fitting, in an irrational manner, by accident, one will have to guess at it as at a riddle" (D 123). But the irrational origins of reason are not an argument against it. Descartes's paragraph on metaphysical certitude shows that reason cannot share in the absolute securities purchased with a presupposition by revealed religion; it can only seem to share them for its strategic advantage. "Let the best minds study this as much as they please": the Cartesian circle seems to be intended to generate reflection on the precariousness of reason.

By undermining metaphysical certitude while appearing to have de-

20. Popkin, *History of Scepticism,* 189–92, 201–2.

sired it and achieved it, Descartes puts a question to the standard of certainty. Metaphysical certitude demands proof of the existence of the things most evident to us and satisfies its demand by presupposing the unprovable existence of a being not evident to us. Moral certainty, however, is something we always have about the existence of the world and this moral certainty can include a kind of certainty attainable without explicitly raising the question of the existence of the world, the certainty of mathematics. Mathematical certainty derives from the constructive operations of the mind, clear and repeatable operations that discover useful truths applicable to the world. The existence of that world may be doubted if one wants to entertain the outrageous, being in the grip of a vivid and express dream; it may also be doubted that two plus three equal five if one demands some absolutely certain standard of measure, or presupposes a being capable of absolutely anything. But Descartes seems to acknowledge the impossibility of actually possessing an ultimate standard of metaphysical certitude in his reply to an objection raised by Mersenne. When asked for a clear and distinct explanation of his principle of clear and distinct knowledge, Descartes says that he is going to "expound for a second time the basis on which it seems to me that all human certainty can be founded." After describing the firm conviction that comes from thinking that we correctly perceive something, he adds: "What is it to us that someone may make out that the perception whose truth we are so firmly convinced of may appear false to God or an angel, so that it is, absolutely speaking, false" (*AT* VII.144–45; *PW* 2.103). "What is it to us?" It is nothing to us. But it is everything to those who want their convictions to correspond with God's. And for Descartes to yield this point is, absolutely speaking, to yield the fortress so carefully erected in the meditations. No longer can one consistently maintain that clear and distinct ideas are necessarily true of the world. "Why should this alleged 'absolute falsity' bother us, since we neither believe in it nor have even the smallest suspicion of it?" The absence of this standard of metaphysical certitude does not in the least bother Descartes however much its absence may bother Cartesians and anti-Cartesians. Called upon to defend his case for human certitude, Descartes indicates that absolute certitude is an impossible ideal and that its absence is not a cause to despair of reason. The greater candor of the *Replies* thus permits Descartes almost to admit that metaphysical certitude is impossible, just as it permits him to admit to "the philosopher" that his argument for God's existence is invalid in another way: one can arrive at the idea of God's infinite understanding by indefinitely extending the idea of one's own finite understanding, the idea of the more perfect thereby arising from and depending upon the less perfect (*AT* VII.188; *PW* 2.132).

The question of the two certainties in the *Discourse* is related to the question of the two foundations and both questions can be resolved in the same way. The metaphysical foundation invokes a standard of certitude with a single necessary ground: presupposing God exists. Descartes allows his reader to gaze into that groundless ground in the very part that purports to provide the foundation for his whole philosophical undertaking. In contrast to this metaphysical foundation stands Descartes's foundation of a mathematical physics which construes the world as matter in motion, the actual foundation of the magnificent structure of science and morals Descartes aims to erect. Those who presuppose that God exists can say: it is possible to doubt that foundation and standard. To which Descartes can reply: possible, yes, but morally outrageous and any greater security must be based on a presupposition. This can seem a draw only to those used to surrendering their reason.

This paragraph in the *Discourse* directed at the skeptical temperaments and inviting the reflection of the best minds exhibits a Descartes willing to run a Montaignian risk with his readers. Addressing his reader directly while giving instructions on how to read his book, Montaigne speaks vaguely of some indeterminate "they" who ruin his work by substituting a false meaning and twisting him to their own view. "They" refers ostensibly to typesetters supposedly responsible for crimes with his text. By blaming the typesetters Montaigne implicitly raises the question: what is Montaigne's own in his printed text? Fair-minded readers must judge for themselves, Montaigne says, when the thought is not up to Montaigne's strength and for his sake reject it as not his own. Indirect communication with readers capable of judging for themselves the relative strengths of the thoughts expressed became necessary for Montaigne because of his setting, for it is here that he describes his age as worse than any iron age known to the ancients. Montaigne's age stands to their age in darkness and naturalness as the bottom of a mine shaft stands to a mere cave. A writer at the bottom of a mine shaft cannot be free of dangers and must count on the ability of his readers to judge for themselves what is worthy of him (*Essays* iii.9, "Of Vanity," 737). It is not a difficult judgment that the blunder of the Cartesian circle is a thought not up to Descartes's strength. However, the discussion of absolute certitude in which it is embedded is Descartes at his strongest. Here the prophet of the new dream lets it be seen that the gods who spoke to him did not come to him in his sleep.

The lip service Descartes paid to religious authority has made it difficult in a sincere age to glimpse the hostility and strategic combat behind
that lip service. But like Bacon, another whose deference hides an advertisement touching holy war, Descartes defers in order to win the upper
hand against what Rousseau could call "the most violent despotism in
the world."[21] This outstanding theme for a Nietzschean history of philosophy is illuminated by Leo Strauss's remark that "the whole series of
political thinkers who succeeded" Machiavelli "were united by the fact
that they all fought one and the same power—the kingdom of darkness
as Hobbes called it; . . . that fight was more important to them than any
merely political issue. This will become clearer to us the more we learn
again to understand those thinkers as they understood themselves and
the more familiar we become with the art of allusive and elusive writing
which all of them employ, although to different degrees."[22] Descartes
employed "allusive and elusive writing" to show that his most important
fight was against the tyrannical power of those whose presuppositions
allowed them not just absolute certitude but absolute exercise of their
certitude, absolute rule. In this fight Descartes is united not only with
Bacon but with another of the post-Machiavellian thinkers for whom
this fight was more important than any merely political issue, Montaigne, for Montaigne goes out of his way to show the place this fight
occupies in his thought: it lies quite literally at the center.

Approaching the center of his first book, Montaigne states that he
has chosen to imitate the way of a painter who places his most important paintings in the best location and lavishes all his skill on them: he
puts them at the very center and surrounds them with all sorts of grotesques to draw attention to them (*Essays* i.28, "Of Friendship," 135). If
we follow Montaigne's guidance and look to the centers of his books for
matters of special importance, we find that he painted at the very center
of each of the three books essays on tyranny, the first by Etienne de la
Boétie, the other two by himself.[23] La Boétie entitled his work "Discourse on Voluntary Servitude" and Montaigne says it was "rebaptized"
as "Le Contre Un," "Anti One," and it becomes clear on studying it that
the ultimate One is God. The first of Montaigne's own central essays
(ii.19, "Of Freedom of Conscience") celebrates freedom of thought in
the face of thought control by praising the Emperor Julian, a philosopher

21. Rousseau, *Social Contract*, bk. 4, chap. 2, "On Civil Religion."
22. Strauss, *Thoughts on Machiavelli*, 231. On the kingdom of darkness, see Strauss,
Spinoza's Critique of Religion, 3.
23. Platt, "In the Middle of Montaigne," 124–43.

branded "the Apostate" by "our religion," but to Montaigne a wholly admirable man. Montaigne begins his essay by calling attention to one of the crude forms of thought control exercised "when our religion began to gain authority with the laws": in its zeal to destroy every sort of pagan book it did more harm to the learning Montaigne admires most highly than did all the fires of the barbarians. Among the books thought too threatening to exist was Julian's own *Against the Galileans*. Montaigne's anti-Christian essay implicitly contrasts an anti-Christian emperor with "the most Christian King," Henry III.[24] It had been prepared by the "grotesque" that described the freedom exercised by ancients to tell their tyrants to their face just what they thought of them and to give the lie to the fraudulent claims of rulers (*Essays* ii.18, "Of Giving the Lie"). That freedom no longer exists, Montaigne says, and he knows what caused the change but he will put off telling it. Till when? The very next essay, the central essay, describes an instance of that freedom with a Christian Bishop freely giving the lie, by his lights, to the rule of Julian directly to his face and suffering no consequence but contemptuous words. It is as clear to Montaigne as it is to Gibbon that the loss of this freedom with respect to rulers is due in large measure to the Christian capture of Roman power. The preceding grotesque had also prepared the reader to understand the consequences of Julian's failure to overturn the Christian capture of Rome by emphasizing another difference between ancient and modern stances toward truth-telling: in our age dissimulation has passed from being a vice to a virtue. Montaigne's own virtuous dissimulation enables him to tell the ruling powers just what he thinks of them; although he was warned by Rome he did not change the substance of his essay praising Julian.

But Montaigne paints his finest picture of tyranny and human freedom at the center of the final part. For there, in an essay "On the Disadvantage of Greatness," he contrasts God and man to man's advantage. Throughout the essay Montaigne sustains a contrast between the tyrant and the philosopher that seems to remain at a merely political level, ending on the tyrant's act of attempting to enslave even Plato. But Montaigne is a writer who does not draw the consequences of his stories and thoughts, preferring that his readers do that on their own (*Essays* i.40, "A Consideration upon Cicero," 184–85) and the consequence to be drawn from this central essay is indicated by Montaigne's opening sentence: "Since we cannot attain it, let us take our revenge by speaking ill of it."

24. McGowan, *Montaigne's Deceits*, 118–19.

What is "it"? This sentence and many other sentences in the essay force one to ask this question. "It" is greatness, but what is greatness? And what are its disadvantages? At this center surrounded by grotesques like what "our" religion did in Mexico and Peru, Montaigne paints his portrait of the absolute tyranny of a sovereign God whose servile regents lord it over the rest of humankind. In speaking ill of the tyranny that is God's sovereignty, Montaigne celebrates what is best in humans, the freedom that is rational thought, for the attempt to sell Plato into slavery necessarily fails: Christian Platonism carries forward in its Platonism the truth about its Christianity.

(Could Descartes have followed the way of Montaigne's painter and centered his central thought? The thirty-third of the sixty-five paragraphs gives the definitive ground of Descartes's actions [iii.27]. And the central sentence of the central paragraph—which Nietzsche quoted for *Human, All Too Human*—states that the intense satisfaction of philosophy so filled his mind that nothing else was of any consequence to him.[25])

While sharing Montaigne's profound opposition to our religion, Descartes does not simply follow Montaigne's way which requires "crushing and trampling underfoot human arrogance and pride" (*Essays* ii.12, "Apology," 327). Descartes abandons Montaigne's way in favor of the path blazed by Bacon, a dangerous path of pride which magnified man into the potential lord of the universe and offered an alternative and competing dream in direct competition to the otherworldly dream of Christianity. Following Bacon's lead, Descartes pursued a double strategy with respect to religion: while making a religion of science, he reformed the old religion in a way that made it as far as possible compatible with science. In making a religion of science Descartes elevated the standard of utility to the highest rank. Utility in providing a life of comfortable self-preservation is the standard of charity transformed in the Baconian way. In the face of a religion that promised the other world, the religion of science promised this world—new bodies and a new earth—the Baconian form of useful dreaming and the agency is man's not God's. Furthermore, although he claimed in part one of the *Discourse* that the rational examination of the truths of religion required "some extraordinary assistance from heaven" and that one "be more than a man" (i.8), the man Descartes, with no claim to assistance, presented his own reformed

25. This is the paragraphing of the 1637 edition. *AT* makes two additional paragraphs at v.56–57.

theology in parts four and five, a refitting of the available teaching on the highest beings. Descartes's version of the God of the philosophers prepared the teaching of modern deists (v. 45) through an Epicurean strategy of moving the divine to the margins of human existence, distant enough to be irrelevant, decent enough to keep hands off.

Descartes's metaphysics of God and the soul is far more than simply a "flag to cover the goods" and win a hearing for his physics as claimed by some who are skeptics about Descartes. As Gerhard Krüger has shown (and as was well known in the seventeenth century), Descartes's teachings on God and the soul, while avowing orthodoxy, are in fact not only consciously heterodox but subversive to the old teachings and serviceable to the new.[26] They represent what Caton calls "militant crypto-atheism."[27] With a reformed God made marginal to the project of the mastery of nature, the biblical God would well have become what his pious Calvinist defenders suspected he had become in Descartes's hands: the evil genius with the power to do anything—anything but persuade the solitary thinker that what he is now thinking is false. Liberation from that subrational divinity is cause for an outburst of enthusiasm as heartfelt as it is rare in Descartes's writings (*Meditations* iii.36). The thinker, the sole limit on such an arbitrary and lawless power, seems to reform that evil genius into a rational and truthful God consistent with the order of nature.

When the relationship between philosophy and religion in Descartes is understood as warfare, his role in the great revolution initiating modern times grows still greater. The historian Hugh Trevor-Roper casts essential light on that role in his authoritative study of "The Religious Origins of the Enlightenment." Describing the fate of Erasmus and Erasmianism in a time of polarized religious opinion, Trevor-Roper shows that philosophers may need to associate themselves with religious movements whose fundamental convictions they cannot share but whose political power they can use for their own ends. As Trevor-Roper says in concluding his indispensable study, "A philosopher in a time of crisis, may have to put on a suit of armor. To that suit of armor he may owe his life, and his capacity to go on philosophizing. . . . The virtue of Calvinism, in respect of the Enlightenment, may perhaps be reduced to this. As a suit of armor it proved serviceable in battle, and though more uncom-

26. Krüger, "Die Herkunft des philosophischen Selbstbewusstseins," 225–72; see Caton, "On the Interpretation of the *Meditations*," 224–45; Caton, *Origin of Subjectivity*, 66–73; Dorter, "Science and Religion in Descartes' *Meditations*," 313–40.

27. Caton, *Politics of Progress*, 61.

fortable to wear, proved easier to discard than the archaic ornamentally encrusted chain-mail which protected, but also stifled the philosophers of the rival Church."[28] Descartes of course outfitted himself with the old chain mail but his efforts seem to have been subversive to its cause, without, of course, being wholeheartedly on the side of its most apparent enemy. Like Montaigne in his *Essays,* like Bacon in *An Advertisement Touching an Holy War,* Descartes shows himself to be a philosopher who knows that we pay "dearly and terribly when religions . . . insist on having their own sovereign way" (*BGE* 62).[29]

Part 5: The Creation of the World

Part four serves Descartes's reputation, but part five presents truths "more useful and more important than all I had previously learned or even hoped to learn." These truths derive, Descartes says, from the laws of nature which he was able to discover because they are impressed on our souls. He alone discovered the laws of nature impressed on all our souls because he alone devised the method. Is this the method of part two, the mathematical-physical method whose success will be exhibited in the *Essays* and whose "suppositions" are the laws of matter in motion? Or is it the procedure described in part four, the vicious circle that makes absolute certitude possible by presupposing the existence of God? And if one says, as is the custom, the procedure of part four, then why abstain from showing the connection between the most useful and

28. Trevor-Roper, *Crisis of the Seventeenth Century,* 236–37. In many brilliant books and essays on the later Renaissance, the Reformation, and the Enlightenment, Hugh Trevor-Roper provides a perspective on the fate of philosophy in revolutionary times that seems to me to be in keeping with a Nietzschean reading of the history of philosophy. He traces the fate of the enlightened, moderate views of Erasmus in a time of increasing religious fanaticism and demonstrates the ambition and reponsibility of thinkers both to preserve those enlightened views in a dark time and to effect a politics that would moderate the warring extremes. Although he deals only incidentally with the two thinkers who seem to me most revolutionary, Bacon and Descartes, Trevor-Roper agrees with the seventeenth-century opinion that assigned Descartes a major role in ending the horrifying witch-craze in western Europe, but not because he wrote against it: as Trevor-Roper asks, why court trouble on a secondary, peripheral issue when the battle is for the center, the whole system of beliefs about nature that could make witches seem to be everywhere as enemies of the faith worthy of drowning or burning? ("The European Witch-Craze," in ibid., 181–82.) See also Trevor-Roper, "Francis Bacon," 73–77.

29. Attempts to recover Descartes's active role in the religious politics of Europe during the Thirty Years War have been made by Yates, *Rosicrucian Enlightenment,* 111–17, and Reiss, "Descartes, the Palatinate, and the Thirty Years War."

important truths and the "foundations" of God and the soul? To claim to be able to show the connection between the laboriously produced but traditional-looking conclusions about God and the soul and the radically new conclusions about the world and *not* to show it, not *ever* to show it, is most unusual if there is a connection, for what could better serve the reputation of the new physics than actually exhibiting its connection to the old metaphysics? On the other hand, there is a perfectly good reason for not showing the connection if there is no connection. And there is a perfectly good reason for alleging a connection even if there is no connection: those with control over Descartes's actions require such ornamentation.

To give a first account of the most useful and important truths, Descartes reports on a book he had written but that "certain considerations" had forced him to withhold. His report shows that the book presented a naturalistic cosmology as an alternative to the view of man and nature presented in the Bible. Only after completing his report will Descartes state that the "certain considerations" blocking its publication arose from the Inquisition's trial of Galileo. Descartes thus exhibits his "guilt" before he points to the tribunal that would have pronounced it. As a brief for the defense that presents the most useful and most important truths as matters one must be wary of publishing, part five identifies the crime before identifying the prosecutor and forces the reader to ask, Who is charging whom? And with what?

Descartes had intended to include in what would have been his first book everything he thought he knew about the nature of material things, but he curbed his original intention out of fear and proceeded instead like a painter, highlighting, shading, and omitting (v. 41–42). Writing as an artist paints, he had depicted the material world in six stages beginning with light and ending with man: his book had told a story of the creation of the world alternative to the six-step biblical account.[30] To secure his freedom and to put his view in "a slightly softer light" he pretended to write not of this world but of a new world "somewhere in imaginary space." That world begins in a "chaos" of matter in which laws of motion are present; eventually those laws bring the original chaos to an order identical to the present order. Descartes's imaginary world has laws which hold in all possible worlds, laws to which even God's will must conform (v. 43). While securing for himself the immunity due a fabulist, Descartes describes after all the world disputed by the learned, our world. Nevertheless, his pretense enables him to leave out

---

30. See Davis, *Ancient Tragedy*, 75–77.

all those forms or qualities about which disputes occur in the Schools, and without which the whole order of material things can be adequately described. Leaving aside such imaginings and presenting his own materialistic account of the world as merely imaginary, Descartes can base his conclusions on knowledge so natural that "one cannot pretend to ignore it," though one could well pretend to pretend to ignore it, as Descartes had pretended in part four where outrageous doubt in the service of metaphysical certitude apparently forced him to doubt everything and then to freely use the language of the Schools to get himself out of his outrageous doubt and back to the world of concern to us.

The rest of part five (from v. 42) presents an evolutionary cosmology that changes the order of the original six stages and adds to their number in a way that highlights the trumped up biblical quality of his first list: he does not begin with "Let there be light," he begins with an account of matter and moves to the laws of nature, the laws of motion governing matter. This second account tells how things gradually "make themselves just as they now seem" (v. 45). Beginning in a chaos of matter where matter is of specifiable kinds and motion occurs in accord with stable laws, Descartes's world evolves into a universe consisting of planetary systems similar to the local one. At this point, after the formation of suns, light can be discussed. Without providing a hint of his own Copernicanism, Descartes passes to a discussion of the earth. The earth as we observe it is the outcome of evolutionary history in which all geological formations, plants, and animals came to exist naturally over the course of time. The evolutionary account gives special notice to fire or heat and one isolated phenomenon that Descartes says he took particular pleasure in describing: the transmutation of ashes into glass with the application of heat. He calls this a natural event as worthy of "wonder" as any other event in nature (v. 44–45). Why is this prosaic event so worthy of wonder, the beginning of philosophy according to Plato and Aristotle? One reason could be that this is an event in nature where the useless is transformed into the useful. For a philosopher who aims at a knowledge of everything useful for life (i. 4) such a natural transformation is of particular value. As Ann Hartle argues, Descartes's wonder at the transformation of ashes into glass can be appreciated by studying his practice in the *Meteorology* where another wonder of nature, the rainbow, moves him to conduct the investigations necessary to understand it and the apparatus necessary to reproduce it.[31] Hartle concludes that "Descartes' task . . . is the elimination of this natural wonder at

31. Hartle, *Death and the Disinterested Spectator,* 150–52, 187.

natural things through the explanation of their nature." Natural wonder is transformed into the ability to reproduce the wonderful. *The Passions* makes explicit this reevaluation of wonder: the danger of wonder is the vice of astonishment or stupefaction in the face of the wonderful typical of those who do not have a high opinion of their competence (*Passions* 73, 77). Wonder is the passion which disposes us to the acquisition of the sciences, but we must emancipate ourselves from it by substituting for wonder acts of will that bind the understanding to attend to what we judge to be worthy of attention (76).

But there could be an additional reason for Descartes's particular pleasure in describing the transformation from ashes to glass, for here is an event in nature of which it could be said that "the more perfect follows from and depends upon the less perfect." This was the clear and distinct impossibility alleged in the argument that proved the existence of a perfect being in part four. Here, however, it seems to be a process revelatory of the whole course of natural history. Not God but nature is most worthy of wonder for a philosopher because the more perfect arises from and depends upon the less perfect in a universe that begins in chaos and culminates in human observation. Reflection on the transformation of ashes to glass shows how completely the scientific method must differ from the theological method that has captured philosophy. Theological method presupposes an original perfection of which no complete account can be given and in the face of which we cannot get beyond wonder. In part four Descartes appeared to surrender to this method as if the thinker were simply bound by its self-evidence, bound to presuppose God's existence. But in part five the more perfect is shown to follow from and depend upon the less perfect in the natural processes of the material world—Descartes does not subscribe after all to the metaphysicians' "faith in opposite values" (*BGE* 2). Descartes's view of natural processes makes it possible to imagine a new ideal of perfection: following from and depending upon the less perfect, the more perfect can be viewed as the result of a long natural history to which human beings may now contribute their conscious efforts. Time does not describe a fall away from an original perfection but an ascent to a possible perfection, the dream of which calls forth our efforts. This dream of perfection fosters the scientific method just as the Christian dream of other bodies, other stars, another earth had fostered theological method. The two methods, though presented as harmonious, one the "foundation" of the other, are in fact contradictory. And in a short paragraph which acknowledges that his treatise dealt with the creation and coming to be of the world (v. 45), Descartes draws attention to the difference of the two methods while asserting directly that the method which holds material things to have evolved naturally allows their nature to be conceived more easily.

When the suppressed treatise turned to its final topic, human beings, Descartes suspended his evolutionary principle. Instead, he imagined a being called into existence all at once, a being exactly like ourselves both inwardly and outwardly, but purely material, lacking any of the forms of soul attributed to alive things by Aristotle. Descartes accounts for aliveness by "one of those fires without light," a new animating principle of heat maintained by respiration, a natural principle like spontaneous combustion that renders superfluous any other explanation of aliveness such as soul. At the beginning of the *Passions,* the mistake of making the soul the animating principle of the body is called a very serious error, the main reason why no one has yet been able to explain the passions correctly (*Passions* 5). On the supposition that human bodies resemble animal bodies, Descartes found that he could account exactly for all of human behavior except what is dependent on thought, on our soul as Descartes understands it, that part of us distinct from the body whose nature is only to think. To account for human behavior insofar as it *is* dependent on thought, Descartes will add, after all, one of those forms about which disputes occur in the Schools, the rational soul. By dividing his account of the human into these two parts, Descartes forces his reader to be attentive to the mechanistic description of the human animal and to pay special attention to what comes last and is not mechanistic, thought: does the new philosophy have to revert at this high point to the old philosophy it explicitly set aside in order to gain knowledge of the world? Will Descartes be content to graft a Scholastic head to a Cartesian body? In the *Passions,* Descartes speaks strictly as a "physicist" and gives an account of "the entire nature of man" without ever making use of the rational soul (*Passions,* Reply to Second Letter; title, First Part)— but what of the *Discourse?*

The *Discourse* presents a mechanical account of the human heart and arteries, saying that it provides the basis for "what one ought to think of all the rest."[32] He wants his serious readers to do what he has done: have dissected in their presence the heart of a large animal that has lungs (v.47), an experimental disposition he emphasizes throughout (v.50). Toward the end Descartes announces the general principle of his account (v.54–55): the heart performs all its functions in accord with the laws of mechanics and these "are the same as the laws of nature." The laws of nature are the laws of matter in motion—three kinds of matter and

---

32. On humans as machines, see Carter, *Descartes' Medical Philosophy.*

three laws of motion as Descartes will later explain in the *Principles*. They are laws of force in which the greater force inexorably dominates the weaker; in that process the more perfect can follow from and depend upon the less perfect; moreover, that process can become predictable and potentially controllable by one who can calculate force.

At the end of his account of the human as a machine in a mechanical universe Descartes turns at last to what is not mechanical. First he deals with automata, man-made machines, and distinguishes humans from machines; then he moves to nature's alive machines, animals, and distinguishes humans from the animals; finally he adds the rational soul in the last paragraph of part five. Descartes's arguments and examples cite without acknowledgment Montaigne's famous demonstration of the resemblance between humans and animals which aimed to bring humans down to join the ranks of all living creatures (*Essays* ii.12, "Apology," 336). And the final paragraph shows that Descartes too follows what has been customary among philosophers according to Montaigne, that they speak for the sake of the well-being of the public especially on matters of religion (*Essays* ii.12, "Apology," 379), for Descartes acknowledges that he introduced the rational soul to protect the virtue of the weak-minded: it is of the greatest importance for their sake to seem to hold that humans are elevated above flies or ants in unique possession of an immortal soul.

The actual effect of Descartes's discussion of the nonmechanical, for those who take seriously his invitation to study Montaigne, is to indicate his agreement with Montaigne and the philosophers before him: there is a greater distance between human and human than between human and beast (Ibid., 342; i.42, "On the Inequality That Is between Us"). That distance is based on qualities of mind, its strengths and weaknesses— for the differences between human and human are in fact the theme of the discussion of machines and animals. The issue of a rank order of human beings is obviously a most sensitive matter, and Descartes treats it with due caution, lacking the freedom to say openly what Plato and Nietzsche, for example, dare to say much more openly, that only the rational are truly free, only those guided by reason are free to act non-mechanically, only they are, as Descartes says at the beginning of his argument, *vrais hommes*.[33] For this is what Descartes's discussion actually distinguishes: true humans and humans.

The discussion of humans and machines opens with the assertion that there is no way to distinguish monkeylike machines from monkeys but

---

33. I owe this point to a suggestion made in an unpublished paper by Janet Rash.

that there are two "very certain means" for distinguishing humanlike machines from "true humans." The first is this: "Never are they able to use words, or other signs to compose words, as we do in order to declare to others our thoughts." Descartes uses what *he* is doing, composing words and signs to declare his thoughts to others, as the first means of distinguishing true humans from humanlike machines. Language itself is *not* the criterion, for one can conceive of a machine that can pronounce the words appropriate to certain corporeal actions which have caused some change in its organs. Insofar as words are a response to stimuli received in the body they can be understood as the products of a machine. However, a machine could "never arrange them differently in order to answer to the sense of all that is said in its presence which the dullest of humans are able to do." But of course the dullest of humans are not at all able to arrange their words in such a way as to answer to the sense of all that is said in their presence; only the few are capable of arranging their words so that they say different things to different people, answering what they are asked in different ways.

The second means is related to the first, for it too concerns the capacity to adapt to circumstances, but the issue now is not the tools of adaptation, words and signs, but its ground, reason. "Although they do many things as well as, or perhaps better than, any of us, they would inevitably fail in others, by which one would discover that they do not act by knowledge but only by the disposition of their organs." To act on the basis of knowledge is to employ reason, "a universal instrument" that can serve in all possible circumstances. Does Descartes hold that all human beings act on the basis of reason? This is a "discourse on the method for rightly conducting one's reason," a fable showing how one man made the heroic effort to ground all his thoughts and actions on reason after seeing that almost all are by nature prey to their appetites and preceptors, bound to think and act on the basis of the laws and customs to which their belief binds them. Reason as a universal instrument of adaptation to circumstances is contrasted immediately with organs requiring a particular disposition for each action and therefore limited in the flexibility of their response. In the *Passions* this difference is treated openly as a difference among human beings; there, the only possible human freedom comes from winning rational control over what had hitherto been prey to the disposition of the organs of the body. What in the *Discourse* serves ostensibly as a means to distinguish humans from humanlike machines, in the *Passions* serves as a means to distinguish the free from the bound, rational from nonrational human beings.

Descartes's discussion has been elaborated under the standard invoked at its beginning and end, moral impossibility. For a second time, at a crucial point in the argument, a moral or practical qualification is introduced in a way that forces the reader to wonder about its status (see iv.37–38).[34] Here Descartes has imagined a practical impossibility, machines invented by humans having the organs and external shape of a human, in order to intimate an actual state of affairs: human machines developed by nature differ from the few true humans in the way they use language and in reason; the few true humans are those who act only on the basis of reason and who use language in such a way as to have it answer to the sense of all that is said in its presence. By emphasizing the flexibility with which a rational human being acts and writes, Descartes suggests that the difference between those who are at the disposal of their organs and those who use the universal instrument of reason is insurmountable in any practical way.

But it is possible, on the basis of the new physics, to imagine an infinity of devices for adjusting the disposition of the organs of the body (vi.62) and for adjusting the world to respond to those dispositions. Furthermore, given the vast powers of the principle of habituation, "there is no soul so weak that it cannot acquire an absolute power over its passions," not, in most cases, by reason, but by being "well guided," by being trained as setters are trained not to shy when they hear a shot, not to run when they spot a partridge (*Passions* 50). Descartes is as far as possible from *introducing* the principle of habituation, for he shows it to be the basic principle of human nature whereby appetites and preceptors frame the dispositions of the organs of the body. What Descartes *does* introduce is rational direction of the principle of habituation and while this does not make machinelike humans rational, it aligns our dispositions for the first time with reason. Reasonable machines. Descartes's vast training program for our species seems to aim at this. And the novelty derives from the word *reasonable,* not from the word *machines.*

Descartes thus seems to have made the step that Nietzsche denied him. In his own best aphorism placing humans back among the animals, *Antichrist* 14, Nietzsche says that "as regards the animals, Descartes was the first to have dared, with admirable boldness, to understand the animal as *machina:* the whole of our physiology endeavors to prove this claim." But Nietzsche's praise does not go far enough for he adds, "And we are consistent enough not to except humans, as Descartes still did: our knowledge of the human today goes just so far as we understand it

---

34. See Descartes's letters to Mesland (2 May 1644) and to Hyperaspistes (Aug. 1641).

mechanistically." Descartes in fact did not except humans, and if he did except the few *vrais hommes* he was like Nietzsche in understanding the life of reason as a long struggle to win freedom from loyalties formed by appetites and preceptors, a struggle to which one is disposed by some unasked for spiritual fate.

After distinguishing true humans and machines on the basis of "two certain means," Descartes applies these means to humans and animals.[35] And now he speaks in a comic vein, invoking examples used by Montaigne to draw precisely the opposite conclusions to those Descartes draws. Descartes begins with the extreme claim that there are no humans so dull and backward, "without excepting even the insane," who are incapable "of composing a discourse by which they make their thoughts understood"—even the insane can do what Descartes is doing and compose a *Discourse*. Montaigne used similar words for a different purpose. In the midst of his discussion of humans and animals Montaigne spoke of humans, foreigners, who could not put *French* words together to make their thoughts understood and were therefore taken to be subhuman (*Essays* ii.12, "Apology," 343). Similarly, Montaigne employed magpies and parrots, and the deaf and dumb, and the languages of animals to make the opposite points to those Descartes employed them to make (Ibid., 335–57). No one could consider Descartes's extreme assertions adequate answers to the arguments of Montaigne that they invoke. On the contrary, by using Montaigne's examples and by making his own case so extreme, Descartes makes his own distinction seem questionable. But then, his distinction is no more radical than the old one between the sensitive and the rational soul which, in its Christian usage, meant that animals have no tincture of the rational while every human has it "whole and entire" (i.3). By deriving his examples of difference from Montaigne's examples of continuity, Descartes excuses himself for having to introduce the old distinction among living beings according to which humans differ absolutely from the animals. And when in the next paragraph he introduces the rational soul, he announces his real reason for distinguishing human and animal in the old way: "If we had no more to fear nor to hope for after this life than have flies or ants" the ground of moral virtue for all but the rational few would vanish. But Descartes is building a new palace of morals and like any prudent architect he provides a temporary shelter while the new one is being built. Therefore the

35. On Descartes's "monstrous thesis," his "irredeemably fatuous belief" that animals are machines, see the reasonable response by Peter Harrison, "Descartes on Animals."

old fictions of a moral God and immortal souls will have to be sustained as a provisional code of morals for a transitional period. But the new building will be constructed by reason, and while all its inhabitants will not be simply rational, they will be trained in accord with reason.

Descartes acknowledges that these references at the end of part five are to Montaigne in the one and only place in all his surviving writings in which he names Montaigne, the remarkable letter to the Marquis of Newcastle, 23 November 1646. There, he reduces to one the two certain means in the *Discourse* for distinguishing humans from machines and animals. In the final paragraph he recites many examples of animal behavior similar to human behavior, which might lead one to conjecture that such behavior derives from thoughts similar to our own if of a much less perfect kind. Descartes has nothing to reply to this conjecture except that "if they thought as we do" they would have immortal souls as we do. And if some have them, all have them. But for imperfect animals such as oysters and sponges, "this is not credible": lest we attribute immortality to the soul of a sponge we must say that no animals have any thoughts like the thoughts of every human. Or am I boring you with this discussion?—says Descartes to the Marquis in bringing it to an abrupt close. On the contrary, we can imagine this philosophical comedy being most entertaining to a correspondent who was the patron of philosophers.[36]

The *Passions* part one, like the *Discourse* part five, contains a discussion of the heart, blood, and animal spirits, but it does not conclude with arguments for the rational soul, the soul's immortality, or the difference between human and animal. On the contrary it raises these three themes in what seems like a precise corrective to what it had been necessary to feign in the *Discourse*. The rational soul is mentioned in order to be refuted by Descartes's more adequate account of a soul without parts (47). The soul is not the place of a struggle among warring parts; rather, reason struggles with body, and "it is by the outcome of these struggles that everyone can tell the strength or weakness of his soul" (48). When the weak-souled enter Descartes's discussion this time, no fiction of immortality is introduced for their well-being. Instead, emphasis is placed on the proper weapons of the soul, judgments. Only a very few completely lack judgments with which to control their passions, but most battle passions with judgments that are false. This is not entirely to be

---

36. *Aubrey's Brief Lives,* 149. The Marquis had commissioned Hobbes to write the *Elements of Law* (1640) and been the private audience for Hobbes's political teaching. Strauss, *Political Philosophy of Thomas Hobbes,* 75–76, 78.

condemned, though only judgments that rest on knowledge of the truth spare one regret or repentance (48, 49). Just here, when reflecting on strong and weak souls and the means to control the passions, "it is useful to know" the power of habituation to break old attachments and to form new attachments (50). So great is that power "that there is no soul so weak that it cannot acquire an absolute power over its passions, when well-guided." For such guidance it is useful to know the similarities between humans and animals, for animals provide examples of the power of habituation over natural inclinations: "Since with a little skill one can change the movements of the brain in animals bereft of reason, it is plain that one can do it even better in men." The *Passions,* with its greater candor, supplies the definitive commentary on the provisional conclusions of the *Discourse* about God and the soul as grounds of moral behavior.

Laughing at the "Silly Errors of the Great Descartes"

Posterity: Never believe the things said about me unless I have divulged them myself.—Descartes (Discourse vi.70)

La Mettrie, his own argument that humans are machines freed by a century of successful struggle against the political necessities governing Descartes's argument, simply took it for granted that Descartes held the same view. La Mettrie took up the apologetic task that needs to be repeated on Descartes's behalf: defending the great Descartes against all those who have taken to laughing at him for his silly errors. La Mettrie's defense places Descartes in a century he had to enlighten and makes enlightenment require a ruse. Descartes got the theologians to swallow a poison hidden in an analogy whose point everyone but the theologians could see: distinguishing humans from animals in the way Descartes appears to, succeeds best in exemplifying the vain pride that most distinguishes this animal from others. It is obvious to La Mettrie that Descartes's manner of refuting Montaigne confirms Montaigne for all true judges and thus confirms Montaigne Montaignianly.[37]

Montaigne is ignored in our current histories of philosophy. So too is Bacon. Is that a worse fate than the indignity visited on the father of modern philosophy today wherever introductory philosophy classes meet? Novices in philosophy who will never again pick up a philosophy

---

37. Vartanian, *La Mettrie's L'homme machine,* 191–92. Similarly, Vico takes the *Meditations* to be Descartes's strategy "to rein in the cloisters" (*Autobiography,* 129).

book are taught to laugh at Descartes's silly errors and to find themselves more rational than the rational man who helped father the spiritual world they occupy. Montaigne, Bacon, and Descartes were the greatest minds of their time, but we have believed bad accounts of them even though we possessed their writings and could have seen for ourselves what they divulged. A Nietzschean history of philosophy recovers the role played by the great rational men in our past.

Any defense of the great Descartes (or the great Montaigne or the great Bacon) against those who laugh at him for his silly errors presupposes acknowledging the intellectual virtue of honest dissimulation, as Redondi called it, as well as its corollary—that Descartes's practice of dissimulation does not make him our moral inferior. With the access to Descartes gained by recognizing his esotericism, we can begin to take pleasure in laughing with him rather than at him. His great weapon of ridicule gives immense pleasure and consolidates the conspiracy: we too can laugh at the positions he opposes by seeming to adopt. Descartes belongs in a Nietzschean history of philosophy as one who knows the power of laughter, for in the long run, as Nietzsche says, every one of the great teachings of purpose "was vanquished by laughter, reason, and nature: the short tragedy always gave way again and returned into the eternal comedy of existence" (*JS* 1). The history of philosophy as the victory of comedy over tragedy, a victory very long in coming, a victory that traces a trajectory from teachings of purpose in the universe or in human history to what Nietzsche hoped could be a final outcome in "the innocence of becoming": *that* would be the way in which a Nietzschean history of philosophy could recover the monumental past and give it its due. The triumph of the spirit of Descartes over the spirit of the Dean and Doctors of the Faculty of Sacred Theology, a triumph even Plato could appreciate, for he kept a copy of Aristophanes under his pillow (*BGE* 28).

But if Descartes is to take an honorable place in a Nietzschean history of philosophy as one of the laughers, complete reevaluation of his famous dualism is necessary: the dualism constructed with the theological and ontological sophistries once necessary to make his reputation now threatens to ruin it. What was required at the bottom of the mine shaft that he shared with Montaigne and Bacon has become an embarrassment in the world formed by the physics he fathered, a world whose history of philosophy neglects the memory of the mine shaft.

Descartes's famous ontological dualism of mind and body dissolves with the recognition of his virtuous dissimulation. Mind and body as substances belong solely to the metaphysical meditations, for substance is one of those forms disputed in the Schools which can have no place in Descartes's actual physics of matter in motion. What might be called Descartes's onto-theological method begins with absolute doubt leading to the certainty of the self, a doubt usefully exercised on previous opinions in the onto-theological domain but not practiced in any account of how Descartes actually proceeded in the sciences for it ignores "what one cannot even pretend to ignore" (v.43). From the certainty of the self, these meditations arrive at God via the vicious circle of clear and distinct ideas certified as true by presupposing God. This circular reasoning allegedly provides the foundation from which to deduce all the truths of the world, but these truths, "more useful and more important" than their alleged foundation (v.41), are arrived at without it. In *The Passions of the Soul* Descartes passes up every opportunity, of which there are many, to mention a dualism of substances regarding body and soul. The soul remains "distinct" from the body but hardly separable, 'for it is the consciousness "joined" to the whole body which arises in its earliest prenatal experiences and "departs" the body at death into oblivion.

Descartes's actual method is an improved Baconianism that abandons Bacon's view of essence and form in favor of matter in motion calculable by the new mathematics. This inductive and experimental method begins with what is simplest and easiest to know; it uses sense information while determining (in the *Dioptrics*) the conditions of its possibility and hence its ontological limitations; it proceeds on the basis of hypotheses tentatively formed that it calls suppositions; it tests the hypotheses with experiments devised to elicit countercases or negative instances. And it produces results like those in the *Meteorology* with its wholly demythologized sky. The method of the new science of nature produces conclusions that make an ontological dualism laughable. The natural, evolutionary universe of Cartesian science is quite evidently monistic. Insofar as that science implies an ontology it would clearly be a monistic materialism or naturalism. And if someone says, this "may appear false to God or an angel, so that it is, absolutely speaking, false . . ." (*AT* VII.144–45; *PW* 2.103)? Who cares? When Descartes said privately that the *Meditations* contain all the foundations of his physics, he warned Mersenne not to tell anyone because it would make it harder for supporters of Aristotle to approve them: precisely on these grounds we should now tell everyone.

But is this not betrayal? Is the assiduous public disclosure of what Descartes artistically and for good reason hid behind a mask of conformity not betrayal? Montaigne supplies a marvelous warning on betrayal near the end of the *Essays,* in "On Physiognomy" (iii.12), an essay on appearances. Berating "a certain scholastic probity" that insists on saying everything just as it was, Montaigne tells two tales of his apparent vulnerability to forces that invade his privacy and threaten his ruin. In each, marauders actually take possession of Montaigne's possessions and turn him out, exposed to the elements. Ruin does not occur, however, because the leaders of the invaders, bent at first on harm, each become Montaigne's friends, transformed by his open nature and his way with his possessions. Montaigne is not reduced to begging for safety from those who penetrate his solitude and realize his possessions are unguarded. Taking possession of them without force because Montaigne willingly shares them, obliges those with whom they are shared to share them in the Montaignian manner. Montaigne's openness with his possessions disarms the intruder of any intended treachery—or it disarms the leader in each case: the others shake their heads at the leader's refusal to carry off what has fallen into his hands.

An identical lesson on betrayal is given by Francis Bacon in "On Friendship." As opened by the brilliant analysis of Stanley Fish, the essay becomes a reflection on solitude and betrayal.[38] "There is little friendship in the world" (*Essays,* "Of Followers and Friends") as Bacon's examples show, for they are all examples of secret trust betrayed. But all are also political examples among men of high ambition; in each, the trusting possessor of power is ruined by the friend in whom trust was placed. But is there friendship in the world of those who come to possess the truth and desire to entrust it to others? Bacon can trust his friends as Caesar could not for they have been made his friends by being entrusted with the gift of what he discovered. The discoveries of Bacon and Montaigne are possessions enlarged by being shared—unlike property and power they increase with their dispersal. Betrayal consists in opening such possessions to those who think them a crime.

But if betrayal once meant exposing Montaigne's or Bacon's or Descartes's reticence on things not fit to utter, have the times not made betrayal the opposite—*not* exposing that reticence? This is a question that necessarily presses upon a Nietzschean history of philosophy. Could the history of philosophy guided by open probity be condemned as the "certain scholastic probity" judged betrayal by Montaigne? Quite obviously, it seems to me that probity must now bring into the open what once had to be kept hidden; so far from betrayal, it is an act of loyalty,

38. Fish, *Self-Consuming Artifacts,* 134–55.

a service on behalf of philosophy that could aid in the warfare brought into the open by Nietzsche: the rule of religion over philosophy or of philosophy over religion. It is both pleasant and edifying to learn how Descartes fought covertly the battles fought overtly by Nietzsche.

When Descartes's virtuous dissimulation is brought into the open, he begins to look more and more like his greatest follower, Spinoza. His view too points to a complete immanentism. How far does Descartes go on this route of immanentism? Does he travel it to its Spinozistic end, the intellectual love of God or Nature, *amor fati,* that is also its Nietzschean end?

It seems to me that a beginning can be made in answering this question by looking again to Francis Bacon. In 1622, Bacon wrote to a young professor of philosophy and mathematics who had initiated a correspondence and who held promise of becoming a most valuable follower: "Be not troubled about the Metaphysics. When true Physics have been discovered, there will be no Metaphysics. Beyond the true Physics is divinity only" (letter to Father Baranzan, June 1622, *Works* XIV.377). This sounds like the physicist Descartes speaking to Burman. But what about divinity? How does the true physics construe divinity? It seems to me that one must study *The Passions of the Soul* again in order to put this question to it, for only there did Descartes—who died too soon— have the opportunity to describe the moral fruit of the new tree of philosophy, or, in his other image, describe the new palace of morals to be erected on the firm foundation of the new science. But the *Passions* must be read with care for Descartes remains as virtuous as ever, assiduously tending to his necessary dissimulation. Still, after twelve years of preparing the reader, Descartes did not need as much pious masking and could much more obviously advocate the moral teachings of the ancient pagans and clarify their opposition to the teachings of our religion. The *Passions* shows how the new view of the universe generates an edifying teaching which includes an idea of divinity and which can serve as the definitive code of morals for all humankind and not just a few philosophers—and do so without dualism.

Descartes described to Elizabeth (15 Sept. 1645) and Chanut (6 June 1647) and suggested in the *Principles* (iii.1–3) the edification implied in the true view of the immensity of the universe. And in the *Passions* he elaborated the comprehensive moral teaching implicit in his scientific naturalism, a moral teaching wholly free of Platonism's lie of moral gods and immortal souls. Morality does not depend upon belief in an invisible distributive justice legislated by forces we cannot see; it does not require the belief that they'll get theirs and we'll get ours when the final reckoning comes. The Cartesian universe is not a moral order, but it is conducive to human moral behavior just as it is.

Descartes leaves it to his Parisian friend to describe how the new philosophy gratifies; he describes in his own name how the new philosophy edifies. Only in the preface is Descartes's Baconianism elaborated, its promise of health and material well-being through the mastery of nature again serving as the argument to explain why Descartes must publish. The *Passions* itself emphasizes mastery over our own nature, intellect's dominion over will (152), the management of the passions such that we derive joy from them all (212). While our nature is in some sense defective because of what was denied us at our birth—rational control over our desires—we are not radically fallen and our subjection to appetites and preceptors can be broken, its consequences overcome wholly without divine intervention. The crucial question of divine intervention allows Descartes to unveil the place of divinity in the new physics.

Descartes follows Montaigne in this important matter, for he speaks of God or Nature (*Essays* iii.6, "Of Coaches," 686), though neither Montaigne nor Descartes was as explicit about identifying God and Nature as was the atheist Spinoza. Descartes brings God or Nature together when he recoils from the impertinence and absurdity of extending the passion of indignation "to the works of God or Nature" as is done by those who "find fault with the governance of the world and the secrets of Providence" (198). Providence. What does Descartes mean by this theological term? What is the secret governance of the world? Near the end of the second part of the *Passions* (145), Descartes raises the question of how to remedy vain desire, desire being the passion that must especially be regulated by moral philosophy (144) because desire faces the future (57) and disposes one to will the things one believes appropriate (86). Reflection on divine Providence is one of the means Descartes recommends for the remedy of vain desire, the other being generosity.

The sections aiding reflection on divine Providence (145–46) have a single aim: to make clear the difference between divine Providence and Fortune, a difference Descartes summarizes at the end as the difference between Fate and Fortune. Providence is fate or immutable necessity; Fortune is what breaks into the necessary, bringing its recipient good or ill. The thought that edifies distinguishes absolutely between Fate and Fortune by abolishing Fortune: everything that happens belongs to an unbreakable continuum of causes that rules out Fortune. Belief in Fortune depends on ignorance of causes, and Descartes's physics is the science of causes, the new science of divine Providence, the science of natural necessity which goes as far as possible to show the particular causes of particular phenomena. Its method depends in principle on refusing Fortune's intervention in the network of causes. Descartes calls the causal whole "divine Providence" but his view excludes the possibility of a particular Providence, of divine intervention into a universe of natural necessity on behalf of a few human beings. Reflection on divine Providence, in Descartes's sense, leads to the conclusion that miracle is impossible and petitionary prayer folly, but this is no cause for despair because desire can be redirected to possible goals and the universe and the human affirmed as they are—as Descartes will show in his account of generosity.

But Descartes also shows that reflection on Fate and Fortune can lead to a great moral gain when one considers just what has transpired under the moral view that God can intervene in nature. Not only is belief in Fortune false, it is morally inferior to the view that recognizes nature as an unbreakable network of causes into which no transcendent force can intrude. Descartes makes this clear with a startling denunciation of those who believe in transcendent forces and who further believe that they can discern its goals and act at its behest. Descartes's denunciation occurs in his discussion of self-satisfaction, a natural disposition of the soul befitting human beings who habitually follow virtue. This disposition is experienced as a passion when one has just performed some action which one thinks is good; this passion is a species of joy "which I believe to be the sweetest of all, because its cause depends only on ourselves" (190). Just here, describing the sweetest natural joy, Descartes turns suddenly to the satisfaction based on unvirtuous actions. It is observed particularly in those satisfied that they are "the great friends of God" for in their delusion that "everything their passion dictates to them is righteous zeal," they are capable of "the greatest crimes man can commit, such as betraying cities, killing Princes, and exterminating whole peoples just because they do not accept their opinions." Here are the starkest extremes Descartes ever draws in his continuous if never wholly explicit contrast in part three between naturalistic virtue and Christian virtue. The religious wars had continued for Descartes's whole mature life and were now temporarily halted in the reciprocal exhaustion of 1649. Such wars, Descartes says, are possible only for the friends of God—Zebedaeus and his kin—not those who base their actions on natural self-esteem. As both Montaigne and Bacon had argued, no pagan whose self-esteem begins with self, could commit the crimes of the friends of God whose self-esteem begins with God. God or Fortune, a power capable of initiating action in the world independent of natural necessity, is an arbitrary power and the moral teaching consequent on presupposing such an irrational power is morally inferior to the teaching founded on natural necessity. Can Fortune be mastered, Machiavelli asked? Fortune must be killed, Descartes answers, with a true view of divine Providence as natural necessity.

But if Nature as uncovered by the new physics can be named Fate or divine Providence, can fate be loved? Does reflection on divine Providence lead Descartes as it led Spinoza to the intellectual love of God, *amor fati?* There seems to be but a single indication in the *Passions* that it does. Descartes distinguishes the kinds of love on the basis of the esteem merited by their objects (83). Devotion is the love due objects we esteem as more worthy than ourselves, and the principle object of devotion is "without doubt the supreme divinity to which we cannot fail to be devoted when we know it as we should." How should we know it? As divine Providence or natural necessity. What is due natural necessity is devotion, a love based on knowledge, an intellectual love. And the love that originates from knowledge when this knowledge is true cannot be too great and it never fails to produce joy (139). This may be a love of God still paler than the one Nietzsche finds in Spinoza, "*amor intellectualis dei . . .* what is *amor,* what *deus,* if there is not a drop of blood in them?" (*JS* 372), but it is, nevertheless, a very large step in the direction of the love of the earth that Nietzsche's Zarathustra teaches. Yirmiyahu Yovel's *Spinoza and Other Heretics* helps open a way to this Descartes of the *Passions.* [39] Although he does not discuss the heretic Descartes at length, Yovel casts light on his work by making Spinoza's view clear: it is wholly consistent, from its highest reaches for the rational intellect to its most popular expressions on behalf of "the multitude." Yovel shows how a philosopher can take seriously his responsibility for directing the multitude to a view of things that enriches and ennobles just where it threatens to sadden and bring harm. The "emotive and cognitive halo" (140) surrounding the truly rational view is, as Yovel shows, far more than simply a ruse because it translates the highest passion, the intellectual love of God, into a worthy popular idiom.

Generosity is the other general remedy for the vain desires that most trouble human beings; along with reflection on divine Providence, it can overcome the moral teaching based on belief in Fortune. Descartes

---

39. Yovel, *Spinoza and Other Heretics,* vol. 1, *The Marrano of Reason.*

makes generosity the central theme of part three from beginning to end, the key to all the other virtues (161), the virtue that grounds a wholly un-Christian and anti-Christian system of virtues. Generosity is the virtue founded on an appropriate human self-esteem; as such it can trace its roots as a passion back through esteem to wonder, the sole passion which is beyond good and evil, beyond the immediate sense of harmful pain and beneficial pleasure. As a word, *générosité* derives its appropriateness from its etymological tie to *génétique* and *généalogie:* generosity springs from genesis and genealogy, the natural origins of natural virtue. "Genesis" surely means much more than local origins, being born to privilege in a French provincial town, say. It must mean everything that goes into the formation of what Nietzsche called the "lucky hits," all the personal, familial, social, historical accidents that come together in forming a thinker of the magnitude of a Descartes. But just how little generosity is a *laisser aller* that leaves itself at the disposal of its genesis and genealogy is shown in the fable of the *Discourse:* heroic resoluteness is necessary to free oneself from the natural attachments that form in a stimulus-response mechanism while it is under the tutelage of appetites and preceptors prior to the birth of reason. As Descartes acknowledges at the end of the *Passions,* his two remedies for distorted desire correct "our constitutional difficulties" (211); reflection on natural necessity and human merit correct the problems bequeathed to us by nature as body-soul composites which come late to the use of reason.

Generosity, in Descartes's sense, defines a natural nobility as hard to credit in a Christian setting as it is to speak about openly. Generosity is the key virtue or disposition in a naturalistic view which holds that there is a natural order of rank among human beings, that there are perspectives natural to the opposing poles in that order of rank, and that there is a natural warfare between the perspectives of those opposing poles. *The Passions of the Soul* part three is Descartes's *On the Genealogy of Morals.* Although it cannot be as explicit as Nietzsche's *Genealogy,* it presents the stark contrast between master morality and slave morality, a morality of generosity and a morality of servility in Descartes's words, and it advertises warfare against the morality of servility.

Generosity is founded on legitimate human self-esteem—Descartes's moral teaching rejects the Christian beginning point that we are so fallen that we can do ourselves no good without grace. And Descartes's statement of legitimate self-esteem is provocatively anti-Christian. Speaking of "wisdom" for the only time before the two concluding sections, Descartes calls "one of the principal parts of Wisdom" knowing "in what

manner and for what cause anyone should esteem or scorn oneself"
(152); the single legitimate cause of self-esteem is "the use of our free
will and the dominion we have over our volitions." The conclusion then
focuses the conflict between his view and the Christian view: "And in
making us masters of ourselves, it renders us like God in a way, provided
we do not lose by cowardice the rights it gives us." We cannot be like
God in any way if cowardice surrenders our dominion over ourselves to
God's dominion over us. We have no right to self-esteem if we embrace
our preceptors' cowardly view that surrendered the rights of man to the
sovereignty of God.

Having generosity makes one esteem oneself; and generosity itself is a
combination of understanding and feeling, understanding one's free control of one's volitions and feeling within oneself the firm and constant
resolution to use that freedom well (153). Such understanding and feeling lead naturally to a fellow-feeling (154), a sense of the natural kinship
among humans, all of whom are endowed with this capacity along a scale
from strong to weak. On Descartes's view, those who commit errors
are not scorned and blamed but are seen rather to lack understanding.
Descartes thus shows how generosity can ground a social ethic that does
not depend on guilt or the assignment of blame. To complete his brief
outline of how generosity and its attendant virtues can replace Christian
ethics with a more salutary view, Descartes shows that generosity leads
to a virtuous humility based on a recognition of the universal human
(155) and the human place in nature (164). Such generosity inclines one
to do great things; it leads the naturally noble to expect noble deeds
of themselves that do not outstrip their actual power to perform them
(156): Descartes derives his comprehensive moral view from the Greek
universalism of the law of nature and nations, and as Bacon showed in
Holy War, that view contains an imperative to act on its behalf. In the *Passions,* Descartes shows how generosity requires great deeds of opposition
to the Christian teaching.

Descartes thus turns from self-esteem to its opposite and contrasts the
virtues of generosity and a fitting humility with the vices of pride and
servility or abjectness (157–59). Pride, vicious pride in its most unjust
form, is characteristic of those who think they have no merit and who
think it more strenuously than the rest thus creating a difference in rank
between themselves and others; such men imagine that there is no natural
merit, that glory is nothing but usurpation, theft of a glory belonging to
another (157). These viciously proud, acknowledging no natural merit,
try to bring down the naturally high while themselves slaves to their

desires, agitated by hatred, envy, jealousy, or anger (158)—is there a more scathing analysis of Christian humility and its historic effects in the *Antichrist?* Servility is defined by dependence and the servile see themselves as wholly dependent on fortune—"grace" would not have been a good word for Descartes to have used here, and not because he is a coward afraid to say what he means: in the penultimate section of the book (211), he acknowledges that his actions have been tempered by the principle of prudence appropriate in any contest that is very unequal. Those who depend on grace or fortune believe we cannot survive by ourselves. The most servile are the most arrogant but they abase themselves around those from whom they expect some profit or fear some evil (159). The contrast between master morality and slave morality continues in this vein throughout part three. "Soul," "divine Providence," "humility,"— Descartes, like Bacon, is "studious to keep the ancient terms" (*Advancement, Works* III.352). But like Bacon he knows how to make those terms work for his own ends. If they appear at first to endorse the old dualism, study of their use shows that they subvert it.

But if the principle utility of moral philosophy is the regulation of desire (144), has Descartes not developed after all a moral philosophy useful only to the very few? Is Descartes not after all like the ancient pagans who failed to instruct us sufficiently on how to know the virtues (i.8) or like the ancient philosophers who secured their own happiness while leaving the rest of the world to their misery and bondage (iii.26)? His morality too could seem to be an Epicurean retreat from the prevailing morality which it can refute but which it lets be. When Descartes refers in the penultimate section to "A General Remedy for the Passions" (211), he admits "that there are few people" who could apply his remedies for they require "forethought and skill." Although Descartes then goes on to define what he calls "the most general remedy," it too is a remedy of self-control and discipline that one might think too intellectual and austere to be practical in any general way. But at the end of part three who will have forgotten the end of part one, with its affirmation of the principle of habituation or conditioning and its arresting example of the power of conditioning to break the natural attachments and forge new ones in those who are well-trained? It belongs to a teaching on the rank order among human beings to recognize that the highest is rarest. If the virtue of generosity is possible in its most exquisite forms only for a very few, it can nevertheless, with its associated and derivative virtues, provide the grounds for a new teaching on morals for everyone. And at the end of part three who will have forgotten the preface with its inflated account of the global benefits of the Baconian-Cartesian teaching, a teaching attentive to the dream in whose midst it finds itself because it openly redirects to earthly ends the fully awakened desires for ease and immortality? Descartes knows where he is and how he must speak; he knows that the new morality of generosity must adopt in altered form the ends of the firmly implanted morality of servility.

In that part of "the eternal comedy of existence" (*JS* 1) which is western civilization on the planet Earth, the few philosophers have mounted the stage to play a role on behalf of the rational. As an actor in those special comedies playing themselves out in Christian Europe in the first half of the seventeenth century, the rational man Descartes had to adopt the local mask of gravity, and that mask can make it look now as if he had been a dualist who compromised not only with the irrational but with its morality of servility. But in masking himself Descartes looked to his reputation, and in looking to his reputation he looked to the reputation of philosophy and to its active philanthropy on behalf of the human. Peering back from this point in the long run of the eternal comedy, we can recover Descartes as one of the masked actors who vanquished our own teaching of purpose with "laughter, reason, and nature." By teaching a few to laugh where it was absolutely forbidden to laugh, Descartes initiated the "waves of uncountable laughter" that overwhelmed "even the greatest of these tragedians." "Consequently?"—Nietzsche asks— "Do you understand me, my brothers? Do you understand this new law of ebb and flood? There is a time for us, too." There is a time for the laughers, for a joyous science of the innocence of becoming.

Before taking leave of Descartes let us enjoy one last laugh prepared for us by the mocker whose outward calm and inward joy contrasts with those enemies turned pale by the inward revenge they plot (200). How can those who are accustomed to reflecting on their actions react when unexpectedly attacked by some enemy (211)? If they feel the desire for revenge inciting them to pursue their attackers, they have to "recall that it is imprudence to lose oneself when one can save oneself without dishonor." *The Passions of the Soul* ends on this moderate advice echoing earlier, more extreme advice about the soul: "For whosoever will save his life shall lose it: and whosoever will lose his life for my sake shall find it" (Matthew 16:25–26). For Descartes it is imprudent to lose oneself, better to save oneself "if the contest is very unequal." And what is more unequal than one mocker against a whole world of zealous believers with control over his actions? Rather than "expose oneself senselessly to certain death" in such a contest "it is better to make an honorable retreat or ask quarter." Descartes does not retreat, he "asks quarter." In the Thirty Years War "ask quarter" was the cry made famous at the battle of Magdeburg where the helpless population asked quarter and no quarter was given. In revenge for that horrifying slaughter, "Ask quarter!" became the cry of the slaughterers to the slaughtered. "Magdeburg quarter" it was called, "Ask quarter!" the slaughterers cried and gave no quarter. Descartes asks quarter. And I prefer to think that Descartes asks Magdeburg quarter: "Ask quarter!" cries the lone mocker as he descends upon the mocked and he gives no quarter.

Gratitude, says Descartes, is a species of love excited in us by some action on the part of the one to whom we are grateful, by which we believe he has done us some good (193). Gratitude toward Descartes befits a Nietzschean history of philosophy. And if that gratitude must be tempered by recognition of what the Cartesian project has engendered, it can, in thinking through those consequences and a possible remedy for them, follow the naturalism of Descartes to the naturalism of Nietzsche.

Part 3

Another Genuine Philosopher

Chapter 10

Nietzsche and the History of Philosophy

We are Hyperboreans. We know the road, we have found the exit out of whole millennia of labyrinth. Who else has found it?—*Nietzsche (A 1)*

No Windelband or Copleston, Nietzsche as a historian of philosophy is beyond writing précis on the great philosophers of the Western tradition fitting them into some perspective still local to that tradition. No Hegel, Nietzsche is far from supposing that our history can all be knit into a great seamless garment of self-praise for us who stand, happy and wise, at its end. No Heidegger, Nietzsche refuses to resign himself to the ineffable, that gift-giving something or other, neither he, she, nor it, granting the thinker that which is to be thought. No, Nietzsche as a historian of philosophy is a "Hyperborean": he dwells beyond the north wind and takes the view from there.

A Hyperborean? In this nice image befitting a philologist Nietzsche lays a pleasant claim to something audacious, a perspective on the past both unique and true. "*We* are Hyperboreans," Nietzsche says, but he admits elsewhere that "I say 'we' out of politeness" (*TI* Reason 5). Pindar gave up ever finding a way to the Hyperboreans: "Neither by land nor by sea shalt thou find the road to the Hyperboreans" (*Pythian Odes* 10)—and they became a beautiful symbol of the inaccessible. As himself a Hyperborean, Nietzsche claims to know the road, but more than that, he claims that knowing it opens the whole geography of the past: "We have found the exit out of whole millennia of labyrinth."

Bacon, Descartes, and Nietzsche

If the aim is to understand the history of philosophy from a Hyperborean perspective, why leap from Bacon and Descartes to Nietzsche? Because to do so brings one whole stretch of the road into clearer view: modern times. The leap from Bacon and Descartes to Nietzsche is a leap from two founders of modern times to the first postmodern thinker. As a historian of philosophy, Nietzsche shares the virtue of Bacon's Cassandra: he knows where he is. He knows he does not stand in some ideal republic nearing the end of history but in the dregs of Bacon and Descartes. Nietzsche is the first philosopher to re-think the Baconian and Cartesian project from the perspective of its relative completion. He allows us to observe the consequences of the Baconian ascendancy, for in his writings the character of modern times is luminously articulated: our progressive view of history, our heed-less rape of nature, our fiction of scientific certainty via a method of counting, and, most comprehensively, our ideal of the common good. In Nietzsche, modern times are revealed as embodying a comprehensive myth construing time as progress, beings as malleable, and human well-being as the meaning of the universe. From a Hyperborean standpoint outside modern faith, modern times can be evaluated as perpetuating a philosophical tradition that can be traced through Bacon and Descartes back to Plato. And always with the Nietzschean disposition: "Let us not be ungrateful."

There is a second reason for leaping from Bacon and Descartes to Nietzsche when the goal is understanding the history of philosophy: together they illumine the respective ranks of philosophy and science. Bacon advocates the ascendancy of Salomon's House while recognizing the supremacy of philosophy; Descartes surrenders glory to the prac-titioners of his method without surrendering the supremacy of phi-losophy. They share the "Nietzschean" view of philosophy according to which "genuine philosophers . . . are commanders and legislators" who "first determine the Whither and For What of humanity" (*BGE* 211). Nietzsche's understanding of the philosopher helps to recover these advocates of science as revolutionary philosophers who elevated science to the first public rank knowing philosophy's actual first rank. Recipro-cally, the monumental examples of Bacon and Descartes make plausible Nietzsche's extravagant claims for philosophy.

Furthermore, the philosopher's art—not just philosophy's rank—is illuminated by juxtaposing Bacon and Descartes and Nietzsche: all three are master practitioners of the esoteric. "Too little philology"—with re-spect to Nietzsche we are still guilty of the crime of which he convicted his contemporaries. "I tell every one of my friends to his face that he has never considered it worth his while to *study* any of my writings" (*EH* Books *CW* 4). Study of Nietzsche's writings brings appreciation of his own brand of esotericism. It differs from Bacon's and Descartes's partly because they succeeded: Nietzsche lived in times dominated by public science and hence by "the youngest virtue," honesty or intellectual probity. Nietzschean esotericism does not consist in some masking process of noble lying. It consists, first, of insight into the distance separating perspectives, a distance of rank; and, second, of communicating that insight in such a way as to elevate to the high, to school in the esoteric. Just how problematic this task is in a democratic age can be seen, amusingly enough, in the refusal of almost all of Nietzsche's advocates to see themselves as "philosophical laborers," a Nietzschean term of high praise, if not the very highest praise (*BGE* 211). Instead, they want to think of themselves as a band of "genuine philosophers," though where in our work are there paragraphs worthy of inclusion in *Beyond Good and Evil,* to say nothing of a *Beyond Good and Evil* itself, or whole decades of such works? One of the tasks of Nietzschean esotericism is to school in the unavoidability of esotericism, to demonstrate a fact unwelcome to a democratic age: philosophers like Plato, Bacon, and Descartes are so sovereign that they could presume to become educators of humankind—and succeed.

Reading Nietzsche should be like reading Bacon and Descartes: the reader I deserve, Nietzsche says, "reads me the way good old philologists read their Horace" (*EH* Books 5)—and good old philologists did not mistake themselves for Horace. "It is not for nothing that I have been a philologist," Nietzsche says, describing the gains of his long discipline: "Philology is that venerable art which demands of its votaries one thing above all: to go aside, to take time, to become still, to become slow. . . . It teaches to read *well,* that is to say, to read slowly, deeply, looking cautiously fore and aft, with reservations, with doors left open, with delicate eyes and fingers" (*D* Preface 5). Nietzsche's lost art of reading presupposes his discovery of the lost art of writing. Having rediscovered that art in the great thinkers of the past, Nietzsche wrote to share his rediscovery with his readers, opening the history of philosophy, the whole history of culture, in a new way. Reading Bacon and Descartes slowly and deeply prepares the reader for Nietzsche's own enigmatic or esoteric style.

And here we encounter a final reason for leaping from Bacon and Descartes to Nietzsche: the study of Bacon and Descartes opens the road into Nietzsche's true radicalism. They aimed to shelter philosophy from the public and the public from philosophy—Nietzsche aims to bring philosophy out from behind its shelters and to construct a new accord between philosophy and the public. Nietzsche's openness, his rashness, his betrayal of Platonic sheltering, forces a confrontation with perhaps the most profound and problematic of all the issues of Nietzsche's thought, his true radicality: Can a human community be built on the deadly truths known to philosophy? Bacon and Descartes shelter philosophy in a global, post-Christian scientific humanism, but Nietzsche aims to make philosophy not only post-Christian but posthumanism, to free society from all forms of humanism based on myths of special origins that confer on humankind special rights of dominance and mastery over nature. Nietzsche's thought is a post-Baconian naturalism, a complete immanentism affirming the natural order, an ecological philosophy dubbed "joyous science" by Nietzsche. "My Mission: the dehumanization of nature and then the naturalization of the human after it has gained the pure concept of nature" (*KGW* V 11 [211]). Nietzsche's destruction of the many humanizations of nature—shadows of dead gods—is far better known than the other, constructive part of his work, the naturalization of the human—his groundwork for a human society that affirms the natural order as it is.[1]

Can a human community be built on a thoroughgoing naturalism or immanentism? Study of Bacon and Descartes prepares the student of philosophy to pore over Nietzsche's writings with this core issue of Platonic philosophy constantly in mind. Why abandon the intellectual virtue of honest dissimulation and betray its practice in the greatest minds who have ever lived? No mere probity or moralism governs the first immoralist's choice: the times dictate what is necessary for philosophy. The rise and dominance of modern science makes Nietzsche's "experiment with the truth" (*KGW* VII 25 [305]) unavoidable. So far from being the whim of a rash philosopher who would rather risk everything than practice a little caution, Nietzsche's experiment is a task thrust upon him by the history of philosophy. He did not choose his task, he was given it—if in a sense different from what Heidegger meant by this judgment. The new history of philosophy made possible by Friedrich Nietzsche includes understanding the present task of philosophy, Nietzsche's work, as an undertaking on behalf of art and truth. Nietzsche's great politics of philosophy exceeds in scope even the philosophic politics of Bacon and Descartes, and it does so because it inhabits a world reordered by Baconian politics.

1. Georg Picht's *Nietzsche,* one of the most instructive books on Nietzsche, exhibits this radicality and defends it. While demonstrating the inner coherence and comprehensiveness of Nietzsche's thought, Picht defends it against the misunderstanding of its most influential interpreter, Heidegger.

Appreciation of the high politics of Bacon and Descartes—their way of having the whole future of humankind on their conscience (*BGE* 62)—prepares one to appreciate Nietzsche's high politics. The prim view is still heard that the philosopher Nietzsche did not lower himself to mere politics, but the study of his writings confirms that he is a political philosopher on the grandest, the Platonic scale: he writes as an enemy of nihilism, as a philologist and philanthropist. A Nietzsche scarcely discovered yet can be enlisted for the only possible long-term politics, the global politics of a planet about 4.5 billion years old, with about 4.5 billion more years to go before our expanding sun vaporizes it and transforms every molecule. Nietzsche's thought grounds a postnationalist politics that loves the earth as humanity's home, a politics that could no more side with modern humanism and the now appalling rights it has granted humans over the community of life that sustains it, than it could side with dead theisms that single out the human as the one thing worth saving from an earth worth damning. Nietzsche's language and themes are very different from those of Aldo Leopold, say, or Wendell Berry, eloquent voices for a land ethic and love of the local; nevertheless, Nietzsche provides a comprehensive grounding in ontology and history, being and time, for the love of the earth. Nietzsche's perspective—cosmic, evolutionary, enlightened, combining philosophy with art—grounds a deep ecology and a new sense of the edifying for the human species.[2]

The argument of my book is that a new history of philosophy can be written on the basis of Nietzsche's thought, one that can make a defensible claim to know the road, the exit out of whole millennia of labyrinth. That history is based on a comprehensive new understanding of the human and of nature: it is not simply a reordered look at the past. The Hyperborean view of the human and of nature cannot be considered in isolation before turning to the history of philosophy; nor can the new history of philosophy be considered in isolation from the new view of the human and nature. The Hyperborean view is historical in its essence and treats culture as a whole: "What matters most is always culture" (*TI* Germans 1).[3] Nietzsche's style is dictated by the indivisibility of his themes: aphorisms on the history of philosophy are always embedded in a setting of aphorisms on culture, psychology, history, religion, the free spirit, as well as the old themes of epistemology and ontology in their

2. See Hallman, "Nietzsche's Environmental Ethics."

3. Blondel, *Nietzsche*, 51: "The problem of culture in Nietzsche has been underestimated, and yet it forms the origin and center of his thought."

new Nietzschean form. Nietzsche could not compartmentalize either his thought or its presentation: because so much was new and odd, everything had to be said at once. A proper presentation of Nietzsche's history of philosophy seems to require that it be considered in the settings Nietzsche himself provided. Therefore, in turning to Nietzsche himself, this fragment of a Nietzschean history of philosophy turns to two of Nietzsche's works, one pre-*Zarathustra,* the other post-*Zarathustra.* The great differences between the two serve notice that *Thus Spoke Zarathustra* is both the turning point and the high point of Nietzsche's writings. *On the Use and Disadvantage of History for Life* sets out a civilizational project in the teeth of the essential and perhaps fatal problem of truth, deadly truth. *The Joyous Science* Book Five intimates a resolution of that problem in a new stance toward truth. The first work is an artistically crafted essay on the theme of remembering and forgetting. The second seems to be a haphazard shoveling together of random thoughts at the end of an already completed book. In fact, however, it is typical of Nietzsche's later assemblages: its coherently developing argument represents a consistent and comprehensive viewpoint. Together these works show that Nietzsche is an affirmative thinker with a comprehensive philosophical perspective who aims at nothing less than a spiritual renewal of the now global West and whose art of the aphorism is the proper means of enticing others to his task.

Chapter 11

Philosophy and the Deadly Truths

Leering out of the writings of my first period is the grimace of Jesuitism: I mean the conscious holding on to illusion and forcibly incorporating that illusion as the basis of culture.—Nietzsche (KGW *VII 16 [23]*)

But Nietzsche was never a Jesuit. Even as early as the *Use and Disadvantage of History for Life*—a work whose basic ideas come from a time prior to *The Birth of Tragedy* (*HH* II.Preface)—Nietzsche expressed his anti-Jesuitism: he did not advocate the conscious holding on to illusion. He stated openly what Jesuitism hushes up, that truth is deadly: "The teachings of the sovereignty of becoming, of the fluidity of all concepts, types and kinds, of the lack of any cardinal difference between man and the animals—teachings I consider true but deadly" (*UD* §9). Nietzsche did not conclude that these deadly truths could be covered up and some illusion, new or old, forcibly incorporated as the basis of culture. Instead, his book is an appeal to find some way to reconcile truth and life.

From the holy lies of the law of Manu, to Plato's noble lies, to Jesuitism itself, Nietzsche was a student of the history of salutary lying, of the "pious fraud" of moralists and "improvers of mankind" (*KGW* VIII 15 [45]; *TI* Improvers). Though perhaps tempted to continue the fraud, believing as he did in the "deadly" character of the three basic truths, Nietzsche's "experiment with the truth" began early. And he knew the stakes were high: "Perhaps humanity will perish of it," says his Zarathustra in an unpublished note (*KGW* VII 25 [305]). The *Use and Disadvantage of History* is an early and important probe in this experiment. It depicts the conflict as one in which life lies and truth kills. Truth and life are never reconciled in the book, but their conflict is presented as the greatest problem of modern life, one that must be solved if a recovery of cultural vitality is ever to occur. The book is therefore "pre-Nietzschean," it antedates the reconciliation of truth and life that *Thus Spoke Zarathustra* exists to present. Still, it exhibits *the* Nietzschean problem with great force and relates it to the history of philosophy.

As one of four *Untimely Meditations*—"assassinations," Nietzsche called them (*EH* Books, The Untimely Ones 2)—the *Use and Disadvantage of History* describes modern times and kindles spiritual warfare against it, against "the historical sense" in particular, or, more broadly, the contemporary understanding of science. Can one stand against one's time? Can a scientific and historical man like Nietzsche stand against his time in its regard for science and history? In claiming to be *unzeitgemäss* Nietzsche claims to have achieved what the *zeitgemäss* hold to be impossible: to have leapt over his own shadow, in Hegel's image; to have become a stepchild of his time and place, in his own image; to have understood his age other than it understands itself and to have understood it truly. How did he do the impossible? How did he change his parentage? By becoming a child of the Greeks, Nietzsche says, and of Schopenhauer and Montaigne, educators who inspired in him an ideal of philosophy other than the *zeitgemäss* one that bound philosophy to its times as their summation in insight. Monumental exemplars of the possibility of transcending one's place and time in understanding bred an offspring in Nietzsche.

No solution to the problem of "too much history" can come from having less. As Nietzsche said explicitly in his 1886 preface to volume two of *Human, All Too Human,* "What I had to say against the 'historical sickness' I said as one who had slowly and with great difficulty learned to convalesce and who was in no way willing to do without 'history' just because he had suffered from it." Historical education is itself the precondition of resolving the modern problem of history, science is the precondition of resolving the modern problem of science. Nietzsche later recognized that his early attempt to transcend his age was not fully successful: "This sort of lament, enthusiasm, and dissatisfaction" shows that in fact he belonged "to the most modern of the moderns" (*KGW* VIII 2 [201]). But that recognition is no surrender; he does not deconstruct the very attempt to transcend his age and reappraise youthful excess as youthful folly. Rather, the confession of early failure presupposes later success.

The *Use and Disadvantage of History* is a systematic and sustained argument with the details filled in. Nevertheless, Nietzsche's friend Rohde criticized this essay because "You deduce all too little, instead you leave more up to your reader than is fair or desirable" (letter to Nietzsche, 23 March 1874). Jorg Salaquarda cites this letter as one of two critiques of his essay that gave Nietzsche pause, forcing him to reflect on his future as a writer.[1] It must have seemed even less fair or desirable to Rohde, but

1. Salaquarda, "*Studien zur zweiten unzeitgemässen Betrachtung,*" 1–45, citation p. 12. On *UD* see especially, Müller-Lauter, *Nietzsche,* 34–65.

the direction Nietzsche took as a writer was to leave still more up to the reader.

I have changed Nietzsche's order of presentation to focus on the themes especially relevant for the history of philosophy. I begin with Nietzsche's presentation of the present age as "the end of history," a still timely view, Hegelianism gone to cynical seed. This historical fiction leads to Nietzsche's description of the three uses of history; if these three were fused, Nietzsche suggests, the recovery of the past could be more adequate. But the uses of history raise the problem of justice, a pervasive problem in Nietzsche's work which here receives a paradigmatic formulation. Justice, giving things their due, opens the decisive perspective on truth and life. If our philosophic tradition is grounded in Platonism, a kind of self-conscious Jesuitism, where has its offspring, modern science, left modern humanity in the old conflict between truth and life? How can advocates of life also be advocates of the true?

The End of History (chapters 5–9)

Modernity's self-interpretation is debilitating and false, contrary to life and contrary to truth. A now-forgotten book by a now-forgotten Hegelian bears the brunt of Nietzsche's timely blast in its final crescendo, but the view attacked is anything but forgotten: it is the interpretation of the modern as the fulfillment of history, the interpretation which received its most fundamental expression in Hegel, was carried forward by Marx and subsequent defenders of modernity as "the end of history," and is now reaching the newspapers as if it were the latest flash of insight.[2] According to this view, history is linear and meaningful as the progress of human freedom and enlightenment culminating in a global society free and wised-up. Nietzsche follows Hegel in seeing this self-interpretation of modernity as a Christian inheritance. But these two philosophical sons of the Protestant manse differ in that Nietzsche views Christianity as "a" religion, not the ultimate and final religion. Both well know that all religions are destined to leave godless heirs, but for Nietzsche Christianity leaves its godless heirs believing dangerous fictions about themselves.

Modern belief in progress is "disguised theology" (§8), a Christian reform movement whose mission includes destroying older forms of Christian belief, in particular the Christian God. Using the tools of modern science, especially modern historical or philological science, it

2. See Kojève, *Introduction to the Reading of Hegel*; Cooper, *End of History.*

triumphs over those older forms by killing their myth of origins with philological weapons, by demythologizing their sacred text. Privileged to witness the death of Christianity at the hands of historical science, Nietzsche poses a general question: can art or religion as spiritual powers survive the historical sense?

According to Nietzsche, the death of the Christian God will be experienced by liberated former believers as self-confirmation. Products of Christian prophecy, they will believe that they have been born into the fullness of time, that they stand at the end of long historical struggles as history's last possible outcome, history's chosen people. This is a mature variant of the Baconian religion which holds time to be meaningful when construed as progress toward the future achievement of the common good: that future has come, we are the posterity for which our forebears sacrificed themselves. Thus, Nietzsche's answer to his own question, "Can religion survive the historical sense?" is yes; religion survives the historical sense *as* the historical sense. Modern historical science demonstrates the mythic character of nonmodern beliefs, but it is carried forward by its own mythic faith that history is progress and modernity the desirable end of history (§8). Nietzsche raises five points of opposition to modern historical society (§5) culminating in the final item, modern presumption or arrogance which wants to believe that the universe exists for the sake of creating modern humankind.

But modern plundering of the past to confirm its faith in the present cannot last because it harbors contradictory beliefs. Belief in historical study is bound to destroy belief in history as progress; the historical conscience is bound to destroy its own unhistorical assumptions. Therefore, at the "culmination" of history, modern historical humans will judge history's efforts not worth the cost. Modern religion breeds its own proper heretics, cynics of the new faith whose self-knowledge justifies their cynicism: if we are the select of history, history has labored in vain. The cynic thus provides the service to the philosopher of history that Nietzsche described in *Beyond Good and Evil* (20), for in the cynic's words one hears the truth behind the modern religious fictions. This truth is bound to persuade the most spirited moderns to despair of their own time and place; spiritual decrepitude inherits the very age taught to believe itself highest and best.

Nietzsche's analysis of modernity culminates in an expression of concern for modern youth: given the surfeit of history that cost us religion and art, youth will come to believe that the only worthy pursuit is serving one's own interests. Modern individualism culminates in small ego egoism. Modest, self-interested pursuit of personal gratification follows necessarily from the myth that the actual as lived by modern humankind is the ideal: there is nothing great or magnificent left to do. Further, the modern myth elevates the state as the instrument facilitating prudent egoism among equal citizens; it rereads the whole of the past as egoism, drawing a moral distinction between the foolish or ambitious egoisms of the past and the prudent egoism of moderns (§9). This early version of Zarathustra's speech on "the last man" is offered as a description of what young moderns are subjected to by their educational institutions. And just here Nietzsche comes into the open as a participant in this debate among believers: neither Christian nor modern nor cynic, he is a friend of the young, one who knows what it is to be young and spirited, and—not incidentally—one who knows how to inflame the young with provocative words that ridicule their authoritative teachers and seduce them to himself.[3]

Nietzsche does not mourn the disappearance of the sacred past of Christianity, and he does what he can to disparage the sacred present as understood by the historical sense, but he becomes an active participant in the debate only in his refusal of complicity in the death of the future. The passion of Nietzsche's book stems from that refusal, as does its rhetoric: he too must find or create coconspirators. As a participant he is buoyed by optimism—we can conspire to assassinate the debilitating lies told by our teachers.[4]

Part of Nietzsche's appeal to youth, *his* corruption of the young, redirects their understanding of the past. History written under the influence of the modern myth reads the whole of the past as a struggle for freedom and enlightenment against slavery and ignorance. This history is written from "the standpoint of the masses" as a justification for modern mass democracy; it aims to discover the "laws" that have governed historical change, the primary law being that the masses are the moving agent of history while the exceptional ones, great men thought once upon a time to have been responsible for historic change, are mere "bubbles that become visible on the flood" (§9). Nietzsche aims to write the history of the West from the perspective of the "bubbles"—masters, though masters must be understood in a Nietzschean and not a Hegelian sense: the greatest thoughts are the greatest deeds and the great think-

---

3. The significance of Nietzsche's appeals to youth in modern democracy is beautifully set forth in Cavell, *Conditions Handsome and Unhandsome,* 33–63.

4. Dürr, "Young Nietzsche," conclusively refutes Paul de Man's historicist reading of this essay.

ers have played a legislative role in history. Philosophy, though always embedded in a setting to which it responds and which it aims to alter, is a decisive player in the history of culture, as Nietzsche recognized from the beginning. It is not its age summed up in thought; it is not as inoffensive as an owl; it comes late but not always too late.

Gathering the means to successfully overcome Hegel and the Hegelians on the meaning of history took most of Nietzsche's mature life, for it was a philosophical, psychological, and historical task of the first magnitude. Only with the complete genealogical method in hand could Nietzsche recover "that eternal basic text of *homo natura*" (*BGE* 230) and undertake the comprehensive rethinking of the Western past required by his opposition to Hegel. This informed anti-Hegelianism demonstrated that philosophy had been an active participant in culture and not a re-active contemplation of it, and it required that philosophy become active again, with one of its first tasks being the destruction of Hegelian stu-pidity. Gilles Deleuze's *Nietzsche and Philosophy,* one of the best books ever written about Nietzsche, shows how successful Nietzsche was in this re-gard while advancing the fight against Hegel's contemporary advocates.[5] A Nietzschean history of philosophy contests the predominant Hegelian view on all the major issues, in particular the social role of philosophy itself.

Nietzsche's Uses of History (chapters 2–3)

The monumental, antiquarian, and critical uses of history arise from three different dispositions: to act and strive, to preserve and admire, to suffer and liberate. But the three can be united in the disposition toward the past characteristic of the man of the greatest "plastic power."

> The stronger the roots of the inmost nature of a man, the more of the past will he assimilate and appropriate; and were one to con-ceive the most powerful and colossal nature, it would be known by this, that no limit of the historical sense would exist for it by which it could be overwhelmed and damaged; the whole of the past, its own and the most foreign, it would draw to itself and incorporate into itself and as it were transform into blood. (§1)

This ideal of spiritual strength takes concrete form in Nietzsche's later writings. For a brief but almost indelible moment, it bears the name

---

5. E.g., Deleuze, *Nietzsche and Philosophy,* 162, 195.

"superman," but later it becomes the "complementary man" (*BGE* 207, 28; *GM* 1.12). Always it is Nietzsche's ideal of the philosopher, the thinker of the most comprehensive strength, who bears responsibility for the future of humankind (*BGE* 62). Nietzsche's history of philosophy necessarily focuses on these legislative thinkers.

Monumental history belongs to those who aspire to great deeds; they are elevated and sustained in their sense of what is possible for them by great exemplars from the past. These men of action may at first seem to be political and military leaders and monumental history to be the mirror of princes, but Nietzsche's examples are Schiller and the men of the Renaissance, examples that emphasize the monumental character of thought and art. The man of action in the highest sense is the philosophical educator and the greatest monuments for the greatest actors are the writings of philosophers: "It is important to learn from such men as Heraclitus that they once existed" (*PTG* 8), for they are the monumental models of what is possible for a thinker. One of the dangers faced early by such solitary actors is the awareness of not having a single friend of their own kind (*SE* 3). As Montaigne said, such men are so rare that friendships between them are still more rare, perhaps once in three centuries. Therefore such men must find their friends, their like, in the past—as Nietzsche himself was still discovering for he was just beginning to study intensely an educator whom he now ranked above even Schopenhauer: Montaigne. Five years later, in the final aphorism of *Assorted Opinions and Maxims* (408) Nietzsche gave poetic expression to his gratitude toward his own monumental examples:

> I too have been to the underworld, like Odysseus, and will be there often again; and I have sacrificed not only rams to be able to talk with the dead, but have not spared my own blood as well. There have been four pairs who did not refuse themselves to me, the sacrificer: Epicurus and Montaigne, Goethe and Spinoza, Plato and Rousseau, Pascal and Schopenhauer. With these I have had to debate when I wandered long alone; from them will I accept judgment, to them will I attend when they judge one another. Whatever I say, resolve, think out for myself and others, upon these eight will I fix my eyes and find theirs fixed on me.

The antiquarian nature emphasizes preservation of the local, a sustaining familial history grown sacred to memory and dignifying even the small—this pathway, this gate, this sign of my continuity and rootedness. But Nietzsche's two examples of the antiquarian spirit are Goethe and the founders of the Renaissance and these examples attest to the highest task of antiquarian history: preserving in human memory what is great. The primary example of antiquarian history comes late in Nietzsche's book, when he describes the task of history as keeping open the dialogue among philosophers (§9). The few philosophers are the highest exemplars of humanity, the goal of humanity, and they constitute a kind of bridge across the stream of becoming. Preserving the past makes it possible for such thinkers to live in "timeless simultaneity," a "republic of geniuses." The highest task of history is to keep open the possibility of renewing that spiritual dialogue and undertaking such great deeds again.

But for monumental and antiquarian history to become possible again in the way Nietzsche describes, an act of liberation is required: critical history must be exercised on the historical sense itself and the bulk of Nietzsche's book does just that: it drags the present myth of the past before the bar of judgment, interrogates it, and condemns it (§3). Neither justice nor mercy guide the judgment of such a critical historian—life itself does. Such a condemnation of the present can endanger a whole age. But reckless acts are part of the life of the human species for "human nature" itself is the product of such acts: human nature is always only an acquired "second nature," a transformed "first nature" which itself was also at some earlier time an acquired second nature. Viewing human history as these sequential transformations, Nietzsche launches a transformation of what now seems like human nature, an undertaking dangerous for the whole age. It is dangerous for him too: he will seem like a teacher of evil and his teaching will seem to deprive the age of everything honorable or moral. Still, it is a monumental deed for which there are noble precedents.

The massive outlines of Nietzsche's lifework take recognizable shape at this early point. His anti-Hegelian understanding of the philosopher allots the philosopher an active role that Hegel's historical piety assigns to Providence or Logic—to magic at work in the unconscious actors of history like Alexander or Caesar or Constantine. What is the current task of the philosopher? Not composing some *Heilsgeschichte* on the wising-up of the universe and collective entry into eternal rest at the End of History. Rather, disclosing the unholy spiritual history of the West and setting forth a new understanding of time and beings. Nietzsche's mature thought combines monumental, antiquarian, and critical history: while attempting to preserve the whole of the natural past in human memory, it abolishes the myth of providence, and it generates a perspective which enables humankind to celebrate its natural place among beings. Opposition is bound to arise: if modern historical culture "had any courage or resolution at all," as it sometimes does, it "would banish philosophy" (§5). Modern opposition to philosophy subverts philosophy by calling *itself* the true philosophy: at the end of history any change is change for the worse. Philosophy *verwirklicht*, Hegelian science or wisdom, tolerates no rivals: mere philosophy belongs in the dustbin of history.

Justice (chapter 6)

Nietzsche's decision to come forward as the first "immoralist" submerged his insistence on justice despite its presence in his work from beginning to end.[6] Justice lies at the heart of Nietzsche's work but as something more than condemnation and punishment: justice is giving things their due. In the *Use and Disadvantage of History,* justice is considered in its narrow aspect of giving the past its due, but the book also reflects on justice in the broadest sense.

Justice first appears in the troubling reflection on the unhistorical in chapter one: it is troubling that the man with a wider horizon, a man of greater justice than the man with a narrow horizon, is less able to act and less sure of the justice of his actions because more attuned to nuance and the likelihood of error. Made tentative by his greater learning, made forgiving by his greater justice, historical man lacks the single-minded vigor of unhistorical man. Life itself seems to favor the ignorant and the unjust by granting them decisiveness and self-assurance. How can an age "justifiably proud" of its knowledge and its justice be lively and healthy?

Justice is the theme of chapter six. Its first paragraph puts a genealogical question to the celebrated justice of modern objectivity: is the motive of justice really fundamental here? Before pronouncing his no, Nietzsche describes justice in what is perhaps the most remarkable paragraph of the whole book. What is the relationship of the true and the good— fact and value in diminished contemporary usage? This question is at the core of Platonism and will remain at the core of Nietzsche's thought. By examining this question, the second paragraph of chapter six provides a clear portrait of Nietzsche's understanding of the philosopher.

Nietzsche elevates justice to the highest rank: justice is constituted of the highest and rarest virtues. Because they are themselves highest and rarest, nothing beyond them can give them warrant. Human justice is

6. Picht frees Nietzsche from Heidegger's slanders on the issue of justice by interpreting the aphorisms Heidegger misinterpreted (*Nietzsche*, 96ff., 122ff.).

unfathomable or ultimately ungrounded because men are not gods: they cannot base their deeds on certain knowledge. Even the most sublime man cannot know his justice is grounded in the true, he cannot be a god or a superman. Nietzsche's text is full of singular superlatives—there is no higher man or measure than what he here describes. What raises a man to "the most solitary height" and makes "him the most venerable exemplar of the species" is the ascension in excellence from the rare to the most rare, from generosity to justice: higher and rarer than open-handed giving is justice, giving what is due. Clearly Nietzsche is speaking of a justice grander than the application of some already present code of just and unjust; he is speaking of the giving of such codes, the bringing of a new good and evil or good and bad, the founding act of the philosophic legislator.

Such legislation is always brought as the truth and Nietzsche says that the highest exemplars of humanity desire truth but that they desire it in a form foreign to modern truth-seeking, for they are anything but dispassionate. Nietzsche finds dispassionate objectivity entirely appropriate for science's "factory workers," but he is speaking of quite different beings here. The highest exemplars desire truth in order to legislate; truth provides the sacred legitimation of their justice. The rank order is clear: the passion for truth can be worthy of great respect only where it is driven by the unconditional will to be just. That apparently most Nietzschean of questions here comes to the fore: Why have truth at all? Why not much rather untruth?—For the sake of justice, for the sake of the highest good.

The highest men are those whose love of the truth serves their pure will to justice. These solitary few are further reduced in number by Nietzsche's final claim: the pure will to justice is accompanied in only the rarest cases by the strength to actually *be* just—a strength of judgment and not of will, a strength that distinguishes the highest exemplars from their look-alikes, *fanatics* whose will to justice is not guided by the strength of judgment that reveals the just to them. Again, Nietzsche is categorical: humanity has suffered most at the hands of fanatics whose passionate justice lacked judgment. The abyss opens: if justice is grounded in judgment and if the highest exemplars of justice are legislators distinguishable from fanatics only by the strength of their judgment with respect to the truth, who can separate Judge from Fanatic?

The *Use and Disadvantage of History* reaches its deepest point in this seemingly irresolvable predicament: how can anyone avoid being reduced to silence or to arbitrary words in separating the Judge from the Fanatic? The rest of the book makes no pretense to solve this issue, but having opened a perspective on it, Nietzsche invites others to share it as a predicament whose solution must be attempted. One further specification is made before the book falls into its necessary silence: modern times masked the predicament in a fraudulent solution; it welcomed a reduced understanding of truth as disinterested inquiry by an army of inquirers equipped with the proper method. This modern ideal of truth served the modern ideal of justice as the common good of all men, understood as comfortable self-preservation.

The *Use and Disadvantage of History* is pre-Nietzschean: having glimpsed the fundamental task of philosophy as love of truth and justice, Nietzsche can criticize the injustice of the modern ideal without grounding that critique in a more adequate understanding of either truth or justice. Still, even fragmentarily glimpsed and inadequately grounded, justice makes one inexorable demand—disloyalty to fraudulent solutions. Nietzsche's call to break faith with modern religion aims to produce the real heretics of modern times: not mere cynics but critics whose attack looks to a still unformulated ideal. If deconstruction is the highest form of justice that Nietzsche can yet formulate, he nevertheless calls his drive for a new understanding of truth and justice a *Bautrieb,* a drive to construct (§7), an active drive in religion and art.

Science (chapter 10)

The *Use and Disadvantage of History* argues that modern historical science is bound to expose its own contradiction and dissipate its energy in egoism and cynicism. But already Nietzsche's question is, what next? What follows the end of history? In posing this problem—the problem of nihilism in his later vocabulary—Nietzsche points to an aspect of Platonism that he found neglected.

In his final chapter, Nietzsche turns to Plato's account of the noble and necessary lie in the *Republic* (iii.414b–415a), the most famous instance of "Jesuitism" in the tradition, of forcibly incorporating conscious illusion as the basis of culture. Nietzsche does not call the lie noble, it is simply "a mighty *necessary lie*" forced on the first generation of the perfect city. And when the lie comes to be believed? "Impossible to rebel against such a past! Impossible to go against the work of the gods." Emphasizing Plato's belief in the necessity of false belief, Nietzsche announces his anti-Platonism: Plato aims to educate a first generation of believers whereas Nietzsche aims to educate a first generation of unbelievers. He wants to wreck modern faith in history as progress, to smash a faith with the truth about it.

Plato's definitive account of the necessity of belief in lies did not end with the noble and necessary lie, for he returned to this theme as the last item in his account of the philosopher: a defining mark of the philosopher is the capacity to endure the necessary lie. Socrates' speech grew passionate as he gazed at Philosophy herself and saw her spattered with mud because of those who bore her name unworthily (*Republic* vii.535c, 536c). The tale of the changeling child that he then told made it beautifully graphic that the citizen's virtue is founded on a lie of origins and that tampering with that lie—telling the citizen the truth of origins—wrecks his virtue and wrecks the city. Only a maimed soul, only a bastard philosopher, would insist on telling the truth under those conditions (vii.535c–539b). The philosopher, lover of truth, will have to learn to endure the necessary lie and not become incensed when others hail as truth what he well knows is a lie. Platonic philosophers like Bacon and Descartes are marked by such endurance. Nietzsche is not. From the perspective of Platonic philosophy Nietzsche is a maimed soul recklessly bent on publicizing deadly truths.

The question to put to Nietzsche from the perspective of Platonic philosophy is: why was he not able to endure the necessary lie? He saw its necessity: the *Use and Disadvantage of History* is a long meditation on the deadly character of truth. His intellectual conscience forced him to conclude that it is a stupidity to suppose that the universe exists for the sake of one species of beings on one small planet. But if this is a life-supporting stupidity is it not necessary to endure it? Why insist on the rash and immoderate course of creating a generation of unbelievers in the faith of their fathers?

Is it just personal taste, personal defect, that made it impossible for Nietzsche to endure the lie? The answer is obviously No. Just as Nietzsche is hardly responsible for the death of God whose consequences he charts, he is not responsible for the now unendurable character of the lie: he is not responsible for the rise of science as a public enterprise or for its explosion of the mythic foundations of all societies including its own. It is no longer a question of enduring a public lie—the public lie is in the process of being publicly exposed by the intellectual conscience of science. The philosopher Nietzsche knows that he dwells in the dregs of Bacon and Descartes where a public science earnestly and inevitably destroys the faith on which it was built. Voltaire said that the high clergy of his time could hardly look at one another without laughing. What Nietzsche described as the high clergy of his own time, the authoritative believers in science, could exercise no such ironic levity towards themselves; they permit no gap between what they believe and what they are taken to believe. In the novel setting created by a successful public science, a new problem is posed for the philosopher who retains the Platonic conviction that the truth is deadly. And in the *Use and Disadvantage of History* Nietzsche *is* a Platonic philosopher in this sense: he holds that the sovereignty of becoming, the fluidity of all concepts, types, and kinds, the lack of any cardinal difference between human and animal, are all true but deadly for if they were flung at the people for one more lifetime, Nietzsche says, the people would perish of petty egoism and greed and cease to be a people (§9). But Nietzsche is the first Platonic philosopher who knowingly refuses to cast his lot with the salutary liars. He refuses any form of Jesuitism.

Honesty or intellectual probity is the youngest virtue, Zarathustra said (*Z* 1.3), and virtues are marked by jealousy (*Z* 1.5). Caring only for its own supremacy, youthful honesty wreaks havoc with established virtue. Virtuous havoc is inflicted by the sublime ones (*Z* 2.13), modern truth-seekers willing for the sake of their virtue to cause all others to come into what the Nietzschean poet William Butler Yeats called

> the desolation of reality:
> Egypt and Greece good-bye, and good-bye, Rome.[7]

Nietzsche sees this happening, helps it happen, and describes what happens next: when the virtue of honesty loses its power to sustain hope without losing its power to sustain action, the result is bitter cynicism for the wise few and petty egoism for the wised-up many. Nietzsche judges the time for Platonic esotericism to be past; its necessary presuppositions have been destroyed by the intellectual conscience of modern science which had long fed on the Christian belief that "the truth shall make you free" (John 8:32).

But Nietzsche has a second reason for telling the truth about modern faith: it is unsalutary. Belief in ourselves as the end of history is not merely a stupidity bound to collapse because it is untrue, it is a debasement of humankind that endangers what is best in it. And when virile modern faith collapses into egoism and cynicism, the situation will not have improved; the nihilism that supplants modern faith will itself have to be overcome.

Nietzsche's fully articulated response to the death of Platonism appears first in *Zarathustra,* but the pre-Nietzschean response of the *Use and Disadvantage of History* is valuable for its anticipations of that later

7. William Butler Yeats, "Supernatural Songs, Meru," *The Poems,* 289.

view. Not necessary lies, Nietzsche says, but necessary truths provide the foundation for educating the new generation. But if truth is deadly, how can truth be medicinal? Medicinal truth appears here as the "unhistorical" and the "suprahistorical," medicines that science is bound to regard as poisons. The unhistorical is the ability to forget and to fold oneself within a horizon; the suprahistorical is art and religion that bestow the character of the eternal and stable upon life. No wonder science views these as hostile powers, for they seem in principle to place limitations on science as inquiry. And when Nietzsche then goes on to say that "science requires superintendence and supervision" he seems to surrender science to the hostile powers. Is this where Nietzsche leaves science, under the jurisdiction of powers that would limit its inquiry? Nowhere does Nietzsche come closer to Jesuitism, masking the truth in some conscious illusion.

The book is over except for one final injunction addressed to those now hypnotized by its theme: Consider the Greeks. The Greeks were a people open to all the influences of their neighbors, and they were the people who invented science. While open and inquiring, they were powerful enough to organize the resulting chaos of perspectives into a unitary artistic whole. The book ends giving no new principle of organization, no positive means for overcoming modern chaos, but recommending the Greek conception of culture "as a new and improved *physis*" which "every increase in truthfulness must also assist to promote."

New and Truthful Greeks

Nietzsche leaves science in apparent conflict with the unhistorical and the suprahistorical while expressing a pious hope for the advancement of culture through the advancement of truthfulness. What happens to the opposition between science and the unhistorical and suprahistorical in the rest of Nietzsche's work? Book Five of *The Joyous Science* will show that Nietzsche never abandoned truthfulness or science, and that he never abandoned the suprahistorical as art and religion, but that he did abandon the unhistorical or what looked like the need for forgetting. In the *Use and Disadvantage of History* Nietzsche is dubious of the possibility of living with science's aim "to abolish all limitations of horizon and launch humankind upon an infinite and unbounded sea of light whose light is knowledge of all becoming" (§10). But this very image of the "open sea" comes to define Zarathustra and Nietzsche himself. So far from a willed forgetting, the later work is a call to remembering, a genealogy open to the whole of natural history and holding it in memory. Nihilism—not Nietzsche's thought—is forgetful, "unfaithful to its memories, it lets them fall, lose their leaves" (*KGW* VIII 10 [43] = *WP* 21).[8] Nietzsche's later work sets a task for which there is no precedent and against which precedent argues: a society founded on the deadly truth about origins and ends.

But what about the suprahistorical? What about art and religion? Could the eternalizing powers of art and religion exist in harmony with science as inquiry and even contribute to science's love of inquiry? Is there an art and religion of the unbounded? Nietzsche defined the suprahistorical—art and religion—in what seems to me an unparalleled way in another of his pre-Nietzschean books, *Richard Wagner in Bayreuth.* Humankind is put in need of art, Nietzsche says, because of human suffering, which is defined in a remarkable way: "That all human beings do not share knowledge in common, that ultimate insight can never be certain, that abilities are divided unequally." These three represent "the greatest suffering that exists for the individual" and all three derive from a kind of injustice bound up with what humanity simply *is* as the species conscious of life: the knowing that defines humanity's being cannot be ultimately fulfilled and it cannot, even in partial fulfillment, be equally shared. The profound injustice of life makes it impossible for the being conscious of life to be simply happy, moral, or wise:

> We cannot be happy so long as everything around us suffers and creates suffering; we cannot be moral so long as the course of human affairs is determined by force, deception, and injustice; we cannot even be wise so long as the whole of humankind has not struggled in competition for wisdom and conducted the individual into life and knowledge in the way dictated by wisdom. (*RWB* 4)

How can life be endured? By recognizing "in our struggles, strivings, and failures something sublime and significant." Just here the art of tragedy enters: tragedy contributes to the ability to endure by teaching us "to take delight in the rhythm of grand passion and its victim." Tragedy is the art that aims, in Nietzsche's image, to retie the Gordian knot, to draw together the single chaotic strands of a diverse cultural heritage and secure them in a cultural unity. Of course, tragedy simplifies and

---

8. Bernard Yack argues that "self-conscious forgetfulness" persists as Nietzsche's "paradoxical" demand throughout his work (*Longing for Total Revolution,* 334–36, 340–41). But Yack's citations (*SE* 6, *A* 3) do not justify his claim that Nietzsche's revolution depends upon making ourselves willing dupes of ignorance.

abbreviates but it does not refute or contradict "the endlessly complex calculus of human action and desire." Modern times make the problem of tragic art still more difficult for the individual, not simply because of increasing complexity but because simple beliefs in the meaning of life are now unbelievable. And "the harder it becomes to know the laws of life, the more ardently do we long for this appearance of simplification . . . the greater grows the tension between general knowledge of things and the individual's spiritual-moral capacities. Art exists *so that the bow shall not* break."

Art has an indissolvable bond to knowledge and to the human character as knowledge-seeking. Art does not relax the tension between the "general knowledge of things" and "the moral-spiritual capacities" of human beings; rather, it makes it possible to live in that tension. So far is Nietzsche from being a utopian who dreams that art should translate us out of a deadly reality. Tragedy, not comedy, is the highest form of art: no comedy like the Christian comedy can be supposed true given modern knowledge, nor can the modern comedy of Baconianism. "May sane reason preserve us from the belief that humanity will at any future time attain to a final ideal order of things. . . . No golden age, no cloudless sky is allotted to the coming generation . . . neither will suprahuman goodness and justice span the fields of this future like an immovable rainbow" (*RWB* 11). Increasing knowledge forbids us the utopian modern dreams heir to utopian religious dreams: the whole of section four of *Richard Wagner in Bayreuth* argued that eclipse of the dreams of oriental antiquity, particularly those of Christianity and its heirs, requires a return to the Greeks: "The earth which has now been sufficiently orientalized, longs again for the Hellenic," and in particular for Greek tragic art. But how can tragic art be revived in a modern setting? How can modern knowledge and the sufferings it brings be transfigured in tragic art?

> The individual must be consecrated to something higher than himself—that is the meaning of tragedy; he must be free of the terrible anxiety which death and time evoke in the individual: for at any moment, in the briefest atom of his life's course, he may encounter something holy that endlessly outweighs all his struggle and all his distress—this is what it means to have *a sense for the tragic*. (*RWB* 4)

The knowledge made public property by modern science gives this sense for the tragic a precise focus:

> And if the whole of humanity is destined to die out—and who dares doubt that?—so the goal is set for it that is its supreme task, so

to grow together in one and in common that it sets out as a whole to meet its coming demise with a sense for the tragic. (*RWB* 4)[9]

If Platonism or Jesuitism sheltered us from our mortality by letting us believe ourselves immortal, modern science makes it plain that our very species is destined to extinction. But such knowledge assigns us a task.

All the ennoblement of humankind is enclosed in this supreme task; the definite rejection of this task would be the saddest picture imaginable to a friend of humanity. That is my view of things! (*RWB* 4)

Nietzsche's hope rests on the birth of modern tragedy. Modern tragedy incorporates modern knowledge, insight into that greatest of dramas, the innocence of becoming. If Nietzsche's hope still rested on Wagner when he wrote this soaring passage, he later recognized his mistake as being "the absolute certainty about what I am projected on some accidental reality" (*EH* Books *BT* 4).

The *Use and Disadvantage of History* ends with the pious hope that truthfulness can be served by art and religion. *Wagner in Bayreuth* defines the hope with greater precision but imagines it could be met by Wagner. Part one of *Thus Spoke Zarathustra* reenacts these preliminaries: it depicts a still young Zarathustra buoyed by hopes that someone else, some future superman, could perform the "impossible" task. But *Zarathustra* continues past the point where the young philologist Nietzsche had to stop, for it describes the discovery of the anticipated teaching. In setting the task for his contemporaries in the hortatory close to the *Use and Disadvantage of History,* and in describing Wagner's task throughout *Wagner in Bayreuth,* Nietzsche set forth his own task, one that he would begin to fulfill in the summer of 1881 when the thought of eternal return took him over. For eternal return is, in Platonic language, the new highest good, the sun of a new fundamental moral judgment and highest standard of value (*JS* 7), but one that beautifies and makes sacred the hitherto deadly truths.

In the winter of 1883–84 Nietzsche sketched the outline of a book to be titled *The Eternal Return.* Balancing its italicized subtitle, *A Book of Prophecy,* is its italicized conclusion: *Antithesis of Jesuitism* (*KGW* VII 24 [4]). The teaching of the eternal return is the birth of modern tragedy, the artistic transformation and celebration of the deadly truth. It is the antithesis of *Jesuitism* because it too embodies an educational politics which

---

9. Unfortunately, this sentence is omitted from the Hollingdale translation.

aims to provide a "basis for culture"; but it is the *antithesis* of Jesuitism because it is an "education to a universally human politics" which celebrates the truth of nature instead of forcibly incorporating a conscious illusion.[10]

The *Use and Disadvantage of History for Life* has this outcome: Nietzsche opposes Platonism. This triviality gains weight as soon as Platonism is understood as Nietzsche understood it: Platonism is the tradition of politic philosophy which judged that truth is deadly to community and must be covered in salutary lies grounding moral behavior. And Platonism enjoyed unrivaled supremacy in ancient and modern versions: lies of transcendence and lies of progress through mastery. But ancient Platonism and modern Baconianism share a refusal of sovereign becoming in favor of being, a refusal of the fluidity of all concepts in favor of timelessly true concepts, and a refusal of the human kinship with the animals in favor of some cardinal difference between human and animal. Such lies have now become completely transparent and untenable but at great cost: cynicism and egoism justly conclude our tradition of salutary lying. Refusing that outcome while exposing its logic, Nietzsche opposes Platonism by raising again the fundamental question of the true and the good. And he does so in the name of an experiment: can a people be built on the deadly truths? Instead of the still cautious conclusions of the *Use and Disadvantage of History,* Nietzsche's later view reflects what Wolfgang Müller-Lauter calls "a change in the evaluation of the worth of history."[11] Nietzsche's mature "philological genealogy"—to use Eric Blondel's shorthand—requires the wholesale reconstruction of the history of humanity, the truthful view of our natural past. And in that new view, the history of philosophy comes to light in a Hyperborean way.

10. On Jesuitism, see *HH* I.55, 441; *WS* 158; *BGE* Preface; "Homer's Wettkampf," *KGW* III, vol. 2, p. 283; VII 25 [263].
11. Müller-Lauter, *Nietzsche,* 51.

Chapter 12

Joyous Science I:

The New History of Philosophy

You ask me about the idiosyncrasies of philosophers? . . . There is their lack of
historical sense, their hatred of even the idea of becoming, their Egyptianism.
Be a philosopher, be a mummy, present monotono-theism while dressed up as
a grave-digger.—Nietzsche (TI Reason 1)

Nietzsche's history of philosophy breaks with the old idiosyncrasies
while having some fun with them. But fun aside, humanity "has
paid dearly" for taking the old philosophers seriously, and Nietzsche's new history of philosophy helps reckon the cost: Nietzsche
never supposed that philosophy was an idle enterprise with little
effect on what humans actually do. His new history of philosophy
traces its causes and effects from a wholly new vantage point, one
that the *Use and Disadvantage of History* could only hope would be the
achievement of some still future explorers and adventurers.

But having become a Hyperborean who knows a wholly new
road, Nietzsche now faces the problem of having to say everything
at once. Recovery of philosophy's past depends upon seeing it as
part of the larger history of culture. And glimpsing the great events
in that comprehensive human past depends upon a new view of the
human soul and of humans in groups—a new psychology and a new
sociology. And these in turn depend upon solving—to a degree at
least—that oldest and most difficult of philosophical problems, "the
way of all beings," Zarathustra called it (Z 2.12). And all of these
together require solving the problems of interpretation: the situ-
atedness of the interpreter, the limits of insight, and the limits of
communication.

Nietzsche's way of presenting his history of philosophy acknowledges these great difficulties: his history is always embedded in settings that address the whole nest of problems faced by a Hyperborean interpreter. *Joyous Science* Book Five provides such an account

of the history of philosophy. It does not contain all the details of Nietz-sche's thoughts about philosophy and its history, nor does it provide all the grounds necessary for the judgments it does contain. But Book Five is typical of Nietzsche's procedure of enucleating philosophy within the setting of issues that made its enucleation possible. Book Five shows how Nietzsche tried to solve his problem of having to say everything at once.

The Joyous Science Book Five

The Joyous Science occupies a special place in Nietzsche's writings, as noted on the back cover of the first edition (1882): it is the last of a series of writings whose common goal is to erect a new image and ideal of the free spirit. Given some of the flightier connotations of "free spirit," it seems better to translate *Geist* as mind: Nietzsche's ideal is the free mind, mind unencumbered by the heart, by mere loyalty, by faith or ob-stinacy. When Nietzsche said the series on the free mind was complete, he knew exactly where his own work was taking him: seven months earlier, in August 1881, on long walks from Sils Maria, his thought of eternal return had appeared to him, and in the following winter, on long walks from Rapallo, Zarathustra had waylaid him as the vehicle for the thought of eternal return. *The Joyous Science* ended on these themes, the first intimation of eternal return (341) and the first appearance of Zarathustra (342). The last of the series on the free mind is the first post-eternal-return book, the first book to be written in the awareness of that fundamental and transforming experience. Eternal return is present ex-plicitly only at the very end, but it is present implicitly throughout as the ground of good cheer; the thought of eternal return makes *The Joyous Science* the book of a convalescent.

In bringing the series on the free mind to a close and preparing for *Thus Spoke Zarathustra,* does *The Joyous Science* mark the end of Nietz-sche's long submission to the impersonality and objectivity of science, their abandonment in favor of the personal and subjective? Many have read Nietzsche this way. But *The Joyous Science* itself suggests that the turn is a turn into the grounds of science, a deepening of Nietzsche's understanding of science and by no means an abandonment of it. The turn is nevertheless both personal and prophetic: personal because it is in Nietzsche's own experience as a thinker that the grounds of science became accessible, and prophetic because what *Zarathustra* teaches is the future grounding for science that enables it to carry forward what is highest in humanity, open inquiry into the enigma of beings. The form of *Zarathustra,* its being a fable rather than a treatise, has made it appear unscientific despite the advocacy of science throughout and the culminating debate on the meaning of science in part four.

But if *The Joyous Science* is special due to its place in the sequence of Nietzsche's writings, Book Five is *very* special. It too is the last of a series—the series of retrospective reflections of the late summer and fall of 1886 when Nietzsche spent months rereading his books and producing new prefaces for most of them. Having pondered his whole authorship, Nietzsche turned last, in October and November 1886, to *The Joyous Science.* Its new preface begins: "This book may need more than one preface . . ." Consequently, Nietzsche added not only a new preface but a whole book, Book Five, and an appendix of songs, "Songs of Prince Vogelfrei," and a new subtitle, "la gaya scienza," staking a claim to Provençal roots, and a new motto that says in part "I never took nothing from nobody," which we would do well to disbelieve given that this new motto replaces the previous motto taken from Emerson—and taken again to make a crucial point in *Zarathustra* (2.11). Book Five is special because it makes clear where Nietzsche stands with respect to science after writing *Thus Spoke Zarathustra* and after rethinking his whole authorship. These are the reflections on science after Nietzsche became Nietzsche, after he became a Hyperborean by solving the problem of deadly truth set out in the *Use and Disadvantage of History.* Deadly science becomes joyous science because will to power has come to light as the fundamental fact and eternal return as the highest value—Book Five is grounded in this insight and this affirmation even if they become explicit only very briefly. An invitation reverberates throughout the whole Book: study *Zarathustra* for the grounds of what is here mere assertion. Book Five is a satellite to *Zarathustra,* a provocation to enter it from the perspective of science. Fascinated by the new understanding of science, the free mind can enter *Zarathustra* prepared to find in its fabulous events the grounding perspectives of a joyous science.

Nietzsche is, emphatically, an advocate of science. Nevertheless, he knew his advocacy was bound to net him the hostility of science (*KGW* VII 2 [127] = *WP* 1) because it rejected science's reigning paradigm. Baconianism in its refined form of Cartesianism, assumed a mechanical universe and elevated physics as the model science while avowing its own certitude and the social benefits of its pursuit. Nietzsche attacks this mechanistic worldview, with its elevation of physics, its claim to certitude, and its claim to social benefit—and he does so as a friend of science.

In place of physics as the paradigm science, Nietzsche offers philology, the art of interpretation or hermeneutics: nimble Hermes supplants club-footed Vulcan, mysterious oracles from a sacred order replace hammer and tongs. And this is not arbitrary, a result of some accident of Nietzsche's aptitudes or the classes he liked as a boy: philology supplants physics because the mechanistic worldview inadequately accounts for the richness of the phenomena.

If philology supplants physics, the probable supplants certitude as a standard of measure. Joyous science does not cease to think of itself as making progress in insight, but it counts as progress a new modesty: its shifts in perspective replace "the improbable with the more probable, though perhaps one error with another" (*GM* Preface 4). Book Five sounds like a new *New Organon* or a new *Discourse on the Method,* investigating the nuances of a method in which the "unnatural sciences" (*JS* 355; *GM* 3.25) place their appropriate curbs on the natural sciences— a new psychology and a new critique of the elements of consciousness force all the other sciences to respect the limitations placed on their conclusions by the mind's categories of organization and interpretation. "Psychology is once again the path to the fundamental problems" (*BGE* 23) because it concerns itself with the critique of the elements of consciousness while probing the inner world of drives and passions in order to understand not just the inner world but the world simply (*JS* 355).

But of all the issues bound to net Nietzsche the hostility of science, and not only of science, the most explosive is his attack on the ideal of the common good in modern technological science, comfortable self-preservation. Book Five is consistent with the *Use and Disadvantage of History* in its critique of this ideal as the greatest danger to science and philosophy. But Book Five goes far beyond that early essay in the crucial respect: it sets out, if still only fragmentarily, a new ideal as the ground of a new social order, a new ideal of loyalty to the earth that aims to ground the human community on the affirmation of nature. The advocate of science becomes the advocate of the order uncovered by science and the advocate of a "great politics" to build a new social order on that natural order. Book Five is special because it presents the comprehensive teaching of the new philosopher as the advancement of science.[1]

---

1. On Nietzsche and science see Eden, *Political Leadership,* 74: "Nietzsche's politics is, in the first instance, leadership of science."

The 1886 Preface: Convalescence and Gratitude

Herr Nietzsche had become healthy again and *The Joyous Science* chronicled his convalescence. So said Nietzsche in his 1886 Preface and he added on behalf of his reader, "Who cares?" We cannot care that it is Nietzsche, but we can care about convalescence, the Preface argues, because convalescence is a recovery from the spiritual sickness shared by all modern Europeans. Both sickness and recovery belong to the greatest events: if "the greatest recent event" is the death of God whose consequences are traced in Book Five, the great event *subsequent* to it is convalescence from it—and not only from it, for the death of God is an event in a long logic of events that constitute Western spiritual history. We can care about Herr Nietzsche's convalescence as the convalescence of a thinker from a cultural sickness we take to be health.

But how should the convalescent share his convalescence? The first words of the 1882 edition are a little rhyme entitled *Einladung*. The "Invitation" is to a feast and Nietzsche who prepared it now invites its guests. The feast will not be to their taste, so the invitation is a dare: risk it anyway, he says; it will not taste good at first but tomorrow it will taste better, and the day after tomorrow it will taste so good you will want more. But how can the host provide more for tastes altered by readings they have just learned to savor? Read them again, he says, and the proverbial seven old things, the things already read, will become seven new things whose presence had not been suspected. By transforming the reader into a gourmet with the acquired taste to savor the feast, *The Joyous Science* practices an artistry like that of Bacon and Descartes. It creates the audience it needs by transforming tastes through the act of reading—through the toil of reading, for Nietzsche's book, like Bacon's and Descartes's, is written for those who combine good sense with study and who will spend years poring over it. And then? Enticed to Nietzsche's feast and transformed by its fare, Nietzsche's guests will be the means of changing the "general taste" (*JS* 39). The "explosive one," the "subtle seducer," sets off a chain reaction through the seduced (*JS* 38): they will change the general taste and teach all of us to say with him, "This thing here?—it's ridiculous. That thing there?—it's absurd."

To what will Nietzsche educate the educated? *Heiterkeit,* cheerfulness. And cheerfully, in the scientific spirit, the 1886 Preface offers a proof of the need for cheerfulness in its final section. The old passion for truth, humorless, driven by gravity, lacking levity, transformed even boys into old men: they panted for a glimpse of truth, they wanted to look at her naked. The convalescent is cured of this passion of the eye—the chaste passion described by Zarathustra in "On the Immaculate Perception" (Z 2.15)—and even if the old art of Schiller raised it to an admirable plane, the convalescent brings the hardest possible judgment against it: it's in bad taste. On matters of taste there is the most fundamental disputation. The new taste abandons the old belief that truth is still truth when stripped of its veils. Convalescence is training in decency. Experience takes a lesson from innocence:

> "Is it true that God is everywhere?" a little girl asked her mother;
> "I think that's indecent"—a hint for philosophers.

This little girl is parent to truth who is a woman. And if truth is a woman (BGE Preface), we have good reason to suppose that the most passionate truth-seekers, the philosophers, have failed to find the proper means to win her heart. Has the convalescent done better? "Perhaps truth is a woman," he says, "who has grounds not to let us see her grounds? Perhaps her name, to speak Greek, is Baubo?" Baubo? This seems a strange name for truth, for Baubo is the old woman in the Eleusinian mysteries who unveiled the naked truth. Her role so shocked Clement of Alexandria that that Christian author revealed Baubo's role in the mysteries in order to discredit Greek religion. After telling the tale of Baubo raising her skirts for the grieving Demeter, Clement quotes "the very lines of Orpheus":

> This said, she drew aside her robes, and showed
> A sight of shame; child Iacchus was there,
> And laughing, plunged his hand below her breasts.
> Then smiled the goddess, in her heart she smiled,
> And drank the draught from out the glancing cup.[2]

Demeter, grieving for her loss of Persephone to Hades, is restored to hope by the sight of Iacchus drawn on Baubo's belly. So how can Nietzsche use Baubo as the name for truth? How can decency regarding nakedness bear the name of the one who indecently raised her skirts? Perhaps—and what but a "perhaps" could introduce any suggestion regarding such matters?—perhaps Baubo lifted her skirts only once, only for Demeter, and only for Demeter in despair at the loss of what she is, her fertility, her Persephone. Baubo belongs to the mystery profaned by Clement

2. Clement of Alexandria, *Exhortation to the Greeks* II.16–18.

who worshipped a sky god and wanted to kill off the gods of the earth. As a part of the mystery, Baubo symbolizes what the mystery treasures as something to be *known,* something never to be forgotten even when the beloved seems lost to Hades: life generates and generates through the sexual organs. *That* was what Clement and his like wanted to forget. Baubo, so understood, would be a fitting Nietzschean name for truth: she preserves what needs to be known in the appropriate way—there *is* that which needs to be known and there is a way to shelter it and share it.

If this is the meaning of "Baubo," no wonder the convalescent ends celebrating the Greeks: "Oh those Greeks! They knew how to *live.*" Those Greeks knew the relationship between truth and life: they knew that truth and life require the "superficial"—superficialities like the mysteries or like Attic tragedy and Aristophanic comedy. And we come back to that Greek experience, Nietzsche says, we convalescents who have recovered from our youthful coarseness, the rational optimism which taught us to believe that we could gaze on Artemis and Athena bathing naked and remain alive and sighted. The convalescent is a philologist who recovers, in part, by recovering the view of the older Hellenes. Nietzsche's history of philosophy will expand the claim here put in terms of the Greek mysteries: early Greek thinkers, including the philosophers of the tragic age of Greece, had been superseded by decadents, Socratics, rational optimists who reported that truth, so far from being a woman, was eternal forms, or ideas in the mind of God, or mechanical law— and needed no sheltering dress. For centuries such reports inflamed passionate youths in love with truth and led them to suppose that truth was something to be gazed upon with the eye. But now—a convalescent claims to have recovered from that lie about naked truth and, in his recovery, to have learned the need for an art of cheerfulness modeled on the old Hellenic worship of forms, tones, and words, an art that is "superficial—out of profundity!" *The Joyous Science* is a work of such cheerful art. And with a Preface that ends seeming to recommend that one stay at the surface, it taunts its reader to plumb its profundity.

Fundamental to the new history of philosophy is a new understanding of philosophy's origins and history among the Greeks. Socrates, the vortex and turning point of all so-called world history (*BT* 15), marks a turn downwards, down and away from the height achieved by a Heraclitus or a Democritus (*KGW* VII 36 [11]; VIII 14 [116]). And yet there is something in the convalescent that was also essential to Socrates.

Corrupting the Young with Ignorance

The forty-one sections that make up Book Five of *The Joyous Science* constitute an ordered structure, each section contributing an element to the whole by its placement as well as its content.[3] Toward the end, the sections grow more personal, identifying the author in ways that assist the reader. One section in particular fulfills this function, and although it does violence to the structure to consider it at the beginning, it is useful to do so because it describes both Nietzsche and his esoteric style.

Section 381, "On the question of being understandable," is the third from the last. Its purpose is to revive the "long forgotten and unknown" virtues of what Nietzsche calls, in the final section, "right reading" (383). Right reading presupposes acquaintance with the esotericism Nietzsche had discovered in philosophers before the modern age of equality (*BGE* 30). For Nietzsche, "the difference between exoteric and esoteric" does not consist of an inside and outside, some Jesuitism masking deadly truths; it consists rather of a level of rank distinguishing high and low and preserving the high. His argument echoes Plato: the highest insights will "sound like follies and sometimes like crimes when they are heard without permission by those who are not predisposed and predestined for them." Follies or crimes—"useless or dangerous" in Plato's words (*Republic* vi.487a–e). Therefore, philosophers must invent an art of speech that performs many tasks at once: shelter the highest thoughts from those not predestined for them, deflect the condemnation of the philosophers by the nonphilosophical, protect the nonphilosophical from useless or criminal thoughts, and communicate those thoughts to those predestined for them.

"On the question of being understandable" focuses on the intention of the author: Nietzsche holds that *auslegen* is *einlegen*—exegesis is eisegesis—but he holds too that an author's intention can be grasped. An author of the sort Nietzsche describes knows his reader as well as his subject and can select his audience, opening his work to some while closing it to others. Discrimination or choosiness has been practiced by "every noble spirit and taste" and has given rise to "all the refined laws of style." The purpose of style is to communicate inward states and good style communicates inward states well (*EH* Books 4): so little is Nietz-

---

3. Robert Ackermann is insightful on the "coiled," "spring-loaded" tension of the aphoristic style, but his claim that "the rain of aphorisms is designed to produce chaos" is refuted by the architectural unity of Nietzsche's final books (*Nietzsche*, 38). On the aphoristic style, see Picht, *Nietzsche*, 44–45.

sche a skeptic about the possibility of communication that he makes successful communication of inward states the defining feature of style. Writer and reader both have responsibilities: "Philology is . . . the art of reading well—of being able to read off a fact *without* falsifying it by interpretation" (*A* 52).

Nietzsche may not want to be understood by everybody, but he does not want to be *mis*understood by those few for whom he writes:

Stylistic Caution
A: But if *everyone* knew this *most* would be harmed by it. You yourself call these opinions dangerous for the endangered and yet you share them publicly?
B: I write in such a way that neither the mob, nor the *populi,* nor the parties of any kind want to read me. Consequently these opinions will never become public.
A: But how do you write then?
B: Neither usefully nor pleasantly—for the trio named. (*WS* 71)

Usefully and pleasantly then for those others by whom he wants to be understood. His work's usefulness depends upon its being understood by those whom it aims to please.

Nietzsche's "friends," he says in section 381, are not to be misled by two features that will tempt everyone to dismiss his work as lacking seriousness: ignorance and jauntiness. Nietzsche has to speak knowingly and almost in earnest about his jaunty ignorance. Such speech is not a sign of the failure of his style, for it possesses its own jauntiness and ignorance—and all the artists of writing, even Bacon and Descartes, found it necessary to speak almost directly about their indirect speech. Furthermore, what Nietzsche here says is not a substitute way of stating what is most profound in his work; it is only a statement "among us" about how he had to formulate what is most profound.

Jauntiness comes first—and why not in a book on science that begins with sixty-three little rhymes entitled "Joke, Cunning, and Revenge" and ends with fourteen poems called "The Songs of Prince Vogelfrei." His jauntiness—his *Munterkeit,* his cheerfulness, liveliness, joyfulness, brightness—follows from his temperament; it is a given. But what is given in his temperament accords with his subject matter: he is naturally fitted to give word to the most profound, and he makes it appear, throughout *The Joyous Science,* almost a little jaunty. Many will be put off by this appearance, thinking it superficial, and Nietzsche drives them further off by likening his style to a quick plunge in and out of a cold bath. "The 'Thorough.'—Those who are slow to know suppose slowness is the essence of knowledge" (*JS* 231). They do not know what the ignorant Nietzsche claims to know: deep cold generates swiftness. A second analogy offers a second club with which to attack him: such issues are not eggs that have to be incubated day and night and made to hatch—they're birds, shy birds glimpsed, if at all, only obliquely and in darting flight and never brooded or captured.

Nietzsche's brevity links style to substance, claiming commensurability between seeker and sought. This kinship of hunter and hunted is a frequent theme of Nietzsche's poetry when it turns to the essential matter, as it does in the central section of Book Four of *The Joyous Science,* "Will and Wave" (310), or in the final poem of the book, "To the Mistral." But this requires of the reader what was scorned by the writer: Nietzsche's reader surely has to brood night and day on these poems in order to penetrate them. Nietzsche's style encourages the opposite of mimicry in its student. The drama of *Zarathustra,* with its making and unmaking of disciples, shows that there are no Zarathustras among them. As Georg Picht argues, Nietzsche is not the exemplar of a new genus to be replicated among his followers; as a "genuine philosopher" he has a singular style.[4]

Before passing to his ignorance, Nietzsche reflects on a final advantage of his brevity: it spares the innocent. To be "heard still more briefly" than the brief way he speaks is not to be heard at all: the immoralist goes out of his way to avoid doing harm. His brevity duplicates Socratic justice by doing good to friends who are good without harming anyone. Nietzsche is an immoralist like that model of immoralism, Plato (*D* 496), for not only does he avoid harming the innocents, he aims to inspire them and ennoble them and encourage them to virtue: Nietzsche is an immoralist who teaches virtue. But of course Nietzsche does not shrink from flaunting the harm his thought will inflict on established order— his rhetoric is far more open than Bacon's or Descartes's, who chose to hide the harm they intended the old order even while inflicting it.

Who are the innocents Nietzsche's rhetoric spares? "Asses and old maids of both sexes." In *Beyond Good and Evil* Nietzsche describes scholars as old maids (206; see *JS* 357 for old maids). But special guidance for identifying asses and old maids is provided at the end of Nietzsche's description: "und 'das habe ich gesehen'—also sprach Zarathustra." These words are not in *Also Sprach Zarathustra* but Zarathustra does see some-

4. Picht, *Nietzsche,* 114, 297.

thing like asses and old maids excited to virtue by his teaching: in part four the superior men are moved to virtue, to a celebration of life, Nietzsche's new virtue, by Zarathustra's teaching. Kept from the ground of Nietzsche's teaching by a form of his brevity, they nevertheless participate in the virtue built upon it. If this is the meaning of "thus spoke Zarathustra" here (and it should be remembered that *Zarathustra* part four had as yet been circulated to only a few friends), then the phrase is a kind of compliment: you asses and old maids for whom I really write, you innocents, I wouldn't want to corrupt your morals. What could be more corrupting?

This first matter of style, his jauntiness, makes Nietzsche Socratic in his way of speaking; the second makes him Socratic in his way of knowing: he openly acknowledges his ignorance. "Worse" than his brevity is his ignorance, but he makes no secret of it, especially to himself for "our task"—the task of a philosopher today—"is and remains above all, not to mistake ourselves for others." "Know thyself" remains the task of the philosopher even if perfect self-knowledge is ultimately impossible.[5] This much the philosopher today can know, Nietzsche says: science grows and with its growth comes the discovery by the most scholarly among the philosophers that they know too little—the growth of science occasions philosophic recognition of its limitations. And recognition of ignorance is an advance, for it would be worse if philosophers knew too much—if they took themselves to be knowers as the gods were once held to be knowers.

There are precedents for Nietzsche's account of an advance in scientific knowledge accompanied by philosophical skepticism. In the *Phaedo* Socrates describes his discovery of the limitations of scientific explanation (96a–100a); that discovery led to Socrates' life's work on behalf of philosophy, his "second sailing," for he recognized that his own experience of the limitations of science would be shared soon enough by others and would lead to an aggressive antiscience reaction: "misology," hatred of reason for trust betrayed. And misology would lead to misanthropy (88c–91c), hatred of the human which had been thought to be crowned by reason. Socrates' second sailing seems to be an effort to preserve philosophy from disappointment in science, a service performed by the already ignorant on behalf of the soon-to-be ignorant. On the last day of his life, in his private review of his life for his friends, where all thought and emotion are focused on what can be preserved

5. See Strauss, "Note on the Plan of Nietzsche's *Beyond*," 182.

from what is passing, Socrates brings his young scientific admirers to this acknowledgment: philosophy with its recognition of ignorance is the most precious possession, and it must be preserved from science's misplaced faith in knowledge and it must be preserved for reasons of philanthropy.

And the recognition of ignorance, or more politely, of the limitations of knowledge, occurs at another high point in the Socratic tradition. Just where he seems to be asserting absolute certainty, Descartes acknowledges that such claims can always be based only on a prejudice (*Discourse* iv.37–39). Faced with a powerful opponent claiming absolute knowledge for itself and its science, the philosopher Descartes quietly acknowledges ignorance while openly claiming absolute certainty for his new science, thus starting it off on the same footing as the old science—"be a philosopher, be a mummy—present monotono-theism while dressed up as a grave-digger."

If philosophers have previously known the distinction between esoteric and exoteric, they customarily employed the exoteric to mask their ignorance; they claimed knowledge just where they knew they lacked it. Book Five will show that Nietzsche took Plato to be the great philosophical model of feigned knowledge. But now, surrounded by a Cartesian faith bound to founder, the new philosopher flaunts a salutary ignorance—he becomes Socratic by again claiming that the highest human wisdom is ignorance. In his jaunty argument for ignorance, Nietzsche maintains that the signs distinguishing the mere scholar from the scholarly philosopher—the philosopher aware of his ignorance—are physiological: needs, growth, digestion, taste. Today's Socratics are not Platonists; they make no claim to having minds purified by detachment from their source in the appetites, or to having grasped the good as such (*BGE* Preface). The taste of the new philosopher conduces to his most characteristic wish—that his spirit grow to resemble a dancer, for the dance is his ideal, his "divine service." Assault monotono-theism while dressed up as a dancer. Nietzsche is a jaunty Socratic, a philosopher scholarly enough to be aware of his ignorance who wants it understood that the highest wish now is the dancer's spirit, a philosopher's spirit that accords with the dance of things. He corrupts by tempting others to his own jaunty ignorance. And he invites himself to be put on trial knowing he will not lack Meletuses.

From Old Caterpillars, a New Butterfly

In its accord with the ideal of the dance, Nietzsche's style is attuned to its precedents, notably "la gaya scienza," the Provençal style promised in the subtitle and in the description of *The Joyous Science* in *Ecce Homo*. Nietzsche's prose attempts to recapture the style of the troubadour that stands as the fountainhead of modern European poetry, a style that possesses as its distinguishing quality what Matthew Arnold called "rapidity." Is rapidity consonant with gravity? The Albigensian Crusade, aimed in the first instance at crushing the Cathars and the Poor Men of Lyons, crushed and burned as well the poesy of the troubadour. Nietzsche's revival of their art revives a graceful gravity the church found it necessary to crush. In rethinking the history of Western culture, including the Medieval church, Book Five adopts in prose the jaunty style of the troubadour. And because "style *an sich* is pure folly" (*EH* Books 4), revival of the style of the troubadour is an act of spiritual warfare against enemies that attempted to crush its first appearance and stamp Europe with their own gravity and grace. Given his choice of weapons Nietzsche chooses wisely: he chooses what will please. Nietzsche is "a musician and an artist in the *irreducible* sense that he gives his reader *pleasure*."[6]

Jauntiness, brevity, and ignorance result in a certain minimalism or compression of content that Nietzsche describes as "my sense of style, for the epigram as style." In such a style, "every word—as sound, as place, as concept—pours out its strength left and right and over the whole." Through "this minimum in the extent and number of signs," Nietzsche attains a "maximum in the energy of the signs" (*TI* Ancients 1). Nietzsche's jaunty minimalism is especially evident on the most basic matters, will to power and eternal return, his teaching on beings and on worth. Not how often and how long he treats these matters, but where and how, determines their weight and measure. In Book Five they are glimpsed in just the right way—at the weightiest moments and fleetingly, shy birds glimpsed in flight out of the corner of the eye.

As a strategist of style no less acute than Bacon, Nietzsche fit his style to a purpose still more radical than Bacon's: a complete change in the public image of the philosopher. A concise statement of that revolutionary change occurs in Nietzsche's reflections on the ascetic priest:

> Let us compress the facts into a few brief formulas: to begin with, the philosophic spirit always had to use as a mask and cocoon

6. Blondel, *Nietzsche*, 39.

the previously established types of the contemplative man—priest, sorcerer, soothsayer, and in any case a religious type—in order to be able to exist at all: the ascetic ideal for a long time served the philosopher as a form in which to appear, as a precondition of existence—he had to represent it so as to be able to be a philosopher; he had to believe in it in order to be able to represent it. The peculiar, withdrawn attitude of the philosopher, world-denying, hostile to life, suspicious of the senses, freed from sensuality, which has been maintained down to the most modern times and has become virtually the philosopher's pose par excellence—it is above all a result of the emergency conditions under which philosophy arose and survived at all; for the longest time philosophy would not have been possible at all on earth without ascetic wraps and cloak, without an ascetic self-misunderstanding. To put it vividly: the ascetic priest provided until the most modern times the repulsive and gloomy caterpillar form in which alone the philosopher could live and creep about. Has all this really altered? Has that many-colored and dangerous winged creature, the "spirit" which this caterpillar concealed, really been unfettered at last and released into the light, thanks to a sunnier, warmer, brighter world? Is there sufficient pride, daring, courage, self-confidence available today, sufficient will of the spirit, will to responsibility, freedom of will, for "the philosopher" to be henceforth—possible on earth?—(GM 3.10)

Do "the emergency conditions under which philosophy arose and survived" still hold? Nietzsche risks everything on the answer being No. Not the caterpillar but the butterfly; not the priest but the dancer; not the ascetic but the troubadour—these are the Nietzschean poses of the philosopher, poses that accord with the thinker's inwardness, his movement, his levity, his intense pleasure. Pleasure and a love of life—at last the philosopher can state directly what the Platonic Socrates and Bacon and Descartes could only hint at: life is choiceworthy for itself and philosophy is choiceworthy as the highest form of human life, the most pleasant pleasure. Can philosophy so proclaimed survive? Can it provide the grounds for nonascetic virtue in those who are not philosophers, virtue that recognizes the fundamental and affirmative character of earthly pleasure—though hardly identifying the pleasant with the easy? Can philosophy publicly attack the old keepers of public virtue instead of accommodating itself to them? This is the meaning of Nietzsche's anti-Platonism, his opposition to the otherworldliness with which philosophy had to align itself to survive.

Nietzsche breaks with the whole past of philosophy's necessary ascetic lie, the noble lies of Platonism which affirmed a permanence behind the changing things, arguing that public virtue depended on belief in moral permanence, God and the soul. Who but a maimed soul would be so short-sighted as to destroy the public virtue on which philosophy itself depended, to destroy the conditions of civility that made insight into the truth and lie possible? Is the maimed soul not a suicidal soul, Aristophanes' Socrates its prototype, a thinker too airy to see that Strepsiades is right to burn down his thinkery?

"That's all over now," Nietzsche judges. The setting for philosophy has been irrecoverably altered by philosophy's collusion with asceticism. The success of Baconian and Cartesian science has changed the public world in which philosophy arises. To avoid the error of Cassandra, the philosopher must know where he is—and Nietzsche is the first philosopher to assess modern times from a standpoint outside of it. "God is dead"—all that means in a literal sense is that yet another religion fulfills the natural cycle of religions. It would be boring but for the fact that with the death of this God "Platonism lies on the ground." The death of Platonism is a far more significant event, for it signals the end of belief in moral permanence and the end of the old asceticism in which philosophy had to shelter itself. Nietzsche's public style is unheard of in philosophy; his jauntiness and ignorance appall the gravity of Platonists from the Aristotelians to the Cartesians. No matter. If they once wisely took their guidance from a world to which they had to conform in order to survive, they now foolishly fail to recognize that that world is passing. The setting for philosophy has changed and philosophy itself must change. In Nietzsche's historical judgment, the emergency conditions under which philosophy arose have given way under the force of modern times to the global community at "the end of history"—the world of last men. And the end of history is the end of philosophy: there is no need for ignorance, for mere love of wisdom, if all men are wised-up. Hence the new philosopher flaunts his ignorance and makes possible a history of philosophy attuned to philosophy's historic ignorance, its recognition of the limitations of knowledge while tolerating impossible knowledge claims for the sake of its own survival. Philosophy's ignorance is consonant with genuine knowledge of its present world and its past, and hence with profound and deeply informed actions, like those of Bacon or Descartes. Nietzsche's deeply informed acts of corruption aim to communicate a knowledge of where we stand. Nietzsche's jaunty ignorance is compatible with his being a Hyperborean and seeing "the end of history" for what it is, an earnest public faith grounded in ignorance, passing for knowledge, fatal to philosophy.

Opposition to the end of history and the end of philosophy force philosophy out into the open, baring its scandalous past as a history of necessary lies masking its ignorance. That scandal hides what is not scandalous: philosophy's philanthropy. Philanthropy now causes philosophy to run its greatest risk: telling the truth about philosophy in order to ground a public philosophy on the sovereignty of becoming, the fluidity of all concepts types and kinds, and the lack of any cardinal difference between human and animal. Nietzsche's history of philosophy assassinates Platonism while drawing its inspiration from the same source as Platonic philosophy: philology and philanthropy, love of the logos and love of the being that houses the logos.

"We the fearless"—the whole of Book Five bears this significant title. But is there a disparity between author and audience in fearlessness? The cunning motto to Book Five suggests there is: "And if you, carcass, knew where I am taking you, you would really tremble." The fearless and knowing mind addresses a taunt to the trembling and unknowing body. But is the knowing mind of the author not also addressing a taunt to the unknowing, carcasslike mind of the reader? Would we really tremble if we knew where he was taking us in Book Five?

Chapter 13

Joyous Science II: The Hyperborean History of European Philosophy and Religion

The hidden history of the philosophers came to light for me.—Nietzsche *(EH Preface 3)*

The hidden history of philosophy, the Hyperborean view brought to light in Book Five, differs radically from any tale philosophy has yet told of itself. Philosophy's origins in the tragic age of the Greeks surpassed what philosophy became in Greece's decline, beginning with Socrates. "The most beautiful growth of antiquity," Plato, corrupted perhaps by Socrates, gave philosophy a stamp and tenor that put all subsequent philosophers and theologians on the same track, the track of a "higher swindle." Epicurus attempted to preserve the perspective of the older Hellenes, protecting philosophy from the Socratic moralizing which had turned philosophy itself against science. But Epicurus too was finally defeated by a kind of Platonist, Augustine, a theologian whose motives are as suspicious as Plato's are not. Augustine and his like captured Socratic philosophy for religion, forcing other forms of philosophy almost wholly underground. A series of renaissances attempted to recover the original joyous spirit of Greek inquiry, but each fell prey to religious revival, to crusades and inquisitions, the most fateful being Luther's for it helped give rise to "modern ideas." Nevertheless, within modern culture and against great resistance, Europe slowly won back for itself the methods devised by the ancients for understanding the world and founding a civilization on knowledge—especially the incomparable art of reading and its disposition of intellectual integrity. But modern science, for all its gains, served modern politics; Spinoza's view that life seeks self-preservation became our orthodoxy, cementing philosophy's collusion with the highest ideal of modern politics, comfortable self-preservation. Modern German philosophy—Leibnitz, Kant, and Hegel—made essential and permanent advances which undermined the religious and political perspective to which they remained loyal. Schopenhauer made the decisive break with that religious narrowness and began where all must now begin, with the greatest recent event, the death of God. That event broadens inexorably into the death of Platonism, and the road to the Hyperboreans becomes clearer, the exit out of whole millennia of labyrinth—recovery of the older Hellenes, recovery of the methods of science, and recovery *from* the much larger phenomenon of which philosophy became a late symptom: the moral misreading of nature and history.

That is a short summary of the elements of the Nietzschean history of philosophy presented in *The Joyous Science* Book Five. Such history is warfare against monotono-theism—gallant, daring, exhilarating. It is warfare on behalf of an affirmative view of our spiritual past, an exercise in gratitude that summons from their underworld spiritual predecessors akin to Nietzsche but profoundly misunderstood—"For that is the nature of human gratitude: it misunderstands its benefactors" (*TI* Skirmishes 44). Out of gratitude, Nietzsche's history of philosophy wants to understand benefactor and malefactor properly, to acknowledge what we owe to the accidental appearance of genius, and to appreciate how much our history has been stamped by great legislative thinkers.

For Nietzsche, the history of philosophy cannot be presented in a vacuum because it did not occur in a vacuum; it must employ the "historical sense" hitherto ignored by the monotono-theists. For the historical sense, everything changes—but "death, change, age, as well as procreation and growth" are not "objections" or "refutations" (*TI* Reason 1). Proper employment of the historical sense depends upon a "proper physio-psychology" that understands the springs of human action (*BGE* 23). Even this physio-psychology, however, depends upon something still more foundational: the truly basic insight in Nietzsche's thought that "the world viewed from inside, the world defined and determined according to its 'intelligible character' . . . would be 'will to power' and nothing else.—" (*BGE* 36). This insight and just how it is possible—this "ontology" and its "epistemology" in the old language—are broached indirectly in Book Five. Similarly, the great affirmation arising out of the foundational insight—the affirmation of eternal return—is glimpsed only once here. It could seem, therefore, that the foundations of Nietzsche's thought—being, knowing, valuing—are not elaborated in this Book. But while making it evident that these *are* the foundational matters, Nietzsche shows nicely that such matters dictate their own imperatives of method. With respect to the foundational matters, Nietzsche's method is always oblique, suggestive, taunting. Here as elsewhere, it always tempts to proper *Versuche:* attempts to glimpse the most elusive, most hidden, but most alluring matters through experimental inferences based on what can be best known—"know thyself." And it sets out to provoke further experiments in refutation and confirmation.

The Joyous Science Book Five is an appropriate focus for the study of Nietzsche's history of philosophy because it presents that history Nietzscheanly: one important thread in a tapestry of threads, the history of philosophy becomes visible only with the coclarification of other main threads—philosophy, psychology, and philology combine with history to provide a new comprehensive view, the insights of each buttressing and supplementing the insights of the others. For Nietzsche's new philosophy is "a system in aphorisms," as Karl Löwith said,[1] and the forty-one aphorisms of Book Five present Nietzsche's "system" "systematically." Not architectonically, of course, as a timeless structure of knowing, acting, and valuing, and not in numbered paragraphs presenting the whole science of wisdom. "Systematic" in application to Nietzsche's works means that they are thematic and dramatic unities, however much they bristle with asides, taunts, objections and replies, jokes, insults, and puzzles. Book Five gathers breadth, strength, and urgency as its aphorisms accumulate, as its sequential and interconnected insights fuse and fission into a comprehensive and affirmative perspective.

Philosophy and the Greatest Recent Event: From Good Cheer to Nihilism (343–44)

What it is with our cheerfulness (343). God is dead and it cheers us. The author, it seems, is not the Madman of section 125 announcing despair at the death of the God. A born guesser of riddles, he seems to share with the free minds their sense of liberation at God's death: detaching the earth from its old sun, entirely wiping away the old horizon—this has made us cheerful rather than fearful. But could it be that we are cheered and fearless because we have not yet fathomed everything that this event may bring in its train? Will it cost *us* something too—our cheerful morality perhaps? The author *could* be the Madman after all.

By opening this way Nietzsche suggests the prophet's role he is to adopt in the coming sections, for who is "compelled to play the teacher"? —he is. Nietzsche is no spoilsport—he would hardly want to ruin the

---

1. Löwith, *Nietzsche's Philosophie der ewigen Wiederkehr des Gleichen*, 15.

party celebrating the death of God. But our cheerfulness and fearlessness will have to be earned by facing the coming consequences of the death of God. When gods die, men play with their shadows for centuries in caves (*JS* 108), and those "gruesome shadows" will themselves have to be vanquished. We will therefore have to strain to understand the consequences of an event that initially cheers us, for the death of a God has a logic but it is a "monstrous logic of terror" and the meaning of it is less apparent than the fact of it.

At the entrance of Book Five stands this announcement of the necessity of playing the teacher of the meaning of European nihilism. *Nihilism* is a word that began to appear in Nietzsche's writings only after *Zarathustra* (*BGE* 10; *BT* Preface 7), and it is analyzed for the first time in Book Five.[2] Understanding European nihilism requires a new understanding of the past—that non-Hegelian, non-Christian historiography called for in the *Use and Disadvantage of History*. Consequently, the coming sections attempt unfamiliar but coherent readings of Greek philosophy, Christian origins, the Medieval church, the Renaissance, the Reformation, modern philosophy, and modern religion—readings free of faith in progress and of belief in the present as the end of history. But given that the traditional readings of these events are unjust to the past and false, as Nietzsche everywhere argues, can his own readings be any more just and true? Nietzsche repeatedly forces his reader to pose this question—his question—by claiming justice and truth for his reading while challenging the grounds of such claims.

According to the "first post-nihilist thinker,"[3] the European past presages European nihilism and makes this historic spiritual event inevitable and understandable. Having ruined good cheer by forcing us to confront European nihilism, Nietzsche leads his reader to believe that the European past could presage something else as well, something that could come later and ground legitimate good cheer. Joyous science ventures first into contemporary nihilism and then out onto "open seas," the like of which have never been glimpsed. By ending the introductory section on this image (see also 289, "All Aboard"), Nietzsche reminds his reader of earlier uses of it in the *Use and Disadvantage of History* and *Thus Spoke Zarathustra*. (As Nietzsche informs the reader of his *Genealogy*, he expects that the reader "has first read my earlier writings and has not

---

2. On the sources of Nietzsche's concept of nihilism see Ottmann, *Nietzsche*, 329ff., and Müller-Lauter, *Nietzsche*, 66–68.

3. Ottmann, *Nietzsche*, 373.

spared some trouble in doing so" [*GM* Preface 8)].) In the former, the image stood for a threat, the deadly openness of science that destroys the closed atmosphere necessary for sustaining life (*UD* 10). In the latter, the image stood for a promise, the liberating openness of Zarathustra's marriage song (*Z* 3.13) which heralds a new understanding of earth and sky and grounds a new and open inquiry into them. Book Five of *The Joyous Science* repeats that promise and in the soberer form of Provençal gaiety reaffirms the open seas.

The way in which even we are still pious (344). One of the frightening shadows cast by the greatest recent event threatens to eclipse science: science, Nietzsche argues, arises from a conviction, a pious choice that can have no scientific justification even if it has a completely understandable historical lineage. Not all gods are dead for the godless ones, for the grounding conviction of science is a sacred relic, a carryover from a Christian and Platonic faith in the commensurability of the true and the good. But the very piety of the free minds will oblige them to probe their piety; their morality will force them to investigate "Morality as Problem" (345). And "Our work" will clarify itself as "Our Question Mark" (346): are we nihilists?

The drama of these opening sections carries the reader with characteristic rapidity through the events about to unfold in the "monstrous logic of terror" implied in the greatest recent event. Nietzsche himself assumes the standpoint of a driven inquirer forced for the first time down a spiral of inexorable questions into the abyss of nihilism. But Nietzsche is the inquirer who had already completed *Thus Spoke Zarathustra* three years earlier: the rhetorical purposes of *The Joyous Science* Book Five require that Nietzsche feign ignorance of what was gained in *Zarathustra* in order to end up there again via a new route along which he carries the reader. A historian of future events, a "soothsaying bird-spirit who looks back when he explains what is to come" (*KGW* VIII 11 [411]), Nietzsche must give his reader many opportunities to be persuaded.

The way in which we are still pious—being pious would hardly be viewed as a virtue by the free minds to whom Nietzsche addresses his opening reflections on science. He could have used other language: given that the "piety" in question is a conviction about science as inquiry into truth, Nietzsche could very easily have spoken, as he usually does, of "intellectual conscience" or of "honesty, the youngest virtue" had he wanted to make his point in a way more attuned to his readers' virtue. But such virtuous speech would have inhibited Nietzsche's rhetorical point, for he aims to rouse piety against itself and force the pious to question their piety—piously. The "wholly objective," having submitted themselves to the demands of objectivity, now submit themselves to its next demand: recognition that that very submission is not itself objective. But recognition of the moral or pious origins of science does not entail their repudiation. Nietzsche's genealogy of science leads to an affirmation of both its pious origins and what grows out of them. At the opening of Book Five, Nietzsche shows where scientific questioning now leads: to the question of its own grounds.

"One says, with good reason" that the propositions of science are not convictions but hypotheses, provisional perspectives that stand under the perpetual police supervision of mistrust. The nurture of the scientific spirit would seem to begin when it permits itself no more convictions. And Nietzsche ends his statement of the self-image of science with a properly scientific tentativeness: that is probably the way it is. But how can the nurture with which science begins begin? By choosing this nurture. But this choice is based on a conviction whose worth cannot be certified in advance. The conviction that moves one to test the worth of all convictions is immune to its own standard; one chooses on the basis of a conviction to do without convictions. Even science rests on a faith, one whose principle tenet is, "Nothing is more needed than truth, and in relation to it, everything else has a value of the second rank."

What is this unconditioned will to truth? It is either, Nietzsche says, the will not to allow oneself to be deceived or the will not to deceive. These two alternative answers are presented as mutually exclusive and exhaustive—and as having completely different grounds, the first being grounded in an assumption, the second in a moral conviction.

The first alternative implies that it is harmful to be deceived and that science, as discovery of the truth, is a prudent endeavor with a long-term utility. This is the view of science defended by science's advocate in *Zarathustra* part four (*Z* 4.15), the dedicated specialist who believes that science is enlightenment which replaces ignorant fear with informed well-being. But it is easy to counter that this claim is itself based on ignorance: it begins with a claim that it cannot possibly know to be true at the start—that knowledge is good for the knower. And as it gains experience it should learn that untruth is as important for life as truth. The conviction that truth is of supreme value could not have arisen from calculations of the utility of truth if both truth and untruth constantly proved themselves useful—"as is the case." Ignorance grounds the first alternative, curable ignorance because the disutility of truth has always been evident.

The second alternative—"I will not deceive, not even myself"—makes the will to truth a moral phenomenon in which one subsumes oneself under the moral universal. The argument now makes a rapid dash through a series of implications ending with the conclusion that God, long the guarantor of truth, is our oldest lie. Why *not* deceive if it should appear—"and it does appear!"—as if life favored appearance, and when the great sweep of life shows itself to have been on the side of the most unscrupulous *polytropoi?* This word from the first line of the *Odyssey* describes Odysseus as a man of "many guiles" or a man "much traveled," a versatile man who lived by deceiving and by avoiding being deceived (see *Odyssey* x.330). The imperative of science, "I will not deceive," conflicts with what life favors in the unscrupulous Odysseuses. Science could thus be the expression of a destructive principle hostile to life, a concealed will to death. Faith in science rests on a "metaphysical faith," the faith of Christianity and Platonism, that God is truth and truth godlike, but "if God himself proves to be our longest lie" then our cheerful science loses its very ground.

Nietzsche's dramatic dialectic leads to a conclusion familiar to students of Bacon and Descartes: modern science as a faith heir to Christianity and Platonism is grounded in an unjustifiable rational optimism which believes that the truth can be known and that the truth will set one free. Nietzsche adds his own characteristic judgment about this moral enterprise: in aiming to create a new world better than this one, it is moved by revenge against this world. If modern science itself harbors a kind of noble lie of the commensurability of true and good, how can it avoid perishing of its own virtue? Moreover, as a consequence of science's death at its own hands, are error, blindness, and the lie about to become godlike? Is that what a *fröhliche Wissenschaft* would enthrone? Barbarism in place of the civility of science? Would Jesuitism not have been a better course after all?

Nietzsche will provide answers in Book Five to the questions raised by this opening section—and they will not abandon the discipline of science or embrace some new noble lie. But what of those polytropoi most favored by life? This one word seems to provide a clue to Nietzsche's argument, a Homeric clue befitting a philologist who sides with Homer's army in the ancient quarrel between Homer and Plato, "the complete, the genuine antagonism" (GM 3.25).[4] Plato examined the question of the polytropoi in *Lesser Hippias* or "On the Lie," a Socratic reflection on

---

4. On *polytropos* see Clay, *Wrath of Athena*, 29–34, 64, 96.

what Homer esteemed that asks, who is the best man in Homer? Is it straight Achilles with his truthful ways or "polytropic" Odysseus with his lying ways? The sophist Hippias defends the moral interpretation of Homer, arguing that Achilles is the best man because he holds that "one must speak out without regard to consequences" (365a, quoting *Iliad* 9.308–12). Achilles finds hateful one "who hides one thing in his mind but says something else," and Hippias finds it hateful too. Both seem to think or hope that the true and the good are related, and that the good will come to the aid of the true. But Socrates demonstrates that Odysseus is the best man in Homer and best because he belongs to the polytropoi. Odysseus's voluntary lying, his speaking with regard to consequences, shows that he is both capable and knowing (375d) and that he is not willing to entrust the outcome of his actions to the pious hope that some moral order enforces the true. Odysseus is the just man where justice is understood as a combination of capacity and knowledge (375d); his justice requires his lying. Socrates notes that Homer is no longer present and cannot be asked what he was thinking when he composed his lines (365d), but the dialogue seems to show that Hippias, who thinks he knows what Homer was thinking, does not, while Socrates, who makes no such claim, does. Homer's greatest man, Odysseus, knows the necessity of treachery and so does Plato whose Socrates is almost openly treachery's advocate. At the very end of the *Republic*, a dialogue that shows at length the necessity of lying, Plato likens his Socrates to a reborn Odysseus, an improved Odysseus free of the love of honor, free to apply his wisdom and guile to the private and unsung life of philosophy, to sing its praises as the new foundation of the moral life. As Book Ten of the *Republic* suggests, the poetry of that new Odysseus supplants the poetry of Homer and establishes the rule of the new philosopher as the teacher of rational optimism and of moral gods and immortal souls.[5]

"A complete skeptic about Plato" could learn that skepticism from *Lesser Hippias* and judge Plato too one of the unscrupulous polytropoi most favored by life. Himself beyond good and evil, Plato established

---

5. On the great theme of Plato's esotericism, Patrick Coby has shown that it is necessary to study the *Protagoras*: Protagoras's own form of esotericism is shown to be inadequate by a Socrates who argues for esotericism esoterically—he even concocts a history of wisdom on its behalf and calls in the aid of the Spartans, the wisest of Greeks because they have hidden their wisdom so well that Socrates alone knows of it (Coby, *Socrates and the Sophistic Enlightenment*). On the kinship of Plato and Nietzsche with respect to esotericism see the insightful article by Stanley Rosen, "Suspicion, Deception, and Concealment."

the reign of a new good and evil by fostering Platonism, a belief in the commensurability of the true and the good that he cannot possibly have held himself, not being as naive as Achilles. Homer and Plato, those great antagonists, do not differ with respect to the superiority of Odysseus over Achilles, of the polytropoi over the merely moral. But now the latest form of moral Platonism, modern science with its conviction about the goodness of truth telling, threatens the whole apparatus of Platonism. Public truth telling—whole institutions of truth-tellers following brave Achilles and speaking without regard to consequences—demands finally that the deadly truth about truth telling be seen: truth is antilife, life favors the lie. But just here, another of the unscrupulous polytropoi most favored by life appears. And how does this new Odysseus improve on the old? On the Platonic Socrates, that is, whose unscrupulous ways made him the one turning point of all so-called world history through the establishment of a morality based on rational optimism? The new Odysseus insists on truth telling, on the piety of conscience as the measure of what is acceptable.

Nietzsche does not side with the polytropoi in the *way* of the polytropoi for he calls attention to those ways. But why insist on truth telling if life favors the polytropoi? Surely no one will answer that Nietzsche is as straight as Achilles, that he speaks without regard to consequences, hating the one who hides one thing in his mind but says something else. Nietzsche seems to insist on truth telling precisely because he admires wily Odysseus; versatility requires the new Odysseus to align himself with the virtuous truth-tellers of science because of the public presence of that science. The first immoralist takes the side of public morality and is polytropic in that respect: public morality having changed because of the world-historical impact of Platonism, philosophy must change with it. But of course it is necessary to stay wary: one who flaunts his own truth telling while uncovering the history of lying keeps a finger pointed at himself.

Can science be detached from its Platonism, its rational optimism, a faith that makes it antilife, antinature, antihistory? Can it peer into its own moral foundations, its piety, without simply succumbing to the horrified judgment that science itself is nihilism? Nietzsche's fundamental argument is with Platonism where Platonism is understood as a faith in "the pure mind and the good as such" (*BGE* Preface), in the commensurability of the true and the good. Nietzsche's argument with Platonism arises inevitably in the setting created by modern Platonism, a public faith in an unsustainable belief. Nietzsche's thought arises in the crisis of Baconianism. In a setting where honesty, the youngest virtue, determines what is possible for science, Nietzsche invites his reader to reflect on the age-old question faced by the most unscrupulous polytropoi, by Homer and Plato, by Bacon and Descartes, the question of the truth and the lie. If the greatest recent event has been the death of God at the hands of the pious, as Nietzsche concludes, then his great question is, what next? What happens when the pious turn their piety on themselves, when their intellectual conscience probes itself? Nihilism happens, the great event of the coming two centuries. And next? To overcome the nihilism consequent upon science's inquiry into itself, it will be necessary to run the greatest risk with truth telling. It will be necessary for philosophy, which is suspicious of knowers, to align itself with the knowers in order to overcome their incipient nihilism. This is the odyssey on which the rest of Book Five will carry its readers.

Philosophy, Morality, Nihilism (345–46)

Morality as problem (345). If science is a form of morality, the question, why science? implies the question, why morality at all? This section does not answer that question but lays claim to it: the problem of morality is "our work." But how will we work at our work? The scientific method is itself part of what needs to be questioned and cannot simply be adopted as the means to an answer. This section therefore opens with one of the strongest challenges that the joyous science puts to the reigning science, the refined Baconian, Cartesian method that its founders recognized as the democratization of science, reduction of its dependence on genius. The method of the reigning science requires stripping off "personality" to allow problems to be approached objectively, in a way that in principle any investigator can duplicate. Its "selflessness" is its version of the virtue of humility espoused by its parent, as Nietzsche argued in his genealogy of the ascetic virtues of science (*GM* 3). Joyous science on the contrary requires that problems of the greatest magnitude, like our problem of morality, be addressed by their lovers, those consumed by passion for the problem. The problem must be worthy of such love, and the lover worthy of such a beloved. For Nietzsche as for Plato, "philosophy" could be thought a misnomer: Sophia demands not philia but eros; the lovers of wisdom are the supreme erotics.

It is clear to Nietzsche that he runs a great risk when speaking of his method this way, the risk of appearing to be antiscience. Acknowledgment of that risk appears with paradigmatic clarity when Zarathustra confronts the superior men over this very question (*Z* 4.14–16). If the objective method of the specialist with its repeatable procedures and goal of certainty is not the whole method of science—as the specialist in the brain of the leech argues it is—and if science itself is understood as a moral choice uncertifiable by the canons of science, then science itself is reduced to one choice among others; science itself is threatened by individual caprice and whim, and all the gains of Enlightenment are threatened by a slide back into ignorance and superstition. For this dramatic moment of *Zarathustra* part four, which depicts the consequences for science of the greatest recent event, Nietzsche peopled his stage with other figures representing world-historical forces bound to appear under the monstrous logic of nihilism unfolding in that event. Science's self-critique is welcomed, even celebrated, by artists and geniuses of invention who take it to be their own liberation into wholesale deconstruction. They dismantle all claims to shareable knowledge and make their own arty playing around paradigmatic: everybody's only playing around, even those who take themselves seriously, like the scientist— or like Zarathustra. "Only fool, only poet"—in this song the great artist deconstructs Zarathustra as merely an artist like himself, except that Zarathustra lacks irony. "And all present flew unwittingly like birds into the net of his cunning"—when Nietzsche wrote that this was the reaction of the superior men to the deconstruction of Zarathustra by the Old Sorcerer (*Z* 4.15), could he have thought that the interpreters of his own work would follow them into that net by supposing that Nietzsche was deconstructing himself? Zarathustra tries to persuade them otherwise and his defense of science parallels the more elaborate program for the advancement of science set out in *The Joyous Science* Book Five. How can science survive the coming nihilism—how can a place for science be secured between an impossible dream of certainty and a nihilistic play of deconstruction?

In "Morality as problem," a preliminary approach to this issue, Nietzsche says that he has met no one, "not even in books," who is consumed by passion for this problem. "Not even in books"—this cannot mean that Plato or Montaigne or Schopenhauer lack profound reflection on the issue of morality. Rather it must mean that for them morality always became part of the solution, part of the "medicine" regardless of how little they themselves were simply moral in the senses they prescribed. The problem of the worth of moral judgments arises now for the first time, and it falls to the philosopher Nietzsche as *his* problem—and he is "medicynical" about the whole medicine of morals (*EH* Books 5).

The greatest recent event alters the problem of morality, a problem coeval with philosophy as the problem of nature and convention. What had become part of the solution—convention or morality grounded in the philosopher's discourse about nature, some noble lie or other—becomes part of the problem when "God himself proves to be our most enduring lie." The death of God shows itself philosophically as the death of Platonism, a far more significant event. Like Bacon and Descartes, the philosopher Nietzsche takes his bearings from his times and for Nietzsche that means the past two millennia of Platonism and the coming two centuries of nihilism. The radical character of Nietzsche's thought follows from the times and not from his temperament.

Having discovered the problem of morality to be his problem, Nietzsche did what he could, he says, to encourage others to take it up in the way it deserves but had little success. When restating this point in the Preface to the *Genealogy of Morals* (7), Nietzsche described how he encouraged his friend Paul Rée to make his problem Rée's problem: instead of "gazing around haphazardly in the blue after the English fashion," Nietzsche counseled Rée to concentrate on the color which "is a hundred times more vital for a genealogist of morals than blue: *gray,* what is documented." Gray—a proper genealogy of morals submits to the rigors of the historical sense or the philological conscience; what is recoverable about the past will ground all its judgments.

English genealogists, not anchored in documentary gray, rushed to childish conclusions: either the fiction of some moral universals shared by all peoples or a more realistic moral skepticism that recognized the actual diversity of morals. The more refined among the latter thought that they had refuted the moral worth of any value when they uncovered the ignobility of its origins. But for the genealogist Nietzsche, ignoble origins do not refute a thing's worth; genealogy is not a reductive process satisfied with bringing shame to what had held itself noble. Plato had argued for complicity with the lie of noble origins fundamental to a people's pride and well-being; but Nietzsche had argued in the *Use and Disadvantage of History* that that lie can no longer be endured—not because of the private umbrage felt by a philosopher but because a public science had made the virtue of honesty the virtue of the educated. Lies of noble origins are no longer credible as proof of nobility, not even that last possible form of a noble lie of origins according to which the whole of history is a noble struggle for the freedom and wisdom of which we are the exemplars—perhaps even the history of the universe: some contemporary cosmologists would like us to believe that the universe exists for the sake of their becoming conscious of it.

The lesson Nietzsche drew from the demise of the lie of origins is not that moral values built on it are worthless. Uncovering origins does "not so much as touch the problem of the worth of values"—Nietzsche's inquiry into origins is not a weapon of debunking; it is the necessary prelude to a harder task: discernment of worth. Unflinching insight into the natural origin of values is a now unavoidable requirement of our science—our pious science about to be horrified by its penetrating gaze into its own groundless ground. A horrified science, nihilistic science, is part of our fate according to Nietzsche, a necessary stage that may perhaps prove to be a "pathological transition stage" to something possible but not necessary: joyous science (*KGW* VIII 9 [35] = *WP* 13).

"Our" great problem is the problem of morality. Such problems require fit temperaments for their solution, and Nietzsche has found no one but himself fit for this problem. The same embarrassing situation at the end of the *Use and Disadvantage of History* led Nietzsche to summon fellow workers to complete the task. Has nothing changed in twelve years? *Thus Spoke Zarathustra* shows that very much has changed: beginning as a teacher engaged in a vain search for his like who will become his superiors, Zarathustra discovers that he has to strike out on his own to solve the historic problem that fell to him. No more than Bacon or Descartes could the philosopher Nietzsche entrust his essential work to followers. And *Zarathustra* shows that it was not necessary for Nietzsche to defer to followers: parts two and three recount Zarathustra's solitary discovery of the solutions to the fundamental problems that presented themselves to him, the problem of morality—of the last man and nihilism. Subsequent sections of Book Five of *The Joyous Science* make clear that Zarathustra's solutions are Nietzsche's possessions. Book Five is one of Nietzsche's attempts to fulfill the task left open even at the end of *Zarathustra* part four, the task of making Zarathustra's problem our problem and Zarathustra's solution our solution. This Book comes early, before it has even dawned on us that this problem is our problem; but it comes late as well, after Nietzsche had fully traversed that problem and come out on the other side. In this section first things come first, and Nietzsche tempts others to share a problem that had been his alone: if we have to put in question the greatest of all medicines, morality itself, "Let's get on with it! For this is our work.—" But "our work" leads to "our question mark."

Our question mark (346). The dash bringing the previous section to an abrupt end anticipates the question opening this one: "You don't understand this?" "Our" question mark turns out to be a question about nihilism, but a part of *our* question is surely about Nietzsche. So he asks at the beginning, "Who are we anyway?" recognizing that free minds cheered by the death of God, will be asking "Who are you anyway?" In answer Nietzsche will have to describe just where we all stand in a spiritual history that can now be "fully surveyed" (357).

Nietzsche is not simply what we have thought—godless, an unbeliever, an immoralist—for these labels, while correct, are inadequate because he is these things in such an advanced form that, being mere negations, they cannot even hint at what is positive in his thought. And even with respect to these negatives it is necessary to explain "how it feels to one at this point." "One"—the singular "*Einem*" and not the general "*man*"—has lost all the bitterness and suffering consequent on being torn away from one's belief, all the necessity to make a belief out of one's unbelief. We have interpreted the world to ourselves far too long in a false and lying way—but Nietzsche makes it quite clear, as Descartes had, that this lying interpretation has had a perfectly reasonable basis in our nature: "Man is a revering animal!" Revering, however, is only one part of human nature, for we harbor a contradiction within ourselves: the revering animal is a mistrustful beast. Nietzsche thus begins to give content to the seemingly dogmatic claim made earlier that "much trust and much mistrust" are both necessary (344). Mistrust has now led humankind to trust at least this: the world does not have the worth we trusted it to have. This leads to a quiet lament: "So viel Mistrauen, so viel Philosophie." Philosophy, our exercise of mistrust, has made us dubious of all reverence, even though it belongs to our nature to revere. Philosophy opposes a part of our nature. Could philosophy encompass the whole of our nature? Could philosophy be conducive to reverence?

If the most mistrustful now know that the world does not have the worth we believed it to have, Nietzsche is certainly one who refrains from saying that it has *less*. And at this point laughter breaks out. And laughter continues until called to account by the severe ones cheered by the death of God. What is laughable is humankind's presumption in inventing values that were supposed to *exceed* the value of the actual world. We can now see this impertinence for what it is: "An extravagant aberration of human vanity and unreason." Moreover, we can have a clear view of its contemporary consequences: having been fully in the grip of an aberration spawned by vanity and unreason, we are tempted now by mistrustful philosophy to spurn both vain humanity and wretched world. Schopenhauer is the final expression of this vain aberration, the last possible Platonist, and our whole history of vain hope and hope dashed can now be surveyed and judged from its end. Nietzsche judges it according to the highest category, taste: the monstrous tastelessness of this whole attitude finally comes home to us and we're sick of it—and we break out laughing.

"Who are we anyway?" Nietzsche is one who stands beyond a whole history of reverent evaluation that took philosophical form in Platonism. He stands beyond the death of God that signals the popular demise of that tradition, and beyond the mere cheerfulness that greets the death of that God as liberation. And he stands beyond the final philosophical form of Platonism, Schopenhauerian despair. And he breaks out laughing.

But as a laugher has he not simply taken one long stride deeper into contempt for humankind and for existence as far as we can comprehend it? Is the laugh at the end of this whole trajectory of reverence and mistrust not simply a further downward turn in that trajectory—cynical bitterness and hatred at finally knowing what humanity and the world actually are? By exposing himself to this line of interrogation Nietzsche explicitly raises the issue of his own nihilism. Has the laugher too fallen into the opposition between two worlds, the world of our reverences and another world consisting of himself alone? If his act of destruction is based on "another world," even a world no more substantial than his own mistrustful, laughing self, is he not, after all, a metaphysician whose faith in another world makes it possible for him to deny the world that has been our home (344 end)? This opposition between the world of our reverences and the mistrusting self as world is the "inexorable, fundamental, and deepest suspicion about ourselves." When this suspicion becomes clear enough to articulate itself, it will confront future European generations with a terrifying Either-Or: "Either abolish your reverences—or *yourselves*." In this historic choice between faith and reason, Nietzsche is categorical about one of the possible choices: to abolish *ourselves,* to abolish mistrustful reason that got us into this dilemma, *that* would be nihilism. But about the other possible choice, the abolition of our reverences, there still seems to be uncertainty: would that too be nihilism?—"that is *our* question mark."

Are these the only choices of the European future after the fully surveyable history of European reverence and mistrust? *Either* the abolition of the mistrustful ones, of philosophy without reverence, leaving at the end of history a world of reverence minus mistrust. *Or* the abolition of our reverences, leaving at the end of history only mistrust without reverence. Must Europe choose between one or other aspect of humankind's animal nature, reverence or mistrust? That is the question mark Nietzsche invites us to put to himself as the one who breaks out laughing at the end of this whole history, and it points to a more complete possibility arrived at by the one who is laughing. For the coming sections will intimate that the laugher harbors a possibility beyond the twin nihilisms here set forth, a mistrust that opens onto reverence, a philosophy that facilitates religion in an entirely new key. Both of Nietzsche's previous books—exercises in mistrust—had culminated in the mysterious return of Dionysos, a philosophizing god, an enigmatic union of mistrust and reverence. Nietzsche's claim to have overcome nihilism is implicit in this first use of the term: the terrifying either-or is in fact not exhaustive; neither philosophy nor religion need be sacrificed if a new conception of philosophy and religion can be generated out of the seemingly hopeless nihilism at the end of European religion and philosophy.

The present section opened with a question: "Who are we anyway?" And it ends with a precise form of that question: Is Nietzsche a nihilist? It is an arresting and almost amusing fact that Nietzsche's first substantial use of the term *nihilism* contains what amounts to an invitation to use it as a club with which to attack him.

Opening with these reflections on the European present and future, Book Five shows how the new history of philosophy arises out of the latest consequence of philosophy's history, nihilism, or the death of Platonism popularly experienced as the death of God. Modern nihilism makes the new recovery of the past possible, just as it makes it imperative.

Philosophy's New Method: *Versuche* (347–48)

Nietzsche now turns to our reverences with what looks like a desire to abolish them. And our reverences include not just our religion but our science. His brief and skeptical look at the origins of scientists and scholars, and of religious men and religions, exhibits a new mode of explanation, a genealogical mode tracing the manifest to the latent. But while presuming to explain our dominant modes of explanation, science and religion, by tracing them to psychic and social factors, Nietzsche's method is employed without explanation. Has Nietzsche forgotten to write a *New Organon* or *Discourse on the Method*? Nietzsche's employment of psychological and sociological genealogies to destroy the authority of other modes of explanation simply forces his reader to wonder about the psychic and social grounds of his own mode of explanation. Nietzsche's way of presenting his method of suspicion is calculated to arouse suspicion.

Believers and their need for belief (347). Nietzsche's analysis of the coming age of nihilism continues in these sections, beginning with a seemingly paradoxical phenomenon already analyzed by Zarathustra: the age of nihilism will be an age of belief. In "On the apostates" (*Z* 3.9), Zarathustra watched his erstwhile audiences, though trained in skepticism, fall prey to a wide array of beliefs, the fracture of uniform authority granting permission to belief rather than forbidding it. Need drives most to retain the old Christian beliefs, Nietzsche says, while the "metaphysical need" made famous by Kant and Schopenhauer drives others to metaphysical faiths. Still others need the typically modern form of the "demand for certainty," the Cartesian, scientific-positivistic form. But in the anarchy of authority where science too is seen as a piety, entirely new beliefs spring up, like the three to which even "the most intelligent contemporaries" are prey: *Vaterländerei, naturalisme,* and nihilism of the Petersburg strain. These localisms, German, French, and Russian diseases destined to bedevil the European future, are beliefs that abolish the unbeliever and much else besides as Nietzsche's accounts of *Vaterländerei* anticipate.

But to trace belief to need is only a provisional explanation: what is the basis of need? Nietzsche now provides the reader of *The Joyous Science* with glancing access to his fundamental explanation of need, the will to power, though the phrase itself will only be used once in Book Five, two sections later (349). The discovery of will to power had been set out with characteristic jauntiness and brevity in *Zarathustra* and *Beyond Good and Evil,* and Nietzsche does not abandon his style here or in any subsequent presentation of this basic matter.

Belief denotes a deficiency of will; and will, as the affect or phenomenal component of command, is the decisive sign of sovereignty or might. This definition of will is then restated in a formula that echoes what Zarathustra had stated only to "you who are wisest," the very few philosophers, after he had discovered the extent of the will to power: the less one knows commanding, the more one covets commands. This is all Nietzsche says here about his fundamental conception; he does not yet go as far as he had three years earlier in *Zarathustra* where commanding and obeying were presented as principles basic not only to all human action but to all life and ultimately all action or motion (2.12). He has not changed his mind as many of his interpreters would have preferred: he repeated the comprehensive view of will to power in *Beyond Good and Evil* and he will repeat it two sections later in *The Joyous Science* and again in *On the Genealogy of Morals* and subsequent books. And he will repeat it in the notes he prepared and polished for the planned major work that he announced but was not able to complete. Nietzsche's brevity about this the fundamental matter follows from his view of philosophy, a view he seems to share with Descartes: "I do not wish to persuade anyone to philosophy: it is inevitable, it is perhaps also desirable, that the philosopher should be a *rare* plant" (*KGW* VII 26 [452] = *WP* 420). Philosophy concerns only a few and for them to be trained in the principles of the new philosophy they will have to be tempted into becoming its codiscovers. If any matter can be described as a shy bird glimpsed only in flight, will to power would seem to be it. Count the mentions of will to power in the post-*Zarathustra* books and it seems to have become a relatively minor subject. Reflect on those mentions, their placement and style, and it is obvious that here is that coldest of baths.

The rest of this section applies the genealogical principle of explanation to the origin and spread of two world religions, Christianity and Buddhism: the whole of human history will have to be reinterpreted in light of the new principle of will and the need to believe. Nietzsche's account of Christianity and Buddhism as two world-dominating fanaticisms shows little trace of the respect with which philosophers had previously treated noble lies, despite the fact that Nietzsche has just said that most people still need such beliefs. But if almost all covet being commanded, what future is there in a public speech that debunks "God, prince, class, physician, father confessor, dogma, party conscience"? Is Nietzsche's attack on authority inattentive to its own recognition of the need for authority? Just why Nietzsche thinks it desirable to end philosophy's toleration of the dominant religion will have to be sought in the coming sections—it is not because the tenets of religion have become unbelievable for a philosopher: philosophers have never been believers (351).

Nietzsche ends with a contrast. Those who need to be commanded are contrasted with those who find pleasure and strength in *self*-determination; the latter's freedom of will leads them to take leave of every wish for certainty and to abolish their reverences. The last sentence is thus a literal match for the first: the hold or security necessary for most is set against the willed insecurity of those Nietzsche now calls "the free minds par excellence," the free minds a new definition of which has been the aim of the whole series of books now coming to a new end in the post-*Zarathustra* conclusion to *The Joyous Science*. Zarathustra had said that the risk of adventure was the true basis of science, refuting the scientist's claim that science is based on a need for security (*Z* 4.15). If adventure and experiment are the foundations of science, and if *Versucher*—experimenter, attempter, tempter (*BGE* 42)—is the name with which to baptize the new scientist,[6] then Nietzsche will have to question the old science: What is the genealogy of *its* commitment to science? The next sections begin this genealogical inquiry with a look at unfree minds, commanded minds.

On the origin of scholars (348). The origin of scholars is treated in two separate sections with the same title even though, taken together, they are shorter than many single sections. The break into two sections also seems curious because it separates two points that seem connected, both being about Jews. Also, the sections both practice a hidden reflexivity: the reader is virtually taunted to apply the author's critique to the author.

The first section begins with a claim the basis and importance of which will be made visible only much later: European scholars have a political loyalty as "essential and involuntary" as the dependencies of a plant. They are advocates of a politics that came to dominate modern Europe, "bearers" of the democratic ideal which Nietzsche's politics oppose. To win European scholars to a new politics, Nietzsche will either have to afford them a consciousness superior to that of a plant such that they can choose his politics, or he will have to nurture new plants. For now, he simply states a claim: if one sends one's view to school—if one's view becomes more voluntary than a plant—one learns to detect the family origins of a scholar's work.

What counts for proof for a scholar depends "almost always" on family traits. Consequently, what counts for proof takes many forms among scholars: classification systems for the offspring of bureaucrats, the appearance of persuasiveness for the offspring of lawyers, and, for the sons of the Protestant manse, claims stated from the heart with feeling. Such sons of Protestantism spring from fathers and grandfathers used to being believed for their earnestness alone. The son and grandson of Pastors Nietzsche and Oehler surely derived a little extra pleasure from this description of his own strain of scholarly plants: he will have aroused a little indignation for speaking his claims from the heart and with warmth and expecting to be believed. The indignant will wonder if he knows what he is doing: presuming to have left the plant kingdom while accusing the rest of breeding true, his style seems to betray that he has bred true. But his last example, the offspring of Jews, opens a new perspective on Nietzsche himself.

Jews spring from forebears used to never being believed because they

---

6. Picht's insightful analysis of this baptism (*Nietzsche*, 61–69) is a crucial component in his comprehensive picture of Nietzsche's revolutionary philosophy.

found themselves a small minority in a setting shaped by the hostile majority; consequently, their scholarly books take recourse to a universal instrument that compels belief, logic. This is the only scholarly trait Nietzsche here praises, and it is the only one that is more than a matter of local style. Logic has Greek and not Hebrew origins, origins on which Nietzsche reflected from the very beginning to the very end of his work. Logic, Nietzsche says, is a cleansing rational discipline that has schooled the European and especially the German mind. Schooled under this form of persuasion, one learns to draw more far-reaching distinctions, to make sharper inferences, and to write more clearly and cleanly. Now Nietzsche himself had become a minority of one in a hostile environment of believers in other faiths, and he had become used to never being believed. In sending his view to school, has he learned to choose a style refined by Jews who have schooled Europe, a logical style of intellectual cleanliness drawing from Greek and Hebrew alike?[7]

What constitutes proof for Nietzsche? More particularly, how has he availed himself of the one refining instrument of proof that compels persuasion in those predisposed to *disbelieve* what is spoken because the speaker is an outsider? In the next section, Nietzsche speaks of the logical method of the logical Jew Spinoza, the outsider who persuaded Europe of a fundamental but erroneous view of life. Nietzsche had discovered in Spinoza a kin, a precursor, for he found himself in "five main points of [Spinoza's] teaching" (letter to Overbeck, 30 July 1881): Spinoza "recovered the innocence of the world" (*GM* 2.15).[8] Still, Nietzsche differs from Spinoza on the fundamental matter, "the will of life." And this is to differ from Spinoza on what made his teaching persuasive, not its logic after all, but shared origins, shared experiences. These shared experiences, Nietzsche will argue, tied modern science to modern politics, Spinoza's view of life serving to undergird the political program of modern democratic movements. If Nietzsche's solitary account of the fundamental will of life, will to power, is ever to persuade and become as pervasive as Spinoza's once solitary account, it will, presumably, likewise depend on auditors with shared experiences.

---

7. On Jews and Greeks and their contribution to the European mind, see *HH* 1.475.

8. On the kinship of Spinoza and Nietzsche, see Deleuze, *Spinoza*, and Deleuze, *Nietzsche and Philosophy*, 62, 206n18.

Spinoza and the History of Philosophy:
Will to Power Not Will to Self-Preservation (349)

Once again the origin of scholars (349). Spinoza's teaching on the nature of life captured the whole of modern science including Darwin: the fundamental life drive is self-preservation. Nietzsche's opposition to the reigning scientific orthodoxy is stated in a counterprinciple: the actual fundamental life drive is the expansion of power, self-preservation is only a symptom of that drive under conditions of distress; "the will to power is the will of life." Spinoza, Nietzsche claims, was obliged to view life as a drive to self-preservation because he himself lived life under conditions of distress; he judged all of life from himself—he acted as a philosopher in the manner stated by Descartes (*Discourse* i.5). Modern natural scientists followed Spinoza not because they were persuaded by his logic, by "the hocus pocus of mathematical form," "the mail and mask" in which he clothed his philosophy (*BGE* 5), but because they were his spiritual kin—they too sprang from such conditions of distress, from corners and caves that made "life is self-preservation" ring true for them.[9]

But Nietzsche says a natural scientist should abandon the human corner that dictates a personal perspective and view nature in a way that is true to nature. What way is that? Nietzsche's way—viewing the will to power as the will of life. This is the only time Nietzsche names will to power in this whole Book addressed to science, but it is hardly a casual occasion: will to power is the *rival* of the view that took over modern science and grounded modern politics.

In differing with Spinoza, Nietzsche sets out a new foundational view, a competing view that aspires to win kin for itself. Will they be persuaded by his logic, or will they have shared his experiences? Nietzsche emphasizes the latter but both are present. His writings pry open a perspective on a different experience of life and exemplify it throughout: classical Greek experience as agonistic, the history of morals as a contest between two dispositions toward life, the spirited life of philosophy, and ultimately the comprehensive teaching of will to power. The aphoristic manner of setting forth this agonistic perspective is a logic of presentation loyal to the inner logic of its content: it tempts to an experience

---

9. Ottmann, *Nietzsche,* 267. On the social origins of Spinoza's thought, its metaphysics, politics, and artful presentation, see Yovel, *Spinoza and Other Heretics,* vol 1. Volume 2 of this important work traces the "Adventures of Immanence" in Spinoza's successors and provides a sympathetic study of "Spinoza and Nietzsche: *Amor dei* and *Amor fati*" (104–35).

articulated in Nietzsche but still inchoate and wordless in his kin. Nietzsche seems to view his relation to subsequent science on the model of
Spinoza's relation to modern science—and modern science does not trace
its view to Spinoza but to the evidence.

By giving expression to experiences only beginning to be felt by
others, Nietzsche makes himself attractive not simply on the model of
Spinoza, but on the model of the very archetype of philosophical seduction, Socrates, the philosopher who initiated the rule of logic. When
speaking for the last time of the lure of the ugly Socrates, Nietzsche
emphasized the appeal of "rationality at all costs" as the revelation of
kinship: in the dying Socrates, Greek youth glimpsed one who had mastered the impulses they were beginning to feel inchoately in themselves
(*TI* Socrates 8–11). When Nietzsche says that his books after *Zarathustra*
are a search for kin (*EH* Books *BGE* 1), he places himself with Spinoza
and Socrates: he seduces through the appropriate means—the logic of
aphorisms—to a view which came early to himself.

In differing from Spinoza and challenging Spinoza's kin has Nietzsche done what he says they never did, left his own human corner? Can
anyone ever leave their corner? The two sections asserting the familial
rootedness of scholars never directly claim that anything but plant life
is possible. Nevertheless, in the very midst of his sociology of knowledge and his psychology of knowledge, Nietzsche intrudes with his own
view of nature, soberly reporting it as if it were simply true and not
some family loyalty. Surely he means to evoke an indignant response:
"But this too is only your forefathers speaking." To which Nietzsche
would surely respond once again, "You will be eager enough to make
this objection?—well, so much the better" (*BGE* 22). Better that those
secure in a scientific orthodoxy, believing in their certitudes about life
as self-preservation, replace those certitudes with genealogical relativity.
But is that all that is possible? Could the son of the Protestant manse
who sent his view to school actually have done what he alleges here?
Could he have left his own human corner and arrived at a view of nature
free of humanization and in some fundamental sense true to nature?

Nietzsche's single presentation of will to power in *The Joyous Science*
parallels his first mention of will to power in *Beyond Good and Evil* (9)—
and a brief look at that presentation will provide a useful supplement on
this foundational issue, about which Nietzsche always speaks with extreme economy. In *Beyond Good and Evil* too, will to power is introduced
as a comprehensive teaching about nature within a critique of a different
account of nature traceable to the needs of its originators, the Stoics.

After his critique Nietzsche generalizes: "Philosophy always creates the world in its own image: it cannot do otherwise. Philosophy is . . . the most spiritual will to power." This generalization disparaging philosophy's hubris ends the very section in which Nietzsche had presented his own account of nature. What warrant can *that* account have? Many have supposed that such self-reflexive playfulness amounts to Nietzsche's deconstruction of his own claims. But would the philosopher with the whole future of humankind on his conscience (*BGE* 61) have spent his years preparing little snares for the entertainment and justification of literary and philosophic critics who would in the coming century suppose that they had discovered the complete relativity of texts? Is that all Nietzsche had on his mind, a little relativism long pondered by philosophy, a little free spiritedness of the sort he himself criticizes as lacking seriousness? The aphorism (*BGE* 9) presenting his own most serious view in the very midst of a critique of the possibility of such views is, it seems to me, not a deconstructive end but a constructive beginning—subsequent aphorisms on will to power build the case that must begin so dubiously and against such disbelief. Rather than positing will to power in order to say, to our relief, "I can't mean it either," these aphorisms initiate the reader gradually into the most comprehensive and fundamental conclusions—conclusions that cannot be welcomed: "When a philosopher these days lets it be known that he is not a skeptic . . . everyone is annoyed" (*BGE* 208). Nietzsche's aphoristic method of *Versuche* suits his end; his logic aims at a shared authentication of his claims; and because any authentication of his fundamental teaching must begin with a clear sense of the implausibility of such claims and a clear sense of the suspicions that must be satisfied before such claims can become plausible, Nietzsche himself sets his view under suspicion.

If "philosophy is this tyrannical drive itself, the most spiritual will to power" (*BGE* 9), Nietzsche's own account of nature is an act of the most spiritual will to power. But is it simply the willful imposition of his own drive to tyranny? An open act of philosophical rage following insight into all the others? The marvelous structural coherence of *Beyond Good and Evil* suggests something different and better: in its own "will to power," the most spiritual form of what is—philosophy—glimpses in what *it* is its continuity with everything that is. And that glimpse leads to the affirmation both of itself and of everything that is.

In *Beyond Good and Evil* Nietzsche begins his presentation of nature as will to power with an invitation containing both these elements, insight and affirmation: "Think to yourselves of an essence such as nature is, wasteful without measure, indifferent without measure, without purposes and consideration, without pity and justice, fertile and desolate and uncertain at the same time, think to yourselves of indifference itself as power—how *could* you live according to this indifference? (9)" How is this insight possible? How is this affirmation possible? Sections 13 and 22 show that what is at stake here are the fundamental views of modern science, biology and physics, the sciences of life and nature. If only interpretations are possible (22) perhaps the most adequate interpretation is accessible through the science nearest to us, psychology, the study of the soul or self (23). Any such study will have the encrusted prejudices of the heart against it; nevertheless, "free minds" will inexorably pursue the dangerous and painful inquiry, driven by their very "conscience of method" (36). Beginning with a study of the self that never forgets "the phenomenality of the inner world too" (*KGW* VIII 11 [113] = *WP* 477), a strict methodological monism will require that it "determine *all* efficient force univocally as—*will to power*" (36). Such a conclusion will draw the objection that it demonizes nature; in fact, however, it is a vindication of god or the gods (37). And that vindication will ultimately express itself in willing the eternal return of all that was and is (56). The valuing being thus brings its valuing into accord with what is; the affirmation of eternal return arises out of insight into will to power.

Beyond Good and Evil charts this course of insight and affirmation but *Thus Spoke Zarathustra* is Nietzsche's master work because it shows the connection in greatest detail between his two basic teachings, will to power and eternal return, the connection between the way of nature and its affirmation.

The Joyous Science Book Five is, in its own way, a repetition of the pattern of insight and affirmation present in Nietzsche's two previous books. The foundational ontological claim of will to power is presented as the rival to Spinoza's view, the view basic to modern science and modern politics. The epistemological limitations on any such ontological claim will be presented when the limits of consciousness are considered (354). The consequent affirmation of eternal return will be broached only after the limitations of method are fully faced (370). And the whole of human history will have to be reexamined in the light of this new fundamental teaching, for if the will to power is "an innovation as a theory—as a reality it is the *primordial fact of all history*" (*BGE* 259).

No new dogmatism lurks in Nietzsche's view of nature as will to power for precisely it necessitates "our new infinite" (*JS* 374), the infinity of possible interpretations. But in understanding interpretations as themselves enactments of will to power, does Nietzsche give himself license to impose his own willful construction on interpretations? Everywhere in Nietzsche's work one encounters the responsibility to be attentive to what is unspoken in interpretations, to hear what is actually present within them. What sounds so willful—interpretation as will to power—itself practices an *allowing* that lets what is present come to the ear. What sounds so lawless legislates philological responsibility for itself, a responsible attentiveness that permits no violence to the thing heard. The great spiritual achievements of culture that are the most frequent themes of Book Five—Science, Art, Religion, Philosophy—are approached in a way that permits them to be heard as what they are. The most spiritual will to power aims to recover the text of our spiritual past as it really was; while uncovering the history of interpretive willfulness, its own willfulness is a passion to allow them to speak as they are. And that allowing which permits the recovery of our historical and cultural past is prelude to the ultimate act of allowing by the most spiritual will to power, the act of letting be that wills the eternal return of beings as they are.

Philosophy and Religion: Understanding Philosophy's Pride and Modesty (350–53)

In honor of the homines religiosi (350). The pair of sections on believers in science is followed by a pair of sections on believers in religion. "In honor of. . ."—the titles lead one to expect tributes honoring the parties named, "homines religiosi" and "priestly natures." In fact, honor is accorded in the first section to only one of the two types of religious men depicted, while honor is accorded in the second section not by Nietzsche but by the people. Here Nietzsche begins rewriting the spiritual history of Europe to accord with his new canons of interpretation, a rewriting to be carried forward by scholars and scientists with minds retrained in Nietzsche's school.

"In honor of the *homines religiosi*"[10] praises the Roman church. One must forcibly remind oneself that Nietzsche views the triumph of Christianity over the classical world as an unspeakable catastrophe: "The whole labor of the ancient world *in vain:* I have no words to express my feelings about something so monstrous" (*A* 59). This section concerns historical events that occurred within that catastrophe to deepen it and secure it.

10. On *homines religiosi*, see *JS* 358; *BGE* 45, 59; *KGW* VIII 7 [5].

The Roman church not only gave harbor to but was in fact founded upon profound suspicion about the worth of existence and about the worth of one's own existence: its Jesuitism long preceded Loyola, for it was heir to the deep and contemplative unfaith of the orient. This is high and astonishing praise from Nietzsche, and it is prelude to an equally remarkable critique of Protestantism: Protestantism is a fervent rebellion by true believers whose literalism and dogmatism precluded the refinement necessary to grasp the profound suspicions the church harbored. And the French Revolution is a further step into dominance by shallow and simple believers. Nietzsche's judgments here are all comparative and intra-Christian: praise of the Roman church springs from insight into Protestantism and its consequences. A broader perspective will appear soon enough and encompass the whole of Christianity in a more comprehensive field.

In honor of priestly natures (351). Rather than honoring priestly natures, this section honors philosophy for being different from the priestly wisdom the people honor. It is difficult to distinguish the philosopher from the priest today, Nietzsche maintains, because everyone has come to share the perspective of the people. From this perspective only one kind of wisdom is recognizable, one that sacrifices itself for the ends of the people. This section reflects on the "emergency conditions" under which philosophy arose and the protective coloring in which it had to shelter itself (*GM* 3.10)—but it removes that protective coloring and describes philosophy in its own, nonpriestly terms.

Priestly wisdom serves the people; it is remote from the way of the philosopher, the way of living passionately in a thunder cloud of the highest problems and heaviest responsibilities. The responsibilities of these passionate solitaries differ from those of priestly wisdom, for priestly wisdom provides certainty and security to the people. Nietzsche's thought is close to Bacon's: priestly wisdom is provided by both the Governor of Strangers' House and the Father of Salomon's House whose religion and science claim certainty for themselves and afford certainty for their dependents.

But claims to certainty make philosophers suspicious—and Nietzsche now offers a penetrating gaze into the philosopher as he understands him. The priest cannot count as a knower for a philosopher because philosophers do not believe in "knowers"—the title "knower" bespeaks a pride unbecoming a philosopher. *Modesty* invented the word *philosopher* in Greece, and left the presumption of calling oneself wise to the "sophists." But the modesty of a philosopher is an odd sort of modesty because it was "the modesty of such monsters of pride and sovereignty as Pythagoras, as Plato—." The monsters of pride and sovereignty who invented the modest word *philosophy* and gave it its most influential definition did not presume to call themselves "knowers" or "wise." Nietzsche knows full well that Pythagoras and Plato made claims to knowledge, Pythagoras fixing knowledge in number and Plato in ideas. Why choose these two as examples of *modesty* in knowledge?

Nietzsche seems to share the philosopher's view of philosophers given clear expression by Montaigne: "I cannot easily persuade myself," Montaigne says, "that Epicurus, Plato, and Pythagoras gave us their Atoms, their Ideas, and their Numbers as good coin of the realm. They were too wise to establish their articles of faith on anything so uncertain and so debatable." Montaigne, like Nietzsche, is a skeptic about philosophers' claims to knowledge and says why: "They wanted to consider everything, to weigh everything, and they found that occupation suited to the natural curiosity that is in us." Philosophy accords with the nature of human beings, but the free pursuit of this natural inclination puts both society and philosopher in jeopardy. Consequently, "Some things they wrote for the needs of society, like their religions; and on that account it was reasonable that they did not want to bare popular opinions to the skin, so as not to breed disorder in people's obedience to the laws and customs of their country. Plato treats this mystery with his cards pretty much on the table" (Montaigne, *Essays* ii.12, "Apology," 379). And Nietzsche repeats this Montaignian view: "In the case of philosophers . . . their entire trade demands that they concede only certain truths: namely, those through which their trade receives public sanction . . . 'Thou shalt not lie'—in plain English, *take care, philosopher, not to tell the truth*" (*TI* Skirmishes 42).[11]

When Nietzsche asked to be forgiven his ignorance at the end of Book Five (381), he had long since made clear that ignorance belongs to the philosopher as such—even to Pythagoras and Plato. Philosophers have never believed in "knowers" but have always been surrounded by "knowers" and have had to adopt the mask of knowers as Bacon and Descartes did. Philosophy had to adopt the appearance of priestly wisdom for its own survival, and that survival history can now be charted by a

---

11. Nietzsche's view is taken over by Leo Strauss who calls for a "future sociology of philosophy" in order to demonstrate that "what unites all genuine philosophers is more important than what unites a given philosopher with a particular group of non-philosophers"—Maimonides and Spinoza with Jews, for instance, or Bacon and Descartes with Christians (Strauss, *Persecution and the Art of Writing*, 7, 8).

Nietzschean history of philosophy as the history of Platonic esotericism. "Ignorance" belongs to the philosopher as openness to the enigmatic whole but such "ignorance" had not been permitted. "The emergency conditions under which philosophy arose and survived at all" (*GM* 3.10) required a priestly mask; philosophers, too, provided the people with security and certainty. "Has all this really altered?" Can the philosopher now appear in the open free of Jesuitism? Can he appear in public as the passionate seeker of knowledge he has known himself to be in private? "The truth must be told though the world crumble!" Nietzsche assents to this "great shout by the great Fichte" (*D* 353) but adds a proviso: "One would have to know the truth first." Philosophy's ignorance is consistent with its knowing the truth about truth and with telling that truth. With Nietzsche philosophy becomes publicly "ignorant" again; it becomes Socratic again, knowing that it will again be put on trial.

The next two sections apply Nietzsche's genealogical method to the need for morality and the origin of religions. Morals and religion are matters about which philosophers "wrote for the needs of society," Montaigne said, because they wanted to preserve obedience. But Nietzsche incites to disobedience, preserving morality as intellectual conscience and religion as an earthly loyalty different from the prevailing religion.

The way in which morality is scarcely dispensable (352). Morality is scarcely dispensable because it clothes our nakedness. But Nietzsche seems bent on flaunting the naked truth and spoiling the party he alludes to: the fun stops when a magician causes us all to see one another naked. The nakedness Nietzsche wants to uncover is an old story in his writings: if morality was once scarcely dispensable as the veneer of civility over a natural beastliness, it is now scarcely dispensable as a veneer over our domestication. The long history of moral discipline altered the natural dispositions by taming and gentling them. Nietzsche is of course no advocate of primal beastliness despite what many have been pleased to say about him; there is no suggestion here or elsewhere that "beyond good and evil" means a return to some premoral, presocial condition.

Nietzsche does not end with nakedness: Zarathustra counsels his disciples never to look on their admired friends naked lest they despair of them; and they are to dress themselves in noble clothing for their friends in order to inspire them (*Z* 1.14). Indispensable morality has changed its look because of the change in the heart of man. The new morality emphasizes spiritedness and combativeness; it elevates the virtuous envy prescribed by Zarathustra: vie with one another for supremacy in a contest of mistrust and reverence, curiosity and decency.

On the origin of religions (353). Religions originate with founders, sin-gular individuals gifted with insight and invention. They invent both a practice and an interpretation, but the interpretation is often more important because the practice is often already in place, as it was with Christianity and Buddhism. Jesus and Buddha were foundational inter-preters who saw something special in an already present way of life, selected it out as the one way that counted, guessed to what end it could be put, and succeeded in generating single-minded fanaticisms about the newly interpreted way. Nietzsche generalizes from these two examples: founders of religions must possess a psychologically infallible knowl-edge of the soul that enables them to recognize likeness in souls thought disparate; in establishing that likeness the founder initiates a historic pro-cess, a long festival of recognition that elevates to the highest importance an already present but neglected quality.

Morality can scarcely be dispensed with. Can religion? This section on religion does nothing more than demythologize two victorious fanati-cisms but *Zarathustra* and *Beyond Good and Evil* had ended on the myste-rious reappearance of Dionysos and Ariadne. *Beyond Good and Evil* (295) had acknowledged a grave difficulty in such religious speech: it comes at the wrong time. Nietzsche had been told, he says, that his "friends" no longer like to hear of God and gods—the God now dead seems to have given religion itself a bad name. Nietzsche's cautious speech about religion in later sections of Book Five is mindful of this restraint.

Philosophy's Means: Consciousness and Its Limitations (354–55)

Philosophy requires a prolegomena, an investigation of consciousness, its sole instrument. This perennial problem, philosophy's self-examina-tion and self-certification, is in some ways an absurd project: "How should the tool be able to criticize itself when it can use only *itself* for the critique? It cannot even define itself!" (*KGW* VIII 2 [87]).[12] Neverthe-less, that project is unavoidable. Nietzsche's Prolegomena to Any Future Metaphysics That Will Be Able to Come Forth as a Joyous Science is, in one of its essential aspects, an evolutionary history of consciousness (354) that shows the impossibility of any metaphysical or transcenden-tal deduction of universal and necessary categories. In its other essential aspect, Nietzsche's Prolegomena is an investigation of the motives be-

12. For a list of such passages and a rewarding discussion of them, see Blondel, *Nietz-sche,* 240ff.

hind the drive for knowledge (355). These social and psychic genealogies make philosophy so precarious that it is always open to doubt.

On the "genius of the species" (354). The *Genius der Gattung,* consciousness, is the defining feature both of the species as species and of individual members of the species singled out by their high degree of consciousness. The few philosophers, those whose conscious passion it is to make everything conscious, stand at the pinnacle of the species as exemplars of what defines it.

Consciousness or "becoming conscious of oneself" arises as a problem when we realize that we could get along just as well without it. As the *Use and Disadvantage of History* had shown, life is stronger without self-reflection. But if life and consciousness appear to contradict one another, what is the purpose of consciousness? Nietzsche proposes an evolutionary answer that begins with the "perhaps extravagant surmise" that the subtlety and strength of consciousness is proportional to the capacity to communicate, a capacity itself proportional to the need to communicate. Nietzsche's evolutionary perspective presupposes that we are an animal species formed over millennia, and still being formed, by our adaptive strategies. In some respects that perspective is a very up-to-date neo-Darwinianism: *homo sapiens* is an accidental appearance in an evolutionary history of life that is not a ladder existing for the sake of its top rung but a bush branching into equally adaptive forms. "We oppose the vanity that the human [was] the great hidden purpose of the evolution of animals. The human is by no means the crown of creation; every living kind stands beside it on the same level of perfection" (*A* 14). Nietzsche possessed what Henning Ottmann calls "astonishing familiarity with the discussions surrounding Darwinianism,"[13] but he refused the Darwinian principle that the preservation of life is *the* force behind adaptive strategies (*BGE* 13); having traced this principle to Spinoza, Nietzsche grounded it in the more fundamental and active principle of will to power.

Speaking of the species as a whole, Nietzsche says that the origin and development of consciousness is explicable as a "net of communication" for "the most endangered animal": it needed to communicate with its peers because it needed to act in concert with them in order to survive. Survival—life—required the development of communication in this species; what one needed had to be learned and relayed quickly through signs in the form of words.

13. Ottmann, *Nietzsche,* 353.

Nietzsche relays his own conclusion ironically: "my thought" is that all thought is social. "Our thought is constantly, through the character of consciousness—through the commanding 'genius of the species' in it—*majorisirt* ["majoritied," out-voted] and translated back into the perspective of the herd." Action cannot help but be individual and particular; thought cannot help but generalize. "Individual thought" is almost an oxymoron: striving to refine, isolate, particularize, thought mixes, blends, generalizes, because thought is consciousness formulated through language. Furthermore, because it is consciousness *communicated* through language, thought must be apprehended by others in its mixed, blended, generalized form. As Müller-Lauter puts it: "Crudification is simply unavoidable in the representation of anything at all." [14] Philosophy or the highest refinement of thought attempts the impossible: to experience and express what is irreducibly singular by a means irreducibly general; philosophy, in Kierkegaard's image, is an attempt to paint the god Mars in the armor that made him invisible. But it is an unavoidable attempt made by the ultimate "artists" of the species, individual latecomers in the history of the species, "orators, preachers, writers," who squander the species' hard-won resources of communication on an effort judged by others to be superfluous and known by itself to harbor a contradiction. "Know thyself" is Apollo's imperative, but in giving the gift of beautiful speech as its means, Apollo gives a gift inappropriate to its task. Philosophy came too late in the history of consciousness to have a Muse of its own. [15]

"This is the real phenomenalism and perspectivism as *I* understand it"; it is no Kantianism; it does not hold that an articulable and timeless network of categories maps an unrepresentable reality. Refusing to compile a list of categories, Nietzsche's phenomenalism and perspectivism lay bare the quality of all possible categories: they render "shallow, thin, relatively stupid, general." And Nietzsche's phenomenalism permits, it even demands, that *Versuche* be made to grasp what is true of the world on the basis of our experience of it, Versuche that Nietzsche follows through to the conclusion that "the world defined and determined according to its 'intelligible character'—it would be 'will to power' and nothing else" (*BGE* 36). Because of the shifting, historical quality of

14. Müller-Lauter, *Nietzsche,* 34.

15. Blondel's *Nietzsche* is a rigorous and illuminating reflection on the limitations of language and Nietzsche's efforts to exploit them for both insight and communication; see especially, 148–53, 201–38. See also Del Caro, *Nietzsche Contra Nietzsche,* 252–58.

all categories, Nietzsche's phenomenalism can never share the Kantian aim of justifying the certitude of Newtonian science. And because of the refusal to accept complete skepticism about "the way of all beings" (Z 2.12), it can never share the Kantian dodge of exploiting ignorance to postulate God, freedom, and immortality of the ever-unknowable and shore up an old morality.

Nietzsche's phenomenalism and perspectivism argue that all attempts to become aware of what is fundamentally the case employ an instrument that fixes what is flowing and makes the unlike like. Thinking and saying are, as Müller-Lauter argues, a *Gleichmachen* and *Festmachen* of items neither *gleich* nor *fest*.[16] This is a cardinal point: philosophy is not simply hampered by this great plight, its discovery is the essence of philosophy, the ground of philosophy's modesty, the primordial awareness of enigma that sets philosophy off from all other forms of awareness and makes it suspicious of all "knowers" (JS 351). In obeying its patron Apollo in the passionate pursuit of self-knowledge, philosophy comes to "know" that complete self-knowledge is impossible. These are the grounds of Nietzsche's "ignorance" for which he asks forgiveness: his ignorance is forgivable because its grounds are the very grounds of philosophy as such.[17]

Just here lies the greatest danger for philosophy. "Ultimately the growth of consciousness is a danger; and one who lives among the most conscious Europeans knows in fact that it is a danger." The danger is not some issue local to academic philosophy, the fraternal philosophical debates of post-Kantian epistemology and ontology. It is not a philosophical but a political danger, one generated by the nature of consciousness as a communal instrument and made acute in the historical stage now arrived at by the development of consciousness. Consciousness, an adaptive tool evolved in the survival struggle of the most endangered species, seemed eventually to render life safe and even make it comfortable. After a long history of increasing safety and comfort, human consciousness has arrived at a point where it "knows" what is good for safety, it "knows"

16. Müller-Lauter, *Nietzsche*, 12.

17. Stanley Rosen, in a series of essays on Nietzsche, finds his ignorance unforgivable. Both Nietzsche's "critique of the elements of consciousness" and his claim that "the total character of the world . . . is in all eternity chaos" (JS 109) are understood by Rosen as so extreme in their implications as to make simply contradictory any assertion about anything. Moreover, Rosen finds Nietzsche taking advantage of this total flux to engage in arbitrary creative acts imposing his own imprint on things, a merely willful will to power bearing no further warrant than Nietzsche's will to tyranny. See especially *Ancients and the Moderns*, 209–34, and *Quarrel between Philosophy and Poetry*, 183–203.

what is useful. "Utility" to the community—"the law that obliges us to procure as best we can the common good of all men"—is what we now know to be good; and that law, that highest good, has become a global law obliging all. Nietzsche describes the danger from a perspective outside the law, a treasonous perspective of a lawbreaker questioning the binding character of the fundamental law: what moderns call "utility" and claim to know is "ultimately only a belief, an imagining, and perhaps precisely that most calamitous stupidity of which we will one day perish." "We"—this is the voice of philosophy, that "modesty" aware of the impossibility of ultimate knowledge. Philosophy may fall victim to "truth," to a "knowing" that philosophy knows to be a set of authoritative opinions passing as knowledge. No philosopher has ever believed in "knowers" but now philosophy is faced with a global race of knowers backed by a uniform scientific method and the authority of universal acknowledgment. Perhaps one day we will perish of this stupidity; perhaps one day philosophy will be abolished by this new religion which "knows" the end of man, the Baconian Cartesian religion. The once most endangered species will, through its genius of communication, have made the world safe for itself and in that safety abolish what still endangers it, philosophy.

Zarathustra's rash speech in the marketplace after ten years of solitude made the same accusatory point about modern faith by quoting "the last man," the citizen of the universal and homogeneous state at the end of history: "No shepherd and one herd! Everybody wants the same, everybody is the same: whoever feels differently goes voluntarily into the madhouse" (Z Prologue 5). Philosophy, necessarily opened onto uncertainty because it treats the enigma of being with an instrument evolved for survival, faces the danger from which it might perish in a universal "knowledge" that derives from the philosophers Bacon and Descartes. Leo Strauss makes Nietzsche's point in the great debate in which Alexandre Kojève advocates the modern and Strauss the nonmodern: "The coming of the universal and homogeneous state"—the rule of the last man, of "the autonomous herd" (BGE 202)—"will be the end of philosophy on earth." [18]

Nietzsche's understanding of philosophy is a modern form of Socrates' "human wisdom" (Apology 20d–e): philosophy knows its own ignorance and learns its vulnerability to public faiths ignorant of their ignorance. Philosophy's task with respect to the now dominant reli-

18. Strauss, On Tyranny, 211.

gion parallels philosophy's task as understood by the Socratics Bacon and Descartes: to preserve threatened philosophy or the pursuit of the rational by bringing religion under the rule of philosophy. Philosophy is modest; it knows its ignorance. But philosophy is immodest; it knows the scope of what it must undertake on its own behalf. That such modesty is wholly consonant with such immodesty is shown by the modesty of such monsters of pride and sovereignty as Plato and Pythagoras (351), or as Bacon and Descartes and Nietzsche.

The aphorism showing the place of philosophy in the history of consciousness ends on the politics of philosophy, emphasizing its present endangered state within the consciousness of advanced modernity. But the core of this section is an epistemological, not a political argument: recognition of the evolution of consciousness forces modesty on the highest consciousness. Philosophy's phenomenalism and perspectivism dictate that it can become conscious only of "a surface- and sign-world, a world made common and meaner" by the sole instrument with which we can apprehend it. We are locked into "mere" phenomena, and into this or that perspective. But if we are, how can we possibly claim that our perspective is "true," that it somehow corresponds to what can never become an object for it? Nietzsche made just such a claim a few pages earlier with respect to the most fundamental matter: the will of life is "the will to power" (*JS* 349). How does Nietzsche's phenomenalism and perspectivism permit such statements? The next section too reflects on this matter and makes this question even more acute.

The origin of our concept of "knowledge" (355). The genealogy of knowledge now turns from an evolutionary history to a psychological one: "knowledge" originates in a species-wide desire that is not a desire for knowledge but a desire to tame fear. Our philosophy, like our religion, has served this motive by generating reasons for eliminating fear. Taking its guidance from what is most natural among the people, philosophy has proven its utility: it is not useless or dangerous, folly or crime, for it can assuage the primary fears. But that too is all over now; philosophy now strikes out on a path that looks "unnatural," a path leading to the most feared.

Nietzsche marks his territory with a nice Socratic opening: like Socrates, he will begin with an explanation picked up from the streets, and like Socrates, he will argue that the street explanation is deficient and needs to be rethought from a nonstreet perspective. But Nietzsche will argue that on the crucial issue of knowledge philosophers since Socrates have been stuck on the street view: for them too knowledge is the assimilation of the strange to the familiar, beginning in "the instinct of fear," it establishes "a sense of security."

Nietzsche's argument against this old alignment of philosophy with the people's fears points a finger at "this philosopher" who was all "too easily satisfied" because he followed the people's inclination and fancied that "the world was 'known' when he had led it back to an 'idea.'" Which philosopher? Plato, surely, the Plato of the *Phaedo*. There, Plato's dying Socrates explains how he abandoned the mechanistic and teleological explanations of Greek natural science in favor of a "second sailing" (99d), a safe method of philosophical inquiry that begins with the *logoi* or words and speeches about things (99e) and traces their explanation to an "idea": the Platonic Socrates learned to begin with explanations picked up from the street and to trace them to ideas. And Socrates himself suggests that this is to be "too easily satisfied": on his dying day Socrates says that with respect to any of his explanations, if no one objected he was satisfied. But while recommending this easy satisfaction to his interlocutors (101d) he adds a quiet proviso: if *they* themselves are not satisfied they are to keep pressing until they are (107b). Was Socrates *himself* satisfied with an answer if no one objected? Or is this not an example of his famous irony? Plato's Socrates stops talking when he has given a satisfactory answer, one to which no one objects. Plato's Socrates differs from Aristophanes' Socrates or the Socrates killed by his city because he knows when to stop talking and appear satisfied: *he* is satisfied when *they* are satisfied and they are satisfied when their fears are settled, when they are told by the wise philosopher—What? That he knows he is ignorant and can show they are too? Plato's Socrates has abandoned that rash indiscretion. No. He tells the people there are good reasons for believing what they want to believe, that their souls are immortal, say. He can even prove it if they are willing to grant, as Simmias is, that learning is recollection (91e–95a), or, as Cebes is, that there are *eide* that cause the things to be what they are (102b–107a). He is even willing to say his imperative came from "a speaker trustworthy to you," their Apollo, though he fears they will take this for irony (*Apology* 20e, 37e–38a).

Here is a major event in Nietzsche's history of philosophy that he will develop in later sections. Plato's Socrates adapted philosophy to the way of the people. This philosophy opposed "Sophist culture . . . realist culture" whose greatest representative is Thucydides, "the grand summation, the last manifestation of that strong, stern, hard matter-of-factness instinctive to the old Hellenes." Plato is the great figure in this turn: "Plato is a coward in the face of reality—consequently he flees into the ideal" (*TI* Ancients 2)—into what calms people's fears. Philosophy became therapeutic. It dressed itself up in monotono-theism.

Philosophers who follow "this philosopher"—and since Plato all philosophers are on the same track (*BGE* 191)—are all too easily satisfied. Their satisfaction with ideas as explanatory principles reduced the individual and unique to what is purportedly common to all things, familiar matters such as our multiplication tables, or our logic, or our willing, or our desiring. Their reduction of the singular and flowing to the common and fixed went far beyond what was simply necessary for consciousness (*JS* 354), because they made more real than the singular and flowing the conceptual devices that inadequately represent this reality. Philosophy not only acceded to the generalizing character of consciousness, it elevated the abstractions of consciousness over the concrete, rendering the strange familiar. The four items in Nietzsche's list—multiplication tables, logic, willing, desiring—have all served as metaphysical principles purporting to explain by leading the singular and strange back to the common and familiar. These four items recount a rough historical sequence beginning with the Greeks and ending with Schopenhauer, the philosopher who led explanation back to "our desires" and was satisfied that he could stop, having led it to the familiar, the "inner world" and "the facts of consciousness." But Nietzsche calls this the "error of errors"—the assumption that what is most familiar is best known, that privileged access to our own will means "that the will alone is really known to us, absolutely and completely known, without subtraction or addition" (*BGE* 19). Despite this error of errors, Nietzsche does not renounce the way of Schopenhauer, the way back to our desires—he takes that way himself but without committing the error of errors. Instead, "I maintain the phenomenality of the inner world too" (*KGW* VIII 11 [113] = *WP* 477)—Nietzsche makes the nearest and "familiar" strange. But he does so without abandoning knowledge and embracing skepticism.

Only "a proper physio-psychology" can provide a "path to the fundamental problems" and it can only do so if it does not suppose one already knows oneself. Nietzsche's method, his way in to the fundamental problem of "the way of all beings" (*Z* 2.12), begins with one's own being—as *un*known but as more knowable: "Many drives struggle to predominate in me. In this I am the image of everything living and I explain this to myself." [19] Nietzsche explains this to others in the methodologi-

---

19. Quoted by Blondel, *Nietzsche,* 233. Blondel provides the best account yet of Nietzsche's "epistemology," his *Versuche* investigating possible knowledge of self and world.

cal rigor of *Beyond Good and Evil* §36, a lengthy *Versuch* which begins with the unknown self, and by a strict "conscience of method" moves to what must be posited about oneself, about "our entire instinctual life," and from there to what must be posited about "all organic functions," and finally about "all efficient force univocally." This most programmatic aphorism on will to power sets the direction for the investigation of the fundamental phenomenon carried out most extensively in notes which Nietzsche's breakdown left unorganized and unpublished. But *Thus Spoke Zarathustra,* Nietzsche's elaborate vehicle for reporting this fundamental discovery and its consequences, had already set out the issue in the way Nietzsche never abandoned—a way that explains the extreme economy of all references to will to power in the post-*Zarathustra* books. After the poetic portrayal of Zarathustra's preparation for the discovery of life's secret ("The Dancing Song," Z 2.10), "On Self-Overcoming" (Z 2.12) extends a private and urgent invitation to "you who are wisest": they are to undertake with him the vast new set of investigations which test the truth of what life revealed to him, that it can be fathomed as will to power.[20] A fundamental philosophical teaching can only take root the way Spinoza's did (*JS* 349): as the insight of a solitary, it can only become persuasive if the solitary can entice those whose kinship with it impels them to confirm it or refute it through their own investigations.

The familiar is the most difficult to know or to see as a problem. Nietzsche takes the opposite way to Socrates' safe way: he aims to make the familiar strange. Philosophy thus breaks its tie with the people: it is not moved by fear to restore a sense of security, nor is it satisfied with the first explanation to which no one objects. Philosophers are never satisfied. Precisely *this* condition Nietzsche holds to be most desirable— he replaces the old highest ideal, divine contemplation of the already known, with a new ideal, insatiable pursuit of what always eludes knowledge. The gods too philosophize. "Profound aversion to reposing once and for all in some total view of the world; enchantment of the contrary way of thinking; not permit oneself to be robbed of the goad of the enigmatic" (*KGW* VIII 2 [155] = *WP* 470). The new science is joyous because it inhabits a universe infinite in a new way (*JS* 374) which satisfies the philosopher's craving never to be satisfied (*JS* 382). Nietzsche aligns himself with Lessing: if some god were to hold truth in his right hand and the passionate drive for truth in his left hand he too would gratefully choose the gift in the left hand.

In breaking with Platonism and its concessions to the people's fears,

20. I analyzed these crucial chapters in *Nietzsche's Teaching.*

Nietzsche grounds a new science the character of which he describes in his last sentence, an open-ended sentence whose closing ellipse invites further thought. "The great security or certainty" of the natural sciences contrasts with the uncertainty of "psychology and the critique of the elements of consciousness," two sciences one might "almost" call "unnatural sciences." It seems unnatural not to pursue security, not to fear fear—but it is only "almost" unnatural. Where does its naturalness lie? In the nature of one who is not *Volk,* one who finds himself driven to inquire. Nietzsche had given this lesson in the natural in *Beyond Good and Evil* (229–31): what *das Volk* call "spirit" Nietzsche called "the basic will of the spirit," the desire to calm fear and achieve security. Opposed to it is the spirit of the knower that contains "a drop of cruelty" but that carries forward its task of inquiry loyal to its nature, to what is given in it.

This is where the joyous science leads its trembling carcass, this is where it leads "the fearless." It opposes the powerful urge to security that arises naturally from the people and it opposes the religion and philosophy that have served that natural urge. To the people and to the old philosophy complicit with it, Nietzsche's joyous science will be a grim science threatening the secure ramparts of a world just now becoming inviolable.

Philosophy's Ends: Master-Builders and Modern Times (356)

Philosophy's pride presupposes its modesty. Aware of the limitations of its means, consciousness, it sets for itself vast ends of knowing and acting.

As Nietzsche sets out his program for philosophy in the transition time of modern nihilism, it becomes evident just how radical a philosopher he is as the first thinker to break completely with the safe way of Plato's Socrates—to break the Platonic alliance that enabled philosophy to feed the need for sacred origins and permanent truths. But Nietzsche's radicalism is grounded in the times, not in the personal iconoclasm of an unwary thinker.

"That's all over now" (*JS* 357). These simple words pronounce Nietzsche's judgment on Platonism. "Platonism lies on the ground" (*BGE* Preface). But why? Not because a few philosophers saw through it: Nietzsche's history of philosophy shows that genuine philosophers have always seen through it and been able to endure it. Platonism lies on the ground because a Platonism for the people struck it down. Christianity inculcated the virtue of truthfulness in the most conscientious till they could not endure the lies of their religion. And if Christian religion is the public victim of Christian virtue, so too is Platonism. Modern faith in reason, the Baconian version of Christian faith, killed God and killed as well the philosophic strategy of Platonism. That's all over now because intellectual conscience is against it. The first immoralist holds that our fate is dictated by our conscience.

The way in which things will become ever more "artistic" in Europe (356). If philosophy is fated always to be provisional in its grounds, it must nevertheless be resolute in its actions. Those geniuses of the species who aim to make everything conscious and who know how problematic knowledge is—they must nevertheless aspire to be master-builders. And such builders must look to their materials—to human nature and to what humans hold about themselves.

Is there such a thing as human nature? Or is humankind as malleable as the born actor who can assume any role? While emphasizing the malleability of humanity through history, Nietzsche is far from holding that humans are simply their history in any individualistic way. Nietzsche is no existentialist, for he ridicules long before its promulgation the existentialist faith that we are free to create ourselves and the existentialist morals that condemn as bad faith identification with one's role. On the other hand, Nietzsche, a psychologist who aims to recover the basic eternal text of *homo natura* (*BGE* 230), is far from thinking that that text is somehow independent of the evolutionary adaptive process to which our species is subject.

In the "transition time" after the greatest recent event we are no longer forced to believe that what we are has been granted by grace—by God or nature—and that our happiness comes in realizing what had been granted. Europe is becoming more "artistic": we believe now that we are free to make ourselves whatever we fancy, that we are at our own disposal as artists whose own best work is ourselves. Nothing is given by nature that cannot be altered by art—this is the belief characteristic of the two transitionary ages Nietzsche cites, Periclean Athens and modern America, democratic periods of cocky faith that I can become anything I set my mind to, that I am not bound to some level in a pyramid as earlier, benighted ages believed. American faith is not an indigenous growth; it began as a European faith transferred to non-European proving grounds: Baconian faith in man's mastery over nature took practical shape in Locke's teaching that America is wild and uncultivated, a waste given to the industrious and rational to be subdued and improved and turned into property.[21] Contemporary American faith applies the Baconian faith in mastery over nature to the frontier of one's own nature and in this form threatens to recolonize Europe. Nietzsche fears that the ancient Greek example, visible in all its consequences, foretells the modern future: this transitionary age may end as ancient Greece ended, with the "actor" as the highest human form, with the Americanization of the globe.

These reflections on the artist and actor introduce one of Nietzsche's principal themes: the contemporary quarrel between philosophy and poetry. The issue will often seem local—Nietzsche contra Wagner—but in Nietzsche's hands it becomes global. Wagner is "a man of the theatre and an actor, the most enthusiastic mimomaniac, perhaps, who ever existed" (*NCW* "Objections"). As the actor writ large, Wagner is an unparalleled occasion for reflection on "the way in which things will become ever more 'artistic' in Europe," and a philosopher must be grateful for proximity to such an occasion: "the case of Wagner is for a philosopher a *windfall*" (*CW* Preface). The Wagner case, studied closely, takes one out of "the narrow world to which every question of the worth of *persons* condemns the spirit" for it opens onto the question of the modern, the age of the actor (*CW* Epilogue).

The age of the actor poses a problem for the master-builder. Such builders—Plato, say, or Bacon or Descartes—have the perspective of millennia and aspire to create a new society; they are prudent legislators who found peoples. Any such aspiration today must face the fact that all people believe themselves capable of everything. Such a faith is most unpromising for the builder whose projects require a very different fundamental belief: that worth derives from being a part of a whole, "a stone in a great structure." To become a stone, one has to become "solid"; only on the basis of this kind of faith can a new society be built in the ancient sense of the term *society*. "*All of us are no longer material for a society:* that is a truth whose time has come."

Can material for a society be fashioned from modern humanity? Intimations of Nietzsche's affirmative answer can be heard as early as *Human, All Too Human:* the cocky faith of the age of the actor must be countered with "true modesty": "recognition that we are not our own work" (*HH* I.588). Philosophy's ignorance is consonant with the recognition that we owe our being to nature and history, that we are not our own but belong, like stones, to a great structure of being and time. A new gratitude loyal to the earth can be built on this recognition.

21. Locke, *Two Treatises of Government*, 2.5, "Of Property."

Schopenhauer and the History of Philosophy (357)

On the old problem: "What is German?" (357). This section may look like a turn from a global ambition to a merely local concern. But Nietzsche turns to the German in order to show that the very latest German philosophy is pan-European and, given the Europeanization of the globe through Baconian and Cartesian philosophy, global. The theme of the master-builder continues.

Is the philosopher simply the child of his place and time or can he become their stepchild (*SE* 3)? The German philosophers, Leibnitz, Kant, Hegel, and Schopenhauer, were no more free of their place and time than was Joabin, a Jew and a Bensalemite in a time of European expansion. But Joabin became a stepchild to his place and time: his insertedness into his own particularities did not preclude his coming to understand them and aspiring to take a hand in global events—thus Francis Bacon, a late-Renaissance Englishman, exhibits his own aspirations as a stepchild of his time. In arguing that Leibnitz, Kant, and Hegel were more tied to their times than Schopenhauer was, Nietzsche opens a perspective on a European philosopher still more free, some unnamed post-Schopenhauerian German philosopher with the perspective of millennia and the task of a master-builder.

Leibnitz, Kant, and Hegel are accorded great honor for their advances in philosophy. Leibnitz's insight into the accidental status of consciousness, Kant's insight into the limits of scientific knowledge, and Hegel's insight into the evolutionary character of thought, are genuine and lasting gains to be built upon by subsequent thinkers. This is not a history of philosophy that looks at fundamental advances as mere paradigm shifts. Still, unlike Goethe and Bismarck, "exceptions" to the German spirit, Leibnitz, Kant, and Hegel are "without any doubt" Germanic in their essential insights. Their thought is rooted in their German context and gives expression to it. Its significance, however, is not reducible to these origins: the uncovering of origins does not so much as touch the worth of what has sprung from those origins (*JS* 345). These German philosophical events are now a European fate.

Is Schopenhauer a German event? No, his anti-Christian atheism and pessimism take their bearings from a pan-European setting; he is the decisive player in the greatest recent event. But if Schopenhauer cannot be tied to his particular German context, his advance is as far as possible from being noncontextual for it is rooted in the broadest sweep of European spiritual history. So contextual is Schopenhauer's thought that a proper physio-psychology could have predicted it in advance: "an astronomer of the soul could have calculated the very day and hour" in which the old constellation set, as it sets in Schopenhauer's thought. If its time was predictable, its place was not, for Schopenhauer's thought is not characteristically German: he was the first genuine German atheist and in this he so opposed the German spirit that the Germans, Hegel in particular, could be called the great delayers of this signal event in the astronomy of the European soul.

What does Schopenhauer mean to the history of philosophy? He represents a triumph of "the European conscience" that Nietzsche makes singular and superlative: "the most fateful act of two thousand years of nurture and discipline for truth that in the end forbids itself the *lie* in the faith in God." Schopenhauer is the greatest of those described in the Preface (4) and at the beginning of Book Five (344) as lovers of the truth at all cost. His thought is an act of intellectual conscience (*JS* 2) in which "Christian morality . . . translated and sublimated itself into the scientific conscience, into intellectual cleanliness at any price." Schopenhauer's atheism is a victory of the new morality over the morality which had invested nature, history, and experience with the signs and hints of divinity. In Schopenhauer, scientific conscience triumphs over its very progenitor. It kills the God that bore it but it does so in despair.

Nietzsche's history of philosophy treats this event in the history of conscience with the greatest seriousness. Christianity may have been a "Platonism for the people" but the severity of its conscience regarding truth was *non*-Platonic. Platonism as Nietzsche understood it not only endured the noble lie, it encouraged it and grounded it and went so far as to define as nonphilosophic anyone who could not endure it. Every great Platonist from Aristotle to Bacon proved capable of such endurance. But that endurance is impossible for the scientific conscience heir to Christianity. Christianity insisted on its beautiful truth or nothing at all and in Schopenhauer the Christian conscience pronounces its Last Judgment on the earth: Nothing at all. Nietzsche's history of modern German philosophy comes to its penultimate stage in Schopenhauer, the moralistic heir to a religious morality. How will post-Schopenhauerian philosophy stand with respect to this piety of conscience?

Good Europeans will do what Schopenhauer did and forcefully shove away from themselves the Christian interpretation—but they will then be faced with Schopenhauer's question in a fearful way and will ask themselves for the next two centuries, has existence any meaning at all? Assuming the mantle of astronomer of the European soul, Nietzsche predicts that the post-Schopenhauerian treatment of this question will abandon Schopenhauer's answer that meaningless existence must be renounced as worthless. That judgment too is a vestige of the Christian dream; Schopenhauer's atheism is Christian despair. Nietzsche asks forgiveness for his judgment against his educator: Schopenhauer was hasty and youthful, a believer just where he seemed to lack belief; he too was stuck fast in a localism, if a broader localism than the one that held Leibnitz, Kant, and Hegel. Post-Schopenhauerian philosophy will abandon his belief that the world should be other than it is, but it will not abandon his intellectual conscience.

But do the German philosophers influenced by Schopenhauer not prove that he was, after all, merely a Germanic phenomenon? No, Schopenhauer-influenced Germans are simply German and therefore neither Schopenhauerian nor European. But what about that most prominent Schopenhauer-influenced German philosopher, the one omitted from the list but educated by Schopenhauer into a "good European" and into forgivable judgment against him? "Nietzsche will claim to be for Schopenhauer what Schopenhauer had wanted to be for Kant: someone who completes a legitimate *Versuch* that was arrested along the way." [22] *Beyond Good and Evil* had already argued that the pan-European phenomenon Schopenhauer had prepared the way for a still more comprehensive, supra-European view, a view from an Asiatic eye, or even "a supra-Asiatic eye" that can only be the eye of the old Asiatic Zarathustra. Freed of the ascetic ideal that still trapped Schopenhauer, the comprehensive view he made possible opens the philosopher "to the opposite ideal," the ideal of eternal return (*BGE* 56, see also 55). The same history of contemporary philosophy is presented in *Zarathustra:* the nightmare caused by the teaching of the Soothsayer Schopenhauer prepares the way for the essential vision of eternal return (*Z* 2.19, 20). Neither Schopenhauer nor Nietzsche are German phenomena; they belong to a European and global fate. But the post-Schopenhauerian Nietzsche sees further; his new teaching of eternal return represents a new departure for Europe even though it is necessarily rooted in its European past and present.

Nietzsche frequently tied the explicitly European experience to the Greek and to Dionysos and pitted the European against the Asian, the dominant successful form of which was Christianity (*KGW* VII 41 [6, 7] = *WP* 1051). This geographical way of picturing the greatest events of Western history links Nietzsche with Bacon and Descartes: schooled

---

22. Blondel, *Nietzsche,* 59.

in the history of philosophy, the master-builder with a supra-Asiatic eye will attempt to recover a pre-Platonic Greek past and marshal its spiritual resources against an Asianized, Platonized, Christianized Europe. The new pan-European philosopher will continue the great work of Bacon and Descartes but he will have to confront European religion still more directly than they did.

Philosophy and German Religion: Luther and the Renaissance (358)

German philosophy is a European fate. So too is German religion. By altering and ultimately ruining that earlier pan-European fate, the Roman church, it played the decisive role in the creation of modern Europe. Modern German philosophy stands against modern German religion and makes it possible to survey its history and consequences. And beyond that, modern German philosophy makes possible a comprehensive reinterpretation of the whole sweep of Western spiritual history by focusing on the relationship between philosophy and religion. It can do so because it is free, finally, of the religious perspective dyed into those offspring of Reformation piety, Leibnitz, Kant, and Hegel. It is free of the view that the Reformation and its consequences are an advance in the spiritual progress of humankind. But while putting the Roman church on a higher spiritual plane than the Reformation and its consequences, the new interpretation of Western history views the Roman church as itself a spiritual decline from an earlier higher plane. German philosophy therefore presents a new interpretation of European religion: so far from being the highest or final religion, it cost humankind its highest spiritual achievements. The view backward is a view upward.

With characteristic brevity, Nietzsche continues to sketch his alternative to the progressive interpretation of Western history. The new interpretation makes prominent the order of rank separating philosophy and religion; it abandons the pious fraud endured by Bacon and Descartes that religion is a higher form of spirituality than philosophy, that believing is higher than knowing. Nietzsche has to alter this classical wording and make the *search* for knowledge higher than any claimed revelation, because philosophers "simply do not believe in any 'men of knowledge' " (*JS* 351). Nietzsche's candor about philosophy and religion retells the history of their intimate relationship in our culture—with a view to severing it. He carries the Baconian and Cartesian holy war into the open, and for their reasons: philanthropy and philology, love of humanity and love of reason. Still, Nietzsche is far from being simply antireligious and will open a perspective on new religious possibilities that recover what was central to Greek religion, gratitude (*BGE* 49).

The peasant rebellion of the spirit (358). The theme of the previous section is continued: what is German about modern European history? Good Europeans schooled by the latest German philosophy will view European religion as in a state of decline traceable to German religion. They will reassess the last Roman construction, the Roman church, as a building carefully constructed with an understanding of human needs and the requirements of power but now destroyed by those who misunderstood such matters, pious Germans who believed they were recovering the church's essence through reformation.

Nietzsche repeats his earlier charge that the Germans failed to recognize the nature of a church, whereas the Romans understood it well (*JS* 350). But his repetition alters and expands his description by emphasizing two traits of the church: suspicion about nature, humanity, and spirit; and freedom and enlightenment of the spirit. The Lutheran Reformation was the indignation of simplicity against such multiplicity; it was a crude, *biederes* misunderstanding of the church triumphant and saw only corruption; it misunderstood the luxury of skepticism and tolerance that every triumphant self-conscious power permits itself; and it set out to replace freedom and enlightenment with its own passionately held religious convictions.

Friedrich Nietzsche speaking out on behalf of the freedom and enlightenment of the Medieval church? This is of course not all he has to say about the Roman church—the very next section will add the decisive consideration. But for now, the event under scrutiny is the Reformation and it must be seen as a relative decline. (This had not always been Nietzsche's view: earlier he had expressed a more conventional view, praising Luther as a "great benefactor" for arousing mistrust against the *vita contemplativa* of Christianity thereby making possible again in Europe an un-Christian *vita contemplativa* [*D* 88]. Earlier still, while under Wagner's influence concerning things Germanic, Nietzsche praised Luther's hymns as the first tempting call of a new Germanic spring [*BT* 23].)

German reformers misunderstood the church triumphant because they were "not spiritual enough" and "not mistrustful enough"—to lack spirit and mistrust is to lack the two qualities Nietzsche attributed to philosophy in the sections that intervene between the two discussions of the Roman church. In contrast to the cunning of the old spider that spun the Roman work, Luther misunderstood "all cardinal questions of power" as shown in his teachings on the Bible, the church, and the priest—the founding documents, the institution, and the functionaries. The first is especially important to a philosophical-philological interpretation of the Reformation: "He surrendered the holy books to everyone." Confident in his own true belief, Luther felt free to expose the sacred core to profane vision—he betrayed to those with a learned suspicion of writings the mysteries of a religion based on writings.[23] And he made the now open sacred writings the sole authority by destroying the concept of the church as the locus of a continuing revelation and by destroying the mysterious authority of the priesthood resident in part in its superman celibacy. "Everyman his own priest" is a formula, Nietzsche claims, for a hidden hatred of the "superior man," for a peasant revolt against the rule of *homines religiosi*.

The consequences of the Reformation lead Nietzsche to repeat Jesus' prayer of forgiveness for those who crucified him: Luther knew not what he did (Luke 23:34). The European spirit grew shallower as a result of Luther's revolt against a spiritual hierarchy—there is no doubt about that, Nietzsche says. Other features of the post-Reformation spirit are more ambiguous: the mobility and restlessness of the spirit, its thirst for independence, its faith in a right to freedom, its "naturalness." This is a list of the very features emphasized by advocates of modernity as liberation and enlightenment—and Nietzsche praises them in later sections. Nietzsche is no enemy of enlightenment: as Georg Picht argues, he wants to deepen and broaden the European Enlightenment "and force it to take the next step . . . to enlightenment about the Enlightenment itself."[24] But in assessing the Reformation, Nietzsche takes even the legacy of Enlightenment to be ambiguous because of the danger represented by the enlightened "last man." With respect to what he had put in quotation marks—"naturalness"—Nietzsche says that one could claim on behalf of the Reformation that it contributed to "naturalness" by preparing what "we today revere as modern science." But such praise must immediately be tempered by blame: the Reformation shares responsibility for "the

23. In Walter Kaufmann's translation, here as elsewhere, comments deriding the text he is translating exhibit how little he has understood Nietzsche's point. On the demystifying power of philology in the history of German letters after Luther, see Del Caro, *Nietzsche Contra Nietzsche*, 130–32. Del Caro cites Novalis: "Luther treated Christendom capriciously, failed to recognize its spirit, and introduced another letter and another religion, namely the sacred inviolability of the Bible. Therewith, unfortunately, another extremely foreign temporal science was mixed in to the affairs of religion—philology— whose consumptive influence becomes unmistakable from then on" (132).

24. Picht, *Nietzsche*, 163.

degeneration of the modern scholar." The freedom and enlightenment of the Medieval church permitted a suspicion and skepticism unknown to modern scholarship.

Praise of modern science evokes blame of modern scholarship: scholarship has fallen under the sway of science to its detriment. The Reformation cannot simply be praised for its contribution to the modern science we now revere because modern science itself must be assessed for its spiritual consequences and science has captured scholarship: trades that once led to a permitted skepticism and enlightenment now produce simple believers, spokesmen for the new science. Nietzsche's books are a "school for the *gentilhomme,* taking this concept in a more spiritual and radical sense than has ever been done" (*EH* Books *BGE* 2)—they are a school for scholars who have, under the influence of modern science, degenerated from the high, skeptical Medieval model.

Joyous science will need its scholars, and they will have to be gathered from the decayed specimens that now prevail and are here insulted. Just as Nietzsche begins to exhibit himself as a philosopher in the Platonic sense, a master-builder whose plan for the future depends on a reinterpreted past, a question is raised about his sagacity. Is it wise to insult the scholars he needs? The answer is surely yes. Modern scholars may be simple believers but they are moved by modern faith in truthfulness, and Nietzsche entrusts his case to their virtue: goaded into refuting a suspicion about themselves that is less than flattering, modern scholars will have to confront the evidence on how far they are still pious. Finding the charges true, what can the pious do but side with the truth—and with Nietzsche? The new master-builder begins conscripting his crew.

In condemning "modern ideas" as consequences of the northern peasant revolt against the mistrustful spirit of the south, Nietzsche goes so far as to describe the Christian church as the greatest monument to that mistrustful spirit. To make this amazing claim plausible, Nietzsche says again: do not forget what a church is. A church can be understood by contrasting it with its modern rival, the state—as Zarathustra had done when describing the modern state as "the new idol" (*Z* 1.11). The state is the construct put together to advance "modern ideas" of equality and enlightenment; it is founded on "the sword and a hundred appetites" and not on a "faith and love." Defining a church, Nietzsche attributes to it "above all" what moderns will have thought the prerogative of a state: it is "a structure for ruling," a construct founded by "the more spiritual human beings" to enable them to rule and to place highest what they hold highest.

Nietzsche's next thought is especially arresting and puts his conclusion in proper perspective: a church "so *believes* in the power of spirituality that it forbids itself all the cruder instruments of force." Coming as it does at the end of his praise of the now-destroyed Roman church, this emphasis on spirituality over cruder instruments of force compels his readers to remember what their protestant, enlightened history will have trained them to remember best about that particular spiritual institution: there were no cruder instruments than those instruments of death and suppression invented by the Roman church to perpetuate and extend its rule against spiritual rivals. Students of *The Joyous Science* will remember that the Roman church employed those instruments to annihilate the very Provençal culture invoked and celebrated by the new title page of the book, the culture of "la gaya scienza" that flourished briefly until burned out root and branch by the frenzy of the Albigensian Crusade and by the Inquisition subsequently invented to remedy the crusade's failure to break every Cathar and purge every troubadour.

Provençal troubadours, part of what is now called "the Renaissance of the twelfth century," were one expression of that Mediterranean, southern, sunlit spirit Nietzsche celebrates in this section. Another expression broke out in the Renaissance of the fifteenth and sixteenth centuries only to be destroyed by that "calamity of a monk, Luther" (*EH* Books *CW*). Nietzsche traces all such expressions of that southern spirit ultimately to Greece, to the Dionysian experience which was "the first great union and synthesis of everything Near Eastern, and on that account the inception of the European soul" (*KGW* VII 41 [6–7] = *WP* 1051). That Greek experience, the birth of tragedy in a spirited, agonistic society, had been revived and nurtured at identifiable points within Western history, but each renaissance had been defeated by what Nietzsche calls in the title of this section, the peasant revolt of the spirit. Renaissance or rebirth of the Greek experience had been at the core of Nietzsche's work from its inception, as had its enemy, identified in his first book with Socratic rationalism. In one of his later and most extended accounts of this long spiritual warfare, Nietzsche refers to it as "Rome vs. Judea, Judea vs. Rome" and says "there has hitherto been no greater event than *this* struggle, *this* question, *this* deadly contradiction" (*GM* 1.16). The Reformation, a German religious event so decisive for modern European history, is an outbreak of this much longer and more fundamental opposition. Nietzsche sides with the Roman church against Luther not because he is a simple advocate of the church but because the church harbored a Renaissance. Luther attacked the Roman church when it was becoming the church of Erasmus and when "Caesar Borgia as Pope" was imaginable. "Luther *restored the Church:* he attacked it" (*A* 61). Luther's zeal precipitated a counterzeal that squeezed out Erasmian latitude and tolerance and ruined the promise of a more permanent rebirth of Greek experience. Luther "cheated Europe out of the last great cultural harvest which Europe could still have brought home—the *Renaissance*" (*A* 61). *The Joyous Science* is "la gaya scienza" and its new advocate is not ignorant of what destroyed "la gaya scienza" in its brief, beautiful first appearance. Nevertheless, Nietzsche can place the Roman church higher than Luther's church and higher than the modern state even though it is responsible for annihilating the Provençal culture that Nietzsche's book celebrates and revives.[25]

Nietzsche's history of philosophy is thus obliged to assess the spiritual institution that dominated European spiritual life since its capture of Rome. How has philosophy fared under Christian dominance?

Philosophy and Roman Religion:
Augustine and Platonism (359)

The revenge against the spirit and other hidden foundations of morality (359). Nietzsche's praise of the Roman church is cast in a new light by this section, connected to the previous one by a thread, the name "Saint Augustine," the name of the single most important father of the Roman church. Praise of the Roman church will have to be tempered by the perspective set forth here: Augustine helped found a spiritual institution on revenge against the spirit, and he did so by perverting the moral teachings of the philosophers to suit his own vengeful ends. As one of "the Christian agitators known as the Fathers of the Church" (*GM* 3.22), Augustine was "shrewd, shrewd to the point of holiness" (*A* 59) and nowhere more than in his use of philosophy.

The repellent portrait of the one pointed to as "there" at the be-

25. An important dimension is added to this history of renaissances by *HH* I.475: "In the darkest periods of the Middle Ages, when the cloudbanks of Asia had settled low over Europe, it was the Jewish freethinkers, scholars and physicians who, under the harshest personal constraint, held firmly to the banner of enlightenment and intellectual independence and defended Europe against Asia; it is thanks not least to their efforts that a more natural, rational and in any event unmythical elucidation of the world could at last again obtain victory and the ring of culture that now unites us with the enlightenment of Graeco-Roman antiquity remain unbroken. If Christianity has done everything to orientalize the occident, Judaism has always played an essential part in occidentalizing it again: which in a certain sense means making of Europe's mission and history a *continuation of the Greek*."

ginning of this section is said to fit Augustine. The details resound of Nietzsche's conclusions about the *Confessions,* a book he had been reading "as relaxation" the previous year. He reported his reactions to his church historian friend Overbeck, an expert on Augustine and his declared enemy. Speaking with "the curiosity of a radical physician and physiologist," Nietzsche accused Augustine of "psychological falsity" in his story of the pears and "revolting dishonesty" in his resolve to go on living after the death of his best friend. More important, Nietzsche interpreted Augustine's work as "*vulgarized* Platonism" with "zero philosophical value." It was, nevertheless, of extreme historic importance: Augustine "adjusted to suit slave natures" the Platonic way of thinking "which was invented for the highest aristocracy of soul." "One sees the guts of Christianity in this book," and one sees in these comments Nietzsche's view of the Christian appropriation of philosophy (letter to Overbeck, 31 March 1885).

"There is a man who turned out badly": his deficiency of spirit has led to self-hatred because he possessed enough education to know that there exist those whose spiritual equal he is not, a process Zarathustra had described in "On the Tarantulas" (*Z* 2.7). He has read books to which he had no right, presumably the books of his spiritual superiors, the philosophers discussed at the end of the section, and his spirit has turned to poison in the form of a will to revenge. Powerlessness corrupts, for Nietzsche, absolute powerlessness absolutely. Perfected revenge against the spirit takes the form of a strict morality, misappropriating "justice, wisdom, holiness, virtue" for vengeful ends. "Don't get me wrong," Nietzsche says, such "enemies of the spirit" can belong to "those rare pieces of humanity" honored by the people as saints or wise.[26] (Two other fathers of the Roman church, Tertullian and Aquinas, are later singled out with respect to revenge [*GM* 1.15], as is Luther [*KGW* VIII 9 [124]].)

But if the Christian religion, a "Platonism for the people," is Platonism poisoned by the vengeance of an Augustine, what about the philosophers themselves? Do they share the revenge expressed by Christianity's greatest "Platonist"? "Among ourselves" Nietzsche asks, what lies behind the morality of *philosophers* who claimed wisdom, the maddest and most immodest of claims? Plato was such a philosopher, the immodesty of his claim being completely compatible with the modesty of knowing

26. Elaine Pagels argues in *Adam, Eve, and the Serpent* that Augustine effectively invented the teachings on original sin and sexuality that became the dominant Christian teaching; she also shows how Augustine's sexual politics, the politics of universal depravity, consolidated and justified complete spiritual and temporal rule over the depraved.

he was not a knower (*JS* 351). In moving up from Augustine to Plato, Nietzsche traces the medicine morality to a desire for a hiding place and not to the sickness of revenge. Philosophers are extremely rare and their need for a hiding place is attributable to their always being solitaries and never having "a single friend of their own kind" except in the underworld of the dead. Two reasons are given for philosophers seeking a moral hiding place, the first more rare than the second. Sometimes the morality taught by a philosopher claiming wisdom has an educating intent: out of solicitude for those in the process of becoming, a philosopher allows disciples to believe in him for their own good. Faith in a philosopher's claim to wisdom is always an error but a permissible error for the sake of education, the cause that "sanctifies so many lies." This lie makes the teacher believable on matters to which the taught can never ascend and shelters the taught against themselves. A philanthropic motive forces the philosopher to endure a salutary lie about his own wisdom eagerly believed by disciples.

But in most cases, the hiding place of the philosopher who claims wisdom has a different if still philanthropic reason. These cases are likened to animals who creep away to die in solitude. In choosing this hiding place, those who claim wisdom actually "become *wise*" in a way that follows the instincts of the animals. Such hiding is a natural wisdom because what is hidden would shock those from whom it is hidden; it spares the unphilosophical the necessity of facing up to the profound shock of a wisdom that knows its own ignorance. With the grace of an animal dying alone, the philosopher spares others what he has had to bear; it is wise that such unwise call themselves wise.

"What? Wisdom a hiding place of the philosopher from—spirit?—" The final question concerns the philosophers alone, but the point of the question derives from its setting: if Augustine's moral teaching involves revenge against the spirit, then the Roman church too, like the Reformation, embodies an attack on the spirit: religion in the West is antispirit. But are the philosophers also enemies of the spirit? What *is* the relationship between philosophy and spirit? Philosophy is "the most spiritual will to power" (*BGE* 9), the highest form achieved by what is. By claiming wisdom, philosophy hid its character as spirit or spiritedness; philosophy let it be believed that reason is higher than spirit and independent of it and capable of grasping the permanent truth of permanent being. It let it be believed that reason and its corresponding virtue, wisdom, are higher than spiritedness and its corresponding virtue, courage. "What? Wisdom a hiding place of the philosophers from—spirit?—"

Yes, philosophy had to hide its spiritedness in order to educate and shelter; it had to deny its very character in order to exist in the world. And that strategy of survival made it vulnerable to appropriation by those utterly different from philosophers, vengeful enemies of the spirit like Augustine, true ascetics rather than apparent ascetics, makers of history whose antilife teachings begin in a hatred of themselves.

This sharp distinction between our religion and our philosophy clarifies the purpose of these two sections on religion as part of a complete revaluation of the spiritual present and past. The German philosopher who claims to be a pan-European phenomenon in his understanding of the philosophic past and future of Europe reinterprets the religious history of Europe from a standpoint outside it. The move backward from modern ideas to the Reformation to the Roman church to Platonism is not a move downward from a spiritual high point to earlier, spiritually inferior stages. This trajectory backward and upward is made to focus on a fundamental event in the philosophical-religious history of the West, Christianity's appropriation of philosophy, Jerusalem's capture of Athens. In Nietzsche's view, that capture was the victory of revenge over the highest possible spiritedness. Freeing our past from the theologizing of history still present in Hegel and his followers, Nietzsche can openly be what Bacon and Descartes were covertly: un-Christian and anti-Christian.

Western morality has different roots in philosophy and religion. The good and evil of Platonism and Augustinianism may seem almost uniform when their hidden sources are ignored, but a proper physiopsychology employs a genealogical method to disentangle radically different motives. It distinguishes Augustine from Plato on what will soon come to light as the basic matter of health and sickness (*JS* 370, 382). Otherworldly morality has now become wholly a sickness from which we need a cure, but Plato can be excused in a way Augustine cannot: for Plato morality was a philanthropic tool, for Augustine a tool of revenge.

These sections with their harsh view of the spiritual past aim to alter the convictions of believers in the modern Enlightenment and its progressive interpretation of the past. Success in this project depends upon intensifying the "sixth sense" developed by modern German philosophy, the historical sense (*JS* 357). Nietzsche refuses to surrender the historical sense to a radical historicism or skepticism as Heidegger and other twentieth-century thinkers do. To view Western history as the unintelligible unfolding of mere mystery, inscrutable fate, or as a sequence of paradigms each employing standards certifiable only by itself, is, from

Nietzsche's perspective, to accede unnecessarily to ignorance. Unlike contemporary Heideggerians and Kuhnians, Nietzsche is not ready to surrender the conclusions of historical science—or the conclusions of modern cosmology and evolutionary biology—to the status of a mere worldview. Nietzsche's defense of science recognizes the probability of its conclusions—shifting conclusions subject to alteration and held under the police supervision of mistrust. "When a philosopher these days lets it be known that he is not a skeptic . . . everyone is annoyed" (*BGE* 208). Nietzsche risks annoyance in defense of a science that can understand itself as pursuing questions to which true and false answers can be given. Is the earth fixed at the center of creation under the sphere of the moon as Augustine seemed to believe? Is it a damnable lust of the eye to want to know if that belief could possibly be false (*Confessions* 10.35)?

But Nietzsche's historical sense goes beyond such questions whose answers are now obvious. Nietzsche asks: what moved Augustine to argue for scientific ignorance? And does the Augustinian monk who founded the Reformation share those motives? In Nietzsche's view, history has in part been made by humans and can in part be understood by a disciplined historical science using a proper physio-psychology. Its tools will sound risky and unreliable, an art of hearing, for instance, that Nietzsche called "second hearing" or a "third ear" (*BGE* 247), an "evil ear" (*TI* Preface) that refuses to do what most readers do, put their ears away in a drawer (*BGE* 247). This art of hearing or reading, this art of nuances (*BGE* 31), refuses to take the past as infinitely malleable at the hands of interpreters. It listens attentively to the great historic figures in order to hear what lies behind their advocacies. The new physio-psychology and the new view of the past that results from it make claims that aspire to be true and testable. As Alan White says at the end of a book that argues for this perspective: Nietzsche's "post-moral world" is a "less dogmatic, *less relativistic*" world.[27]

Nietzsche's genealogical history is now taking shape: European modernity is a decline of the spirit traceable, in part, to great events in philosophy and religion; its misinterpretation of itself as the progressive advance of the whole of history threatens to make that decline permanent as the actual end of history. The human past and present come to light as knowable because we can, to a degree, know ourselves—but just here an issue of human self-knowledge arises that has bedeviled Nietzsche's writings: knowledge of our selves as male and female. The next

27. White, *Within Nietzsche's Labyrinth*, 118, 147 (italics added).

sections raise this most controversial matter of human psychology in the context of understanding modern times.

A Central Issue: The Genealogical Physio-Psychology of Woman and Man (360–62)

There are forty-one sections in *The Joyous Science* Book Five. If one counted them, §363 would be the central, twenty-first section, separating two halves of twenty sections each. Could the "central" section, devoted to man and woman and their different perspectives on love, have central significance?

Does Nietzsche play little number games like this? Such play has a dignified past: Montaigne, Bacon, and Descartes, among many others, played such games; their centering often gave a studied prominence to items that at first sight appeared negligible. And Nietzsche plays related number games, perhaps the most striking being the elaborate numbers game in *Thus Spoke Zarathustra*. The book had appeared in three parts, the first two consisting of twenty-two chapters each. Notes indicate that twenty-two was in no way accidental (see e.g. *KGW* VII 16 [83, 84], 20 [3, 8], 21 [3], 23 [10]). But part three contained only sixteen chapters. The sixteenth chapter, however, is "The Seven Seals," the image of a sealed book that Nietzsche borrowed from *Revelation,* a book of twenty-two chapters and the final or sixty-sixth book of the Bible, and a book promising annihilating warfare between opposing views of the earth. Fifteen chapters and seven seals total twenty-two, and three sets of twenty-two total sixty-six: Nietzsche's little play with numbers parodies the old revelation by playing games with its most deadly symbols. And the game suggests a new apocalyptic clash between opposing views of the earth.

Is *The Joyous Science* Book Five another example of structural playfulness, numerically centering the central issue? Certainty cannot be expected in such matters but an affirmative answer is indicated by the centrality of the subject matter, the subtle preparation for it in the sections leading to the central section, and the abrupt break after it that begins the second half of Book Five.

Here in particular Nietzsche has to say everything at once: contemporary events misconstrued by those immersed in them come to light as items in a millennia-long sequence of events visible in its coherence only to the one who combines a proper physio-psychology with the longest view backward and forward. Here, Nietzsche's psychology and his history of philosophy and culture combine to interpret both the nearest and the most comprehensive: first, one of his most essential advances in psychology (360), then the problem that has troubled Nietzsche longest (361), then, Napoleon, nationalism, and renaissance (362), and finally, man, woman, and nature (363). When the inquiry enters the deepest matter, nature, the conclusions serve as the ground for the history Nietzsche has been unfolding.

Two kinds of causes that are often confounded (360). This section, coming after Nietzsche's psychological genealogies, turns to a general rule of method and begins a series of sections that lead up to perhaps the most important claim in the new psychology: there exists in the human soul a groundedness and givenness that is the result of the accumulated history of the race and of the history of life itself. That givenness, that now sedimented accumulation of innumerable generations of experience, that basic text of *homo natura,* confirms once again the ground of the new modesty: we are not our own.

The opening of this section states its importance: it deals with one of Nietzsche's most essential advances in analyzing the causes of human action. All goals that give a human life a particular direction Nietzsche counts among "the little accidents" that cause the fundamental and undirected energy of life to course this way rather than that, into revenge, say, or into shelter. The closing questions suggest that even the apparent causes of direction are caused, even the apparent steersman is steered. And the final sentence contains the essential reflection: we need a "critique of the concept 'goal' "—Kant's third critique with its account of goal grounded in autonomy is inadequate. In Nietzsche's psychology, is autonomy always only a vanity?

With his censure of Augustine still reverberating in our ears, Nietzsche shows how far he is from holding individuals responsible for the calamity of millennia (*EH* Wise 7). One of Nietzsche's most essential advances took him beyond the psychology of individual responsibility, the hangman's psychology that affixes praise and blame to individuals, and which Nietzsche had studied throughout his mature life, the definitive elaboration coming in the second treatise of *On the Genealogy of Morals.* The new psychology freed itself from the long-dominant moral claim that one can be held responsible or blamable for one's actions; it is as far as possible from believing the American fiction that one can make oneself whatever one fancies (*JS* 356). This essential advance in the study of the soul is evident in Nietzsche's three-stage history of moral evaluations: "good and evil" were at first judgments made on the basis of the beneficial or harmful consequences of an action; then, during the long "moral" period of our history—"the last ten thousand years or so"— good and evil named what were thought to be the decisive motives for action; yet to come is a third stage, beyond good and evil, in which actions are recognized as part of the whole network of events into which they are inserted (*BGE* 32; *HH* I.39, 207).

Nietzsche stands at the head of this third stage advocating a revolutionary change, an alteration in conscience. The original formation of conscience, bad or guilty conscience, was an evolutionary event of such magnitude that it could be likened to the transformation from sea animals to land animals (*GM* 2.16–18). The socialization and pacification of our species is pictured by Nietzsche as occurring under the force of "the most involuntary, unconscious artists there are," the natural dominators and masters who first created the "state" out of formless populations of nomads. The novel conditions created by being "finally enclosed within the walls of society and peace" meant that "the instinct for freedom" was "forcibly made latent" for those so enclosed and was "able to discharge and vent itself only on itself." This internalization of natural aggression marks the beginning of guilty conscience. The soul was born of this process, "the most fundamental change" the human animal has undergone, the change that makes humans the interesting animal worthy of a god's wonder. "All *protracted* things are hard to see, to see whole" (*GM* 1.8), and these events are protracted in the extreme, involving millennia of human history and demanding that past trajectories be projected into the future, now the future of an alteration in conscience.

Given this long perspective, the whole history of philosophy must be understood as a somewhat parochial phenomenon—"only two millennia"—falling within the much broader moral period of humankind. In its dominant forms philosophy has appeared as the servant of morality, the means of grounding morals rationally. Plato and Augustine—and, as will be seen, Democritus and Epicurus—can only be understood when they are inserted into this greater history, the history of the human soul. And Nietzsche sets his own work into this broader process of natural and human evolution: it marks a revolution in conscience—the recognition that we are not our own but the evolutionary consequence of a long natural history now becoming accessible.

Nietzsche's extreme radicality forces him to stand against what looks radical, modern revolutionary teachings that can now be understood as extending the millennia-long fiction of individual self-making, the fiction of responsibility and its attendant notions of sin, guilt, and punishment. Nietzsche abandons these moral fictions in the name of the basic text of *homo natura*. One aspect of that basic text, the one Nietzsche chose to single out both here and at similar junctions in other works, is the natural difference between woman and man, natural bisexuality. Nietzsche is notorious for his opposition to the modern revolution as it applies to man and woman. His opposition is anything but accidental, for it is grounded in his genealogical method, his historical perspective, and his advocacy of nature. It accuses the modern revolution of applying to man and woman the old moral fiction of self-making and of understanding male and female as alterable states, either because sexuality is a convention that can be overcome, or because it is natural but faulty according to the modern, antinatural ideal of equality or sameness. The theme of woman and man is one of the themes that provides access to the deepest matter in Nietzsche's thought, the nature of nature. Nietzsche's revolutionary opposition to modernity can be understood as the conservation of natural difference, the recovery and affirmation of human nature.

On the problem of the actor (361). The sections leading to the central section turn from one of Nietzsche's most essential advances in psychology to the problem that has troubled him longest, the problem of the actor. Here Nietzsche folds into a single paragraph his lifelong concern with one of the great issues of modern times and ultimately of philosophy itself. For while the problem of the actor may seem incidental for a philosopher, it is in fact one form of the problem of appearance and reality, the problem of distinguishing the true from the false. Moreover, the problem of the actor, as Nietzsche had already said (356), raises the problem of the European future and these sections root that problem in the natural artistry of woman (361), in the natural activity of man (362), and in the natural difference in their prejudices about love (363).

The actor—the *Schauspieler* or player who puts on a show—exemplifies a condition in which delight in appearance and adaptation to circumstance overpower any given stability of "character." This condition links the actor with the last man, modern adaptable man who believes we can make ourselves whatever we fancy. Rather than linger over the features of this modern condition, Nietzsche inquires into its origins and the inquiry again indicates something general about the joyous science: its conclusions do not attain the rank of certitude. Unlike Freud, Nietzsche never tries to make it easy for his psychology by arguing that it is only a part of the already authoritative scientific Weltanschauung. On the contrary, its uncertainties shake the foundations of that orthodoxy and replace mathematical certitude with a police force of suspicions.[28]

Nietzsche's genealogy traces the hypertrophy of the actor's art to historical conditions that forced humans into adaptive role playing. In settings marked by brute power, the powerless achieved their ends via an actor's resourcefulness; cleverness offset power by shaping appearance to the wishes of the powerful. Nietzsche's list of adaptations begins with dependent classes who took on appearances pleasing to those on whom they depended; it passes to ruling classes and their typical forms of diplomatic acting; then it turns to Jews, a minority always required to receive permission to exist from an alien majority; and it ends with women. What is said about women reinforces what had been said about the other three groups: what is given in women and is now "instinct" is the result of a long history in the formation of character. Human nature is the result of a long process of making and self-making in which nature or what was given was always already the result of prior change and always proved malleable to persistent forces of change. We humans now have a nature determined by our history. Such human self-making opposes the notion that individuals have been free to make themselves or are now free to do so—Nietzsche's thought concerns "whole races and chains of generations" (354).

Modern belief in human malleability traced through four different but complementary roots in the history of acting, the history of the need to please others through appearance, ends with this judgment: "Woman is so artistic . . ." The reader is commanded to provide the grounds for this judgment: "think about" the whole history of women; "listen to" their most unguarded thoughts; "love" them and experience their nature in that love. Nietzsche's conclusion suggests Zarathustra's concise judgment: the happiness of women has depended upon their success in winning over men; men are only the means to their real happiness, the child, but men had to be flattered into thinking that they are themselves the end and meaning of a woman's life (Z 1.18). Such judgments appear frequently in Nietzsche's writings in locations that attest to their inseparability from Nietzsche's most basic thoughts.

Is the issue of woman and man really that important? "A thinker who

---

28. The use to which Freud put Nietzsche is illuminated by an important study of Nietzsche's place in twentieth-century social science generally, Stauth and Turner, *Nietzsche's Dance,* see 6–7, 125–50.

proves himself shallow in this dangerous spot—shallow in instinct—may be considered altogether suspicious, still more, betrayed, exposed: probably he will be too 'short' for all the fundamental questions of life, of the life to come too, and incapable of attaining *any* depth" (*BGE* 238). Nietzsche not only invited the reader to judge him on this issue, he taunted the reader to judge him—and readers have, for the most part, agreed: here Nietzsche is shortest. A book on his politics which prides itself on looking scrupulously fair before pronouncing its prim denunciations, treats Nietzsche quite automatically and without argument or documentation as "an unabashed misogynist" whose "views on women need no comment except to say that they are probably the most thoroughly discredited aspects of his thought."[29] Refusal to consider any of the passages of this "most thoroughly discredited aspect" makes it quite easy to continue to sully Nietzsche's reputation while appearing to be so tasteful as hardly to mention the unmentionable.

"Unabashed misogynist"—in fact, Nietzsche's judgments on woman and man, among the most subtle in his writings though accompanied by unsubtle and provocative phrases, demonstrate the contrary, and they are judgments now being recognized as worthy of the most serious consideration: Is there a female nature developed and shaped over the millennia of herstory? Has mothering played a special role in the formation of that nature? Are women today heirs to a disposition that carries with it typical perspectives on the world that are especially valuable in a time of unparalleled dominance and pillage? Nietzsche's analysis raises questions that have taken a hundred years to become, if not respectable, at least in some circles not criminal. But Nietzsche's thought here requires special attention because it is so dangerously open to prejudiced misunderstanding. There are no denser sections in the whole of Book Five, none that more reverberate with Nietzsche's essential ideas, none where his extreme brevity more demands being heard at great length. As Nietzsche said in introducing another important concept, such matters are "not easy to bring to hearing and need to be pondered, lived with, and slept on for a long time" (*GM* 2.16).

If all of Europe is becoming more artistic (356), it is becoming more female. The antidote to Europe's becoming more female in this sense

---

29. Detwiler, *Nietzsche and the Politics of Aristocratic Radicalism,* 15, 193. Other recent books also accept this issue as simply settled: Thiele, *Nietzsche and the Politics of the Soul,* 16–17; Staten, *Nietzsche's Voice.* For opposing views see, Graybeal, *Language and 'The Feminine,'* 27–39 (an illuminating discussion of earlier sections in *JS* dealing with woman and man); Bertram, "God's *Second* Blunder"; Ackermann, *Nietzsche,* 122–31.

is its becoming more manly. Because this is a development in which Nietzsche would very much like to believe, the next section outlines a faith.

Our faith in the masculinization of Europe (362). Nietzsche's faith sounds perverse to modern ears. Faith in warfare that culminates in a war between the sexes sounds like an enemy faith. Nietzsche's faith is also a hope, expressed here with an assurance befitting a confession of faith— the hope that the warfare now breaking out would create a new future that would look back on these times with envy and awe as the decisive centuries in which the battle for humankind was fought and won.

The hero of the faith is Napoleon whose great deed is represented as a renaissance bringing back "a whole slab of antiquity, perhaps the decisive slab" that will overthrow modernity. Napoleon is an early hero in another renaissance, another upsurge of the Greek and Roman. The German philosopher who expresses faith in this renaissance holds that an earlier one failed because of German religion; German philosophy can serve this renaissance as a *Wiedergutmachen* for the fatal blow German religion dealt that one. The new renaissance takes a perspective on nineteenth-century history that aligns its different forces as armies in a protracted struggle. Some had traced the war-glory of contemporary nationalist movements in Europe to Napoleon, but Nietzsche reads nationalism as anti-Napoleonic and destined to come into conflict with the antinational pan-European spirit that is the true heir to Napoleon's aspiration to a unified Europe.[30] Nietzsche's faith makes it possible for him to view the present from the perspective of the distant, postwar future; that future looks back on Napoleon with gratitude because it owes its being to the success of Napoleon's heirs. The report from the future on the "classical age of war" is given in Nietzschean shorthand: "Man" or the real man of Nietzschean manliness became master over the competing modern ideals of man, of which two are named, the businessman of the commercial republic, and the philistine of modern education. Perhaps, Nietzsche adds, that real man will even become master over "woman," over the modern ideal of woman. That ideal sprang from Christianity, from the enthusiastic spirit of the eighteenth century, but especially from "modern ideas"—sources against which he makes open war.

Warlike Napoleon considered modern ideals almost a personal enemy, a *Feindin* worthy of manly opposition, and in this opposition he proved

30. But: "Napoleon made nationalism possible; that puts a limitation on him" *KGW* VIII 10 [31]. For Napoleon, see Ottmann, *Nietzsche*, 273–75.

himself one of the greatest protagonists of the Renaissance. Nietzsche, a philosophic student of ancient and modern, will not have taken his guidance on renaissance from the warrior Napoleon however much Napoleon's warlike model serves as an inspiration. Nietzsche knows better than Napoleon what is worthy of rebirth; through his own revival of the ancient, the philosophic Napoleonic man sets out to triumph over the nationalist movements that now fraudulently trace themselves to Napoleon while being the vehicle only of modern ideas. He aims at Napoleonic goals, a united Europe, a *Europa* that would become "*Mistress of the Earth.*" Nietzsche lays claim to being Napoleon's philosophic "heir and continuator," disputing the claim of the one who heard Napoleon's guns outside Jena while putting the finishing touches on his own history of the European spirit.

Nietzsche praises Napoleon in a similar setting at the end of the first treatise of the *Genealogy:* Napoleon represents a decisive event in the history of the battle between good and evil and good and bad (1.16) and the Napoleonic is carried forward by Nietzsche (1.17). But it is in *Ecce Homo* that Nietzsche at last gets blunt and tells "a few hard truths" about modern history: "*Who else would do it?*" (*EH* Books *CW* 2), who else possesses "the grand perspective" on history that all narrower visions proscribe? The "German interpretation" of modern history is such a proscription, Nietzsche charges, as shown in its interpretation of the Renaissance and Napoleon. Germans, who robbed Europe of the harvest of the last great age, the Renaissance, are now attempting to rob Europe of the great event of nineteenth-century European politics by falsifying the meaning of Napoleon. A pan-European force that aimed to create a European unity has been transformed into a force for the petty politics of nationalism, a dead end that Nietzsche identifies as "the most *anticultural* sickness and unreason there is." Nietzsche's hard truths end with this: "Does anyone besides me know the way out of this dead end? A task great enough to *unite* nations again?" (*EH* Books *CW* 2). *The Joyous Science* Book Five shows Nietzsche's right to this audacious judgment about himself: he is the master-builder with the perspective of millennia for whom contemporary events become visible as episodes in the longest spiritual struggles. "The classical age of war" dawns in Nietzsche's writings, and it dawns on spiritual warfare "without powder and smoke" (*EH* Books *HH* 1).[31] And it dawns as "the means to real peace" that knows the history of warfare:

31. Ottmann's *Nietzsche* definitively corrects the long-standing misrepresentation of Nietzsche's views on war and nationalism. "Nietzsche was a preacher against the sicknesses

The doctrine of the army as a means of self-defense must be re-nounced just as completely as the thirst for conquest. And perhaps there will come a great day on which a nation distinguished for wars and victories and for the highest development of military discipline and thinking, and accustomed to making the heaviest sacrifices on behalf of these things, will cry of its own free will: *"we shall shatter the sword"*—and demolish its entire military machine down to its last foundations. *To disarm while being the best armed,* out of an *elevation* of sensibility—that is the means to *real* peace, which must always rest on a disposition for peace: whereas the so-called armed peace such as now parades about in every country is a dispo-sition to fractiousness which trusts neither itself nor its neighbor and fails to lay down its arms half out of hatred, half out of fear. (*WS* 284)

"Our faith in the masculinization of Europe," with its account of new Napoleonic wars for Europe and the globe, touches many of the deci-sive themes to which Nietzsche turned again and again at the core of his work, though each time with a brevity true to Zarathustra's resolve not to do anything for the reader they can do for themselves (*Z* 1.7). But with the fragments of Nietzsche's view of Western history begin-ning to cohere with the help of this Napoleonic or manly section, one of its essential elements is expanded and deepened in the next section where the manly is contrasted with the womanly on the issue of love. Nietzsche's "faith" for Europe is grounded in his most basic psychology. His study of the soul now opens onto the soul's loves—what is loved or the lovable—and heralds Nietzsche's most basic affirmation: love of the earth.

The Central Section: Love and Gratitude (363)

How each sex has its prejudice about love (363). The central section deals with the central matter, for if the title speaks of prejudice, the text speaks of nature. The "prejudices" man and woman harbor about love are rooted in the difference between male and female, a "natural opposition" be-tween the sexes that Nietzsche thinks no social contract, no good will to justice can ever get around. *The Joyous Science* has emphasized the mal-

---

of Europe, against nationalism and power politics, against racism and anti-Semitism. . . . But who has heard this Nietzsche? Who has listened to him, in the face of his *Wirkungs-geschichte,* as a hope for Europe?" (127).

leability of humankind through history by tracing fundamental features of modern times to historic accidents like the ignorance of a German monk or the revenge of an African bishop. But here a kind of bedrock is reached, something given by nature though nature is always understood historically.

"Love, thought whole, great, and full, is nature." Because it is nature, love is, "in all eternity," something "immoral," beyond good and evil. At the very center of Book Five of *The Joyous Science* lies an account of human nature that dares to say that "love . . . is nature." Nietzsche can say this while being far from any romantic notion that nature is love. Nevertheless, the love or *eros* that is nature in human beings shares in nature as such—nature as universal will to power in Nietzsche's sense. Joyous science uncovers nature and human nature; it becomes joyous in that uncovering. Still, it will not do, Nietzsche says, "to remind oneself constantly how harsh, terrible, enigmatic, and immoral" nature is in the antagonism of the sexes in love. Nature must in a way be beautified by art, by beautiful speech loyal to nature that does not falsify nature.

This is the third section in sequence to have spoken about *das Weib*. The first (361) dealt with the problem that had troubled Nietzsche longest, the problem of the actor or artist, and it ended with the statement, "Woman is so artistic." In the central section, that art of appearance of which woman is master is shown to be rooted in the very nature of woman, the artistic being par excellence whose love is a yielding to the beloved as the means to her happiness. The next section (362) dealt with a renaissance of manliness, a faith which wants to believe that it could perhaps master even woman corrupted by modern ideas of equality and sameness. In the central section, that manliness is shown to be rooted in the very nature of man, the restless being driven to possession, whose love is a will to possess the beloved. That manly will to possession is now *the* problem of love.

Not Napoleon but the French Revolution gave rise to the particular issue from which Nietzsche sets out: "*equal* rights in love." A campaign for such equal rights is contrary to the nature of man and woman as regards love. Each sex understands love differently, Nietzsche argues, and built into the understanding of each is an expectation of the other, an unspoken demand that love be reciprocated in a different way from which it is given. Beginning then with woman's love, Nietzsche describes a dialectic of gift and expectation that is like a dance or a dancing song, a play of complex complementarity.

What woman understands by love is "clear enough"; what man understands by love will be the problem. For woman love is total devotion, an unconditional renunciation of rights—though one dare not forget what Nietzsche said two sections earlier: "Woman is so artistic." Man expects total devotion but cannot offer it himself without the result being "an empty space." Not only does duality fall into nullity in such a response but, Nietzsche maintains, for a man to offer total devotion is to become a slave while for a woman it is to become "a more perfect woman"—and not a slave. "Slave"—this word indicates that man's surrender of his own concept of love has world-historical connotations, given Nietzsche's analysis of Christianity as a slave religion that defeated the manliness of classical antiquity. The only real man in Christianity is the imaginary one, God, to whom all humans offer total devotion and an unconditional renunciation of rights. And in Nietzsche's history of the spiritual trajectory of the West, the French Revolution is a "Christian" phenomenon which renounced the one Man, the Shepherd, with the goal of becoming an "autonomous herd" (*BGE* 202). This process can hardly be viewed as the victory of woman: woman's love requires that man *be* something.

Woman demands of man that he not surrender everything, her love is given to be taken. "Woman gives herself away, man acquires more"—this is Nietzsche's summary of the condition he calls an "opposition of nature." It withstands every attempt to get around it "by means of social contracts or with the best will in the world to be just." Nature rules convention in the fundamental matter of love. But Nietzsche immediately warns that it is *not desirable* to flaunt this natural opposition or "remind oneself constantly how harsh, terrible, enigmatic, immoral this antagonism" is. This cautionary statement comes as a distinct surprise in a thinker who seems bent on reminding us constantly of this very antagonism. He even adds a further limpid sentence to what we ought not constantly remind ourselves of: "For love, thought whole, great, and full, is nature, and as nature in all eternity something 'immoral.' "

This reminder of something we ought not always remind ourselves of brings to a special focus one of the central themes of Book Five and of Nietzsche's thought generally: the boundary between truth and art, or nature and convention. As desirable and involuntary as it is to seek to possess the truth, it is not desirable to simply expose it in the way that it is possessed. Exposing it opens a private possession to inspection by others that violates what one has come to possess for oneself. Truth and art are both necessary and where naked truth harms or is deadly it is not to be masked in some noble lie that denies it but bodied forth in art that beautifies it. Does Nietzsche insist on reminding us constantly of the deadly truth? Not constantly. For if the deadly truth must be known, the constant insistence on its deadliness is deadly. But Greek tragic art proves the possibility of beautifying the deadly truth without denying it in noble lies. And that art was a public art: if only for a moment, a glorious moment, a people lived the beautified truth. And Nietzsche's art too is Greek or Dionysian art as he stated emphatically in two retrospective accounts of his work, the "Attempt at a Self-Criticism" introducing the new edition of the *Birth of Tragedy,* and "What I Owe to the Ancients" the chapter at the end of *Twilight of the Idols* balancing the "Problem of Socrates" at its beginning. In both essays Nietzsche shows how Dionysian art beautifies and celebrates the natural antagonisms without constantly reminding us of their harsh, terrible, enigmatic, immoral character.

Seen from this perspective Nietzsche's writings have two aims: discovering the deadly truth and beautifying it in art. With respect to nature and convention, the cautionary statement in the central section suggests that the natural difference in love can be sustained without constant reminders of its harsh qualities. A teaching that accepts the natural strife of the sexes would do well not to simply flaunt that strife or kindle strife or insist on the fraudulence of harmony or concord. A new social contract and will to justice could secure and celebrate the natural opposition in ennobling ways. One thing Nietzsche insists on: modern equality of rights in love reflects a social contract and will to justice that aims not at the harmony but at the eradication of natural difference. Nietzsche anticipates, without dictating, a new social contract that could be seen as a renaissance of the ancient Greek symbolism of Dionysos and Ariadne. One of his last descriptions of that symbolism emphasized its sexual character.

What Nietzsche owes to the ancients is most profoundly the Dionysian experience to which he lays claim as an insider, the last initiate and disciple of Dionysos. The Dionysian mysteries are orgiastic; they represent a will to life that recognizes and sanctifies life's origins in sexuality. For the old Hellenes, "the sexual symbol was the venerable principle par excellence, the real profundity of the whole of ancient piety. Every single element in the act of procreation, of pregnancy, and of birth aroused the highest and most solemn feelings" (*TI* Ancients 4). Nietzsche emphasizes the sanctification of childbirth and particularly of the pain experienced by the mother in giving birth: "the pangs of the woman giving birth hallow all pain; all becoming and growing—all that guarantees a future—involves pain. . . . I know of no higher symbolism than this *Greek* symbolism of the Dionysian festivals." Its height, its sublimity, arises from its experience that life is not refuted by pain and that life is not to be idealized as affirmable only if pain is subtracted. Nietzsche ends on the contrary symbolism of Christianity "which first made something unclean of sexuality." Nietzsche could make jokes about this hatred of sexuality: "Christianity gave Eros poison to drink: he did not die of it but degenerated—into a vice" (*BGE* 168). Or he could ridicule its high representatives like Pope Innocent III whom Nietzsche quotes for his disapproval of his "impure begetting, disgusting means of nutrition in his mother's womb, baseness of the matter out of which man evolves" (*GM* 2.7). But Nietzsche knows where this loathing of being born of woman leads: to the misogyny of Schopenhauer who hates women metaphysically for having bodies that carry within themselves the reproductive principle (*GM* 3.7). In the language of the central section of Book Five, Schopenhauer can be understood as the metaphysical male on whom it dawns that complete possession is impossible; male resentment finds this intolerable and resigns the whole wretched game claiming superior virtue. Nietzsche's new spiritual history of the West necessarily includes the history of sexuality, its sanctification in the old Greeks and its demonization in Christianity. The rising tone of Nietzsche's attack on Christianity seems to derive in no small measure from growing clarity of what the advocacy of Dionysos required of him: denunciation of the high and holy, celebration of the deep and sacred.

"Love is nature" is a thought not usually associated with Nietzsche. To be understood in a Nietzschean way it must be thought together with other statements about nature. In *Beyond Good and Evil*, Nietzsche described nature as immoral and pilloried philosophy for moralizing nature (9). "Love is nature" does not moralize either nature or human nature, for love is strife. *Beyond Good and Evil* named nature "will to power" even though the name offended its audience of free minds trained to a Christian understanding of nature (36–37). Insisting on an inescapable, natural bisexuality, an inescapable warfare between the sexes, again runs the risk of offending free minds—"free" minds having been schooled in the modern teaching of equality according to which any difference is difference in rank or worth because there is only one unit of measure and schooled too in the modern teaching of malleability according to which any difference can be eradicated by adjustments to the social contract. The teaching on will to power requires that minds be reschooled to what is given by nature and reschooled to the desirability of limits to the human urge to alter nature. Rather than falsifying nature, that teaching culminates in a new love of nature, *amor fati*.

But "love is nature" must above all be thought together with *Thus Spoke Zarathustra,* the book that contains Nietzsche's most complete expression of the view that love is strife. In a book with many dramatic elements, the decisive drama is the relationship between a man and a woman, Zarathustra and Life. The drama begins in a way that seems almost conventional, the warrior symbolism of "On Reading and Writing" (*Z* 1.7). But it expands and deepens into a dance involving the most enigmatic elements of being and knowing (2.9–11). If the dance leads to insight, insight is not enough (2.20): it leads too, by an inexorable logic, to actions—in the symbolism of the book, to declarations of love and ultimately to marriage (3.13–16). The erotic dance with life leads to the love of life that affirms its eternal return.

The relationship between Zarathustra and Life is an analogue in Nietzsche's poetry for the relationship expressed religiously in Dionysos and Ariadne, as comes clear in the climactic songs at the end of Part Three.[32] As enigmatic as Dionysos is in Nietzsche's writings, this much he says directly: Dionysos is a philosophizing god (*BGE* 295). As such, Dionysos expresses the nature of man in the highest manliness: he is possessed by the restless desire to possess the truth while recognizing that the truth cannot be possessed fully. His love for Ariadne grows even after her surrender—he would be the last to concede that she had nothing more to give him. Ariadne is still more mysterious than Dionysos but in her appearances in Nietzsche's writings she expresses the nature of woman in the highest womanliness: as Life in *Thus Spoke Zarathustra,* she yields to Zarathustra only at the end of a courtship in which she has her way with him, and she yields only because of his possession of the whip. This most notorious of Nietzsche's symbols is no symbol of cruelty or a will to harm, nor is it a symbol of the modern desire to master nature; it is a token of Zarathustra's forcefulness, his spirited will to possess Life as she is. Man's love is the opposite of the artistic yielding which Nietzsche sees as characterizing woman's love. But Life as a woman does not yield to the yielding; she yields to Zarathustra only in stages and only to his forcefulness. Only late in a lifelong dance does she yield the secret of her nature, that she is will to power, and she yields it as a test of his manliness and promising her ultimate capture of him (2.12). To yield her secret is not yet to yield herself and she yields herself only after his understanding of her secret has led to his affirmation of what she is— only after he whispers in her ear that he wills eternal return. This affir-

---

32. I analyzed these songs in *Nietzsche's Teaching.*

mation confirms to her that he loves her as she is and desires to possess her as she is. Only then will Life accept from Zarathustra the name he desires to bestow upon her in marriage: Eternity. Only then will Life and Zarathustra—Eternity and Zarathustra—produce the offspring both long for, children of the human affirmation of life.

When *Zarathustra* is considered from the perspective of *The Joyous Science,* it becomes clear that Life yields to Zarathustra only after he has solved the problem of man's love, disloyalty, the problem to which Nietzsche turns at the very end of the central section of Book Five. Nietzsche approaches the problem of man's love through an essential component of woman's love, loyalty. Loyalty or being true—*Treue*—follows from the very definition of woman's love, and although it *can* be a feature of man's love, it is so far from being its necessary feature that "one might almost speak with some justification of a natural antagonism or counterplay between love and loyalty in man." This antagonism between love and loyalty follows from the very nature of man's love which Nietzsche finally defines: it is a *Haben-Wollen,* a wanting to have, that comes to an end every time with *having.* Man is not loyal to what he loves after he possesses it; man is a faithless marauder, hunting down then letting fall whatever he comes to possess. Continued loving depends on continued wanting, on remaining unsated. But unsatedness *can* become a feature of man's love, a "finer and more suspicious thirst to possess," which arrives only rarely and late in his "having" and which alone allows love to persist. To the degree that this thirst remains present, man's love can still grow after woman's love surrenders and flowers in loyalty. Mutual growth of love depends on solving the problem of *man's* love, and Nietzsche's final words suggest his solution: that a man "not readily concede that a woman should have nothing more to give him." A man learns the limitations of possession by learning subtlety, by learning that there exists that which is always beyond his grasp—woman's surrender is her artistry; it is desirable that the beloved exceed his grasp and draw his grasp.

Psychology is the path to the fundamental problems and this description of human love opens onto the fundamental issues of philosophy, knowing and being. Love is nature and it has now become apparent how the most spiritual love, philosophy, is not only natural but the most spiritual form of nature: love of wisdom is an insatiable passion to possess the most artistic of beloveds; the philosophers are the never-satisfied. Nature accords with philosophy, it merits the love of the wise as always having more to give; as "our new infinite" (*JS* 374), it is lovable in itself.

The new philosophy has a responsibility to instruct in the new ideal of love and counter the old antinatural ideal. The new philosophy generates an ideal in accord with nature; not rest but motion, not satiety but more, not being but becoming. Its opposition to the old Platonic ideal can be expressed simply: "Plato is boring" (*TI* Ancients 2). This is not a judgment against the dialogues but against their ideal: the good in itself—unchanging, eternal, transcendent, boring; the pure mind—severed from passion, all eye and immaculate perception, boring. Persuasive opposition to the old ideal will have to take many forms, as Nietzsche illustrates on one of the rare occasions on which he raises the veil of the new beloved (*BGE* 36–37). Having shown how the new method forces the conclusion that "the world viewed from inside, the world defined and determined by its 'intelligible character'—it would be 'will to power' and nothing else," he hears an objection: "What? Doesn't this mean, to speak with the vulgar: God is refuted, but the devil is not?" This is the voice of Platonism, of the old view of the lovable, and it reacts in horror at the destruction of its high ideal and the elevation of what it had lowered: process, becoming, the insatiable. Nietzsche responds as a theologian to this Platonic theological horror: "On the contrary! On the contrary, my friends." The devil is refuted and God is not. But this new view of the divine is no simple reversal of the old view: "And the devil—who forces you to speak with the vulgar?" That old vulgarity of God and devil, built on a false idea of what is lovable, yields to a new subtlety built on a sense of the lovable that accords with human love.

Sexual complementarity or the war between the sexes is no accidental whim of Nietzsche's thought. It is the countermove to Platonism in the language of love where love is nature and nature is will to power. Diotima was never Nietzsche's teacher on matters of love, as Plato alleged she was Socrates'. In Diotima's tale, Eros is conceived by Poverty and Plenty on the night Aphrodite was born. There is a hierarchy of loves for mortals, but all take direction from the nature of love as the desire to possess the good forever (*Symposium* 206a) and from the nature of mortality to strive to exist forever and be immortal (207d). The highest form of eros is the philosophic eros visible in what Eros inherited from his parents: he is shoeless and homeless like his mother, but a schemer after the beautiful and the good like his father (203b–e)— he is like Socrates, though on this occasion scheming Socrates put on his fancy shoes (174a). According to Diotima, erotic desire in mortals can move them upward from the immortality gained through the reproduction of children, to the immortality gained through the undying fame accorded poets and the founders of peoples, to the highest of all possible erotic satisfactions, the vision of unchanging being, of what always is, of the Good and the Beautiful and the True (210d–211b). Of the Boring. Philosophy entered the city in the form of the beautified Socrates (*Symposium* 173b), in the poetry invented for Socrates by the immortal Plato. That poetry beautified philosophy by civilizing it, giving it a fresh bath and new clothes (174a), and allowing it to talk in an edifying way of the Good and the Beautiful and the True. A short note expresses Nietzsche's dissent: "For a philosopher it is disreputable to say that the Good and the Beautiful are one; if he goes on to add 'the True too' he should be thrashed" (*KGW* VIII 16 [40, §6]). After two millennia of Platonism, Nietzsche thrashes Plato for sanctifying a lie contrary to nature on the highest themes of love and the lovable.

Diotima could say that no god is a philosopher because the gods are wise; they possess the permanently true (204a). But Nietzsche says "the gods too philosophize" (*BGE* 295).[33] This "far from innocuous novelty" transforms our understanding of the highest, of the beings most worthy of emulation, the gods. But the new understanding thrashes Plato not only on his theology but on the whole array of philosophic themes, replacing "*moral values* with purely *naturalistic* values" (*KGW* VIII 9 [8]). Metaphysics no longer masquerades in eternal ideas but becomes a joyous science celebrating the primacy of becoming. Epistemology no longer alleges the adequacy of pure mind for apprehending the good as such but revels in the inescapability of enigma, of "open seas" that draw on the explorer. Art no longer claims that "Beauty is truth, truth beauty" because it looks "at science in the perspective of art, but at art in the perspective of life" (*BT* Attempt 2). Theology no longer speaks a monotono-theism— and certainly not of God "the father," "the judge," "the rewarder" (*BGE* 53) for it knows "the greatest advantage of polytheism" (*JS* 143). This whole complex of philosophy, art, and religion is what Nietzsche celebrated in the New Year's resolution that followed his insight into eternal return the previous summer. January 1, 1882: "I want to learn more and more to see as beautiful what is necessary in things: then I shall be

---

33. Leo Strauss says Plato shared this view, "Note on the Plan of Nietzsche's *Beyond*," 175. Strauss's compacted essay strikes me as perhaps the most profound piece ever written on Nietzsche. The fruit of a lifetime of penetrating reflection on Platonic political philosophy and Nietzsche's place in that philosophy, its greatest service—exhibited throughout and almost declared at the end—is to show how Nietzsche replaces Plato. Like all of Strauss's later work, however, it is not constructed to be easily understood.

one of those who make things beautiful. *Amor fati:* let that be my love henceforth!" (*JS* 276): Let my love be loyalty.

But man's love lacks loyalty as an essential feature. And the core of Nietzsche's moral teaching is loyalty to the earth. How can loyalty to the earth take root when it depends upon a feature inessential to man's love and almost contradictory to it? Nietzsche states that loyalty "*can easily develop in the wake of love*" in a man, and he names two ways in which this can occur: through "gratitude" or through "an idiosyncrasy of taste." Gratitude and taste are essential to Nietzsche's thought, gratitude as a virtuous word for amor fati, taste as refined sensibility both inborn and acquired, the result of both natural history and schooling in nature. Gratitude and taste rebel at modern man's extreme lack of loyalty, a lack Nietzsche described in a remarkable passage:

> Our whole attitude toward nature, the way we rape her with the aid of machines and the heedless inventiveness of our technicians and engineers, is *hubris;* our attitude toward God as some alleged spider of purpose and morality behind the great captious web of causality is *hubris* . . . ; our attitude toward ourselves is *hubris,* for we experiment with ourselves in a way we would never permit ourselves to experiment with animals. (*GM* 3.9)

Here is a Nietzsche yet to be heard, the advocate of love who traces the modern rage to alter and possess nature to the natural propensity of male eros. The death of nature is an act of males whose love lacks loyalty for what nurtured them. Loyalty to the earth is an imperative that arises out of insight into nature and history. In gratitude and taste Nietzsche protests the spiritualized and organized aggression of male sexuality goaded into vengeance against humankind and the earth by the long and now ignoble Platonic lie of their defective or fallen character.

The central section of Book Five emphasizes, against modern fictions of sameness and equality, that love is strife. But it points to a harmony as well, a harmony of faith. Nietzsche had said in the previous section that "our faith" rests on the increasing manliness of Europe (362). And here he says that woman's love in its absence of conditions is "a *faith:* woman has no other." The common faith of woman and man lies in the recovery of nature in man and woman, in allowing woman and man their natural difference. The future of Europe desirable for both men and women of this faith is therefore not the future prepared by the French Revolution (362) with its talk of equal rights (363), but the future prepared by

Napoleon as a renaissance of perhaps the decisive slab of antiquity. Male and female have an equal stake in this unique warfare of ancients and moderns in which the ancient is *pre*-Platonic and the "modern" a Platonism for the people. To take the side of these ancients means to break faith with one's own, to practice disloyalty to the modern in which one is raised. But disloyalty is harder for women. Nietzsche must appeal to women to break faith with what has come to seem the sole means of women's emancipation, modern ideas of equality. And how shall a mere man make such an appeal and presume to teach women their very nature and call them back to their nature? Nietzsche has to break Zarathustra's prohibition—"About women one should speak only to men" (Z 1.18)—and do so in a way calculated to have effect. He seems to have calculated that the effective way is the offensive way. If love is strife, recovery of the ancient strife depends upon sowing strife. Make love, make war.

"We the fearless" have "our work": putting the worth of morality into question (345). But the question of the worth of morality has led Nietzsche necessarily to the question of nature as the only standpoint from which to judge morality's worth. Here in the central section Nietzsche speaks as one who has access to the nature of nature, and who judges that in humans love is nature and that it takes two complementary forms. Zarathustra had said that "Everything about woman is a riddle and everything about woman has one solution: that is pregnancy." But here man is a riddle who needs a solution: male love is a *Haben-Wollen* terminated in every case if possession occurs. Another way of putting this is that man would rather will nothingness than not will (*GM* 3.1). But this will to nothingness has grounded two thousand years of thought and action: "This hatred of the human, and even more of the animal, and more still of the material, this horror of the senses, of reason itself, this fear of happiness and beauty, this longing to get away from all appearance, change, becoming, death, wishing, from longing itself—all this means—let us dare to grasp it—*a will to nothingness*" (*GM* 3.28).

Inquiry into our history must be grounded by insight into our nature and Book Five, in its central section, secures its various probes and sorties into the history of philosophy and the history of culture with this insight into our nature. The implicit question of the central section is how the nihilism at the core of man's being can be avoided, the nihilism of *Haben-Wollen* that ends with possession. The answer actually given points to a more refined and suspicious sense of possession which recognizes and exults in the fact that possession is always incomplete, that what eludes possession enchants and draws the will. Everything about man is a riddle and everything about man has one solution: that his play be inexhaustible. Unlike Diotima whose ideal transcends generation and repudiates it on the way to the highest, Nietzsche remains true to the Hellenic or Dionysian symbolism; he too is a warrior in Homer's army; his ideal enhances the sexual symbol as the venerable symbol par excellence. Nietzsche's "idealism," so to speak, magnifies and sanctifies the natural processes of life. In this most natural way, the strife of male and female finds its common solution in concord or concourse—without disloyalty, without the surrender of art, and without modern ideas. *Europa* in this sense, the unified *Europa* of Napoleon's philosophic heir, would be worthy of being the mistress of the earth.

Chapter 14

The Joyous Science III: Hyperborean
Politics or European Antinihilism

Nothing shall keep me from becoming blunt and telling . . . a few hard truths:
who else would do it? . . . *This most* anti-cultural *sickness and unreason
there is . . . this perpetuation of European particularism, of petty politics. . . .
Does anyone besides me know the way out of this dead end street?*—*A task
great enough to* unite *nations again*—*Nietzsche (*EH *Books* CW *2)*

"The last anti-political German" (*EH* Wise 3) plotted a pan-
European, global politics, a "great politics" on the scale of a Bacon
or Descartes, the scale of a Plato. The history of philosophy provided
Nietzsche with monumental examples of a philosophic politics the
end of which was a reordered society, the motive of which was philanthropy and philology, love of the human and love of the logos.
The politics of such loves led Nietzsche to unprecedented attacks on
the established good and evil, and many have asked, what moved
Nietzsche to such attacks? Ignoring both his monumental examples
and his psychology of the genuine philosopher, they have found no
better answer than a love of fame or even a love of mayhem and
cruelty. It is embarrassing to proclaim oneself a paragon of virtue,
and Nietzsche did what he could to avoid it: call him the first
immoralist. But what moved Nietzsche moved the great philosophers: the passion Zarathustra first named "the gift-giving virtue"
(*Z* 1.22) but which he later permitted to be seen immorally, as "the
three evils," erotics, the lust to rule, and selfishness (*Z* 3.10). Such
passion is *bound* to be misunderstood, bound to draw down on its
exemplars a fear and hatred impenetrable to persuasion, even when
the three evils can easily be seen as belonging to the very definition
of the genuine philosopher and as worthy of virtuous names.

What to do? If fear and hatred are inevitable, accede to their inevi-
tability but plot a strategy against them. The gift of the new teaching
kindles spiritual warfare as consuming as the warfare kindled by

Bacon and Descartes. That war was not won by Bacon and Descartes but by Baconians and Cartesians who took up the new teaching persuaded of its desirability. Nietzsche declared a spiritual war he could not win but that he could kindle and plot and, to some small degree, direct. Like Descartes in part six of the *Discourse,* Nietzsche stood at the head of an army not yet mustered and outfitted, an army formed for public battles still a long way off though already fought and won in the mind of their instigator. Nietzsche's great politics is not simply a new teaching meant to supplant the pervasive old teaching: "This is war, but war without powder and smoke" (*EH* Books *HH* 1).[1]

In its second half, *The Joyous Science* Book Five turns more explicitly to the practical tasks of politics and war—recruitment to the new view set out in the first half. Its first sections break sharply with the fundamental themes of history and nature, time and being, that peak in the center of Book Five. The solitary inquirer now returns to society to form the alliances that will be necessary if the new understanding is ever to be more than the solitary experience of one lone thinker. Scholars are the special target (364–66), and they are led to ponder a new perspective on art and truth (367–70). The new future (371–72) reestablishes the proper relationship between science and philosophy by reinterpreting the history of philosophy and in particular, Epicurus (373–76). But for all its grandeur, the new politics must linger over what looks most local and personal: just who is Nietzsche anyway (377–83)?

---

1. Nietzsche's politics has been set out in unprecedented scope and detail by Henning Ottmann in *Philosophie und Politik bei Nietzsche.* "Basically only legends circulate about the politics . . . which Nietzsche named 'great politics,' demonizing or sanitizing legends" (236). Ottmann, at last, explodes those legends and treats Nietzsche's great politics sympathetically and responsibly—and in a way that constantly informs. Still, as grateful as one must be for Ottmann's achievement in presenting Nietzsche's "new political Platonism" (148), even he understands such politics, whether Plato's or Nietzsche's, as merely "utopian." This limitation of Ottmann's presentation is corrected by Alex McIntyre's far-reaching and insightful essay, " 'Virtuosos of Contempt.' " On Plato as the model for Nietzsche's educational or cultural politics see Blondel, *Nietzsche,* 56. Bergmann's *Nietzsche: "The Last Antipolitical German"* describes Nietzsche's development into "the prophet of an unwanted Europeanism" (169). Informative and valuable for its many details of Nietzsche's political awareness, Bergmann's book, it seems to me, misses the core of Nietzsche's great politics because it makes him subject to the local politics of his time and imagines him resigning into the "antipolitical."

Entering Society in Alliance with the Scholars (364–66)

In the first two of these sections, a solitary ends his solitude to address others, and in the third he addresses his select audience, scholars. Why would one who chooses solitude choose to enter society? And how? The sociability the solitary forces on himself he calls, in his first word, an "art." His art makes him a wolf (364), a ghost (365), and a seducer of scholars (366). In all three forms, his gaiety and sportiveness keep him from falling into the vice implicit in his theme: condescension and insult. Moreover, his very style betrays this solitary's secret: he knows his way around in society.

In different imagery, what Nietzsche here describes is the philosopher's return to the cave, the philanthropy that obliges the apparent misanthrope to take up once again his place among human beings. Having been forced aside by his natural asceticism, the involuntary choice of poverty, humility, and chastity demanded by his "dominating instinct" of inquiry (*GM* 3.8), he finds it necessary to reenter society. But he will not do it quietly and he will not leave it as he found it. He enters society to alter it, to change the images and echoes reflecting from the walls of the cave.

The solitary talks (364). The lone wolf of the first section lacks by nature the wolf's hunger that would permit him to devour his fellow man; he must create that hunger by art. Nietzsche indicates his problem by misquoting a devil: Goethe's Mephistopheles says politely that even "the worst company allows you to feel that you are a human being among human beings." Nietzsche's Mephistopheles changes a single letter—*dich* becomes *sich*—in order to counter that virtuous sentiment: "The worst company allows itself to be felt."[2] Given the setting, that seems to include *all* company. Lacking the wolf's hunger and experiencing distaste at the fare, the solitary who mixes with humanity will have to create an appetite in order to digest his fellow man. Three dietary laws govern this art and show how he does it: alter yourself in order to experience pride at your courage; alter others to make them more palatable; leave everything the same, but follow the standard human practice of self-hypnosis allowing you to absent yourself without leaving and without

---

2. *KGW* goes against the authority of the first edition to change Nietzsche's *sich* back to Goethe's *dich* (*Faust* line 1637). Kaufmann translates *Wolfshunger* "ravenously hungry," losing Nietzsche's image of the solitary wolf preying on the herd.

scandal. This scientific formulation of the art of patience prepares the theme considered next, the extreme demands placed on his patience:

The solitary speaks again (365). The title suggests the main point: "speaking again" means speaking posthumously. The solitary, dead for his contemporaries, sees to his resurrection, his immortality among men, for his thoughts are *sub specie aeterni* (262). All clothe themselves, but the solitary clothes himself as a ghost, as one already dead. Being a ghost has two advantages, it frightens the fearful and incites the fearless. The solitary ghost looks to the fearless for his resurrection, such calculated immortality being "the art work par excellence of the posthumous men." They will be raised from the dead or visited in their underworld as were the four pairs of posthumous men Nietzsche visited: Epicurus and Montaigne, Goethe and Spinoza, Plato and Rousseau, Pascal and Schopenhauer (*AO* 408). Inventing a speech for such a posthumous man, Nietzsche shows how he has to work at the common virtue, patience. The long perspective of the posthumous makes them look very patient, patient enough to die unknown, but in fact they would never be able to hold out without assurance of the resurrection.

The solitary Nietzsche welcomes the visits of those who risk the journey to his underworld, for being raised from the dead depends on their reports. He is not directly the cause of his own rebirth though he prepares it by a calculated dependence on others whom he forces to do what they delight in doing: bringing back reports from the dead. This solitary can leave his *Umgehen mit Menschen* to these trustworthy characters; he will be introduced into polite company by those who belong to it and who will see to it that others come to recognize that the banished solitary belongs too.

While he expected to be brought into the open by those whom Zarathustra called "nutcrackers" (*Z* 3.6), Nietzsche seems to expect a modicum of decency in their handling of his solitude. Perhaps he even guarantees it by means of the chair he props politely against the door to his privacy. This does not mean that some conspiracy of silence is to be maintained by those who think they have discovered some esoterica behind the ghost costume. It means rather, the preservation of privacy regarding the merely personal or accidental, the refusal to invade that privacy in the customary way at which Nietzsche took offense and which he, for all his physio-psychology, never indulged: psychological or sociological reductionism that supposes that the dress, the teaching, owes its being to some little personal fact, some idiosyncrasy making the solitary like everyman; such impertinence presumes to explain away unique achievement by shared triviality. Nietzsche warned his friends against such psychohistory: "The worst readers of aphorisms are the friends of their author who are bent on tracing the general back to some particular to which the aphorism owes its origin: for through such pot-peeking they negate the whole effort of the author and so they only deserve it when they receive, instead of a philosophical mood and instruction, nothing more than the satisfaction of a common curiosity" (AO 129). Enticing the nutcrackers into his underworld by the lures of his text, Nietzsche keeps the chair propped politely against that door, propped against impertinence not against probity.

Faced with a scholarly book (366). Enticement of the scholars continues in this section, for if Nietzsche begins critically, measuring scholars by a standard foreign to them, he ends addressing them as friends, praising their virtue, and submitting to their measure. The opening admission that his thoughts come not from books but while walking, leaping, climbing, dancing, plus the admission that "we read rarely," hand over the weapons with which scholars can verbally punish him—while he punishes them for their characteristic traits. But mutual abuse is not the end of the matter, for the section suggests an alliance that would advance their common ends. If the posthumous birth of the solitary depends upon the scholars, one trait above all others assumes importance, their defining trait of "unconditional probity." Nietzsche measures scholars aware that they will measure him; he flaunts his differences confident that he can accredit himself by their standard, for unconditional probity is a quality they share.

Nietzsche's opening seems calculated to discredit him among scholars in the way pictured by *Zarathustra* (2.16): one taste will be enough for them to repeat after Wilamowitz-Moellendorff: "Nietzsche is no longer a scholar." Closing his book they will do so without the gratitude he reports on closing one of theirs. Gratitude for the scholarly spirit does not preclude describing it as crippled—and Nietzsche bases his description, he says, on his own experience with scholarly friends—one wonders what Rohde and Deussen thought on reading this section. Nietzsche is categorical: nothing can be done about the way the scholarly craft deforms the scholar; education cannot cure it because education causes it. But all mastery comes at high cost, and the mastery of the learned is so far from being a disease that it is a form of health compared to a modern growth that has refused the scholar's deforming discipline: the intellectuals or literati Zarathustra described as "flies of the market place" (*Z* 1.12).

The final and most elaborate of the things for which he blesses his "scholarly friends" is their uncompromising opposition to all that is "semblance, half-genuine, dolled up, virtuoso-like, demagogic, actor-like." The solitary and the scholars are allies in opposition to modern times, the time of the actor (361). But uncompromising opposition to everything that smacks of fraudulence will make one wonder about Nietzsche's own work. Audacious claims, seeming scorn of proof or demonstration, heaps of aphorisms, a method whose thoughts come while walking, leaping, climbing, and dancing, comparatively little reading (he says)—all these smack of fraudulence to scholars. Nevertheless, the standards of taste scholars apply align them in the end with Nietzsche, especially their final and highest test of "unconditional *probity* in discipline and prior training." Scholarly accreditation of Nietzsche's writings depends upon certifying his probity and ascertaining whether his discipline and prior training have led him to judgments that scholars can in some measure confirm.

Nietzsche often acknowledged his need for assistance—as in his wistful recollection of how he could have used Paul Rée's "sharp and disinterested eye" for his investigations of the history of morality (*GM* Preface 7), or his vain hope for a whole band of scholars as bloodhounds to be sent into the dark forests of the religious sentiment (*BGE* 45), or his plans for the combined work of all the faculties in a cooperative effort of natural history—the problem of the evolution of moral evaluations (*GM* 1 endnote). The assistance always takes a distinct form: *they* work at *his* tasks. They are philosophical laborers—or philological or psychological or physiological laborers—who work within the horizon provided by the genuine philosopher. Nietzsche recognized that his work could not be pressed upon contemporaries; they could not be persuaded of its worth because they could not be persuaded of *his* worth. Posthumous birth was necessary because no contemporary could be thought supreme enough for the sublime tasks of the genuine philosopher. Posthumous birth in Nietzsche's case is decisively aided by recovering the role played in the history of philosophy by genuine philosophers like Plato, Bacon, or Descartes. They succeeded in doing what Nietzsche sets out to do, open a new perspective for the scientific and scholarly investigation of being and time.

The Joyous Science is not a scholarly book, but it is surely a book that aims to win scholarly accreditation. That accreditation will have to come on Nietzsche's terms. Nietzsche frequently charged that modern scholarship for all its vaunted independence served modern politics, but *The Joyous Science* praises the trait that promises scholars a kind of independence after all, their unconditional probity. That probity will eventually detach them from all their loyalties—except their loyalty to probity. What Nietzsche had earlier called "the degeneration of the modern scholar" (358) seems remediable through the scholars' highest virtue. Still, *The Joyous Science* claims that an honest scholarship will develop new loyalties; while never abandoning its books and its deforming discipline, its very probity will compel it to place itself in the service of the dance.

Nietzsche's parenthetical remark on probity grounds this claim in an argument: a deficiency in probity cannot keep itself masked. Not even genius in this age of the actor can fake probity forever. But if fraudulent probity yields to probity's gaze, so too will probity. And Nietzsche has to entrust everything to this process because there is no other way to authenticate the genuine. "Only fool, only poet"? The time is coming in which the problem of the actor is what will trouble *scholars* most. Exempt from the bad conscience of modern artists, scholars must judge whether the new philosophy shares their own probity as it claims it does. They are caught—they have flown into the net of his cunning (Z 4.15); insofar as they are not fakes, they know their own virtue and hence its possibility. The only question now is whether it can be present in the degree and fashion claimed by a dancer who lays aside their books in gratitude, having achieved a comprehensive perspective from which to view the matters to which they devote their specialized lives. Nietzsche forges an alliance with the scholar as Plato did with the gentleman and Bacon and Descartes did with the scientist. And he does so by counting on their virtue. Now the problem is to change their taste.

Art and Truth: Some Discourses on Method (367–71)

"Nietzsche is the philosopher friendliest to art"[3] and here that friendliness exhibits its grounds. They are old grounds, for if poets have always been hostile to philosophy, philosophers have always been friendly to poets. As Nietzsche noted in an early fragment, "they regard them as bridges from religion to philosophy" ("On the Poet" [1875]);[4] or, as he

3. May, *Nietzsche and Modern Literature,* 1.
4. *Friedrich Nietzsche on Rhetoric and Language,* 243.

stated later, philosophy's independence attracts poets as its valets (*GM* 3.2–5).

All the central sections of *The Joyous Science* Book Five concentrate on the problem that troubled Nietzsche longest (361), the problem of the actor, of art and truth, and what that problem means for method. The current sections (367–71) are devoted specifically to art and they culminate in "What is Romanticism?"—Nietzsche's clearest expression of his resolution of the problem of art and truth. Is there a truthful standard for judging art where "art" includes everything made by human beings? "Is there a measure on the earth?" Nietzsche's thought has Hölderlin's question constantly before it but Nietzsche answers yes, the measure of taste grounded in a healthy body. Nietzsche knows his answer is laughable— it will seem like a joke to those still confident of some standard of truth independent of art and guaranteed by reason or God or history. It will also seem like a joke to those who have lost faith in such grave standards and grown skeptical of any standard. How can the standard of taste— how things smell: "My genius is in my nostrils" (*EH* Destiny 1)—have dignity where one has been used to invoking God as measure? Nietzsche makes it still more laughable: taste has *always* been his standard and it began by getting things all wrong. What he once savored now smells bad. Can anyone have confidence in a new standard so insubstantial and so prone to error? In giving warrant to the new standard, section 370 will bring Nietzsche's discourses on method to their appropriate conclusion, for it will intimate both the ground of the new standard and how it can issue in the highest value, eternal return.

With respect to the history of philosophy, these sections show how the new standard of measure grew, in part, out of reflection on the fate of philosophy in our culture. Epicurus becomes a central figure. Rethinking Epicurus led to essential advances in the new physio-psychology. Reciprocally, those advances required the whole history of philosophy to be reordered.

The first distinction to be made regarding works of art (367). The solitary speaks yet again to introduce a basic distinction: works of art are either "monological art" or "art before witnesses." Only the true solitary, the godless one for whom the ultimate witness is dead, can make this most fundamental distinction with respect to art and truth—Nietzsche knows of "no deeper distinction."

"Works of art" include everything made by human beings, and "monological art" and "art before witnesses" divide everything made into two classes: made for oneself or for others. The distinction applies especially to the highest or most sublime products of heart and mind including "the whole lyric of prayer." The solitary reports that for the pious there is no solitude—a claim exhibited by the encounter of the solitary Zarathustra with an apparent solitary, the old saint in the forest (*Z* Prologue 2). But if solitude and monological art are impossible in religion, are they possible in philosophy? Given the context, the question is: Can heart and mind produce anything grounded wholly in probity? Or does the ascetic standard of truthfulness that Nietzsche says the scholar applies to art require the judgment that there is no honest art, only theatrics, art before witnesses? At issue is "the eye" with which the artist views his own work, not in its completed state but in its coming to be: there is "no deeper distinction in the whole optic of an artist" than the perspective from which he views his art in the making. If he views it with the eye of the witness, his art will be the art of the actor, and probity would always detect in it an inauthentic core, something performed for the sake of being seen. If this is the only art possible, art would be irremediably social and reactive, an act of submission to the other, a conclusion consistent with the view of Hobbes and Hegel that at the very root of human making stands the desire for recognition. To draw this conclusion is to side with what became dominant in modern thought, and to side against the very few thinkers who held that there was something higher than recognition and that philosophy was the monological art par excellence.

In turning to that possibility, Nietzsche returns to those few thinkers. Speaking negatively, in wording left over from Christian asceticism, Nietzsche raises the possibility of an artist who "'has forgotten the world.'" Essential to every "monological art" is a kind of world forgetfulness that resembles the asceticism of the religious, except that it forgets the ultimate witness too. Still, it would hardly be simple forgetfulness for it would hold in memory what is essential to the work itself in its coming to be. Can there be such art? The great battle of *Zarathustra* part four is fought over this question, the Old Sorcerer holding that the artist ultimately recognizes that there is no monological art but only art for witnesses. Zarathustra argues as Nietzsche does in *The Joyous Science* for the possibility of a genuine art of the solitary. In the next section, Nietzsche expands and defends this possibility while speaking explicitly against Wagner.

The artistry of *The Joyous Science*, like the artistry of *Thus Spoke Zarathustra*, is not monological art. *The Joyous Science* is an act of communication addressed to scientists and scholars with the intent of introducing them to a new conception of science; while composing it, Nietzsche surely watched over every sentence with the eye of the witness. The question however remains: is the insight on which it is based a view of things made possible by forgetting the world of witnesses? Unconditional probity will try to answer that question.

The cynic speaks (368). The music of forgetting leads Nietzsche to the music of Wagner which never forgets its witnesses. Nietzsche condemns Wagner's music for a series of physiological reasons: "Why bother to dress them up in aesthetic formulas?" A plausible reason is given at the end: because it is very easy to dismiss the physiological as whims of one kind of body, the sick body of their author as the Wagnerian claims in turning Nietzsche's physiological standard against him. Can the standard of Nietzsche's healthy body be taken seriously, given the history of standards claiming superiority to the body, and given the despair at standards that accompanies the demise of such superior measures? Can taste be elevated as a standard without being trivialized or criminalized as happens in the revenge on which the section ends?

Finding himself with bodily objections to Wagner's music, Nietzsche asks himself a general question: What is it that my whole body really *wants* from music? Nietzsche's method thus grants validity to already present physiological judgments of approbation and disapprobation and wonders about their meaning and implications. Body is weighty and melancholy and seeks the antidote to its gravity in lightness and ease. The goal of music is the beautification of the grave into the light, into dance. Such beautification, so far from being the denial of the "animal functions," is their quickening and elevation. The power of rhythm, referred to earlier as Apollo's most powerful gift which can bind even the goddesses of fate (*JS* 84), is the power that accelerates and elevates the animal functions. But if this is the function of music, music is higher than drama, the theatrical effect into whose service music was pressed by Wagner. Nietzsche claims to be "essentially anti-theatrical," a monologic artist who does not view his work in the first instance from the perspective of the audience.

But the argument with Wagner becomes theatrical at the end as Nietzsche drags a Wagnerian onto his stage. Addressing him with his essential critique of theatre, Nietzsche claims for himself the standpoint of a solitary not forced to abandon his honesty, taste, and courage to the considerations of an audience, and he attacks Wagner not simply for having his eye on his audience but for submitting to the modern mass audience. The Wagnerian makes a fine response to Nietzsche's polemical outburst, and in reporting it Nietzsche leaves a fine challenge to the reader regarding physiological objections. Who is the cynic of "the cynic speaks"? Is it the first speaker, Nietzsche himself, whose body has taught him to be cynical of aesthetic formulas? Or is it the clever Wagnerian, cynical about Nietzsche's tastes because they lack aesthetic formulas and are based on the prior judgments of his body? Erich Heller registers surprise that Nietzsche was "almost infallible in his aesthetic discernment" despite the narrowness of his origins.[5] But Nietzsche himself flaunts the real basis of surprise: he takes his guidance from his body—how can we avoid being cynical about that? What gives warrant to a thinker's judgment? Not only does Nietzsche dare to say that judgment is based on taste and taste on the body, he dares to claim superior taste on the basis of a healthy body—and he dares to claim that that taste is shareable and sufficiently firm to justify all-out warfare against the historic standards that lack taste because they are based on unhealthy bodies. The measuring body is not any body. The argument of Book Five comes to its culmination in "The great health" (382), the final section but for the laughter of the "Epilogue" (383); the great health belongs to a body that has convalesced from the great sickness.

The Wagnerian claims that Nietzsche is simply not healthy enough for their music. With that sally he yields to Nietzsche's choice of weapons thinking he can defeat Nietzsche on his own terms. What a marvelous way for Nietzsche to end a little section on method.

Our side by side (369). Taste and creative power may stand side by side in artists but they develop independently of one another. Taste may contradict creative power or outstrip it. But Nietzsche emphasizes the case in which creative power outstrips and eclipses taste until taste is completely atrophied and unable to judge what the artist creates. This is the relevant question in his own case, the explicit question of the next section where Nietzsche begins with his most serious *mis*judgments about his own work. The whole world of Greek poetry and art serves as Nietzsche's "tremendous example" of his claim that the artist's creative power can outstrip his taste: Greek poetry and art never "knew" what it did. This is the world of poetry and art Nietzsche held in highest regard, and his audacious judgment against it once again forces the question of his own taste or judgment. How does it stand with *his* side by side? Does he, like those he here condemns, utter stupidities about his work, utter

5. Heller, *Importance of Nietzsche,* 175.

them and believe them? The next section dares to admit that he began by uttering stupidities about his work and believing them.

What is romanticism? (370). The long reflection on art and truth now comes to fulfillment in the section that begins with Nietzsche's confession that he had uttered stupidities. Georg Picht says, "There are few texts in which Nietzsche gave such a complete and transparent representation of his basic philosophical stance."[6] For if he begins by confessing his mistakes, Nietzsche here presents the most detailed elaboration of a new method of interpretation that enabled him to correct them, and he ends suggesting—for the only time in Book Five—the teaching with which he identified himself, the affirmation of eternal return. This auto-biographical section—one of the last retrospective products of the half-year devoted almost exclusively to a review of his writings—provides access to the mature intentions and motives of the writer who immediately afterwards speaks of his necessary incomprehensibility (371). Like Descartes's discourse on the method, this one ties the new method to its founder's singular life-history while recommending the method as the new tool for a general science. The new method is introduced putting a question to itself: can a method be at all dependable whose inventor or discoverer began by making great errors with it?

Nietzsche's early errors were a product of his hope—hope for modern pessimism. Hope survived his disenchantment with modern pessimism and attached itself to something uniquely his own, the teaching of eternal return. But if Nietzsche's hopes lie with the teaching of eternal return, why mention it only once and only obliquely? As is typical of the post-*Zarathustra* works, *The Joyous Science* Book Five approaches the deepest discoveries of *Thus Spoke Zarathustra* with remarkable economy and indirection. This section most closely resembles *Beyond Good and Evil* section 56, which also penetrated modern pessimism, bared its roots, and moved beyond it to affirm eternal return. When studied together, the two sections provide indispensable insight into Nietzsche's most important teaching—and into Nietzsche's refusal to do everything for the reader, especially on the most important matters. The reader must build on Nietzsche's suggestions in order to rethink Nietzsche's thought, but the reader cannot proceed alone: both sections suggest, even command, that the reader follow the course set out in *Thus Spoke Zarathustra,* the book that exists to open the way into the teaching of eternal return.

6. Picht, *Nietzsche,* 178.

The origins of Nietzsche's early errors were personal; his misreading of modern pessimism sprang from a desire to fit contemporary phenomena to his instincts. The exact origins of his errors are now inaccessible—"who knows out of what personal experiences?"—they can therefore be of no concern to anyone, not even himself, as far as understanding his errors is concerned. Still, what kind of error it was is both knowable and interesting. While chastened by his earlier errors and flaunting them before his reader, Nietzsche has not become a skeptic of interpretation. Undermining his authority at the beginning, he asserts it throughout by grounding interpretation in his new physio-psychology.

Nietzsche says he misunderstood two great modern phenomena—the most modern philosophy and the most modern art—because he interpreted them as the rebirth of the tragic insight of the Greeks. He attributed to Schopenhauer and Wagner something not due them, a fundamental break with the tradition via a return to its origins. In Nietzsche's later language, he took them to be anti-Platonic, whereas they were in fact the final outbreaks of Platonism. The pivotal term is *romanticism,* and Nietzsche's failure to understand the romanticism of Schopenhauer and Wagner leads him to pose the question: what is romanticism?

To give an adequate answer to this seemingly local question, Nietzsche begins with the widest possible scope: "Every art, every philosophy." And he is categorical, not to say dogmatic, in stating what is true of all art and philosophy: it may be viewed as in the service of growing, struggling life; it presupposes those who suffer; and "there are two kinds of sufferers." Those who suffer from the "over-fullness of life" desire an intensification of life in a Dionysian or tragic art. Those who suffer from the "impoverishment of life" desire release from life; their art is romantic in Nietzsche's sense, and it expresses itself in a desire for rest and redemption or in a desire for intoxication and anesthesia. The "Dionysian god and man," Nietzsche says, can "afford the sight of the terrible and questionable" and even of "destruction, decomposition, negation"; all this "is, as it were, permissible" because of an "excess of procreating, fertilizing energies." Nietzsche's description of the converse—of romanticism—takes up the rest of the aphorism and requires that he refer to his new interpretation of the history of philosophy and religion.

For the most part, romanticism or suffering from the impoverishment of life requires mildness, a God who saves by deliverance from life, or a logic that calms by making existence explicable. Calming logic leads to a reflection on one of Nietzsche's underworld kin, Epicurus, whom Nietzsche had come to understand differently from perhaps everybody else (*JS* 45). For Nietzsche, Epicurus was one who sought deliverance from life—he therefore shared the romantic sentiment with Christianity. As long as Christianity dictated the terms, the atheist Epicurus could seem the opposite of Christianity, and Christianity could even brand all pagan philosophy Epicurean or atheistic. But from the perspective of Nietzsche's physio-psychology, these theisms and atheisms are opposites only superficially; the new method requires that spiritual history be rewritten to make their kinship clear. According to this perspective, Christianity belongs in the camp of the philosophy it singled out as its extreme spiritual enemy. Both seek deliverance from the world. Epicurus's philosophic romanticism sought deliverance through a comforting logic that like the garden wall closed out fear and closed in optimism. Later, Nietzsche will return to Epicurus and show "Why we look Epicurean" but are not (*JS* 375). It was in an earlier section, however, that he stated his essential insight into Epicurus (*JS* 45): he was a sufferer from life who watched, controlled and happy, as the sun set on the ruins of antiquity, on the greatest achievements of human history. Not his atomism or his atheism mattered most to Nietzsche's physio-psychology but his resignation from life, the transformation of bodily passion into the dispassionate eye fixed with resigned happiness on the demise of the highest. For all their differences, Epicurus shared with Christianity a postclassical optimism happy to let the world go.

But if Epicurus shared something with the Platonism for the people that shaped Western spiritual life, he nevertheless retained something anti-Platonic from the Greek philosophers prior to Plato, the scientific naturalism Platonism spurned. Only when this aspect of Nietzsche's new Epicurus is made clear ("Why we look Epicurean" [375]) can we fully appreciate Nietzsche's revaluation of Epicurus and its importance for his new history of philosophy.

Understanding the kinship between Epicurus and the Christian was an essential step in Nietzsche's understanding of romanticism, and Nietzsche credits his advance to his sharpened eye for "that most difficult and most suspicious" form of inference, the retrospective or backward inference, inferring truth from art, inferring what is true of the singer from the song. Retrospective inference is the key element in Nietzsche's method; it alone can legitimate the distinction drawn between an Augustine and a Plato; it alone made possible the new understanding of Schopenhauer and Wagner. Nietzsche captured the implications of this method exactly in the title "how to philosophize with a hammer": what seems like indiscriminate smashing based on nothing more substantial than likes and dislikes, is a listening to human phenomena that aspires to the precision and exactitude of a trained ear as true to pitch as a tuning fork.

Practice in retrospective inference led Nietzsche to a generalization: "regarding all aesthetic values," all art and philosophy, Nietzsche now asks himself, "Has hunger or overabundance become creative here?" This looks like a blunt instrument, but it expresses a major point in the method of the "great health"—the basic condition that makes a new psychological subtlety possible. The new duality, hunger and overabundance, replaces the older and more obvious duality of being and becoming because it is able to subsume the older duality in something more fundamental. What has prompted creation? Nietzsche asks, what has moved the doer to his deed? The old answers of a yearning for being or a yearning for becoming may be more visible, more accessible at a glance, but they are not primary: each is ambiguous because each harbors within itself the new and deeper distinction. Yearning for being, for permanence, could be the expression of either a creative hunger or a creative superabundance, as could yearning for becoming, for destruction or change. Nietzsche treats the yearning for becoming first and very briefly, as if it were less in need of explanation than the yearning for being: the yearning for becoming could be "Dionysian," an expression of overflowing energy that is pregnant with future, or it could express a hatred of everything that exists. Yearning for being requires a longer treatment because understanding this ambiguity enabled Nietzsche to understand Schopenhauer and Wagner as romantics. Furthermore, Nietzsche's clarification brings his teaching of eternal return to light for the only time in Book Five.

Nietzsche discusses the yearning for being under a new term: *der Wille zum Verewigen,* "the will to eternalize." Kaufmann's English translation, "the will to immortalize," is exactly wrong, for not only does it submerge the verbal reference to Nietzsche's own will to eternalize in eternal return, it implies a negation of the mortal through making immortal. The will to eternalize in Nietzsche's thought is anything but a will to immortality: it is a will to the eternal return of the mortal as mortal, the highest affirmation of the mortal. Nietzsche first describes the will to eternalize which is grounded in overabundance: it springs from "gratitude and love." No further description of gratitude and love is given—*Zarathustra* presents the most elaborate display of these passions culminating in their highest expression in willing eternal return. Instead, Nietzsche here describes the art that would spring from gratitude and love as an art of apotheosis—an art that prepares the appearance of the god—and names three examples, the art of Rubens, Hafiz, and Goethe. While these three differ, each is said to share a quality: each is "Homeric." An art that serves the will to eternalize out of overabundance spreads "a Homeric shimmer of light and glory over all things." This is the art to which Nietzsche aspired and which is set forth explicitly in the climactic chapters of *Zarathustra* part three where willing eternal return causes the animals to sing of the light and glory in all things (3.13), and causes the apotheosis of Dionysos and Ariadne (3.14). The will to eternalize out of overabundance ultimately expresses itself in willing the eternal return of mortal beings, the Dionysian affirmation that takes the side of Homer in "the complete, the genuine antagonism" between Plato and Homer, between the advocate of "beyond" and the deifier of the near (*GM* 3.25).

But the will to eternalize can also be an expression of hunger, of the impoverishment of life. As such it is a tyrannical will that takes revenge on all things, transforming its own suffering into a binding law branded into all things. And this is the real meaning of Schopenhauer's philosophy and Wagner's music. So far from representing Greek tragic insight and its affirmation of life, they represent "romantic pessimism," a form of revenge that experiences despair at the loss of the Platonic world of being and knows no better counsel than renunciation of the wretched world of becoming. In *Zarathustra* part four, the Old Sorcerer is introduced singing the most Dionysian of songs with one eye on his audience, Zarathustra (*Z* 4.5). And Zarathustra is tricked by the song just as Nietzsche once was, but when he sees through the pose and discovers the romanticism of the Old Sorcerer, he takes a stick to him, just as Nietzsche now does to both Schopenhauer and Wagner.

Nietzsche calls romantic pessimism "the last *great* event in the fate of our culture"—but he ends with a parenthesis that raises suspicion about the meaning of "last," the same suspicion raised earlier about the next event in pan-European philosophy after Schopenhauer (*JS* 357). The final parenthetical remark refers to what is most Nietzsche's own as a completely different kind of pessimism from Schopenhauer's, a "classical" pessimism that belongs to Nietzsche as a "premonition and vision." "Classical" fits as a description, but the term has been used up by trite interpretations of the Greeks, and Nietzsche renames his classical pessimism "Dionysian pessimism." Nietzsche's thought is a renaissance of the classical, a return of Dionysos, the god of tragedy who appears at the climax of *Zarathustra*, at the end of *Beyond Good and Evil*, and at the end of the *Twilight of the Idols* as the god of the Hellenic affirmation of life, the *philosopher* Dionysos whose last disciple expresses the affirmation of life in the affirmation of eternal return.

If the last great event in the fate of our culture is Schopenhauer, the last possible Platonist, then the Dionysian pessimism Nietzsche sees coming must in some sense transcend our culture. It goes beyond it by going back before it—to the god driven from the stage of our culture by the scourge of Socratic syllogism (*BT* 14). The return of Dionysos signals the end of our culture as Platonism, the vision of Being transcendent to Becoming, of gods or God who do not philosophize because they already possess the permanent wisdom sought by humans—the end of a culture built on suffering from the impoverishment of life. Nietzsche's thought thus achieves in itself what he had once mistakenly attributed to Schopenhauer and Wagner, the overcoming of our culture through a return to its origins. Nietzsche views the history of philosophy as a continuous whole from Plato to Schopenhauer while grounding Platonism in one of the fundamental dispositions of soul illuminated by the new physio-psychology. On the other hand, the pre-Platonic, the post-Platonic, and the subterranean presence that broke out in the renaissances are all grounded in the other fundamental disposition of Nietzsche's physio-psychology, the will to eternalize out of overabundance that sheds a Homeric shimmer over all things.

"I—the teacher of the eternal return" (*TI* Ancients 4). Nietzsche wanted to be identified with the thought of eternal return and yet that thought appears very sparingly in the post-*Zarathustra* works. Fittingly, its single elaboration in *The Joyous Science* (341) serves as the first introduction to Zarathustra (342): *Thus Spoke Zarathustra* exists to present this oddest and most important of Nietzsche's teachings. In *Zarathustra,* "the will to eternalize" appears in the only form possible for one whose fundamental disposition of gratitude and love says to the beloved: Be what you are, be eternally what you are! The beloved is Life herself in the poetic drama of *Zarathustra;* it is "everything that was and is" in the marvelously economical prose presentation of eternal return in *Beyond Good and Evil* (56). For one who says, "Be loyal to the earth," the only respectable form of the will to eternalize is an ecological form that honors earthly things as what they are. As a comprehensive ecological philosophy, Nietzsche's thought unites fact and value on the most fundamental level: when the totality of beings is glimpsed as will to power, this fundamental fact draws forth from the one who glimpses it the new highest value, the lover's yearning that the world as it is *be* as it is an infinite number of times. Such a "yearning to fix, to eternalize, a yearning for being" (*JS* 370), enhances and magnifies the object of its desire, the totality of nature of which humans are a small part. Looked at from the outside, eternal return can appear both odd and arbitrary; when entered in the way Nietzsche's presentations encourage, eternal return possesses its own inexorable logic. Gratitude and love can know no higher desire.

The new science, the joyous science of Dionysian pessimism, reinterprets the whole history of our culture by applying a new fundamental distinction to all the products of spirit: do they spring from hunger or from abundance? From revenge or from gratitude and love? Nietzsche was aware of the danger of the new standard. Perhaps nothing indicates that danger better than the manner in which the new standard has been applied to Nietzsche himself. To take only the most egregious example, Heidegger's interpretation of what lies behind the will to eternalize in the teaching of eternal return: at the end of his lifelong meditation on Nietzsche, Heidegger drew the conclusion that eternal return is a teaching of revenge that expresses hatred of the mortality of beings in a desperate effort to machine them immortal. Lacking Nietzsche's proper physiopsychology and lacking Nietzsche's insight into the historic politics of philosophy, Heidegger risks his own retrospective inference from art to truth, from Nietzsche's writings to Nietzsche's intentions, taking his bearings from his own history of being which consigns the fundamental events in human spiritual history not to human beings but to being, to the unfathomable. Like the Wagnerian at the end of section 368, Heidegger thought he could read Nietzsche's motives by inverting Nietzsche's claims, and he concluded that the teaching of eternal return is the apotheosis only of modern times; no god lies hidden in it, only the will to absolute dominance or planetary mastery.[7] On the contrary, what appears in Nietzsche is what Heidegger sought to achieve via his own *Holzwege,* a human way of being on the earth that permits all beings to be what they are; in Nietzsche's language, the will to eternalize out of love and gratitude.

We incomprehensible ones (371). Who are the incomprehensible ones? After the repeated "I" of the previous autobiographical section reporting a new method unique to Nietzsche and a coming Dionysian pessimism wholly his own, the "we" who never complain about being misunderstood because they fully expect it reduces to the singular Nietzsche. He himself had completely misunderstood Schopenhauer and Wagner before perfecting his novel art of retrospective inference; he himself needed training in Christianity and Epicurus in order to understand what was nearest to him: he can hardly complain about being misunderstood by

---

7. Heidegger, *Was heisst Denken?* 40–47; "Wer ist Nietzsches Zarathustra?" *Vorträge und Aufsätze,* vol. 1, pp. 114–18.

others. Besides, his constant growth has made him still more difficult to understand: he has had to shed the skins in which he first became known, his Schopenhauerian and Wagnerian skins. He expects to be taken for what he is not, but subsequent sections labor to clarify just who he is. *Ecce Homo* calls this his "duty": "Hear me! For I am such and such a person. Above all, do not mistake me for someone else" (*EH* Preface 1).

Nietzsche says it is modest of him to refer to 1901, the dawning of the new century, as the date by which he may cease to be incomprehensible. Referring to Nietzsche's impact on the new century, Eugen Fink says he "disturbed the spirit of the times but did not fundamentally alter it. The reality of technocracy, the world-encompassing spirit of rational planning, and the ever greater efficacy of the principle of equality set in motion by the French Revolution are the incontestable reality in both hemispheres of our globe."[8] For Nietzsche to become comprehensible would mean that his thought be seen as a plausible means of altering these most basic aspects of the times—2001 perhaps?

Nietzsche describes his growth through the image of a tree—an image taken over and expanded from *Zarathustra* (1.7)[9] where it served to clarify for the young student of Zarathustra's speeches what was incomprehensible to him in his own response to those speeches: how could his growth upward into the heavens be accompanied by growth downward into "evil"? Evil there is the envy the young man experiences at Zarathustra's superiority; but the evil into which Nietzsche describes himself as growing in *The Joyous Science* has no such modifier. What appears to be simple, unmitigated evil presupposes the analysis of evil present throughout Nietzsche's writings: evil is what goes against custom (*HH* I.96). "The new is always evil, as that which wants to conquer, to overthrow the old boundary markers and the old pieties." But "the strongest and most evil spirits have so far done the most to advance humanity." Using means such as new religions and new moralities, these evil spirits break up the settled ways of the "good"—"the farmers of the spirit"—earning for themselves the label "evil" (*JS* 4). Simple, unmitigated evil of the most general kind is the inquiry into the grounds of custom that breaks custom's hold. Evil on the grandest scale breaks the hold not just of this or that set of customs but of custom as such; it breaks the hold of the way

8. Fink, "Nietzsche's New Experience of the World," 204.

9. On the image of the tree, see Foster, *Heirs to Dionysus,* 132–34, where it illustrates Foster's insightful analysis of Nietzsche's "aesthetic naturalism."

of the ancestors as Zarathustra did in his war with the spirit of gravity, the ancient way of making things grave.

Nietzsche is evil enough to play with the word *evil,* letting himself be branded with it in order to make it understandable. "Has the famous story that stands at the beginning of the Bible really been understood" (*A* 48)? Understanding it means seeing what *it* brands as unmitigated evil: inquiry, inquiry that violates its primary prohibition by consuming the fruit of the tree of knowledge of good and evil. Such knowledge comes to recognize "God's hellish fear of science." "Science is the forbidden as such . . . the first sin, the seed of all sin, the *original sin.*" Growth in science is growth in evil. Joyous science is joyous evil. Just how far customary authority is willing to go to forbid this evil is beautifully stated in Nietzsche's conclusion: when the growth of science breaks the boundaries of religious control, "the old God makes a final decision: 'Man has become scientific—*there is no other way, he has to be drowned.*' "

The organic growth of the incomprehensible ones into evil saddles them with a grave responsibility: they are no longer free to perform arbitrary acts. A philosopher "has no right to isolated acts of any kind," neither isolated errors nor isolated truths (*GM* Preface 2). Everything is related as the fruit produced by "one will, one health, one soil, one sun." A philosopher is responsible for coherence, for a unified and global perspective consistent with itself and the phenomena. Karl Jaspers maintained that "*self-contradiction* is the fundamental ingredient in Nietzsche's thought" and that it is "the task of the interpreter to be forever dissatisfied until he has *also* found the contradiction." [10] On the contrary, Nietzsche leaves his interpreter the responsibility of finding the organic unity of apparently disparate thoughts.

Nietzsche speaks of growth in all directions but the direction emphasized is upward, into the open sky. And he ends with a consequence of upward growth repeated from *Zarathustra:* it runs the risk of drawing lightning—our fate may become our fatality. What Nietzsche sees coming, the Dionysian pessimism that represents his hope for the European future, could be consumed by forces that necessarily oppose it. What Nietzsche sees coming is not the consequence of some inexorable logic of history in the sense that human beings are bound to adopt it next—"logic calms and gives confidence" (*JS* 370). It is not itself an item unfolding in the monstrous logic of the greatest recent event, however

10. Jaspers, *Nietzsche,* 10.

much it possesses the inner logic of the thinking that arises at the end of Platonism. Its adoption depends upon persuasion, upon its own ability to command assent despite the built-in resistance to "evil."

Plato and the History of Philosophy: Plato's Great Health (372)

Why we are no idealists (372). This intricate and beautiful section argues that the history of philosophy is our essential history, that our "idealism," our Platonism, has molded our character, even our bodies. "We moderns" believe only in the senses, but "the most modern of the moderns" returns to the older view that the world turns silently around the creators of ideas (*JS* 359). Nietzsche's own ideas force a new perspective on the history of idealism: if a relatively uniform idealism springing from Plato has, until recently, dominated our tradition, there is an exception to the uniformity, *Plato himself.* And reflection on Plato inspires the nonidealist to his own historic action.

The theme of the section is blood and ideas, Nietzsche's terms for the traditional dualism of heart and mind. Idealists favor one interpretation of that dualism, whereas "we moderns" favor its opposite. Nietzsche's final suggestion is not a synthesis of these two; instead it returns to the conditions out of which idealism first sprang by reinterpreting Plato.

According to the idealists themselves, they set out from an acknowledged fear of being lured away from the realm of "ideas" by the senses. Nietzsche's example is Odysseus's act of stopping the ears of his friends out of fear for them. By mentioning only "wax in the ears," Nietzsche singles out Odysseus: he did not stop his own ears, he did not fear that he himself would be irretrievably corrupted by hearing the Sirens' song even if he took the precaution of having himself strapped to the mast. Nietzsche's use of wily Odysseus suggests that ancient idealism began with an act of philanthropy, the gracious act of one who feared for his friends. When he turns to Plato at the end of this section, Nietzsche seems to confirm this interpretation.

After stating ancient idealism's fear of the senses, Nietzsche describes the judgment "we tend to incline to today"—and "we" seems to be "we moderns" generally, we believers in the senses. As the exact reversal of the ancient view, it "could be equally false." We moderns judge that ideas are worse seductresses than the senses. We too base our judgment on fear and share the fundamental motive with idealists, differing only on its object; we the fearless are not so fearless after all. Nietzsche shares the modern antipathy to idealism: pale ideas have sucked the philosopher's blood, consuming his senses and his very heart. What could have begun as generosity meant to protect friends from powers too strong for them has turned into a vampire sucking the blood out of the philosopher himself.[11]

But now the rhetoric changes and Nietzsche speaks directly to "you" about the effects of idealism on the body, using the appropriate verbs of what you "feel," "see," or "sense" in order to draw attention to idealism's historic consequences. Spinoza's philosophy is Nietzsche's exemplar of just how idealism tamed the senses by starving them. How is this whole idealist history to be interpreted? Nietzsche's conclusion points to a possibility outside the antithesis of idealists and believers in the senses: "All philosophical idealism to date was something like sickness." But he adds an exception, "the case of Plato."

Plato? Plato is the idealist par excellence of Western philosophy, the very inventor of the realm of ideas as the ground of virtue. How can Nietzsche single out Plato and spare him the general indictment against idealism? Plato is "the most beautiful growth of antiquity" (*BGE* Preface). Idealism may be a sickness but its inventor was a model of health; *his* idealism had three characteristics: First, Plato's idealism is *caution* that springs from an overrich and dangerous health, from precisely what Nietzsche attributes to himself, the great health on which he will bring his self-description to a close (382). Second, Plato's idealism is *fear* of overpowerful senses. Is Plato the Odysseus who graciously stops up the ears of his friends with wax, fearing that they are not equal to the untamed music of their senses after losing the traditional restraints? Third, Plato's idealism is *Klugheit,* the prudence and cleverness of a Socratic. Plato had been "corrupted" by Socrates, taught cleverness and prudence by a mentor less noble than himself (*BGE* Preface, 190); left to himself, uncorrupted, Plato could have "discovered an even higher type of philosophical man who is now lost to us forever" (*HH* I.261).

Nietzsche's Plato is a Plato not found in the textbooks, a Plato like Montaigne's. Caution, fear, and prudence led Plato to invent Platonism as a means of curbing overpowerful passions released into self-indulgence by the death of God, the collapse of the moral order of Zeus. Nietzsche's Plato is a "monster of pride and sovereignty" (*JS* 351) whose idealism became the "dogmatism" that once bestrode Europe, a dogmatism adapted to Augustine's passion for revenge (*JS* 359) and to Spinoza's bloodless love of God (*JS* 372), a dogmatism that now lies on the ground

11. On vampirism, see *EH* Destiny 8.

in ruins (*BGE* Preface). Nietzsche's Plato is modest in the way befitting philosophers (*JS* 351)—he did not believe in "knowers." But he believed in belief in "knowers," choosing "with pedagogical intent" to hallow the lie of his own status as a knower (*JS* 359). Nietzsche's Plato is remarkably like Bacon's and Descartes's, a politic philosopher who wanted to have believed what he himself never for an instant believed (*KGW* VIII 14 [116] = *WP* 428). Nietzsche would not have discovered this Plato in Bacon or Descartes, and probably not even in his underworld kin Montaigne where he is explicitly described. Nietzsche too seems to have rediscovered Plato in the dialogues, as had the other great students of Plato; he seems to have rediscovered Plato through his own ascent to the grandeur and ambition of philosophy, its philology and philanthropy.

The task of philosophy in its contemporary setting seems to be suggested by the final sentences of this section. "Perhaps we moderns are merely not healthy enough, *to have need* of Plato's idealism?" Plato's idealism was once needed and its no longer being needed marks a deficiency in us. But the words Nietzsche italicized are quoted from his discourse on method (*JS* 370), where they serve as one way of describing his art of retrospective inference: "From the ideal to him who has need of it." Nietzsche's physio-psychology has uncovered in Plato himself an exception to the rule of idealism as sickness, and uncovered in us—in our ability to *dispense* with the Platonic ideal—a deficiency of health. No longer endangered by impulses that made idealism necessary, we have been tamed into illness by the cure. As products of two millennia of Platonic caution expressed in a variety of idealist dogmatisms, we inherit numbed bodies; the wax in our ears seems like natural hearing, the blocked out music of the body seems no longer to exist. As Nietzsche suggested earlier (352), our civility, our platonism, has domesticated the beast that once dwelt in our senses. Nietzsche's unparalleled polemical talents gather for this historic occasion, the sick domestication at the end of history that passes for health. The task is to bring us back to our senses. By making an exception of the philanthropic Plato, Nietzsche suggests the dimensions of his own educative task. And if idealism is vampirism, Nietzsche's task is to pump blood back to the senses, to champion war and the battle of the sexes, to advocate walking, leaping, climbing, and dancing as the means of making even science joyous and aligning philosophy with the earth.

But the exact wording of Nietzsche's conclusion carries yet another echo: "Just not healthy enough." This is the retrospective inference about

Nietzsche drawn by the Wagnerian offended at his account of his master
(*JS* 368). Retrospective inference is a dangerous method and health a
dangerous standard because everything depends on subtlety and taste.
Nietzsche follows, in effect, Kierkegaard's John the Climber: he wants
to make things hard, as hard as possible, but not any harder than they
are. How can retrospective inference judge health and sickness without
arbitrariness and without erecting a new dogmatism? The dangerous science that develops under the care of the new philosophy is deprived of
Platonic, Augustinian, and Spinozistic idealism; that means that it is deprived of both dignity and certainty—it cannot tie itself to the high, the
ideal, to certify its own standard. But its self-certification has a wonderful weapon in the history of philosophy itself: at their heights, in Plato
or Spinoza, the old idealisms always knew that their own certification
by the ideal was a pious fraud.

Science and the History of Philosophy:
"Hooray for Physics!" (373–74)

The prejudice of science, absolute spiritual rule by the Fathers of Salomon's House, endangers what a few philosophers have understood philosophy to be, an openness to the enigmatic whole aware of its own
ignorance. For science to pass into the care of the new philosophy means
that even the exact sciences would be contained within the horizon of
the unknowable, and the advancement of science would be accompanied
by a new disposition toward nature and history. The distinction Nietzsche draws in the first of these sections parallels the classical distinction
between knowledge and opinion, but in the place of knowledge Nietzsche puts awareness of "the great problems and question marks," and in
the place of opinion, "prejudice." Nietzsche's distinction is Socratic in
the sense elaborated by Leo Strauss: "Philosophy as such is nothing but
genuine awareness of the problems, i.e., of the fundamental and comprehensive problems."[12] Authoritative modern opinion, "prejudice," is
based on the alleged certainty of Cartesian science. In daring "to speak
out against an unseemly and harmful shift in the respective ranks of science and philosophy" (*BGE* 204), Nietzsche claims that the Cartesian
method of certainty and exactitude brackets and forgets what is richest
in the world it presumes to disclose (*JS* 373). If Cartesian science deprives the world of its rich ambiguity, science under the care of the new

12. Strauss, *On Tyranny,* 196.

philosophy will be open to new possibilities ruled out by Cartesian science, a reenchantment of the world that does not come at the cost of intellectual conscience (*JS* 374).

"Science" as prejudice (373). A philosophy aware of its ignorance condemns science—in quotation marks—as prejudice. But Nietzsche ends his condemnation of "science" addressing the conscience of scientists. To refine and reeducate science means appealing to its greatest strength, its already existing imperative to honesty. Nietzsche does not protest the prejudicial character of science but the character of its prejudices— a joyous science would not cease to harbor prejudice but it would align prejudice with "knowledge," it would align opinion with awareness of "the great problems and questions marks."

The first sentence of this section appeals to a kind of natural law, "the laws of the order of rank." These harsh laws dictate that the learned will not catch sight of the great problems and question marks "insofar as they belong to the spiritual middle class." They need not belong to that class but insofar as they do their view will necessarily be limited by three things: their courage, their vision, and the needs that made them researchers. Their needs limit their courage and vision because they are "inner assumptions and wishes" that things might be other than they are, "fears and hopes" that are satisfied far too soon (*JS* 355). The easily satisfied differ in this decisive respect from the philosophers, the never satisfiable whose intellectual conscience masters their fears and hopes (*JS* 382). The laws of the order of rank are laws of a spiritual hierarchy, of the mind's capacity to tether the heart. And this is the great impediment to the public success of the joyous science: it has the heart against it (*BGE* 23). "What does it mean after all to have *integrity* in matters of the spirit?—That one is severe against one's heart" (*A* 50).

Nietzsche gives two quite different examples of vision eclipsed by needs too easily satisfied, each dealing with a basic aspect of modern science: its idea of the good, and its idea of the method. The first example contrasts the highest ideal of a celebrated scholar with how that ideal appears "to us." Herbert Spencer's ideal of a homogeneous and happy society built on small ego egoism is one of the apotheoses of modern liberalism, the last man from the perspective of its advocate. Spencer shared a great deal with Nietzsche: "Now that moral injunctions are losing the authority given by their supposed sacred origin, the secularization of morals is becoming imperative." But Spencer assumed that European humanity had arrived at "the last stage of evolution," a teleological conception of ethics according to which the end is perfectly peaceful societies and the good is what conduces to that end.[13] Like George Eliot, Spencer belonged to those who "have got rid of the Christian God, and now feel obliged to cling all the more firmly to Christian morality" (*TI* Skirmishes 5). A humanity that had realized Spencer's ideal would be worthy of annihilation, Nietzsche says, because it would mark the end of the spiritual order of rank, of the high and sublime. That Spencer "had to experience" as his highest hope something that could only appear as a disgusting possibility to others—that is one of the great question marks because it could never appear as a question mark to Spencer himself. The inaccessibility of the highest good to legislators of the good is one of the great question marks. In Plato's *Laws*, Kleinias and Megillos are made ready, after a long, ascending conversation, to yield to the Athenian Stranger on what is visible only to him. Could Spencer yield to Nietzsche? Enclosed within a modern ideal to which he was simply subservient, Spencer could not put that ideal into question and any questioning of it by the likes of Nietzsche—someone who finds it a disgusting possibility—would draw from a Spencer, as it draws from later moderns, the judgment that Nietzsche must be a nihilist because he is not loyal to the highest ideal so obvious to everyone else.[14]

Similar limitations hold for the second example of the too easily satisfied, where vision is limited by method. Here Nietzsche refers to materialist natural scientists generally, Cartesians for whom "the laws of mechanics are the same as the laws of nature" (*Discourse* v.54). These strict scientists are adherents of a "faith" in the complete commensurability of thought and being where thought amounts to mechanistic Cartesianism. Their faith too posits another world, "a world of truth" grasped and mastered by human reason stripped down to mathematical qualities. This now dominant Cartesian positivism draws a protest from Nietzsche that bespeaks an entirely new sensibility for science: existence itself is degraded by such a narrow mathematical conception because the fundamentally enigmatic character of existence is lost to an appearance of clarity and distinctness. Nietzsche's protest is framed in terms of what we should want and not want: a mechanistic world is what is wanted by the adherents of such a faith. But "above all, one should not want to disrobe existence of its rich ambiguity." Nietzsche gives only one reason for not wanting to strip existence naked: "*good* taste" defined as rever-

13. Spencer, *Data of Ethics*, iv, 21; see also Rachels, *Created from Animals*, 64ff.

14. Nietzsche says "the primeval law of things" assures that the greatest question marks remain closed to all but the highest inquirers (*BGE* 213). See Eden, *Political Leadership*, 92–94.

ence for everything that lies beyond one's horizon. Reverence is a key ingredient in the joyous science, replacing the complete lack of reverence for nature presupposed by the mechanistic view that wanted naked nature to be a masterable machine.

But why *want* a world that cannot be revered? Nietzsche's reasoning depends on his history of philosophy and his physio-psychology: in its lack of reverence for nature, modern physics serves modern politics which in turn serves a passion of revenge similar to Augustine's. Modern physics wanted a world that could not be revered because "the democratic instincts of the modern soul" wanted "everywhere equality before the law; nature . . . is no better off than we are" (*BGE* 22). Modern democratic humanism elevated the human by denigrating nature, and it was aided by a physics that offered the fitting world-interpretation. Overturning Platonism's resistance to obvious sense-evidence, mechanistic physics expanded its dependence on the senses into a metaphysics; it set itself under the anti-Platonistic imperative that where humankind finds nothing more to see or grasp it has no further business, the appropriate imperative for an industrious race of machinists and bridge-builders with nothing but rough work to do (*BGE* 14). That not even the world is to be revered strikes Nietzsche as "a second and more refined atheism" extending to nature itself modern antagonism against the laws of an order of rank (*BGE* 22). Wanting a world that cannot be revered imposes a "naively humanitarian emendation" on nature that a joyous science is bound to attack—and its attack on this now dominant modern humanism is bound to be interpreted as antihumanism. In fact, however, it is only posthumanism just as it is posttheism; in neither a biblical nor a modern sense are humans the meaning of the world. The joyous science is a blow to the modern form of human vanity that supposed the whole of nature to be prey to human categories and prey to human mastery—and unworthy of reverence.

Nietzsche's appeal to good taste includes a tirade against the tastelessness of materialistic natural scientists: "your" view is an imperialist world-interpretation that permits only what justifies the positivist worldview, information based on counting, calculating, weighing, seeing, and touching, and nothing more. Such a dogmatism is a crudity and naivete, assuming that it is not mental illness, not idiocy. And its simplistic method is bound to result in simplistic conclusions, a world-interpretation that would be the dumbest yet. Nietzsche confesses that his tirade is addressed to the *consciences* of Cartesians who consider the mechanistic worldview and its method of counting to be comprehensive:

can they in good conscience insist on the universality of a method that fails to grasp anything subtle or nuanced? What would one have understood about *music* after calculating everything countable in it? Nietzsche argued in the previous section that the "music of life" could not reach idealist philosophers who had their ears blocked against it. Here music falls completely outside the competence of a method that takes itself to be omni-competent.

Nietzsche risks his whole strategy on conscience, on stirring the conscience of the conscientious against itself: if belief in a method serves the deeper belief that the method can discover the truth, then the conscience of truth-seekers can be aroused against their method. Nietzsche invites Cartesianism to die of suicide, its belief in truth killing its belief in the method as the means to truth. Cartesianism is not the first faith to die of suicide, of virtuous war between its truthfulness and its truths: the Christian God died by that very means as Nietzsche frequently took pains to argue (for example, *GM* 3.27).

But this is more than a conflict of consciences: conscience for truth is pitted, still more fundamentally, against the *wants* of the conscientious for a world that cannot be revered. These wants elevate the human until it becomes the very meaning of nature and history—and wants characteristically overpower the conscience for truth (*JS* 347). Joyous science at first seems grim indeed because it costs us the modern route to human dignity as well: there *is* no cardinal difference between man and the animals, evolution is not a ladder to the human. Acceptance of this antihumanistic conclusion depends upon the power of conscience over the power of wants, of intellect over heart. It depends on a spirited control of the passions where the spirit can make no appeal beyond its own imperatives nor give any warrant for its imperatives other than their own integrity. The greatest recent event disallows any shadow of the old fiction that conscience represents some transcendence, that it derives the warrant for its cruelty to wants from any source other than itself.

But then there *is* a difference between human and animal, if not a cardinal difference: humans are the animals that fell under the sway of conscience, the animals bred to keep promises, as Nietzsche put it in his next book. "It is sickening and dismaying," as Frithjof Bergmann says, "it is a travesty," that this genealogy is still read as if "Nietzsche's central message was a sermon in praise of ruthlessness,"[15] as if Nietzsche advocated a return to some precivil or presocial animality and brutality. On

15. Bergmann, "Nietzsche's Critique of Morality," 44.

the contrary, Nietzsche discovers in the natural history of conscience, in this difference between human and animal, grounds for a conscientious celebration of both human and animal, and of the whole natural order that for a cosmic instant evolved into life on this planet. Grim science transforms itself into joyous science with this way of understanding the human. But if it does, then physics, branded a prejudice in this section, is not simply a prejudice but part of the means to celebration. "Hooray for physics!" Nietzsche says in *The Joyous Science* (335).

But has Nietzsche contradicted himself then, criticizing modern physics as prejudice while relying on a worldview certified by modern physics to ground an affirmation of humanity and world? Section 373 emphasizes the profound limitations of modern Cartesian physics with respect to its idea of the highest good and its idea of the method, both of which express a passion of revenge against nature. But Nietzsche is far from indicting the whole of physics or natural science. His attack on the prejudices of modern science must not be allowed to obscure the fact that he is wholly a modern man with respect to the general worldview of science: even the fabulous Zarathustra stands under an open sky in which the sun is merely our star and on a planet that has given birth to life as an evolutionary process. With respect to science and philosophy Nietzsche is as far as possible from Wittgenstein's ahistorical, acultural insularity that could claim: "The Darwinian theory has no more to do with philosophy than any other hypothesis of natural science."[16] An early writing expresses the cosmic perspective presupposed throughout Nietzsche's work:

> In some remote corner of the universe that is poured out in count-less flickering solar systems, there once was a star on which clever animals invented knowledge. That was the most arrogant and un-truthful moment in "world history"—yet indeed only a moment. After nature had taken a few breaths, the star froze over and the clever animals had to die. ("On Truth and Lying in the Extra Moral Sense" [1873])

It is wholly immaterial that contemporary cosmology anticipates, in-stead of the earth freezing over, its being encompassed and vaporized by the expanding sun as the sun passes through the fuel consumption stages of a star in the main sequence on its way to becoming a white dwarf and then "freezing over" into a black dwarf. Just how the clever ani-

---

16. Wittgenstein, *Tractatus,* 4.1122.

mals come to their end within the cosmos is interesting but immaterial; but that *humanity* is part of a natural process which includes its own extinction as a species is completely material. Nietzsche expresses himself exactly on this matter and indicates what he thinks of the relationship between cosmology and philosophy in a passage that bears repeating:

> The individual must be consecrated to something higher than himself—that is the meaning of tragedy; he must be free of the terrible anxiety which death and time evoke in the individual: for at any moment, in the briefest atom of his life's course, he may encounter something holy that endlessly outweighs all his struggle and all his distress—this is what it means to have a *sense for the tragic*. And if the whole of humanity is destined to die out—and who dares doubt that?—its supreme task for all time to come is placed before it as the goal, so to grow together in one and in common that it sets out as a whole to meet its coming demise with a sense for the tragic: all the ennoblement of humankind is enclosed in this supreme task; the definite rejection of this task would be the saddest picture imaginable to a friend of humanity. That is my view of things! (*RWB* 4)

"Hooray for physics!" because it educates humanity to its place in the natural order. Physics is essential to what Nietzsche described as "My Mission" in a note from the time of the first appearance of eternal return: "The dehumanization of nature and then the naturalization of the human after it has gained the pure concept of 'nature'" (*KGW* V 11 [211]). The naturalization of humanity requires that humanity recognize its place in the cosmos:

> We can defend ourselves only slightly in the great matters: a comet could at any moment smash the sun, or an electrical field arise that could all at once melt the solar system. What do "statistics" mean in such matters! We have for earth and sun perhaps a few more million years in which such a thing will *not* happen: that proves nothing. Readiness for the absolutely sudden and annihilating belongs to the naturalization of humanity. (*KGW* V 11 [228])

"Hooray for physics!" because it places controls on what we can allow ourselves to think. These controls derive not only from cosmology but also from evolutionary biology, a science that falls within "physics" in the broad, Greek sense presupposed in section 335. Physics there plays the part of a conscience overseeing conscience. The account of nature given by physics demonstrates that natural conscience develops in human beings via traditions ignorant of nature. Natural conscience, the voice of forefathers and gods, is placed under suspicion by physics, its role as the giver of imperatives compromised by a new imperative based wholly on insight into the natural process of its formation. Conscience matures into independence under the tutelage of physics: with knowledge of the natural process whereby conscience was formed, conscience curbs conscience conscientiously. Physics as the conscience of conscience is thus doubly affirmed: it provides an understanding of what is true about the natural order, and it bears within itself the felt imperative to live in accord with nature.

But "Live in accord with nature" is quoted by Nietzsche as the Stoic imperative—and then ridiculed. The Stoic understanding of nature is a humanitarian emendation of nature that "creates the world in its own image." Besides, who "could live in accordance" with nature when nature is "wasteful beyond measure, indifferent beyond measure, without purposes and consideration, without mercy and justice, fertile and desolate and uncertain at the same time" (*BGE* 9)? The philosopher who accuses philosophy of imperialism in reading its own interpretation of nature into nature thus gives his own interpretation of nature. And who could live in accord with *that?* Who indeed? Nietzsche's whole philosophy, his mission, flowers beautifully into its ultimate aims in this fine ironic setting: to give an account of nature that is in some sense true (while kept under the police supervision of mistrust), and to create the music and poetry that make it possible to live in accord with nature. In Nietzsche truth and art combine into an ecological philosophy post-theistic and posthumanistic. Post-God and post-Man, it would not have beings be other than they are.

"Hooray for physics!" implies "Down with metaphysics!" the old lies about nature that humanized it. After announcing that a part of our mission or "new battles" includes vanquishing the shadows of the dead God on the walls of our cave (*JS* 108), Nietzsche gave shape, in one of the most memorable sections of *The Joyous Science* (109), to some of the forms those shadows have taken in science. The section could be Nietzsche's expanded final version of his note "My Mission" because it provides an extended account of ways in which nature must be de-humanized and ends with a call for the naturalization of the human. "Let us beware" of thinking of the world as a living being, or of believing that the whole is a machine, or of positing that the elegant movement of neighboring stars holds everywhere in the universe, or of attributing heartlessness or unreason or their opposites to the world, or of saying there are laws in nature, or of saying that death is opposed to life, or of thinking that the world creates eternally new things. All seven items are like shadows of God that darken our minds with respect to the natural order. Nature dehumanized and dedivinized, liberated from such scientific myths, provides the basis for the other half of Nietzsche's work, the "naturalization" of humanity in accord with the purified view of nature.

Science that passes into the care of philosophy in Nietzsche's sense is a thoroughgoing naturalism in keeping with the best scientific traditions of antiquity and modernity. Like Bacon and Descartes, Nietzsche explicitly aims to recover the scientific traditions of the early Greeks that were almost lost to Socratic philosophy. In many notes from the spring of 1888 (*KGW* VIII 14), Nietzsche reflected on the extraordinary fact that Greek philosophy set itself against Greek science, especially in Socrates and the Socratic schools but even in Epicurus and Pyrrho. One of the longest of these notes (14 [141] = *WP* 442) describes the hatred of science exercised by philosophy, a moralism that cannot tolerate the cleanliness of science, its objectivity and refusal of mere utility. "The concept of guilt and punishment, the entire 'moral world-order,' was invented in *opposition* to science" (*A* 49). The church inherited the whole arsenal developed by Greek moral philosophy against science, as did modern moralism. Nietzsche sets himself wholly within the scientific camp; his history of Western philosophy and religion is bent on uncovering the role played by the fear of science. It treasures a public science, historical and natural, that brings authoritative opinion into accord with a thoroughly natural science.

But because it necessarily attacks the imperialism and bias of modern science, joyous science is bound to rouse the ire of its believers and draw the absurd charge that it is antiscience. In fact, its attack on modern science aims to rid science of its humanistic, theological, and metaphysical dogmas. Some have thought that Nietzsche's adoption of the prophetic mantle of Zarathustra required laying aside his mission on behalf of science. But not only does Book Five of *The Joyous Science,* like other post-*Zarathustra* endorsements of a refined science right up to the last pages of the *Antichrist,* refute this notion, *Zarathustra* itself is one of the means of fulfilling Nietzsche's mission on behalf of science. Zarathustra himself does not say "Hooray for physics!" but he does say "Hooray for science!" His praise is not permitted to be heard because the superior men of modern culture—having grown suspicious of science, thinking it only poetry—shout "Zarathustra!" where he shouted "Science!"

(4.15). But Nietzsche is emphatically a friend of science as his history of philosophy and religion makes clear: the disaster of Christianity derives from its costing humankind the harvest of classical science and almost permanently blotting out a scientific view of things (for example, *GM* 3.22).

> All the prerequisites for a learned culture, all the scientific *methods,* were already there, the great, the incomparable art of reading well had already been established—the prerequisite for a cultural tradition, for a uniform science; natural science, in concert with mathematics and mechanics, was on the best possible road—the *sense for facts,* the last-developed and most valuable of all the senses, had its schools and its tradition already centuries old! Is this understood? . . . Everything *essential* for setting to work had been devised . . . the free view of reality, the cautious hand, patience and seriousness in the smallest things, the whole *integrity* of knowledge—was already there! already more than two millennia ago! (*A* 59)

"The Christians unlearned *reading,* and how the ancients had taken pains themselves, in their philologists, to learn it! But the Bible!" (*KGW* V 4 [235]). Nietzsche's thought depends upon the modern recovery of science, of methods of inquiry destroyed by Christianity and "won back for ourselves today with an unspeakable amount of self-mastery" (*A* 59). As a friend of science, Nietzsche brings science within the sphere of a "modest" philosophy with no pretensions to absolute truth and no desire to fake such pretensions. Such a philosophy can say "Hooray for physics!" because of the probability with which physics can discover that human life occurs in a setting of billions of galaxies on a planet roughly 4.5 billion years old as a part of an evolution of organisms that relates humankind to all other species bound up in a process of evolution and extinction. Such a philosophy finds the human unique as the species bred to keep promises, including now the promise to be true to an informed conscience. And such a philosophy assents to the natural order and aspires to the highest form of assent, willing the eternal return of beings as they are.

Our new "infinite" (374). So far from being accessible to the simple method of counting, existence eludes even the most scrupulous and subtle analyses: the too easily satisfied will have to learn from the unsatisfiable ones that no simply satisfactory interpretation is possible. Beginning with Nietzsche's radicalized perspectivism that emphasizes the limits of knowledge and the unavoidability of interpretation, this section ends putting a Kantian issue in the Nietzschean way of temptation: what might be postulated about the new infinite? Is it amenable to divinization? Can we have Religion within the Limits of Joyous Science Alone?

Nietzsche's statement on the limits of intellect is categorical, but he puts its implications in an open, problematic way. The first implication is that we are now—"I should think"—far from "the laughable immodesty" of decreeing from our little corner that perspectives are permitted only from this corner. But the previous section acknowledged just how firmly we still stand within a laughable immodesty, the decrees of Cartesian mechanism. "We" in this section denotes those few who are already beyond that modern scientific faith—and for them the world has become infinite again. Their experience echoes Zarathustra's: "Day-wisdom mocks all 'infinite worlds.' For it says 'Where there is force, *number* will become queen: she has more force'" (Z 3.10). Day wisdom refuses the infinite and, in its Cartesian form, construes the world from the perspective of finite forces that can be mastered through their calculability—but day wisdom is less wise than the night wisdom with which Zarathustra casts his lot.

The new infinite holds that the world encloses within itself infinite interpretations. But this new infinite has a consequence "we the fearless" may fear. Having been stripped of the comforting certainties of the modern scientific faith, and been shaken "once again" by the face of the infinite, "who would really desire to divinize immediately again *this* monster of an unknown world in the old way? And even to worship the unknown henceforth as the 'Unknown One'?" The Apostle Paul reported that the Athenians once worshipped the "Unknown One" (*Acts* 17:23) and Nietzsche himself addressed the "Unknown One" in his graduation day poem "Dem unbekannten Gott." But Nietzsche has placed three qualifications on the desire to divinize: who would have such a desire "in the old way"—and "immediately"—and "again"? Could the desire to divinize express itself in ways other than the old way, and not immediately but after time had passed and the shadows of the old god lifted, and not simply "again" but for the first time under a new sense of the divine as open in the way of the new infinite?

The section ends with a sentence fragment in which the desire to divinize is overshadowed by the fear to demonize: "Ah, too many *ungodly* possibilities of interpretation are counted in with this unknown, too much devilry, stupidity, foolishness of interpretation—our own human, all too human itself, which we know . . ." What do we know about our own human, all too human interpretation? Is Nietzsche's own *Human, All Too Human,* his own pre-*Zarathustra* ungodly interpretation, included among these ungodly interpretations? Whatever the answer to that specific question, it is clear that the new infinite opens itself first to ungodly interpretations, because of the long shadows cast by the greatest recent event. The death of our God persists as the death of divinity, as the impossibility of gods.

This section is something special—"Listen closely," Nietzsche says on another such occasion, "for I rarely speak as a theologian" (*EH* Books *BGE* 2)—here Nietzsche speaks as a theologian on the contemporary crisis. Any new divinization of the world is constrained by the demonization of the world in the biblical religions, their curse on the world assigning it to the powers of darkness. The old God is dead but his shadow dictates that no one liberated from that last monotono-theism would want immediately to divinize this monster of an unknown world again in the old way. Nietzsche's own desire to divinize advertises him as the last disciple and initiate of the god Dionysos; Nietzsche's greatest work, *Thus Spoke Zarathustra,* comes to its stunning climax in a modern repetition of the ancient mystery, the apotheosis of Dionysos and Ariadne (*Z* 3.13–16). When he speaks more openly of Dionysos at the very end of *Beyond Good and Evil,* he excuses himself for daring to talk about gods at all in deference to those he addresses, free minds who—he has been told—"no longer like to hear of God and gods" (295). Restraint attentive to the scruples of an audience still under the shadow cast by the greatest recent event explains why *The Joyous Science* says so little about the greatest issues of *Thus Spoke Zarathustra:* will to power, eternal return, and Dionysos and Ariadne. The introduction of the joyous science to free spirits demands respect for "the strict habits of their ears" (*BGE* 295) especially regarding the desire to divinize. Nevertheless, the open horizon of the new infinite recognizes "the greatest advantage of polytheism" (*JS* 143): unlike monotheism's tyrannical doctrine of "one normal human type"—"perhaps the greatest danger that has yet confronted humanity"—"in polytheism lay prefigured the freespiriting and manyspiriting of humanity: the strength to create for itself new eyes, its own eyes, and ever again new ones still more its own, so that for humanity, alone among the animals, there exists no eternal horizons and perspectives." Here is the difference between humans and animals: animals other than human are natural Platonists; alone among the animals, humans can free themselves from Platonism.

What scholars and scientists will like least about Nietzsche is his talk of divinizing, his seeming embrace of what they set beneath themselves. The newly disenchanted will not want to open themselves to reenchantment—and Nietzsche suggests some reasons why in his reflections on Epicurus.

Epicurus and the History of Philosophy (375–76)

Why we look Epicurean (375). Yes, Nietzsche says, he is proud to experience the character of Epicurus differently from perhaps everyone else (*JS* 45). But not only is Nietzsche's experience different, so too is his means of sharing it, for he offers only occasional and fragmentary glimpses of his interpretation of Epicurus even though it was a major element in his rethinking of the history of philosophy. With Epicurus, as with other of his underworld kin (*AO* 408), Nietzsche does not want to do everything for his reader. But the portrait of Epicurus that can be drawn from Nietzsche's scattered reflections provides a crucial element in understanding his history of philosophy.

Nietzsche experienced the character of Epicurus as marked by happiness—and he says so in the center of three sections discussing happiness (*JS* 44–46). The claim to have understood Epicurus differently is a claim to have understood him correctly, to have seen through the general mechanism of misunderstanding described in the first of these sections: "Happiness or misery come to human beings" on the basis of "the fictitious or fanciful motives" they ascribe to conduct (44). Epicurus's happiness did not come from Epicurean *ataraxia,* the indifference to all passions, it came from a passion, from *Wollust* grown modest and transformed into the observing eye that watched the sun set on the magnificence of antiquity. In the afternoon of antiquity, Epicurus achieved a happiness that could have been invented only by one who suffered continuously, a happiness "that now can never weary of the surface" (45). Epicurus was a Greek artist who knew how to live (*JS* Preface 4).

Can Nietzsche's private understanding of a passionate and happy Epicurus be true? The third of these sections (*JS* 46) expresses amazement at the happiness science brings, "the deep and fundamental happiness" based on the power of science to grasp things that hold their ground against the constant flux of human laws and concepts—things like the happiness of Epicurus which remains accessible to the scientific inquirer and occasions his own *Wollust* of amazement. In an age in which nothing seems firm and "the fickleness of everything human" has taken over our judgment, we experience the sensual pleasure of amazement at things that can be shown by science to stand—like the experience of Epicurus, still recoverable from the misunderstanding of almost everyone.

The happiness with which Epicurus experienced late antiquity is described in a meditation perhaps as beautiful as anything in Nietzsche's writings, "Et in Arcadia ego" (*WS* 295). The idyllic Arcadia Nietzsche paints is not identical to the one painted by Poussin but the title links Nietzsche and Poussin as inhabitants of paradise who know its mortality but have experienced a moment of revelation, a feeling at one and the same time idyllic and heroic. Men have actually *lived* in that idyllic and heroic manner, Nietzsche claims, and "among them was one of the greatest of men, the inventor of an idyllic-heroic mode of philosophizing, Epicurus." This is the Epicurus of Lucretius as well, heroic Epicurus likened to a god (*De rerum natura* 3.1–30) though it is perfectly clear to Lucretius that gods of the old sort do not exist (2.581–660; 5.1–54) and that Epicurus's main service was to have freed humans from service to them (1.62–78).

How have others experienced the inventor of the heroic-idyllic mode of philosophizing? Though the practice of taking Epicurus for someone he was not began during his own lifetime (letter to Köselitz, 3 August 1883), the misunderstanding that became dominant is perhaps most graphically expressed by Jerome's judgment on Epicurus's greatest follower, Lucretius. Jerome, exponent of desert monasticism, spread the tale that Lucretius "was driven mad by a love-potion, and having composed several books in the intervals of his madness . . . committed suicide in his forty-fourth year." Happiness for Christians in the desert depended in part on believing in the misery of Lucretius in his walled garden, and in the misery of his atheist master, Epicurus.

Nietzsche emphasized this difference between the Christian view of Epicurus and Lucretius's view of him in a later reference to Epicurus, one that is wholly consistent with the portrait drawn earlier (it is in part a repetition of what Nietzsche had already said in *Daybreak* 72) and that makes explicit a very important element in Nietzsche's interpretation of Epicurus. Nearing the end of his attack on Christianity, Nietzsche invokes Epicurus as an ally (*A* 58). "One should read Lucretius to comprehend *what* Epicurus fought; *not* paganism but 'Christianity.' " Lucretius makes Epicurus accessible as a heroic Hellene who fought against the mystery religions that were so foreign to the classical spirit and that corrupted souls "via the concepts of guilt, punishment, and immortality." "And Epicurus would have won" against all the subterranean cults including Christianity, for "every respectable spirit in the Roman

Empire was an Epicurean."[17] But the Apostle Paul succeeded in translating Christianity into a popular form of redemption that triumphed over antiquity. One of the perks of victory was the freedom to rewrite history and create a miserable Epicurus and a mad Lucretius—and to guarantee this interpretation by burning the evidence. Lucretius survived in a single manuscript rediscovered in 1418, but not one of Epicurus's three hundred books got through—and they were among the books that "one could still read" in pre-Christian Rome and "for whose possession one would nowadays exchange half of some national literatures" (GM 3.22).

But in Nietzsche's history of philosophy, the victory of Christianity was the victory of Platonism, a philosophic politics that did not blush to employ the lies of guilt, punishment, and immortality. Platonism triumphed over Epicureanism despite the best efforts of the garden god (BGE 7) which included "the most venomous joke" known to Nietzsche: Epicurus permitted himself to call Plato and the Platonists *Dionysiokolakes:* they prostrate themselves before the tyrant Dionysius, and they do so as *actors.* Platonism is part of the victory of the actor in the Hellenistic world (JS 356), and Epicurus's venomous joke strikes at the heart of the matter: Plato's politics for philosophy proved victorious, not because of Dionysius but because of Plato's willingness to employ the very lies Epicurus did his best to explode. Platonism triumphed over Epicureanism through the medium of Christianity but now, after modern science has reconquered the teaching of life after death in favor of the idea of "definitive death," Nietzsche can say: "And Epicurus triumphs anew!" (D 72).

The opportunity granted Christian Platonism to write the spiritual history of the West meant that Epicurus was lost as one of the thinkers (Pyrrho was the other) who carried forward into an uncongenial age what was best in Greek thought, the achievement of thinkers prior to Socrates (KGW VIII 14 [99–100] = WP 437)—not mere "pre-Socratics" as if Socrates were the definitive advance over them, but "the philosophers of the tragic age of the Greeks." "The height attained in the disposition of a Democritus, Hippocrates, and Thucydides was not attained a second time" (KGW VII 36 [11] = WP 443). Nevertheless, Epicurus shared "with all the profound natures of antiquity" disgust at "the philosophers of virtue" who sprang from Socrates and his moralizing (KGW VIII 14

---

17. As Cicero shows, however, even self-respecting Romans like Atticus, a character in his *Laws,* had to mask their Epicureanism behind a view thought more salutary, the Stoic teaching on natural law. See Strauss, *Natural Right and History,* 154–55.

[129] = *WP* 434). That moralizing harbored a fundamental hostility to science in the one culture that had given birth to science (*KGW* VII 36 [11] = *WP* 443), and that hostility made it congenial to the God with the hellish fear of science (*A* 48). To experience Epicurus in a way different from perhaps everybody else meant experiencing him as heir to what was best in Greek science. More generally it meant experiencing the whole of Greek philosophy from the perspective of science: the Platonic Socrates marks a decline into moralism unfriendly to science. Nietzsche's history of philosophy recovers its fundamental events from a perspective friendly to science; that perspective marvels at what stands firm amid the flux of things and recovers Epicurus despite all the efforts to drown him.

But Nietzsche must go beyond Epicurus—post-Christian spiritual warfare must abandon the walled garden. It can no longer content itself with winning over the few Memmiuses, the few self-respecting Romans; and it can no longer honor gods who withdraw into happiness and silence, tired of humankind and its love affairs (*D* 150). Just here, in taking the divine hammer in hand and fighting in a general warfare (*BGE* 62), it has to take a page from Plato, his philosophic politics, though not, of course, the fully unbelievable concepts of guilt, punishment, and immortality that are the height of bad taste. And the new Epicureanism has to abandon something fundamental in Epicurus's philosophical teaching as well. Epicurus's doctrine was, in the end, related to the religions of redemption against which it fought; even though it contained "a generous admixture of Hellenic vitality and strength of nerve," it was "the pagan doctrine of redemption" (*A* 30). Epicurus was a romantic in Nietzsche's sense whose romantic pessimism would have to be replaced by a Dionysian pessimism (*JS* 370). Even with respect to his kin Epicurus, Nietzsche maintains that "we must overcome even the Greeks" (*JS* 340).

"Why we look Epicurean," one fragment in Nietzsche's general picture of Epicurus, focuses in an affirmative way on Epicurus's bent for knowledge. "We moderns" mistrust final explanations, the deceptions of conscience intrinsic to every strong faith. Our mistrust can in large part be explained as the once-burned-twice-shy syndrome of erstwhile believers (*BGE* 59). But a positive and not a negative consequence of having been burned interests Nietzsche most: a jubilant curiosity. Jubilant curiosity is appropriate to former inhabitants of a small corner of conviction now liberated from the narrow tyranny of that perspective into a new infinite. Nietzsche's anatomy of this "jubilant curiosity," a near synonym of joyous science, describes an almost Epicurean happiness. Possessing it depends upon developing "a nearly Epicurean bent for knowledge," and "an aversion to the big moral words and gestures." And possessing it brings pride, a particularly Epicurean pride based on self-mastery, mind's mastery of the heart, the mastery on which Epicurus insisted in the face of Plato's concessions to the heart.

Epicurean pride is the conscious experience of what Nietzsche called one of his most essential advances (*JS* 360), the distinction, with respect to the causes of an action, between the stored-up energy and the direction given to that energy. "Our pride" is based on the control we exercise over "our forward streaming drive for certainty," a drive fostered by the faith of Christianity and the faith of modern science, the two dominant forms of certitude that have formed us but no longer direct us. The "new infinite" of uncertainty may draw a shudder (*JS* 374) but we take pride in not being subject to our shudder either. Our senses may have grown bloodless under the vampire idealism (*JS* 372) but now as then we have "mad and fiery animals under us"; we know we cannot still them but we think we can direct them.

Modern pride is a virtue, a historic achievement which understands its genealogy to include kinship with a few proud Greeks as well as tutelage in a corner of conviction from which it now knows itself liberated. Nietzsche's flattery of modern pride seems to be a goad bent on engendering it and exploiting it. Proud modern riders, controlling and directing their passion for certainty, plunge into the new infinite hesitating least of all in the face of danger.

Nietzsche's recovery of Epicurus is a key element in his new history of philosophy because it provides another means of access to its all-important themes: the philosophic and scientific tradition prior to Socrates which Epicurus attempted to preserve; the meaning of Platonism as a philosophic compromise with moralism; Platonism's vulnerability to capture by an alien religion with a passion for revenge and an ultimate enforcer; the struggle within Roman culture between two philosophic traditions, one susceptible to such capture, the other not; the still all-pervasive influence of the victor's interpretation of that history; the meaning of modern history as—in part—the warfare which wins back from popular Platonism the methods of inquiry already firmly founded by the Greeks and preserved by Epicurus; and, finally, the need to adopt a Platonic politics for philosophy and not an Epicurean one. Part of that politics is the very act of recovering the history of philosophy for an Epicurean perspective and exploding its Platonic misrepresentation.

Our slow times (376). This quiet section is a reflection on death appropriate for an Epicurean. "Our" is limited to a single type, those like Nietzsche himself who are "motherly" in giving birth to works. Their slow periods arise from the belief that with the completion of a work they have arrived at the goal of their lives. They "hesitate" not in the face of danger but having completed their work. Such artists seem to be exemplars of natural mortals, accepting mortality as the finite completion of a natural goal. Like mothers, they yield their being to their work. Such a yielding generates "a faith"—faith in a longer tempo, in a life extending beyond the death of the maker. Unlike Christianity which places the whole weight of life on its final hour (*UD* 8), Nietzsche's *memento mori* is the remembrance of "a stupid physiological fact" (*KGW* VII 25 [226]) that ends existence without refuting it and without requiring redemption, and in the best case, after its full ripening.

Great Politics, or Just Who Is Nietzsche? (377–83)

Nietzsche's politics is a new Athenian universalism that aims to overcome all the fraudulent fusions of Athens and Jerusalem. Another renaissance, it claims kinship with the "gaya scienza" renaissance of the twelfth century, and the Renaissance of the fifteenth and sixteenth centuries that almost put the Greek spirit on the Pope's throne, and the renaissance of Napoleon with its rebirth of manliness and pan-European aims.

Who is this political Nietzsche? He is homeless in modern Europe (377). But he remains who he is despite attempts by friends and enemies alike to make him something he is not (378–80). He works at being as clear as possible while recognizing that the complexity of the subject matter and the novelty of his approach may look like willful obscurity (381). He aspires to create a new European home for the homeless (382). And if this seems all grim and ponderous, laughter breaks out and ends the joyous science joyously (383).

We the homeless (377). Nietzsche has a proper audience: those driven out of their European home by its present loves and hates. He is emphatic: his "secret wisdom and *gaya scienza*" is "laid expressly on the hearts of precisely these." His "gaya scienza" is a *geheime Weisheit* which provides a *Heim* for the *Heimatlose*. Just how far off that future home lies is evident from the seismic tremors set off by a section like this. What look like permanent features of European politics—"conservative," "liberal," "progressive"—are only temporary categories of a "breakable broken transition time"; they cannot exhaust the politics of Europe for they cannot encompass what Nietzsche called his "great politics."

But the hold of the old politics becomes evident from Nietzsche's attack on it. Borrowing images from a parallel but more elaborate account of his politics, Zarathustra's speech "On the Old and New Tablets" (Z 3.12), Nietzsche likens the seemingly permanent to ice covering a flowing stream and the new teachings to a thawing wind that melts the ice. The image is doubly apt: not only does Nietzsche melt the ice, he draws the outrage of those dumped into the cold stream. This section and others like it raise profound suspicions about Nietzsche's politics for it will seem to have no foundation of its own, no ice, and yet be willing to risk destruction of the traditional foundations. Leo Strauss put it this way: Nietzsche "used much of his unsurpassable and inexhaustible power of passionate and fascinating speech for making his readers loathe, not only socialism and communism, but conservatism, nationalism and democracy as well." [18] Is there any defense for a "great politics" that flaunts its abandonment of "equal rights" and "free society" while reinstating war, danger, conquest? Nietzsche even goes so far as to praise slavery in a time that understands the very meaning of history to be its triumph over slavery and its deliverance of humankind into freedom. How can a new politics promising war and slavery win a hearing? Does it deserve a hearing?

Modern times promise "the most humane, the mildest, the most righteous" future yet. But these beautiful words evoke an ugly suspicion voiced by Zarathustra in "On the Tarantulas" (2.7) that the sustaining passion of such teachings is a hidden revenge. "On the Tarantulas" places this unsettling suspicion in the broader context also evoked by this section of *The Joyous Science:* Are these righteous teachings our true European heritage? Are we at home in the European tradition, are we faithful to our Greek past, when we are at home in these teachings?

Nietzsche's analysis of contemporary European politics focuses on two phenomena, a love and a hate, love tied to French national politics, hate to German. Rather love than hate, rather modern France than modern Germany, but for the homeless, neither nor. The cultural themes of the *Use and Disadvantage of History* here receive more penetrating expression partly because the modern options are more starkly separated and Germany more presciently blamed, but also because the model presented by ancient Greece now achieves precision as a relevant if still alien possibility. The contemporary "religion of pity" ("the only religion preached nowadays" [BGE 222]) stems from revolutionary French

18. Strauss, *What Is Political Philosophy?* 55.

politics originating in Rousseau (*SE* 4). "We are no humanitarians," Nietzsche says, "and we would never allow ourselves to dare to speak of our 'love of humanity.'" But Nietzsche's view is posthumanitarian, not subhumanitarian, and if he does not permit himself the phrases of modern humanitarianism, his politics is moved by philanthropy on the Platonic model.

Nietzsche does not love in the modern French way, but he most certainly does not hate in the modern German way, a racial hatred that draws from Nietzsche the most emphatic denunciation long before it became evident to others and unleashed its greatest damage on the world, blotting even Nietzsche's reputation. German racial hatred is "doubly false and indecent" because Germans are the people of "the historical sense"—and Nietzsche will eventually lay claim to that proper German inheritance on behalf of the homeless. For now, German racial hatred drives the *unzeitgemäss* from their European home, forcing them to find a home in past or coming centuries.

The homeless are mixed in their race and descent and aspire to be called "good Europeans," heirs to thousands of years of the European spirit. Part of that heritage is Christianity: Christianity is part of our blood (*KGW* VIII 15 [30]), and two features of that blood still obligate: cruelty and faith. In outgrowing Christianity we have grown averse to it but that very aversion carries forward the uncompromising rectitude characteristic of it. For the sake of their faith our Christian ancestors "willingly sacrificed possessions and blood, position and fatherland." And we, their heirs averse to their faith? "We—do the same." But why? For the sake of our unbelief? "You know better than that, my friends," Nietzsche says. We too do it for the sake of our faith, a faith that grounds our uncompromising rectitude and allows us to do no other, a faith Nietzsche describes as "the hidden Yes" in the homeless ones that overpowers their nos and maybes, a faith expressed in the morality of science.

The hidden yes behind Nietzsche's great politics has seemed hidden indeed, obscured by nos, untempered by maybes. Where *does* Nietzsche stand in the political spectrum and how can his stance be affirmative? He is not content with European liberalism, the blind commercialism tied to a rape of the planet for immediate profit and ease which tempts the whole world to do the same in the ignorant conviction that everyone can go on doing it forever; nor is he persuaded by European progressivism that supports itself with myths of freedom and equality dependent upon machinery. Nietzsche has seemed to belong to those spiritual critics of modernity who turned "conservative" in ways as varied as those of Wagner and Eliot, of Heidegger and Pound, and of Leo Strauss. But

Nietzsche is no conservative, "we don't want to return to any past." He does not "shrink down before the Cross" like Wagner and Eliot. He does not aver the timeless superiority of Plato's wisdom like Strauss. He does not take up nationalism and most assuredly not German nationalism: Nietzsche is no Martin Heidegger who paraded his swastikas on his lapels during his 1936 visit to the penurious apartment in Rome of one of his best students, Karl Löwith, a cultured and philosophic German of Jewish descent driven out of Germany three years earlier by the swastika wearers.[19] If not conservative or liberal or progressive can Nietzsche have a politics with any contemporary relevance other than destruction?

Nietzsche's politics broadens the political perspective instead of shrinking itself into some modern option. "Good Europeans" in Nietzsche's sense are heirs of the European spirit: hard heirs of Christianity's uncompromising rectitude, they are heirs too of Greece, of the scientific spirit of jubilant curiosity suppressed by Christianity, revived in the renaissances, and carried forward in modern Europe's spiritual warfare. Aided by the cruelty of a probity schooled in physics—"Hooray for physics!"—good Europeans view themselves as heirs to the whole natural history of the race, a natural history first come to conscious awareness among a few European thinkers. They view that history as wholly natural without falling into the superstition that it existed in order to produce them.

This is the rootedness of the new politics: arising in multicultural Europe with its mixed inheritance of biblical religion and Greek thought, it reads its genealogy in the whole history of the race and in the history of life on this planet and in the history of the universe whose course will some day extinguish it—"and who dares to doubt that?" This rootedness gives meaning to Nietzsche's talk of slavery. What seems like reckless speech is an attempt to curb reckless modern talk of freedom. Nietzsche understands freedom as an always problematic obedience to what is given as one's own fate, a historical as well as a natural givenness among whose imperatives one finds oneself or comes to oneself. Freedom as the deepening and broadening awareness of fatedness culminating in the love of fate, Nietzsche's highest love (*JS* 276)—such an understanding of freedom, though it is to be found in Spinoza, can scarcely be credited in an age that imagines itself the first to experience mass freedom. But it is precisely the fiction that all men and women are free by virtue of citizenship in the universal and homogeneous state at the end of history that creates the homeless few on whose hearts Nietzsche presses his writ-

19. Löwith, *Mein Leben in Deutschland*, 57.

ings. To them he speaks of a new slavery, the recognition that we are not our own, that we have not made ourselves (*HH* I.588) but are the products of nature and history. This great politics of natural rootedness experiences a responsibility toward its past that grows out of gratitude; the gratitude of the antiquarian spirit now encompasses the whole of the natural order as the history of its kind. History becomes genealogy, the tale of our family.

Nietzsche's politics lays claim to the past. It is the local politics of a "good European" who affirms his European home as heir to Christianity and Greece, to hardness and intellect. But that local politics broadens out as this particular past makes possible the recovery of the whole of the human and natural past; a local loyalty expands into loyalty to the earth.

Nietzsche's politics lays claim to the future. It is a global politics that arose in Europe, in Sils Maria on walks that began at the Durisch house and that ended in insight into eternal return, and on walks from Rapallo along "the magnificent road to Zoagli" where Nietzsche was waylaid by Zarathustra. It spreads out of Europe as Descartes's politics spread out from the *poêle* near Ulm, but it spreads out as a future global politics of loyalty to the earth, ecological or "green" politics that has only begun to formulate its agenda but that finds in Nietzsche's thought a comprehensive means of affirming the earth.

This politics finds no European home in conservative or liberal or progressive Europe with its various theisms and humanisms. As post-humanism, Nietzsche's politics has to face the profound Platonic question present behind the theisms and humanisms of the past: "Can a society be built on deadly truth?" How could a postmodern society be built on anything else? Nietzsche's politics takes its bearings from its times, from its long view backward and forward, and it takes its bearings from a proper physio-psychology. The new politics of earthly affirmation is tied to a reformed and joyous science. It breaks cleanly with the Platonic Socrates who argued on his dying day that love of the logos and love of the human, philology and philanthropy, required abandoning the deficient formulations of natural science in favor of the deficient formulations of the community of speakers and required falling silent when the questioner was satisfied. Science as a public project has made the Platonic strategy seem immoral: who can love a noble liar nowadays? And who can believe that only a belief in just gods and immortal souls can ground a society? Not good Europeans surely.

The new politics is bound to appall. For Nietzsche that means that it is bound to be taken for what it is not, that *he* is bound to be taken for what he is not. The next sections give an uncanny anticipation of some of the ways in which Nietzsche would be mistaken for somebody else. But they also anticipate his posthumous birth as himself.[20]

"And become clear again" (378). How will the times treat a gift-giver whose gift it cannot know it needs or wants? In a single extended metaphor, Nietzsche describes what must befall a teaching on metaphysics and divinity that is necessarily as political as his own. Fundamental teachers, teachers of evil to contemporaries, are like fountains whose depth and persistence allow them to survive all the attempts to poison them and ultimately to dispense their clarity and purity to distant generations, the posterity of which Descartes spoke. Distortion and vilification come not only from the enemies of a new teaching, "the good and the just" who have the laws on their side, but from its supposed friends as well, "apes" and "fools" who feed on its contempt while lacking its love or longing (Z 3.7). What Zarathustra learned from the poisoned friends of his teaching is "to pass by"—all the while retaining the hopes for the future of his teaching that Nietzsche expresses here.

"Unfortunately," Nietzsche says, "we don't know how to defend ourselves where we want to." The actual history of attempts to poison Nietzsche's teaching makes one wonder what Nietzsche might have done differently to defend himself. At the very least, he could have put less trust in his readers' ability to appreciate ironic excess on delicate subjects. *Vergiss die Peitsche nicht!* And no one has forgotten. Nietzsche himself expressed amazement to an acquaintance embarrassed by this statement, "But please, I beg you, that can't have given you any difficulty! I mean, it's clearly understandable, that that was only a joking, exaggerated, symbolic mode of expression."[21] The next section suggests another way to poison Nietzsche's fountain that Nietzsche might have taken greater pains to forestall.

The fool speaks up (379). Is Nietzsche the fool? A fool speaks up in *Zarathustra* proclaiming himself an advocate of Zarathustra's teaching (Z 3.7). The people believe him and call him "Zarathustra's ape," but Zarathustra

20. One thinker who did not mistake Nietzsche for someone else was William Butler Yeats. His profound appreciation of Nietzsche appears, for instance, in "The Statues" where Nietzsche's cultural history of Greece and Christianity finds expression worthy of it in the vivid conciseness of Yeats's matchless images; or in "A Dialogue of Self and Soul" where Yeats reenacts the historic struggle of the self to win freedom from the soul for an affirmation of itself and finally for that highest of all affirmations, eternal return; or in *A Vision* with its elevation of the singular hero Nietzsche and the graceful claim staked by Yeats himself to "the magnificent road to Zoagli," the road on which Nietzsche was waylaid by Zarathustra. See my essay, "Yeats's Nietzschean Dialogue."

21. Gilman, ed., *Begegnungen mit Nietzsche,* 410. On this "over-determined" image, see Graybeal, *Language and 'The Feminine,'* 55–56.

calls him a "fool" and repudiates his would-be follower after listening to enough of his speech to recognize how far it is from his own and how it will taint his reputation. Is the fool who speaks at the end of *The Joyous Science* another ape, to be repudiated in the name of Nietzsche's own teaching? So it seems to me.

The fool reflects on what sounds like a Machiavellian theme: it is better to be hated than held in contempt, and the times are worthy only of contempt. The fool's contempt is his taste and privilege, his art, his virtue perhaps—Nietzschean standards applied to a contempt that grows increasingly tasteless. And the fool adopts Nietzsche's terms as his own— we most modern of moderns, we the fearless. Secure in his superiority, the fool taunts his contemporaries: they will hardly behead us or jail us or send us into exile; they will not even ban our books or burn them. The fool is a poor prophet, for Nietzsche's books were in fact banned in Naumburg and Leipzig, the very cities that gave him his classical education. The fool seems to think that he can get away with anything because he is needed: not only does his speech lack "that impish and cheerful vice courtesy" (*BGE* 284), it lacks Nietzsche's realism about just how little his age would recognize a need for his teaching, just how precarious the future possibilities were for the joyous science. But above all, the fool's speech lacks the taste Nietzsche claimed for his contempt. Zarathustra's fool spits and vomits his response to the stench of the great city outside of which he stations himself; Nietzsche's fool ostentatiously holds his nose in proximity to everything human.

The last item of what the fool says he loves perhaps gives a perspective on the whole of this section that distances it from Nietzsche himself. The fool loves "the artist's mockery of himself." Though it requires that the fool be taken in this one instance as expressing Nietzsche's own view, the whole section can be viewed from this final phrase: Nietzsche permitted himself an artist's mockery of himself, a view of himself as a fool with contempt for the whole of the human and not just its decadent modern forms, a view of himself from the eye of an enemy. A small outcry in a letter to an old friend may indicate what Nietzsche expected: "How is it no one ever rises up to protest? That no one ever takes exception to my being insulted?" (letter to Baron von Seydlitz, 12 February 1888.) The outcry serves as a motto for a fine book published in France in the 1930s to protest one of the worst insults, that Nietzsche was tainted with German racial hatred.[22]

22. Nicolas, *From Nietzsche down to Hitler.*

"The Wanderer" speaks (380). Another character from Nietzsche's past speaks here—one closer to Nietzsche—and suggests that the perpetual wanderer, old Odysseus, has arrived home, at a new European home. "The Wanderer" seems to address his question to his Shadow—to one who has shadowed him—and the question could, to any third party, appear wholly enigmatic (see the *Wanderer and His Shadow,* introductory dialogue). The focus is European morality and the question is two-fold: Can one ever leave one's European home to view its moral towers from a non-European height—with "an Asiatic and supra-Asiatic eye," as Nietzsche said in *Beyond Good and Evil* (56)? And can one ever cease wandering and arrive at a new moral home?

Four titles or near titles from Nietzsche's books form part of the argument and suggest that the *Wanderer (and his Shadow)* have completed their quest and can measure European morality from a standpoint outside it and offer a new moral home. In order for *Thoughts on Moral Prejudices (Daybreak)* to be more than prejudices on prejudices, a *Beyond Good and Evil* must have been arrived at free from European prejudices. That very undertaking begins in irony, in "a minor madness": while aiming at a free, unencumbered view of moral things, it begins unfree, encumbered by its own moral imperative. The examination of conscience is a directive of conscience; will chooses intellect's rule over will, wills its subjugation. Can such an encumbered beginning achieve the height? Nietzsche's answer assumes that it can, that one's "specific gravity" permits breaking free of "the spirit of gravity."

To transcend one's place and time requires creating two things for oneself, a view and a quality of vision: eyes to survey millennia but also clear sky in those eyes—the clear sky of Zarathustra's song to the open sky, a song of gratitude that prepares him for his blessing on earthly things (*Z* 3.4). In the present section Nietzsche describes this creation as the overcoming of revulsion against the times, the overcoming of his *Zeit-Ungemässheit* (a variation on the title *Unzeitgemässe Betrachtungen*) which makes it possible to become timely again. Nietzsche's timeliness seems to be hinted at in what he names as his final overcoming: "his Romanticism"—overcoming Romanticism prepares a Dionysian pessimism (370). The Wanderer speaks courteously to claim for himself what Nietzsche ended claiming more boldly: he is a Hyperborean, he knows the road. Amidst all the poisonings and misunderstandings, is this understandable?

On the question of being understandable (381). Nietzsche can now speak in his own voice about his intentions in writing. Like previous philosophers, he lures and forbids and is attentive to his times. But, while placing himself in the small company of philosophers, Nietzsche calls attention to his singularity, to two features of his refined style that his intended readers will have to learn to appreciate. His jauntiness and ignorance may at first provoke the very readers by whom he wants to be understood, because they have been trained in a sober way of knowing assured of its correctness. But his style is no accident; not only is it grounded in his nature, it accords with the objects of inquiry; jauntiness and ignorance belong to the joyous science as essentially as somber rational optimism belonged to Platonic science or Cartesian science (*BGE* 14). Still, jauntiness and ignorance are going to be hard for modern "knowers" to swallow as virtues; what Nietzsche claims is that with the proper jauntiness inquiry can at last become serious without ever becoming grave (*GM* 3.11), and with the proper recognition of ignorance—our new infinite of interpretive possibilities—inquiry can at last set out on open seas with a fitting mix of pride and modesty. The highest aspiration of the new philosopher, Nietzsche says, conjoins his ideal, his art, and his piety in the spirit of a dancer. "To those who think as we do, all things themselves are dancing"—thus spoke the animals to Zarathustra at the climactic event of *Thus Spoke Zarathustra,* as they described the dance of the eternal return of things, a playful, ecstatic, rhythmic dance that has no purpose beyond itself (*Z* 3.13). Zarathustra himself sings of the dance of Dionysos and Ariadne, divinities whose return gives focus to the new celebration of the earth. *The Joyous Science* nears its end by invoking the ideal of *Zarathustra* and expressing its own form of optimism: the accord of thinker and thought.

The great health (382). This last section before laughter breaks out as a symptom of health epitomizes the spirit of the whole book and expresses the new ideal. Great health is a risky ideal, placing the whole weight of the ultimate criterion on something that looks merely subjective and personal. It runs the risk of refutation by counter-charge—"So you're just not healthy enough for our music" (*JS* 368). But great health is neither subjective nor accidental; it is a historic event in the spiritual history of humankind whose meaning comes to light through genealogy: great health follows convalescence from the great sickness. This is the fitting conclusion to *The Joyous Science,* for Nietzsche's reflections on our spiritual history culminate in a convalescence that grounds joy.

"The great health"—Nietzsche is not defiantly recommending his eyesight or his migraines. Great health is the name given to a primary shift in the natural history of morals that will gradually bring to an end the "moral period" of human history. During that period—"the last ten thousand years in a few large regions of the earth"—the worth of an action came to be fixed in its origins, its intentions. The polite history of this event in *Beyond Good and Evil* (32) is deepened in the second treatise of *On the Genealogy of Morals* where the first immoralist gets quite rude about it: "Here is sickness . . . the most frightful sickness that has raged in humans," the sickness of *ressentiment* (it's your fault) and bad conscience (it's my fault).[23] The ten-thousand-year period includes the two millennia of philosophy and its attempt to ground guilt and punishment rationally. Socrates, formerly "the one turning point and vortex of so-called world-history" (*BT* 15), becomes one turning point among others within that larger history; he furthers the already present moral sickness by using dialectic to secure "the most bizarre of all equations," reason = virtue = happiness (*TI* Socrates 4, 10) and corrupting even Plato into employing the lies of punishment, guilt, and redemption. In Nietzsche's comprehensive perspective, the history of philosophy can only be understood when it is set within this larger historical phenomenon whose valet it has been. The third treatise of *On the Genealogy of Morals* singles out one main feature of the moral period, ascetic ideals, as "the true *calamity* in the history of European health" (3.21). The ascetic ideal blossomed under the careful cultivation of ascetic priests into the whole baroque apparatus of punishment, guilt, and redemption, even creating for itself the spectacle of a god who would take upon himself what was rightfully ours, eternal damnation for the sin of having been born—"here is sickness." The history of philosophy is marked by accommodation to this sickness, the mendacious employment of reason to secure a "moral" universe like the one that doles out eternal punishment.

Is modern science the cure for this sickness? Science achieved a victory over the "theological astronomy" employed by ascetic priests as the cosmic framework for the drama of human punishment. Nevertheless, "the self-belittlement of humankind, its *will* to self-belittlement . . . has progressed since Copernicus" (*GM* 3.25). "Since Copernicus, humankind seems to have got itself on an inclined plane" sliding into nihilism and self-contempt. But if Galileo's apparatus assisted this human slide downward, modern science can still be celebrated for the will to truth at work in it, that remnant of the ascetic ideal that "finally forbid itself the lie involved in belief in God" (*GM* 3.27). Conscientious refusal of God is an "awe-inspiring *catastrophe*" because it carries forward a still older

23. Deleuze, *Nietzsche and Philosophy*, 21.

trajectory, not simply the death of a two-thousand-year-old God but the passing of the whole moral period of human spiritual evolution.

> As the will to truth thus gains self-consciousness—there can be no doubt of that—morality will gradually *perish* now: this is the great spectacle in a hundred acts reserved for the next two centuries in Europe—the most terrible, most questionable, and perhaps also most hopeful of all spectacles. (*GM* 3.27)

What is the hope? Great health. Philosophy is the means of convalescence, convalescence through insight into our spiritual past, insight into the way of all beings as will to power, affirmation of time and beings grounded in those insights, and great politics on behalf of the new view of things.[24]

Zarathustra's war with his archenemy, the spirit of gravity, presents philosophy's overcoming of the ten-thousand-year moral period and the achievement of great health as a fable. When *Ecce Homo* relates "the history of *Zarathustra*" or the circumstances surrounding Nietzsche's being waylaid by Zarathustra on the roads out of Rapallo, it quotes the whole of "The great health" from *The Joyous Science*. It is no contradiction, rather it is essential to his main point, that Nietzsche laconically reports that he was taken over by the great health during a winter in which "my health could have been better." The great health was not a cure for his headaches but for something much more serious and historic. "The great health" runs a risk of sounding merely therapeutic and local, but even the circumstances of its appearance show how little this is the case; as Nietzsche said, "we have neither the time nor the inclination to rotate around ourselves" (*KGW* VIII 14 [28] = *WP* 426).

Nietzsche's history of philosophy shows that great health, recovery from ressentiment and bad conscience, is not the end of conscience; it is not a move backward into the premoral or submoral but a move forward into the postmoral. Just as the conscience of physics destroys the old theological astronomy, intellectual conscience destroys the foundations of the moral period of human history. Unconscionable now is what is contrary to nature. "It is *not* error as error that horrifies me at this sight [of the ascetic ideal] . . . it is the lack of nature, it is the utterly gruesome fact that *antinature* itself received the highest honors" (*EH* Destiny 7).

Nietzsche's history of philosophy shows how the conflict between

---

24. On the great health in the *Genealogy of Morals,* see the exhilarating and edifying essay by Alphonso Lingis, "Black Stars."

health and sickness can be expressed religiously: "Have I been under-stood?—Dionysos versus the Crucified.—" Dionysos and the Crucified, two gods who suffer, die, and are reborn. "The Crucified" is the Apostle Paul's label for Jesus of Nazareth (I Corinthians 11:13, 23; 2:2; Galatians 2:30), shorthand for Paul's interpretation of Jesus' role in the transaction that bought our redemption by paying off God's just demand for eternal punishment of the guilty. On Nietzsche's reading of the New Testa-ment, Jesus' teaching—a "peace movement" that "had abolished the very concept of 'guilt'" (A 42)—was perverted into its opposite when Paul interpreted Jesus' death as a sacrifice promising life after death. When Jesus became "the Crucified," the gospel was transformed into "the *im-pertinent* doctrine of personal immortality" (A 41), impertinent because it is the ultimate in personal vanity to suppose that what is important in the universe is my salvation: "The 'salvation of the soul'—in plain lan-guage, 'the world revolves around *me*'" (A 43). The whole spectacle of the subsequent worldly success of "the Crucified"—"Christianity owes its triumph to this miserable flattery of personal vanity" (A 43; GM 1.8), an argument made again and again in Gibbon's matchless chapters on the rise of Christianity in the *Decline and Fall of the Roman Empire* (chaps. 15, 16)—this "is really a *spectacle for the gods,* for those gods who are at the same time philosophers" (A 39).

The sufferings of Dionysos, his death and rebirth, are the polar oppo-site of the sufferings of the Crucified and differ from them as health differs from sickness. The death and rebirth of Dionysos sanctify life by recognizing suffering as a part of life and life as irrefutably good even in its suffering. The Dionysian festivals make "the *sexual* symbol . . . the venerable symbol par excellence" and sanctify "every single element in the act of procreation, of pregnancy, and of birth." In summarizing the Dionysian festivals, Nietzsche says "I know no higher symbolism than this *Greek* symbolism of the Dionysian festivals. Here the most profound instinct of life, that directed toward the future of life, is experienced religiously" (*TI* Ancients 4).[25]

In Book Five of *The Joyous Science,* the great health appears as a fully natural condition where nature is understood as wholly flux. Its "new goal," the ideal of the dance, is not a state of rest that delivers it from its condition, but a state of sublime motion that perpetuates and gives joyous expression to its condition. The pervasive image of this section is of argonauts driven by their health to explore the whole coastline of

---

25. See "Dionysus and Christ" in Deleuze, *Nietzsche and Philosophy,* 14–17.

a *Mittelmeer,* till every cove of their landlocked sea of idealism is known to them. Suddenly, without really meaning to do so, they open their eyes on a wholly new shoreline, a land without boundaries that accords with their own boundless, unsatisfiable natures. Nietzsche thus ends on an uplifting note that contrasts gravity and grace and presents nature as in accord with human nature. *The Joyous Science* does not go as far in this direction as *Thus Spoke Zarathustra* where the new land that opens before the argonaut Zarathustra is glimpsed as the boundless, enigmatic world of will to power which receives the boundless affirmation of eternal return. But this section points the reader back to *Zarathustra* for it ends saying, "The tragedy *begins* . . . ." *The Joyous Science* of 1886, like *The Joyous Science* of 1882, is a prelude to *Thus Spoke Zarathustra,* the fable in which Nietzsche felt freer to present the victory of grace over the spirit of gravity.

An additional note from *Zarathustra* is sounded in this section, for Nietzsche uses the word made prominent by its placement at the very beginning of Zarathustra's teaching, *Übermensch,* a word that almost drops out of Nietzsche's vocabulary after *Zarathustra.*[26] Nietzsche's use of it here acknowledges the risk run by the word: the new ideal of a *menschlich-übermenschliches Wohlsein und Wohlwollen* often enough appears *unmenschlich.* The new health will appear to be an old disease. Nevertheless, Nietzsche defiantly describes it in a way that would force the old philosophy to condemn it: glimpsing the new land evokes an impassioned outcry: "From now on nothing will sate us!" This is a state of bliss for the new health, the state of misery for the old sickness with its Platonic ideal of perfect rest or dreamless sleep. The most spiritual of the most modern rejoice at the enigmatic and unfathomable; a new concord between human and nature appears; in this world gods too philosophize. Here is Nietzschean theodicy: the world accords with the deepest spiritual nature of the most spiritual human beings; the joyous science justifies the ways of nature to man. But as Gilles Deleuze says, theodicy becomes cosmodicy.[27]

The new beginning and the new ending of *The Joyous Science* are meditations on convalescence or the great health. As such they belong to the many post-*Zarathustra* commentaries on *Thus Spoke Zarathustra,* intimations of what it really contains as *"Incipit Tragoedia."* If *Thus Spoke*

---

26. The only other uses are *GM* 1.6; *TI* Skirmishes 37; *A* 4; and *EH* Books 1; *EH* Books *Z* 6; *EH* Destiny 5.

27. Deleuze, *Nietzsche and Philosophy,* 25.

Zarathustra is Nietzsche's real birth of tragedy, he claims unparalleled importance for it. Being "involuntary parody," it may look like parody only. But parody is its by-product, an even regrettable opposition to what humans have taken as serious during the protracted moral period of their life on this planet. What is not a by-product is its aspiration to the "great seriousness" of the postmodern, post-Platonic, postmorality task. Aspiring to the birth of tragedy on a global scale, it dares to paint the real question mark: Is the wisdom of the wisest wise? It marks the turning in the history of philosophy with which Nietzsche's name will be associated: the end of philosophy's collusion with morality and the beginning of philosophy's advocacy of a healing, postmoral vision of humankind and nature. Can humankind live unsheltered by noble lies of divine origin and divine purpose that have housed it until now and that have been taken over by ressentiment and bad conscience? Can our gravity, our Platonism in the decayed forms of romantic pessimism and Baconian dominance of nature, be overcome by a Dionysian pessimism, the affirmation of eternal return that celebrates the purposelessness of nature and humanity's place among the animals?

Epilogue (383). Nietzsche ends the new edition of *The Joyous Science* as he began it, pointing back to the still more important book with which he had painted the fundamental question mark. Or rather, Nietzsche *intended* to end *The Joyous Science* this way, inviting one to enter *Thus Spoke Zarathustra,* but he found that the great seriousness made him willing to add one last section as a service to his readers, a set of instructions on how to read *Zarathustra,* an account of forgotten and unknown virtues, "the virtues of right reading." [28] But the thought of a reader's manual to *Thus Spoke Zarathustra* violates the gaiety of *The Joyous Science* and the spirits of his present book just won't permit it. Nietzsche was thus forbidden to write his sober essay on a forgotten kind of writing.

Instead *The Joyous Science* ends gaily, the sobriety of further instruction giving way to music for a dance to joy. But while allowing the laughter of the spirits of his book to deflect him from the sober instruction he might otherwise have given, Nietzsche has a last laugh on the laughers: the songs they induce him to sing, Songs of Prince Vogelfrei, provide music for their dance, but in their cunning way the songs slip in the fundamental lessons as well. The singer may suffer "the Singer's

---

28. *KGW* returns to the *Lesens* of Nietzsche's *Druckmanuskript* instead of the *Lesers* of the first and all later editions.

Curse" of not being understood by the dancers for whom he sings and this inattention to his words may even make the dancers better able to hear his music and his manner and to dance to his Dionysian pipe. "Is that what you want? . . ."

Well, yes and no. Yes for those whose dance is not simply dependent upon understanding. No for those whose dance *is* the dance of under-standing, those goaded by his challenge to understand the singer's song despite the missing instructions. For them, the Songs of Prince Vogel-frei turn out to be exemplary Zarathustrian songs hiding within their gaiety the great seriousness befitting a *Zukunftsmusikant*. And with that painful word from Nietzsche's past, the playful spirits of his book make sport of him again, but in a way that is playfully fitting for one who aspires to compose the fundamental music of the future. The fourteen songs of Prince Vogelfrei look like parody and are, but they too paint again the real question mark: Can humankind live under an open sky of purposeless play?

Chapter 15

Epilogue: The Nietzschean Renaissance

Every great human being exerts a retroactive force: for his sake all of history is placed in the balance again, and a thousand secrets of the past crawl out of their hiding places—into his sunshine.—Nietzsche (JS 34)

The sunshine of Nietzsche's thought brings the hidden history of philosophy to light. A thousand secrets of the past crawl out of hiding places—some even chosen by great thinkers in our history like Bacon and Descartes. "What matters most . . . is always culture" (*TI* Germans 4) and philosophers such as Bacon, Descartes, and Nietzsche are students of what matters most, the thousand goals, as Zarathustra called them, the thousand tablets of good and evil that humankind has placed over itself. All such tablets live out of their past, embodying an interpretation of their past. Nietzsche's thought affirms culture in the deepest sense by placing history in the balance again, by recovering the past, and building a future on that past, the thousand and first goal.

But not just any past: if rootedness in a past is necessary for any people with a present and future, Nietzsche makes it clear that the European past, for all its vulnerability to interpretations that do it violence, is both unique and to some degree recoverable as it was—though always under the police supervision of mistrust. Nietzsche's recovery of our past is one of many renaissances that have erupted in our tradition and always as spiritual warfare. Like the others, from Provençal "gaya scienza" to Napoleonic pan-Europeanism, Nietzsche's renaissance depends upon a recovery of the Greeks—with Nietzsche, the thinkers of the tragic age of the Greeks, a philosophic, scientific, artistic, and literary tradition eventually overlaid with the most bizarre of all equations: Socrates' reason = virtue = happiness. Lifelong meditation on the problem of Socrates led to clarity on this one turning point in the paradigm of cultures. Before Socrates: Homer, tragedy, Democritus, Thucydides, the older Hellenic instinct, Dionysos. After Socrates: the Platonic higher swindle, the losing battle of Epicurus and Pyrrho, a powerful Platonism for the people that drove the whole Homeric army into Hades.

In Nietzsche's "genealogy" our family history is at stake. In a late reflection on "the great, the *uncanny* problem which I have been pursuing longest," Nietzsche recounts how the genealogical pursuit began for him: through discovery of "the so-called *pious fraud*," the right to lie morally that the great philosophers and priests granted themselves in their task of schooling humankind (*TI* Improvers 5). Esotericism proved to be but the first handle on a problem that became Nietzsche's lifework, the cultural history of humankind and its grounding in pious lies of difference—whether it be the difference of our clan, our tribe, our nation, or our species, lies of difference have always grounded our primary claims to dignity. Nietzsche is an immoralist: he spares himself shock at this past and attempts to understand it as a philosopher with the whole future of humankind on his conscience.

Genealogy forced Nietzsche into holy war. The war is not fundamentally against pious fraud but against its outcome at the end of history, the modern fraud of a free and equal global society as the meaning of history. Against the inner ridiculousness of any such theology of history, Nietzsche advances a nontheistic, nonhumanistic naturalism bound to sound immoral but by no means a novelty in the philosophic tradition. The world-affirming immanentism of laughing Democritus—the subversive teaching of inarticulate giants according to the divine Plato (*Sophist* 246a–250d)—necessarily became a subterranean tradition in philosophy after the Christian capture of Rome. The heroic effort to effect its renaissance can be appreciated in Francis Bacon, witness to the death of a Renaissance at the hands of zealots. Bacon's science masquerades as the recovery of King Solomon's science while actually recovering pre-Socratic Greek science; with Nietzsche that recovery comes into the open, ending its complicity with its opposite, world-denying transcendentalism. Some are born posthumously—not only Nietzsche but Democritus and Epicurus, or Bacon and Descartes. And some can be posthumously buried, Augustine, say, and other agitators against the affirmative spirit.

Genealogy as holy war possesses a powerful weapon in the hidden history of philosophy. The underworld of great thinkers can, to a degree, be brought into the sunlight as part of the argument on Nietzsche's behalf. If esotericism was philosophy's once necessary compromise with the only form of spiritual authority enjoying public favor, then publicizing the esoteric is a renaissance weapon in a postascetic age. Democritus and Epicurus have largely been lost to us, but one manuscript of Lucretius got through. Plato was saved by what was light and frothy in his writings. And Bacon and Descartes survive as do Montaigne, Machiavelli, Spinoza, Hobbes, Locke, Rousseau: their mighty works are subversive weapons that can be brought into the open on behalf of a rational understanding of the European past.

That rational understanding is no rationalism. Reason came into the world by accident, a survival tool of the most endangered species. With Nietzsche, reason rejects the old "safe way" of Plato's Socrates and the belief it fosters in the commensurability of pure mind and the good as such. With Nietzsche, reason becomes jaunty and ignorant again, publicly suspicious of all knowers; its philology and philanthropy take up the first sailing again, inquiry into the causes of all things. If joyous science severs ties with Baconian mastery and Cartesian method, "let us not be ungrateful" to them: their historic compromises subverted and destroyed the enemy to whom they had to look friendly.

Can a future human society be built on joyous science? Joyous science possesses the great advantages of a powerful virtue, honesty, and a powerful ally, public science. Together they can ridicule the ridiculous and attract those educated to scientific virtue: philosophy continues to be useful for harming stupidity, for turning stupidity into something shameful (*JS* 328). Ridicule can recover as an ally that master of the enigmatical style, Francis Bacon, the Lord Chancellor who advertised holy war while seeming to promote peace. And it can recover as an ally that comic dualist, Descartes, one of the greatest minds that ever lived, though ridiculous sobriety still prefers to judge him confused rather than ironic. With allies like that, joyous science can help to alter the general taste: "This thing here?—it's ridiculous. That thing there?—it's absurd" (*JS* 38).

Perhaps even more important for the social ends of the new philosophy than honesty and science is another old notion shared among philosophers: gratitude. The old teaching that we are not our own, that we owe our being to something infinitely greater than ourselves, achieves in Nietzsche's thought a new expression wholly consistent with honesty and science. Genealogy generates gratitude: we come to ourselves in an evolving universe that has made us what we are through a stupendous sequence of events that we can to some degree investigate and comprehend, though always under the supervision of mistrust. Hooray for physics, a tradition of inquiry that is our true heritage. Recovery of the natural and human past within the mystery of the whole enlarges our memory of the things worth memorializing. A culture built on joyous science would be a remembering culture aware of its place in the immensities of space and time, aware of its place on earth among species that evolve and fall extinct, aware of its heritage as a spirited species bent on surpassing.

Aware too that our spiritual heritage, in its dominant tradition, expresses "hatred of the human, and even more of the animal, and still more of the material" (*GM* 3.28), joyous science is necessarily martial on behalf of the human, the animal, and the material. Martial or manly, in love with possessing, joyous science unites with a love that is womanly and true, loyal to the beloved. This marriage of loves treasures what it possesses, grateful for what is given and always unsatisfiable.

Works Cited

Bacon's Works

Farrington, Benjamin. *The Philosophy of Francis Bacon.* Chicago: University of Chicago Press, 1964. Contains *The Masculine Birth of Time, Thoughts and Conclusions, The Refutation of the Philosophies.*

The Works of Francis Bacon. Edited by J. Spedding, R. L. Ellis, and D. D. Heath. 14 vols. New York: Garrett Press, 1968 (1857–74).

Descartes's Works

Oeuvres de Descartes. Edited by C. Adam and P. Tannery. 13 vols. Paris: L. Cerf, 1897–1912.

The Passions of the Soul. Translated by Stephen Voss. Indianapolis: Hackett Publishing, 1989.

The Philosophical Writings of Descartes. Edited and translated by J. Cottingham, R. Stoothoff, D. Murdoch, A. Kenny. 3 vols. Cambridge: Cambridge University Press, 1984–91.

Nietzsche's Works

Werke. Kritische Gesamtausgabe. Edited by Giorgio Colli und Mazzino Montinari. Berlin: Walter de Gruyter, 1967–78.

Briefe. Kritische Gesamtausgabe. Edited by Giorgio Colli und Mazzino Montinari. Berlin: Walter de Gruyter, 1975–84.

Beyond Good and Evil. Translated by Walter Kaufmann. New York: Vintage, 1966.

The Birth of Tragedy and the Case of Wagner. Translated by Walter Kaufmann. New York: Vintage, 1967.

Daybreak, Thoughts on the Prejudices of Morality. Translated by R. J. Hollingdale. Cambridge: Cambridge University Press, 1982.

The Gay Science. Translated by Walter Kaufmann. New York: Vintage, 1974.

Human, All Too Human. Translated by R. J. Hollingdale. Cambridge: Cambridge University Press, 1986. Contains *Assorted Opinions and Maxims* and *The Wanderer and His Shadow.*

On the Genealogy of Morals and Ecce Homo. Translated by Walter Kaufmann. New York: Vintage, 1969.

Philosophy in the Tragic Age of the Greeks. Translated by Marianne Cowan. Chicago: Regnery, 1962.

The Portable Nietzsche. Translated by Walter Kaufmann. New York: Vintage, 1954. Contains *Thus Spoke Zarathustra, Twilight of the Idols, The Antichrist, Nietzsche Contra Wagner,* and an abridged version of *Homer's Contest.*

Selected Letters. Translated by Christopher Middleton. Chicago: University of Chicago Press, 1969.

Untimely Meditations. Translated by R. J. Hollingdale. Cambridge: Cambridge University Press, 1983. Contains *David Strauss: The Confessor and Writer, On the Uses and Disadvantages of History for Life, Schopenhauer as Educator, Richard Wagner in Bayreuth.*

The Will to Power. Translated by Walter Kaufmann and R. J. Hollingdale. New York: Vintage, 1968.

Works by Other Authors

Ackermann, Robert John. *Nietzsche, a Frenzied Look.* Amherst: University of Massachusetts Press, 1990.

Anderson, Fulton. *The Philosophy of Francis Bacon.* Chicago: University of Chicago Press, 1948.

Andrewes, Lancelot. *The Private Devotions of Lancelot Andrewes.* Translated by F. E. Brightman. Gloucester, Mass.: Peter Smith, 1978.

Ansell-Pearson, Keith. *Nietzsche Contra Rousseau: A Study of Nietzsche's Moral and Political Thought.* Cambridge: Cambridge University Press, 1991.

Aubrey's Brief Lives. Edited by Oliver Lawson Dick. Ann Arbor: University of Michigan Press, 1949.

Bergmann, Frithjof. "Nietzsche's Critique of Morality." In *Reading Nietzsche,* edited by Robert Solomon and Kathleen Higgins. New York: Oxford University Press, 1988.

Bergmann, Peter. *Nietzsche: "The Last Antipolitical German".* Bloomington: Indiana University Press, 1987.

Bertram, Maryanne. "God's *Second* Blunder—Serpent, Woman, and the *Gestalt* in Nietzsche's Thought." *Southern Journal of Philosophy* 19 (1981): 259–77.

Blondel, Eric. *Nietzsche: The Body and Culture, Philosophy as a Philological Genealogy.* Translated by Seán Hand. Stanford: Stanford University Press, 1991.

Bossy, John. *Giordano Bruno and the Embassy Affair.* New Haven: Yale University Press, 1991.

Briggs, John. *Francis Bacon and the Rhetoric of Nature.* Cambridge: Harvard University Press, 1989.

Brinton, Crane. *Nietzsche.* Cambridge: Harvard University Press, 1941.

Brunschvicg, Leon. *Descartes et Pascal, lecteurs de Montaigne.* Paris: J. Vrin, 1944.

Burger, Ronna. *The Phaedo: A Platonic Labyrinth.* New Haven: Yale University Press, 1984.

———. *Plato's Phaedrus: A Defense of a Philosophic Art of Writing.* University: University of Alabama Press, 1980.

Carter, Richard B. *Descartes' Medical Philosophy: The Organic Solution to the Mind-Body Problem.* Baltimore: Johns Hopkins University Press, 1983.

Castiglione, Balthasar. *The Book of the Courtier.* Translated by George Bull. Harmondsworth: Penguin Books, 1976.

Caton, Hiram. "Descartes' Anonymous Writings: A Recapitulation." *Southern Journal of Philosophy* 20 (1982): 299–312.

———. "On the Interpretation of the *Meditations*." *Man and World* 3 (1970): 224–45.

———. *The Origin of Subjectivity: An Essay on Descartes*. New Haven: Yale University Press, 1973.

———. *The Politics of Progress*. Gainesville: University of Florida Press, 1988.

———. "The Problem of Descartes' Sincerity." *Philosophical Forum* 2 (1971): 355–70.

Cavell, Stanley. *Conditions Handsome and Unhandsome: The Constitution of Emersonian Perfectionism*. Chicago: University of Chicago Press, 1990.

Choniates, Niketas. *O City of Byzantium, Annals of Niketas Choniates*. Translated by Harry J. Magoulias. Detroit: Wayne State University Press, 1984.

Cicero. *De divinatione*. Translated by W. A. Falconer. Cambridge: Harvard University Press, 1923.

———. *Tusculanae disputationes*. Translated by J. E. King. Cambridge: Harvard University Press, 1927.

Clarke, Desmond. *Descartes' Philosophy of Science*. University Park: Pennsylvania State University Press, 1982.

Clay, Jenny Strauss. *The Wrath of Athena: Gods and Men in the Odyssey*. Princeton: Princeton University Press, 1983.

Clement of Alexandria. *Exhortation to the Greeks*. Translated by G. W. Butterworth. Cambridge: Harvard University Press, 1919.

Coby, Patrick. *Socrates and the Sophistic Enlightenment: A Commentary on Plato's "Protagoras"*. Lewisburg: Bucknell University Press, 1987.

Cole, John R. *The Olympian Dreams and Youthful Rebellion of René Descartes*. Urbana: University of Illinois Press, 1992.

Cooper, Barry. *The End of History: An Essay in Modern Hegelianism*. Toronto: University of Toronto Press, 1984.

Couissan, Pierre. "The Stoicism of the New Academy." In *The Skeptical Tradition*, edited by Myles Burnyeat. Berkeley: University of California Press, 1983, 31–63.

Curley, E. M. *Descartes against the Skeptics*. Cambridge: Harvard University Press, 1978.

d'Alembert, Jean Le Rond. *Preliminary Discourse to the Encyclopedia of Diderot*. Translated by Richard N. Schwab. Indianapolis: Bobbs Merrill, 1963.

Daniel S.J., Gabriel. *A Voyage to the World of Cartesius*. London: Thomas Bennet, 1692.

Davis, Michael. *Ancient Tragedy and the Origins of Modern Science*. Carbondale: University of Southern Illinois Press, 1986.

Del Caro, Adrian. *Nietzsche Contra Nietzsche*. Baton Rouge: Louisiana State University Press, 1989.

Deleuze, Gilles. *Nietzsche and Philosophy*. Translated by Hugh Tomlinson. New York: Columbia University Press, 1983.

———. *Spinoza*. Translated by Robert Hurley. San Franscisco: City Lights Books, 1988.

Descartes' Conversation with Burman. Translated by John Cottingham. Oxford: Clarendon Press, 1976.

Detwiler, Bruce. *Nietzsche and the Politics of Aristocratic Radicalism*. Chicago: University of Chicago Press, 1990.

Dewey, John. *Reconstruction in Philosophy*. Enlarged edition. Boston: Beacon Press, 1948.

Dorter, Kenneth. "Science and Religion in Descartes' *Meditations*." *Thomist* 37 (1973): 313–40.

Dürr, Volker. "The Young Nietzsche: Historical Philosophizing, Historical Perspectivism, and the National Socialist Past." In *Nietzsche: Literature and Values*, edited by Volker Dürr, Reinhold Grimm, Kathy Harms. Madison: University of Wisconsin Press, 1988.

Eden, Robert. *Political Leadership and Nihilism*. Gainesville: University Presses of Florida, 1983.

Eusebius. *The Life of the Blessed Emperor Constantine*. In *A Selected Library of Nicene and Post-Nicene Fathers of the Christian Church*, 2d ser., vol. 1, edited by Philip Schaff and Henry Wallace. Grand Rapids: Eerdmanns Publishing Co., 1952 (1890): 481–559.

Ferguson, John. *The Heritage of Hellenism: The Greek World from 323 B.C. to 31 B.C.* New York: Harcourt Brace Jovanovich, 1973.

Fink, Eugen. "Nietzsche's New Experience of the World." In *Nietzsche's New Seas*, edited by Gillespie and Strong, 203–19.

Fish, Stanley. *Self-Consuming Artifacts: The Experience of Seventeenth-Century Literature*. Berkeley: University of California Press, 1972.

Foster, John Burt, Jr. *Heirs to Dionysus: A Nietzschean Current in Literary Modernism*. Princeton: Princeton University Press, 1981.

Galileo Galilei. *Dialogue concerning the Two Chief World Systems*. Translated by Stillman Drake. Berkeley: University of California Press, 1967.

Gibbon, Edward. *The History of the Decline and Fall of The Roman Empire*. New York: Modern Library, n.d. (1776–78).

Gillespie, Michael Allen, and Tracy B. Strong, eds. *Nietzsche's New Seas: Explorations in Philosophy, Aesthetics, and Politics*. Chicago: University of Chicago Press, 1988.

Gilman, Sander L., ed. *Begegnungen mit Nietzsche*. Bonn: Bouvier Verlag, 1987.

Gilson, Etienne. *Discours de la méthode, texte et commentaire*. Paris: Librairie philosophique, J. Vrin, 1925.

Graybeal, Jean. *Language and 'the Feminine' in Nietzsche and Heidegger*. Bloomington: Indiana University Press, 1990.

Hallman, Max O. "Nietzsche's Environmental Ethics." *Environmental Ethics* 13 (1991): 99–125.

Harrison, Peter. "Descartes on Animals." *Philosophical Quarterly* 42 (1992): 219–27.

Hartle, Ann. *Death and the Disinterested Spectator: An Inquiry into the Nature of Philosophy.* Albany: State University of New York Press, 1986.

Heidegger, Martin. *Nietzsche.* 2 vols. Pfullingen: Neske, 1961.

———. *Vorträge und Aufsätze.* 3 vols. Pfullingen: Neske, 1967 (1954).

———. *Was heisst Denken?* Tübingen: Niemeyer, 1961.

Heller, Erich. *The Importance of Nietzsche.* Chicago: University of Chicago Press, 1988.

Hobbes, Thomas. *Leviathan.* Edited by C. B. Macpherson. Harmondsworth: Penguin Books, 1968.

Hume, David. *An Enquiry concerning Human Understanding.* Edited by Eric Steinberg. Indianapolis: Hackett Publishing Co., 1977.

Jaspers, Karl. *Nietzsche: An Introduction to the Understanding of His Philosophical Activity.* Translated by Charles Wallraff and Frederick Schmitz. Tucson: University of Arizona Press, 1965.

Jones, R. F. *Ancients and Moderns: A Study of the Rise of the Scientific Movement in Seventeenth-Century England.* New York: Dover, 1982 (1961).

Joy, Lynn Sumida. *Gassendi the Atomist: Advocate of History in an Age of Science.* Cambridge: Cambridge University Press, 1987.

Judovitz, Dalia. *Subjectivity and Representation in Descartes.* Cambridge: Cambridge University Press, 1988.

Kant, Immanuel. *Critique of Pure Reason.* Translated by Norman Kemp Smith. New York: St. Martin's Press, 1965.

Kedar, Benjamin Z. *Crusade and Mission: European Approaches toward the Muslims.* Princeton: Princeton University Press, 1984.

Kennington, Richard. "Descartes' 'Olympica.'" *Social Research* 28 (1961): 171–204.

———. "Descartes and Mastery of Nature." In *Organism, Medicine, and Metaphysics,* edited by S. F. Spiker. Dordrecht: Reidel, 1987, 201–23.

———. "Rene Descartes." In *A History of Political Philosophy,* edited by Leo Strauss and Joseph Cropsey, 3d ed. Chicago: University of Chicago Press, 1987, 421–39.

Klein, Jacob. "Plato's *Phaedo.*" In *Lectures and Essays.* Annapolis: St. John's College Press, 1985, 375–94.

Klug, Brian. "Lab Animals, Francis Bacon and the Culture of Science." *Listening* 18 (1983): 54–72.

Kojève, Alexandre. *Introduction to the Reading of Hegel.* Translated by James Nichols, Jr. New York: Basic Books, 1969.

Krüger, Gerhard. "Die Herkunft des philosophischen Selbstbewusstseins." *Logos* 22 (1933): 225–72.

Lachterman, David. *The Ethics of Geometry: A Genealogy of Modernity.* New York: Routledge, 1989.

Lalande, A. "Sur quelques textes de Bacon et de Descartes." *Revue de métaphysique et de morale* 18 (1911): 296–311.

Lampert, Laurence. *Nietzsche's Teaching: An Interpretation of "Thus Spoke Zarathustra."* New Haven: Yale University Press, 1986.

———. "Yeats's Nietzschean Dialogue." *Yeats: An Annual of Critical and Textual Studies* 11 (1993).

Laymon, Ronald. "Transubstantiation: Test Case for Descartes' Theory of Space." In *Problems of Cartesianism,* edited by Lennon, Nicholas, Davis, 149–70.

Lea, Charles. *A History of the Inquisition of the Middle Ages.* 3 vols. New York: Russell and Russell, 1955 (1887).

———. *A History of the Inquisition of Spain.* 3 vols. New York: American Scholars Publications, 1966 (1906–7).

Leiss, William. *The Domination of Nature.* Boston: Beacon Press, 1974.

Lennon, Thomas M., John W. Nicholas, John W. Davis, eds. *Problems of Cartesianism.* Kingston and Montreal: McGill-Queen's University Press, 1982.

Lingis, Alphonso. "Black Stars: The Pedigree of the Evaluators." *Graduate Faculty Philosophy Journal* 15, no. 2 (1991): 67–91.

Livy. *Histories.* Translated by B. O. Foster. Cambridge: Harvard University Press, 1919.

Locke, John. *Two Treatises of Government.* Edited by Peter Laslett. New York: New American Library, 1965 (1960).

Löwith, Karl. *Mein Leben in Deutschland vor und nach 1933: Ein Bericht.* Stuttgart: Metzler, 1986.

———. *Nietzsches Philosophie der ewigen Wiederkehr des Gleichen.* 3d ed. Hamburg: Felix Meiner Verlag, 1978 (1935).

Lucretius. *De Rerum Natura.* Translated by W. H. D. Rouse. Cambridge: Harvard University Press, 1975 (1924).

McGowan, Margaret. *Montaigne's Deceits.* London: London University Press, 1974.

Machiavelli, Niccolò. *The Prince.* Translated by Harvey C. Mansfield, Jr. Chicago: University of Chicago Press, 1985.

———. *The Prince and the Discourses.* New York: Random House, 1950.

McIntyre, Alex. "'Virtuosos of Contempt:' An Investigation of Nietzsche's Political Philosophy through Certain Platonic Political Ideas." *Nietzsche Studien* 21 (1992): 184–210.

Maimonides, Moses. *The Guide of the Perplexed.* Translated by Shlomo Pines. Chicago: University of Chicago Press, 1963.

Maritain, Jacques. *The Dream of Descartes.* Translated by Mabelle L. Andison. New York: The Philosophical Library, 1940.

May, Keith M. *Nietzsche and Modern Literature.* New York: St. Martin's Press, 1988.

Medawar, P. W. "On 'the Effecting of All Things Possible.'" In *The Hope of Progress.* New York: Anchor Books, 1973, 119–38.

Merchant, Caroline. *The Death of Nature: Women, Ecology and the Scientific Revolution.* San Francisco: Harper and Row, 1980.

Meyendorff, John. "Byzantine Views of Islam." *Dumbarton Oaks Papers* 18 (1964): 115–32.

Montaigne, Michel de. *Essays.* Translated by Donald Frame. Stanford: Stanford University Press, 1965.

Müller-Lauter, Wolfgang. *Nietzsche, seine Philosophie der Gegensätze und die Gegensätze seiner Philosophie.* Berlin: Walter de Gruyter, 1971.

Nancy, Jean-Luc. "*Larvatus pro deo.*" *Glyph: Textual Studies* 2 (1977): 14–36.

Nicolas, M.-P. *From Nietzsche down to Hitler.* Translated by E. G. Echlin. Port Washington: Kennikat Press, 1970 (1938).

Friedrich Nietzsche on Rhetoric and Language. Edited and translated by Sander L. Gilman, Carole Blair, David J. Parent. New York: Oxford University Press, 1989.

Norton, Grace. *The Influence of Montaigne.* Boston: Houghton Mifflin, 1908.

Norwood, Gilbert. *Greek Comedy.* New York: Hill and Wang, 1963 (1931).

Ottmann, Henning. *Philosophie und Politik bei Nietzsche.* Berlin: Walter de Gruyter, 1987.

Pacheco, Juan Manuel. "Un amigo de Descartes en el Nuevo Reino." *Revista Javeriana* [Bogota] 51 (1959): 315–21.

Pagels, Elaine. *Adam, Eve, and the Serpent.* New York: Vintage Books, 1988.

Paterson, Timothy. "Bacon's Myth of Orpheus: Power as a Goal of Science in *Of the Wisdom of the Ancients.*" *Interpretation: A Journal of Political Philosophy* 16 (1989): 427–44.

———. "On the Role of Christianity in the Political Philosophy of Francis Bacon." *Polity* 19 (1987): 419–42.

———. "The Secular Control of Scientific Power in the Political Philosophy of Francis Bacon." *Polity* 21 (1989): 457–80.

Patrick, Max J. "Hawk versus Dove: Francis Bacon's Advocacy of a Holy War by James I against the Turks." *Studies in the Literary Imagination* 4 (1971): 159–71.

Penrose, S. B. L. "The Reputation and Influence of Francis Bacon." Ph.D. diss., Columbia University, 1934.

Perez-Ramos, Antonio. *Francis Bacon's Idea of Science and the Maker's Knowledge Tradition.* Oxford: Clarendon Press, 1988.

Philo of Alexandria. *On the Contemplative Life.* Translated by F. H. Colson. Cambridge: Harvard University Press, 1941.

Picht, Georg. *Nietzsche.* Stuttgart: Klett-Cotta, 1988.

Plato. *Alcibiades I.* Translated by W. R. M. Lamb. Cambridge: Harvard University Press, 1917.

———. *The Apology of Socrates.* Translated by Thomas G. West and Grace Starry West. In *Four Texts on Socrates,* translated by Thomas G. West and Grace Starry West. Ithaca: Cornell University Press, 1984.

———. *Euthyphro*. Translated by H. N. Fowler. Cambridge: Harvard University Press, 1914.

———. *Laws*. Translated by Thomas L. Pangle. New York: Basic Books, 1979.

———. *Lesser Hippias*. Translated by James Leake. In *The Roots of Political Philosophy: Ten Forgotten Socratic Dialogues,* edited by Thomas L. Pangle. Ithaca: Cornell University Press, 1987.

———. *Phaedo*. Translated by H. N. Fowler. Cambridge: Harvard University Press, 1914.

———. *Phaedrus*. Translated by H. N. Fowler. Cambridge: Harvard University Press, 1914.

———. *Republic*. Translated by Allan Bloom. New York: Basic Books, 1968.

———. *Sophist*. In *The Being of the Beautiful: Plato's "Theaetetus," "Sophist," and "Statesman,"* translated by Seth Benardete. Chicago: University of Chicago Press, 1984.

———. *Symposium*. Translated by W. R. M. Lamb. Cambridge: Harvard University Press, 1925.

Platt, Michael. "In the Middle of Montaigne." In *The Order of Montaigne's Essays,* edited by Daniel Martin. Amherst: University of Massachusetts and Hestia Press, 1989, 124–43.

Popkin, Richard H. "Cartesianism and Biblical Criticism." In *Problems of Cartesianism,* edited by Lennon, Nicholas, Davis, 61–81.

———. *The History of Scepticism from Erasmus to Spinoza*. Berkeley: University of California Press, 1979.

Rachels, James. *Created from Animals: The Moral Implications of Darwinism*. Oxford: Oxford University Press, 1990.

Redondi, Pietro. *Galileo Heretic*. Translated by Raymond Rosenthal. Princeton: Princeton University Press, 1987.

Reiss, Timothy J. "Descartes, the Palatinate, and the Thirty Years War: Political Theory and Political Practice." *Yale French Studies* 80 (1992): 108–45.

Rosen, Stanley. *The Ancients and the Moderns: Rethinking Modernity*. New Haven: Yale University Press, 1989.

———. *Hermeneutics as Politics*. New York: Oxford University Press, 1986.

———. *The Quarrel between Philosophy and Poetry: Studies in Ancient Thought*. New York: Routledge, 1988.

———. "Suspicion, Deception, and Concealment." *Arion* 3d ser., vol. 1, no. 2 (1991): 112–27.

Rossi, Paoli. *Philosophy, Technology and the Arts in the Early Modern Era*. Translated by Salvator Attanasio. New York: Harper Torchbooks, 1970.

Roth, Leon. *Descartes' Discourse on Method*. Oxford: Clarendon Press, 1937.

Rousseau, Jean-Jacques. *On the Social Contract*. Edited by Roger D. Masters and translated by Judith R. Masters. New York: St. Martin's Press, 1978.

Salaquarda, Jorg. "Studien zur zweiten unzeitgemässen Betrachtung." *Nietzsche Studien* 13 (1984): 1–45.

Santillana, Giorgio de. *The Crime of Galileo*. Chicago: University of Chicago Press, 1955.

Schaefer, David Lewis. *The Political Philosophy of Montaigne*. Ithaca: Cornell University Press, 1990.

Scott, J. F. *The Scientific Work of René Descartes*. London: Taylor and Francis, 1952.

Sessions, William A. "Francis Bacon and the Classics: The Discovery of Discovery." In *Francis Bacon's Legacy of Texts,* edited by Sessions, 237–53.

——— , ed. *Francis Bacon's Legacy of Texts*. New York: AMS Press, 1990.

Simpson, David. "Putting One's House in Order: The Career of the Self in Descartes' Method." *New Literary History* 9 (1977): 83–101.

Spencer, Herbert. *The Data of Ethics*. New York: A. L. Burt, 1879.

Starnes, Colin. *The New Republic: A Commentary on Book I of More's Utopia Showing Its Relation to Plato's Republic*. Waterloo, Ont.: Wilfrid Laurier University Press, 1990.

Staten, Henry. *Nietzsche's Voice*. Ithaca: Cornell University Press, 1990.

Stauth, Georg, and Bryan S. Turner. *Nietzsche's Dance*. Oxford: Blackwell, 1988.

Stephens, James. *Francis Bacon and the Style of Science*. Chicago: University of Chicago Press, 1975.

Strauss, Leo. *The Argument and the Action of Plato's "Laws."* Chicago: University of Chicago Press, 1975.

——— . "How Farabi Read Plato's *Laws*." In *What Is Political Philosophy?* 134–54.

——— . *Natural Right and History*. Chicago: University of Chicago Press, 1953.

——— . "Note on the Plan of Nietzsche's *Beyond Good and Evil*." In *Studies in Platonic Political Philosophy,* 174–91.

——— . *On Tyranny*. Edited by Victor Gourevitch and Michael S. Roth. Rev. and expanded ed. New York: The Free Press, 1991 (1948).

——— . *Persecution and the Art of Writing*. Glencoe, Ill.: The Free Press, 1952.

——— . *Philosophy and Law: Essays toward the Understanding of Maimonides and His Predecessors*. Translated by Fred Baumann. Philadelphia: The Jewish Publications Society, 1987 (1935).

——— . *The Political Philosophy of Thomas Hobbes*. Translated by Elsa M. Sinclair. Chicago: University of Chicago Press, 1952 (1936).

——— . *Spinoza's Critique of Religion*. Translated by E. M. Sinclair. New York: Schocken Books, 1965 (1930).

——— . *Studies in Platonic Political Philosophy*. Chicago: University of Chicago Press, 1983.

——— . *Thoughts on Machiavelli*. Chicago: University of Chicago Press, 1978 (1958).

——— . *What Is Political Philosophy? and Other Studies*. Glencoe, Ill.: The Free Press, 1959.

Studer, Heidi. " 'Grapes Ill-Trodden . . .' Francis Bacon and the Wisdom of the Ancients." Ph.D. diss. University of Toronto, 1992.

Tacitus. *The Histories*. Translated by Clifford H. Moore. London: William Heinemann, 1925.

Temple, William. *Nature, Man and God*. Gifford Lectures, 1933–34. London: Macmillan and Co., 1934.

Thiele, Leslie Paul. *Friedrich Nietzsche and the Politics of the Soul*. Princeton: Princeton University Press, 1990.

Toland, John. *Tetradymus*. London, 1720.

Toulmin, Stephen. *Cosmopolis, the Hidden Agenda of Modernity*. New York: Free Press, 1990.

Trevor-Roper, Hugh. *Archbishop Laud*. London: Macmillan, 1965 (1940).

————. *Catholics, Anglicans and Puritans: Seventeenth Century Essays*. Chicago: University of Chicago Press, 1988.

————. *The Crisis of the Seventeenth Century: Religion, The Reformation and Social Change*. New York: Harper and Row, 1968.

————. "Francis Bacon." *Encounter* 18, no. 2 (Feb. 1962): 73–77.

————. *Men and Events*. New York: Harper and Brothers, 1957.

————. *Renaissance Essays*. Chicago: University of Chicago Press, 1985.

Urbach, Peter. *Francis Bacon's Philosophy of Science*. La Salle, Ill.: Open Court, 1987.

Van de Pitte, Frederick. "The Dating of Rule IV-B in Descartes's *Regulae ad directionem ingenii*." *Journal of the History of Philosophy* 29 (1991): 375–95.

Vartanian, Aram. *La Mettrie's L'homme machine: A Study in the Origins of an Idea*. Princeton: Princeton University Press, 1960.

Vico, Giambattista. *The Autobiography of Giambattista Vico*. Translated by Max Harold Fisch and Thomas Goddard Bergin. Ithaca: Cornell University Press, 1963.

Vitoria, Francisco de. *Political Writings*. Edited and translated by Anthony Pagden and Jeremy Lawrance. Cambridge: Cambridge University Press, 1991.

Watson, Richard A. "Transubstantiation among the Cartesians." In *Problems of Cartesianism*, edited by Lennon, Nicholas, Davis, 127–48.

Webster, Charles. *The Great Instauration: Science, Medicine, and Reform, 1626–1660*. New York: Holmes and Meyer, 1976.

Weinberger, Jerry. "Introduction." In *New Atlantis and The Great Instauration*, edited by Jerry Weinberger. Rev. ed. Arlington Heights, Ill.: Harlan Davidson, 1989.

————. "On Bacon's *Advertisement Touching a Holy War*." *Interpretation: A Journal of Political Philosophy* 9 (1981): 191–206.

————. *Science, Faith, and Politics: Francis Bacon and the Utopian Roots of the Modern Age*. Ithaca: Cornell University Press, 1985.

Wheeler, Harvey. "Francis Bacon's *New Atlantis*: The 'Mould' of a Lawfinding Commonwealth." In *Francis Bacon's Legacy of Texts*, edited by Sessions, 291–310.

————. "The Invention of Modern Empiricism: Juridical Foundations of Francis

Bacon's Philosophy of Science." *Law Library Journal* 76 (1983): 78–120.

White, Alan. *Within Nietzsche's Labyrinth*. New York: Routledge, 1990.

White, Howard B. *Peace among the Willows: The Political Philosophy of Francis Bacon*. The Hague: Martinus Nijhoff, 1968.

Whitney, Charles. *Francis Bacon and Modernity*. New Haven: Yale University Press, 1986.

———. "Francis Bacon's *Instauratio*: Dominion of and over Humanity." *Journal of the History of Ideas* 50, no. 3 (1989): 371–90.

Wittgenstein, Ludwig. *Tractatus Logico-Philosophicus*. Translated by D. F. Pears and B. F. McGuiness. London: Routledge and Kegan Paul, 1963 (1921).

Woodbridge, Benjamin M. "The *Discours de la méthode* and the Spirit of the Renaissance." *Romantic Review* 24 (1933): 136–42.

Yack, Bernard. *The Longing for Total Revolution: Philosophical Sources of Social Discontent from Rousseau to Marx and Nietzsche*. Princeton: Princeton University Press, 1986.

Yates, Frances. *Astraea: The Imperial Theme in the Sixteenth Century*. London: Ark, 1985 (1975).

———. *Giordano Bruno and the Hermetic Tradition*. Chicago: University of Chicago Press, 1982.

———. *The Rosicrucian Enlightenment*. London: Routledge and Kegan Paul, 1978.

Yeats, William Butler. *The Poems*. Rev. ed. Edited by Richard J. Finneran. New York: Macmillan, 1989.

———. *A Vision*. New York: Macmillan, 1956 (1937).

Yovel, Yirmiyahu. *Spinoza and Other Heretics*. 2 vols. Princeton: Princeton University Press, 1989.

Zagorin, Perez. *Ways of Lying: Dissimulation, Persecution and Conformity in Early Modern Europe*. Cambridge: Harvard University Press, 1990.

Index